Walker Art Center   Painting and Sculpture from the Collection

Walker Art Center

Painting and Sculpture from the Collection

Essays on the Collection
Martin Friedman
and
William C. Agee
Edward F. Fry
Joseph Masheck
Carter Ratcliff
Diane Waldman

Collection Entries
Lucy Flint-Gohlke
and
Elizabeth Armstrong
Peter Boswell
Ann Brooke
Constance Butler
Mildred S. Friedman
Marge Goldwater
Donna Harkavy
Nora Heimann
Lawrence Rinder
Nancy Roth
Joan Rothfuss

Walker Art Center, Minneapolis
Rizzoli International Publications, Inc., New York

This publication was made possible by generous grants from:

The Andrew W. Mellon Foundation

Luce Fund for Scholarship in American Art, a program of The Henry Luce Foundation, Inc.

National Endowment for the Arts

First edition

© 1990 Walker Art Center

Published in 1990 by Walker Art Center, Minneapolis, and Rizzoli International Publications, Inc., 300 Park Avenue South, New York, N.Y. 10010. All rights reserved. No part of the contents of this book may be reproduced without the written permission of the publishers.

Walker Art Center .
Walker Art center : painting and sculpture from the collection / introd. Martin Friedman : essays William C. Agee [et al.] : catalog entries Lucy Flint-Gohlke [et al.] .
p.   cm.
Includes bibliographic references.
ISBN 0–8478–1267–7. —
ISBN 0–935640–33–9 (pbk.)
1. Walker Art Center—Catalogs. I. Friedman, Martin L.
N583.A884 1990
708.176'579—dc20   90–34587
                            CIP

Printed and bound in Japan.

Editorial supervision by Mildred S. Friedman

Edited by Sheila Schwartz

Designed by Glenn Suokko

Dimensions are in inches and centimeters; height precedes width precedes depth.

Contents

Essays on the Collection

Introduction

Martin Friedman

The Walker Art Center's collection, like that of many American museums, began as a reflection of one man's taste. Thomas Barlow Walker (1840–1927) was a successful Minneapolis lumberman and entrepreneur who, having made a sizable fortune, ennobled his status in the community by becoming a noted patron of the arts. To his opulent residence on Hennepin Avenue, in what is now downtown Minneapolis, he added a substantial wing in 1879 for a gallery whose walls were soon covered with ornately framed European paintings. Aware of the art collections being amassed by East Coast captains of industry such as Andrew Mellon, Henry Clay Frick and Andrew Carnegie, he was determined to accumulate his own treasures.

Walker's taste in art was broad, but like other nineteenth-century tycoons who collected on a grand scale, he concentrated on highly representational imagery, especially when it exemplified virtuoso technique. His eye was not always informed, however, and in more than a few instances he acquired paintings attributed to Renaissance masters whose provenance turned out to be cloudy. He was on surer ground when buying romantic nineteenth-century French Barbizon and American landscapes. Walker's keen eclecticism also led him to collect late eighteenth- and early nineteenth-century Chinese jade and porcelain, Syrian glass, Greek vases, American Indian pottery, and Japanese ivory netsuke. Portraits of the Napoleonic era were his particular enthusiasm, and within a short time he assembled quite an array, including several of the Little Corporal himself and other members of the Bonaparte family.

As the second president of The Minneapolis Society of Fine Arts (the governing body of The Minneapolis Institute of Arts), from 1888 to 1893,

9

T.B. Walker's fondest dream was to see his collection permanently installed in a special wing of the Institute. When fellow trustees declined his offer to donate his entire collection, Walker resigned from the Society to create his own museum on Lyndale Avenue, directly opposite the Hennepin Avenue Methodist Church, of which he was a prominent member. On 22 May 1927, at the age of eighty-seven, T.B. Walker proudly opened the doors of the new Walker Art Gallery to the public. During the Gallery's first few months, the patriarchal Walker would occasionally conduct dazzled visitors through his Moorish-style palace of art. But his pleasure in his great accomplishment was brief, for he died in October of that year.

In successive decades the Walker Art Gallery was operated under the auspices of the T.B. Walker Foundation, the family-governed organization Walker had established in 1925. But during the Depression the resources of the Foundation were virtually nonexistent. Archie D. Walker, T.B.'s youngest son, oversaw the daily operations of the Gallery, with the assistance of his children, Hudson D. and Louise Walker. The only museum professional and non-Walker was Reuben Adams, who performed basic curatorial tasks related to the collection. In 1939 the Federal Arts Project, a Works Progress Administration program, was granted temporary control of the Gallery by the Walker family. Thanks to the WPA, designed to provide employment opportunities for artists throughout the country, the Walker Art Gallery suddenly had a new lease on life. In June 1939, under the auspices of the FAP, Daniel Defenbacher, who had been trained in art and architecture at the Carnegie Institute of Technology, became the Director of the Gallery. Defenbacher had worked as a field director for the WPA, and with his activist leadership the Gallery became the regional headquarters for the FAP and, commensurately, a lively forum for contemporary art. Its name was changed to the Walker Art Center to reflect the new diversity of activities initiated by Defenbacher: an imaginative program of special exhibitions utilized many objects from the permanent collection, particularly its decorative arts material such as ceramics and jade. He also established an art school that welcomed wide public enrollment and presented exhibitions of works by local artists. In 1943, when the WPA returned control of the museum to the T.B. Walker Foundation, which by then was able to resume its financial support, this emphasis on regional and contemporary art was preserved.

Defenbacher, with the support of Hudson Walker, a serious collector in his own right, added a group of nineteenth-century American landscapes to those acquired by T.B. In the spring of 1934, Hudson served briefly as the first curator of fine arts at the University of Minnesota Art Gallery. In 1936 he had opened his own art gallery in New York City, but his interest in the institution built by his grandfather remained strong. Hudson was especially effective in persuading members of the T.B. Walker Foundation of the importance of building a contemporary collection. As head of the museum's acquisition committee, he continued his efforts to help the Walker acquire key works, among them Franz Marc's 1911 German Expressionist masterpiece *Die grossen blauen Pferde (The Large Blue Horses)* and Lyonel Feininger's 1926 *Barfüsserkirche II (Church of the Minorites II)*.

Particularly noteworthy during Defenbacher's tenure was the addition of a substantial group of early-to-mid-twentieth-century examples of American realism. Among the earliest of these is John Sloan's 1907–1908 *South Beach*

Bathers, a quintessentially proletarian depiction of a crowded public beach. Other examples of such reportage of the American proletariat acquired in these years are George Luks's celebrated 1921 *Breaker Boy of Shenandoah, Pa.*, and Jack Levine's *The Neighborhood Physician* of 1939. The most important example of American Regionalist painting in the Walker's collection remains Edward Hopper's moody urban tableau of 1940, *Office at Night*, acquired in 1948. Not all artists were caught up in social or psychological issues, or even in the precise rendering of the American scene. Utterly devoid of topicality are John Marin's watercolors of the Maine coast. The crystalline spatterings and frothy washes in his 1932 *Rocks, Sea and Boat, Small Point, Maine* were laid down with little concern for either specific locale or spatial logic. Rather than descriptions of place, they are evanescent impressions—memories of visual events.

In March 1951, after twelve years of developing the Walker Art Center into a respected national artistic resource, Daniel Defenbacher left the museum. Succeeding him was H. Harvard Arnason, who had come to Minneapolis in 1947 from Northwestern University, where he had been a professor of art history, to become chairman of the art department of the University of Minnesota. By arrangement with both institutions, Arnason was able to divide his time between the Walker and the university. Within a few years his effect on the museum's direction became apparent: he considerably expanded its exhibition and collecting activities to emphasize current American and European art. Because his special interest was sculpture— of which the Walker had few examples—he set about acquiring key works by early twentieth-century European masters and, at the same time, those of young Americans whose production was beginning to attract serious critical response.

Among the pioneer modernist European works Arnason purchased were two figurative bronzes, Aristide Maillol's full-bodied female nude, *Study for La Méditerranée* (circa 1905) and Picasso's 1905 *Le fou (The Jester)*. Also under Arnason's directorship, Duchamp-Villon's cubistic bronze *Le grand cheval (The Large Horse)* (1914/1957) took its place in the Walker's collection along with other sculptures, primarily female nudes and heads from the 1920s, that reveal the diverse influences of Cubist abstraction. The sleek Art Moderne, or Deco, style is perfectly exemplified in Elie Nadelman's delicately poised, lyrical marble *Figure* (circa 1925), and Gaston Lachaise's bronze female *Head* of about 1928, a work that recalls the stately bronze heads of Nigeria's Ife culture.

The stylistic extremes of European figurative sculpture during the mid-1920s are revealed in bronzes by two German artists, Rudolf Belling and Georg Kolbe. The facial features of Belling's gleaming 1925 *Kopf in Messing (Head in Brass)*, a highly sophisticated depiction of a modish flapper, are so mechanized as to be virtually robotlike. By contrast, Georg Kolbe's *Junge Frau (Young Woman)* of 1926 offers an introspective, spiritualized depiction of an adolescent girl on the brink of womanhood.

One of Arnason's most ambitious acquisitions was Jacques Lipchitz's monumental bronze *Prometheus Strangling the Vulture II*, modeled in 1944 and cast in 1953. Originally installed at the east entrance of the Walker Art Center's 1927 building, this massive neo-Baroque work, with its rounded volumes, is now located in the Minneapolis Sculpture Garden.

The use of direct metal welding techniques to construct form was a particularly important phenomenon in American sculpture during the 1940s and 1950s. Thanks to Arnason, the Walker now owns major works in that technique by David Smith (*The Royal Bird*, 1947–1948) and Theodore Roszak (*Cradle Song Variation No. 2*, 1957–1960).

Arnason continued the American emphasis initiated by Defenbacher in the Walker's painting collection by adding a number of early twentieth-century examples, several of which illustrated the growing influence of European modernist ideas on American art. Marsden Hartley's *Storm Clouds, Maine* (1906–1907) recalls the brooding romanticism of German Expressionism. At the same time, its subject and technique are reminiscent of Cézanne's images of Mont-Ste.-Victoire. Arnason's interest in Cubism's effects on young Americans who ventured abroad in the early 1900s led to his acquisition of paintings by Morgan Russell (*Synchromy Number 4 (1914) to Form*, 1914) and Stanton Macdonald-Wright (*Synchromy in Green and Orange*, 1916), the cofounders of the short-lived Synchromist movement. Mondrian's legacy is evident in two works purchased in the 1950s, a thin painted metal column by Ilya Bolotowsky and a circular abstraction by the Swiss-born Fritz Glarner that employs classic De Stijl red, yellow, and blue rectangles.

Among the mid-twentieth-century American paintings that entered the collection in the 1950s, the most cohesive group documents the Precisionist tendency. Precisionism's unique synthesis of regional themes and sharp-edged geometry is nowhere better exemplified than in Charles Sheeler's 1949 *Buildings at Lebanon* and his 1954 *Midwest*. Also acquired by Arnason in that decade were Niles Spencer's 1951 *Wake of the Hurricane* and Charles Demuth's drawing *Two Acrobats* of 1918. Arnason sought as well less "classic" examples of Precisionism and its heritage, as in the works of Stuart Davis, whose 1954 *Colonial Cubism*, acquired the year after it was painted, indicates that he had no qualms about abstracting his themes. Among Precisionist-related works of an earlier period acquired by Arnason were Joseph Stella's *American Landscape*, painted in 1929, and Georgia O'Keeffe's elegantly delineated 1926 *Lake George Barns*.

In 1961, when Arnason resigned to become Vice President for Arts Administration at the Solomon R. Guggenheim Museum, I succeeded him as Director of the Walker Art Center. Among my objectives were to build a strong public constituency for contemporary art and to make the Walker's programs reflect and interpret significant current artistic directions in this country and abroad. This approach would emphasize special exhibitions as well as lectures, classes, and related programs in film, music, and dance. The Walker's operating funds, voted annually by the T.B. Walker Foundation, were fairly modest, and though many excellent works by young artists were purchased, it was determined that the priority for the immediate future would be programs, rather than collection. By the mid-1960s, however, the museum's financial situation had begun to improve, and more attention could be paid to building the permanent collection.

While no formal acquisition policy was adopted at that time, some general goals evolved from discussions between the Walker's staff and the Board of Directors. The museum would seek to acquire important works by living artists, particularly those at the beginning of their careers, a policy that would benefit the artist, identify the museum as a supporter of new creativity, and closely relate the Walker's collecting focus to that of its exhibition program, which has consistently reflected a broad range of ideas relevant to current art. Retrospective and thematic exhibitions of the work of major living artists, exhibitions that examine significant twentieth-century movements in the arts, and exhibitions documenting works in progress came to characterize the Walker's program. Of course, the relative affordability of works by younger artists was a factor in shaping the museum's buying patterns. In addition, efforts were made to acquire key paintings and sculptures by artists of international stature, especially those who were pioneers of major mid-twentieth-century stylistic phenomena such as Abstract Expressionism, Assemblage, Minimalism, and Pop Art. Fortunately for the Walker's collection-building efforts, the 1960s was a particularly fertile decade for American art, which in variety and quality was gaining considerable international respect. Indeed, it could be argued that the Walker's evolution into a major center of contemporary art was largely attributable to this burgeoning art scene. Paintings and sculptures in a wide range of styles by young American artists were being eagerly collected, and, like other museums here and abroad, the Walker sought significant examples of these works.

Purchases for the collection were made from several Walker exhibitions documenting aspects of 1960s movements. A 1963 retrospective of paintings by Adolph Gottlieb, one of Abstract Expressionism's progenitors, led to the acquisition of two key paintings: *Blue at Noon* (1955) and *Trio* (1960). Closely related to the Abstract Expressionist ethos are the symbol-laden, black-painted walls, towers, and boxes of Louise Nevelson, such as the monumental wall piece *Sky Cathedral Presence* (1951–1964), acquired in 1969. The acquisition of Richard Stankiewicz's untitled piece of 1962, and Lucas Samaras's 1965 sculpture of two chairs, one totally executed with pins, the other sheathed in fluorescent colored yarn, considerably broadened the Walker's Assemblage holdings.

The elementary geometry of Minimalism—the diametric opposite of Assemblage in attitude and form—is well represented at the Walker. Its emergence as a full-fledged stylistic movement was in large measure foreshadowed by the work of two older luminaries, David Smith and Tony Smith. The Walker acquired David Smith's *Cubi IX* (1961) in 1966 and, two years later, Tony Smith's cubistic 1965/1968 *Amaryllis*. A series of exhibitions organized by the Walker from the mid-1960s to the early 1970s highlighted the Minimalist approach. The galvanized metal boxes of Donald Judd were displayed on the museum's floors and walls in the 1966 *Ambiguous Image* exhibition, from which the red, hingelike untitled wall sculpture was purchased. In 1969, while the museum was undergoing a major building program, it presented *14 Sculptors: The Industrial Edge*, a broad survey of the Minimalist development, in the commodious auditorium space of [Dayton's department store] in Minneapolis. As a result, several works entered the collection, including Ellsworth Kelly's 1968 *Green Rocker*; Sylvia Stone's *Untitled* (1971), and Robert Murray's *Track* of 1966. The southern California variation on the Minimalist aesthetic is represented in the Walker's collection by two mid-1960s Robert Irwin paintings and a 1967–1968 Larry Bell glass cube.

Throughout the 1960s, the Walker also purchased art that represented the two-dimensional aspect of Minimalism, exemplified in the hard-edged

geometry of painters such as Frank Stella (*Sketch Les Indes Galantes*, 1962), Ellsworth Kelly (*Red Green Blue*, 1964) and Kenneth Noland (*Track*, 1969). But not all practitioners of pure abstract painting during those years employed such pristine, hard-edged geometry. During the 1960s and 1970s, the Walker's collection was enriched by acquisitions of paintings by Morris Louis and Helen Frankenthaler, whose works, despite obvious predilections for elemental forms, retained aspects of Abstract Expressionism's freely brushed quality and incorporation of accidental effects.

Exuberant manifestations of Pop Art began to enter the collection during the 1960s, often in the very year they were completed: among these were Oldenburg's monumental 1966 soft sculpture *Shoestring Potatoes Spilling from a Bag* and George Segal's *The Diner*, finished in 1966. Andy Warhol's *16 Jackies* (1964) and Robert Indiana's *The Green Diamond Eat* and *The Red Diamond Die* (1962) were purchased within a few years of their completion. Life after Pop, in the form of New Realism, is also well traced in the Walker's collection. This fascinating stylistic footnote of the late 1960s reached its apogee in Chuck Close's gigantic face-scapes. The first of these, his 1968 *Big Self-Portrait*, was acquired in 1969. Strengthening the collection's representation of American art of the early 1960s is an especially important "combine" painting by Robert Rauschenberg, the three-part 1960 *Trophy II (for Teeny and Marcel Duchamp)*; ten years later, James Rosenquist's mural-size *Area Code* (1970) was a significant addition.

By the end of the 1960s, it was evident to the Walker Board of Directors and staff that the museum's collection and extensive exhibition program were expanding at such a rate that they could no longer be housed in the existing building. And after exploring several options for adding space, the dramatic decision was made to tear down the original structure and build a new one on its site. Edward Larrabee Barnes, the New York-based architect selected for the job, came up with an elegant, highly functional scheme, which he developed working closely with the Walker staff. In response to the museum's request for flexible spaces where large contemporary works of art could be displayed, and, on occasion, even be created, he proposed a cubelike building using simple warehouse construction techniques. The galleries would be laid out in a rising helix configuration around a central elevator and staircase core; approximately half of this space would be reserved for displays of the permanent collection.

Barnes's proposal was accepted, fund-raising for the new building began, and in January 1969 the wrecking ball struck the building that T.B. Walker had so proudly inaugurated in 1927. Prior to construction of the present Walker Art Center building, however, the trustees of the T.B. Walker Foundation, most of whom lived in California, made another decision that would radically affect the development of the collection: they authorized the sale of a large number of historical paintings and decorative art objects owned by the Foundation and in the possession of Walker Art Center. There was precedent for such action: in 1946 the Foundation had disposed of a number of primarily decorative art objects of secondary importance in a massive sale conducted by the Victor Hammer Gallery and held at Gimbel's in New York City. The new series of sales, which began in 1969, reflected the Foundation trustees' realization that the Walker Art Center, as a modern museum, had little use for such historical material and that funds realized from their disposition could be

used to acquire contemporary works of art. These sales, held at Sotheby Parke Bernet in New York City, included seventeenth-century European paintings, Barbizon landscapes, Chinese porcelains, and such diverse material as eighteenth-century miniatures, Near Eastern jewelry, and Syrian glass. However, the celebrated collection of late Chinese jades, so carefully assembled by T.B. Walker, was placed on long-term loan to The Minneapolis Institute of Arts. Of the Walker's original pre-twentieth-century collection, only the nineteenth-century American landscape paintings were retained. With funds realized from these sales, important pieces by several stalwarts of modernism could be purchased. Among the earliest of these acquisitions were Alexander Calder's 1964 black stabile *Octopus* and Isamu Noguchi's 1959 bronze *Mortality*.

The 1970s was an especially significant decade in the development of the Walker Art Center's collection. On 15 May 1971 the new building was inaugurated with a presentation of major works from the permanent collection, and a special exhibition, *Works for New Spaces*, featured a number of large-scale commissioned pieces made specifically for the Walker's new galleries. Several of these commissioned works were purchased by the museum, including Donald Judd's series of six metal cubes and Robert Irwin's scrim piece designed for one of the Walker's galleries, where it has since been reinstalled a number of times. Sam Gilliam's stained canvas *Carousel Merge* was also acquired in 1971. Its voluminous yardage is periodically suspended in graceful folds beneath the skylight in the lobby between the Walker and the Guthrie Theater.

Two works by Joan Miró were acquired following an exhibition of his sculptures organized by the Walker in 1971: *Femme debout (Standing Woman)*, an imposing 1969 goddess figure in black patinated bronze; and another primitivistic work of 1967, *Tête et oiseau (Head and Bird)*, a bronze cast of an Aztec-like stone head that Miró had carved in wood years earlier.

In addition to the spacious galleries provided by the Barnes scheme, the museum gained three roof terraces for the display of sculpture. Installed on these at the time the new building opened were Tony Smith's *Amaryllis*, Calder's *Octopus* (1964), the embattled *Prometheus* by Lipchitz, and a 1960–1961 *Reclining Mother and Child* bronze by Henry Moore. Shortly afterward, Claes Oldenburg's blue-and-yellow 1969/1971 metal sculpture *Geometric Mouse—Scale A* joined this high-rise collection. The lawn at the east end of the Walker site was a second location for large outdoor works; in 1971, Calder's magnificent *The Spinner* of 1966 was installed there. Its jaunty red, yellow, and blue forms still wave to endless lines of passing traffic.

As the Walker began to fully utilize its new building for special exhibitions and installations of the permanent collection—and for its rapidly growing education, performing arts, and film programs—it became apparent that considerably more annual support would be required than originally had been projected. It was also evident to the T.B. Walker Foundation's trustees that the annual operating funds they provided would be insufficient to underwrite these burgeoning activities. In light of these realities, the Foundation trustees, in their concern for the future of the Walker Art Center, accepted an offer made by the museum's locally based Board of Directors that it assume full responsibility for the Walker's governance and financial security. The result was a transfer of assets in 1976 from the Foundation to

the Walker Art Center itself, which included the museum and Guthrie Theater buildings, the collection, and a major share of the Foundation's capital. As a result of this generous act, the Walker Art Center's status as a publicly governed institution was permanently assured, a fact that subsequently has helped attract significant local and national financial support. Through successive endowment campaigns, the museum's financial position was gradually improved; consequently, more attention could be directed to the growth of the collection, to special exhibitions, and to other activities.

Since the early 1970s, a number of artists who have had retrospective exhibitions at the Walker have made generous gifts of their work to its permanent collection. Significant among these, Isamu Noguchi gave the museum five sculptures from the 1930s and 1940s, including the bronzes *Swimming Pool for von Sternberg* (1935), *Avatar* (1947/1980), and *Judith*, the latter cast in 1978 from the carved balsa-wood tent poles that comprised the 1950 set Noguchi designed for a Martha Graham dance piece. Also included in Noguchi's gift was the original 1947 balsa carving for *Cronos*. In 1973 Louise Nevelson, the doyenne of Assemblage, presented the museum with fourteen pieces, ranging from small quasi-abstract terra-cotta sculptures from the mid-1940s to tree-and-column pieces of the mid-1970s. Her gift included a 1947 wood-relief sculpture and *End of Day Nightscape III*, a large 1973 wall piece constructed of printers' type cases. Thanks to the Nevelson gift, the Walker's collection of Assemblage grew significantly. Works by other artists in this fertile idiom were also added during the 1970s: Joseph Cornell's *Andromeda (Sand Fountain)* (1953–1956) and Mark di Suvero's 1965 *Stuyvesantseye*, a remarkable mobile "combine" of improbable elements, including an ancient wood barrel and a battered chair.

The Walker's coverage of the Minimalist movement in sculpture also increased during the 1970s with the addition of Sol LeWitt's white grid, *Cubic Modular Piece No. 2 (L-Shaped Modular Piece)* of 1966 and Christopher Wilmarth's glass and steel *Trace*, a 1972 standing floor piece.

By the middle of the 1970s, young sculptors, equally disenchanted with the cool rigor of Minimalism and with Pop Art's deadpan glorifications of everyday icons, began seeking alternatives. Many of them also rejected the notion of large, public-scale imagery in favor of an intimate, indeed miniature, scale. From a 1977 Walker exhibition, *Scale and Environment: 10 Sculptors*, a group of small works entered the collection, including a 1975 generic bronze house on a metal plane by Joel Shapiro, and Siah Armajani's 1970 *Bridge for Robert Venturi*, one of several bridge models executed by the artist in the early 1970s. Also acquired from the exhibition were two red-clay sculptures by Charles Simonds depicting stages in the life cycle of an imaginary Neolithic village.

Turning to painting acquired during the 1970s, the Walker's collection was enriched by the addition of key works by several leading modernist figures. The patron saint of many artists associated with Minimalist sculpture was the Abstract Expressionist painter Barnett Newman, whose uncompromising view about stripping form to its barest essentials helped set the scene for Minimalism. The Walker's documentation of Abstract Expressionism gained considerable stature with the arrival of Barnett Newman's red-orange canvas, *The Third*, painted in 1962. Another significant addition to this group was the imposing, densely painted 1950 abstraction *Untitled*, by

Clyfford Still. On the other side of the coin are those Abstract Expressionists whose later work was affected by the simplifying impulses of Minimalism. The Walker's representation of this tendency in American art was augmented by its acquisition of Robert Motherwell's large 1971 canvas *Untitled*, purchased from the museum's 1972 exhibition of Motherwell's paintings.

An especially strong tendency in the Walker's acquisitions since the 1950s has been for paintings and sculptures whose imagery reflects early twentieth-century European abstraction. Two decades after Arnason began to acquire such works, the museum purchased Burgoyne Diller's *First Theme* of 1963–1964, whose planar rectangular forms mirror the influence of Piet Mondrian. Such carefully calibrated De Stijl-based compositions gave way in the 1970s to the reductionist geometric abstraction of such artists as Agnes Martin and Brice Marden; both are represented with paintings acquired in the 1970s.

Toward the end of the 1970s, new approaches to painting and sculpture were making themselves felt in the work of young artists on both sides of the Atlantic. Variously characterized as Neo-Expressionism and New Figuration, this emotive new direction in painting recalls many historical sources, ranging from various tribal arts to early twentieth-century German Expressionism. The works of Susan Rothenberg, such as her 1979 *Tattoo*, a primal linear image of a charging horse, acquired the year it was painted, eloquently exemplify this impulse in recent American art. By the early 1980s, expressionistic figuration attained new visibility in American and European painting. The style runs the gamut from atmospheric evocation of form to aggressive delineation of figures, interiors, and landscapes, a range apparent in several paintings recently acquired by the museum, among them Jennifer Bartlett's 1979 long, friezelike abstraction *Swimmers at Dawn, Noon and Dusk* and Donald Sultan's brooding, monochromatic *Forest Fire, April 13, 1984*. Other variations on figuration are seen in newly acquired paintings such as Richard Bosman's enigmatic depiction of drowning men clinging to a tree branch (*Crossing*, 1984), and a biomorphic canvas in the shape of a teacup by Elizabeth Murray (*Sail Baby*, 1983).

In 1985 the Walker's Abstract Expressionist holdings were again broadened by the Mark Rothko Foundation gift of four large paintings and a watercolor representing crucial periods in Rothko's stylistic evolution. At the same time, the museum continues its tradition of collecting works from exhibitions organized by its staff. In this way, the Walker acquired two important David Hockney works from the 1983 *Hockney Paints the Stage*: the large gouache *Hollywood Hills House* (1980), and *Les mamelles de Tirésias (The Breasts of Tirésias)* (1983), an environmental work based on Hockney's set for the opera by Francis Poulenc.

The Walker's important collection of Assemblage works is now being reinforced by the acquisition of new pieces that reveal that the movement still has strong proponents, as in *Portrait of a Mother with Past Affixed Also*, a collaborative work by Edward Kienholz and Nancy Reddin Kienholz made in 1980–1981. Decidedly in the Assemblage spirit of creative improvisation is Jim Dine's monumental *The Crommelynck Gate with Tools*, a large, linear 1983 bronze purchased in 1984. Among the works acquired by younger sculptors who use the Assemblage method are Deborah Butterfield's 1981 evocation of a horse resting on the ground (*Rosary*) and Michael Singer's *Cloud Hands Ritual Series 1982–83* (1982–1983), an intricately

21

constructed abstraction dealing with the transitory character of nature. Like Singer, the English sculptor Richard Long employs natural forms, and much of his work is made for outdoor sites. Among pieces Long has created for specific indoor installations is the romantic circle of red Vermont slate, *Minneapolis Circle*, completed and acquired in 1982. Another European work recently added to the collection is Anselm Kiefer's 1985–1987 *Die Ordnung der Engel (The Hierarchy of Angels)*, a powerful mixed-media painting with lead elements.

In an effort to enrich the Walker's holdings in what are now perceived as "historic" movements in American art, the museum during the 1980s acquired early works by pioneer artists associated with Minimalism. The theoretical direction Robert Smithson's art would take is already apparent in his 1968 *Leaning Strata*, a painted white-metal construction. Other works of this type recently acquired include metal sculptures by Peter Forakis and David Novros. Also working in this tradition is Robert Mangold, who is represented by *Pink X within X*, a 1980 shaped canvas purchased in 1983.

Making sculptures that are utilitarian rather than purely aesthetic objects is a concern of many artists today, and none more so than the late Scott Burton, whose stone and marble chairs, benches, and tables perfectly express this new direction. Two 1983–1984 angular Burton armchairs in polished granite are installed on the Walker's roof terrace, where they are intended for visitors' use. A somewhat more symbolic approach to public art characterizes several works by Siah Armajani, whose projects include plazas, classrooms, and designs for bridges but also individualistic objects constructed of wood, such as *Dictionary for Building: The Garden Gate* (1982–1983) and a tall, boxlike 1984–1985 mirrored construction *Closet under Dormer*, which suggests a doorway.

In its quest for works by established modernist masters, the museum found an exceptional three-dimensional painted piece by Richard Artschwager—his 1984 *Low Overhead*, which, like most of his works, defies ready classification. Here he combines a wood-grained plastic laminate with painted wood grain to create an enigmatic doorway to nowhere. Roy Lichtenstein's 1973 painting *Artist's Studio No. 1 (Look Mickey)*, a virtual compendium of the artist's motifs since the 1960s, was one of the Walker's major acquisitions of the 1980s. Frank Stella's third major work in the collection is the 1986 *Loomings 3X*, a monumentally scaled three-dimensional painting whose pinstriped silver surfaces recall his early *Sketch Les Indes Galantes* of 1962. The documentation of various phases of an artist's development has become a distinctive factor in the Walker's approach to building its collection. In addition to groups of works by pioneer modernists such as Isamu Noguchi, Louise Nevelson, Mark Rothko, and Alexander Calder, the Walker has acquired a number of works over the past twenty years that show the development of many other artists, among them, Jennifer Bartlett, David Hockney, Donald Judd, Claes Oldenburg, Frank Stella, Robert Irwin, Sol LeWitt, Morris Louis, Roy Lichtenstein, Ellsworth Kelly, Siah Armajani, Tom Rose, and Susan Rothenberg.

Several recent events at the Walker have indelibly affected the scale and character of the collection. The first was the substantial addition to the museum in 1984 of the McKnight Print Study Room, designed by Edward Larrabee Barnes. This commodious two-level area for the care and study of the museum's collection of works on paper is adjacent to two new galleries. Coinciding with this construction was the acquisition of the Tyler Graphics Archive, a collection of some fourteen hundred images, including many one-of-a-kind prints from Kenneth Tyler, the founder of Tyler Graphics Ltd., one of the country's leading print workshops. Thanks to this acquisition, many important artists whose paintings and sculptures are in the Walker's collection are now also extensively represented by their graphic works. The Walker Art Center's agreement with Tyler Graphics provides that an example of each print issued by the Tyler workshop will be received by the museum for its Tyler Archive. Thus, a significant new collecting emphasis has evolved at the Walker. A two-volume publication devoted to the Tyler Archive, including scholarly essays and a catalogue raisonné, was published in 1987. The addition of these new physical facilities led to the Walker's first commission for a permanent work of art for its interior. As a transition from his 1971 building to the new spaces, Barnes designed a small lobby directly next to and a few steps below the Walker's main lobby. This new area, it was determined, would be free of displays, and its walls would be used for a mural-scale piece. In response to an invitation to create such an environmental work, Sol LeWitt produced a four-wall, frescolike ink painting, consisting of red and yellow circles and squares that function like great windows through which a brilliant blue sky is seen.

An even more recent construction project will further broaden the scope of collecting at the Walker Art Center: the establishment in September 1988 of the seven-and-one-half-acre Minneapolis Sculpture Garden directly to the north of the Walker-Guthrie Theater complex on land owned by the Minneapolis Park and Recreation Board. Designed by Edward Larrabee Barnes, the Garden, which represents a close collaboration between the Walker Art Center and the City of Minneapolis, contains a number of permanent features. Its exhibition spaces include four 100-foot-square tree-lined plazas, a 65-foot-high glass conservatory, a fountain sculpture, and a 320-foot-long steel pedestrian bridge that spans a broad state highway to connect the Garden to Loring Park and thus to downtown Minneapolis.

The Walker Art Center's agreement with the Park and Recreation Board ensures that the museum will purchase and own all works of art permanently installed in the Garden, whose maintenance and security will be the responsibility of the City of Minneapolis. The two large squares closest to the Walker are designated for temporary exhibitions; the other two are reserved for sculpture from the Walker's permanent collection. Several important works have already been acquired for the Garden through purchases and commissions, including large-scale steel sculptures by Richard Serra (*Five Plates, Two Poles*, 1971) and Mark di Suvero's *Arikidea* of 1977–1982, which serenely dominates a northern plaza. This sculpture is an especially welcome component of the Garden; from the apex of its eight-legged tepee structure is suspended a large flatbed swing that visitors are encouraged to ride. A major bronze sculpture, *Goddess with the Golden Thighs*, by the Abstract Expressionist master Reuben Nakian is a work of 1964–1965, newly cast for the Garden.

At the north end of the Garden is *Spoonbridge and Cherry*, a site-specific fountain by Claes Oldenburg and Coosje van Bruggen. Its form is that of a giant aluminum spoon whose bowl rests on an island in the middle of a 125-foot-wide amoeba-shaped pond that lends itself admirably to the sailing of toy boats. Another ambitious commissioned work is by Siah Armajani. His Irene Hixon Whitney

Bridge is composed of two giant arcs, one curving upward and the other downward, which overlap at the center of the structure. Access to the bridge on the Garden and Loring Park sides is via ramps that also serve as viewing platforms. Like the fountain-sculpture by Oldenburg and van Bruggen and di Suvero's giant swing, the bridge is a work the public can use as well as view. Permanently installed in the high central house of the Cowles Conservatory is *Standing Glass Fish*, a witty and imposing work by the Los Angeles architect Frank Gehry. This 22-foot-high glass-and-wood leviathan was made for a 1986 retrospective of Gehry's work organized by the Walker, with the intention of later installing it in Barnes's transparent building.

To emphasize the close relationship between the Walker Art Center and the Garden, and to welcome visitors to the museum, a tall brushstroke sculpture, *Salute to Painting*, by Roy Lichtenstein, was commissioned in 1985 for installation on the granite stairs along the museum's north side, opposite the Garden. *Salute to Painting* is the second permanently installed exterior work next to the building, Calder's *Spinner* being the first, now rising from a granite plaza on the museum's east side.

The development of its permanent collection remains a high priority for the Walker Art Center. While considerable progress has been made in filling important historical gaps, especially in post-World War II American painting, particular attention has been devoted to purchasing works by artists whose production exemplifies seminal new stylistic directions. The collection, through its chronological span and variety, lends itself admirably to many special installations, from small groups of works by one artist to presentations of major themes and styles of twentieth-century art. Among such themes might be the course of American realism, from the gritty early twentieth-century reportage of Sloan and Luks to Pop Art's ironic commentaries on contemporary consumer culture. The Walker can offer as well authoritative installations of several mid-twentieth-century movements; Assemblage, Minimalism, and Pop are particularly well represented. The extensiveness of the Walker's collection also provides a continual framework against which its temporary exhibitions can be considered. Installations from the permanent collection are often presented to expand upon a theme posited in a special exhibition. Thus in 1980, when *Picasso From the Musée Picasso* was on view, the Walker staff selected for an adjacent exhibition a wide variety of paintings and sculptures from the collection to illuminate the great master's enduring influence on successive generations of European and American artists. In American art, the effects of Cubism were apparent in paintings by such pioneer modernists as Charles Sheeler and Stuart Davis, as well as in sculptures by David Smith and Donald Judd. A mid-1980s loan show of drawings that explored the effects of Surrealist imagery on the formative stage of Abstract Expressionism was supplemented by an installation of sculpture from the Walker's collection that followed this same theme.

Developing the collection of a contemporary museum such as the Walker Art Center is at best a subjective process, dependent upon the availability of works and the predilections of the director and curatorial staff. Unlike institutions that collect works of venerable pedigree, those associated with today's artistic production must often make judgments on the basis of immediate responses to images and ideas. This, however, is far from a purely intuitive process, because no matter

Surrounded by giant palm trees, Frank Gehry's *Standing Glass Fish* (1986) is the focus of the central house of the Cowles Conservatory, Minneapolis Sculpture Garden.

how original a work of art under review may seem, it must also be considered historically in terms of the stylistic direction it represents. While we seem to have left the era of great sweeping artistic movements, Abstract Expressionism being the last of these classical phenomena, the collective memory, filled with information about virtually all styles of the twentieth century, remains extremely active and affects the work of many young artists today.

There is no shortage of youthful painters and sculptors experimenting with a broad spectrum of images and techniques. Painting, prematurely declared dead by some critics in the 1970s, has assumed fresh vitality as its new practitioners daub and slash away with neo-expressionistic gusto on the one hand, and rediscover the cool elegance of geometric abstraction on the other. Today sculpture has taken on a rich new personal quality as legions of young artists bend, twist, slice, and glue diverse materials to make forms that are antithetical in spirit to the purist orthodoxy that ruled previous decades. Making sense of this dizzying abundance is not easy; nor is determining which works are of consequence. Therein, however, lies the undeniable lure of shaping a contemporary collection.

The international art world has undergone convulsive changes since Thomas Barlow Walker wrote to his favorite New York City galleries asking them to ship a few crates of paintings to Minneapolis for his inspection. The Walker Art Gallery he established in 1927, transformed into the Walker Art Center in the late 1930s, has made radical changes in its physical plant, its programs, and its attitude toward collecting. The direction of the institution he founded has shifted from that of a nineteenth-century *Wunderkammer,* where all manner of objects ranging from painting to decorative arts were juxtaposed, to that of a museum fully committed to the art of its time.

In large measure, the Walker's seemingly inexorable impetus toward the collecting and exhibiting of contemporary art is attributable to the presence of its sister institution, The Minneapolis Institute of Arts, whose comprehensive collection deals admirably with the march of art history. Given its mandate to focus on the art of this century, the Walker's collection has become a lively index of ongoing artistic activity. Thanks to the support of its Board of Directors, the generosity of many individuals who share the museum's desire to build a collection that illuminates contemporary art's outstanding achievements, and the commitment of its staff to the work of today's artists, the Walker Art Center continues to pursue this goal.

Vine-covered arches are on permanent display as part of the Regis Gardens, designed by Barbara Stauffacher Solomon and Michael R. Van Valkenburgh in 1988 for the Cowles Conservatory.

Modern European Art

Edward F. Fry

The significant European collections of the Walker Art Center fall into six quite distinct groups: French Symbolism; Cubist pictorial ideas extended to sculpture and to non-French contexts; German Expressionism; the sculptural consequences of French Surrealism; Italian modernist classicism; and the diverse, but predominantly late Surrealist, crosscurrents of the School of Paris from 1950 to the recent past.

Late nineteenth-century Symbolism, of which the Walker possesses four important examples, has always eluded short, easily graspable definitions or explanations. The Symbolist world of the 1880s and 1890s included not only Gauguin and the young Nabis such as Bonnard and Paul Ranson but also the late Monet and the young Picasso. Yet unlike the empirically perturbed classical realism of the Impressionists or the radical anti-Cartesianism of Cézanne, Symbolism was a movement, an era, and a sensibility rather than a style or a specific mode of visual cognition. The Symbolist movement may be seen in retrospect as an attempt, ultimately unsuccessful, to fill the void left by the decline of Christianity in the wake of Enlightenment secularization. Christian absolutes and traditions had so controlled European consciousness from the fourth century onward that the secularized modern world sought post-Christian equivalents of the old metaphysical order. Late nineteenth-century French Symbolism was the fullest and most far-reaching attempt to compensate for the loss; most explicit were the iconographic curiosities of the period, which ranged from Maurice Denis and Puvis de Chavanne's disguised new versions of traditional Catholic symbolism to Ranson's efforts to invent new esoteric signs for a seemingly new set of beliefs. But the two most radical aspects of Symbolism were the artist's elevation of sensory and psychological experience of all kinds to the position formerly occupied by the intensity of religious emotion, and the ambition of the artist, as well as the need of the spectator, to confer upon art and the aesthetic experience an exalted and absolute role comparable to the certitude of traditional religious transcendence.

These post-Christian acts of substitution were doomed to fail at the tasks assigned to them, but in the years from Seurat's experiments with the indirect but programmatic expression of primal emotions in the early 1880s to Matisse's pre-1910 evocations of the harmonious pleasures of mankind reunited with Edenic nature, the Symbolist enterprise dominated European art in general and French art in particular. Odilon Redon's *The Sybil* (circa 1900; p. 550) epitomizes the convergence of the multiple strands in Symbolist art. A woman, whose features are those of Redon's 1882 portrait of his wife, in the Louvre, holds a bowl as if to lay it on an invisible altar. Absolutely immobile, frontal, and symmetrical, the figure is depicted in a setting enclosed with an arched upper border, as if the painting were a neo-Quattrocento religious icon. The moment chosen is static and ambiguous, although directed: the spectator is given the task of receiving and completing the figure's votive offering, thereby entering into complicity with the artist's nominally but surreptitiously neo-Christian fantasy.

Auguste Rodin's *Le baiser du fantôme à la jeune fille (Girl Kissing a Phantom)* (circa 1895; p. 551) attains Symbolist objectives of a different sort. If we bear in mind that the Walker's marble is a less faithful reflection of the artist's touch than of his ideas, we still have ample evidence both of its explicit iconographic content and of its implicit Symbolist orientation. Iconographically, the subject is a variation on the theme of Cupid and Psyche, as in Canova's Neoclassical sculpted version in the Louvre. But in Rodin's group, Psyche is replaced by a spectral figure, which shifts the manifest subject toward an ambiguous yet pessimistic conflation of sexual awakening and somnolent desire—the life force—with the fatal mortality of earthbound existence: the kiss of desire awakens woman to her eternal, procreative role, yet also reinforces our awareness of the finiteness of biological life. But this post-Christian, Bergsonian, and ultimately gloomy vision, which appears in the 1890s most vividly in the work of Munch and Hodler, is given a special twist in Rodin's art. A modeler in clay, Rodin endlessly formed with his hands small-scale images and figures such as these. He became through this working method a surrogate, life-creating god, creating mankind yet standing apart from its fate. Rodin was, in fact, the greatest example in nineteenth-century France of the artist as divinity: the contemplation and public reception of his works became an aestheticized substitute for religious experience.

The curious role of the classicist revival during the French Symbolist era was a minor issue in Rodin but assumed major proportions in the quarter century lasting from Puvis and Seurat to Denis, Matisse of the *Bonheur de vivre*, and the Ingres revival in the years just after 1905. This classicist presence emerged with full force in the work of Aristide Maillol at the beginning of the twentieth century, notably in his *Study for La Méditerranée* (circa 1905; p. 332). Maillol began as a painter and tapestry maker within the Symbolist milieu of the 1890s, but his Mediterranean upbringing was never far beneath the surface of his art. His first important works in sculpture, done before a trip to Greece in 1908, are probably his most significant achievements. At best Maillol attained a personal version of classicism in these years, which, as in the Walker torso, simultaneously recalls the classical yet also establishes a remoteness from it, particularly by confining the figure within arbitrary rectilinear spatial volumes—a common academic, rather than strictly classical, precept that Maillol intensified to an extreme degree. We become aware both of the classic itself and of its unbridgeable distance from us: *Study for La Méditerranée* is an elegiac version of classicism, widespread in French art during the first decade of the twentieth century. Yet there is more to Maillol's sculpture than the sheer evocation of a lost classical past. For in works such as *L'Action enchaînée (Action in chains)* (1906) the tensions to which he subjected his classicized figures engender in the viewer a powerful self-awareness of the human body, detached from any iconographic necessity—a primal, absolute experience, which, along with Maillol's often explicitly erotic imagery, fulfills the quintessential Symbolist goal of generating new absolutes of feeling comparable to those of a lost Christian faith. The Walker torso displays two further strategies: the partial figure, recalling unearthed statuary, and the summary modeling also evoke the loss of the classical—characteristics seen in Rodin, Bourdelle, and numerous other contemporaneous sculptors.

The Symbolist enterprise of late nineteenth- and early twentieth-century European art provides an invaluable frame of reference for a wide cross section of artists and works, including the young Picasso in Barcelona and Paris from 1898 through much of the Blue Period of 1902–1904. His 1905 *Le fou (The Jester)* (p. 549), however, is not overtly Symbolist in the nineteenth-century sense, but rather in Picasso's unique ability to compress a world of allusions and emotions into an indirect or oblique visual metaphor. Sir Roland Penrose, a close friend of the artist and a scrupulously reliable source, reports that Picasso conceived the work after an evening at the circus—probably the Cirque Médrano in Montmartre—with his close friend the poet Max Jacob.[1] Picasso began the sculpture as a portrait of Jacob, but the image gradually changed, notably with the addition of a jester's cap. This anecdotal basis detracts in no way from the sculpture's expressive power, particularly that of its sunken eye sockets, which recall Picasso's earlier obsession with blindness in his 1903 Barcelona works, where the themes of disease, poverty, and inner vision are intertwined. More immediately interesting is Picasso's fascination with circus entertainers and their marginal lives, a fascination that reveals not only his partial identification as a poor artist in 1904–1905 with harlequins, clowns, and acrobats, but also his awareness of the masks and roles an individual assumes. *Le fou* nevertheless marks the end of one period in the artist's life, shortly after which he started on the long and complex route to his invention of Cubism.

Raymond Duchamp-Villon's *Le grand cheval (The Large Horse)* (1914; p. 194), one of the most important works of so-called Cubist sculpture, also marks a crossroads of ideas and historical traditions in European art on the eve of World War I. The motif is a horse that has undergone a partial metamorphosis into a machine, resulting in the juxtaposition of hoof, dynamo, and the cams and drive shafts of a steam engine. This mixture of traditional and mechanical imagery appeared at the same time in the works of the sculptor's brothers, Marcel Duchamp and Jacques Villon, the Franco-Italian painter Severini, and as early as 1910 in those of the Italian

1. Roland Penrose, *Picasso: His Life and Work* (New York: Harper & Row, 1971), p. 119.

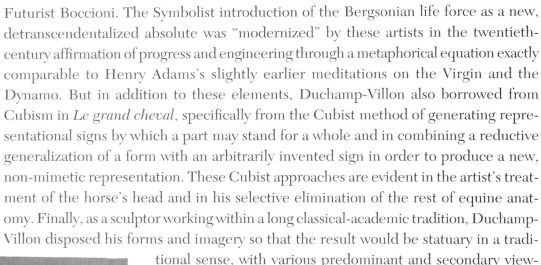

Futurist Boccioni. The Symbolist introduction of the Bergsonian life force as a new, detranscendentalized absolute was "modernized" by these artists in the twentieth-century affirmation of progress and engineering through a metaphorical equation exactly comparable to Henry Adams's slightly earlier meditations on the Virgin and the Dynamo. But in addition to these elements, Duchamp-Villon also borrowed from Cubism in *Le grand cheval*, specifically from the Cubist method of generating representational signs by which a part may stand for a whole and in combining a reductive generalization of a form with an arbitrarily invented sign in order to produce a new, non-mimetic representation. These Cubist approaches are evident in the artist's treatment of the horse's head and in his selective elimination of the rest of equine anatomy. Finally, as a sculptor working within a long classical-academic tradition, Duchamp-Villon disposed his forms and imagery so that the result would be statuary in a traditional sense, with various predominant and secondary viewpoints apparent when seen in the round.

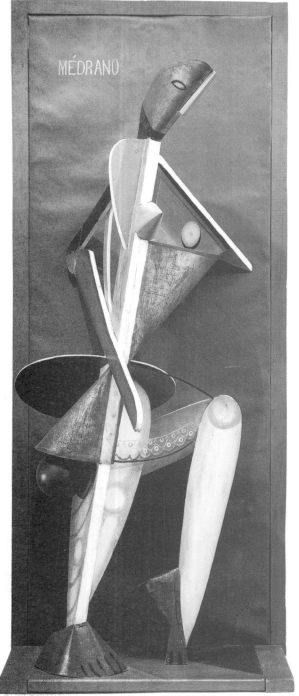

Alexander Archipenko
Médrano II 1913
painted tin, glass, wood,
oilcloth
50 (127) high
Collection Solomon R.
Guggenheim Museum,
New York

In contrast, Alexander Archipenko's *Turning Torso* (1921/1959; p. 531) is a mannered version of sub-academic realism, and at a far remove both intellectually and aesthetically from his own outstanding, early work such as *Struggle* (1914) or his Médrano constructions, which are comparable to Duchamp-Villon's *Le grand cheval* in their Cubist-derived, but ultimately non-Cubist, rationales. A similar dilemma, arising from mixed or conflicting impulses, underlies the sculpture Rudolf Belling produced in Germany during the 1920s, as in the Walker's *Kopf in Messing* (*Head in Brass*) (1925; p. 134). Belling, who began as an Expressionist, responded to Archipenko's pre-1914 Cubist-inspired sculpture and then, in the first half of the 1920s, to Bauhaus and Constructivist versions of Cubism. By the mid-1920s, however, Belling and many other French and German artists turned toward a new, highly stylized version of realism. The Walker's head, with its evocation of the mannered elegance of a fashion mannequin, is a prime example of this new realism of the brittle decade of the Weimar Republic, the crumbling underside of which was brilliantly depicted in the art of Dix, Grosz, and Beckmann, and in film by directors such as Fritz Lang. The sculpture of Georg Kolbe, however, as in the Walker's *Junge Frau* (*Young Woman*) (1926; p. 290) was relatively independent of this Weimar ethos and remained within the confines of a somewhat gothicized and elongated academic realism. The long and relatively stable career of Gerhard Marcks is similarly definable by the limits of a provincial, if often highly energized, version of French classicism, as in the Walker's *Mélusine III* (1949/1951; p. 342).

From about 1915 to the later 1920s, the influence of Parisian Cubism spread throughout Central and Eastern Europe. For artists such as Malevich and

Alexander Archipenko
Struggle 1914
painted plaster
23¾ (60.3) high
Collection Solomon R.
Guggenheim Museum,
New York

Mondrian, with strong, independent points of view and with roots in indigenous traditions, Cubism would serve as a creative catalyst for the transformation and restatement of those traditions. In Germany, Cubism played a similar role for several artists of the Blaue Reiter group in Munich, formed in the years immediately before World War I by Kandinsky, Marc, Klee, Jawlensky, and others. The Blaue Reiter group had no programmatic manifesto comparable to that of the Futurists, although its members shared a desire to liberate art from the world of external appearances in favor of inner states of mind, feeling, and spirit, and thereby to reestablish a transcendental unity with nature and the cosmos. Such aspirations represented a reaction against the alienation of individuals from each other and from nature in the industrial society of Wilhelmine Germany. Moreover, they signaled the reemergence of an older German romantic and pantheist tradition, which, focused by the Reformation, gave priority to the individual and to his direct access to the divine through nature. To further their ends, the Blaue Reiter artists drew heavily on sources ranging from folk and tribal arts to French Fauvism; Klee was strongly, if briefly, influenced by Cubism, both directly and through the intermediary of Robert Delaunay.

One of the most important works in the Walker collection is Franz Marc's monumental canvas *Die grossen blauen Pferde* (*The Large Blue Horses*) (1911; p. 340). It is inconceivable without Matisse's Fauvism, yet its animist pantheism places it at the center of Blaue Reiter attitudes. Its anti-naturalistic colors declare an independence from academic realism in favor of subjective empathy between inner emotional states and the external world. The horses, functioning as empathetic protagonists, offer the viewer entry into the world of animals unalienated from and at one with nature and, through that empathy, the experience of a metaphorical unity with nature. The artist underlines this intention by his careful use of rhythmic curves,

Henri Matisse
Blue Nude ("Souvenir of Biskra") 1907
oil on canvas
36¼ x 55¼
(92.1 x 140.3)
The Baltimore Museum of Art: The Cone Collection, formed by Dr. Claribel Cone and Miss Etta Cone of Baltimore, Maryland
BMA 1950.228

which not only join the horses to each other but also, by means of an almost musical echoing and repetition like that in Matisse's 1907 *Blue Nude*, unite them to the plants, trees, and background hills of the landscape.

Although he exhibited with the Blaue Reiter, Lyonel Feininger's art at first encounter seems to have little in common with that of Marc or other members of the Blaue Reiter circle. But Feininger also borrowed from contemporary French styles in order to reinterpret older German traditions. His personal reformulation of Delaunay and Parisian Cubism is evident in the Walker's

Barfüsserkirche II (Church of the Minorites II) (1926; p. 198). Light and the crystal-line spatial planes that begin as architectural structures, but also function autonomously, are the central elements of this painting. The small scale of figures in relation to architecture, the subdued, meditative quality of light, and Feininger's frequent references to Gothic style all contribute to the emotional expressiveness of the work but also indicate the cultural traditions that informed his art. Feininger reinterpreted the same transcendental impulses of the German Middle Ages that had nourished Caspar David Friedrich in the early nineteenth century, with the difference that Feininger's art is predominantly urban in motif and borrows from the formal vocabulary of French Cubism for its own profoundly anti-Cubist and anti-classical purposes.

These German appropriations of Fauve and especially of Cubist style for the restatement of indigenous traditions have their counterparts in later twentieth-century French art. The power of the Cubist paradigm in particular was so persuasive that even artists who had ostensibly rejected or outgrown their Cubist beginnings never fully escaped from its style, intentions, or both—the prime example being Picasso himself, even in his supposedly neoclassical and Surrealist phases. By contrast Braque, who contributed substantially to Picasso's invention of Cubism and participated briefly in its realization, remained only partially within the Cubist universe and in his later life was drawn back toward the normative traditions of French painterly representation. Fernand Léger, however, never fully understood Cubism, but he created by 1912–1913 a personal, somewhat literal and physical version of it to which he remained faithful throughout his life. In the 1941 *Plongeurs sur fond noir* (*Divers on a Black Background*)(p. 542) Léger used the outlined bodies of his bathers as if they were elements in a Synthetic Cubist composition of interlocking planes, to which he added the decorative effects of his color areas and their bleeding across and behind the figures in his theme.

More curious is the post-Cubist career of Amédée Ozenfant, whose well-known collaboration with the architect Le Corbusier culminated in the influential review *L'Esprit Nouveau* of the 1920s. Ozenfant was an early critic of Parisian Cubism, which he found too intuitive and wished to supplant with a highly geometric and ordered version he called Purism. While in exile in America during World War II, Ozenfant moved toward an almost Surrealist version of Purism, possibly as a result of the presence in New York of many Parisian Surrealist refugees. The unusual painting *The Sleeping Canyon* (1945–1946; p. 416) is an important example of his post-Purist style. Its evocation of a moonlit cityscape, filled with references to urban geometries but also with grotesque, thrusting organic forms, marks a rapprochement with the Surrealist dreamscape, a mode perfected by his fellow exiles Max Ernst and Yves Tanguy.

Jacques Lipchitz, more complex in thought and evolution than Léger and Ozenfant, and a far greater figure in the history of art, also began as a Cubist, translating the ideas of Picasso and Gris into sculptural equivalents. Lipchitz's volumetric Cubist statuary of 1915–1918 gradually evolved toward pictorial relief as the artist came to terms with the inner logic of Cubist representation. During the middle and later 1920s he turned from what he called the "golden cage" of Cubism, and by the 1930s he had become a new artist, openly acknowledging Rodin and the great Western sculptural tradition of symbolic and allegorical subjects. At the same

time he also attempted ever more ambitious statements in both scale and theme. In the context of European history during the 1930s, it is no surprise that Lipchitz's work began to focus on the crisis of human freedom and the survival of Western civilization.

This second phase of Lipchitz's art suffered from critical neglect during the 1960s and early 1970s, when contemporary art in America and Europe was concerned primarily with formal, stylistic, and phenomenological issues. But the later Lipchitz is destined to return to prominence, if only because the issues of stylistic modernism have been overshadowed by renewed threats to the Enlightenment traditions of freedom in thought and action. *Prometheus Strangling the Vulture II* (1944/1953; p. 314) is a sequel to a work of the same theme the artist made for the 1937 Paris World's Fair—at the time of the Spanish Civil War and also of Picasso's *Guernica*, which was exhibited at the same fair. But unlike Picasso, who translated his intensely personal *Minotauromachia* etching of 1935 into the political domain, Lipchitz addressed his age with a more direct political engagement, even while choosing the classical and allegorical guise of Prometheus as the symbol of man's urge for freedom and the tormenting vulture as the agent of totalitarian powers. In 1937—both in the world and in Lipchitz's monument—the outcome of that struggle was uncertain at best. But by 1944, when Lipchitz began the Walker bronze, the balance had tipped in favor of freedom and Prometheus was victorious. This work, with its mighty theme, would not be the masterpiece it is without Lipchitz's early involvement with Cubism. The compaction of dramatic masses, the summary yet evocative treatment of detail, and the perfect equivalencies of solid and void are, like Cubism itself, the result of a profound understanding and reinvention of the classical tradition within the conditions and demands of a post-Cubist modern world.

In comparison with Lipchitz, Marino Marini created sculpture that seems untouched by virtually every issue, social and cultural, of the twentieth century. His equestrian figures, such as the outstanding *Cavaliere (Horseman)* (circa 1949; p. 348) inhabit a cisalpine world in which Roman and even Etruscan antiquity is still alive, if moribund. Whereas Marini's point of reference, like so much Italian culture, is centered on antiquity, Giacomo Manzù's universe is that of a medieval Catholicism which remains as much a part of twentieth-century Italy and its burdens as does the classical heritage. *La grande chiave (The Large Key)* (1959; p. 544) makes a deliberate reference to the enormous, handwrought iron keys carried and used by church doorkeepers everywhere in provincial Italy to this day. But Manzù's reference is perhaps also to the seat of Catholic Christendom, the Church of St. Peter's, whose doors he was commissioned to sculpt in bronze. Among modern European artists, Manzù was, under Pope John XXIII, one of the few who was esteemed and accepted by the Vatican.

The last great European artistic movement was probably Surrealism, beginning in Paris in the 1920s and 1930s. Subsequent, post-1945 developments in European art, from Tachisme, Art Brut, and COBRA, to Group Zero and Neo-Expressionism, all originated primarily in Surrealist or proto-Surrealist movements. Surrealism itself was based on the attempt, by a wide variety of means, to liberate the human mind from the arbitrary limits of external social conditions and of internalized cultural restraints. This emancipatory and implicitly revolutionary set of goals never came anywhere near realization, but the tensions between ambitions and means generated whatever lasting interest the Surrealist movement still retains in the late twentieth century. The Dada and Dada-derived anarchism and sensationalism of the earliest phases of Surrealism soon revealed that bourgeois society was able to absorb any disruption, turning anticonventional actions and attitudes into succès de scandale and radical chic. André Breton and other leaders of the Surrealist movement realized by the mid-1920s that if direct, political revolutionary action was to be ruled out, the only feasible way of changing external social conditions was to change the thought and consciousness of society's individual members. This shift to the radical transformation of the subjective world permitted the flowering of Surrealism in literature and the visual arts. Surrealism thus became yet another milestone in the long modern tradition of bourgeois consciousness achieving self-awareness by subverting itself from within.

There are only a finite number of ways for the mind to achieve these goals at any time; and within the specific historical tradition of secularized French Cartesian culture, the possibilities crystallized around a strategy of the subversion of a priori rationality and of the institutionalization of social norms arising from that rationality. Thus the prime strategies of Surrealism became the shock of the accidental, the unexpected, and the incongruous; the subversion of structured consciousness through the exploration of the Freudian world of dreams, clinical insanity, and the libido; and the rediscovery of the primal dimensions underlying the rationalized human condition, be they biological, tribally primitive, animistic, or infantile. That the entire Surrealist enterprise was a willed undertaking reveals it as a characteristically self-conscious modern attempt to come to terms with the human mind. The furthest possible frontier for the mind thus still remained within the bounds of an extended if perturbed reason, which, if unable to free itself from itself, at least achieved partial emancipation by revealing its own characteristics within a given set of cultural and historical conditions for all to see, as if for the first time.

These various Surrealist strategies often appeared together in a single work. Thus Miró's *Tête et oiseau (Head and Bird)* (p. 354), though dating from 1967, assembles disparate elements into a bizarre object in a manner favored by Surrealists during the 1930s—by Miró himself as well as by Picasso, Magritte, Breton, Giacometti, Bellmer, and many others. In this example, Miró used both the juxtaposition of the unexpected and incongruous, and a reference to the primitive world of pre-Columbian civilization. He also drew on his own previous paintings: the whimsical placement of a bird atop the head and the elusive, personal version of Cubist representation are found in his paintings as early as 1923. *Femme debout (Standing Woman)* (1969; p. 356) also has precedents in Miró's early Surrealist paintings, particularly in the proportions of the female body, distorted and exaggerated in order to emphasize biological and sexual functions: the tiny head and arms are dwarfed by the enormous hollow womb-vagina that traverses the entire figure.

This sexual and biological metaphor is part of the Surrealist strategy of subverting rationality by an emphasis on the primal and the libidinal; it also marks the return, now in an intensified and concentrated mode, of the Bergsonian theme of life force that first emerged in nineteenth-century Symbolism. This biomorphism, in which forms mimic the processes of life and growth, appeared in Miró's paintings during the early 1920s, but Jean Arp's Dada reliefs of 1916–1918 in Zurich

Jean Arp
The Forest 1916
painted wood
12⅞ x 7¾ x 3
(32.7 x 19.7 x 7.6)
Collection National Gallery
of Art, Washington, D.C.
Andrew W. Mellon Fund,
1977

mark the true beginning of modern biomorphism. It was a metaphorical strategy that proved itself from the start to be especially well suited for sculpture, even as early as Brancusi's quasi-biomorphic ovoid volumes of 1912–1914. Arp became the master of biomorphic sculpture from the latter 1920s to the end of his life. His 1953 *Aquatique* (p. 116) is a late example, in which the overall character of the forms as well as the marble's extreme polished smoothness suggest, mimetically, the general qualities and motion of a fish, seal, or other waterborne creature, while the gently convex protuberance on the upper side is a more general biomorphic metaphor for life and growth.

Biomorphism reached its fullest, most monumental sculptural form not in Arp, however, but in the works of the English sculptors Barbara Hepworth, and above all, Henry Moore. By the early 1930s, both had responded to the new representational language of Surrealist-inflected Cubism, especially the Cubist equivalence of solid and void. Hepworth's 1952 *Figure: Churinga* (p. 240) shows her characteristic care in the choice and handling of materials and her sensitivity to the evocativeness of organic volumes and the expressive power of the concave depiction of solids. Moore's *Reclining Mother and Child* (1960–1961; p. 362) is a distinguished example of the artist's preference for horizontal figural compositions. But Moore's art, here as elsewhere, contains additional Surrealist elements. He often used, as a point of departure, old bones, pebbles, and other found objects, which suggested themes and images to him, and which, when enlarged and reworked, became the basis for monumental sculpture. This deliberate circumvention of cognitive conventions for representation appeared in Parisian Surrealism as early as the mid-1920s, both in the guise of found objects incorporated unchanged into works of art and through the visual free associations underlying Surrealist "exquisite corpse" collaborative drawings. More significant in Moore, however, is his long-standing practice of evoking the primal instincts of life itself through his frequent choice of the mother and child theme, and in his treatment of this theme through the juxtaposition of large and small biomorphic forms. This latter conceit appeared briefly in Arp's work in 1930–1931 and first emerged, probably independently, in Moore's sculpture during the later 1930s. Such primal evocations, which subvert all a priori logical and social structures, underwent a transformation when crossing the Channel to England. In their original French Surrealist context, they function in a critical, disruptive manner, whereas in Moore and Hepworth they become an affirmation of life itself and of that deep bond between man and nature that lies just below the surface of the Anglo-Saxon mind.

Alberto Giacometti, one of the greatest artists of the twentieth century and a preeminent figure in Surrealism, had two if not three careers in his relatively short life of sixty-five years. The first is represented by his work as a Surrealist sculptor, the second by his sculpture from the late 1930s to his death, and the third by his achievements both as a draftsman and a painter. Giacometti's works of the early

42

1930s, though still too little known, are among the landmarks of the Surrealist movement. His inventions of the tabletop tableau and of the space cage, combined in such masterpieces as the *The Palace at 4 a.m.*(1932–1933), exerted a long and enduring influence on sculptors in both Europe and America. The later Giacometti, renowned for his emaciated, solitary figural works of the 1940s, was nevertheless a direct outgrowth of the Surrealist period; the brilliant compositions of the early 1930s are but restated in his maturity. The tabletop tableaux became empty city squares traversed by isolated figures; while the early space cages, inhabited by grotesque or incomprehensible forms that contrast to their geometrical frameworks as the Freudian id does to the rational ego, similarly evolved into Giacometti's later treatment of the human image. The mature, isolated single figures, along with the many series of portraits of his relatives and friends—notably that of his brother Diego (circa 1954; p. 214)—take as their space cage the experiential space of everyday life, within which are depicted figural wraiths who seem to have no mass. There is thus a second, conceptual framework—that of the normative human figure—within the outer spatial context of the real world. Within this double space cage, now mentally internalized, Giacometti made figures by a process of modeling based at least as much on subtraction of mass as on the building up of representational volumes. The result is a vision of the human condition that has never been excelled in its fusion of exterior likeness and internal psychic presence.

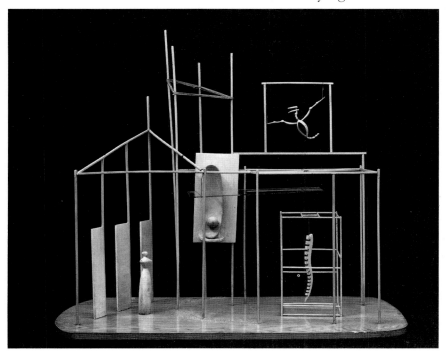

Alberto Giacometti
The Palace at 4 a.m.
1932–1933
wood, glass, wire, string
25 x 28¼ x 15¾
(63.5 x 71.8 x 40)
Collection The Museum of
Modern Art, New York
Purchase

What great art emerged after the end of World War II in Europe was almost without exception the work of established masters of the first four decades of the century—Picasso, Matisse, and Giacometti in France, or Moore in England. The only major new figures to appear were Francis Bacon in England, Joseph Beuys in Germany, and Jean Dubuffet in France, each of whom was indebted in one way or another to Dada and Surrealist traditions. In Paris during the late 1940s and the 1950s, however, many new talents flourished briefly, among the most promising of whom was the sculptor Germaine Richier. Her sculptures ranged from hallucinatory images of spectral figures and Surrealist-inspired predatory insects to fantasies based on children's games, as in the somewhat Giacomettiesque *Don Quixote of the Forest* (1950–1951; p. 550). But the great hope for the future of French painting in the early 1950s was Nicolas de Staël. His *Le ciel rouge (The Red Sky)* (1952; p. 174) is a distinguished and characteristic example of his art at its best: a rich, thickly impastoed surface, broad areas of color perfectly balanced and harmonized, and a subtle yet sensuous counterpoint between color, texture, and image, which here as elsewhere was preferably landscape. But de Staël's strengths were also his weaknesses, for it was precisely his mastery of the rich cuisine of the French painterly tradition, from

43

Chardin to Braque, combined with a treatment of the motif that descended from Vuillard, Bonnard, and Matisse, which suggested that he stood at the end of an entire era of French art. De Staël's work came to represent the civilized repetition of a seemingly completed culture and sensibility, which no amount of nostalgic aesthetics could ever reconstitute, rather than explorations in a postwar world filled with new and uncertain energies.

The career of Jean Dubuffet, who rose to stellar prominence in the world of French art in the 1960s, was fueled in part by those for whom he represented a sophisticated rebuttal to American Abstract Expressionism, in part by those within the gravitational pull of Parisian culture who saw in him the legitimate extension of French Surrealist hegemony over the international avant-garde. Among many members of the art worlds of Paris and New York, Dubuffet was what Pollock might have become if only he had been a cultivated European rather than an awkward and often embarrassingly provincial American. After the premature death of the neo-Dadaist Yves Klein (who was strongly influenced both by Pollock and the early Rauschenberg), Dubuffet thus became the touchstone for those Europhiles on both sides of the Atlantic who were unable to concede that the project of French twentieth-century aesthetic modernity had been completed and who were also unwilling to grant that a different yet comparable modernism had emerged in American art. What is beyond dispute, however, is that Dubuffet, who was an exact contemporary of Giacometti but who became a serious artist only during the early 1940s, was uniquely able to exploit the Surrealist strategy of the primal and the primitive during the post-1945 era in France, when all other aspects of the Surrealist heritage were exhausted. Almost from the beginning of his work, Dubuffet sought to primitivize himself, drawing upon the imagery of the naive, the insane, or of children, so as to negate both Cartesian classicism and its modern sequels. This negation included the use of raw materials, earth, and other "matière brute" as neo-Duchampian ready-mades intruding into the context of pictorial high art. In his Hourloupe series, beginning in the early 1960s, Dubuffet drew upon yet another vintage Surrealist strategy, automatic writing and drawing, and expanded it into a monumental style in both painting and sculpture. *Les péréquations (The Levelings)* (1971; p. 192) and *Tour (Tower)* (1975; p. 536) demonstrate the innate flexibility of such an anti-hierarchical and random set of graphic principles; yet ironically, this Hourloupe phase also represents a social and cultural assimilation of what began in Breton's circle of the 1920s as a radical, intellectually and artistically subversive practice.

One further new development in post-1945 European art was the COBRA movement, a loosely affiliated group of such artists as Asger Jorn from Copenhagen, Pierre Alechinsky from Brussels, and Karel Appel and Corneille from Amsterdam, the name of the group being an amalgam of the first letters of their native cities. At one time Dubuffet was also within the COBRA circle, but for the most part these artists were involved with a revival of Northern expressionist traditions in combination with imagery borrowed or translated from Fauvism, Matisse, and the later Picasso. The Belgian Alechinsky, born in 1927 and thus the youngest member of COBRA, has shown himself to be its most durable talent, despite his very evident debt to Dubuffet's sophisticated primitivism and mixing of words and images. In such works as *Referendum* (1963; p. 530) he satirizes the endless discussions that took place in France in 1962 on Charles de Gaulle's establishment of a presidency by universal suffrage.

From the vantage point of the early 1990s, Bacon, Dubuffet, and Beuys appear to be the only twentieth-century masters to have emerged in European art since 1945. To this short list one might possibly add, with suitable and in some cases stringent qualifications, Lucio Fontana in Italy, Yves Klein in France, the sculptor Anthony Caro and the painter Richard Hamilton in England, and Anselm Kiefer in Germany; however, in almost every instance this list reflects tendencies that *extend*, rather than transform or revivify, well-established strategies and innovations of early twentieth-century modernism. Beuys stands out as an important if partial exception, who has dramatized both the strengths and limitations of the Dada-Surrealist heritage by forcing himself to act out that heritage, and to test art against life, in the alien context of his own life in postwar Germany. In the overall landscape of recent European art, such efforts assume a possibly disproportionate stature, however; for the Europe of the last three decades, divided and still deeply traumatized by the enduring effects of World War II, has been hard pressed to reestablish a semblance of its former political and social institutions. This struggle has until recently provided too meager a base to support simultaneously both the recuperation of a past heritage and the creative extension and transformation of that heritage in the uncertain world of the late twentieth century. With the emergence, at the beginning of the 1990s, of the possibility of a unified Europe and the end of the cold war, the prospects have suddenly brightened for major European talents of the future once more to address the world at large from within a reconstituted political and cultural heritage.

From 1985–1987 Edward F. Fry was co-director and American commissioner of *Documenta 8*, Kassel, Germany. Since 1985 he has been the curator of the Morris Arboretum sculpture park of the University of Pennsylvania, Philadelphia. In 1987 Fry was a guest curator at the Tel Aviv Museum, Israel, and he was an advisor on *Picasso and Braque: Pioneering Cubism*, the 1989 exhibition at The Museum of Modern Art, New York. He is currently studying the art of the 1930s.

Modern American Art: The First Half-Century

William C. Agee

At the beginning of this century, American artists initiated a tradition of modernism that we have only recently come to understand. While once we viewed American art as crude, awkward, and unabashedly direct by contrast to European finish and polish, we now see that these qualities are, in part, precisely those that endow American art with its own special character and strengths. And, rather than exist as secondary products of an insular culture, the best American art was an integral part of the complex, hybrid internationalism of modern art. Still, we are far from having discovered just who the truly good American artists were; nor have we yet completely defined the nature and depth of their distinctive accomplishments. The Walker's collection, while not encyclopedic, gives us a clear sense of some of the directions taken by American art from 1900 to 1955. This essay, then, is not an inclusive history of the period; rather, it attempts to define these directions and suggest some of the themes sounded by American artists during these years—themes that often continue to inflect our art and life.

Historians have tended to characterize American art as virtually bereft of real vitality as the country entered the new century. This is something of an exaggeration, for many of the true giants of American art were working vigorously, and some were even at the height of their powers. Certainly, Winslow Homer and Thomas Eakins were artists whose accomplishments can be ranked on a worldwide scale. Although grounded in the nineteenth century, their work was not completely without relevance for the twentieth century. Homer's art of the early 1900s, for example, corresponds to contemporaneous expressionism, and the internal rhythms of Albert Pinkham Ryder's art echo throughout the painting of Marsden Hartley and,

Stuart Davis
Colonial Cubism 1954
(detail, see p. 170)

47

later, in the linear webs of Jackson Pollock. William Merritt Chase's slashing brush-work influenced an entire generation in the handling of paint. With one exception, however, these artists represented the culmination and last formulation of an older tradition that could not sustain the aspirations of a younger generation. The exception was Eakins, whose unflinching examination of the world around him struck a responsive chord in artists from Robert Henri to Edward Hopper.

Eakins lived and worked in Philadelphia, the city to which we can trace the birth of modernism in America. There, in the 1890s, a group of independent artists, including William Glackens, Everett Shinn, and George Luks, formed around Robert Henri and John Sloan. Inspired by Eakins, Henri championed a native American art, rather than the sentimental romanticism that characterized much of the art popular in America at the time. These men all started as artist-journalists for the Philadelphia newspapers, a livelihood that honed their instincts for the vitality of the modern city. By 1900 they had all moved to New York City, signaling the subsequent shift of the country's art center from Philadelphia. Henri established himself as an influential teacher—indeed, his famous book *The Art Spirit*, which urged artists to capture the immediacy of life around them, still is read by today's art students.

In 1908 the group exhibited together as The Eight. The press termed their daring contemporary subject matter "Ash Can" realism. Their styles, however—amalgams of Manet and early Impressionism, as well as Hals, Velázquez, and Goya—were far from revolutionary. Morever, as the Ash Can works in the Walker collection demonstrate, no single style or subject matter united the group. Glackens's early *Fourth of July* (1896; p. 537), with its highly charged linear movement encompassing the multiplicity of street activity, recalls his training as an artist-reporter. Later, in New York, Glackens adopted a softer, Impressionist style to portray more bucolic images of American life, as in *The Swing* (1910; p. 537). Indeed, the painters of The Eight, for all their supposed realism, often perpetrated the very sentimentality of popular painting they believed they were opposing. John Sloan's *South Beach Bathers* (1907–1908; p. 478) captures the myriad pleasures of the beach with a high-keyed palette and richly painted surfaces. Far different in mood and color, though also richly painted, is George Luks's *Breaker Boy of Shenandoah, Pa.* (1921; p. 328). Luks's deep, luminous blacks recall Goya, and he uses them to present a penetrating depiction of a young coal miner, seemingly just emerged from the depths of the earth. The only pictorial relief to the stark reality of the portrait is provided by the glowing spots of color from the boy's cigarette and helmet light. A second generation of Ash Can realists, most notable among them Reginald Marsh, was influenced by the teaching of Kenneth Hayes Miller at the Art Students League during the 1920s. In the Walker's *Girl Walking* (1948; p. 545) Marsh adapts a style dependent on Rubens and Delacroix for his own robust view of the city scene.

The continuing fascination with the city's tempo and rhythm, its life and its artifacts, has extended deep into American art in diverse ways. In the fall of 1909, for example, Stuart Davis, then only seventeen years old, enrolled in Henri's class in New York. Davis learned to capture the pulse of the city, first in a realist vein, then by the mid-1920s in an increasingly abstract manner. His brilliant *Colonial Cubism* (1954; p. 170) embodies the essence of the urban tempo and represents a continuing link with Henri and Sloan, an introduction and conclusion to this chapter in American art. At the same time, Davis represents a younger generation, which, though often building on the teaching of Henri and Sloan, began to absorb more radical art. The Armory Show of 1913 has been frequently identified as the birth of modern art in this country. However, while the exposure to van Gogh, Cézanne, Matisse, Picasso, and Duchamp spurred on American artists, its most evident influence was on public awareness of modern art. In fact, the first American modernists had been educating themselves in the new art, primarily in Paris, since 1904. By that year, Alfred Maurer (see his circa 1927 *Self-Portrait with Hat*; p. 352) had learned of Picasso and Matisse through the collections of Gertrude and Leo Stein, and of Sarah and Michael Stein, whose weekly salons were crucial forums for American artists visiting Paris. Patrick Henry Bruce was also in Paris by 1904, to be followed in rapid succession by Max Weber and virtually every major artist of early American modernism. In addition to the Steins, Walter Pach, an American artist and critic living in Paris, and Edward Steichen, the painter and photographer, were well-informed contacts for the young Americans abroad. Direct contact with Matisse was afforded through his school, which opened in January 1908, and his art and teachings quickly exerted a strong influence on American art.

In this country prior to 1913, Alfred Stieglitz provided fundamental spiritual, aesthetic, and financial support to the growth of modernism by holding major exhibitions of the work of Cézanne, Matisse, and Picasso, as well as by showing the work of the young American modernists at his 291 gallery. Although modernism in the United States is unthinkable without Stieglitz, after 1914 the salon hosted by Mabel Dodge and the circle around Walter and Louise Arensberg also became centers for American vanguard art.

Forging individual styles from Cézanne, Fauvism, Cubism, Orphism, and Futurism, our first modernists often sang the praises of the American urban landscape. Unlike The Eight, who preferred intimate glimpses of human activity in the city, they gravitated to the forces embodied by the icons of the twentieth century, the bridges and skyscrapers that were radically altering New York. By 1912 John Marin's loosely brushed watercolors showed the influence of Cubism and even Futurism in their rectilinear grids of tall buildings merging with bustling crowds in the street. After 1920 Marin's urban interpretations, such as the 1936 *New York, Downtown No. 7* (p. 544), were defined by an internal frame and broader, more distinct planes, but the fusion of buildings with the movement of the street remained a lifelong fascination. The directness of watercolor gives it a uniquely American stamp, and Marin was one in a line of great American watercolorists dating back to the nineteenth century. Yet it was Cézanne's watercolors that gave Marin his immediate impetus, one more example of how distinctly American elements combined with European styles to give American modernism its own flavor, while establishing it as an integral part of international art.

From its very beginnings to the present day, American art has been immeasurably enriched by the influx of artist-immigrants. Chief among the modernists was Joseph Stella, whose odes to the glories of the Brooklyn Bridge, such as *American Landscape* (1929; p. 502), are among the most memorable images in American art. In his virtually seamless surface of urban structures, the bridge and the skyscrapers appear gigantic and elongated, ascending into a limitless space that bespeaks a boundless optimism in the future of America and the modern city.

The city also afforded quieter sources of visual stimulation for the modern artist. Charles Demuth, another of America's great watercolorists, frequently painted vaudeville performers in the café-concert-cabaret tradition established by Manet, Degas, Seurat, and Toulouse-Lautrec. *Two Acrobats* (1918; p. 172) fuses a remarkably delicate touch with an intricacy of graphic design rarely equaled.

The natural landscape, too, provided a major theme for the first American modernists. The greater proportion of Marin's work after he discovered Maine in 1914 was landscape, especially the seascape off the rugged coast. In the Walker's 1932 *Rocks, Sea and Boat, Small Point, Maine* (p. 346), Marin combines a natural serenity with an unsettling sense of the potent forces of nature, capable of momentarily unleashing a terrible fury. The resultant pictorial tension underlies the success of his art, whether in watercolor or oil.

Marsden Hartley, perhaps the most gifted and accomplished American artist of the first modernist generation, demonstrated an early and ongoing affinity with the natural landscape. Hartley returned to the mountains of his native Maine as the source for many of his most powerful paintings. His *Storm Clouds,*

Marsden Hartley
Portrait of a German Officer
1914
oil on canvas
68¼ x 41⅜
(173.4 x 105.1)
Collection The Metropolitan
Museum of Art, New York
The Alfred Stieglitz
Collection, 1949

Maine (1906–1907; p. 230) shows his nascent grasp of modernist principles, as he allows the paint texture to diverge from the nature of the object depicted, thus imbuing the picture with a painterly crust and abstract patterning that have their own inner expressiveness. Here, as later, the clouds and sky are as strongly painted as the mountain itself, with the same gravity and weight. Hartley was nurtured by Stieglitz and the art of Cézanne, Matisse, and Picasso that he saw at 291. In 1912 he traveled to Paris, and by late that year he had done his first abstract paintings. The personal Cubist vocabulary Hartley developed marks the great German Officer series of 1913–1914 as among the best American pictures of the time, as well as original contributions to international art.

A lonely and restless soul, Hartley frequently traveled back and forth between America and Europe. By 1916 he had returned to the United States and begun a series of abstractions, including the Walker's *Movement No. 9* (1916; p. 232). These paintings consist of fewer, broader, and more tightly woven shapes, with a darker palette than that in the earlier paintings. Here Hartley is at the very forefront of international vanguard art, part of the first move toward a more stable and clearly structured type of Cubism. It is part of a classicizing drive that would be made famous by Léger and Le Corbusier after 1918 but had its first manifestations in 1916.

Three American artists who remained in Europe for more extended periods made significant contributions to modernism. Morgan Russell, Stanton Macdonald-Wright, and Patrick Henry Bruce had all settled in Paris by 1908 and become active and well-known members of the international avant-garde. Russell and Macdonald-Wright banded together in 1913 as the Synchromists, committed to an abstract art based on brilliant spectral color interacting according to the laws of color theory developed in the nineteenth century. Although not a Synchromist, Bruce used the same color principles to create a very different kind of abstract painting. Twenty-five years ago, historians assumed these artists were merely followers of Robert and Sonia Delaunay and Frantisek Kupka. We now know that the Americans had been independently investigating the properties of light and color since 1907 in a parallel yet distinct endeavor.

Russell was a pioneer of abstract art. In a note of 7 July 1912 he urged himself to "forget the objects forming the subject: make little spectrums of color and sharp encounters between them . . . and let the form result."[1] His *Synchromy Number 4 (1914) to Form* (1914; p. 552) is possibly based on the formal rhythms of Michelangelo's *The Dying Slave*, interpreted by contrasting patterns of spectral color. Figures derived from Renaissance painting and sculpture were also the basis for Macdonald-Wright's paintings, as seen in *Synchromy in Green and Orange* (1916; p. 330), done after he had returned to the United States. His art, however, was always more diffused and softer than Russell's.

Michelangelo
The Dying Slave
1513–1516
marble
90 (228.6) high
Collection Musée du
Louvre, Paris

After World War I both American and European artists pulled back from the pursuit of color- or Cubist-based abstractions, which were viewed as too hermetic, no longer appropriate for the new realities of a changing world. In American art this is often perceived as a failure of modernism, as a "retreat" or a loss of confidence. In fact, despite the isolationist politics of the time, modern American art during the 1920s developed in new ways that paralleled developments in world art. The best of the early generation—Hartley, Marin, Bruce, Dove, and Demuth, among them—continued to produce art of the first order throughout the 1920s and 1930s, often reaching the very height of their powers during those decades. Moreover, new forums for contemporary art appeared: in 1917 the Society of Independent Artists held its first exhibition; in 1920 the galleries of the Société Anonyme, founded by Katherine Dreier, Marcel Duchamp, and Man Ray, opened as the first museum of modern art. By the end of the decade, The Museum of Modern Art and A.E. Gallatin's Gallery of Living Art had opened in New York, followed shortly by the Whitney Museum of American Art.

Hartley himself produced a large and powerful body of art after 1920 that is as compelling as his earlier work. His *Still Life* (1920; p. 539) explored the possibilities of 1908–1909 Cubism and Matisse's high-keyed color and provided the pictorial grounding from which he evolved his later, personal expressionism, a modernism of another order. In the late 1920s, Hartley reached back further into modernist history by renewing his contact with Cézanne, as if to reaffirm his early commitment to the animating sources of modernism. In a series of landscapes of 1926–1930, including those done in Maine in

1. Morgan Russell, unpublished papers; collection Montclair Art Museum, Montclair, New Jersey, gift of Henry Reed.

Paul Cézanne
Mont Sainte-Victoire
1896–1898
oil on canvas
30¾ x 39 (78 x 99)
Collection Hermitage
Museum, Leningrad

Marsden Hartley
*Beaver Lake, Lost River
Region* 1930
(see p. 539)

1930, Hartley openly appropriated Cézanne's facture, including his bleeding planes and open contours. They may at first strike us as literal derivations and, to be sure, they are an open act of homage. At the same time, however, they possess a heavier, broader touch, a more condensed image than may be found in Cézanne, as well as a virtuosity in color and light effects that is Hartley's alone. The color in some is a florid combination of reds, pinks, yellows, and purples; in the Walker's painting of 1930, *Beaver Lake, Lost River Region*, (also p. 539) Hartley goes to the opposite end of the spectrum, using only cool greens and grays, with the surface texture permeated by countless inflections of silver light.

In the 1920s a younger generation of artists continued the American fascination with the city and the machine. But, unlike Joseph Stella, they largely rejected the painterly, multiple planes of prewar Cubism. Instead, they adapted a hard-edged, crisp linearity, in dispositions ranging from Cubist realism to full-blown realism, a style now known collectively as Precisionism. The sources of Precisionism can be traced to Morton Livingston Schamberg's distilled machine paintings of 1916 and Demuth's linear Cubist watercolors of 1917. Charles Sheeler was the artist responsible for the flowering of Precisionism—indeed, it has been argued, he was the only true Precisionist. From his 1915 photographs of Bucks County barns, Sheeler distilled the unadorned planar shapes that informed his drawings of 1917 and paintings of 1920, the first truly Precisionist works. Like many artists linked with Precisionism, Sheeler embraced both rural and urban architecture, the old and the new, the simple clarity of Shaker design and the complexity of modern industry. Above all, his art celebrates America.

After 1929, encouraged by the Neue Sächlichkeit (New Objectivity) movement in Germany, Sheeler largely discarded Cubist planes for a finely wrought veristic style. A decade later, however, he began to reintroduce the planar structures and intersections indebted to Cubism, as found in *Buildings at Lebanon* (1949; p. 468) and *Midwest* (1954; p. 470). These late examples demonstrate just how pervasive the Precisionist strain was in American painting. Because of its crisp detailing, Precisionist painting frequently causes objects to appear far lighter and less massive than in fact they are. One could argue that this effect extends through much of American art, from the sharp delineations in the portraits of John Singleton Copley, to the fluorescent colors and tensile materials of Donald Judd's Minimalist structures.

An almost palpable stillness, suggesting a moment frozen in time, often permeates art linked with Precisionism. George Ault's *Sullivan Street, Abstraction* (1924; p. 120) is shrouded in an eerie light and a mysterious quietude. (Nocturnal scenes appeared with increasing frequency in cityscapes of the time.) As in the Joseph Stella night scene, we are confronted with a vast space, here created by

Morton Livingston Schamberg
Telephone 1916
oil on canvas
24 x 20 (61 x 51)
Collection Columbus
Museum of Art, Ohio
Gift of Ferdinand Howald

the precipitously receding street and the vertical canyon soaring dramatically between the murky buildings. These areas of space and shadow are rendered with the same density as the buildings themselves. The architecture, unlike that found in Sheeler's work, does not describe a specific site; it is generalized and devoid of realist details. The mood and setting suggest that not all Precisionist-related art was an unqualified celebration of the city; uncertainty and a sense of the dehumanizing effects of urban life are readily apparent.

In Louis Lozowick's *New York* (1925–1926; p. 326), as in Stella's conception of the Brooklyn Bridge, we are suspended high in space, viewing a structure set against looming skyscrapers. Lozowick, however, adds a distinctly Futurist element in the multiple patterns of the tracks of the elevated train that hurtles through the city. The geometry of the buildings also relates Lozowick's art to Russian Constructivism, a movement with which he was familiar after exhibiting in Berlin in 1920 and then in 1922 after visiting his native Russia. That Lozowick's surfaces, such as those of the bridge, are sometimes relatively painterly in handling indicates that Precisionism was subject to multiple stylistic as well as thematic mutations. Certainly it was far from being a homogeneous movement, or even a movement at all in the sense we usually construe that term. Rather, we can most usefully consider Precisionism as part of the worldwide search for a more stable, classicizing art, a drive born from the chaos of World War I.

During the 1920s Georgia O'Keeffe moved freely between organic abstraction and the planar structuring and crisp detailing associated with Precisionism. Her painting also alternated dramatic views of the city with quiet rural scenes, often of barns. *Lake George Barns* (1926; p. 402) clearly recalls Sheeler's motifs and their directly frontal disposition. However, distinct evidence of O'Keeffe's hand appears in the brushed surfaces and atmospheric effects, so unlike Sheeler's, that describe the background.

American sculpture did not fare nearly so well as painting in the early years of this century. It long remained tied to a commemorative function, celebrating great events, civic virtues, and public heroes by means of academic styles that lingered long into the modern age. Thus, sculpture was unable to establish aesthetic autonomy until well after painting had gained the freedom to explore new and independent avenues.[2] The Armory Show had virtually no effect on American sculpture, and there were no other catalysts or centers that nourished alternate modes of a more adventurous nature.

The only sculptor to achieve major stature was Gaston Lachaise, who must be considered this country's most important sculptor until his early death in 1935. Lachaise immigrated to the United States in 1906 and served as an assistant to Paul Manship before developing his singularly powerful style. He

---

2. This history has been well chronicled by Daniel Robbins, "Statues to Sculpture: From the Nineties to the Thirties," in Whitney Museum of American Art, New York, *Two Hundred Years of American Sculpture*, exh. cat., 1976, pp. 112–159.

obsessively directed his vision to an idealized, even exaggerated, conception of the female body, but his portraits too exude an earthy sensuality and depth of feeling (*Head*, circa 1928; p. 294). Lachaise far surpassed Manship, whose allegorical and mythological themes were articulated by streamlined forms distilled from sources in Archaic Greek sculpture (*Europa and the Bull*, 1924, p. 544). The "moderne" style employed by Manship became enormously popular and was used extensively as architectural ornament during the 1920s and 1930s. Elie Nadelman's *Figure* (circa 1925; p. 374) also apparently makes classicizing references, although he departed from these canons by condensing the body into a series of elongated and flattening curves. Nevertheless, even such indirect references to classical art demonstrate once more just how hard it was for sculpture to distance itself from its old roots.

It remained for the younger generation that first appeared in the 1930s—David Smith, Alexander Calder, Isamu Noguchi, and Ibram Lassaw among them—to assert for sculpture a new direction, a new freedom in technique and subject that had long since been claimed by painting.

No period in American art is more complex than the years 1929 to 1941. Nor has any period been subject to greater misunderstanding or more intensely emotional interpretation. Only recently have we begun to sort out the myriad currents that constitute American art of this time. The turbulent forces of the 1930s—the Great Depression, the rise of Fascism, radical politics, the approaching war—so clouded our perception of the period that it was all too easy to assume that art of the 1930s was exclusively dominated by regionalism, American scene, or social protest painting. To be sure, numerous artists were involved with creating an art reflecting the social and political issues of the time. But their responses were far more varied than was formerly supposed, as the contrast between Ben Shahn's *Italian Landscape* (1943–1944; p. 553) and Jack Levine's *The Neighborhood Physician* (1939; p. 298) readily demonstrates: both were socially oriented artists but of very different aesthetic persuasions.

In one sense, the American scene painters should be seen as another, albeit radical, manifestation of a generation reacting against the private world of Cubist-based, abstract art of the World War I period. These artists sought to reintegrate art more closely with life in terms that would appeal to the public at large, going so far as to renounce modernism altogether. Thomas Hart Benton's art at its best has a distinct rhythmic power, but many other artists trapped in the merely topical, were unable to transcend the limits of a specific time and place. Far more successful and far more meaningful to us today were those artists whose work was drawn from the American scene but who were not limited by locale. Rather, they captured something deeper about the American experience. Charles Burchfield used loosely brushed but controlled watercolors to depict the profound quietude of nature and the barren solitude of rural or small-town architecture. With the limited range of grays and blacks in *Blackbirds in the Snow* (1941–1945; p. 533) we can virtually feel the icy chill of a winter day, what it is like to live in rural America. Yasuo Kuniyoshi, working in the spirit of his first teacher, Robert Henri, conveys another facet of American life: his isolated women, stiffly arranged in anatomically improbable poses, are situated in indeterminate locations, seemingly overcome by the ennui of modern urban life as in his *Lay Figure* (1938; p. 542).

Without question, the figurative artist who most tellingly captured essential truths about the American experience and, indeed, the human condition, was Edward Hopper. Trained by Henri and Miller, and influenced by the honesty of style and approach of Eakins, Hopper portrayed the isolation, detachment, and loneliness felt by ordinary people in everyday settings both in the city and country. In the condensed, powerful *Office at Night* (1940; p. 252), the two figures are physically close but psychologically and emotionally distant, even estranged, despite the obvious sexual overtones. The painting may be taken as a metaphor of individual alienation in the modern city. And Hopper's meticulously constructed composition imbues the painting with its poetry and drama. In his compelling and haunting images, Hopper touched a chord that still rings true today. He shows us the American dream gone sour, a recurring theme in recent figurative art.

Milton Avery, whose art began to mature after 1930, found another kind of poetry, the lyrical poetry of chromatic fluency and harmony. Although he most often painted landscapes and the figure, either isolated or in groups, he was at a far distance from the American scene painters. Rather, he sought the quiet, intimate side of the personal life of family and friends around him. He rendered these scenes through carefully adjusted areas of color indebted to Matisse, and an expressive contouring he learned from Picasso. Avery showed a younger generation of Americans how to incorporate the lessons of Matisse's later, broader decorative style to their own ends, and he was an important catalyst for the color conceptions of Mark Rothko and Adolph Gottlieb. In *Seated Blonde* (1946; p. 122) Avery's choice of hues—yellow, orange-red, and magenta—played against the white of the figure and the black frame of the chair is luxurious, daring, and startling. Even more remarkable is how he varies the touch, texture, and weight of each hue and area, thus establishing shifting balances throughout the chromatic field.

At the opposite pole from 1930s realism is the work of abstract artists who believed that their art had a revolutionary mission that could be the agent of profound social change. Thus, non-objective painting—based on Russian Constructivism, Dutch De Stijl, and the Bauhaus—established itself as a strong current in our art. Important examples of non-objective painting could be seen at A.E. Gallatin's Gallery of Living Art, including a Mondrian that entered the collection in 1933; at The Museum of Modern Art, especially during its great exhibition *Cubism and Abstract Art*, held in 1936; and then at the Solomon R. Guggenheim Museum, which opened in 1939 as The Museum of Non-Objective Art. Josef Albers, who came to the United States in 1933 after the Nazis closed the Bauhaus, was the first major proponent of non-objective art to teach here. He was widely influential in spreading the principles of an art based on openness, clarity, and strict economy of means. Later, in 1937, Moholy-Nagy founded the New Bauhaus in Chicago, an institution that had an enormous impact on art and design in this country. The American Abstract Artists, founded in 1936, provided a forum, through their annual exhibitions, for artists working in a geometric vein.

With the outbreak of war and Mondrian's move to New York in 1940, the international center for non-objective and geometric art shifted to New York. Fritz Glarner was particularly affected by Mondrian's *Victory Boogie Woogie*, done in New York. In 1944 Glarner made his first *Relational Painting: Tondo*. From

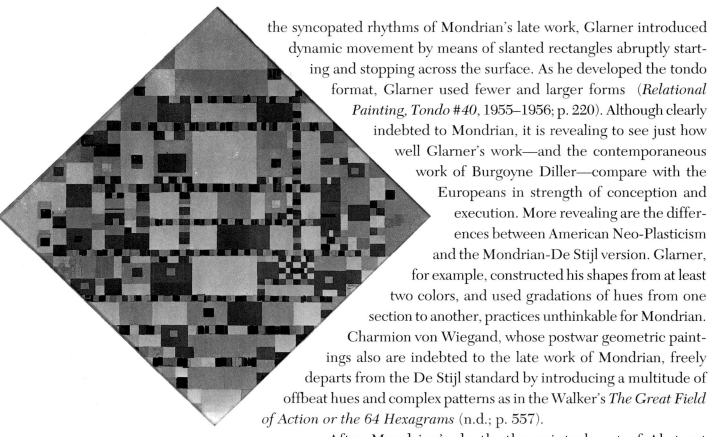

Piet Mondrian
Victory Boogie Woogie
1942–1944
oil, colored paper, colored
tape on canvas
50 x 50 (127 x 127)
Collection Mr. and Mrs.
S.I. Newhouse, Jr.

the syncopated rhythms of Mondrian's late work, Glarner introduced dynamic movement by means of slanted rectangles abruptly starting and stopping across the surface. As he developed the tondo format, Glarner used fewer and larger forms (*Relational Painting, Tondo #40,* 1955–1956; p. 220). Although clearly indebted to Mondrian, it is revealing to see just how well Glarner's work—and the contemporaneous work of Burgoyne Diller—compare with the Europeans in strength of conception and execution. More revealing are the differences between American Neo-Plasticism and the Mondrian-De Stijl version. Glarner, for example, constructed his shapes from at least two colors, and used gradations of hues from one section to another, practices unthinkable for Mondrian. Charmion von Wiegand, whose postwar geometric paintings also are indebted to the late work of Mondrian, freely departs from the De Stijl standard by introducing a multitude of offbeat hues and complex patterns as in the Walker's *The Great Field of Action* or the *64 Hexagrams* (n.d.; p. 557).

After Mondrian's death, the painterly art of Abstract Expressionism, first nurtured in the 1930s, was increasingly in the ascendancy. However, geometric and non-objective art remained a strong current in American art after 1945. In fact, it formed an unbroken tradition that only became apparent with the emergence of hard-edged painting in the 1960s.

Ralston Crawford was an important figure in sustaining that tradition. By 1942 he had largely purged his art of its Precisionist qualities of illusionist modeling and increasingly emphasized the flatly patterned shapes that he saw as constituting the world around him. As his art grew more and more abstract, he often reordered and recombined the shapes and colors of disparate places and events. Yet no matter how abstract his post-1945 art may appear, Crawford always based his work on something seen, something known or remembered. The structure of his art was never purely invented, although his color took on a life of its own. In *Third Avenue El* (1949; p. 166), Crawford combines patterns of light with the shapes of the tracks and steel girders, viewed through the tracks from directly below. The brilliant color—except for the suggestions of sky and sun in the blue and yellow—has little to do with the urban grayness we would normally associate with the scene. Crawford's move from Precisionism to broadly conceived Cubist forms also marked the course of his friend Niles Spencer. The solidly constructed *Wake of the Hurricane* (1951; p. 492) shows Spencer's version of late Cubism, although its somber palette relates more to Juan Gris than to the contemporary chromatic brilliance of Crawford's art.

From 1909, when he joined Henri's class, until his death in 1964, Stuart Davis touched virtually every important aesthetic, social, and intellectual issue affecting American art. The Armory Show had demonstrated for Davis the universal validity of French modernism. After absorbing the lessons of Gauguin, van Gogh, and Matisse in landscapes and portraits from 1913 to 1920, during the 1920s

56

Stuart Davis
Egg Beater #3
1927–1928
oil on canvas
25 x 39 (63.5 x 99.1)
The Lane Collection,
courtesy Museum of Fine
Arts, Boston

Davis assimilated Synthetic Cubism related to Picasso, Braque, Gris, and Léger. In his Egg Beater series of 1927–1928, he created virtually abstract paintings that gave new impetus to advanced American modernism. He insisted even then, however, that his purpose was to make realistic pictures despite their abstract nature. As he wrote to Ralston Crawford in 1950, his art was always drawn from the "immediate experience of the tempo of life today." Davis's fully mature style, based on a personal Cubist syntax, evolved in the early 1930s. After 1940, from the example of Matisse, Davis's color became even stronger, reaching a new height of brilliance in *Colonial Cubism*. Davis, it can be said, influenced and was influenced in turn during the 1940s by certain developments shared with Abstract Expressionism: his painting evolved toward an allover format in which the entire surface had equal intensity. After 1950 the scale, and thus the impact, of his paintings increased; furthermore, his painting began to incorporate fewer and larger forms. Nevertheless, as in *Colonial Cubism*, Davis remained committed to the objective order of his own brand of late Synthetic Cubism. During the 1950s his increasing use of words, signs, and letters derived from the commercial world around him served as an important precedent for the development of Pop Art.

Davis seems the quintessential American artist—upbeat, breezy, even offhand. Yet, at the same time, he was a methodical and disciplined worker, often basing new themes on older configurations—*Colonial Cubism* derived from a 1922 composition. Originality for Davis was not a function of form but rather of the painting's unity and internal logic. His strident color and forms may belie his long search to create major art by uniting American subject matter and American realism with an original variant of an international pictorial language.

Postwar American art has often been viewed as a phenomenon distinct from early American modernism. But by now it is clear that changes in postwar American art did not occur overnight. The art of Davis, Glarner, Marin, and others of their generation emphatically demonstrates that there was an ongoing tradition. Although we still have much to learn about the exact nature of the relation between earlier and postwar modernism, we now understand that such chronological divisions are arbitrary at best, that the course of our history has been fluid and continuous. And it was this continuity which helped to ensure the vitality of a modernist tradition that has not yet ended.

Art historian William C. Agee was Director of the Museum of Fine Arts, Houston, from 1974 to 1982 and a visiting scholar at the Smithsonian Institution from 1983 to 1985. Agee is the author of a number of catalogues on the work of American artists, including Donald Judd, 1968, Patrick Henry Bruce, 1979, and Morton Livingston Schamberg, 1982. He is the editor of the forthcoming Stuart Davis catalogue raisonné.

Abstract Expressionism and Assemblage

Diane Waldman

The artists who participated in the formation of the now-historic movement known as the New York School first came to prominence after World War II. Although they worked in extraordinarily diverse styles, they were and continue to be categorized simply as Abstract Expressionists. The term "abstract expressionism" was first used in 1919 to describe a certain period of Kandinsky's work; it was employed again in this context in 1929 by Alfred Barr. In 1946 the critic Robert Coates applied it to the work of certain young New York-based painters, particularly Willem de Kooning and Jackson Pollock. Partisans of the movement coined other terms, such as "Action Painting" (Harold Rosenberg) in an attempt to describe the new idiom. While no one label seems an adequate designation for this momentous and highly varied movement, both Abstract Expressionism and the more neutral New York School continue to be used frequently and interchangeably.

      In addition to de Kooning and Pollock, advocates of the revolutionary art included the renowned painters Franz Kline, Robert Motherwell, Adolph Gottlieb, Clyfford Still, Mark Rothko, and Barnett Newman, and such masterful sculptors as David Smith. These artists created a new aesthetic without manifesto, without program, but with a heady sense of risk and of limitless possibilities. They exemplify a spirit of adventure, of drama, and a grandeur of vision unparalleled in twentieth-century American art. Although diverse in many aspects of style and attitude, the members of the New York School were united in their rejection of the realism that had prevailed in American painting and sculpture during the 1920s and 1930s, and in their ambition to forge a new and heroic American art that would rival that of the early twentieth-century European modernists.

Adolph Gottlieb
Blue at Noon 1955
(detail, see p. 222)

Thomas Hart Benton
Cradling Wheat 1938
tempera, oil on board
31 x 38 (78.7 x 96.5)
Collection The Saint Louis
Art Museum, Missouri
Museum purchase

The realism these young artists had inherited was represented by the Regionalism of Thomas Hart Benton, Grant Wood, and John Steuart Curry; the American Scene Painting of Reginald Marsh, Isabel Bishop, the Soyer brothers; and the Social Realism of Ben Shahn, Philip Evergood, and others. Whatever the form, realism had triumphed over earlier American experiments in abstract painting. Indeed, Benton (who would be the teacher of Pollock) had turned violently against the abstraction he himself had embraced after World War I. His reaction was symptomatic of the country's isolationism, its social, political, and aesthetic conservatism, its mood of hopelessness and despair, born of the war and deepened by the Depression. Although a small number of Americans— Arthur Dove, Morgan Russell, and Stuart Davis among them—and Josef Albers and Hans Hofmann, Europeans who came to the United States in the early 1930s, continued to work in advanced styles, the majority of painters here during this period were more concerned with depicting the disillusionment of the downtrodden urban masses or heralding the virtues of rural life than they were with celebrating the glory of abstract painting. American painting in the 1920s and 1930s was typically an unrelenting document of an era of abject poverty, economic upheaval, and social strife.

None of the forces in play during this period, however, proved to be lasting deterrents to vanguard art. In a reactionary time, artists devoted to the cause of abstraction continued to paint. In 1937, a number of them formed the American Abstract Artists, a group committed to geometric abstraction. Among the artists who participated in meetings or exhibitions were Stuart Davis, Burgoyne Diller, Ilya Bolotowsky, and Charmion von Wiegand. Their art was based upon the European De Stijl, Constructivist, and Bauhaus movements, whose central premises were rational aesthetics and ethical ideals. After war broke out in Europe, the ranks of the American Abstract Artists were strengthened by the immigration of many of the major proponents of these movements. Piet Mondrian, the most influential among them, became something of a prophet for artists working in New York.

Yet despite Mondrian's importance, it was the Surrealist émigrés who freed the future painters of the New York School from the provincialism that had dominated American art throughout the 1920s and 1930s. The presence in New York of Max Ernst, André Masson, Yves Tanguy, Roberto Matta, and the poet laureate of the movement, André Breton, provided a major catalyst for the development of new American art. While personal contact with the Surrealists was limited, Americans had direct access to their work, which assured the fledgling painters and sculptors that these legendary artists were, after all, real people whose art was within reach. For the young American artists it was an exhilarating time, a moment when

Piet Mondrian
Composition 1933
oil on canvas
16¼ x 13⅛
(41.3 x 33.3)
The Sidney and Harriet
Janis Collection
Gift to The Museum of
Modern Art, New York

they finally gained the confidence and momentum to challenge their provincial past. In the researches of Freud and his exploration of the subconscious, the Surrealists had found some ideal tools for their experiments. Although, unlike Freud, they accepted dream images as significant realities rather than as mere symbols of unconscious life, they appropriated Freud's theories on the role of language in dreams and dream interpretation. Out of these theories the Surrealists developed the technique of automatism, which they applied to both poetry and painting. In 1924 Breton first described Surrealism as "pure psychic automatism, by which it is intended to express, verbally, in writing or by other means, the real process of thought. Thought's dictation in the absence of all control exercised by reason and outside all esthetic and moral preoccupations."[1]

Although Surrealist imagery, with its sexually charged subject matter and its ambiguous thematic content, found its way into American painting and sculpture in the 1940s, it was automatism and the concepts it engendered that radically altered the course of American art. Automatism liberated the painters of the New York School from the external world of reality and freed their art from conscious control, allowing them to explore the inner universe of the subconscious. Like the Surrealists before them, the Abstract Expressionists exploited the irrational and the elements of chance and accident. Unlike the Surrealists, who remained committed to a form of representation and narrative, many of the Abstract Expressionists used automatism as their point of departure in the formation of a radical new abstract imagery. Automatism made it possible for them to transcend representational subject matter, consolidate process and end product, and fuse inner vision and external phenomena.

Like many of his colleagues, William Baziotes was drawn to Surrealism and accepted its concepts and methods as the fundamental premises of his mature art. In the 1940s, in conjunction with Matta, Masson, and Motherwell, he began to explore aspects of Surrealist automatism and to concretize imagery drawn from the imagination. For Baziotes, as for many artists of the New York School, the elemental forces of nature, particularly marine and plant life, became a viable alternative to imagery drawn from the external world. Baziotes now invented a cohesive language of biomorphic forms upon which he drew throughout his life. Paintings such as the Miróesque *Opalescent* (1962; p. 130) exemplify an oeuvre in which graceful evanescent forms float in a luminous liquid field. Like Rothko's images, Baziotes's undulating biomorphic forms are invested with a mythical quality that defies absolute definition. Nevertheless, it is possible to see in these images references to biological and botanical forms and traces of such natural phenomena as dawn or dusk. His virtuoso technique, an adaptation of the watercolor medium to oil painting, reinforces the illusion of a world in which inanimate forms appear mobile and animate forms are cloaked in enigma.

1.   André Breton, *What Is Surrealism?* (London: Faber & Faber, 1936), p. 59.

While many painters, most notably Arshile Gorky, found their true style through Surrealism, several members of the New York School, in particular Rothko, Newman, and Gottlieb, developed a body of archetypal images based on Jungian theory, which they believed to have universal significance. They substituted these symbols or signs for the Freudian dream imagery of Surrealism, although without abandoning their belief in the power of the subconscious. Gottlieb and Rothko, working closely together in the 1940s, dedicated themselves to the expression of mythic content. Removed from their primitive contexts, however, the Abstract Expressionists' symbols lost their original meanings and functions; they became, instead, virtually abstract signs without mythic significance. But it was this progression from ancient myth to abstract sign that led to the formulation of a new abstract imagery. Rothko's *Ritual* (circa 1944; p. 438) is a key example of this important transitional phase in New York School painting. Here, as in other paintings of the period, Rothko creates a series of totemic images that vaguely suggest animal forms, human figures, birds, and aquatic life. The animated twirling or revolving forms, subtle color harmonies, and emboldened calligraphy are unexcelled in the artist's work to that date and reveal a new and heightened confidence and sophistication. In *Ritual*, Rothko retains the clearly defined zones and registers that he had first employed in his figurative paintings of the 1930s. Now, however, in his introduction of floating, amorphous shapes skillfully integrated with the flat field of the canvas, he signals his determination to relinquish all forms of overt realism and seeks instead an imagery that negotiates the "middle ground between abstraction and surrealism."[2]

Joan Miró
Dutch Interior II 1928
oil on canvas
36⁵⁄₁₆ x 28¹³⁄₁₆
(92.2 x 73.2)
The Peggy Guggenheim
Collection, Venice
Solomon R. Guggenheim
Foundation, New York

In his search for a new imagery, Rothko, like his colleagues, drew upon Surrealist prototypes. While he has acknowledged the influence of Dali, de Chirico, and Ernst, it is the Surrealist-inspired Miró who figures importantly in paintings such as *Ritual*. Miró's characteristic ears and flamelike forms are reinterpreted and recast as prominent features of Rothko's paintings. New, too, is the Miróesque element of play, which relieves the painting of the somberness and melancholy more typical of Rothko's work. Like Miró, Rothko retains the semblance of an image, in this instance a figure, and fragments of abstract forms—dislocating, shifting, and reassembling them into a new "portrait," one that is evocative, mysterious, and, ultimately, elusive. In its title *Ritual* signals Rothko's abiding interest in myth, while its organic shapes, commonly associated with biological life and marine organisms, speak for his involvement with the elemental forces of nature. Yet his imagery is both too complex in its derivation and too ambiguous in its final form to be strictly interpreted as nature- or myth-derived.

Gottlieb's Pictographs, which he began to develop in 1941, combine a latticelike grid, derived from Cubist precedents, with a highly charged vocabulary of signs and symbols. References to an eye, a hand, a face, to teeth, and

2. Quoted in Art of This Century, New York, *Mark Rothko: Paintings*, exh. cat., 1945.

62

other parts of the human anatomy constitute the residual data of his earlier involvement with the figure. They are part of a repertory of image-symbols (including snakes, birds, masks, and eggs) that he discovered in earlier art forms that appeared to him to have universal significance as part of the "collective unconscious."

The grid provided Gottlieb with a fecund working formula for over a decade. He would select a form, such as an eye, at random and place it in one of the grid's numerous compartments. Both the random pattern of the grid and the equally random selection and juxtaposition of images were based on techniques of chance and automatism. As Gottlieb's work evolved during the late 1940s and early 1950s he gradually abandoned all but the most subliminal references to representation; he did not, however, relinquish his interest in nature or natural phenomena. Throughout his life he retained a conviction that the forces of nature and those of the subconscious were inextricably intertwined and that together they served as the wellspring of the imagination.

Blue at Noon (1955; p. 222) verifies that the grid continued to play an important role in Gottlieb's mature painting. Here, however, the grid merges with other shapes; it lacks the strict definition that was such a pronounced feature of the earlier work. The compelling tracery of black lines, the network of white signs and the lustrous blue field juxtaposed in shallow layers combine to produce an intense luminosity and a perceptible, if ambiguous, depth. The vigorous allover pattern, an adaptation of automatism, shares certain affinities with the interlacing forms of Pollock's classic drip paintings. Gottlieb, however, never fully relinquished either the scale of easel painting or the need to separate figure and ground.

Although Gottlieb subsequently rejected the grid, its structure is implicit in the series called Imaginary Landscapes, of which *Trio* (1960; p. 224) is a brilliant example. But it is Gottlieb's feeling for radiant color and powerful form that is given its fullest expression in works of this period. They reveal a new love of pigment that in its sensuous expansiveness is reminiscent of Impressionism. Gottlieb's emphasis on the primacy of color allowed him to reduce the number of shapes and to float them in a field, a schematic arrangement that culminated in the series of paintings known as Bursts. As in *Trio*, Gottlieb's late style conforms to his concept of "polarities," wherein one or more smooth, closed concentric forms are contrasted with a like number of exploding centrifugal forms with open contours and jagged edges. The resolution of these polarities establishes the equilibrium of the painting by bringing the conflicting forces of nature into harmonious accord. If the Pictographs, as Gottlieb stated, "stem from introspection, free association and automatism," then the paintings of the last decades of his life reflect a greater emphasis on external phenomena and on the act of painting.[3]

By the early 1950s many of the Abstract Expressionists had arrived at their mature styles. Despite the diversity of their approaches, it is possible to discern two major tendencies that emerged within the movement after a protracted period of experimentation and change. One direction, gestural painting, emphasizes surface, texture, and physical manipulation of pigment. For the earlier gestural painters—Pollock, de Kooning, and Kline—the mark, the drip, the brushstroke were vital

3. Quoted in Selden Rodman, *Conversations with Artists* (New York: Devin-Adair, 1957), p. 91.

Jackson Pollock
Autumn Rhythm 1950
oil on canvas
105 x 207 (266.7 x 525.8)
Collection The Metropolitan
Museum of Art, New York
George A. Hearn Fund,
1957

evidence of the artist's activity, documents of the process of painting. Although improvisation and accident were integral parts of the painting of many New York School artists, it was the drip technique that enabled Pollock to capitalize to the utmost on chance and spontaneous effects. Moreover, the drip technique involved the use of his entire body and inevitably led him to abandon easel-sized pictures in favor of monumental mural-scale canvases. Unlike Pollock, de Kooning retained the easel scale, the figure, and the traditional figure-ground relationship. But in his idiom, this relationship and the figures themselves represent monumental pictorial tensions that issue from his dynamic, expressive brushwork and broad, sweeping gestures. In his 1950s paintings of women, de Kooning achieved a radical synthesis of figuration and abstraction. Although he had produced a notable body of abstract paintings during the 1940s, his canvases of the 1950s speak of an artist who was prophetic in his exploration of the abstract potential of the human form. He was then and is now the one New York School painter for whom the term Abstract Expressionist had and continues to have the most relevance.

Franz Kline's vigorous architectural compositions are structured primarily in black and white, with forms interlocked so as to integrate both colors with the picture plane. His large and rugged but precise forms, his powerful brushstrokes, and his bold calligraphy reflect an approach that is at once thoughtful and impulsive. A similar synthesis of abandon and control is revealed in the work of Hans Hofmann (*Elegy*, 1950; p. 540). His reliance on the principle of "push-pull" allowed him to establish dynamic tensions between figure and ground without compromising the emphasis on the two-dimensional picture plane that was a fundamental premise of Abstract Expressionism. Within the limits of this flat plane, Hofmann was able to explore a broad range of sensations and moods, as well as atmospheric and spatial effects and variations in density and transparency of medium. Among his other achievements were his early innovations in the realm of color alignment, which influenced the development of the Color Field painters Morris Louis and Kenneth Noland.

Franz Kline
Painting #7 1952
oil on canvas
57½ x 81¾
(146.1 x 207.6)
Collection Solomon
R. Guggenheim Museum,
New York

The other major tendency within the Abstract Expressionist movement is epitomized in the large-scale chromatic abstractions of Still, Newman, and Rothko. Such masterful paintings as Still's *Untitled* (1950; p. 504), Newman's *The Third* (1962; p. 388), and Rothko's untitled (#2) (1963; p. 442) exemplify an art that conveys a profound sense of the transcendental and the sublime. All three painters share a commitment to the large canvas, to vast expanses of space, and intense color sequences. They purified their art by rejecting the decorative surface qualities of paint, by ridding their canvases of complex relationships of color, form, and structure. Color becomes volume, form, space, and light in their work. Having emptied their canvases of the superfluous, they were able to express both the material reality of abstract painting and the incorporeal reality of the sublime. For all of them painting was an act of revelation, of exaltation, an embodiment of universal truth.

Newman achieved his characteristic, mature style of single color fields interrupted by vertical stripes, or "zips," of another color or tone as early as 1948. By 1949 he had enlarged his canvases to heroic scale; indeed, Newman was ultimately to develop the idea of the expansive field further than either Rothko or Still. Whereas Rothko usually presented horizontal bands of color within a vertical or nearly square field, Newman chose, by about 1950, to orient his paintings horizontally and subdivide them vertically with one or more zips. And in his mature paintings, such as *The Third*, he eliminated much of the texture that had marked the grounds of his earlier canvases. Thus he created fields more neutral than those of Rothko or Still; their canvases remained, respectively, atmospheric and heavily impastoed. Despite Newman's rejection of pronounced texture, his fields are not entirely flat or unmodulated: he activated his surfaces with subtly differentiated brushstrokes and with his zips, produced by masking off a section of the canvas, painting over the tape, and allowing the pigment to bleed underneath the tape. The pronounced frontality and verticality of the zip works against the lateral expanse of the field to create an illusion of deep space and a sense of the void.

Newman relished austerity. He restricted his palette to a few saturated hues, especially red, orange, and blue. Color was as expressive and emotive for him as it was for Rothko, but in Newman's work color functions in an ordered and reasoned manner. The measured calm that Newman obtained from his vast fields of color endows his canvases with a heightened grandeur that evokes analogies between man and the forces of nature, man in relationship to nature and the sublime.

From the late 1930s to the mid-1940s, Still, like Rothko and Newman, sought inspiration in Surrealist precedents and was concerned with ritualistic subject matter and archaic forms. Later in the 1940s, however, he renounced all ties to European artistic movements and also chose to work apart from the New York School painters. Although he disdained identification with Abstract Expressionism, his work clearly belongs within the movement. His skillful manipulation of color, shape, and texture, as in the 1950 *Untitled*, and his ability to create an illusion of flickers of light by placing small areas of color at the canvas edges and throughout the field are among the most notable features of his work. Still's highly individualistic style is characterized, too, by shapes with hooked and jagged contours, the consistent use of large areas of black that suggest cavernous depths, by sharp and dramatic contrasts of positive and negative forms and light and dark areas, and by the thick skin of a heavily encrusted paint surface. And, although the essentially transcendental nature of his art links him most directly with Newman and Rothko and bears analogies to the primal forces of nature, the marked rawness and brutality in his work aligns him as well with the gestural Abstract Expressionists. Like Kline, whose muscular forms burst forth from the canvas, Still's jagged shapes appear to rend its very fabric. If Gottlieb's paintings are a statement about the harmonious resolution of the conflicting forces of nature, Still's paintings are about chaos and upheaval. Nature is harsh, often brutal, but always awesome.

Both Still and Newman developed their mature idioms before Rothko. By winter 1949–1950, however, Rothko achieved a breakthrough with the introduction of his luminous color paintings, in which he enlarged and neutralized his shapes, allowing color to breathe and stand alone. From that time on, his color ceased to refer to particular nature- or myth-derived images, or to serve as a secondary element that supported shape. Not only did disembodied color now represent form, it became the very substance of Rothko's art. His method of paint-handling—a watercolor technique translated into oil—was crucial to the development of his color forms: he achieved the effect of dematerialized color by allowing paint to soak into the canvas. Yet the color retains its intensity as an all-encompassing sensation. Indeed, Rothko's color is often surprising because he refused to accept its conventional limitations. His ambition was to express with color both area and volume, as well as complex moods and human emotions. In his evocative and emotionally resonant painting, color became the vehicle for exalted, transcendental experience.

In the 1963 untitled (#2), Rothko's mature style attained unparalleled heights. As in his other paintings of this period, large floating color shapes are anchored by one or two bands of glowing color. The soft pastel palette of his 1950s paintings, influenced by Matisse and by Rothko's friend and mentor Milton Avery, was replaced in the 1960s by a light-suffused dusky palette that recalls Rembrandt and by a superb command of form inspired by the powerful figures of Michelangelo. The viewer, enveloped within its boundaries, experiences sensations that Rothko equated with religious experience. Like Still's awesome *Untitled* and Newman's majestic *The Third*, Rothko's untitled (#2) is both a singularly personal statement and an expression of the universal meaning of life and the life of the spirit.

The New York School produced fewer important sculptors than painters, yet the same spirit of adventure and sense of limitless possibilities vitalized the artists working in three dimensions. The muscular, heroic, and highly inflected work of David Smith, the preeminent sculptor of the Abstract Expressionist movement, achieves in the realm of sculpture the epic vision of New York School painting.

Like the painters, Smith was initially influenced by the Surrealists: his art of the mid-1930s to mid-1940s is indebted to the sculpture of Alberto Giacometti. Ultimately, however, Smith rejected Surrealist allegory and allusion in favor of a more formalist aesthetic exemplified by Picasso's welded steel sculpture and the forged iron pieces of Julio González. In particular, González's feeling for materials and his consummate ability to draw in space provided crucial inspiration for the young American artist. Smith's capacity to expand on González's imagery and skillfully adapt the Spanish artist's "flying iron drawings"[4] to formulate his own mature style is evident in *The Royal Bird* (1947–1948; p. 480). Notable for its imaginative form, horizontal emphasis, and the resolution of figure and base, it constitutes one of the many motifs in Smith's vocabulary of the late 1940s. The figure in part represents the artist's distillation of a prehistoric bird he had seen in the American Museum of Natural History in New York. Although the bird of prey is a highly charged subject with ominous and mysterious overtones, Smith's interpretation indicates his shift away from sources in nature and Surrealist imagery toward a more abstract conception. *The Royal Bird* reveals his unsurpassed ability to define form and delineate space in a way that anticipates his extraordinary achievements of the 1950s and 1960s.

Isamu Noguchi, a contemporary and friend of the Abstract Expressionists, successfully synthesized Eastern and Western artistic traditions in his sculpture. Like his New York School colleagues, Noguchi was initially drawn to Surrealism, and sculptures such as *Cronos* (1947; p. 394) and *Avatar* (1948; p. 396) fuse Surrealist archetypes with traditional Japanese forms. Noguchi, however, like Smith, ultimately turned to more strictly formal concerns. *Mortality* (1959; p. 398) reveals the sense of ordered calm and quiet authority and the profound love of materials that inform all of his mature work.

From the 1930s until his death in 1988 Noguchi designed gardens, bridges, and plazas and produced sets for dance and theater (Model for *Play Mountain, New York*, 1933; p. 547, and theater set piece from *Judith*, 1950/1978; p. 548). His lean and spare forms reflect a highly cultivated aesthetic, based on Zen tradition, in which every garden signifies an entire landscape and sand and stones evoke the sea. In keeping with this tradition, Noguchi limited his intervention in both nature and natural forms. His investigations of wood, stone, brass, marble, iron, steel, and aluminum speak of the traditional Japanese reverence for materials, whereas the specific forms with which he endowed these materials constitute a unique, highly personal, and distinctly modern contribution. In his sculpture, he crystallizes ancient tradition and modern innovation in timeless forms.

4. David Smith, "González: First Master of the Torch," *Art News*, vol. 54 (February 1956), p. 37.

One of the most notable features of Abstract Expressionism was its emphasis on process and materials. This emphasis was crucial to the development of Assemblage, an art form that emerged as an important force in the late 1950s. Although ultimately derived from the two-dimensional medium of collage, Assemblage, as William Seitz has pointed out, is more immediately descended from Dada and Abstract Expressionism. Seitz noted, however, that Assemblage is distinct from its forebears in its orientation: "it marks a change from a subjective, fluidly abstract art towards a revised association with environment."[5]

Seitz defined Assemblage as "a generic concept that [includes] all forms of composite art and modes of juxtaposition."[6] Thus Assemblage artists as diverse as Joseph Cornell, Louise Nevelson, Robert Rauschenberg, and Mark di Suvero are united not only by their common ancestry in Abstract Expressionism but also by a shared indebtedness to the Dada master Kurt Schwitters. By appropriating fragments from the real world and transforming them into evocative poetic statements in his collages and *Merzbau* constructions, Schwitters provided the Assemblage artists with a crucial source of inspiration.

Although Cornell neither subscribed to the more esoteric theories of the Surrealists nor participated in the group's activities, he acknowledged the importance of the Surrealists in the development of his work, citing in particular André Breton and Max Ernst. His work clearly reveals the influence of Ernst's collages, Marcel Duchamp's objects and altered readymades, and Schwitters's *Merzbau* constructions. Cornell accepted the Dada and Surrealist concept of the box as an object whose detailed and often intricate construction was contradicted by the absence of any true function. His major innovation in his boxes was to combine the associative power of the estranged object with a rare and formal power. He made of the box construction a realm in which real and imagined worlds coexist, combining in them objects that had delighted him as a child with those that spoke of his adult obsessions. Thus, in works such as *Andromeda (Sand Fountain)* (1953–1956; p. 162), seashells, stamps, toys, marbles, and clay pipes are juxtaposed with ballerinas, sky charts, driftwood, or cordial glasses. His objects came from everywhere: "Everything can be used, says Cornell—but of course one doesn't know it at the time. How does one know what a certain object will tell another?"[7] Cornell's dreams, contained within the walls of his glass-paneled boxes, are ultimately elusive. However rational the formal ordering of his box constructions may be, their imagery flows from his unconscious, to remain deeply personal and forever mysterious.

Louise Nevelson's magnificent *Sky Cathedral Presence* (1951–1964; p. 382) and her equally classical *Relief* (1956; p. 546) and *Case with Five Balusters* (1959; p. 386) epitomize the Assemblage idiom she evolved in her mature constructions. Nevelson accumulated found objects, which she assembled into poetic constructions that range in size from a diminutive box to a massive wall. Painted a uniform matte black, white, or gold, they resonate with the forcefulness of great theater. Like Cornell, Nevelson found inspiration for the use of random objects in the

Kurt Schwitters
Merzbau mit blaues Fenster (Merzbau with Blue Window) 1933
Collection Sprengel Museum, Hannover

5. William Seitz, in The Museum of Modern Art, New York, *The Art of Assemblage*, exh. cat., 1961, p. 87.
6. Ibid.
7. Howard Griffin, "Auriga, Andromeda, Cameoleopardalis," *Art News*, vol. 56 (December 1957), p. 64.

Surrealist juxtaposition of disparate elements. Again like Cornell, she was able to enhance the provocative associative power of each object by combining it with other, unrelated elements. Her constructions, despite their composite nature, are unified totalities with a majestic presence and the magic force of primitive, archetypal forms that relates them to the monumental paintings of Newman, Rothko, and Still. She ennobled the commonplace elements of her walls and, like these transcendent painters, created a resonant and heroic art.

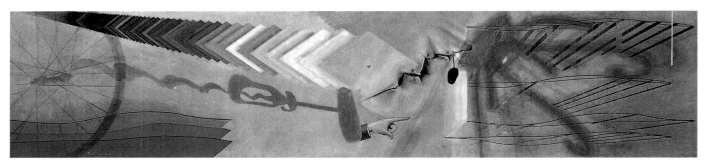

Marcel Duchamp first elevated the common object to the status of art. As a longtime resident of New York, Duchamp's influence on American artists working there from the 1940s through the 1960s was profound. Along with Schwitters, Duchamp rejected the concept of the art object as a unique entity, and it is to this precedent that Robert Rauschenberg owed his initial experiments with junk and Assemblage. Rauschenberg incorporated clippings, photographs, and, more important, three-dimensional objects from the real world into his paintings and constructions. In the major combine painting *Trophy II (for Teeny and Marcel Duchamp)* (1960; p. 422), for example, the canvas surface, inflected with dynamic Abstract Expressionist brushwork, is enhanced by the addition of ordinary objects such as a tie, a glass, and a spoon. In their appropriation of the detritus of everyday life, Rauschenberg's combine paintings are reminiscent of Schwitters's collages and constructions, yet they are indebted as well to the evanescent imagery of Cornell. They differ from Dada works, however, in their presentation of the quotidian, in their painterliness and large scale, and in their juxtaposition of images from different eras to create a fictive time within the real time of the painting's own existence.

The sculpture of Mark di Suvero exemplifies the neo-Dada attitudes of a younger generation of artists that came to prominence in the late 1950s and early 1960s. The impressive *Stuyvesantseye* (1965; p. 176), which incorporates a chair and a barrel, is the sculptural equivalent of Rauschenberg's combine paintings. Di Suvero seizes upon found objects and exploits their potential as pure form and volume. Yet he preserves the characteristics of the commonplace objects he uses, forcing us to apprehend their inherent visual qualities at the same time that he transforms them. Thus the commanding physical presence of his sculptures derives in part from his choice of objects, in part from his alteration of them. The cohesiveness of di Suvero's work ultimately depends not on the objects themselves but upon his consummate ability to shape them into significant aesthetic statements.

Many artists figured prominently in the arena of Assemblage during the early 1960s. In this decade the medium of light—an offshoot of the all-pervasive interest in materials—also attracted considerable attention. It is in this domain that Chryssa introduced an intriguing new dimension to sculpture. She first used neon in an aluminum construction, *Times Square Sky* (1962; p. 534). This assemblage of massive metal letters, familiar from her earlier work in bronze, aluminum, and plaster, is effectively offset by the fragile thread of neon tubing spelling out the word "air." As is typical of her work in neon, Chryssa contrasts a concrete form (the aluminum letters) with an ephemeral form (the neon tubing). Light serves to suggest atmosphere and connote place; it functions as color, and it completes our reading of the construction. It also serves to remove the sign from the realm of reality and elevates it to the status of symbol. Despite the visual impact of the aluminum construction, Chryssa's dense metal forms are dependent on light for their full effect. Like her later neon work, *Times Square Sky* plays on the concept of positive and negative forms, shadow, and substance. The evocative poetry of earlier Assemblage constructions is here reiterated in new and arresting form.

Both the Abstract Expressionist and Assemblage movements constitute high points in American art of the twentieth century. The artists who emerged during the postwar period were impelled by a need to challenge tradition and extend the frontiers of art. Their formal innovations, unorthodox subjects, and use of materials enlarged and enhanced painting and sculpture. Their work has contributed to our understanding of these art forms and continues to inspire artists and public alike.

Diane Waldman is Deputy Director of the Solomon R. Guggenheim Museum, New York. She recently completed a major installation of the work of Jenny Holzer for the Guggenheim and is the author of the exhibition's accompanying catalogue, which includes an essay on Holzer and an interview with the artist. Her book *Collage, Assemblage and the Found Object in Twentieth-Century Art* is forthcoming.

Formalism, Minimalism, and Recent Developments

Joseph Masheck

The complexities of Postmodern theory have clearly demonstrated the fact that any developmental order in contemporary art once implied, if not imposed by modernism has finally broken down. This does not necessarily mean that all is in chaos, not even in the special preserve of "pure" abstraction, where the crisis of modernism centered. A kind of root *modernity* persists despite claims that art today is thoroughly atomized in a free-for-all of styles and values. How, then, today, to construct anything more than a list of disjunct artistic "incidents" in the recent past without projecting a false order?

Some order, over time, follows from a working distinction between painting, especially "formal" abstract painting, as a vehicle of metaphoric statement and transcendental aspiration, and sculpture, Minimalism above all, as pertaining more immediately to the literal materiality of things in the world. While extremes do implicate their opposites, I am inclined to cluster the Walker's astutely diverse, undogmatically selective range of abstract paintings and sculpture of the last twenty-five years in sequences wherein one or the other mode or condition is dominant. This allows for alternating emphases, not just swings of a supposed stylistic pendulum; after all, "abstraction" itself was once considered one "style," though by now it has had a diverse as well as continuous history over about seventy-five years. My procedure, then, can be considered a variation, however informal, on the typology of "tender-minded" versus "tough-minded" temperaments articulated in William James's *Pragmatism* (1907), James himself having been aware of the possible subtleties of attendant qualification.

Since the years around 1960 were problematic for new art, especially in the face of the conventionalization of Abstract Expressionism, a good

Sol LeWitt
Four Geometric Figures in a Room 1984
(detail, see p. 302)

73

place to start is with the Walker's *Untitled* (1960; p. 168) Stripe painting by Gene Davis who in the 1950s had worked in a painterly and expressive abstract mode. Here, in a seamless array of taut, abutting bands of vivid color, two very different tendencies of the new decade, the optical sensationalism of Color Field painting and the elemental, built rigor of Minimalism, can almost be said to coincide. The painting compares tellingly with one by Barnett Newman of two years later, *The Third* (1962; p. 388): each has a brace of stripes positioned at extreme left and right, but to quite different effect. If Davis's painting was something of a departure, Newman, in the older generation, had been slicing through fields of color with the strumming vertical bands he called "zips" since the mid-1940s. His *The Third* can be approached as an otherwise scaleless "space" of color made all the more present, and convulsively so, by its inflecting zips. Newman's is a relatively "tender-minded" position, thanks especially to his ongoing pursuit of an affective sublimity akin to that of Romantic landscape; the utter extremism of his mature "simplicity" would also prove inspiring to young Minimalists of the 1960s. What Davis proposes, quite differently, is opaque, vivid yet rigid, and distinctly artificial (and "tough-minded") rather than reminiscent of nature: his dark blue stripes at either end share in, as well as close off, the dark-light alternation of stripes of the image as a whole even as they secure that image precisely as finite. Davis simplifies structure to the point of self-evidence yet keeps it packed so full that almost all there really is in his striped painting is color.

Such painting also eschews the visible painterly fluidity that marks the post-expressionist concern with process as gerundive, as having visibly *gone on*, as in the paintings of Morris Louis, Kenneth Noland, and Helen Frankenthaler. Frankenthaler's *Alloy* (1967; p. 210) is a later example of her pioneering work in staining colors with fluid immediacy into unprimed canvas. This procedure was an obvious extension of Pollock's direct dripping and spattering onto an expanse of unstretched canvas unrolled on the floor. Significantly, the new generation, with its aestheticizing variations on painting as action, profited from the availability of new acrylic paints, which avoid the leached "halo" of oil around a form and which, being water soluble, in fact behave more like watercolor: indeed, many acrylic abstractions are like giant watercolors, with puddling as well as spills and even passages of "muddiness," only writ large. Furthermore, the new colors tended to be lively, if brash, much like the analine dyes introduced about a century before into both industrial and tribal textile production. But whereas critics such as William Morris found the chemical dyes offensively artificial, and connoisseurs of tribal textiles still today tend to see them as corrupt, the juicy analine "bite" of the new acrylic paints had some positive appeal. Painting of this kind offers a specialized, intensified experience of color that entails the integral, even "textile," flatness of design about which so much has been written. But it also involves the framing of painterly incident. In Morris Louis's *#28* (1961; p. 324), vertical stripes of color gather in two clusters, a larger one, unevenly astride the painting's meridian, and a smaller one that splits the exposed field to the right of the first cluster in half. The clustering advances a sensuous experience of the colors vibrating together as if in two rich organ chords. Note that one of the poured paint bands, obviously once a dribble, "leaks" upward and to the left, hinting that the painting, as we confront it, has been inverted. The result is an upward-jetting, fountainous play of sheer pigmental effect.

Orientation is hardly an issue with Kenneth Noland's centered concentric rings of color. As if to stabilize the image in an optimum position, however, *Cantabile* (1961; p. 400) has been stretched slightly taller than it is wide. These bull's-eye paintings, clear in structure yet almost aurorally optical in effect, differ essentially from the Target paintings of Jasper Johns. Noland's concentric rings have some bare canvas, some breathing space, between them. The central disk around which the rings of *Cantabile* so pacifically orbit introduces the first circumference, while the last encircling ring has the special structural role of closing off the series of ever larger rings: a cloudy, fuzzy-edged, vaporous zone of gray swells out into the field, as perhaps in skywriting.

Adapting the polarity of William James, one might say that, simultaneous with all painterly, pliant, or otherwise "soft" abstract painting, there was also, through the 1960s and into the 1970s, an abstraction of "hardness," with its own roots and potentialities. This "hard" abstraction tends toward a chunky, "built" presence, whereas soft abstract painting tends toward an overall pliancy, whether the paint soaks into the canvas or not. In hard painting the canvas is concretely subsumed rather than furnished or inhabited as a fictive or poetic space. Both can be "frontal," but instead of opening anything like a prospect onto a configuration of entities, the hard abstract painting takes the initiative in presenting itself *unto* the viewer.

By itself this typology has a tendency to suspend developmental factors. In seeing Al Held's *Hidden Fortress* (1961; p. 540) and Burgoyne Diller's *First Theme* (1963–1964; p. 184) as similarly hard, one may overlook the fact that Held's painting represents for him a definitive but intermediate step away from Abstract Expressionism, while *First Theme* is one of many moments in Diller's untiring pursuit of Constructivist geometry. Yet, typically for Held's work at that time, *Hidden Fortress* is divided into parts, with fragmentary and whole units coexisting, and this sense of definable, removable sections shares with *First Theme* a thingness that anticipates what was about to come from the younger generation. The structure of *First Theme* looks crisp and solid enough almost to stand as an object; indeed, at that time Diller was also executing very similar compositions in three-dimensional form—plastic laminate over wood.

In Germany, much earlier, Josef Albers had begun in a perhaps surprisingly Expressionist way. But his prolific Homage to the Square series is rigorously simple in its set structure of nested, low-riding squares. The Homages provide, as it were, neutrally standardized, formally self-evident containers in which different (also standardized) colors are juxtaposed in calculated interrelations. Color itself, normally the most irrational part of art, undergoes scrupulous calibration and becomes the substance of the thing. The Walker's *Homage to the Square: "Gentle Hour"* (1962; p. 100) is one of the paintings in which Albers implies by a romantic-poetic subtitle that the *product* of such quasi-experimental control might even carry one away.

Frank Stella's classic Black paintings, begun with their brushy black bands in nested L-shaped or rectangular-concentric arrays, offer a number of parallels to classic modern design, whether Henri van de Velde's famous *Tropon* poster (1899) or building facades designed by the Mondrianesque architect J.J.P. Oud in Rotterdam in the mid-1920s. Stella's *Sketch Les Indes Galantes* (1962; pp. 76 and

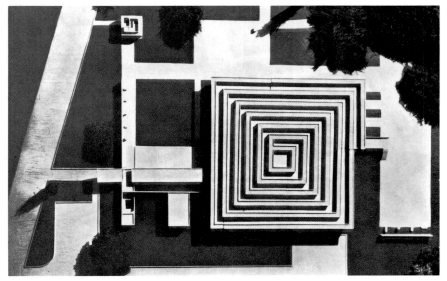

Frank Stella
Sketch Les Indes Galantes
1962 (see p. 496)

Le Corbusier and **Pierre
Jeanneret** 1939
Bird's-eye view of
*A Museum for Unlimited
Growth*
(Plan established for
Philippeville, Algeria)

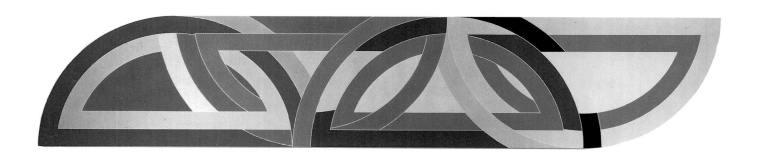

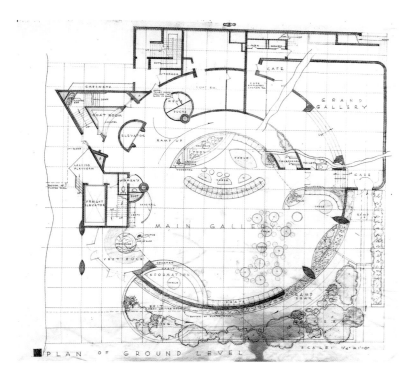

Frank Stella
*Damascus Gate Stretch
Variation* 1968
(see p. 498)

Frank Lloyd Wright
Ground level plan for
Solomon R. Guggenheim
Museum (presentation
drawing) 1958
pencil on tracing paper
40 x 35 (101.6 x 88.9)
Collection The Frank Lloyd
Wright Archives,
Scottsdale, Arizona

76

496), whose gray and white bands shifting at each diagonal axis challenge the eye to grasp concentric squares where there is in fact a continuous right-angling band, recalls Le Corbusier's Algerian museum project of 1939—a squared spiral building designed so that extra galleries could be added indefinitely in ever longer sides. These references are offered suggestively, in view of the obdurate way paintings such as *Sketch Les Indes Galantes* present themselves as built. Stella's *Damascus Gate Stretch Variation* (1968; pp.76 and 498), a large Protractor painting, is inescapably architectural. The title suggests a type of Roman gateway that offers inward recessions of semicircular moldings as well as right-angled recessions in rectilinear elements. Not to be overlooked, either, is the conceptual association of the protractor as an architectural drafting tool; for there also reverberates in Stella's semicircular reversals and interlacing overlaps a basic compositional device of Frank Lloyd Wright's for generating floor plans, as, for instance, in the shapes and placement of such elements as the pool, elevator, and information desk in the Solomon R. Guggenheim Museum. Stella's work is decidedly not picture-making; it is in some sense about paintings as built, *erected* things (as in *Loomings 3X*, 1986; p. 500). No wonder it has so often been seen in relation to the literalism of Minimalist "object" thinking.

Ellsworth Kelly stayed in France after army service in World War II and there developed a typically American sense of painting's built *objectivity* by finding structural pretexts for his works in architectural motifs. To the extent that the geometricity of the formal structure gives itself over to pure color, such works as *Red Green Blue* (1964; p. 274) stand close to Albers's Homages to the Square, though Kelly, unlike Albers, is often sensuously blatant with color and fastidiously tailors the simple forms it occupies. In *Red Green Blue*, the widths of the color zones are sensitively tuned in area and intensity; the colors occur in spectral sequence, but having the green L-shape embrace the rectangle of red, and be embraced in turn by a taller and wider but narrower L of blue, also makes for a strong A-B-A or "tricolor" aspect. With *Green Rocker* (1968; p. 276) the (often neo-Purist) painter renders two planes of color sculpturally concrete enough to be capable of rocking back and forth. Such pieces show a surprisingly enthusiastic physicality of presence for a painter who pursues lithe, if not inhibited, abstract bodily shapeliness.

Fairly irrelevant at the time, even to Americans entertaining farfetched alternatives to formal abstraction, was the Op Art movement associated with The Museum of Modern Art's 1965 exhibition *The Responsive Eye*. Op was populistically nonobjective in its promiscuous exploitation of optical after-images, illusions, and other perceptual tricks. Nevertheless, thanks to the insights of a new generation of skeptical and graphically inclined, rather neo-Conceptual artists, a work such as Bridget Riley's *Suspension* (1964; p. 424) now gets a second chance. *Suspension* is unnerving precisely in its forthright contrivance, and this in a world full of contrivances, not to mention manipulations, of ostensibly aesthetic effects—especially in advertising. Quirkily, but astutely, even its optical dazzle can present itself today as "supercharged," with almost electronically "artificial" effect.

Largely in negation of an established modern tradition that conceived forms in a mutuality of interdependent relations, the 1960s saw a radical revisionism, preeminently in Minimalist sculpture. Minimalist artists set themselves in categorical opposition to transcendent form as enshrined in painting. From the

Minimalist point of view, even such a construct as Anthony Caro's *Sculpture Three, 1962* (p.156) smacks of the pictorial arrangement of forms. True, its main, longitudinal axis thrusts forward from, and is perpendicular to, a highly stable vertical feature rising from an erect trapezoid. This same axis terminates in a leaning element composed of two gentle curves. Space is shot through with formal activity; the whole could even be likened to an ancient chariot sculpture. And yet the structure appears as a system of mutually dependent "touches" that might almost have been brushstrokes happening to occupy real space.

To the new anti-formalist artists, form was to be so elemental as to become in one sense absolutely opaque and mute, while, in another, transparently self-evident. Though only a few years later than Caro's piece, Tony Smith's *Amaryllis* (1965/1968; p. 486) is altogether different—closed, faceted, crystalline, and elemental, like some mineral. This work is constructed of a series of metal planes; although logical, it manages to be a rather architectonically solid *form* even while an evidently hollow *thing*. Tony Smith was no card-carrying Minimalist, and *Amaryllis* is more complex, in its unfolding asymmetry, than most Minimalist works. As with those aptitude tests of volume and conception, you have to remember how the object is seen from one side while seeing it from another. The black painting of the piece does not simply reinforce its unity but heightens a sense of the object as being of mysterious crystalline structure, with angles of such-and-such degree engendering in some determinate but elusive way the planes of a faceted "solid" (and its enveloping void of space, as if in negative).

With the related works *Cubic Modular Piece No. 2 (L-Shaped Modular Piece)* (1966; p. 300), and *Three x Four x Three* by Sol LeWitt (1984; p. 306) one confronts definitively Minimalist works with thoroughly interchangeable modular units. Even Tony Smith's *Amaryllis* seems, by comparison, to consist of a diversity of interresponding elements. Fabricated in steel with a finish of white baked enamel, these two structures are among LeWitt's many three-dimensional grids, each systematically developed within a set of possibilities and open to execution without limit as to scale. These structures are so "abstract" that they suggest for some the sheer structurality of mind itself, while their whiteness can only corroborate a "neoclassically" rational look. Paradoxically, however, their presence is so concrete that they also seem to offer a furniturelike aspect, as though something could be at once a piece of pure thought and, say, in this case, an étagère. If such art may not seem to "say" much, it does evidently speak with utmost clarity. Consider, here, how two vertically stacked wall-like sections interpenetrate where they come together in a right angle: neither stack has to give way to the other, and interpenetration makes for no

uneven emphasis. The structure is simply, clearly, and mutely available to beholding.

To wonder about the concreteness of furniture or architecture—LeWitt's structures also readily suggest the orthogonal girders of building construction—is appropriate when considering works of Minimalist art. Their utter concreteness would make them sculptures practically, whether the artist liked it or not. Robert Murray's *Track* (1966; also p. 372), a carefully conjoined ramplike pair of boxy steel rectangular tubes, has the architectonic of the well-known McMath Solar Telescope at Kitt Peak, Arizona, finished in 1962 to designs of the architectural firm of Skidmore, Owings & Merrill. The assembly detail of *Track* is more to the point than is necessarily the case with Minimalist sculpture, while a spiffy red paint job carries a certain period flavor.

Robert Murray
Track 1966 (see p. 372)

While most Minimalists have continued over the past twenty-five years on fairly unwavering paths, Robert Morris has so transformed his work that one almost has to look down into the lens of time to regain a sense of such a classic earlier piece as the Walker's untitled felt relief of 1968 (p. 366). Here in a single work is much of this new generation's argument against the domination of "beautiful" formal art, especially in respect to painting. Just because the piece does retain sculptural conviction, it may require some retrospective imagination to sense the seeming impertinence with which it once presented itself. The felt relief is tantamount to a mockery of the very status or "standing" of painting as something that hangs ineffectually on the wall. Morris's two layers of limp felt are pliably heavy, "plastic" enough to be basically sculptural; cut through in even horizontal bands (in incidental parody of Stella's Black paintings?) and left to droop, they claim a kind of attention, as well as wall space, from painting.

The desire to take sculpture down to an ultimate materiality has been for Carl Andre much more than a matter of formal "reduction:" it connotes an honest, uncompromised negotiation of a real task—the very work of workers, of "navvies," as well as, say, building contractors. Some find it difficult to grasp, except as irony, how this politically active artist could have produced sculpture in which regular-sized units of industrial metal plate are simply put down on the floor in rows or grids so uninflected as hardly to be configurations at all. Andre's views have a dogged, Yankee literalness. (His plan to charge for floor pieces per square foot can only have shown up cynics.) *Slope 2004* (1968; p. 102) juts out across the floor from the wall at an oblique angle, but to the extent that this generates anything like "composition" it does so only in relation to the given room; also, while the piece stakes a territorial claim, it doesn't "hog" any space because it is okay to walk on it. So, while presenting itself boldly, its hardy materiality is prepared to recede into the condition of floor tiling or other ordinary constructional work that "can take it." The cult of "real materials" (Tatlin) in Russian Revolutionary Constructivism was in this sense renewed by Andre and the other principal Minimalists.

Donald Judd has produced not only individual, boxlike sculptures but also sets of several boxlike units comprising single "pieces." His 1968 untitled (p. 268), an open stainless steel and Plexiglas box, is in every respect unitary; in fact, it simply rests on one unprivileged long side, almost as if merely parked on the floor. Indeed, it bespeaks a culture of inorganic materials and of their (secondary) processing and mobilization in industry. Judd's works are things made without evidence of "human touch." The six sheet-metal boxes of Judd's later untitled (1971; p. 270) are for all intents and purposes identical, marching side-by-side in squared-away file; units of this kind imply the stereotypic. Yet Judd's boxes can reward closer reading: the 1971 units are closed on all four sides but have recessed ends, almost in reinterpretation of the semitransparent, rectangularly tubular, open-ended single box of 1968. Gestalt psychology tells us we can take in up to six units without counting, which may be one reason why the set of boxes can be so clear in its unity as well as its multiplicity.

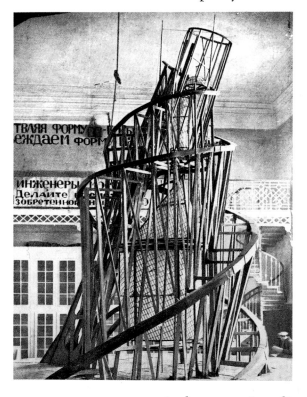

Vladimir Tatlin
Model of the *Monument to the Third International*
1919–1920
Plate from book by
N. Punin: *Tatlin (After Cubism)*, St. Petersburg, 1921

Richard Serra's *Prop* (1968; p. 552) and Dan Flavin's *"monument" for V. Tatlin* (1969; p. 208) advertise the urgency of such materialist matters in Minimalism. In studio teaching, Serra laid emphasis on basic manipulative processes, an approach that is related to "ordinary" body movements in avant-garde dance. In *Prop* this concerns the sheer physical standing of the piece as a function of weight, position, friction, and the force of gravity; more specifically, the forthrightly manipulated, hardly *transformed*, identity of two pieces of sheet metal, one rolled tight into the "prop" that by leaning holds the other against the wall. Considering the likely skewing of the square lead sheet against the wall, there is an inevitable allusion to Kasimir Malevich's then increasingly important *Suprematist Composition: White on White* (1918), with its skewed near-square in a square field. Comparably, Dan Flavin's "monument" declares a Russian modernist affiliation in its very title. Actually, Flavin's piece only resembles the spiraling trusswork of Vladimir Tatlin's projected *Monument to the Third International* (1919–1920) in the narrowing of its skyscraperlike "setbacks." But by its employment of real, industrial fluorescent light, equipment and all, it becomes an outright homage to Tatlin's sculptural materialism, while the glow of its equally real light can only be a comment back upon the poetic fictiveness of painting.

Other sculpture of around 1970 can be located in relation to the new outlook. Sculpturesque works by Robert Irwin dematerialize color, perhaps more than one thought possible, into a phenomenological experience of tinctured luminescence. Irwin's untitled 1965–1967 piece is a simple circular, buttonlike disk hovering before the wall (p. 262).[1] The same artist's 1971 untitled scrim piece (p. 264) is really an installation, that newly prominent sculptural strain, as well as a literalization of the seeming elusiveness of sheer light that for centuries was a definitive property of painting. Irwin's luminous scrim stretching down at a receding diagonal from ceiling to floor and lit from behind, "dematerializing" and diaphanous as it is, bears a resemblance to Minimalist sculpture, whether Serra's insertion of a large rolled steel plate into the corner of a room or, for that matter, Flavin's sculptures with fluorescent light, which are also installed in corners.

In Anthony Caro's *Straight Flush* (1972; p. 534) the rise of heavy-duty architectural steel is overwhelming when compared to the tenser, more epigrammatic recourse to steel in this artist's earlier constructions. The whole assumes a heaving, tumbledown aspect that is not altogether unrelated to minimalistically anti-formal sculpture. Conversely, Charles Ginnever's *Nautilus* (1976; p. 218) consists of six units, like Judd's 1971 row of cubes, here inverted triangular planes. In one sense that is all there is to it. But by raising the question of form—of, say, the chambered nautilus shell as aesthetically fascinating in the rigor of its incremental mathematical expansion—it breaks an anathema, in a way. No wonder the lowest, broadest triangle of the series seems to take up a special punctuating function, almost like the clearly formal role of the clubfootlike trapezoid in Caro's early *Sculpture Three, 1962*.

Two huge abstract paintings of 1971, each with an expanse of canvas subtly marked by straight lines or edges, offer distinctly different artistic alternatives around the turn of the decade. Robert Motherwell's *Untitled* (1971; p. 368) forms a direct link with the New York School in its Abstract Expressionist heyday and also an indirect one with the Matissean strain of European painting. *Untitled*, which belongs to Motherwell's series of Opens, offers an expanse of almost gaseously disembodied color. Yet this field carries not only nuances of pentimenti but structurally attuned inflections: a light ocher square with a hard outside edge and irregular brushwork inside, versus a black irregular "blob" floating free, with a pair of perpendicular lines forming two right angles inside it. The dark patch, itself inflected for a small stretch along its rim by a clinging patch of yellow ocher, recalls the subtly worked abutments in Clyfford Still's *Untitled* (1950; p. 504), while the square might be likened to the pair of vertical bands toward the left and right ends of Barnett Newman's *The Third*—a matched "pair" of elements now seen to demark a ragged, irregular strip of red at the left as against a whole and even one at right.

The other 1971 canvas is by Ed Moses. *ILL. 245 Hegemann* (p. 546) is one of a series of unstretched paintings marked by ranges of parallel lines. These constitute a kind of homemade, adversarial response to mainstream abstraction, whether European or American. The works introduce themselves as something equal to high abstraction, claiming modern self-sufficiency but in an unorthodox way. The canvas has pointedly not been stretched in the normal way over a conventional rectangular stretcher—that 1960s touchstone of the concrete givens of painting. A wide band of poured resin, now yellowed and brittle, frames the heavy drape of

1. Non-titles have something of a prehistory in photography, which has been followed by artists in other media. They were used on occasion by George H. Seeley, whose 1904 work was even exhibited as *No Title* (also known as *The Pines Whisper*) in 1910, while Paul Strand normally used no title at all, not even *that*; see Weston Naef, *The Collection of Alfred Stieglitz: Fifty Pioneers of Modern Photography* (New York: Metropolitan Museum of Art/Viking Press, 1978), pp. 432, 472. No doubt the early photographers meant to stress the formal self-sufficiency of their images, as against the literary significance associated with conventional art-pictures; the later artists would seem, by extension, to lay emphasis on their works' "abstract" facticity.

canvas: not ideal edges as "given" in formalistic theory of the time but something else, something that assumes an "alternative," identifiably West Coast stance while also implicating process. Indeed, the titles of paintings in this series refer to the illustrations in Elizabeth Hegemann's *Navajo Trading Days* (1963), a book dealing with Navajo weaving; but instead of actual textiles, the photographs identified in Moses's titles show weaving as an activity in Navajo life.[2]

One of the most systematic approaches to painting in the 1970s that does bear comparison with Minimalism entails implicit or explicit grid structure. Its apparent structural self-evidence notwithstanding, the grid has an artistic history, from grids as underlying ornamental and modular patterns, through the disassembly of pictorial structure in earlier modern painting, to the latter-day eschewal of "relational" composition. An uncommonly complex example is Jennifer Bartlett's *Series VIII (Parabolas)*, also of 1971 (p. 124), in which a vast, shifting, watery array of repeating sideways parabolas results from the simple filling of fine-lined graphlike grids with single tiny touches of color in a system of linear and incremental repetition. Strikingly labor-intensive, Bartlett's method has a marked feminist aspect, as in analogy with needlework. Over all, *Parabolas* consists of six vertical tiers, each comprising six one-foot-square plates: having the vertical tiers separated by foot-wide blank spaces of wall serves rhythmically to punctuate, like measures in music, what would otherwise be a relentless mega-grid of 2,304 tiny squares.

Agnes Martin started off with a much "tougher," less Jamesian-"tender," approach to painting than that evidenced by work, such as the Walker's *Untitled No. 7* (1977; p. 350), for which she became revered in the 1970s. Her works of about 1960 are as frontal and blocky as anything conceivably Minimal in painting. Of a group of Martin paintings from the early 1960s with rows of bars locked in the surface, Donald Judd wrote: "All of the pieces have a slight border of canvas or paper; the field is that of a rectangle and is not a section of an implied continuum;" and, "in a quiet way, the work is forceful."[3] Despite the subsequent development of Martin's painting through something more elusive and "romantic," Judd's point can help qualify the grid in *Untitled No. 7* as a sufficient entirety and not a sample from an endless, potentially decorative, repetition. The careful, unobsessive hand drawing of Martin's grid keeps us from taking the grid for granted and permits variant readings of the interstices as bars or spaces in shifting alternation.[4] If there is a feminist point here, it must be that Martin effects a large, full, and still affirmatively sensitive totality by means one might have thought limited to an intimistic scale.

Brice Marden's painting is likely to be considered reductive or Minimalist by anyone impatient with such a seemingly simple but thoroughgoing abstraction. If anything, work like the 1971–1972 *Untitled* (p. 344) leaves no room for casual reconnaissance. Certainly a dense materiality is of the essence here: except for a pervasive sentience, the image might almost be masonry pure and simple, three

2. Joseph Mascheck, "Ed Moses and the Problem of 'Western' Tradition," *Arts Magazine*, vol. 50 (December 1975), pp. 56–61.
3. Donald Judd, *Complete Writings, 1959–1975* (Halifax: Press of the Nova Scotia College of Art and Design and New York: New York University Press, 1975), p. 112.
4. Compare the subtleties in gridded building facades by Ludwig Mies van der Rohe, an architect also often misperceived as reductivistic or "Minimalist;" see Joseph Mascheck, "Reflections in Onyx," *Art in America*, vol. 74 (April 1986), pp. 138–151, 203, esp. p. 146.

slabs of dressed stone. However, Marden's materiality is a function of the beeswax medium, which carries an air of almost bodily pliability. But beeswax was also the medium of the Eastern Orthodox icon painting tradition, and if Marden's piece seems built up, even "filled" up, something of the icon's airless frontality or confrontation proffers itself too. The larger point is that a work so palpably material supplies the necessarily "real" occasion for the very transcendence of materiality.

Some of the best American art of the 1970s is sculpture that in one way or another entails thought about painting. Lynda Benglis's work has toyed with, even mocked, the status of painting, as if to show up its special claims or contrived effects. Early on, she made piles of "expressionistic" colored latex heaped on the floor—converting a Pollock idea into one more material, sculptural process, à la Serra—or even had such "painterly" material ooze grossly through venetian blinds (the Albertian "window" of painting theory hilariously literalized?). *Excess* (1971; p. 532) is a Benglis relief that, with its colorism and wax medium, can be counted as painting; on the other hand, the fact that it is built up by the undisguised physical process of dripping makes it *thingly* and sculpturesque before all else. In these now classic pieces, on narrow, yard-long vertical boards, the medium collects in irregular deposits into a kind of reverse vermiculation, a badlands of irregular mesas and crevasses built up crustily rather than eroded away. *Excess* (and note the title) is in highest relief toward the center, culminating in a pair of transverse peaks that could imply a bodily, genital focus (labia) and/or a landscape.

Christopher Wilmarth's steel and glass *Trace* (1972; p. 524) might seem less ambiguously sculpturesque, but Wilmarth's work, while materially grounded and consciously Constructivist, continues the American romance with sheer luminescence—from nineteenth-century landscape painting to Robert Irwin's scrims. Wilmarth produced an aesthetically "soft" constructionality in sculpture through the translucency of his frosted glass, closely matched with plate steel of like dimensions. Having already likened other Wilmarth relief sculpture to the painting of Georgia O'Keeffe,[5] I cannot overlook a similarity here between *Trace* and an O'Keeffe painting in the Walker collection, *Lake George Barns* (1926; p. 402), in which the blue-white glow of a six-paned barn window is distinctly like Wilmarth's surprisingly "poetic" constructional logic, with its (materially) steel binding cable as (ideally) demarcating "line."

The Walker's collection also includes certain drawings—or "works on paper," as they have been qualified in the last decade—that augment some of the more conceptual, yet nevertheless sculpturesque, manifestations of recent art. Jan Dibbets's *Horizon 1°–10° Land* (1973; p.180) is an artwork whose premises are "abstract" in the sense of being essentially intellectual—here, a series of photographic slices, varying systematically in width, of the horizon as warped by the earth's curvature. Concepts of the whole earth as a massive spheroid and of the horizon as being "horizontal" only for a person at some one point on the vast curved surface are concretized in a lateral row of separately framed photographic prints whose varying widths make the curve in question seem curiously different each "time." The great Dutch landscapists of the seventeenth century had to come to terms with an utterly

5. Joseph Masheck, "Wilmarth's New Reliefs," in Wadsworth Atheneum, Hartford, CT, *Christopher Wilmarth: Nine Clearings for a Standing Man*, exh. cat., 1974, n.p.

"minimal" topography: not without wit, Dibbets extends just that sense of the relentless enforcement of the horizon.

Joel Shapiro's prismatic small "house" forms take the generic architectural prism as a pretext for abstract sculpture. His 1975 *Untitled* (p. 462) consists of a slab of bronze with a little "house" implanted in the center, the whole resting on a wooden, tablelike carpentry base with diagonal braces. When, as in the Walker piece, the house form is rendered as if in perspectival diminution, it cannot escape comparison with the qualified, sometimes reversed, perspective rendering of simple chunky houses in the paintings of Cézanne. No wonder the works assume a retrospective overtone of earlier modernity: what may have seemed shy a decade ago proves perspicacious in having managed to embody some sense of doubt and withdrawal in the "late modern" condition. With Richard Nonas's *Razor-Blade* (1977; p. 548) and Robert Mangold's *Pink X within X* (1980; p. 336) sculpture and painting are found practically neck-and-neck. Both are long-armed, cross-shaped constructions in which line subdivides the principal members in a controlled structural ambiguity. That Mangold's *Pink X within X* hangs skewed on the wall as a relief brings it as close as possible to the Minimalist sculpturalism with which Nonas's *Razor-Blade* territorially organizes the floor. Nonas's piece has its own linear, graphic aspect in the thin channels between its abutting steel bars, analogous to the applied graphic lines of Mangold's eccentric but pristine painted surface. Nonas, who has done field research in anthropology, shows something of the logical differentiation of structuralist thought as it emerged from specialized anthropology into general cultural discourse. His piece has one long bar, square in section, extending through or between two short crossbars, also square in section, on either side of the center: lucidly "linguistic," the doubling of the shorter, cut lengths accounts for their being shortened.

The work of the British artist Richard Long has a decidedly conceptual aspect, in that much of it consists of photographs, documentarily presented, of lengthy "walks" undertaken as works of art in various locales around the world. These large projects have deep roots in the very British tradition of amateur topographical art pursued on treks in the wilds. Yet, like Robert Smithson, Long brings nature "home" into the cultural sphere. *Minneapolis Circle* (1982; p. 318) is typical: collected irregular specimens characteristic of the place—here, red slate flags—are freely but fairly evenly distributed within a circular area. As a form, the circle seems meaningfully suggestive of a circuit or "round trip," not to mention its self-containment as independent of confinement. (How does this compare with painting?) A dignified sense of plain labor is also implied, something relevant to the work of Andre but, thanks to Carlyle as well as to Ruskin and William Morris, associated in British culture with a distinguished tradition of social theory. This is a large and obviously heavy work of "stone sculpture" that manages to do without the taint of domination that monumental stone sculpture anciently acquired.

A sense of nature was also important around 1980 to painters seeking new expressive involvement with painting as a special mode of human activity. The horse parts in Susan Rothenberg's *Tattoo* (1979; p. 434) are pretextual in the sense that they seem generated out of a psychological primitivism, pertaining as such to "natural" mental life, and also in that they furnish something to work with, some not unmeaningful "material" for abstract manipulation. Perhaps the title implies concern with tribal body ornament, which was important a century ago to theoreticians who were interested in primitive ornamental art for its proto-abstract stylizations.

Elizabeth Murray's *Sail Baby* (1983; p. 370) is a fully abstract painting that may be invested with, but not consumed by, skepticism. For a solid decade Murray has been producing serious abstract painting of a high order, often almost metaphysically comical. In *Sail Baby*, three bulgy, bulbous forms nuzzle and nudge one another like a kind of papa, mama, and baby bear family of biomorphs, descendants of the "guitar-woman" forms in Cubist painting. The triad is held together by distractingly interesting colored areas that, by reverse camouflage, strive to hold the shimmying cluster together. Most remarkable in Murray's art is the coincidence of beauty and wit, the beauty being, as usual, more difficult to account for.

The sculpture of Scott Burton is as intelligent as it, too, is often ironic. An utter concreteness takes root right where we were used to making do with a mere idea—above all, the generic chair, "the chair," that is, of so much Conceptual Art and general philosophic speculation. While each of the artist's two-part chairs can obviously be sat upon, this instrumentality is incidental. One cannot look at *Two-Part Chairs, Obtuse Angle (A Pair)* (1983–1984; p. 144) and not be led to consider the L-shaped parts in relation to one another, or the negative keystonelike space beneath the seat, or the masses of stone in relation to gravity, or even—to return to the conceptual by a back door—to what degree the very grain of the polished stone, on the most profoundly material level, makes it impossible for two concrete things ever to be absolutely identical.

Finally, Sol LeWitt's mural for the lower lobby of the Walker Art Center, *Four Geometric Figures in a Room* (1984; p.302), confronts us as an architecturally attuned project by a sculptor but in the form of abstract painting. The color scheme, with blue geometric figures banded in yellow against a Pompeian red ground, even recalls the red-grounded Roman murals of the ancient room from Boscoreale, now in The Metropolitan Museum of Art, which Mark Rothko must have pondered a generation ago. The disposition of the Walker murals is clever: four geometric figures occupy two adjacent walls in conjunction with similarly color-banded real architectural features on the others. The set of geometric figures further subdivides logically into one pair of regular figures—circle and square—and another of modified forms—a rhombus and a truncated triangle. LeWitt has used the truncated triangle before in similar sets of elements, no doubt in order to gain for it a greater equality of area with similarly scaled circles and squares. It may not be too much of a conceit to recall that, in purely geometrical terms, this is not unlike the truncated triangular element of Caro's *Sculpture Three, 1962*, that definitively "formal" form so different from the forms purged of relationality in all Minimalist sculpture. The significance of forms, after all, is not intrinsic but contextual, as in the special context of the museum we may have ideal occasion to see.

Joseph Masheck is Associate Professor of Art History and Coordinator of the Graduate Humanities Program at Hofstra University, Hempstead, New York, and a contributing editor of *Art in America*. For the past several years he has been at work on a study of the origins and afterlife of the idea of the "statue in the rock," long associated with the work of Michelangelo and the relationship of form to material. His second volume of essays, *Modern Supplies: Art-Matters in the Present*, is forthcoming.

Pop Art and After

Carter Ratcliff

In *POPism: The Warhol '60s*, the artist recalls the atmosphere at his New York studio, the Factory, where he produced paintings of flowers, Jackie Kennedy, and "some big square Marilyns with different-color backgrounds." Warhol and an assistant worked "with Lesley Gore singing 'You Don't Own Me' and Dionne Warwick doing 'A House Is Not a Home' and bouncy hits by Gary Lewis and the Playboys and Bobby Vee playing."[1]

"The truth is," the critic Max Kozloff wrote in 1962, "the art galleries are being invaded by the pin-headed and contemptible style of gum-chewers, bobby soxers, and, worse, delinquents."[2] That year, the target of Kozloff's outrage had several names, none firmly attached: "The New Realism," "common object art," "Neo-Dada." After a season or two, the New York art world had agreed to call the new phenomenon "Pop Art," a label that still covers Andy Warhol's images of Jackie and Marilyn and Campbell Soup cans, Claes Oldenburg's colossal hamburgers and drum sets, Roy Lichtenstein's blowups of comic book panels, Tom Wesselmann's glossy nudes, and James Rosenquist's evocations of a commercial landscape dominated by billboards.

Some of Pop Art's early detractors later came to see that it had a significant part in the modernist endeavor—that Pop elaborated the potential of the allover field; brought fresh complexities to the negotiations between abstraction

Roy Lichtenstein
Artist's Studio No. 1 (Look Mickey) 1973
(detail, see p. 308)

1. Andy Warhol and Pat Hackett, *POPism: The Warhol '60s* (New York: Harcourt Brace Jovanovich, 1980) p. 70.
2. Max Kozloff, "Pop Culture, Metaphysical Disgust, and the New Vulgarians" (1962), reprinted in Kozloff, *Renderings: Critical Essays on a Century of Modern Art* (New York: Simon and Schuster, 1969), p. 221.

and the figure; and, in general, demanded that the audience expand its notion of aesthetic seriousness. The style not only belongs to modernism, it enlarges the tradition's possibilities. Two signs of its strength: first, Pop has encouraged the human figure to persist in contemporary art, as we see in work as diverse as Chuck Close's portraits and Robert Longo's constructions; second, Pop Art reached beyond itself even in the work of its first practitioners, who have developed their original premises so richly that the Pop label applies only to their work of the 1960s. In place of Pop Art, we now have the mature work of Warhol and Lichtenstein, Wesselmann, Oldenburg, and Rosenquist.

But in the early 1960s those devoted to the accomplishments of the New York School and its European heritage saw Pop Art as a flippant insult to Willem de Kooning, Jackson Pollock, Barnett Newman, and the entire enterprise of modernist art. To some viewers, the unashamed legibility of the style was as offensive as any particular message. Although the New York art world of the 1950s encouraged controversy, a consensus had formed on one point: Abstract Expressionism and its offshoots provided an alternative to the imagery of popular culture. If the commercial landscape assaulted the eye with images all too easily deciphered, serious art would insist on being difficult and, for the most part, nonfigurative. In serious art, human forms had to struggle to be seen. What the critics of Pop objected to was not only the movement's "contemptible style" but as well the prosaic presence of the figure. Yet the struggle to keep the figure was continuous through the

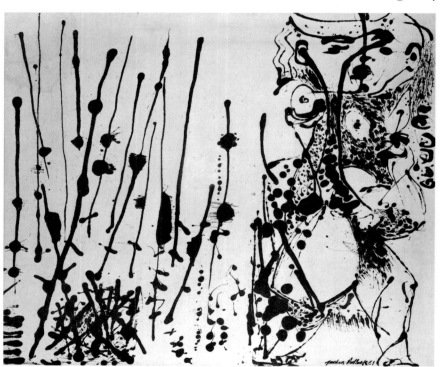

Willem de Kooning
Woman, 1 1950–1952
oil on canvas
75⅞ x 58 (192.7 x 147.3)
Collection The Museum
of Modern Art, New York
Purchase

Jackson Pollock
Number 7, 1951 1951
oil on canvas
56½ x 66 (143.5 x 167.6)
Collection National Gallery
of Art, Washington
Gift of the Collectors
Committee

1950s: in 1951 Pollock let recognizable figures appear in his paintings, and faces and bodies often welled up from de Kooning's painterly lather.

The impress of the world and its inhabitants was so strong in the work of second-generation New York painters such as Lester Johnson, Larry Rivers, and Alex Katz that critics began to talk of a figurative revival. Johnson questions that revival. "For some of us," he has said, "the figure never went away."[3] His dark canvases, with their slashing, dripping brushstrokes, evolved directly from first-generation Action Painting—from the abstract style of Franz Kline, Robert Motherwell, and

3. Conversation with the author, spring 1982.

even de Kooning. But when Johnson attacked the canvas that became *Figures with Columns* (1965; p. 540), he insisted on discovering human presences there. Layering, smearing, and gouging his pigment, Johnson emphasizes the surface and edges of the canvas—the basic geometry of his medium, which finds an echo in the images of angular men and flattened-out Doric columns. Whether delicate or violent, painterly painters like Johnson leave the edges of their forms ambiguous. From the elusive play of figure and ground comes nuances of feeling, subtleties of atmosphere.

Richard Lindner offers refinements of a different kind. Born in Hamburg and a resident of Paris for most of the 1930s, Lindner immigrated to the

Roy Lichtenstein
Roto Broil 1961
oil on canvas
68½ x 68½ (174 x 174)
Private collection

United States at the outbreak of World War II. Fascinated by the billboards and magazine ads, the calendar art and even the pornography of America, he is sometimes seen as a predecessor of the Pop artists. Like them, he invites commercial graphics to cross the border between high and low art. Nonetheless, a wide gulf separates Lindner from the practitioners of Pop. Lindner arranges his paintings according to the dictates of traditional composition (*119th Division*, 1963; p. 312). The Pop artists do not. As elaborated during the Renaissance and afterward, composition employs visual checks and balances to bring the disparate parts of an image into a harmonious balance. By contrast, Andy Warhol's *16 Jackies* (1964; p. 518) imposes a rigid symmetry. In 1961 Roy Lichtenstein filled a square canvas with a rendering of a Roto Broil cooker.

These anti-compositional tactics had a precedent in the allover fields of Jackson Pollock, Barnett Newman, and other members of the New York School's first generation. And Jasper Johns's Flag paintings, which align the edges of an image with the edges of the canvas, showed the Pop artists how to attain an allover effect with figurative imagery.

Lindner's allegiance to high-art traditions of composition also reminds us of his European heritage, which permitted him to view the American city from an imaginary distance even as he lived in its midst. The distance between the artist and America was actual in the case of the British painters who inspired the critic Lawrence Alloway to coin the phrase "Pop Art" in the late 1950s. Oppressed by the dreariness of postwar Britain, enchanted by Hollywood and a world conjured up by rock and roll, these artists made paintings from logos, celebrity images, and the language of billboards. Their homage to America was ironic and often private.

David Hockney filled his version of Pop with diaristic allusions, some of them indecipherable. Joe Tilson evolved a set of enigmatic emblems from everyday images found on television screens, shop signs, and magazine pages (*LOOK!*, 1964; p. 556). Richard Smith pushed aggressive, hard-sell advertising graphics toward an elegant variety of abstraction (*Quartet*, 1964; p. 484). British Pop tells a story of yearning for America and, at the same time, of mocking one's desires. It evokes an imaginary future, a time of fulfillment it knows (with a touch of relief) will never arrive. American Pop, by contrast, reflects the immediate, all-encompassing present generated by a nonstop image-barrage.

Behind the Pop movement in America is a phenomenon of

the late 1950s, the Happening, which Jim Dine helped invent in collaboration with Allan Kaprow, Claes Oldenburg, Lucas Samaras, and others. Happenings were theatrical events designed to extend the improvisatory spirit of Action Painting from two to three dimensions. Supplying props and script, Oldenburg put on his first Happening, *Snapshots from the City*, in 1960. During this period he designed sets and costumes for dance concerts and underground theater pieces. Moreover, his environmental installations—especially *The Street* (1960) and *The Store* (1960)—gave gallery space the atmosphere of a Happening. Bizarre in shape and roughly finished, Oldenburg's sculpture from this period gives off Expressionist heat.

Claes Oldenburg
View of *The Street* as installed in the Judson Gallery, New York, during the *Ray Gun Show*, January 1960

In 1961 Oldenburg began to make life-size sculptures of pastries, hamburgers, and ice cream sodas from painted plaster. As these became more realistic, he took yet another direction. His objects soon grew immense and, astonishingly, soft, as he taught himself to work with kapok-stuffed canvas and vinyl. *Upside Down City* (1962; p.404), one of the artist's first soft sculptures, has the passionately improvised look of the objects displayed in *The Street* and *The Store*. Sagging toward the floor, the city's skyscrapers let go of their architectural form and take on a vaguely organic air. Quickly sprayed dashes of color indicate windows. Oldenburg still feels the pull of abstractions in the Action Painter's style.

His *Shoestring Potatoes Spilling from a Bag* (1966; p. 406) shows him clarifying his imagery. From now on his abstraction will point up sharp visual equivalencies. As the potatoes descend toward the floor, they also appear to reach toward the ceiling. With a dreamlike wit, these soft forms combine monumental presence with hints of human gestures and bodily attitudes. The massive *Three-Way Plug-Scale A, Soft, Brown* (1975; p.410) levitates above us like a weirdly reassuring UFO. During the last decade Oldenburg has turned often to gigantic public works. Designed for outdoor sites, these projects have required his forms to grow rigid again, yet they preserve what might be called their monumental friendliness. *Alphabet/Good Humor, 3-Foot Prototype* (1975; p.548) is a study for a public sculpture. Though it is unified and simple, this object presents remarkably complex articulations—like a body, perhaps, or a convoluted vegetable. Yet it owes its organic presence not to natural form but to the alphabet, as if Oldenburg sees life in verbal abstraction and something like the patterns of language in living beings.

Tom Wesselmann's *Great American Nude #32* (1962; p. 558) shares some of Lichtenstein's and Warhol's themes but not their desire to find a Pop equivalent of an allover image. In a manner reminiscent of Matisse, Wesselmann balances organic form against the shapes of windows, doors, and furniture. The resulting compositions are lush to the point of hedonism. George Segal's *The Diner* (1964–1966; p. 454), built from actual hardware and lighting fixtures, makes a bleak comment on urban life—too bleak to count as Pop Art, which neither condemns nor celebrates its subject matter. Peopling his fragments of the city with awkward, unexpressive plaster effigies, Segal presents ordinary life as mute and alienated. His later bas-reliefs (such as *Embracing Couple*, 1975; p. 456) remove the plaster wrappings used in the casting process. Its flesh unencumbered, the Segalesque body now evokes antique statuary. Like Segal, Lucas Samaras has always refused to cultivate the dead-pan glamour of a Warhol *Jackie* or a Lichtenstein comic book panel. Samaras's sculptures tell stories of grotesque and violent transformations. His untitled chairs (1965; p. 448) defy sitters—one bristles with pins; the other, bearing a tracery of yarn in garish colors, would collapse from one's weight on its tilted legs. Samaras presents us with signs of the emotions that rage behind the facades of Segal's tableaux of anonymous public life.

The bright, solid blocks of color and stencil-like lettering of Robert Indiana's paintings bring us back to the Pop landscape. "EAT" says one large canvas. "DIE" says another (*The Green Diamond Eat* and *The Red Diamond Die*, 1962; p. 258). With a terseness learned from highway signs, the artist presents a full life cycle. Images of the American highway veer close to the realm of abstraction in Allan D'Arcangelo's hard-edge reminders of traffic markers and through-the-windshield perspectives (p. 535). Chryssa's neon and aluminum *Times Square Sky* (1962; p. 534) condenses the Manhattan night into an intricately layered logo. As lettering drifts free of any coherent message, the alphabet's familiar meanings linger like ghosts. Nicholas Krushenick's *Battle of Candy Stripes* (1964; p. 542) exorcises language and, indeed, any image of the world beyond its frame. This is abstract Pop, as is Eduardo Paolozzi's *Silk* (1965; p. 549).

Pop Art redefined the allover field, opening it to the impact of the news, entertainment, and advertisements—the world of images from which the Abstract Expressionists had fled. Dismissed early on as transient and faddish, Pop has been the vehicle for works of major ambition, among them James Rosenquist's *Area Code* (1970; p. 428). As an art student experimenting in an Abstract Expressionist style, Rosenquist supported himself by painting billboards in midtown Manhattan. The artist said in 1964 that he learned the most "from painting signs. I painted things from photos and I had quite a bit of freedom in interpretation, but, still … it felt like I hadn't done it, that it had been done by a machine … [My paintings are] still done the same way."[4] Rosenquist's billboard-scale version of Pop pushes familiar images to the verge of abstraction. Even after the color streaks of *Area Code* resolve themselves into frayed coaxial cables, they continue to work as flurries of red, orange, and purple—especially when distorted by the shiny surfaces of Mylar that appear at one end of the large expanse of canvas. *Area Code* evokes the artist's vision of "the way things are thrust at us, the way this invisible screen that's a couple of feet in front of our mind and our senses is attacked by radio and television and visual communications, through things bigger than life."[5] Submitting to the attack, Rosenquist lets his imagination be absorbed by the "invisible screen" of the media. Making that screen visible in his art, he remakes it on his own, implicitly critical terms. Unlike the other Pop artists, Rosenquist invites us to question the overbearing images that inhabit our cultural landscape.

Roy Lichtenstein is more concerned with ironies of taste than with media power. "It was hard to get a painting that was despicable enough so that no

4. James Rosenquist, "Interview with G.R. Swenson" (1964), reprinted in *Pop Art Redefined*, eds. John Russell and Suzi Gablik (New York: Praeger, 1969), p. 112.
5. Ibid., p. 111.

one would hang it," he said. "It was almost acceptable to hang a dripping paint rag. The one thing everyone hated was commercial art." Having spent the 1950s painting in an Abstract Expressionist manner, Lichtenstein turned first to the advertising pages of the newspapers, then to comic books of love and war. As we have seen, many were appalled. Yet by 1963 the artist could say, "Apparently they didn't hate [commercial art] enough either"[6]—Pop Art was already beginning to achieve critical success. Although Lichtenstein denies any didactic intent, recommending that we focus on the play of color and line, his images of heartbroken heroines and war-mad heroes remind us of the degree to which we define ourselves and others with stereotypes.

Roy Lichtenstein
Woman with Flowered Hat
1963
Magna on canvas
50 x 40 (127 x 101.6)
Courtesy Gagosian Gallery,
New York

Lichtenstein's *Woman with Flowered Hat* (1963) added a new kind of heroine to his repertory: a figure from Picasso's Cubist portraiture, which Lichtenstein found in a book of reproductions. With images borrowed from Mondrian, Abstract Expressionism, Art Deco, Monet, Surrealism, German Expressionism and even, in 1979, American Indian art, Lichtenstein has continued to find his themes in the form of four-color reproductions. In 1973–1974, he recapitulated his Pop career to date in a four-part series of canvases called the Artist's Studio. The Walker's *Artist's Studio No. 1 (Look Mickey)* (1973; p. 308) incorporates his 1961 picture of Donald Duck and Mickey Mouse, a mirror from a decade later, one of the 1964 landscapes, and wall moldings and sofa ruffles, which recall the Entablatures that first appeared in 1971. For Lichtenstein, Pop Art became a means of systematically Lichtensteinizing our visual culture, of capturing and remaking it according to the dictates of his own cool wit.

If Lichtenstein's dots and lines recall the crudities of four-color comic book printing, Los Angeles Pop artist Ed Ruscha's touch mimics the much more elegant look of slick magazine reproduction. In *Steel* (1969; p. 444), the image undertakes its own mimicry—the letters spelling out the title flow over the canvas like some rusty liquid. Deflecting the confrontational aggression of New York Pop, Ruscha cultivates a bemused delight in paradox. *No.1 Mirror* (1971–1973; p. 226) by Robert Graham, also a California artist, looks like a Minimalist environment reduced to portability. An arrangement of severe forms, it is also the habitat of two female nudes rendered with obsessive accuracy. Graham's figures have gotten bigger over the years. For the 1984 Olympics, he sculpted a pair of nude figures roughly twice life-size. But whether large or small, his forms propose a zone of the imagination where sensuousness and monumentality join to produce an atmosphere of meditative quiet.

Siah Armajani learned much from the Minimalist example, yet his art never strives for geometric purity. Inflecting simple forms with memories of vernacular architecture, Armajani evokes the world of frame houses and railroad trestles—a story-laden landscape. The artist's designs for parks and other public places (model for the Irene Hixon Whitney Bridge, 1985; p.114) intermingle his imaginary narratives with the flow of daily life. Donna Dennis, too, uses anonymous buildings as

6. Roy Lichtenstein, "Interview with G.R. Swenson" (1963), reprinted in *Pop Art Redefined*, eds. John Russell and Suzi Gablik (New York: Praeger, 1969), p. 92.

sources (*Station Hotel*, 1974; p. 535), though her art is more private than Armajani's. Reducing the size of her borrowed forms, she transforms them into architectural emblems. The effect is paradoxical: immediate and theatrically present, her sculptures also stand apart in a melancholy region of half-told tales and silence.

The attempt to restore narrative content to Minimalist geometry led other artists—Robert Smithson, Michael Heizer, and Walter de Maria—to put earth-moving equipment to work in the deserts of the Far West. With it they built Earthworks large enough to inflect immense landscapes.

Christo, though not, strictly speaking, an earth artist, also refuses to work within gallery confines. Instead of building new forms, he wraps in fabric and cable a stretch of Australian coastline, a bridge in Paris, or a building such as the Reichstag in Berlin. *Wrapped Reichstag (project for Berlin)* (p. 534), completed in 1980, drew attention to the building's site near the wall between East and West Berlin, and to the memories of Fascism and world war that haunt the site. Leaving the building wrapped for only a few weeks, Christo tried to refocus our vision on a setting too easily overlooked. Bureaucratically complex and carefully designed, his work projects generate much paperwork. This documentary residue helps to shape the narratives implied by his shrouded forms.

Earthworks generate myths, usually of a heroic kind. Charles Simonds sustains the grandeur of myth while shrinking Earthworks to miniature sculptures of architectural ruins. After his earliest pieces appeared in vacant lots and other neglected corners of Manhattan, the artist began to publish fragments of imaginary archaeological lore, always taking care not to tie them too closely to particular sculptures. We must imagine for ourselves how the 1977 landscape called △ *Early* becomes △ *Later* (p. 474). And in looking at Michelle Stuart's books, we must try to intuit a landscape in their rubbed and sometimes battered pages. Stained with the dust of a particular place, Stuart's book sculptures, such as *Every Wave Book (For Melville)* (1979; p. 555), suggest that "reading" does not always involve language.

By enlarging faces, kitchen appliances, and tangles of spaghetti, James Rosenquist invites them to turn into patterns of color. Chuck Close extends a similar invitation to images of faces, his own (*Big Self-Portrait*, 1968; p.158) and those of his friends. First he pencils a grid over a snapshot portrait. On a large canvas he lays down a corresponding pattern. A painting appears as he transfers the contents of the smaller grid to the larger one. Deliberately working so near the surface that he cannot see the image as a picture, only as form and color, the artist obscures his representational intent. Yet the finished work is always an uncannily accurate enlargement of a photographic image—snapshot turned icon, with the shift from focused to unfocused regions of the face rendered with eerie accuracy.

On the one hand, the Photorealism of Chuck Close and others is representational in the spirit of Pop. On the other, its methods recall styles of abstraction such as Minimalism and the Process Art that developed from Minimalist carpentry and metalworking. From that contradiction, Photorealism developed a high degree of artifice. Jerry Ott's *Carol and the Paradise Wall* (1972; p. 549) shows a nude woman in an extravagant, Wesselmannesque pose; the lush woodland behind her is obviously a studio backdrop. This is a painting of a photograph, which, in turn, contains a photomural of "nature"—or was the backdrop of trees and sky an immense painting? Photorealists draw our attention to ambiguities that persist even when a picture is meticulously accurate.

Since the late 1960s, Kay Kurt's subject has always been some variety of candy. *Weingummi II* (1973; p. 542) shows candy fish, birds, and automobiles floating as they could never do in the gravity-bound space of a photograph. Her brushwork shows the obsessive precision, not of Photorealist transfer, but of fidelity to an inward vision. Joseph Raffael's touch blurs form (*Water Painting VII*, 1973; p. 550), producing a pattern of luminous color. The effect recalls photographs taken with the lens out of focus, and yet Raffael works intuitively. Impressionism, no less than the camera, has guided his vision of light.

Photorealists or not, these painters address similar problems. How, after the impersonalities of Pop Art, was it possible to confront the world directly, brush in hand? Was it not necessary by the late 1960s to acknowledge that even the most passionately private image has its conventional, emblematic aspects? And Minimalism's example seemed to require that the painter reveal the process of deploying the medium's conventions. Sylvia Plimack Mangold responded with dark, emotionally charged landscapes that would have looked like a rejection of all these concerns, except for one disconcerting detail. In *Carbon Night* (1978; p. 338), strips of masking tape and other signs of process frame earth and sky to insist that these images are, first of all, arrangements of pigment on canvas. Looking more closely, we see that Mangold's tape strips are also painted. Jud Nelson's *Hefty 2-Ply* (1979–1981; p. 380), the crumpled form of a trash bag faithfully transferred to Carrara marble, offers a comparable set of surprises in three dimensions.

As the 1970s began, Jack Beal and many other painters rejected the modernist imperative to abstraction. They attempted to heal the rift between painting's present and its pre-modern origins. The synthesis of now and then is apparent in Beal's *Nude on Sofa with Red Chair* (1968; p. 532), where play of line and vivid, unearthly color can be read without undue strain as a contribution to hard-edged abstraction.

William T. Wiley appropriates the allover field of Abstract Expressionism and Color Field painting in another spirit. With *I Won't Forget Again One Jillion Times* (1973; p. 522), he treats the canvas like a notepad. Hasty-looking scribbles and arcane symbols drift over the surface, entangling themselves in suggestions of a map. Claiming the allover field for his idiosyncratic ruminations, he turns its vastness in on itself. A West Coast artist, Wiley has established a carefully calibrated distance between himself and New York, the American art capital. So did the Chicagoan H.C. Westermann. Like Pop Art, Westermann's sculpture embraces ordinary imagery and inclines toward brash, iconic forms. Yet his methods and materials were resolutely traditional. Westermann was like an old-fashioned cabinetmaker under a Surrealist spell. *A Piece from the Museum of Shattered Dreams* (1965; p. 520) shows a bulky, enigmatic object (one's imagination keeps coming back to the suggestion of a hand grenade) slung over a scrawny column decorated with reminders of Carpenter Gothic. Two shark fins pierce the upper surface of the pedestal. Westermann conjured threat and disillusionment from our homiest, most comforting images.

Minimalism and Earthworks, Conceptualism and Performance Art—from the late 1960s through the following decade, these developments drew attention away from painted and sculpted images of the body. Yet, to quote Lester Johnson once more, "The figure never went away." For Deborah Butterfield, the figure is not human but animal. Her *Rosary* (1981; p. 146) shows a reclining horse built from metal and wood. As they define the creature's bulk, these materials wrinkle, surge, and jut in ways that recall the brushstrokes of Action Painting. Expressionist impulses have persisted as powerfully as the figure. Joe Zucker's *Pairkeets* (1973; p. 559) shows these same impulses oddly transformed by his decision to use Rhoplex-soaked cottonballs in place of brushstrokes. The resulting surface is unlike that of any other painter, yet we see immediately how to read cottonballs as if they were brushstrokes—the marks of a painterly painter, an Expressionist at that. Yet Zucker's process undermines even the illusion of Expressionist spontaneity. Producing an ambitious variant on the all-over field, his artifice counts, in a way, as entirely sincere.

The heavily painted surfaces of Susan Rothenberg's canvases are sincere in a more usual sense: evidence of the painter's touch conveys the pressures of strong feelings. As forms drift up out of Rothenberg's field of paint—outlines and emblems of horses in *Tattoo* (1979; p. 434)—we are challenged to see the artifice of this secretive, diaristic painting. Haunted and dreamlike, *Tattoo* is also the product of stern formal control. This inward-turning canvas also turns outward to make its contribution to the history of the New York School's allover field. So does Nicholas Africano's painting, *Ironing* (1978; p. 530). Starting with that Minimalist device, the monochrome surface, Africano invades it with a deliberately crude figure in low relief. And he adds a caption, breaking another Minimalist rule. Yet Africano's transgressions are more whimsical than violent. He teases the absolutism of the 1960s.

Richard Bosman's *Crossing* (1984; p. 533) shows a man clinging to a vine that hangs over a precipitous rushing stream; a second man grasps one leg of the first. In Bosman's narrative paintings ambiguities of style and theme are unexplained—as in the "mystery story," a genre of popular literature that provides the painter with his link to Pop Art. The artist's heavy, smeared brushwork recalls Expressionism, though it is not clear whether he has chosen as his ancestry the first generation of the New York School or the German Expressionists of the century's early decades.

Two Humeians Preaching Causality to Nature (1984; p. 534), by the Scottish painter Steven MacMillan Campbell, alludes to the writings of his eighteenth-century countryman David Hume, whose skepticism called into question our routine assumptions about cause and effect. It is not obvious why Campbell's Humeians reverse the philosopher's position as they address nature's denizens, animal and vegetable. Perhaps Campbell feels skeptical about Hume's skepticism. Throwing intellectual doubt into doubt, the artist steps up the power of gesture—that of his brush and of the statuesque figures his brush calls into being. Donald Sultan is an American who stays close to American sources. His *Forest Fire, April 13, 1984* (1984; p. 510) transposes to the medium of watercolor and tar Clyfford Still's heritage of looming, even Gothic forms. Still implied a narrative subject. Sultan spells it out, yet sustains the grandeur of his New York School heritage.

Though a shift from abstraction to explicit storytelling usually appears only when we trace developments from one generation to the next, it has occurred within a single career. Philip Guston was a pioneer Abstract Expressionist;

in 1969, he suddenly shifted to a figurative manner. His delicate touch remained, but now at the service of a purposely crude style of drawing. The leading characters in Guston's late paintings enact a cartoon version of the myth of the alienated artist. T.L. Solien, whose cartoon style likewise invades the realm of painterly refinements, ranges more widely. Evoking themes of birth and death, aspiration and survival, he reaches into memory for a style that looks childish at first glance (*The Bricklayer's Tender*, 1982; p. 490). And at second glance, too. Solien insists that his paintings show the impress of his earliest feelings. With the sophistication of his art—its complex patterns of allusion, its economical management of pictorial space—he suggests that maturity must have a reciprocal influence on all that memory calls forth.

Robert Longo's works, recalling Pop Art in general and James Rosenquist's early paintings in particular, evoke the power of the media images that crowd our attention and sometimes overwhelm us. He sees monumentality lurking in the public images we devise for ourselves. Longo makes drawings, paintings, and sculpture. He puts on performance pieces that employ photography, music, and dance. Whatever his medium, Longo's art feels statuesque. He calls up all that is impersonal—hence oppressive—about the contemporary city, whether it evolves with the speed of fashion in urban clothes or looms on the skyline decade after decade. With *National Trust* (1981; p. 320), he suggests that our image-monuments—of people or of architecture—are fragile and ghostly. Longo persuades the monumental to show where it is vulnerable.

David Hockney, whose early Pop works sought a rapport between images of everyday things and the high styles of European modernism, particularly Cubism and Expressionism, eventually became less interested in the flat, emblematic forms of the commercial landscape. Turning to the world of his immediate surroundings, sharpening his observations, Hockney refined his brushwork and adjusted his palette more precisely to nuances of light. *Hollywood Hills House* (1980; p. 246) evokes the climate of Los Angeles, where Hockney lives. With collage, he flattens space and recalls his Cubist heritage. The palm tree is a Hockneyesque emblem with Abstract Expressionist roots. Yet the painting coheres because a texture of observation, an accuracy that approaches realism, extends into every corner of the image. Of course Hockney's realist impulses are far from detached. He views even quiet interiors as spectacles to be managed pictorially, a way of seeing that led him to work for the stage. The Walker owns a version of the set he designed and painted in 1983 for Poulenc's opera *Les mamelles de Tirésias* (p. 248). In part an homage to Picasso and Cubism, this complex painting with its freestanding figures represents the full range of Hockney's art, from the early Pop phase to his L.A.-style realism. Reminders of the painter's travel sketches fill the work. Above all, it reflects his desire to displace ordinary life with the realm of theater.

In 1976 Jim Dine looked back on his years as a painterly painter closely allied to Pop Art: "Although I was able to draw with a certain degree of efficiency, I denied it. I always wanted to hide it because it wasn't American ... it wasn't in the Duchampian esthetic we all came to admire, which I feel is such an empty one, though very intelligent."[7] Warhol filled the Duchampian emptiness with irony. Dine wanted

7. Quoted in Constance W. Glenn, *Jim Dine: Drawing* (New York: Harry N. Abrams, 1985), p. 198.

his art to make a more direct address, so he began in the early 1970s to teach himself traditional draftsmanship—the technique of modeling and composition so effectively undermined by modernist painting's drive toward flatness. The results of Dine's self-discipline show in *My Studio #One: The Vagaries of Painting, "These are sadder pictures"* (1978; p. 188), a still life composed of small objects with monumental presences. Dine places his teapots, statuettes, and bottles in a panoramic space; a tabletop takes on the dimensions of a stage. Dramatic lighting brings out an extraordinary range of volumes and textures. A skull links this painting to the early still-life theme of *vanitas*, the emptiness of worldly things. Thus, whereas Pop paintings confront us with an all-enveloping *now*, Dine's later style charges the allegorical still life with a sense of time and history.

Yet whatever he says about his early days as a Pop painter, Dine has not completely repudiated his past. Like many Pop canvases, *My Studio #One* counts as a reinvention of the allover field. Though *The Crommelynck Gate with Tools*, a bronze sculpture from 1983 (p. 190), employs a traditional material, its image has the emblematic flatness Dine himself did so much to define in the 1960s. Appearing in many of his drawings and prints, the motif originates in the gate to the Parisian workshop where Dine has made many of his lithographs. Picasso worked there, too, and *The Crommelynck Gate* recalls the sculptural experiments that led to the so-called drawing in space of Picasso and Gonzalez. Moreover, it reminds us that the American David Smith also "drew" with thin metal forms. Dine's mature art does not deny his beginnings so much as extend them in directions unimaginable a quarter of a century ago.

Pop seemed at first to have abandoned the modernist ideal of progress, which usually produced abstract imagery. Now Dine and the others have shown us that Pop Art pursued another and, in many ways, more powerful ideal: not a relentless advance toward an exclusively aesthetic goal but an insistence that art find its meaning in contact with life.

Carter Ratcliff is an art critic and poet. A contributing editor to *Art in America*, he also writes frequently for other art journals. Ratcliff is the author of a number of books of art criticism, including *Art Criticism: Other Minds, Other Eyes, 1974–1975*, *Willem de Kooning*, 1975, *Robert Smithson*, 1979, and most recently, *Komar and Melamid*. He is working on a book about postwar American painting.

Collection Entries

Identification Key	Example
Artist's Name	**Louise Bourgeois**
Title of Work date	**The Blind Leading the Blind** 1989
nationality, birth place, birth date—death date	American, b. France, 1911
medium	**painted and lacquered bronze**
size in inches and centimeters —	**88 x 65 ¼ x 16 ¼ (223.5 x 165.7 x 41.3)**
sculpture foundry	**Modern Art Foundry, Long Island City, New York**
inscription (face and or reverse)	**on base, *L.B.I.***
provenance	**acquired from the Robert Miller Gallery, New York (gift of the Marbrook Foundation, Marney and Conley Brooks, Virginia and Edward Brooks, and Carol and Conley Brooks, Jr. 89.69)**

Josef Albers

Homage to the Square: "Gentle Hour" 1962

American, b. Germany,
1886–1976

oil, acrylic on board

48 x 48 (121.9 x 121.9)

**on reverse, upper right
quadrant in black ink,
*Homage to the Square:/
"Gentle Hour"/Albers
1962/Ground: 6 coats of
Liquitex .../Center:
Winsor White (W+N)/
painting, paints used—
from center:/Naples
Yellow Reddish
(Rhenish)/Cadmium
Yellow Medium (Shiva)/
Naples Yellow ...
pigment,/with addition of
turpentine/all in one
primary coat/Varnish:
Polyvinyl Acetate in
Toluene.***

**acquired from the Sidney
Janis Gallery, New York;
1967 (gift of the T.B.
Walker Foundation 67.28)**

Albers painted this work in his studio in New Haven while his *Interaction of Color* was being prepared by Yale University Press. The book, published in 1963, consists of a didactic text by Albers and a portfolio of eighty-one silkscreens, four-color separations, and photographic offsets of color studies by Albers and his former students at Yale—a complete course in the empirical investigation of color.[1]

This painting illustrates the issues outlined in Chapter V ("Lighter and/or darker—light intensity, lightness") and XXIII ("Equal light intensity—vanishing boundaries"). In Chapter V, Albers describes the difficulty of distinguishing "lighter from darker within close intervals when obscured by contrasting hues or by different color intensities." The sample used to test the student's ability to discern lighter from darker colors presents overlapping rectangles of subtle greens, grays, a mauve, and a yellow and fleshy pink that resemble those selected for *"Gentle Hour."* In the painting, the close coloristic intervals between one hue and another make the differentiation of light intensity even more difficult to perceive. Despite appearances, the light intensity of the outside and inside squares is almost uniform.

Through his selection of hues and the number and proportions of squares, Albers also illustrates the phenomenon of "vanishing boundaries" he describes in his book: "Though rarely perceived, it is a fact that articulate boundaries between colors can be made nearly unrecognizable, or made practically invisible—through the choice of color alone." In certain light conditions, the innermost square appears to merge with the middle square, even though it seems to be lighter in relation to it. At the same time, the middle square seems to be darker than the outer square, an illusion produced by the volume and density of the square surrounding it.

As Albers cautions, the interaction of these squares is not fixed, even once quantity, form, and recurrence of color are established. Interaction will vary according to how much and what part of the image is scrutinized, at what distance and under what quality, quantity, and direction of light. The deceiving simplicity of the picture—the mathematical basis of its composition, the impersonal application of paint, and the reduced palette[2]—allows the complexity of color and its relationship with light to assume the central role. The isolation of that subject is emphasized by the narrow white band that reveals the illuminating

nature of the underlying ground and removes the painting from its surroundings.[3] Albers said that he kept a white margin because "I want my pictures to have a beginning and an end."[4]

Despite his zeal for clarity and procedural explicitness, Albers alludes to the durational aspects and mysterious essence of his paintings in evocative subtitles such as *"Gentle Hour."*

L.F.G.

1. The silkscreens for the book were done by Albers's former student and assistant, Sewell Sillman, who took over the color course at Yale when Albers retired in 1960; the design of the book is by another former student, Norman Ives.
2. The format is one of four basic ones Albers used in the Homage to the Square series, diagrammed by Werner Spies in *Albers* (New York: Harry N. Abrams, 1975), p. 49, lower left. Using as the proportional unit the width of the leftmost vertical band, the relations read 1:2:4:2:1 laterally, and 1½:3:4:1:1½ top to bottom. The ratio of the squares, or more correctly, the implied squares, excluding the white border, is 1:2:2½. As for the application of paint, Albers reported that he spread it straight from the tube with a palette knife, as thinly as possible and in one coat onto the textured side of the Masonite to form what he described as "a durable film," in WAC questionnaire, 14 October 1974, p. 1. Despite the thinness of application, there is variation in surface texture, which decreases in activity from the center square out; the outermost seems to have been sponged on.
3. See Margit Rowell, "On Albers' Color," *Artforum*, vol. 10 (January 1972), pp. 27–37, for a discussion of Albers's understanding of light and color, and its sources.
4. Quoted in Katharine Kuh, *The Artist's Voice: Talks with Seventeen Artists* (New York: Harper & Row, 1960), p. 2.

Carl Andre

Slope 2004 1968

American, b. 1935

hot-rolled steel plate

six units, approximately
36 x 36 x ⅜
(91.4 x 91.4 x 1) each

acquired from the Irving
Blum Gallery, Los Angeles,
1969 (Art Center
Acquisition Fund 69.12)

In 1966 Andre cited the road as his ideal piece of sculpture.[1] The flat path that can be trod on, overlooked or stepped over represented for him the greatest possible challenge to the vertical monolithic structure of traditional sculpture. His definition of a thing as "a hole in a thing that it is not"[2] applies not only to the "road" he lays down, which displaces only a small amount of actual space, but to the three-dimensional channel of space implicitly carved out above it. He calls these visualized spaces "zones."[3] The paths that transform this space through simple intrusion are not simple in themselves. They are composed of unattached rectilinear modules resting side by side, conforming in their flatness to the ground they interrupt, but not fused with it like a road. The course is easily disassembled, the plates reordered and recombined. The fabricated geometric shapes, which Andre refers to as "tiles," have particular properties of color, surface, density, and opacity due to their material and method of fabrication; each one remains integral and independent, linked through temporary position rather than preordained sequence.

Once Andre has programmed the general form and the installer has positioned the pieces, they are held in place by the natural force of gravity, without further artifice. Andre has associated this casual bonding with memories of the shipyards of his native Quincy, Massachusetts, where he saw "acres of flat steel plates lying in the weather."[4]

In the four Slope pieces exhibited together in 1968–1969 at the Irving Blum Gallery, Los Angeles, Andre relinquished two of his fundamental givens, the orthogonal grid derived from the square and the repeated identical unit.[5] As a result the units, uncharacteristically, are not interchangeable. Because one of the 36-inch-square-plates in *Slope 2004* is trimmed on a slant, it directs the chain on a diagonal course from the wall. The diagonal diversion from the perpendicular path is reminiscent of the track switches of trains, a plausible connection given the influence on his work which Andre attributes to his job as freight brakeman and conductor for the Pennsylvania Railroad from 1960 to 1964.[6] He has commented particularly on the process of linking, unlinking, and reordering units to form and alter trains.

A bird's-eye view of the metal path and the floor on which it rests, as diagrammed in the felt-tip on graph paper certificate of authentication for the work, shows the form as sloping or descending, making the title intelligible. With reference to the sculpture as it is perceived by the viewer, the term "slope," implying a deviation from the horizontal, is more ambiguous.

L.F.G.

1. In David Bourdon, "The Razed Sites of Carl Andre: A Sculptor Laid Low by the Brancusi Syndrome," *Artforum*, vol. 5 (October 1966), p. 17.
2. Quoted in Haags Gemeentemuseum, *Carl Andre*, exh. cat., 1969, p. 41.
3. See Phyllis Tuchman, "An Interview with Carl Andre," *Artforum*, vol. 8 (June 1970), p. 61.
4. Quoted in David Bourdon, *Carl Andre: Sculpture 1959–1977* (New York: Jaap Rietman, 1978), p. 18.
5. For Andre's precepts, see his letter to the editor in *Art in America*, vol. 64 (September–October 1976), p. 5; self-interview in Städtisches Museum, Mönchengladbach, West Germany, *Carl Andre*, exh. cat., 1968; and Tuchman, pp. 55–61.
6. See Jeanne Siegel, "Carl Andre: Artworker," *Studio International*, vol. 180 (November 1970), p. 178, and *Artists in Their Own Words: Interviews by Paul Cummings* (New York: St. Martin's Press, 1975), p. 190.

Carl Andre

Aisle 1981

American, b. 1935

redwood

thirty-eight elements
12 x 12 x 36
(30.5 x 30.5 x 91.4) each
36 x 300 x 36
(91.4 x 762 x 91.4) overall

acquired from the artist
through the Paula Cooper
Gallery, New York, 1987
(Walker Special Purchase
Fund 87.17)

Carl Andre's first sculptures, in 1958–1959, were lengths of timber, notched and serrated in a manner inspired by Brancusi's totemlike abstract forms such as *Endless Column*.[1] Before long, he abandoned direct carving, having realized, he said, that "the wood was better before I cut it than after. I did not improve it in any way."[2] Instead of cutting into the material of his sculptures, Andre realized that the sculpture itself could act as a "cut in space."[3] The Element series, to which *Aisle* is closely related, was begun in 1960, incorporating standardized 12 x 12 x 36-inch timbers arranged in various geometric configurations. These sculptures were assembled without glue or nails, the weight of each unit acting as the binding force. In *Aisle*, Andre creates a pattern of alternating vertical and horizontal units whose modular sequence epitomizes the so-called Minimalist aesthetic.

Andre's four years as a freight brakeman and conductor with the Pennsylvania Railroad is often cited as an influence on his use of regimented, interchangeable units. This idea seems particularly apt in the case of *Aisle*, whose rows of wooden beams clearly resemble the seemingly infinite and unvarying progression of railroad ties and boxcars. Andre himself has pointed to his grandfather's profession of bricklayer: "I've always been able to put the elements in place myself, which is the theory of masonry ... being able to make large structures of small units."[4] His attitude about artisanship distinguishes his products from Duchamp's celebrated "readymades," to which they are sometimes compared. Andre has said, "The fault of the Duchamp readymade is that it idealizes an industrial product by severing it from its origins in working class craft and claiming it as a trophy of capitalist cunning."[5]

Andre has been highly vocal and distinctly political throughout his career, believing that an artist must take responsibility not only for the work of art but also for its "propaganda."[6] His statements often echo the bold directness of his art:

> My work is atheistic, materialistic, and communistic. It's atheistic because it's without transcendent form, without spiritual or intellectual quality. Materialistic because it's made out of its own materials without pretention to other materials. And communistic because the form is equally accessible to all men.[7]

Despite the artist's desire to make his work accessible to the common man, he creates forms of such extreme simplicity that sculptures such as *Aisle* often seem, ironically, to be difficult, mysterious, and obscure.

L.R.

1. See Phyllis Tuchman, "An Interview with Carl Andre," *Artforum*, vol. 8 (June 1970), p. 55, and David Bourdon, "The Razed Sites of Carl Andre: A Sculptor Laid Low by the Brancusi Syndrome," *Artforum*, vol. 5 (October 1966), p. 15.
2. Quoted in David Bourdon, *Carl Andre: Sculpture 1959–1977* (New York: Jaap Rietman, 1978), p. 17.
3. Quoted in Bourdon, "Razed Sites," p. 15.
4. Quoted in Jeanne Siegel, "Carl Andre: Artworker," *Studio International*, vol. 180 (November 1970), p. 178.
5. Carl Andre, "Against Duchamp," *Praxis*, vol. 1 (Spring 1975), p. 115.
6. See Siegel, p. 178.
7. Quoted in Bourdon, "Razed Sites," p. 17.

Siah Armajani

Bridge for Robert Venturi   1970

American, b. Iran, 1939

stained balsa wood

14 x 76⅝ x 12¼
(35.6 x 194.6 x 31.1)

acquired from the artist,
1977 (purchased with the
aid of funds from
Mr. Brooks Walker, Jr.
77.67)

Siah Armajani's work has taken many forms over the years, from calligraphic paintings and typewritten pages early in his career to full-scale architectural commissions, such as the Irene Hixon Whitney Bridge connecting Loring Park to the Minneapolis Sculpture Garden. His involvement with this latter project is foreshadowed in *Bridge for Robert Venturi*, an early sculpture. The work's title pays homage to the noted contemporary American architect, who has written at length about vernacular architecture and the need for buildings to relate to their larger environment.

Bridge for Robert Venturi, part of Armajani's third series of bridge models called Limit Bridges, which investigates the accommodation of a bridge to its site, is crudely constructed and stained. It was done shortly before his well-known *Bridge over a Tree*.[1] The basic form of the Venturi bridge derives from the early American tradition of covered wooden bridges and has a distinctly vernacular look. However, as is the case in all Limit Bridges, passage is inevitably blocked. Entry to the Venturi bridge is at the center rather than at either end, so that one can go only from side to side rather than across the length of the bridge. Moreover, if the bridge is designed to span either a valley or water—as appears from its support structure—the actual entrance at the bridge's midpoint would occur in a ditch or in the water. These perverse and illogical departures from the

basic form of a covered bridge, which make passage problematic, force us to think about what it means to pass from one place to another both literally and figuratively, and underscore the bridge's status as metaphor rather than as practical solution.

M.G.

1. Walker Art Center owns a related drawing, *Bridge over Triangle Tree*, 1984, which was executed after both the model and an actual bridge of that design (1970) were realized.

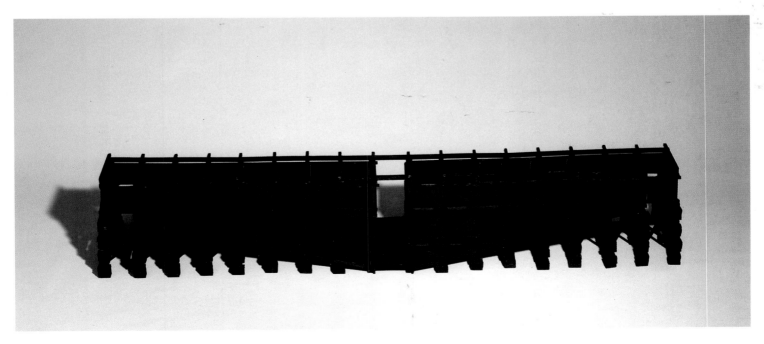

Siah Armajani

Dictionary for Building: The Garden Gate   1982–1983

American, b. Iran, 1939

painted wood

**95⅛ x 32¼ x 74
(241.6 x 81.9 x 188)**

**acquired from the Max
Protetch Gallery, New
York, 1983 (purchased
with the aid of funds from
William D. and Stanley
Gregory and Art Center
Acquisition Fund 83.12)**

Dictionary for Building: The Garden Gate reflects Armajani's abiding concerns with the conjunctions among architecture, sculpture, and language. A painted wooden structure, it is composed of two freestanding, adjacent elements, each a series of several intersecting planes in the tradition of Constructivist sculpture. It is also a functional object, offering a modest bench and reading stand for the viewer. Generally exhibited in the Walker's galleries with a book on its stand, it gently encourages the literacy that is vital to the vision of a democratic society; Armajani consistently comments upon and promotes these ideals in his work.

Garden Gate is ironically titled because one cannot pass through it. Unlike the bench and reading stand, the fence-gate component functions only in the metaphorical sense, like his earlier models for bridges.

The work is part of Armajani's Dictionary for Building, a series of indoor sculptures begun in 1979 that investigates the language of various architectural elements, including doors, windows, and mirrors. The vivid juxtaposition of the blue and ocher doors against the red gate is intended to suggest the development of the more elaborate red gate as a variation on a basic door. As is true in all the Dictionary works, Armajani first dissects the various architectural elements and then puts them back together in a deliberately awkward fashion so that each element—in this instance, the door and the gate—continues to have independent meaning.

M.G.

Siah Armajani

Closet under Dormer   1984–1985

American, b. Iran, 1939

painted wood, shellac, mirror

107½ x 48 x 29¼ (273.1 x 121.9 x 74.3)

acquired from the Max Protetch Gallery, New York, 1986 (T.B. Walker Acquisition Fund 86.78)

Closet under Dormer is one of the works in Siah Armajani's Dictionary for Building, an ongoing series of indoor sculptures based on table-size cardboard models the artist worked on in 1974–1975 that parse the language of architecture. *Closet* is one of six works within the larger Dictionary series that is concerned with the idea of "up and down" and features one major architectural element under another. *Closet* examines several of the recurring images in the series, including doors, windows, and mirrors. The artist isolates the various elements and then recombines them in ways that offer clear evidence of their deconstruction and subsequent reconstruction.

Combining elements from two of the small cardboard models, *Closet* contains all the items one associates with proper closets and dormers—doors, mirror, clothing bar, and, of course, windows. But the curious configurations, beginning with the doors stabilized in a semi-open position, reveal that it is an artist, not an architect, who has assembled the components. The space on either side of the mirror plays a unique role within the overall design, contradicting the standard function of a closet as protective enclosure. The placement of the mirror at the rear of the closet denies its reflective function as it also defies traditional closet design. Walking around the sculpture, we realize that this mirror is a two-sided device, which thus brings the inside out. In the same way, the double window, which looks as though it might have been peeled apart, has a strictly interior element that assumes the more typical position as a viewpoint to the outdoors. Armajani contradicts the domesticity of the closet by assigning it outdoor properties and does precisely the reverse with the window, endowing this element with indoor presence.

Despite its intentionally provocative disharmonies of form and function, *Closet* has the comfortable, familiar feel of Americana that characterizes all of Armajani's work, a quality that is underscored by the work's red, white, and blue color.

M.G.

Siah Armajani

Model for the Irene Hixon Whitney Bridge   1985

American, b. Iran, 1939

basswood, birch

74 x 12 x 4
(188 x 30.5 x 10.2)

(acquired from the artist
in connection with
construction of the
Minneapolis Sculpture
Garden 86.60)

With works such as the Irene Hixon Whitney
Bridge,[1] Siah Armajani fully realizes his ambition
to be a "public artist," to make art that both articulates the values of the community and becomes
a locus for their realization. His largest public
bridge to date, its design incorporates the three
fundamental approaches to bridge building—
beam, arch, and suspension. Each system provides approximately one third of the support. The
model for the Whitney Bridge shows the interlocking arches, one pale blue, the other pale yellow,
which subtly reflect the two distinct areas the
bridge connects—Loring Park and the
Minneapolis Sculpture Garden. The use of two
colors to delineate separate areas reinforces the
idea and experience of passing from one place to
another. Constructed by the artist primarily from
basswood, this model differs slightly from the
final design of the bridge, in which the supporting
beams are spaced farther apart and for which
both stairs and ramps have been built. Unlike the
majority of Armajani's earlier bridge models, intended as sculptural objects and visionary proposals, this is a working model, which served as
the basis for the final design of the realized
full-scale bridge.

M.G.

1. Community leader and philanthropist Irene Hixon Whitney
(1926–1986) lived in Minnesota all her life and owned the
Fawkes Building that overlooks Loring Park. Her family
provided the major funding for the construction of the
bridge.

**Irene Hixon Whitney
Bridge**
Designed by Siah Armajani
Gift of the Minneapolis
Foundation/Irene Hixon
Whitney Family Founder-
Advisor Fund, the
Persephone Foundation,
and Wheelock Whitney,
with additional support and
services from the Federal
Highway Administration,
the Minnesota Department
of Transportation, the City
of Minneapolis, and the
National Endowment for
the Arts, 1988

Jean (Hans) Arp

Aquatique 1953

French, 1886–1966

marble

**13½ x 25⁵⁄₁₆ x 9³⁄₁₆
(34.3 x 64.3 x 23.3)**

**Curt Valentin Gallery,
New York, 1954; acquired
from Curt Valentin, 1955
(gift of the T.B. Walker
Foundation 55.4)**

Aquatique is a modified version of Arp's earlier *Réveil* of 1938, which stands erect on a rounded "tail," with "wing" pinned back and "head" raised.[1] Somewhat reminiscent of Brancusi's transcendental birds, *Réveil* also resembles a crowing cock. In *Aquatique*, conceived fifteen years later, the figure is lowered to a reclining position, the head is bowed, and the tail is bipartite, like that of a fish or aquatic mammal. This tail is made of breastlike forms related to the buds designated in the titles of other works.[2] Although the Walker marble has been consistently exhibited and reproduced in its present orientation, a photograph of the original plaster taken during the artist's lifetime shows it inverted, which makes the reference to marine life more clearly legible. It was not unusual for Arp to consider multiple, variable positionings for his works, and on occasion he would sign a picture in two corners to encourage its rotation.

The forms of the sculpture, although carrying certain connotations reinforced by the title, remain open to alternative readings. H.H. Arnason recalled Arp's remarks about *Aquatique*: "When asked in 1956 about a piece entitled *Aquatic* ... which, reclining, suggests some form of sea life, and standing on end, a particularly sensuous female torso—he commented, 'In one aspect or another, my sculptures are always torsos.'"[3] According to Arp's testimony, he assigned titles to his works after their completion. He did not, therefore, establish the subject for a sculpture a priori and then mold its forms to convey that subject, but allowed associations to emerge spontaneously as the work took shape. This flexible, metamorphic response to abstracted natural form is reflected in his statement that "the content of a sculpture should reveal itself on tiptoe, without pretension, like the track of an animal in the snow."[4]

The marble appears to have been completed in 1953, not long after a plaster model, and was available for exhibition in New York by March of 1954. The plaster is lost, or destroyed (perhaps by Arp himself); no casts have been made. The marble was probably carved with the help of an Italian stonecutter named Pisanelli, who assisted Arp in the 1950s in his studio at Meudon/ Clamart.[5]

L.F.G.

1. Stephanie Poley, *Hans Arp: Die Formensprache im plastischen Werk* (Stuttgart: Verlag Gerd Hatje, 1978), pp. 34–36.
2. Ibid., pp. 36, 85.
3. H.H. Arnason, *History of Modern Art* (New York: Harry N. Abrams, 1968), p. 301.
4. Jean Arp, text of 1955 published as "Memories and Observations," in Chalette International, New York, *Jean Arp: Sculptures, Reliefs, Works On Paper*, exh. cat., 1975, n.p.
5. Greta Ströh, in letters to the author, 7 January 1985 and 10 February 1986, provided the information on the plaster model and the stonecutter.

Richard Artschwager

Low Overhead   1984

American, b. 1923

laminated plastic, latex paint on mahogany plywood and linden

96 x 93 x 18½ (243.8 x 236.2 x 47)

on reverse, *Walt/+/Ted/ Artificers/+/Illusionists/ 1984*

acquired from the Donald Young Gallery, Chicago, 1985 (T.B. Walker Acquisition Fund 85.714)

Richard Artschwager
Explanatory sketch for
Low Overhead (detail)
1987
graphite on paper
11 x 8½ (27.9 x 21.6)
Collection Walker Art Center
Gift of the artist, 1987

Artschwager has compared the furniture-related art he has made since 1962 to objects in still-life painting, whose monumentality is unrelated to their original function: "By killing off the use part, non-use aspects are allowed living space, breathing space."[1] *Low Overhead*, more blatantly surrealistic in character and baroque in form than his work had been for years, is, to use his terms, the "surrogate or effigy" of a doorway. Although the viewer is invited, through the punning title, to imagine putting the work to use, the door does not open, and would in any case open onto the wall; therefore, for all practical purposes, it remains closed. As he has observed, "the properties of 'open' and 'closed' cannot be divorced from the 'geography' of the door, i.e., without reference to that which the door opens or closes."[2] This object, although resembling a door, has none of the purposes and properties of a door, not even its primary function of opening and closing spaces. Rather, it exhibits behavior invented in the imagination of the artist.

Artschwager has likened *Low Overhead's* "herring-bone construction which points upward (fortuitous??) and gets distorted at the top" to "the growing point of a vegetable running into a hard stratum of soil."[3] The notion of mysterious changes of property is most exuberantly pursued in relation to the work's essential material— wood. The surfaces of a Philippine mahogany plywood and linden, a hard basswood, are covered by laminated plastic imitating wood and paint applied to resemble the plastic. The fetishistic implications that Artschwager acknowledges in his objects[4] involve a removal at two stages: not only are things substituted for people, but these things are subsequently replaced or concealed by the diagrammatic representation of their attributes. Artschwager came to like laminated plastic because of its mimetic, ersatz quality: "It looked as if wood had passed through it, as if the thing only half existed … it was a picture of a piece of wood."[5] The "Rotunda Oak" in *Low Overhead* is literally a full-scale photographic representation of wood grain in a plastic laminate.[6] The black and white painted surfaces are like a blown-up depiction of the plastic.

Artschwager reveals further photographic sources for the work:

a scribble of a column in which I [was] imitating a camera with a fish-eye lens … up close so that one was looking up at the capital and down at the base. This

would be an exotic, not average, position from which to look at a column and not surprisingly the scribble metamorphosed into a door where the capital became the supporting arch and the base became steps. The steps got eliminated, making the door more accessible (read: in your and my space) … all this at eye level, a bit low so that you have to duck or would have to duck if you could actually enter.[7]

When the bulging, overhanging arch is viewed frontally, the manner in which it is painted contradicts the way it is carved, creating a planar ambiguity like that encountered in the "parallax of daily life."[8] Although eccentric in contour, the arch is simply formed of two curved planes. Illusionistic shading suggesting multiple planes contradicts the real shadows, both systems appearing equally possible or equally fictitious. Below, the inconsistent gray, white, and black "shadowing" in the grooves of the door planks abets a confusion produced by the tendency of the herringbone pattern to imply rectangles viewed at an angle, an implication that collapses the door forward or backward depending on how the viewer sees it.

L.F.G.

1. Quoted in Jan McDevitt, "The Object: Still Life," *Craft Horizons*, vol. 25 (September–October 1965), p. 30.
2. Richard Artschwager, "The Hydraulic Door Check," *Arts Magazine*, vol. 42 (November 1967), p. 41.
3. Artschwager, in WAC questionnaire, 15 April 1986, p. 2.
4. See McDevitt, p. 54, for Artschwager's comments on his "exotic" reactions to pieces of furniture and their function as "people surrogates."
5. Ibid.
6. The laminated melamine plastic Artschwager used is made by Pioneer Plastics. Technical details and conservation recommendations were provided by the artist in WAC questionnaire.
7. Artschwager, in WAC questionnaire.
8. Artschwager, quoted in Coosje van Bruggen, "Richard Artschwager," *Artforum*, vol. 22 (September 1983), p. 50.

George C. Ault

Sullivan Street, Abstraction   1924

American, 1891–1948

oil on canvas

24 x 20 (61 x 50.8)

lower right, *G.C. Ault 1924*[1]

The Downtown Gallery, New York, 1928 to at least 1935; estate of the artist, 1949; Zabriskie Gallery, New York, 1957–1961; acquired from the Zabriskie Gallery, 1961 (Art Center Acquisition Fund 61.2)

Ault described his artistic endeavor in terms that are both romantic and cerebral: "I do not at all try to 'copy' nature—I make order out of nature and 'crystalize' [sic] its beauty or, rather, my 'reactions' or 'feelings' about nature. That is all that matters—what I—The Artist—feels."[2] More concretely, he painted "the scene that excited my esthetic emotion reduced to the simple forms of which it was composed, leaving out all unessential detail; distortion of those forms when necessary, and the modification of color values. Each component part of the picture thought of in relation to the whole and not for itself alone."[3]

In *Sullivan Street, Abstraction*, Ault replaces the usual crystalline daylit clarity found in the works of colleagues such as Sheeler with an atmospheric nocturnal chiaroscuro. Although related in subject matter to O'Keeffe's contemporaneous nighttime views of Manhattan streets, the canvas shows a more metaphysical approach. The irrational, moody illumination of the empty street and elevated train arose from Ault's need to romanticize the city, to soften what he perceived as its essential grimness. Describing his neighborhood, Greenwich Village, where this picture is set, he said: "The village ... is never romantic at noon.... The city needs haze. In this harsh light you see all the ugly details—you see the city crumbling to pieces."[4] In 1947, neglected by the art world and living in Woodstock, New York, and in many respects—financial, physical, and emotional—crumbling to pieces himself, Ault returned to his imagery of the late 1920s, and painted *Sullivan Street, Abstraction No. 2.*[5] This version is almost identical in composition, but the atmospheric glow of the haloed lamps has disappeared, and the outlines have been hardened, diminishing the sense of mystery and emphasizing the picture's more purely abstract design qualities.

Ault's characteristic blending and alternation of rigor and romanticism have elicited wildly divergent though uniformly respectful responses from critics over the years. In 1928, a reviewer of the last one-man show to be held during Ault's lifetime wrote of his "subtleties of tone and atmosphere ... in the 'Sullivan Street, Abstraction,' in which he takes that term of the modernists and makes of it a lovely and striking urban nocturne."[6] In contrast, an anonymous writer viewing the work in 1950 described it as being "as frightening as a scream in the dark."[7]

L.F.G.

1. The date is not visible to the naked eye, but was discovered by Foy Casper while examining the work for conservation purposes. The work is often dated 1928, the year of its first exhibition.
2. Handwritten note signed "G.C.A." below a review in *The Arts* of his December 1928 Downtown Gallery exhibition (Ault Papers, AAA, Reel D247).
3. Quoted in The Newark Museum, *American Painting and Sculpture*, exh. cat., 1944.
4. Quoted in Louise Ault, *Artist in Woodstock: George Ault: The Independent Years* (Philadelphia and Ardmore, Pennsylvania: Dorrance & Co., 1978), p. 104.
5. Both versions were based on a watercolor called *The El, Abstraction* of 1923 in which the orange cars of the train and the windows of the skyscraper above are clearly identified as such. The retention of the motif of the elevated train in the Walker work is an imaginative transposition: the Sixth Avenue elevated ran parallel to Sullivan Street rather than across it.
6. William B. McCornick, "Ault and Others Return to Local Art Galleries," *New York American*, 25 November 19 (Ault Papers, AAA, Reel D247).
7. Clipping from *Pictures on Exhibit*, 1950, p. 18 (Ault Papers, AAA, Reel D247).

Milton Avery

Seated Blonde 1946

American, 1885–1965

oil, charcoal on linen

52 x 33¾ (132.1 x 85.7)

**lower left, in black paint,
Milton Avery 1946 (last
digit changed from a 5)**

**Paul Rosenberg & Co.,
New York, 1946–1951;
Mr. and Mrs. Roy R.
Neuberger, New York,
1951–1952 (gift of Mr.
and Mrs. Roy R.
Neuberger 52.6)**

In *Seated Blonde*, Avery's frequently cited debt to Matisse is conspicuous in the broad unmodeled areas of high-value color, the uneven contours, and the abrupt change of scale. The interruption and reorientation of the line where floor meets wall, causing the floor to rear up in the background area, is a technique inherited from Cézanne, filtered through the Cubists. Despite his reliance on these adopted devices, however, Avery brings to the work an inventive handling of paint and a subtle, personal understanding of color relationships. The burnt sienna of the floor, thinned with turpentine rather than linseed oil to yield an active, textured surface, harmonizes with the sandy brown wall and goldenrod-yellow chair cushion. The flat chair frame calligraphically cuts through these expanses of warm color. A hot orange-red and magenta combination anchors the upper right corner, where the decoratively incised tapestry and the thickly painted scalloped frame of the adjacent painting balance the monumental, bleached female figure in the foreground. Her volume is flattened in scumbled whites and pale yellow, enlivened by the blue of her halter top, which picks up the somewhat grayer blue of the seascape. The poses of both figures are casual, contained, introspective; they appear to be oblivious to the orgy of rich color that surrounds them.

According to the artist's widow, Sally M. Avery, the model's name is Stella, a "tall, statuesque creature," the daughter of Rudolph Jacobi, a European artist who came to the United States in the early 1940s. During that period, Mrs. Avery stated:

> [We] used to go to sketch class once a week at her father's studio at the southwest corner of 15th Street and Fifth Avenue, and Stella was frequently the model. She never posed nude. From one of the sketches made in class Milton painted Seated Blonde. The paintings hung in the background were simulated. The figure in the background may have been me or one of the other members of the sketch group.[1]

The preparatory sketch shows Avery's method of composition to be one of rearrangement; motifs have been added or deleted for visual effect rather than for any narrative implications. The background figure is immersed in the inactive, private realm of reading, completely withdrawn from the foreground figure, whose attitude is equally remote and noncommittal. The absence of personality description or interaction between

the figures allows the emotional intensity of the painting to reside solely in the actions and decisions of the artist, as expressed in color, brushstroke, shape, line, and texture.

L.F.G.

1. Letters to the author, 12 December 1984 and 13 February 1985.

Milton Avery
Seated Blonde 1946
ink on paper
17 x 11 (43.2 x 28)
Collection Ann Fader
Associates, White Plains,
New York

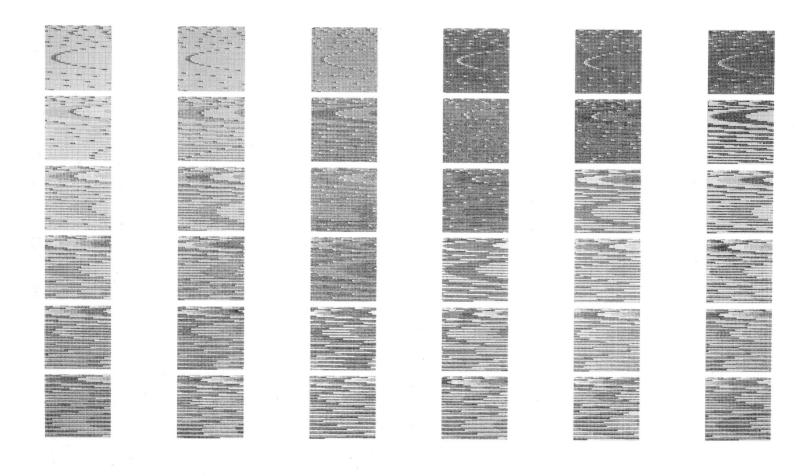

Jennifer Bartlett

Series VIII (Parabolas)   1971

American, b. 1941

enamel on steel

thirty-six plates
12 x 12
(30.5 x 30.5) each
77 x 132
(195.6 x 335.3) overall

acquired from the Reese Palley Gallery, New York, 1972 (gift of the T.B. Walker Foundation 72.16)

Series VIII (Parabolas) and two other works in the permanent collection were shown in Jennifer Bartlett's first major New York exhibition at the Reese Palley Gallery in 1972. She covered the walls in an allover fashion with numerous series of plate works that clearly anticipated the ambition and achievement of subsequent large-scale works such as *Rhapsody*, the 153-foot-long painting which forged her reputation in 1975–1976.

Series VIII (Parabolas), the artist's first work to be acquired by a museum, is comprised of thirty-six 12 x 12-inch plates, hung precisely 1 inch apart in vertical columns, with a 12-inch gap between each column. The paint is carefully applied with quantifiable daubs of unmixed Testors enamel in a manner that recalls Pointillism. The overall pattern that emerges looks as though it had been generated by computer, but Bartlett's systems, generally quite arbitrary and obscure, are very much her own invention. In *Series VIII Parabolas*, a fundamentally abstract work, her elaborate system for adding different colors in varying amounts on each grid confounds its strict organizing principles with a romantic suggestion of a cosmic ocean, a theme she later pursued at great length.

Bartlett had the 16-gauge steel plates that became her trademark fabricated to order: They were coated with white enamel and overlaid with a light gray quarter-inch grid before she began to paint on them—a logical development from the drawings on graph paper she had been making since college. Bartlett hit upon the idea of using steel plates from the station and directional signs she saw in the New York City subways, and for eight years she worked on such plates exclusively. The plates eliminated the need for stretcher bars (which were difficult to build) and, being easily transportable, they suited her Conceptualist-Minimalist orientation as well. By hugging the wall, the plates avoided the illusionism inherent in a more three-dimensional canvas. They also offer an alternative surface on which to make paintings during a period when many considered traditional painting to have reached a dead end.

M.G.

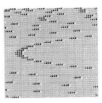
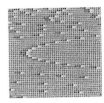

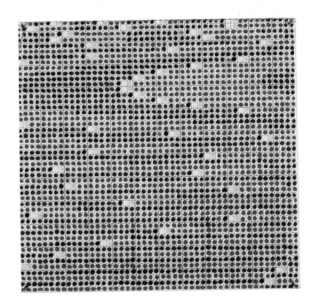

Jennifer Bartlett

Swimmers at Dawn, Noon and Dusk   1979

American, b. 1941

oil on canvas, enamel on
steel plate

seventy-two plates, three
canvases
77 x 297
(195.6 x 754.4) overall

acquired from the Paula
Cooper Gallery, New York,
1985 (gift of Joanne and
Philip Von Blon 85.18)

Jennifer Bartlett's work has undergone major
transformations in the years since she first began
exhibiting her enamel-coated steel plates. However, from her early work, with its leanings toward
Minimalism and Conceptualism, to her recent,
more representational explorations in two and
three dimensions, the conflict between system
and intuition prevails. Moreover, her work continues to retain its environmental scale, as in
Swimmers at Dawn, Noon and Dusk, a painting
that stands midway between abstraction and
figuration.

   Swimmers at Dawn, Noon and Dusk expands
upon the ocean theme that Bartlett first introduced in *Rhapsody*—she grew up on the ocean in
Long Beach, California, and has a sibling who
was an Olympic swimmer. Bartlett has almost
always worked in series and this Swimmer painting is the second of several that culminated in a
major commission, *Swimmers: Atlanta*, created in
1979 for the Richard B. Russell Federal Building
in Atlanta. She first introduced the flesh-toned,
lozenge-shaped swimmer in *Termino Avenue*
(1977), the final work in her House series.

   The swimmer in the Walker work bobs up and
down across an expanse of blues, pinks, yellows
and browns, which is as carefully organized as
Bartlett's earlier, more mathematically inclined
works. She divides the image into thirds (sea,
land, sky) and within each section the brushstrokes are oriented in the same direction (diagonally, horizontally, vertically). Her longstanding
interest in the passage of time as well as her tendency to compare and contrast are registered
here: from the unexpected vantage point of the
sea looking toward land, we see the swimmer
portrayed at different times of day and with different media. However, the limitations of the gridded plate structure, with its surface interrupted
every twelve inches, defines only the right half of
the work, for the left half is traditional oil on canvas. The newfound freedom of the unbroken surface in the Walker *Swimmers at Dawn, Noon and
Dusk* and other early works that incorporate
canvas proved a boon to Bartlett.

   M.G.

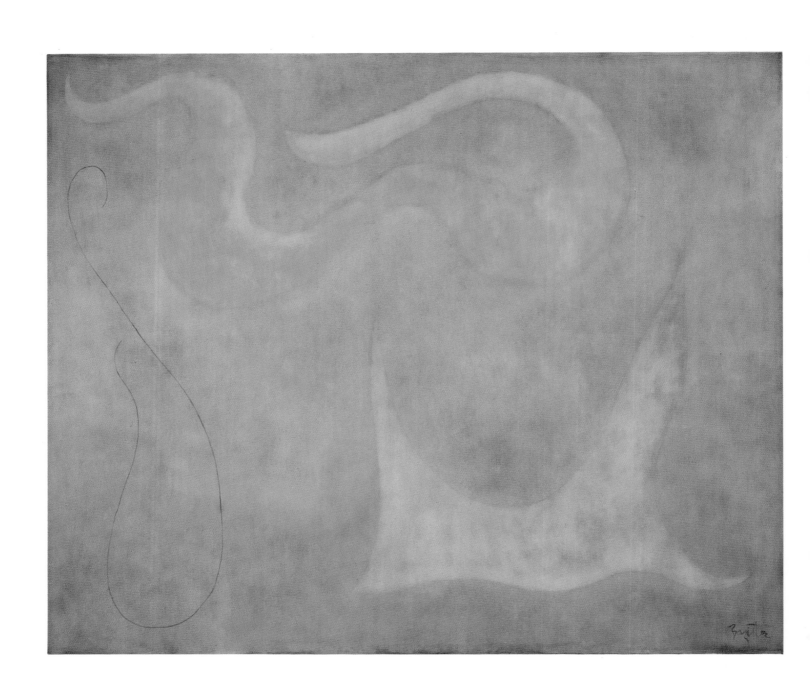

William Baziotes

Opalescent   1962

American, 1912–1963

oil on canvas

42⅜ x 50¼
(107.6 x 127.6)

lower right, *Baziotes*;
on reverse, upper left,
*Opalescent/William
Baziotes/1962*

Sidney Janis Gallery,
New York; acquired from
the Saidenberg Gallery,
New York, 1963
(gift of the T.B. Walker
Foundation 63.5)

Baziotes looked closely at the art of the past as well as that of his contemporaries, and was generous in his acknowledgment of their contribution to his development.[1] One of the modern masters for whom he expressed admiration was Miró, whose work he had apparently known since 1937.[2] In paintings such as *Opalescent*, his attraction to Miró's work is readily felt in the sinuous streamers, calligraphic lines, and biomorphic forms floating discretely on a subtly modulated field. However, Baziotes has dulcified Miró's contours and immersed the motifs in an aqueous environment where they languidly wave and curl. The colors are correspondingly nacreous, their application imitating the technique as well as the palette of pastels. Layer upon layer of thin veils of color (sky blue over a rusty ground, green, yellow, aquamarine) create a delicately nuanced medium. A connection suggested with Redon's pastels, fusains, and paintings seems plausible,[3] given the poetic intention and narcotic mood of Baziotes's work: "It is the mysteriousness that I love in painting. It is the stillness and the silence. I want my pictures to take effect very slowly, to obsess and to haunt."[4]

Baziotes worked intuitively to give shape to his fantasies, reveries, and sensations. The exploratory nature of his method allowed for pentimenti such as the incompletely suppressed line undulating horizontally from the painting's lower left edge to the left edge of the pinkish form at the lower right.

> What happens on the canvas is unpredictable and surprising to me…. Each beginning suggests something. Once I sense the suggestion, I begin to paint intuitively. The suggestion then becomes a phantom that must be caught and made real. As I work, or when the painting is finished, the subject reveals itself.[5]

The title of this work, which suits the milky iridescence of the colors, derives from the word for a water-based gem. Water is frequently evoked by Baziotes's titles (as in the related *Aquatic* of 1961), and by the atmosphere of his images. "Every one of us finds water either a symbol of peace or fear. I know I never feel better than when I gaze for a long time at the bottom of a still pool."[6]

L.F.G.

1. William Baziotes, "Symposium: The Creative Process," *Arts Digest*, vol. 28 (15 January 1954), p. 34.
2. Irving Sandler, "Baziotes: Modern Mythologist," *Art News*, vol. 63 (February 1965), p. 28.
3. Robert Pincus-Witten, "New York," *Artforum*, vol. 9 (April 1971), p. 74.
4. William Baziotes, "Notes on Painting," *It Is*, no. 4 (Autumn 1959), p. 11.
5. William Baziotes, *Problems of Contemporary Art: Possibilities*, vol. 1 (Winter 1947–1948), p. 2.
6. From a letter to Barnett Newman, 22 January 1948, excerpt published in Thomas B. Hess, "William Baziotes, 1912–1963," *Location*, vol. 1 (Summer 1964), p. 89.

Larry Bell

untitled   1967–1968

American, b. 1939

**coated glass and
rhodium-plated brass**

**20¼ x 20¼ x 20¼
(51.4 x 51.4 x 51.4);
59¾ (151.8) overall height
with Plexiglas base**

**acquired from the Pace
Gallery, New York, 1968
(purchased with matching
grant from Museum
Purchase Plan, National
Endowment for the Arts,
and Art Center Acquisition
Fund 68.32)**

To produce the subtle mists of spectral color on the glass planes of this cube, Bell used a mirroring process that took place in a vacuum chamber installed in his studio. It has been described as follows:

> The glass is locked into a removable rack and inverted in a cylindrical vacuum chamber. Immediately below the glass are electrode points attached to a container or "boat" of metal to be applied. The chamber is secured, an air [sic: vacuum] pump run (for some two hours), to produce a partial (nearly complete) vacuum. The electrodes are triggered and in ten seconds the metal is evaporated, the vapor rising upward, coating the surface. This coating is so gauzily delicate, though permanent, that it is measured in hundreds of angstrom units (an angstrom equals one tenth of a millimicron).[1]

The spray of metallic and non-metallic materials, such as quartz, leaves some areas transparent while others become reflective, effects that change according to the quantity and direction of light, the position of the viewer, and the nature of the surroundings. Given particular conditions, light refracted by the metals causes a blue-lavender-red-orange-yellow spectral gamut (varying in sequence) to hover almost imperceptibly in the smokily diffused density of the glass. The color is determined by the thickness, or degree of interference with light, of the thin films deposited in layers on the surface.[2] The incorporeality of the phenomena and their interaction provoke a perceptual confusion regarding boundaries and origins. The cubic volume marked with chrome is modular in a lyrical way, made ambiguous through the replacement of applied color by chromatic light. The metal strips were evidently a technical solution to making a glass box with sharp corners and identical sides,[3] and were later discarded, encouraging Bell's move to freestanding wall-size panels. The Plexiglas base is transparent in order to allow light through all panels,[4] and designed at a height to raise the piece to eye level. The viewer's reflection and any attendant notions about self-awareness were not of concern to Bell.[5]

It seems that the preciosity, ethereality, and precision of Bell's work have had a therapeutic function for him:

> Sensually the works purify my jumbled and unstable emotional condition. The externalization of that which has no other exit.... Intellectually, I feel that being creative is an aggressive and hostile act both objectively and socially. If I think about the position of my work in relation to that of others, then I reflect this aggression and hostility, scheming and planning how and what to do that will change the nature of everything else.[6]

L.F.G.

1. Fidel A. Danieli, "Bell's Progress," Artforum, vol. 5 (June 1967), p. 69.
2. The effect is like that of gasoline on water: mid-spectrum green is 550 millimicrons, or 5,500 angstroms thick; blue is thinner and red thicker. During this period, Bell used quartz for interfering layers and chrome or a nickel chrome alloy called inconel to act as the reflecting layers; letter to the author, 12 December 1986.
3. It is technically impossible to miter together panes of glass this length; see Danieli, p. 69.
4. Letter to the author, 12 December 1986. Bell first intended to use a glass pedestal, but finding it impractical at the time, substituted plastic; letter to the author, June 1979.
5. It has been said that Bell at one time hoped for an ideal presentation of his cubes in an empty white room with the viewer observing them through a peephole; see Michael Kirby, "Sculpture as a Visual Instrument," Art International, vol. 7 (October 1968), p. 35.
6. Statement, a facsimile of which is published in Marlborough Galleria d'Arte, Rome, Larry Bell, exh. cat., 1974, n.p.

Rudolf Belling

Kopf in Messing (Head in Brass)   1925

German, 1886–1972

brass

15¼ x 8¹³⁄₁₆ x8¹¹⁄₁₆
(38.7 x 22.4 x 22.1)

probably H. Noack, Berlin

acquired from the
Flechtheim Galleries,
Berlin, by Josef von
Sternberg, Los Angeles,
by 1931; acquired from
Duveen Graham Modern
Art, New York, 1957
(gift of the T. B. Walker
Foundation 57.2)

Kopf in Messing belongs to the beginning of what Belling described as his third creative period, when he returned to naturalistic subjects after several years of experimentation with pure abstraction. Anti-naturalistic tendencies persisted, however, informed by the *style moderne* that was prevalent in architecture and design in the mid-1920s. In *Kopf in Messing*, the concurrence of fluid curve and sharp edge, the sleekness of surface and its high polish are responses to this style. By reducing observed detail, distorting human proportions, and finishing the surface with machinelike precision, Belling combines his attention to the formal issues of sculpture with the decorative impulses he brought to his architectural sculpture projects. His interest in the relationship between solid and void is described in the penetration of the pristine, armorlike shell in several areas, most dramatically in the eyes. These were cast separately, then fastened by metal stems bolted to the inside of the hollow head through a squarish opening at the back of the head, now covered with a brass plate and scarcely visible.

It has been suggested that the head bears the features of Belling's first wife, the dancer Toni Freeden, whom he married in 1923; a photograph of the period shows her wearing a shining metallic cap and holding the sculpture to her chest.[1] While similarities between Freeden and the brass head can be detected, the generalization of the sculptured face makes absolute identification difficult. Belling himself evidently repeatedly denied that it was intended as a portrait.[2] He apparently originally conceived the head as part of a mother-child group that he abandoned.[3]

The work was first reproduced as a brass cast in 1925; the original plaster appears to have been lost or destroyed in a bombing raid of 1944.[4] The Walker cast appears to be the third, probably made between 1928 and 1930. Subsequently, a number of other casts were made, primarily by the Noack foundry in Berlin.

L.F.G.

1. The connection was proposed by Hans Hildebrandt, *Die Kunst des 19. und 20. Jahrhunderts* (Wildpark-Potsdam: Akademische Verlagegesellschaft Athenaion, 1931), p. 444; the photograph is reproduced in Winfried Nerdinger, *Rudolf Belling und die Kunstströmungen in Berlin 1918–1923: mit einem Katalog der plastischen Werke* (Berlin: Deutscher Verlag für Kunstwissenschaft, 1980), pl. 135.
2. J.A. Schmoll gen. Eisenwerth, *Rudolf Belling* (St. Gall, Switzerland: Erker-Verlag, circa 1971), p. 13.
3. Helga D. Hofmann in Galerie Wolfgang Ketterer, Munich, *Rudolf Belling*, exh. cat., 1967, p. 42; Schmoll gen. Eisenwerth, p. 32. When Belling returned to Germany from Turkey in 1966–1967 he was interviewed by these two scholars, and told them about the larger mother-child conception (Winfried Nerdinger, letter to the author, 13 November 1984; ibid. for the data on the plasters and cast).
4. Nerdinger, p. 194.

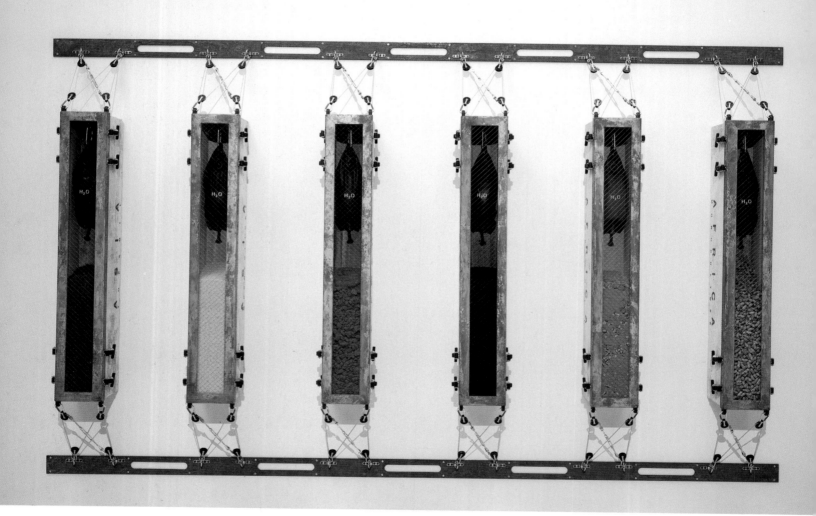

Ashley Bickerton

Minimalism's Evil Orthodoxy Monoculture's Totalitarian Esthetic #1   1989

American, b. West Indies, 1959

steel, concrete, glass, rubber, plastic, soil, rice, coffee, peanuts

96 x 156 x 12½
(243.8 x 396.2 x 31.8)

acquired from the Sonnabend Gallery, New York, 1990
(T.B. Walker Acquisition Fund 90.19)

In this complex wall sculpture, Ashley Bickerton creates a provocative analogy between aesthetics and ecology. The work's six cast-concrete boxes contain soil and crop samples from Africa, Asia, and South America, areas where monoculture—the widespread cultivation of a single cash crop—has become a common practice in the wake of the "green revolution" in agriculture. Bickerton compares this type of artificially restrictive farming with the reductivist aesthetic of Minimalism—the use of simple primary forms to create works whose impact depends on their sheer physical presence rather than on any allusions to the outside world—evoked through the serial repetition of the six identical boxes. He implies that, in their narrow pursuit of a single goal, both Minimalism and monoculture willfully ignore the implications of their endeavor.

In his questioning of Minimalism's assumptions, Bickerton created in the mid-1980s a series of works through which he sought to investigate "the whole implication of the object—as something of social, aesthetic, economic and political value."[1] These "culturescapes," as he called them, mimicked the high-tech finish and serial imagery of Donald Judd's work. But they also incorporated advertising logos, clearly visible handles, protective covers, and elaborate rigging that anchored the works to the wall. These additions served to emphasize the role of the artwork as a transportable commercial product.

Beginning in 1988 Bickerton extended his analysis beyond the bounds of art's relationship to culture in an effort to deal with culture's relationship to nature. "Essentially I had reached a point," he said, "where I realized painting what I refer to as culturescapes was a proposition with an increasingly limited return. In the end it seemed I wanted my work to have the ability to discourse with the world cultural and natural at large."[2]

In *Minimalism's Evil Orthodoxy* Bickerton implicitly critiques what he sees as the single-minded thinking underlying both Minimalism's relentless pursuit of pure, efficient form and monoculture's emphasis on specialized crop production. While admiring the clarity of Minimalist form, he finds the absolutism of its accompanying dogma to be every bit as limiting and poisonous as the effects of monoculture: dependence on chemical fertilizers and pesticides, hybrid crops with a diminished resistance to weather and disease, and the depletion of the agricultural

gene pool. "To me Minimalism suddenly revealed itself as a progenitor or accomplice to the same logic that produces monoculture row planting in national forests, and saturation bombing.... I wanted to do an acrobatic leap between the piety of the Minimalist project and the real world effects of that kind of thinking."[3]

While his earlier works have a glossy, highly finished seductiveness, *Minimalism's Evil Orthodoxy* is comparatively rough and unfinished. "Once I imagined these new objects as containers," Bickerton says, "I wanted to evoke a sense of something which was not produced for gallery walls in the late 1980s. To make a paradox: a futuristic relic ... I wanted to move from art season time (season 87/89) to geological time."[4]

P.B.

1. The artist quoted in Shaun Caley, "Ashley Bickerton: A Revealing Exposé of the Application of Art," *Flash Art*, no. 143 (November–December 1988), p. 79.
2. The artist quoted in "Une conversation avec Mark Dion," *Galeries Magazine*, no. 33 (October–November 1989), p. 142.
3. Ibid.
4. Ibid.

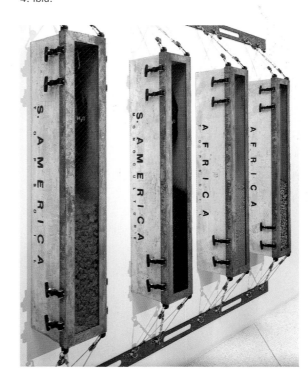

Charles Biederman

Red Wing No. 6   1957–1963

American, b. 1906

painted aluminum

**38⁷⁄₁₆ x 26¼ x 8⅝
(97.5 x 66.7 x 21.8)**

**acquired from the artist,
1964 (gift of the artist
through the Ford
Foundation Purchase
Program 64.31)**

Biederman considers this work a realization of the artistic objectives he has been clarifying since 1937, when he first began analyzing the conceptual ambitions of Western art since Impressionism.[1] He believes that Courbet marked the end of the viability of representational art, and that Monet presented the first real challenge to such art in his conception of nature as light-created color structuring space rather than as solid forms inhabiting space. The most important figure in generating Biederman's own response was Cézanne, whose structuring system emulated the processes of natural creation in an exclusively pictorial way. Cézanne replaced organic curvature with planes of color defined by light that referred to rather than ignored the two-dimensional, linear structure of painting.

Biederman claims that the implications of Cézanne's revolutionary redefinition of the aims of painting were not properly understood until he himself evolved an optical-spatial alternative to the obsolete forms of painting and sculpture. He called this alternative Constructionism, then Structurism and, finally, simply "the new art."[2] He sharply admonishes those artists whose work his own most resembles, such as Mondrian and the Russian Constructivists, for their failure to create what he considers an art appropriate to the age. He accuses them of attempting to destroy structure and form an implacable rejection of nature instead of creating new, uniquely artistic structures reflecting the organizing principles of nature. Identifying nature as the only creative structuring system familiar to man, his aim has been to find a way of expressing that creative process in exclusively man-made, inorganic terms, made possible through machine technology. Since everything painted on a surface introduces the element of spatial illusion, which diminishes the concrete reality of the object created, Biederman makes his compositional elements actual. He considers the backdrop a field of color rather than a pictorial ground; the forms supported by it interact in and penetrate real space. The reflections, shadows, and highlights of the colored planes and their edges shift subtly or dramatically with changes of light.[3] They are frequently painted in the colors of nature, reflecting his view that color is a fundamental structuring element rather than a descriptive feature.

Red Wing No. 6 evolved from rough colored-pencil sketches and a gouache-painted wooden model. The finished piece is made from mechanical drawings, the elements painted with an airbrush and screwed on from the back. Biederman intends the reliefs to project about ½ inch from the wall, to appear to be part of though separate from it.[4] The date of this work applies to an entire series, the first of which was begun in 1957 and completed in 1963. The numbers that appear in the titles, however, were added long after the works were executed and some errors of sequence occurred.[5]

L.F.G.

1. Biederman has published four books and extensive articles on the theory and development of modern art and his place in it. See particularly *Art as the Evolution of Visual Knowledge* (Red Wing, Minnesota: Charles Biederman, 1948), *Search for New Arts* (Red Wing, Minnesota: Charles Biederman, 1979), and numerous articles in the journals *Structure* and *The Structurist*.
2. For a concise explanation of the terms Constructionism and Structurism, see Jan van der Marck in Walker Art Center, *Charles Biederman: The Structurist Relief 1935–1964*, exh. cat., 1966, p. 203, n. 1.
3. Biederman has considered using lights that gradually move over the work in a simulation of the path of the sun, so that the changes in the work in response to light would be perceived in the gallery; conversation with the author, 7 June 1986.
4. Ibid.
5. Conversation with the author, 17 August 1986.

Lee Bontecou

Untitled No. 38 1961

American, b. 1931

iron, welded steel, copper wire, canvas, velvet fabric

56 x 39½ x 21⅛ (142.2 x 100.3 x 53.7)

stamped, upper right, *1961*; lower right, *LB*

acquired from the Leo Castelli Gallery, New York, by the Dwan Gallery, Los Angeles, 1963; acquired from the Dwan Gallery, 1966 (gift of the T.B. Walker Foundation 66.10)

Attached to a frame and projecting aggressively from the wall, Bontecou's reliefs elude definitive categorization as painting or sculpture.[1] During the early and mid-60s their ambiguous status stimulated animated discussion, to which Bontecou responded by succinctly declaring her allegiance: "I want to get sculpture off the floor."[2] In order to do so, she needed a lightweight material, which she discovered in the laundry bags from the establishment under her New York apartment; she later went farther afield to scavenge old canvas, a material borrowed from the domain of painting.[3] From the conventions of sculpture she appropriated the welded armature, building it out from the two-dimensional plane implied by the iron frame (equivalent of the stretcher in painting). She then stretched patches of canvas over the planar segments, gluing or more often "tacking" them together with copper wire. The black hole, her evocative but non-mimetic primary image, is created through the essential cooperation of all parts of the object—it is not drawn onto or carved out of a support. Donald Judd, one of her most passionate supporters, wrote admiringly of her achievement in "making the entire shape, the structure and the image ... coextensive,"[4] a precept crucial to him and other Minimalists.

The worn, improvisational, pseudo-functional qualities of the materials suggest prior use. As containers of a hollow volume, with apertures that permit partial entry to the space within, Bontecou's works conceptually resemble vehicles such as airplanes and boats—visually, their features evoke portholes, engines, machine bodies, and vents. She told a journalist that it pleased her when a viewer compared her work to an Eskimo kayak,[5] which may have sparked a connection in her mind with her father's aluminum canoe business.[6] The related construction of airplanes interested her as well—she made model planes in her studio, and in one piece included part of a World War II bomber. She was also intrigued by Sputnik. This interest in space travel is consonant with her comment that "I like space that never stops. Black is like that. Holes and boxes mean secrets and shelter."[7] The notion of a vehicle containing human voyagers penetrating unknown, vast, and potentially dangerous regions, holds the excitement and sense of mystery Bontecou sought to express. The machine analogy is given sexual overtones in the dentated slit and womblike enclosures, demonstrating her "grasp of the mechanical-biological opposition."[8]

Bontecou has discussed several times the specter of nuclear disaster. In 1963 she reflected that her generation "at least had some years without the atomic fear hanging over our heads. But to be born into that situation in which we can end it all!"[9] The element of danger, inherent in her recorded interests and her images—the saw blades and military camouflage palette of *Untitled No. 38*, for example—is contained within a stable, asymmetrically balanced composition, a contrast paralleled by the disparity between two rectangles of sensuous black and red velvet and the coarse, proletarian canvas. These oppositions may express her frequently quoted aspiration to "glimpse some of the fear, hope, ugliness, beauty and mystery that exists in us all and which hangs over all the young people today."[10]

L.F.G.

1. Significantly, these reliefs began with drawings in soot made with an acetylene torch, a tool more commonly used to weld sculpture; see Tony Towle, "Two Conversations with Lee Bontecou," *The Print Collector's Newsletter*, vol. 2 (May–June 1971), p. 26.
2. Quoted in an unidentified clipping (after 1964), artist's file, The Museum of Modern Art Library, New York.
3. Ibid.
4. Donald Judd, "In the Galleries," *Arts Magazine*, vol. 37 (January 1963), p. 44.
5. Unidentified clipping, artist's file, The Museum of Modern Art Library.
6. For her father's business, see William Wolf, "Bumpers, Wires and Canvas," *Journal*, 9 June 1963, clipping in artist's file, The Museum of Modern Art Library.
7. Unidentified clipping, artist's file, The Museum of Modern Art Library.
8. Carter Ratcliff, in Museum of Contemporary Art, Chicago, *Lee Bontecou*, brochure, 1972, n.p.
9. Quoted in Wolf.
10. From a letter to Dorothy C. Miller, 1960, excerpt published in The Museum of Modern Art, New York, *Americans 1963*, exh. cat., 1963, n.p.

Louise Bourgeois

The Blind Leading the Blind 1989

American, b. France, 1911

painted and lacquered
bronze

88 x 65¼ x 16¼
(223.5 x 165.7 x 41.3)

on base, *L.B.1.*

Modern Art Foundry, Long
Island City, New York

acquired from the Robert
Miller Gallery, New York
(gift of the Marbrook
Foundation, Marney and
Conley Brooks, Virginia
and Edward Brooks, Jr.,
Markell Brooks, and Carol
and Conley Brooks, Jr.,
89.69)

The Blind Leading the Blind is a recent bronze cast of a 1947–1949 painted wood sculpture by this French-born artist, who works in New York City. Its distinctive configuration—consisting in the original of roughly hewn lengths of wood painted in black and deep red—is a horizontal lintel supported by seven pairs of tapered legs. The work in the Walker collection is the first of three casts made in 1989 from the original wood sculpture.

As a part of the earliest body of sculptural work by Bourgeois, *The Blind Leading the Blind* derives its composition from an image that appeared in her paintings and drawings of the late 1940s—a windowless house on stilts. In successive variations, the house disappeared as she focused her attention on the stilts, which, in their ambiguity, were abstract evocations of a single figure as well as of a group of figures.[1]

Bourgeois's use of this multi-legged image is attributable to several sources. According to the critic Kay Larson, its inspiration might have come from the artist's childhood memories of crawling with her brother under the dining room table, from which perspective "all we could see of the world were these legs, very disgusting and very aggressive."[2] Another notion is that her fascination with multiple legs might have its roots in the period when she worked in her parents' tapestry-conservation workshop outside Paris. There she was frequently assigned the task of redrawing the legs of figures at the bottom of huge, often frayed cloths.[3]

But even with such clues related to earlier phases of Bourgeois's life, *The Blind Leading the Blind* lends itself to a variety of other interpretations. It is simultaneously a large hairbrush and an exotic multi-ped creature; it can also be read as a group of figures on the march, a view supported by the artist's comment that the sculpture portrays "people who were fated to be destroyed together" and "women as victims trying to support each other."[4] This reading is reinforced by the title, based as it is on a biblical admonition: "If the blind lead the blind, both shall fall into the ditch."[5]

The Blind Leading the Blind is a theme Bourgeois reworked several times during the late 1940s, making five related sculptures that share the same basic configuration but vary in number of legs, lintel shape, and overall proportions.[6] Cast under her supervision and painted to match the color of the original, the Walker sculpture features a rectangular base added by the artist especially for its placement in the Minneapolis Sculpture Garden.

M.G.

1. Lucy R. Lippard, "The Blind Leading the Blind," *The Bulletin of the Detroit Institute of Arts*, vol. 59 (1981), p. 25.
2. Kay Larson, "Louise Bourgeois: Body Language Spoken Here," *Village Voice*, (24–30 September 1980), p. 83.
3. Bourgeois's parents ran a workshop for the restoration of tapestries, which were then sold in a gallery they also operated.
4. The artist quoted in Lippard, op. cit., p. 27.
5. Matt. 15:14.
6. The first version of *The Blind Leading the Blind* was exhibited and then destroyed by Bourgeois, who reused its various elements in later versions.

Scott Burton

Two-Part Chairs, Obtuse Angle (A Pair)   1983–1984

American, 1939–1989

granite

33 x 24 x 33
(83.8 x 61 x 83.8) each

acquired from the Max
Protetch Gallery,
New York (gift of the
Butler Family Fund 84.3)

Chairs had been a major theme for Burton since his days as a performance artist, when he situated them on the stage in lieu of actors. Later he became more engaged with the everyday world by designing objects—including chairs—that straddle the line between fine art and functional furniture, consciously aligning himself with the earlier twentieth-century De Stijl and Bauhaus traditions. His ongoing fascination with chairs might be explained by their ubiquity in our everyday lives and their ability to symbolize the human form. *Two-Part Chairs, Obtuse Angle (A Pair)* is the first of an edition of two. They are part of a loosely defined series of approximately eight geometric granite works, created between 1982 and 1984, which also includes a chaise lounge, settees, a seat and table, a café table and *Two-Part Chairs, Right Angle (A Pair)*, a more upright, masculine member of the same family whose patriarchs are the imposing granite *Lounge Chairs* (1977–1981).

Burton first worked out the ideas for the chairs in drawings and with cardboard models. Then he had these unconventional works of art made with the traditional materials of a sculptor and the time-honored methods of a craftsman. Their fabrication at the hands of someone other than the artist (a stonecutter) parallels the industrial processes appropriated by the Minimalist artists. The severity of the chair forms also makes reference to Minimalism and specifically brings to mind the well-known L-beam pieces of the mid-60s by Robert Morris.

Matisse envisioned an art that is like a comfortable armchair. Burton had another vision, equally compelling, of an art that provides a direct means of social engagement, an anonymous art which is both functional and subversive. His *Two-Part Chairs* sit on the Walker's sculpture terrace, the quintessence of form and function. They intervene in the lives of all museum visitors, those who recognize them as sculpture as well as those who understand them exclusively as a convenience. Occupying a position of irony and power that Burton intended, the *Two-Part Chairs* offer a place for two friends to rest and chat.

M.G.

Deborah Butterfield

Rosary 1981

American, b. 1949

wood, metal, brick dust

**31 x 95⅜ x 74¼
(78.7 x 242.3 x 188.6)**

**acquired from the Hansen
Fuller Goldeen Gallery,
San Francisco, 1982
(purchased in memory of
Miriam Swenson by her
friends 82.24)**

Before introducing metal into her sculpture, Butterfield had used twigs and mud to make images of horses inspired by the shapes of debris caught on branches and clotted on the banks of Montana rivers that had swollen and receded.[1] By 1979 she felt that her exploitation of the media had become too facile and characteristic, and the figures too refined, and she began using found machine-made junk and industrial refuse. She also attributes the change of media to her then recent move to a neglected farm whose pasture was littered with equipment and metal scraps, and to the detritus produced during the refurbishing of the house.[2]

The materials for the recumbent *Rosary*—a crushed heating duct covered with the pinkish brown dust of shattered bricks and lengths of wood—were gathered from a demolition site.[3] The work is made of four separate parts, allowing for a slight change with each installation. It has a graphic quality, derived from the expressive use of line and contour, which suggests the horse's essential appearance and inner energies. Despite the abstraction of form and the tactility of the metal and wood surfaces, the gestures, tensions, and expressions of the horse are precisely

observed and rendered. While acknowledging her fascination and regard for horses, several of which she owns, rides, and trains, Butterfield is careful to distinguish her undertaking as a transformative process rather than a romantic paean to the horse—a process involving self-expression and formal exploration. She has compared the basic rectangle of the horse's torso to a canvas within which her expressionist marks are contained.[4] The horse, moreover, has also served in Butterfield's work as a psychological self-portrait. In her early hollow plaster horses begun in 1973, the mare is patient, serene, yet powerful, a beneficent alternative to the male warhorse and, as the artist perceives it, an idealized vision of herself. The later horses—more aggressive incarnations in mud and then metal—acknowledge nature's and her own darker side.[5]

Like Degas and Boccioni, Butterfield has studied the horse closely, and knows that a recumbent horse is one that feels comfortable in its surroundings and can permit itself to be vulnerable. She interprets the supine horse in the unnatural environment of the art gallery as a metaphor for her own combined self-exposure and self-assurance.[6]

L.F.G.

1. Statement in The Israel Museum, Jerusalem, *Deborah Butterfield: Jerusalem Horses*, exh. cat., 1981, n.p.
2. Tape-recorded conversation with Graham Beal, Walker Art Center, 10 February 1982.
3. Butterfield, in WAC questionnaire, undated. The site had been that of the Holy Rosary School in Bozeman, which several of Butterfield's best students had attended. The title of the work arose also from "the rose-colored dust and the sainted kind of imagery (piercing sticks);" letter to the author, 26 March 1987.
4. The Israel Museum.
5. Ibid., and typewritten statement prepared by the artist in September 1981 for the Hansen Fuller Goldeen Gallery in San Francisco. The technique is correspondingly aggressive: she crumpled and shaped the metal with a sledge hammer before attaching it with galvanized wire to the welded steel armature. When the work was damaged in transit in 1983—part of the upper neck stake splintered off and the wood was compressed—she repaired it by simply readjusting the stake, feeling that the notion of damage was integral to the piece; letter to Carolyn DeCato, Walker Art Center, 20 May 1983.
6. The Israel Museum.

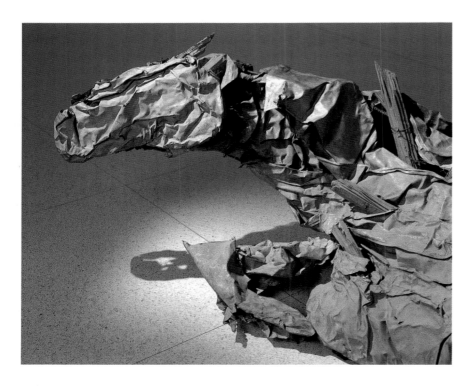

Deborah Butterfield

Woodrow 1988

American, b. 1949

bronze

**99 x 105 x 74
(251.5 x 266.7 x 188)**

**Walla Walla Foundry,
Washington**

**commissioned for the
Minneapolis Sculpture
Garden, 1988 (gift of
Edson and Harriet Spencer
88.375)**

Deborah Butterfield's romance with horses began long before they became the central theme of her work, in the early 1970s. "I loved horses even before I could talk," she told the curator Graham Beal.[1] Initially considering a career in veterinary medicine, she attended the University of California, Davis, which was also known for its art department. Once there, she was able to combine these two interests by making horses the subject of her art.

In the 1980s, having created horses from a diversity of found materials—combining fragments of wood, wire, scrap metal, and even mud—Butterfield began working with cast bronze, largely in response to several outdoor commissions she had received. Her first efforts consisted of using a cast-bronze armature on which she formed the horse's contours with crumpled sheet metal. *Woodrow*, a heroically scaled equine installed in the Minneapolis Sculpture Garden, represents a radical departure in that it is made up entirely of cast-bronze elements. This piece was foreshadowed by several small bronzes, each about three feet high, in which she worked out her technique for grander versions.

In fabricating *Woodrow*, Butterfield sought to remain as true as possible to her usual method of assembling elements improvisationally. But in so doing she went to unusual lengths. Rather than building the sculpture out of a variety of materials and then casting its completed form in bronze, she sent a selection of sticks, tree branches, and bark to the foundry with instructions that each element be cast individually. From these components, she constructed her monumental horse by fitting, then welding, the elements together—a technical feat of some magnitude—in order to build up its complete image. After the sculpture was fully assembled, its separate elements were patinated to resemble the original sticks and branches. The result is a remarkable trompe-l'oeil effect: *Woodrow* constantly astonishes Garden visitors, most of whom are at first convinced that the work is made of wood.

Because the strength and number of bronze elements she used permitted Butterfield to dispense with the usual interior armature, *Woodrow* is a remarkably "open" sculpture that carries a special flowing feeling within its maze of sticks and branches. Its bronze elements function metaphorically, if not literally, as horses' bones and tendons. An accomplished horsewoman, Butterfield is almost as passionate about the art of dressage as she is about making sculptures of horses; she sees analogies between such training and creating her art. "By training a dressage horse," she says, "you're making a sculpture, because you're redistributing the muscle structure of the horse. I find myself building my sculptural horses the way I'd like to build my real horse."[2]

Like many of Butterfield's sculptured horses, *Woodrow* is larger than life-size. "I always enlarge," she says. "You know how when you think of someone with great love and joy you kind of expand them? That's what happens with the horses, and why they're so much bigger than real horses would be."[3] While many of her horses have a somewhat vulnerable air, *Woodrow*, with its great size, resilient materials, and alert, rigid-legged pose, is an unusually assured and monumental presence.

M.G.

1. The artist in conversation with Graham Beal, Walker Art Center, 10 February 1982.
2. Quoted in "Equestrian Mysteries: An interview with Deborah Butterfield," *Art in America*, vol. 77 (June 1989), pp. 155ff.
3. Ibid.

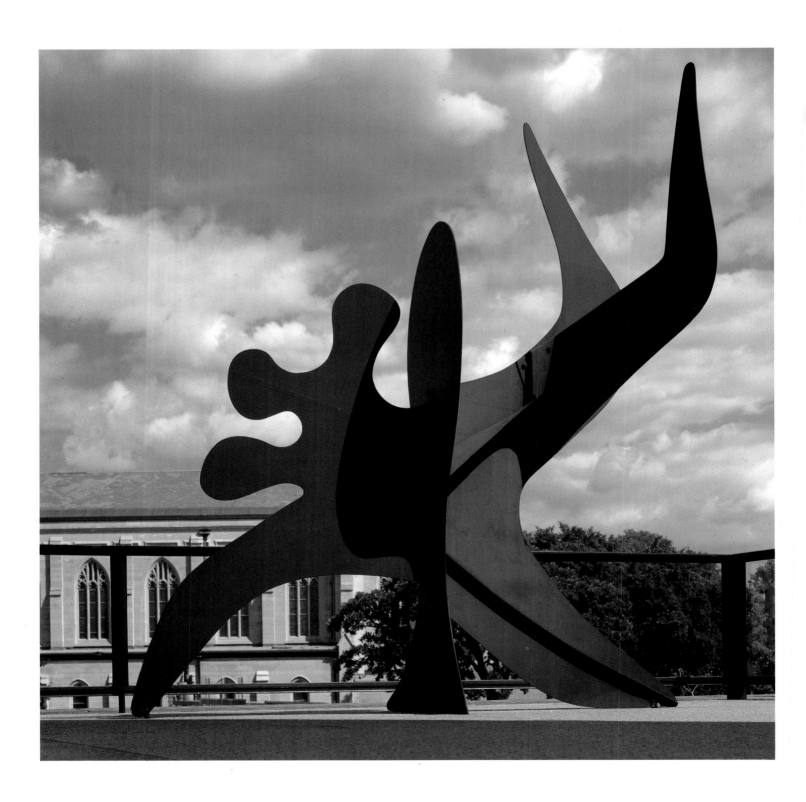

Alexander Calder

Octopus 1964

American, 1898–1976

painted steel

**116½ x 111 x 67¼
(295.9 x 281.9 x 170.8)**

**on middle plate,
monogram, *64***

**Segre Iron Works,
Waterbury, Connecticut**

**acquired from the artist by
the Perls Galleries,
New York, 1964; acquired
from the Perls Galleries,
1968 (gift of the T.B.
Walker Foundation 68.1)**

In works such as *Octopus*, Calder used flat plates of machine-cut steel whose outlines bear a resemblance to cutout elements in the reliefs of Arp (who invented the word "stabile" for Calder),[1] but are removed from any support and bolted together to carry their own weight. One of the most stable balancing systems for a freestanding structure is the tripod—here the "head" and "neck" provide the central fulcrum while two "tentacles" arch and droop to meet the ground on either side. The distribution of weight permits the addition of tentacles waving languidly on one side, and abstracted suckers humorously mimicking the shape of the head on the other. The depicted movement has the multidirectional, gravitationally released quality of underwater life. Like the octopus itself, the sculpture is mostly head and vagrant limbs. However, the soft, spongy texture and the coloristic changeability of the creature have been eliminated, replaced by planes of ungiving metal painted a flat black, rearing stiffly through space. Calder is quoted as saying: "I like a hard shape, something like a fresh fruit, rather than an old, rotten shape."[2]

As in Constructivist sculpture, mass and volume, although rolled into flat planes, paradoxically occupy more space than they displace by virtue of their extension. In this respect, the effect of Calder's stabiles is architectural, while the visibility of the means of construction relates them to engineering, a field Calder had once studied. The bolts, ribs, and gussets were added as needed for support, and were not integral to the initial design of the work:

> I try something new each time. With the model at three meters you can wobble it and see where it gives, where the vibrations occur, and then put your reinforcement there. If a plate seems flimsy, I put a rib on it, and if the relation between the two plates is not rigid, I put a gusset between them—that's the triangular piece—and butt it to both surfaces. How to construct them changes with each piece.[3]

L.F.G.

1. See Katharine Kuh, *The Artist's Voice: Talks with Seventeen Artists* (New York: Harper & Row, 1960), p. 41.
2. Quoted in Richard Schickel and Phillip Harrington, "A Visit with Calder," *Look*, vol. 22 (9 December 1958), p. 56.
3. Quoted in Robert Osborn, "Calder's International Monuments," *Art in America*, vol. 57 (March–April 1969), p. 49.

Alexander Calder

The Spinner   1966

American, 1898–1976

aluminum, steel, oil paint

235 high, 351 diam.
(596.9 high, 891.5 diam.)

on base, monogram *66*

Etablissements Biémont,
Tours

acquired from the Perls
Galleries, New York, by
Dayton Hudson
Corporation, Minneapolis,
1966; acquired from
Dayton Hudson
Corporation, 1971 (gift of
Dayton Hudson
Corporation 71.16)

The Spinner is closely related to the "totems" Calder devised to accompany a group of gouaches he was going to exhibit at the Galerie Maeght, Paris, early in 1966: "I scratched my head and came up with some tall black pyramidal shapes with mobile festoons on their heads. They are made out of steel and their tops of aluminum."[1] In a poem published in the Maeght catalogue, Jacques Prévert compared the new structures with the Eiffel Tower, and both with the physically ponderous, mentally agile artist: "Mobile en haut/Stabile en bas/Telle est la tour/ Eiffel/Calder est comme elle."[2] In the Walker work, mobile and stabile are mediated by a spinning element.

The conical base or trunk of the 1500-pound sculpture is made of four triangular steel sheets, or flanges, attached to anchored clips and bolted to a central shaft. Calder imagined a substance filling in the space between such planes:

> When I use two or more sheets of metal cut into shapes and mounted at angles to each other, I feel that there is a solid form, perhaps concave, perhaps convex, filling in the dihedral angles between them. I do not have a definite idea of what this would be like, I merely sense it and occupy myself with the shape one actually sees.[3]

An effect comparable to his imaginings emerges in the spinning element, which when twirling produces the illusion of a coloristically self-transforming volume. Slipped over the central shaft above the stabilized black cone, the "spinner" has ball bearings at top and bottom to encourage the movement of its four plates, which are furled at their outside corners to catch the wind. They are painted in such a way that, like the base, they appear to be two intersecting plates rather than four on a stalk. One of these intersecting plates is red on one side and blue on the other, and the other plate yellow and black. As they turn, the sequence blue-black-yellow-blue-red-yellow-black-red flashes by, the colors fluidly waxing and waning.

Typically, Calder limits himself to primaries and "non-colors," claiming that the "secondary colors and intermediate shades serve only to confuse and muddle the distinctness and clarity."[4] His preferred opposition, red and black, is used on the respective sides of each plate of the mobile elements dangling from a long arm, which "seems to best approximate ... freedom from the earth."[5] This arm pivots on the top of the shaft and can swing and rock to a limited extent, contributing to the movement of the secondary arms, to produce another kind of occupation of space and another level of animation, with increased possibilities for unpredictable movement and shifting relationships in response to the wind.

Although Calder has denied a conscious connection between his *Circus* (1926–1931) and the mobiles,[6] they have significant features in common. As exemplified by *The Spinner*, these include bright color contrasted with darkness, the simultaneous activity of many parts, the emphasis on movement—involving balancing bars, bodies supporting other bodies, hanging by single points and spinning—and the potential for danger. His explanation for the appeal the circus held for him could apply to his other work: "I've always been delighted by the way things are hooked together.... It's just like a diagram of force. I love the mechanics of the thing and the vast space—and the spotlight."[7]

L.F.G.

1. Alexander Calder, *Calder: An Autobiography with Pictures* (New York: Pantheon Press, 1966), p. 277.
2. "Oiseleur du Fer" in *Derrière le miroir*, no. 156 (February 1966), n.p.; a literal translation was published in Archives Maeght 1, *Calder: The Artist, the Work* (London: Lund Humphries, 1971), p. 24: "Mobiles at the top/Stabiles at the bottom/Such is the Eiffel Tower/Calder is like the Tower."
3. Statement, "What Abstract Art Means to Me," *Museum of Modern Art Bulletin*, vol. 18 (Spring 1951), p. 7.
4. Ibid.
5. Ibid.
6. Cleve Gray, "Calder's Circus," *Art in America*, vol. 52 (October 1964), p. 23, and Katharine Kuh, *The Artist's Voice: Talks with Seventeen Artists* (New York: Harper & Row, 1960), p. 41.
7. Quoted in Gray, p. 25.

Anthony Caro

Sculpture Three, 1962   1962

British, b. 1924

painted steel

78⁹⁄₁₆ x 62⅞ x 148⅝
(199.5 x 159.7 x 375.9)

acquired from the David
Mirvish Gallery, Toronto,
1967(gift of the T.B.
Walker Foundation 67.27)

In his works of this period, Caro's aim was to "make sculpture which is very corporeal, but denies its corporeality."[1] He began *Sculpture Three, 1962* in his one-car garage at Hampstead by raising a railway line to the desired height and inclination with the help of Isaac Witkin.[2] The effort of lifting the tie, present by implication, is belied by the overall structure, in which physically insufficient and unassertive supports serve pictorially as lines through space. Although top-heavy in fact, the sculpture is light and graphic in effect, its elegantly awkward lines and curves suggesting sweeps of paint. "All sculptors have dreams of defying gravity," Caro has said. "One of the inherent qualities about sculpture is its heaviness, its substance. There is an attraction in the dream of putting heavy pieces calmly up in the air and getting them to stay there."[3]

Caro achieved his gravity-defying, substanceless effect through an open-ended and dispersive configuration. Having made the piece in his garage, he did not have enough space to step back from it while it was in progress. The consequence, in his mind desirable, is that he could not compose in a traditional sense, balancing and counterpointing parts within a whole, but had to relate one part to the next additively. Not only are the elements fragments of larger wholes, implying an unconsummated extension, but they do not delineate or enclose a volume. The space of the sculpture and its surroundings function more like those of a Suprematist painting, in which weightless, non-allusive planes appear to hover, pass behind, bump into, and glide over one another within an infinite atmosphere. Although there is no single viewing point from which *Sculpture Three, 1962* can be fully grasped, it seems to have a lateral primary view. One tends

to align the circular penetrations on a single plane as if they were sites, creating the sense of a flat, shallow picture plane in which forms are suspended in different directions. From the end of its long axis, the lines are foreshortened and the space compressed, which again produces a pictorializing effect.

Caro defended his "anti-sculptural" decisions, maintaining that a sculpture can hold "a great deal of pictoriality" without losing its integrity as a medium.[4] Despite their cloak of paint and miraculous suspension, his materials are scruffy, heavy, clearly of this world, and actually penetrating space. Nevertheless, Caro eventually became uneasy about the pictorializing aspects of his work and abandoned them in 1963. Strengthening his structure, he stopped adding color to unify disparate elements and began to make the floor a more integral, formal element.

L.F.G.

1. "Anthony Caro Interviewed by Andrew Forge," *Studio International*, vol. 171 (January 1966), p. 7.
2. Caro, in WAC questionnaire, 8 November 1981, p. 2.
3. Phyllis Tuchman, "An Interview with Anthony Caro," *Artforum*, vol. 10 (June 1972), p. 56. As Caro has acknowledged, there are practical difficulties to this approach: "[The sculpture] has always been a bit shaky.... Trying to suspend a railway line high above one's head was not a very practical thing to do;" letter to Martin Friedman, 8 July 1967. The vertical support that ends in a three-quarter arch appears out of perpendicular alignment in some photographs, which may in part explain the collapse of the work in January 1974; it has since been rewelded and stabilized.
4. "Anthony Caro—A Discussion with Peter Fuller," *Art Monthly*, no. 23 (1979).

Chuck Close

Big Self-Portrait 1968

American, b. 1940

acrylic on canvas

107½ x 83½
(273 x 212.1)

on reverse, lower center, *"Big Self-Portrait" Charles Close 1968 acrylic on canvas*

acquired from the artist, 1969 (Art Center Acquisition Fund 69.16)

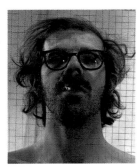

Chuck Close
Study for *Self-Portrait*
1968
photograph, pen and ink, pencil, masking tape, white paint, wash and blue plastic strips on cardboard
18½ x 13¼ (47 x 33.7)
Collection The Museum of Modern Art, New York
Gift of Norman Dubrow

Close has recounted in various interviews the circumstances that led to *Big Self-Portrait*, the first of his mural-scale paintings derived from photographs of sitters' heads. Late in 1967, while photographing a nude he had painted on a vast canvas, he felt dissatisfied both with its content and lack of intrinsic monumentality. He used the remaining sheets of film to record his own head and neck, filling the frame.[1] From the negatives he made contact sheets, and from these he selected a negative to enlarge and print as two "working photographs" for a greatly enlarged painting.[2] One of these was gridded and the squares identified by number and letter for the laborious four-month task of transferring the image to canvas.[3] The Walker's monumental painting, then, can be seen as the culmination of a series of mutations of a single image, beginning with a photographic negative.

In the photographic print the pictorial elements of shape, volume, texture, edge, plane, shadow, and highlight are mechanically recorded as varying areas of black, white, or gray. Precisely emulating this anti-naturalistic effect, Close sprays black acrylic onto the canvas with an airbrush, and permits both subtle and dramatic variations of density, and smooth and abrupt transitions. One of the unexpected, but in Close's mind felicitous, aspects of the photographs of his head was the shallow depth of field, which heightens the contrast between sharp and blurry boundaries. Unlike the eye, which involuntarily concentrates on the areas on which it focuses, the camera lens "sees" near and far simultaneously and records them with equal impassivity. The closest and farthest areas in the self-portrait—the cigarette tip and the hair at the back—have indistinct edges and surfaces, while the rest of the face is sharply defined. This "sandwich" effect had paradoxical spatial consequences that interested Close: "To the degree that something is out of focus, other areas that are similarly out of focus are on the same level in space."[4]

The formal properties of photography are of considerable importance to Close: "I go to a great deal of trouble to get the specific kind of photograph that is going to have the kind of information that's interesting to me—texture, elaborate depth of field—and the distance I shoot them from is important."[5] He is concomitantly unconcerned with the expressive content of the photographs he uses, which "do not have an object status of their own. They are simply a notation system for information to be used later in any number of ways."[6] Although he chooses faces that are personally familiar to him, he explains that this is not for sentimental reasons, but because they serve as barometers of his success in making his marks legible.[7] Just as his scrutiny and analysis of the photographic information must be unimpeded by subjective response, imaginative elaboration or aesthetic considerations in order for him to persuasively translate it into painting, so too the image selected must be as factual as possible.

Close freely admits, however, that his feelings toward the sitter inevitably influence the image. In the case of *Big Self-Portrait*, the manner in which he photographed himself situates the painting within the tradition of the psychologically revelatory, self-aggrandizing or deprecatory self-portrait; referring to the painting, Close himself wryly confesses to "having seen too many James Dean movies."[8] Later, he was to clarify his conceptual intentions by neutralizing the presentation of his sitters, including himself, to more closely correspond with the "snapshot or mugshot quality of a California driver's license,"[9] eliminating the characterizing poses, expressions, and accessories.

L.F.G.

1. Linda Chase and Ted McBurnett, "The Photo-Realists: 12 Interviews," *Art in America*, vol. 60 (November–December 1972), p. 76. Close used a borrowed 4 x 5 view camera with a long lens; conversation with the author, 11 September 1986.
2. Letter from Lisa Lyons to Norman Dubrow, 5 August 1980. One of these photographs, measuring 14 x 11 inches, was given by Mr. Dubrow to The Museum of Modern Art, New York; the whereabouts of the other, slightly larger, is presently unknown—it was traded by Close to someone for two kitchen chairs, about 1970. Although he isn't certain, this photograph was probably ungridded, as it was his practice to work from one gridded and one unmarked photo; conversation with the author, 11 September 1986.
3. For a description of his precise procedures, see Lisa Lyons in Walker Art Center, *Close Portraits*, exh. cat., 1980, pp. 30–33.
4. Chase and McBurnett, p. 77.
5. Ibid., p. 76.
6. Quoted in Amy Baker Sandback and Ingrid Sischy, "A Progression by Chuck Close: Who's Afraid of Photography?," *Artforum*, vol. 22 (May 1984), p. 50.
7. See Cindy Nemser, "An Interview with Chuck Close," *Artforum*, vol. 8 (January 1970), p. 55.
8. Quoted in Lisa Lyons, p. 30.
9. Quoted in "Ten Portraitists Interviews/Statements," *Art in America*, vol. 63 (January–February 1975), p. 41.

Bruce Conner

The Bride 1960–1961

American, b. 1933

wood, nylon, string, wax, paint, candles, costume jewelry, marbles, paper doily

38 x 19 x 23
(96.5 x 48.3 x 58.4)

acquired from the Braunstein/Quay Gallery, San Francisco, 1987 (Braunstein/Quay Gallery and T.B. Walker Acquisition Fund 87.23)

Bruce Conner moved to San Francisco in 1957, where he became closely associated with the artists and poets of the Beat movement. Although he had been experimenting with collage as early as 1954, it was in San Francisco that he began working in earnest in the collage/assemblage medium. Assemblage dominated his output from 1958 to 1964, after which he effectively abandoned the medium.

Conner's Assemblages were heavily flavored by the San Francisco locale; he ransacked the condemned Victorian-style buildings and second-hand stores in his neighborhood for materials.

As a result his work is infused with an air of decaying elegance. Often combining themes of sexuality and violence, Conner's most disturbing and notorious pieces explore what one critic termed "the never-ending dark dialogue of the sexual sickness and the social sickness."[1]

Like many of Conner's Assemblages, *The Bride* features torn and stretched nylon, a material that allowed Conner to at once reveal and conceal the multifarious found objects. While most of his Assemblages are wall pieces, *The Bride* is one of a small number of freestanding sculptures: others include *The Child* (1959), *Portrait of Allen Ginsberg* (1960), *Snore* (1960), and *Catch* (1964). In addition, *The Bride* is among the works that refer to film—Conner is one of the most influential experimental filmmakers of the postwar era. The title *The Bride* is derived from the portrayal of Miss Havisham in the 1946 movie version of Charles Dickens's *Great Expectations*. While working on the piece, Conner began to see similarities between his sculpture and the demented spinster who, having been jilted at the altar, continues to wear her bridal gown, live in a home bedecked with aging wedding regalia, and finally perishes when a candle sets fire to her dress.[2]

Like many of Conner's works, *The Bride* invokes the traditional *vanitas* themes of the transience of human existence and, especially, the loss of youth and beauty. Working in the post-Freudian era, the artist lingers on the sinister aspects of self-delusion, when the gap between reality and projected fantasy becomes too wide to bridge.[3]

P.B.

1. Philip Lieder, "Bruce Conner: A New Sensibility," *Artforum*, vol. 1 (December 1962), p, 30.
2. Conversation with the artist, 29 July 1987.
3. When the piece was originally exhibited at San Francisco's Batman Gallery in 1960, its candles were lit daily. Inevitably, the work caught fire, and was later restored by the artist.

Joseph Cornell

Andromeda (Sand Fountain)[1]   1953–1956

American, 1903–1972

wood, glass, paper, sand, pigment

14 x 7¾ x 3¾
(35.6 x 19.7 x 9.5)

on reverse, lower right, on tape, written backwards in ink,[2] *Joseph Cornell*

acquired from the artist, 1971 (gift of Mr. and Mrs. Russell Cowles [Elizabeth Bates Cowles Foundation] and Judy and Kenneth Dayton 71.1)

Like other examples of Cornell's "philosophical toys," this work was intended to be activated by the spectator. If its condition permitted handling, the box could be rotated clockwise, causing the blue sand to feed into the triangular hopper through an opening at the upper right. After the box was righted, the sinking sand would be visible through the "porthole." As it fell through the aperture at the truncated lower angle of the hopper, it would fill the broken cordial glass before cascading over the edge to return to its bed at the bottom of the box.

The references to time and the ocean released in this operation are appropriate to the subject of Andromeda, whose image as a constellation has been cut out and glued to the back of the interior of the box.

The persistence and intensity of Cornell's use of the Andromeda and Cassiopeia theme in his work may have biographical roots. As a myth, the story of a mother's unwitting abuse of her child may have set off his feelings of hurt and frustration at his own mother's rejection of Christian Science—a faith to which he fervently adhered—as a possible source for a cure for his sickly brother Robert.[3] As a constellation, the theme pertains to his lifelong obsession with astronomy.[4] In his imagination, stargazing was strongly tied to his Christian Science beliefs, associated with spiritual consolation, redemption, the restoration of lost innocence, and eternal life. In his diaries he frequently describes the light shed by the constellations in quasi-religious terms that are reminiscent of passages from Mary Baker Eddy. In analyzing a dream on 9 September 1967,[5] Cornell associated the vision seen through a telescope ("sense of a dark rugged interior + exquisite image of clarity, at the end sky") with the experience of talking with a Christian Science practitioner, and equated his mother's reluctance to look through the telescope with her willful blindness to the "healing truths" of Christian Science.

A definitive interpretation of the Andromeda theme is inappropriate since Cornell's diaries make it clear that the constellations carried multiple associations for him, frequently evoking admired and inaccessible women, whether fictional, historical, or living. Emily Dickinson, with whom he professed a spiritual kinship, identified herself with Andromeda in several poems, as he no doubt knew.[6] That Cornell should interweave a range of meanings is consistent with the

structure of his thinking, in which the objectively perceived world was fully enmeshed with the subjective, literary, musical, and mythical realm of his interior self, forming a complex, internally cohesive but poetically mysterious universe.

L.F.G.

1. This title was not assigned by Cornell, who used the term "sand fountain" as a generic designation in his papers, sometimes distinguishing individual examples by color of sand. The formulation that will be used in the forthcoming catalogue raisonné by Lynda Roscoe Hartigan is "Blue sand fountain (Andromeda)."
2. Cornell favored mirror writing for signatures in works of the 1950s and 1960s; Lynda Roscoe Hartigan, letter to the author, 9 July 1986.
3. In his diary entry of 2 January 1971, Cornell makes the maternal destructiveness of Cassiopeia explicit by conflating her with Medea in the name "Kassomedea;" (Cornell Papers, AAA, Reel 1064).
4. Cornell collected copies of planetarium publications such as *The Sky Reporter*, clippings about astronomy from the *Christian Science Monitor* and New York and Boston newspapers, instrument manuals, advertisements, and books, now on deposit at AAA, and the Joseph Cornell Study Center, National Museum of American Art, Smithsonian Institution, Washington, D.C.
5. (Cornell Papers, AAA, Reel 1064.)
6. Carter Ratcliff, "Joseph Cornell: Mechanic of the Ineffable," in The Museum of Modern Art, New York, *Joseph Cornell*, exh. cat., 1980, p. 51. In the case of this particular Andromeda cutout, Cornell may have observed a formal connection with photographs of the dancer Pearl Lang. He combined clippings on Pearl Lang and Andromeda (the complete figure) in the same dossier (Cornell Papers, AAA, Reel 1073), and in an accompanying note drew a connection between them. In one newspaper photograph, Lang's pose is reminiscent of that of the cutout, which almost directly precedes it in the file.

Tony Cragg

Ordovician Pore   1989

British, b. 1949

granite, steel

five elements
96 x 90 x 124
(243.8 x 228.6 x 315)
overall

acquired from Marian
Goodman Gallery, New
York (gift of Joanne and
Philip Von Blon 89.535)

British sculptor Tony Cragg investigates forms found in nature, believing that the natural world contains "the keys to essential processes and explanations of our existence."[1] While asserting that his relationship with the natural world is the dominant theme of his art, he also refers to man-made objects in his work, aiming to enhance their associative power. Indeed, many of his pieces refer to such natural forms as rock stratigraphy, molecular structure, and the human vascular system, and to such man-made forms as food containers and laboratory vessels. In his sculptures, Cragg seeks to discredit the conventional separation between man and nature, which, he says, "leads us to forget that *Homo sapiens* are also natural objects."[2]

In *Ordovician Pore* Cragg combines five elements to suggest a confluence of the natural and artificial worlds. Two hollow, belled cylinders of cast steel, whose smooth surfaces and symmetricality reveal their man-made origins, are complemented by a pair of biomorphic forms also made of steel. One of these, a bulbous, gourd-shaped mass, seems to be pouring from the mouth of one cylinder onto the ground; the second, a lobed form that suggests a seedpod, rests passively on the rough-hewn chunk of granite that supports the elements.

The title of the sculpture refers to the Ordovician Period, a geological era generally believed to have begun about 500,000,000 years ago. Rock formed during this period contains distinctive marine fossils, especially of algae and trilobites (three-lobed arthropods). The Ordovician Period also saw the introduction of oxygen into the earth's atmosphere, allowing terrestrial life to evolve. The species of algae that produced the oxygen, however, was subsequently destroyed by it.

Cragg likens the two organic forms in *Ordovician Pore* to fossils or polyps, linking them to the natural world of prehistory.[3] But he also alludes metaphorically to the self-poisoning that occurred during the Ordovician Period: the word *pore* denotes an opening for both absorption and emission, and the sculpture's cylindrical shapes bear a close resemblance to the cooling towers of nuclear power plants. Cragg seems to posit a relationship between the evolution of primitive life forms and the rise of technology in the modern world, and to suggest that although pollutants may eventually obliterate human life, this destruction might also permit the development of another form of life.

Cragg worked out the final configuration of *Ordovician Pore* while the piece was being installed in the Minneapolis Sculpture Garden, in December 1989. Its composition is typical of his other recent works in that it is made up of invented, fabricated forms rather than found objects. The steel elements were cast in Düsseldorf, near Wuppertal, Germany, where the artist lives.

J.R.

1. From a statement by the artist published in *Artforum*, vol. 26 (March 1988), p. 120.
2. Ibid., p. 121.
3. The artist in conversation with Martin Friedman, December 1989.

Ralston Crawford

Third Avenue El 1949

American, b. Canada,
1906–1978

oil on canvas

**30⅛ x 40⅛
(76.5 x 101.9)**

**lower left quadrant,
Ralston Crawford**

**acquired from The
Downtown Gallery, New
York, 1951 (gift of the
T.B. Walker Foundation,
Gilbert M. Walker Fund
51.15)**

Although the clarity of design and the urban subject matter of Crawford's work of the late 1940s betray his origins as a Precisionist, he had by this time abandoned that aesthetic and developed a "colonial Cubism" visually related to that of his close friend Stuart Davis. Crawford's interpretation of Cubism was at once intellectual and intuitive. In *Third Avenue El* the forms that appear generally to evoke the overhead train in a synthetic Cubist language in fact derive from specific details of photographs Crawford took, and then subjected to his methodical analysis and imaginative transformation. In 1949, the year *Third Avenue El* was executed, Crawford wrote about his photographs:

> They are sometimes used in relation to my drawings and color studies as sources of specific information concerning the movement of light patterns in relation to the possible effect on picture structure. On many occasions I use the camera as a sketch pad. The endless variations on a theme such as the "El" picture [referring to a related painting, *Elevated with Lahaina Color*, completed the same year] were suggested with a 36-exposure role of 35mm film. Also the various formal combinations arrived at through the enlarging (with various croppings) of a single negative are highly informative.[1]

In several of these El photographs, one of which was first exhibited in April 1949,[2] the elevated train track structure is viewed from underneath, with brilliant light visible through its ties and girders. The ambiguity of spatial relations, the confusion of scale, and the close cropping of the image make each of these photographs an abstract composition rather than a documentary description. They are presented as organizations of rectilinear light and dark forms in

an indeterminate, shallow space. In the sketches Crawford made from the photographs, the process of abstraction is carried a step further. He examines and selects from the photographs certain shapes and passages and draws them, frequently reversing positive and negative areas. In composing the final painting, he makes another selection of forms, which he modifies, organizes, and orients according to pictorial necessity. In determining color, he has recourse to his own memory; in the case of the Walker version, it seems likely that he drew on his recollections of the scene as he first experienced it, with the blue of the sky glimpsed through the tracks, the brilliant yellow of the sun, and the blacks, grays, and whites of shadowed and illuminated metal.

Fidelity to experienced reality, then, is maintained in these pictures in a submerged, invisible way—the objective world is recorded, broken up, sifted through, reordered, enlarged, reduced and re-presented. Crawford's method becomes a metaphor for the process of abstraction.

L.F.G.

1. Quoted in *Modern Photography*, vol. 13 (September 1949), p. 110.
2. The date of the photographic expedition that inspired the El paintings has not been established. The 1948–1949 date assigned to *Elevated with Lahaina Color* in a caption of early 1949 (accompanying a photograph of his studio reproduced in The Cincinnati Art Museum, *Crawford, Cutler*, exh. cat., 1949) argues for a 1948 date. It seems likely that *Lahaina* was painted at the turn of the year, and *Third Avenue El* between February and May of 1949.

Ralston Crawford
*Third Avenue Elevated,
[Horizontal]* 1948
gelatin silver print
6½ x 9½ (16.5 x 24.1)
Ralston Crawford Estate

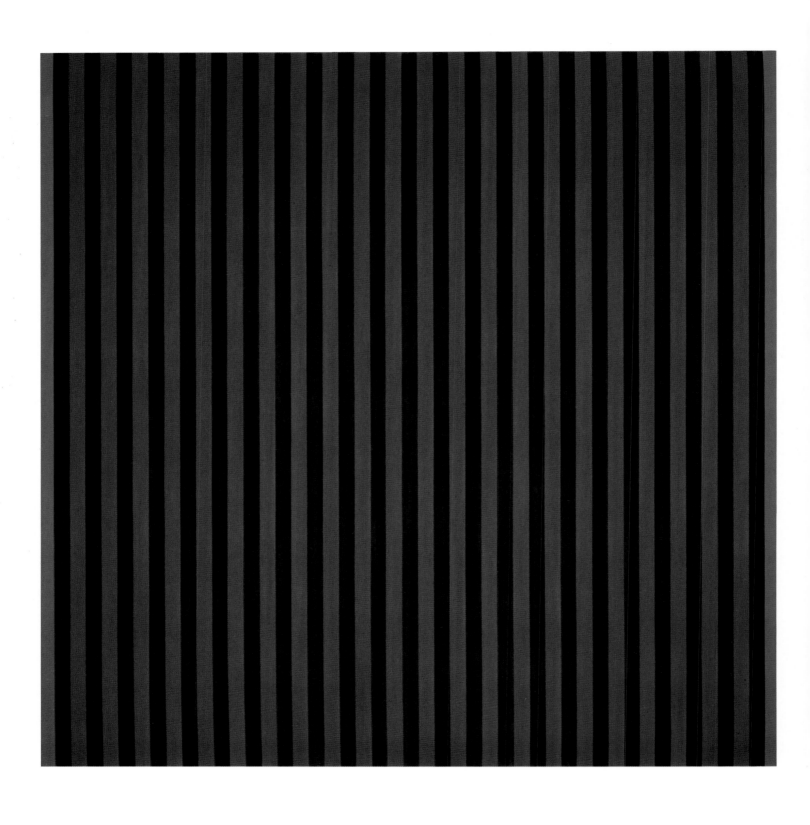

Gene Davis

Untitled 1960

American, 1920–1985

acrylic on canvas

92⅛ x 92⅛ (234 x 234)

acquired from the artist, 1980 (gift of the artist 80.21)

Davis, who once described himself as a frustrated musician, frequently drew analogies between his Stripe paintings and musical forms, calling them both arts of interval.[1] The first Stripe pictures he made, in 1958–1959, were simple alternations:

> I know a certain passage in a Vivaldi bassoon concerto that repeats the same note for what seems like three or four minutes. It goes on endlessly, and, for some reason, it has tremendous appeal for me. Repetition can be hypnotic in the proper context.[2]

He then painted about twenty transitional canvases in which the rhythmic stresses are regular throughout the lateral expanse to the flanking edges, where bars of a contrasting color spring forward from the field. In the Walker's example, stripes of clear, sonorous blue bracket the low-key alternation of olive gray and blackish brown. Davis achieved the regularity with tape and a two-inch brush used to determine the width of the bands, whose geometry is only slightly softened by the bleeding edges.[3]

In a rare interpretive comment, Davis once compared the rigidity of his stripes to bars: "Perhaps they shut other people out, and shut one in."[4] This work is particularly hermetic. Its structure resembles that of his *Narcissus*,[5] in which a sequence of stripes not only reflects itself along a central vertical axis as in the Walker picture, but is duplicated in a second canvas. The self-reflecting, closed and inward nature of these works, conveyed by the *Narcissus* title, distinguishes them from Davis's more open-ended pictures. The emphasis on symmetry was important to Davis at that time for formal reasons as well, as his aim was to generate a simple, instantly absorbed visual sensation.[6] He later reversed this position, abandoning the simpler format to explore more complex coloristic and spatial effects. He never abandoned the stripe, however, considering it the ideal neutral form to contain his color and determine its intervals. He insisted that his

stripe did not derive deductively from the canvas support, contrary to the suggestion of formalist critics such as Greenberg and Fried, and attributed his fall from favor with them to this disagreement.[7] In response to other critics' ridicule of his early works, he felt obliged to provide an artistic pedigree for his stripes that included Klee's "walking line," and Newman's zips.[8] He also defended the subject matter as proto-Pop, comparing it with Johns's targets and locating its sources in the decorative arts, textile design, and other familiar forms.[9]

L.F.G.

1. Barbara Rose, "A Conversation with Gene Davis," *Artforum*, vol. 9 (March 1971), p. 50; see also Gerald Nordland, "Gene Davis Paints a Picture," *Art News*, vol. 65 (April 1966), pp. 46–49, 61–64.
2. Jean Lawlor Cohen, "A Conversation with Gene Davis," *Art International*, vol. 23 (Summer 1979), p. 56.
3. The medium that produced the fragile surface is highly thinned Bocour Magna on unprimed canvas; Davis, in WAC questionnaire, 21 July 1980.
4. Interview with Walter Hopps, in Donald Wall, ed., *Gene Davis* (New York: Praeger Publishers, 1975), p. 120.
5. Reproduced in Steven Naifeh, *Gene Davis* (New York: The Arts Publishers, Inc., 1982), p. 83, where it is dated "1961" in the caption but "1962" in the text.
6. Leslie Judd Ahlander, "Art in Washington: An Artist Speaks: Gene Davis," *Washington Post*, 26 May 1962, p. G7.
7. Gene Davis, "Random Thoughts on Art," *Art International*, vol. 15 (20 November 1971), p. 40.
8. Davis, who had first seen Newman's work in 1951, admitted that "I was attracted to the vertical stripes and not the color fields, which are actually what his work is all about;" quoted in Mary Swift, "An Interview with Gene Davis," *Washington Review*, vol. 4 (December 1978–January 1979), p. 8.
9. Rose, p. 50.

Stuart Davis

Colonial Cubism 1954

American, 1894–1964

oil on canvas

44⅞ x 60⅛ (114 x 152.7)

lower center, *Stuart Davis*

acquired from The Downtown Gallery, New York, 1955 (gift of the T.B. Walker Foundation 55.7)

In the late spring of 1952 Davis found a group of sketches he had made in the early 1920s in Gloucester, Massachusetts, and used one of these to develop a painting, now unlocated, that was closely related to the Walker canvas.[1] Also unlocated is the sketch used, but a 1922 painting derived from it gives some sense of its appearance.[2] The forms, generally evoking landscape features—clouds, rocks, water, perhaps a bridge—are organized and patterned in the manner of Synthetic Cubist painting and collage. Davis considered subject matter irrelevant to the purpose of his pictures, and in the 1922 painting and in *Colonial Cubism* the naturalistic references are submerged.

The theoretical principles Davis had published in 1922[3] were not fully expressed in the painting of that year, but are consummately articulated in the versions of the 1950s. He held that pictures, although expressive of the emotions experienced at the time of painting, were to be impersonal in execution, composed of "positive and direct" unmodulated color planes organized logically on the canvas, ordered by the dominance of a particular "unit of area" to which all other units respond in size, color, shape, and planar relationship to establish an active three-dimensional balance.

The means through which *Colonial Cubism* conveys these fundamental properties of painting are particularly rigorous. The primaries blue and red, the secondary orange, and the "non-colors" black and white are applied with little evidence of brushwork, in flat planes that produce a dynamic but controlled advance-retreat alternation in the pictorial field. All surface patterning, perspectival devices, modeling, and the use of line independent of form have been eliminated. Lines are established by the juncture of color planes and function graphically only in the signature.[4] The massed shapes are centered in a stable composition, like a collage of cutouts on a field.

Although Davis has visually simplified the work, he has complicated it conceptually. Red areas within the "collaged" form can be read as views of the underlying ground, as complete figures on top of it, or as partial figures cut off or interrupted by neighboring color areas. The device of the apparently snipped edge is wittily demonstrated in the star at the lower left: one is instinctively compelled to complete those cut-off points, to reconstitute the familiar emblematic form. Davis implicitly advises the viewer to similarly

extend all straight lines in the composition to construct an imaginary rectilinear scaffolding.

In a somewhat ambiguous statement, Davis suggested that the title *Colonial Cubism* was intended satirically,[5] evidently meaning that while his debt to European Cubism was overwhelming, he had full confidence in the new vision he was communicating; the tone of the title, then, would be ironic rather than deferential. Elsewhere he said that he sought to emulate the French Cubists in this canvas "without becoming too expatriate about it."[6]

L.F.G.

1. Dorothy Gees Seckler, "Stuart Davis Paints a Picture," *Art News*, vol. 52 (June–August 1953), p. 31. Davis confirmed that "*Colonial Cubism* is another product of old drawings made in Gloucester;" Sidney Simon, unpublished interview that took place at Walker Art Center with Davis in 1957, p. 32. In this interview Davis refers to a smaller version, probably not the 1952 canvas but *Memo No. 2*, recently located by William C. Agee, who is preparing a catalogue raisonné of Davis's work.
2. Reproduced in The Brooklyn Museum, New York, *Stuart Davis: Art and Art Theory*, exh. cat, 1978, p. 76.
3. Reprinted in Diane Kelder, ed., *Stuart Davis* (New York and Washington, D.C.: Praeger Publishers, 1971), pp.34–39.
4. For Davis's discussion of the inclusion of his signature as a formal element, see Katharine Kuh, *The Artist's Voice: Talks with Seventeen Artists* (New York: Harper & Row, 1960), pp. 57, 58.
5. Interview with Simon, p. 32.
6. Quoted in National Collection of Fine Arts, Smithsonian Institution, Washington, D.C., *Stuart Davis Memorial Exhibition*, exh. cat., 1965, p. 42.

Two Studies for *Colonial Cubism* (from 50 boxes of Stuart Davis papers) Collection The Fogg Art Museum, Harvard University, Cambridge, Massachusetts Gift of Mrs. Stuart Davis

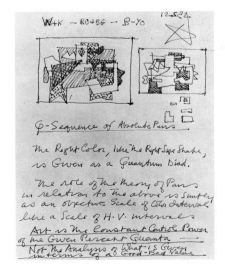

Charles Demuth

Two Acrobats   1918

American, 1883–1935

watercolor, pencil on paper

13 x 8 (33. x 20.3)

lower left, in pencil, *C. Demuth '18-*; lower right, in pencil, *C. Demuth -18-*

acquired from The Downtown Gallery, New York, 1955 (gift of Mrs. Edith Halpert 55.1)

The drawings and paintings of Charles Demuth are distinguished by an assured yet fastidious grace. Possessing a graphic, almost architectonic style, the work of this American modernist reflects a precocious and sophisticated understanding of Cubism and Postimpressionism, which Demuth encountered in several visits to Europe during the first two decades of the century.

After studying in Paris from 1913 to 1914, Demuth returned to the United States, where he associated with avant-garde American and expatriate European artists, including the Parisian Surrealist Marcel Duchamp. With Duchamp, Demuth delighted in attending circuses and costume balls; and around 1915, he began a lively watercolor series of acrobats, dancers, and circus performers, which included a sequence of studies for *Two Acrobats*, and a preliminary version of this work, *In Vaudeville: Two Acrobats No. 2*, (1916).

The high, tilted horizon line of *Two Acrobats*, a common element in the vaudeville series, gives the performers an appearance of immateriality and weightlessness. This incorporeality, heightened by the acrobat's impassive facial expressions and stylized gestures, which are echoed by concentric curves in the landscape, demonstrate Demuth's interest in the ornamental aspect of his work. Such formal emphasis is accentuated by the freely varied washes of color, which Demuth brushed and blotted in layer upon layer, achieving a vibrant textural surface.

A friend and fellow modernist, Marsden Hartley, noted the abstract qualities and technical finesse of Demuth's work, describing it as delicate, decorative, and harmonious. This impulse toward abstraction became increasingly pronounced in the years that followed, as may be seen in Demuth's celebrated images from the 1920s and 1930s of still lifes and industrial landscapes.

N.H.

Nicolas de Staël

Le ciel rouge (The Red Sky) 1952

French, b. Russia,
1914–1955

oil on canvas

**51½ x 64⅛
(130.8 x 162.9)**

lower right, *Stael*

acquired from the artist by Theodore Schempp, New York; M. Knoedler & Co., New York; acquired from Knoedler's, 1954 (gift of the T.B. Walker Foundation 54.7)

Le ciel rouge was painted during a year de Staël considered critical in his artistic life. After a decade of presenting forms as elements entirely removed from the context of observed objects, in the early 1950s he had consciously turned to the objective world to derive the structure of his pictures. In 1952 he painted a pivotal series of pictures from sketches he made of a soccer match at the Parc des Princes in March. Although recognizable as figures, the players are represented as blocky, boldly colored structures whose movement derives from the interaction of color and form as much as from pose and depicted activity. The ragged edges, discrete forms and uninflected color areas of these works and those that followed evoke the technique of collage that de Staël was practicing contemporaneously under the influence of Matisse, whose gifts as a colorist had a profound and acknowledged effect on him.

That same year, de Staël began painting landscapes studied in visits to Chevreuse, Gentilly, Mantes, Honfleur, Bormes in the Var and Le Lavandou on the Côte des Maures. Although *Le ciel rouge* on first viewing does not announce an allusion to such landscapes, the title establishes an equivalence between formal and landscape elements. The structure of landscape is given plastic expression, though its particular forms are simplified beyond recognition. While insisting that all good painting derived ultimately from nature, de Staël observed that "one never paints what one sees or believes one sees. One paints in a thousand vibrations the effect felt."[1] This canvas is primarily an abstract construction of interacting color forms whose drawing, often a single stroke of the palette knife, is co-extensive with their color: the block of color is the form, it does not describe it.

Coinciding with de Staël's return to an active correspondence with nature and vivification of the palette was his expansion of scale—of the canvas and of the strokes. Broadening the tesserae of earlier work, he applied paint like spackle to literally construct the picture plane in bricks of color. His friend Jean Bauret credited himself with having advised the artist to switch from a palette knife to a trowel or spatula to accommodate the greater monumentality of scale.[2] This period of de Staël's work, then, saw changes of subject matter, technique, palette, and scale. He felt deeply about the paintings he undertook in 1952, and in a text for the brochure accompanying his exhibition in New York early the next year wrote that "today I am showing a group of paintings which, in all modesty, mean more to me than any I have done before."[3]

L.F.G.

1. Quoted in Galerie Beyeler, Basel, *De Staël*, exh. cat., 1964, n.p.
2. Douglas Cooper, *Nicolas de Staël* (London: Weidenfeld and Nicolson, 1961), p. 61.
3. Quoted in M. Knoedler & Co., New York, *Nicolas de Staël*, exh. cat., 1953, n.p.

Mark di Suvero

Stuyvesantseye   1965

American, b. Shanghai,
1933

wood, steel

**86 x 89¼ x 95⅞
(218.4 x 227 x 243.5)**

**centered on base front,
*STUYVESANTSEYE***

**acquired from the
Goldowsky and Lo Guidice
Galleries, New York, 1972
(gift of the T.B. Walker
Foundation 72.8)**

Di Suvero once referred to *Stuyvesantseye* cryptically as "a New York history dream-autobiography."[1] The comment strongly suggests some connection between this work and Peter Stuyvesant (1592–1672), the last Dutch governor of New Netherland before the settlement was surrendered to the English in 1664 and given its present name. The nature and degree of di Suvero's personal identification with Stuyvesant or with New York City is largely speculative. At the time the sculpture was made, however, di Suvero's personal history as a resident of New York had already been singularly eventful. He had arrived from California in 1957 and formed a lasting friendship with Richard Bellamy, then director of the Green Gallery. In 1960, a few months before his first exhibition was to open, he suffered nearly fatal injuries in an elevator accident. Surpassing all medical expectations, he not only survived the accident, but continued to work, at first from a wheelchair.[2] In 1963, dissatisfied with the commercial galleries in New York, he joined with several other like-minded artists in opening a cooperative exhibition space, Park Place Gallery. And by 1965, by dint of extraordinary effort and perseverance, he was again able to walk without crutches. *Stuyvesantseye* presents no direct references to these experiences. It is, however, a delicate balance of discarded, "found" objects within one system, a system that moves, being strong and flexible enough to interact with its audience. As such it does seem something of a triumph, a victory of mind over matter, or perhaps of buoyant good spirits over waste and despair.

Consisting as it does of found parts, *Stuyvesantseye* is related to the contemporaneous work of such Assemblage sculptors as Richard Stankiewicz or John Chamberlain.[3] But in contrast to other Assemblage artists, di Suvero is primarily concerned that the found object be invested with a formal value and function within the created piece; the object's former life, the circumstances in which a log or tire might have been found, is a secondary consideration at best. He therefore avoids the shocks of unexpected juxtaposition that might be generated by such Dada-influenced artists as Robert Rauschenberg.

In the mid-60s, di Suvero's interest in Constructivism and especially in the work of Max Bill led him to experiment with reflective materials.[4] The metal sheet rolled into the inside of the barrel in *Stuyvesantseye*, intended to yield an actual eye image,[5] is probably one such experiment. But neither Dada nor Constructivism exerted the kind of force on di Suvero's early development as did the Abstract Expressionist idea of gesture. In fact, as Carter Ratcliff has pointed out, di Suvero actually expanded the possibilities of Abstract Expressionism. For instead of using gesture to mirror a transitory inner state, he was able to direct the gesture outward. In *Stuyvesantseye*, in particular, he has arranged for the work itself to gesture, allowing it a measure of spontaneity within its own space.[6]

N.R.

1. Letter to Don Borrman, Walker Art Center, 27 March 1972.
2. While campaigning against the Portuguese in the West Indies in 1644, Stuyvesant suffered a leg wound. Eventually the leg had to be amputated, and was replaced by a silver-ornamented wooden limb. Later, despite a certain reputation for irascibility, he proved himself a capable and efficient administrator. As di Suvero said of Stuyvesant (conversation with the author, 8 October 1986), "he was driven crazy with his bum leg." Parallels exist, then, between Stuyvesant and di Suvero in that both went on to substantial achievements after having suffered disabling physical injuries.
3. Max Kozloff, "Mark di Suvero: Leviathan," *Artforum*, vol. 5 (Summer 1967), p. 43.
4. Carter Ratcliff, "Mark di Suvero," *Artforum*, vol. 11 (November 1972), pp. 35–42.
5. Conversation with the author, 8 October 1986.
6. Ratcliff, p. 36.

Mark di Suvero

Arikidea 1977–1982

American, b. Shanghai,
1933

Cor-Ten steel, steel, cedar

**316½ x 510 x 450
(803.9 x 1295.4 x 1143)**

**acquired from the Oil and
Steel Gallery, New York,
1985 (gift of Judy and
Kenneth Dayton 85.43)**

Through the 1960s, di Suvero's work, most of it combining wood and steel, tended to incorporate a higher and higher proportion of steel until, in 1967, he produced his first all-steel sculpture. Through the 1970s, as he was gradually able to choose the kind of steel best suited to a given project and to work with bigger equipment and spaces, his work assumed monumental proportions. Large-scale outdoor steel sculpture remains today di Suvero's signature style.

Arikidea belongs to a group of sculptures created between 1977 and 1983 in which certain of the artist's well-established ideas are elaborated. Already in the mid-60s, for example, di Suvero was making work that moved, and he would often include a swing or suspended tire as a means of letting the audience interact with a piece. *Arikidea*, too, moves. The balance of the parts in this case, however, is such that a viewer may move, with a touch, a quantity of steel the sculptor estimates to weigh about three tons.[1] The swing, too, invites a visitor to move in and through the work. The possibility of movement has been further enhanced over that of earlier pieces through a new joint design that allows for motion in more than one plane.

Di Suvero began to construct the suspended portion of *Arikidea* about 1977 at his studio in Petaluma, California; the structural portion of the work was begun later, about 1981. The title evolved by stages from the word arachnid, from the Greek for spider, for di Suvero had come to admire that creature's capacity to create structure in space. The present name, however, has no specific references within the sculpture beyond lending it an ambiguous, archaic flavor.[2]

N.R.

1. Conversation with the author, 8 October 1986.
2. Ibid.

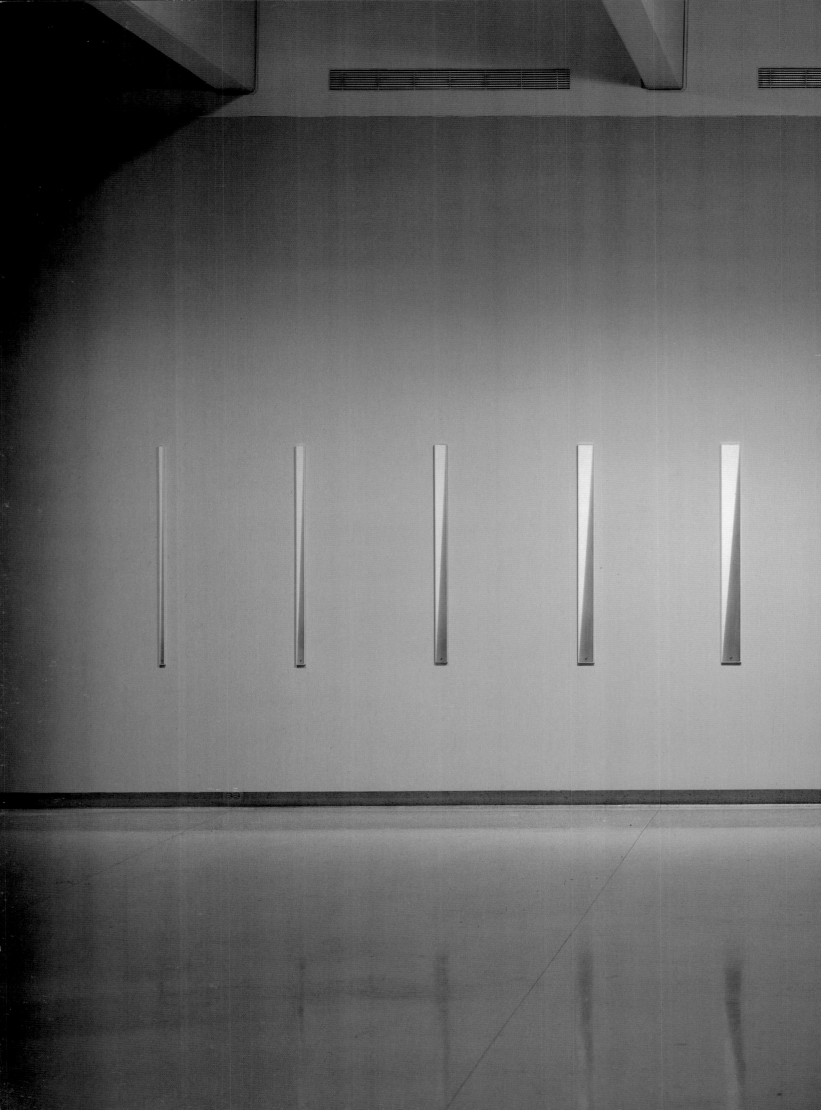

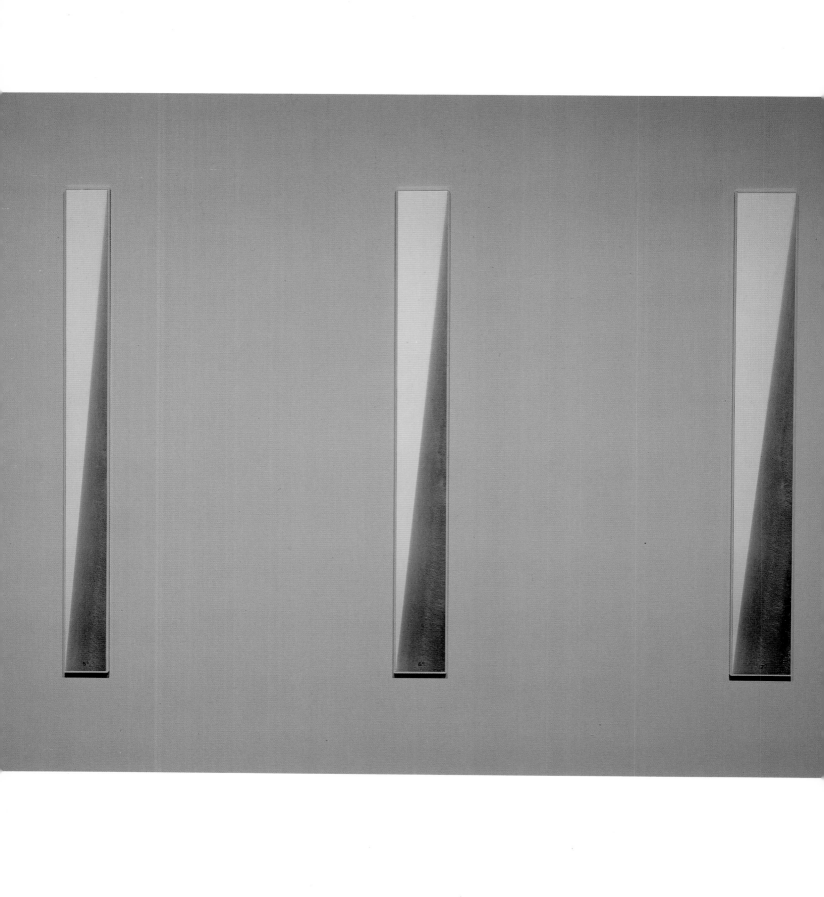

Jan Dibbets

Horizon 1°–10° Land 1973

Dutch, b. 1941

ten color photographs

48 (121.9) high each, total width variable

on reverse, in center of tenth panel, *Jan Dibbets 1973 1°–10° Land*

Leo Castelli Gallery, New York, 1975; Giuseppe Panza di Biumo, Milan, 1976–1977; Leo Castelli Gallery, New York, 1977–1978; acquired from the Leo Castelli Gallery, 1978 (Art Center Acquisition Fund 78.19)

In the late 1960s, after studying in London at the St. Martin's School of Art, Dutch artist Jan Dibbets stopped painting in favor of a more conceptually oriented art. Impressed by the work of English artist Richard Long, Dibbets began working directly with nature.[1] While his involvement with Conceptual and Earth Art was relatively short-lived, his interest in nature has remained constant.

Dibbets's primary medium is photography. He often makes his images by methodically varying the angle of the camera and then juxtaposing the resulting photographs to create panoramas of land and seascapes. In *Horizon 1°–10° Land*, however, the artist used a single image of a landscape horizon, which he printed with an increasingly larger frame to produce ten individual photographs. He altered the standard orientation of land to sky by shifting the horizon line almost ninety degrees from its usual position to create a diagonal line—an ironic twist to the expected horizontal orientation of the flat Dutch landscape. In each successive image, the picture is rotated one degree so that each photograph has a slightly larger angle of horizon to landscape than the one before.

Dibbets's imagery presents visual-conceptual paradoxes, operating in the void between what we see and what we know.[2] Instead of literally documenting the world seen through the lens of his camera, Dibbets transforms the natural environment into abstract imagery characterized by simplicity and clarity. For him, photography is a means to an end. It is a device that allows him to explore the principles of perspective and the properties of line, form, color, and light. From a distance the land and sky in *Horizon 1°–10° Land* lose their definition; their vastness is transformed into flat triangles of color. Only close examination reveals the subject matter. In this way, Dibbets is heir to Piet Mondrian, who abstracted nature into a series of horizontal and vertical lines and planes of primary color. With its pared-down format and measured progression, *Horizon 1°–10° Land* also recalls the elegant serial imagery of Minimal Art.

D.H.

1. See Barbara Reise, "Introduction," in Scottish Art Council and Welsh Art Council, *Jan Dibbets*, exh. cat., 1967, n.p.
2. Barbara Reise, "Jan Dibbets: A Perspective Correction," *Art News*, vol. 71 (Summer 1972), p. 40.

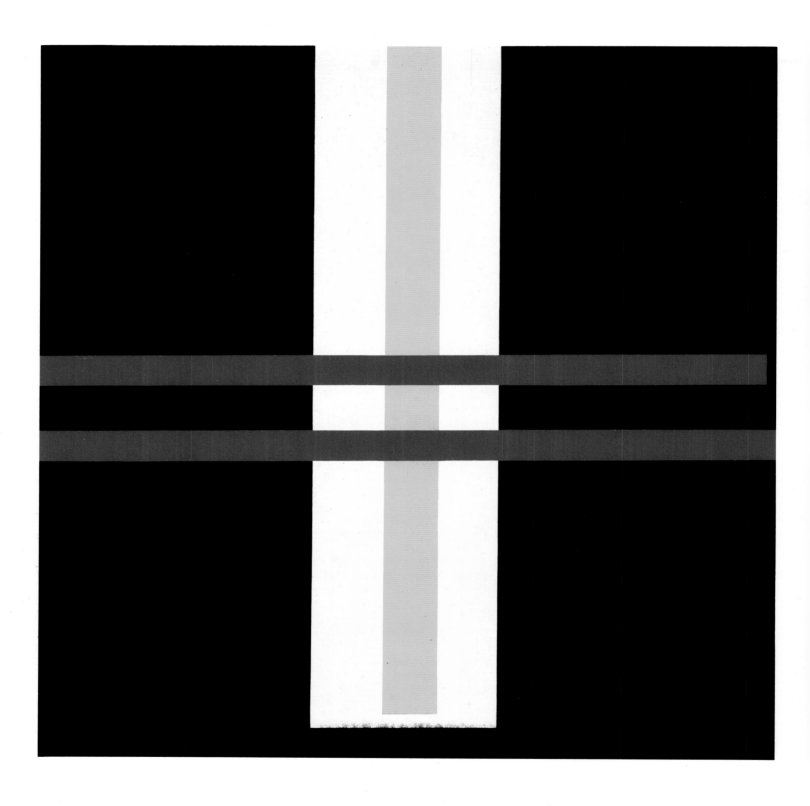

Burgoyne Diller

First Theme 1963–1964

American, 1906–1965

oil on canvas

72 x 72 (182.9 x 182.9)

on reverse, upper left quadrant, *diller—1963–64/1st. Theme*; embossed on plastic tape, upper stretcher member, left, *10/First Theme/Constrution* [sic] *Theme*

acquired from Noah Goldowsky, Inc., New York, 1972 (gift of grandchildren of Archie D. and Bertha H. Walker 72.23)

According to Diller, all of his work could be separated into three compositional categories or "themes," which he described verbally and visually in a notebook of 1961.[1] The first theme is characterized by free elements drawn on a ground, while in the others elements are created through the intersection of lines. Here, for example, the elements overlap without losing their integrity as forms. His approach was deliberate, pondered, and empirical. He first drew in the lines of a composition in charcoal on the canvas, sometimes using a T-square or triangle, and then worked out the general color relationships by pinning pieces of colored paper to the canvas to fill the contours of the planes he had defined. Once these had been adjusted, he mixed his paints to the precise colors he wanted, and painted strips of paper to replace the colored papers. After multiple adjustments and revisions, he took the canvas from the easel and laid it down horizontally. Removing the papers one by one, brushing off the charcoal and re-delineating each area with pencil, he then began filling in the color in short, careful brushstrokes, all in the same direction within a plane.[2] Even with this frequent testing and correcting he sometimes regretted decisions and would scrape down areas of paint in order to rework them, leaving essentially no trace of the alteration in order to maintain the velvety, matte surface.[3]

Given the highly planned, though flexible, nature of Diller's method of composition, the changes that do occur from the initial drawing for this work to the finished canvas are of considerable interest. Of greatest consequence was the decision to prolong the lower red horizontal bar to the edge of the support. In fact, it continues around the corner of the inch-thick stretcher, as does the rest of the composition. Diller clearly intended the work to be exhibited unframed—even the stretcher nails are painted—implying that the lines and planes extend indefinitely and that the canvas edge does not close off the plane. The momentum of the staggered red lines draws attention to other expressions of apparent motion. Like Glarner, another artist influenced by De Stijl, Diller heeds Mondrian's dictum of asymmetrical equilibrium.[4] Although the white rectangle, or U shape, is centered on the square black field, none of the color strips is similarly centered: the yellow deviates to the right, the two red bars are dropped slightly off center, and the central yellow block is not quite a square.

The decision to center the white occurred during the course of painting; in stretching the canvas he pulled it over about an inch on the right side. This painting is one of the earliest to include the so-called U theme, in which a white U interrupts a black field, a scheme he was to use repeatedly from 1963 on.

L.F.G.

1. Diller's notebook is reproduced in Galerie Chalette, New York, *Burgoyne Diller*, exh. cat., 1964, n.p.
2. For detailed technical information on Diller's procedures and materials, see Elaine de Kooning, "Diller Paints a Picture," *Art News*, vol. 51 (January 1953), pp. 26–29, 55, 56.
3. The unvarnished surface was important to him, as he found reflectiveness distracting; if scraped areas showed a sheen, he would sand or pumice them; ibid., p. 55.
4. For the influences on Diller, particularly of De Stijl, Russian Constructivism and the push-pull theory of his teacher Hans Hofmann, see Philip Larson in Walker Art Center, *Burgoyne Diller: Paintings, Sculptures, Drawings*, exh. cat., 1972, pp. 5–15. For a more extended analysis, see Anita Ellis, "Burgoyne Diller: A Neo-Plasticist," M.A. thesis, University of Cincinnati, 1975.

Burgoyne Diller
Study for *First Theme*
1963–1964
crayon and pencil
10⅞ x 8⅜ (27.6 x 21.3)
Collection The Museum of Modern Art, New York
Mr. and Mrs. Milton J. Petrie Fund

185

Jim Dine

July London Sun   1969

American, b. 1935

acrylic on canvas with
wooden easel

five panels:
four 48 x 36
(121.9 x 91.4);
one 10 x 8 (25.4 x 20.3);
dimensions of easel
variable

on reverse of each of four
large panels, *Jim Dine/
1969*; and *A, B, C, D,*
respectively; on panel
marked *A,* diagram
showing disposition of four
panels

acquired from the
Sonnabend Gallery, Paris,
by Mr. and Mrs. Miles Q.
Fiterman, Minneapolis,
1973 (intended gift of Mr.
and Mrs. Miles Q.
Fiterman)

Disassociating himself from so-called Pop artists, Dine has spoken of his emotional attraction to objects, their ability to profoundly move him: "When I use objects, I see them as a vocabulary of feelings.... I think it's important to be autobiographical. What I try to do in my work is explore myself in physical terms."[1] The laconic specificity of the title of this work evokes the sensation of a particular time and place, like a notation in a diary. The easel represents the painter's act of putting this subjective experience onto the surface of a canvas, in this case a back drop of four self-contained but interrelated canvases. The transformation from self to art is signaled by the miniature painting on the easel, whose single stroke echoes one of the same size on a larger panel behind. Through this device, Dine explores questions of how scale is established and how it functions, and observes the fact of a whole being composed of an infinite number of parts that can be isolated and presented as complete in themselves.

When Dine moved to London in 1967, he had not painted for a year; but the experience of London appears to have reawakened his desire to paint. In *July London Sun* he uses a palette reminiscent not only of his own landscape colors in earlier works such as *Long Island Landscape,* (1963), but also of de Kooning's abstract work of the late 1950s related to sensations of the landscape from the highway.[2] The theatrical aspect of Dine's paintings-with-props may have derived in part from his involvement with Happenings in the early 1960s and an ongoing interest in drama and the stage. The inclusion of props is primarily indebted to Assemblage and Rauschenberg's Combine paintings.[3] Looking back on his work of this period, Dine said in a 1981 interview that he found it incompletely formed, evasive of the fundamental issues of painting, and reproached himself for the impatience he revealed by using objects as a shortcut way of completing pictures.[4] Responding to the criticism that his use of objects showed a kind of infantilism, Dine agreed that "if you're a mature artist, you don't need to rely on these theatrical props, and that's what they become. And that's what I was doing. I was skirting the issue of painting and making a kind of inanimate theater."[5] In 1986, Dine was more tolerant of this period of his work, feeling that "anything is fair game," including theatricality.[6]

L.F.G.

1. Quoted in John Gruen, "Jim Dine and the Life of Objects," *Art News*, vol. 76 (September 1977), p. 38.
2. Dine stated in conversation with the author, 29 September 1986, that he has been influenced "by *all* of de Kooning."
3. Ibid. See Rauschenberg's *Pilgrim* of 1960, for example, in which a chair stands in front of a painted canvas. Dine traces the origins of his incorporation of objects from the external world to Picasso, Braque, Schwitters, Rauschenberg, and Motherwell; see "Dine on Dine," in David Shapiro, *Jim Dine: Painting What One Is* (New York: Harry N. Abrams, 1981), p. 210.
4. "Dine on Dine," p. 203.
5. Ibid., pp. 208, 209.
6. Conversation with the author, 29 September 1986.

Jim Dine

My Studio # One: The Vagaries of Painting, "These are sadder pictures"   1978

American, b. 1935

oil on canvas

72 x 228¾
(182.9 x 581.1)

upper right, *Jim Dine*; on reverse, *My Studio # One/ The Vagaries of Painting/ "These are sadder pictures"/ summer 1978/ Jim Dine/ Putney/ 1978*

acquired from the artist through the Pace Gallery, New York, 1982 (gift of the artist 82.167)

Dine has often used real objects in lieu of painted depictions in his work. The easel and small canvas in the Walker's *July London Sun* (1969) exemplify that aspect of this expression. But between 1977 and 1980 he created a group of ten still-life paintings in which he overcame his anxieties about the acceptability of traditional painting.[1] Dine attacked the problems of rendering objects naturalistically in the conventional still-life genre. In these works, including the present example, he made a "serial use" of objects he happened to have around. For the earliest still lifes he arranged the objects and painted them in the traditional still-life manner; but later simply painted one object at a time, arranging them on the canvas as he proceeded. Describing his compositional method, he explained that "I try and find the center in each thing."[2]

In attempting to capture the essence of each object in this canvas, Dine made numerous revisions, erasures, rethinkings, and repaintings that give ghostly highlights and pentimenti. The subversion of verisimilitude is compounded by the irrational, incoherent space, scale, and light. Although Dine himself makes no comment on the content of the picture, others have interpreted it as metaphorical. His friend, the poet David Shapiro, attributes symbolic meaning to several of the objects: the face as a comic mask introduces the theme of replication, the skull is a memento mori, the severed hand alludes to artifice and the dangers of detachment, the plaster statuette of the Venus de Milo is an amatory or sexual symbol threatened by the menacing boots.[3] Dine does not find this analysis "applicable," and attributes symbolic content only to the statuette,[4] which he bought—and incorporated into paintings and sculpture—because it was "a distant subject matter that's in the public domain…. I wanted to feel like an artist. So I went in an art store and there was the Venus de Milo…. It speaks about art."[5] Otherwise, he describes his primary efforts as the search for a neutral theme that would allow him to maintain painting as the subject.[6]

Dine made his first series of still lifes in 1977, completing them in the winter. He returned to the subject in the summer of 1978 with this work and *My Studio # Two*, in which a conspicuous addition is a suggestive Jamaican conch shell. He made the canvases as big as he could, the scale and proportions being dictated by the dimensions of the two walls of his studio in Vermont on which they hung.[7] The Walker picture contains many of the same motifs as *The Studio Near the Connecticut River* (1977), which may immediately precede it in the sequence.

L.F.G.

1. See John Gruen, "Jim Dine and the Life of Objects," *Art News*, vol. 76 (September 1977), p. 38; it was not until Dine was in his thirties that he redirected his attention to art of the past, making frequent visits to The Metropolitan Museum in New York; see Thomas Krens, "Conversations with Jim Dine," in *Jim Dine, Prints: 1970–1977* (New York: Harper & Row, in association with the Williams College Artist-in-Residence Program, 1977), p. 21.
2. Quoted in David Shapiro, *Jim Dine: Painting What One Is* (New York: Harry N. Abrams, 1981), p. 203.
3. Ibid., p. 46.
4. Conversation with the author, 29 September 1986.
5. Quoted in Michael Edward Shapiro, "The Sculpture of Jim Dine," in the Pace Gallery, New York, *Jim Dine: Sculpture and Drawings*, exh. cat., 1984, p. 8.
6. David Shapiro, p. 207.
7. Conversation with the author, 29 September 1986.

Jim Dine

The Crommelynck Gate with Tools 1983

American, b. 1935

bronze

108 x 132 x 36
(274.3 x 335.3 x 91.4)

Bronze Aglow, Walla
Walla, Washington

acquired from the Pace
Gallery, New York, 1984
(gift of Mr. and Mrs.
Edson W. Spencer, the
R.C. Lilly Foundation,
Clarence Frame, Ann
Hatch, and John A.
Rollwagen and Beverly
Baranowski 84.5)

The inspiration for this work was the early nineteenth-century gate outside 172 rue de Grenelle, the Paris studio of Aldo Crommelynck, the master printer of much of Picasso's late graphic output, who is also Dine's collaborator and friend.[1] With the assistance of his students, Dine conceived and cast the gate, about twice the size of its source, as part of a course in casting he taught at Otis Art Institute in Los Angeles in the winter of 1982–1983. The tool forms were cast in bronze from a selection of sixty wax castings, some bent and some not, of real tools belonging to Dine. The placing of the elements was determined through Dine's usual process of intense experimentation. Begun in January, the project was interrupted by a five-month sojourn in London, where Dine mused on its assemblage in five collages. On his return, *The Crommelynck Gate* was put together in three days and patinated on the fourth.[2] The initial edition of three was later enlarged to six, each one with variations.[3]

In *The Crommelynck Gate*, Dine's use of objects retraced and renovated his preceding work. The literal transformation of actual things into the materials of art and the modification of their appearance through casting represented a fusion of his incorporation of objects and his painted depictions of them. Formally, *The Crommelynck Gate* may be seen as a partial rehearsal for works such as his 1962 *Black Tools in a Landscape*, a floor piece in which real tools attached to a rectangular support imitate its actual source, and negative spaces and textured, calligraphic sculptural lines are repainted with vigorous, expressionistic strokes. In the *Gate*, the plane has been raised vertically replacing the flat ground and painterly marks of the 1962 assemblage. The tools have been handled and changed in the wax stage of their transubstantiation. The branches at right and left allude perhaps to the analogy with tree forms Dine was introducing into his arsenal of "primary forms" at the same time. In terms of past art, the bronze recalls David Smith's early open sculpture and that of their mutual predecessor, Giacometti, both his linear works of the 1930s and the scabrous, extenuated figures that followed.[4]

The subject of Crommelynck's gate had appeared to Dine in a dream in 1981. It appealed to him since it permitted him "finally to make something abstract, or something near to it,"[5] and to pay homage not only to Crommelynck but to French culture in general. Although he claims not to know what the tools mean, he has intimated that in certain instances they serve as surrogate human beings, though they lack the immediacy of the portrait: "The figure is more loaded. A hammer is an inanimate object that you could charge with certain power and is a metaphor for other things.''[6] Dine says that his use of tools invariably has sexual connotations, since sex is the most natural, comfortable, and familiar subject to him.[7] His familiarity with tools, which provide the sublimated, fetishistic charge in his work, dates to his childhood, when he fixed on them as powerful, evocative, and emotionally satisfying objects in his environment. Both his grandfather and father had stores in which they displayed and sold tools that he admired and handled: "From the age of nine till I was eighteen I worked in these stores. I was completely bored by the idea of selling but in my boredom I found that daydreaming amongst objects of affection was very nice."[8] He has recently contradicted his earlier statement that he seized on the objects to avoid interacting with his father, attributing the obsession to boredom alone.[9]

L.F.G.

1. See Pat Gilmour, "Symbiotic Exploitation or Collaboration: Dine & Hamilton with Crommelynck," *The Print Collector's Newsletter*, vol. 15 (January–February 1985), pp. 194–196.
2. Maurice Tuchman in Los Angeles County Museum of Art, *Jim Dine in Los Angeles*, exh. cat., 1983, n.p.
3. Ibid., for details of the project.
4. Dine included Giacometti in a list of artists in whom he was interested; see John Gruen, "Jim Dine and the Life of Objects," *Art News*, vol. 76 (September 1977), p. 42.
5. Quoted in Los Angeles County Museum of Art, *Jim Dine*.
6. Quoted in Susan Hennessy, "A Conversation with Jim Dine," *Art Journal*, vol. 39 (Spring 1980), p. 175.
7. See Alan Solomon, "Jim Dine: Hot Artist in a Cool Time," in Art Gallery of Ontario, Toronto, *Dine Oldenburg Segal*, exh. cat., 1967, n.p.
8. Quoted by John Gordon in Whitney Museum of American Art, New York, *Jim Dine*, exh. cat., 1970, n.p.
9. Conversation with the author, 29 September 1986. The earlier statement was from an interview by David Shapiro, in his *Jim Dine: Painting What One Is* (New York: Harry N. Abrams, 1981), p. 209.

Jean Dubuffet

Les péréquations (The Levelings) 1971

French, 1901–1985

vinyl, acrylic on polyester resin panel, polyester, fiberglass

128½ x 193½ x 6 (326.4 x 491.5 x 15.2)

lower right, *J.D. 71*; on reverse, upper right, *29/ Les péréquations* (recorded 1973)

acquired from the artist through the Pace Gallery, New York, 1974 (gift of the T.B. Walker Foundation 74.8)

Les péréquations is a late manifestation of Dubuffet's Hourloupe, the "graphic script" he developed in 1962 that became a philosophical principle he applied consistently to his art until 1975. Dubuffet's Hourloupe separates forms within a visual continuum, but unlike language does not categorize or particularize them. Although *Les péréquations* is composed of eleven parts assembled and interlocked and has sometimes been seen as a figural group, it functions just as readily as an allover, undifferentiated rhythm of jigsaw-puzzle piece contours. The irreducible units, the ghosts of figurative detail, have identity only in relation to the matrix in which they are lodged, and which they at the same time constitute.

Slightly over a week before he made the drawing for *Les péréquations*, Dubuffet noted:

> The language of the Hourloupe, since it is based on a very allusive and very arbitrary transcriptional handwriting, lends itself to denoting objects and forms that are more and more dubious, and it lends itself even, conversely, to presenting involuntary combinations leading the mind to corresponding visions.[1]

The conceptual nature of reality and man's use of signs to denote its illusions were notions consciously invoked by Dubuffet's technique of transferring his images from paper to canvas by projecting a diapositive slide.[2] After being traced, the panel on which the canvas is mounted was sawn along the contour as if it were being excised from a page. The black edges recall the object's origin in the figures glued to black sheets in the little Hourloupe book Dubuffet had made years earlier, whose genesis in turn was the distracted ballpoint pen doodlings outlined and filled in with striations or solid fields during telephone conversations of late July 1962.[3] Half-conscious creative impulses are recorded in a more architectural way in such *praticables* as *Les péréquations*. He imagined these works as mounted on rolling wheels and serving as animated stage props and sets in an alternative theater expressing the Hourloupe state of awareness: "I conceived the *praticables* in order to create free figures and independent grounds and subsequently assemble them in any combination."[4] Completed in September 1971, *Les péréquations* was early in the sequence of one hundred *praticables* made between May 1971 and July 1973.

In *Coucou Bazar*, performed at the Solomon R. Guggenheim Museum in New York in 1973, Dubuffet was able to realize what he had visualized, combining *praticables* with actors in Hourloupe costumes and masks whose stiff, mechanical movements suggested an equation with the props in a demonstration of his theory that all manifestations derive from the same impersonal universal energy.[5] The word *"péréquation,"* which in French has the comical staccato sound of many of Dubuffet's neologisms, means "equal distribution," "equalization," or "levelings," and is thus consistent with the entropic nature of his vision. It has been convincingly argued that the restricted palette of the Hourloupe series was not natural to Dubuffet, in view of the vitality of his previous coloristic and textural experiments, but rather represents a deliberate purging of expressive or evocative elements in his paintings to complement the "continuum of ciphers—or visual equation—that graphically articulates their surfaces."[6] The renunciatory, theoretical aspect of this decision was confirmed by Dubuffet in a statement made in the waning moments of the series, in which he describes it as "nothing but impersonal lines and coloring laid on with summary flatness" and explains that without "farewells to what one loves, without these departures toward entirely new lands, one can expect nothing but a long wearing away and extinction."[7]

L.F.G.

1. Quoted in Andreas Franzke, *Dubuffet* (New York: Harry N. Abrams, 1981), p. 179.
2. Details of the process are provided in Franzke, p. 210.
3. See Margit Rowell, "Jean Dubuffet: An Art on the Margins of Culture," in the Solomon R. Guggenheim Museum, New York, *Jean Dubuffet: A Retrospective*, exh. cat., 1973. p. 32, and Franzke, p. 159.
4. Quoted in Rowell, p. 34.
5. For a more extensive presentation of these ideas, see Dubuffet's frequently reprinted "Anticultural Positions" (1951), in *Arts Magazine*, vol. 53 (April 1979), pp. 156, 157. For his description of the *praticable*-based spectacle as he envisioned it, the effects he hoped would be achieved, and his dissatisfaction with the production of *Coucou Bazar* at the Grand Palais in 1973, see Max Loreau, ed., *Catalogues des travaux de Jean Dubuffet: Dessins 1969/1972, Fascicules XXVI* (Paris: Weber Editeur, 1975), pp. 211–219.
6. Rowell, p. 31.
7. Letter to Claude Renard, spring 1975, quoted in Max Loreau, pp. 171–172.

Raymond Duchamp-Villon

Le grand cheval (The Large Horse)   1914/1957

French, 1876–1918

bronze

39⅝ x 39⅝ x 20¾
(100.7 x 100 x 52.7)

rear of base,
Duchamp-Villon/1914 4/6

Susse Frères, Paris

acquired from the Galerie
Louis Carré, Paris, upon
completion of casting,
1957 (gift of the T.B.
Walker Foundation 57.6)

Raymond Duchamp-Villon
Photograph of the
armature for the projected
enlargement of *Le Cheval*,
1914, taken in Duchamp-
Villon's studio.
Collection The Museum of
Modern Art, New York
Gift of Jacques Villon

This sculpture is an enlarged version of a work called *Le cheval*, which Duchamp-Villon completed in 1914.[1] The earliest surviving modeled sketches are stylized but comparatively organic studies of a horse and rider in various positions, followed by clay and plaster models, and sketches on paper, in which a machine morphology became increasingly dominant. Probably in August 1914, before he was mobilized for World War I, Duchamp-Villon undertook the 44cm plaster version of a fully synthesized horse-machine, which, according to his friend and patron Walter Pach, he completed during military leaves in the second half of 1914.[2] When the sculptor died he left in his studio not only the plaster, but also the armature for a 100cm enlargement.[3] Jacques Villon oversaw the realization of the larger version, first cast about 1930–1931.[4] In 1955 Louis Carré had the edition to which the Walker cast belongs begun by Susse Frères.[5] The execution of an even more monumentally scaled version, known as *Le cheval majeur*, was supervised by Raymond's other brother, Marcel Duchamp, in 1966.

In *Le cheval*, Duchamp-Villon abandoned the literal representation of natural form to suggest its inner forces, which he associated with the latent energy of the machine. As he wrote to Pach in January 1913: "The power of the machine imposes itself and we can scarcely conceive living things without it anymore."[6] In the sculpture and studies for it, Duchamp-Villon sought to maximize the expression of "superior dynamism" by opening up, displacing, and counterpointing sculptural volumes for the greatest visual and spatial interaction.

The artist closely studied the dynamics of animal locomotion during military service in the Cuirassiers and in the late nineteenth-century photographic studies of Eadweard Muybridge and Etienne-Jules Marey. While the ambiguous pose of *Le cheval* suggests both a rearing horse and a horse with hooves gathered, the anecdotal content has been purged—the visual movement of the pistons, wheels, and shafts that have replaced the limbs transforms a creature of nature into a poised mechanical dynamo. It has been observed that the natural function and rhythm of the horse's motion are "plastically dissected" out, divorcing the subject of the horse from the "plastic-poetic" intentions of the sculpture.[7]

The issue of the posthumous versions and their casts and how well or poorly they serve the artist's intentions has been raised by several scholars. It is known that Duchamp-Villon actually had envisioned the image in steel,[8] and he implicitly experimented with the present scale by building the armature, but he did not clearly specify his intentions for the final realization of the work.

L.F.G.

1. For a detailed review of the state of research on all aspects of the piece, and numerous reproductions of studies and various versions, see Angelica Zander Rudenstine, *Peggy Guggenheim Collection, Venice* (New York: Harry N. Abrams and the Solomon R. Guggenheim Foundation, 1985), pp. 270–281.
2. Walter Pach, *Raymond Duchamp-Villon: Sculpteur (1876–1918)* (Paris: Jacques Povolozky Editeur, 1924) , p. 15. For a discussion of Villon's inconsistent memories of the completion date, see Rudenstine, p. 271 n. 1 and p. 273 n. 6.
3. The 44cm plaster that remained in the studio (now apparently lost) was later acquired from the artist's widow by John Quinn, who had it cast in bronze a few years later. The image at this scale is recorded in two extant plasters and various casts. The armature is reproduced in a photograph Jacques Villon gave to The Museum of Modern Art in 1938 with a letter to Alfred H. Barr, Jr., 30 August 1938, stating that it appears as it was when war was declared in August 1914; Rudenstine, p. 273.
4. Ibid.
5. According to Dina Foy, "Jacques Villon had further plasters made from the original model in 1954 and asked Louis Carré to publish an edition of six, plus one artist's cast;" see Ronald Alley, catalogue of *The Tate Gallery's Collection of Modern Art Other Than Works by British Artists* (London: The Tate Gallery, 1981), p. 193.
6. Quoted in R.V. Gindertael, "L'Oeuvre majeure de Duchamp-Villon," in "Chroniques du jour," supp. to *XXe Siècle*, no. 23 (May 1964), n. p.
7. Carola Giedion Welcker, "New Roads in Modern Sculpture," *Transition*, no. 23 (July 1935), p. 203.
8. Letter from Villon to Barr, cited above, n. 4: "The only thing I couldn't do was to cast it in 'STEEL' (POLISHED), and had to content myself with a 'bronze,' given the difficulty of realizing it in steel, which my brother would have preferred."

John Duff

Red Queen 1985

American, b. 1943

enamel, wood on painted fiberglass

87¾ x 22 x 32⅝ (222.9 x 55.9 x 82.9)

acquired from the Blum Helman Gallery, New York (T.B. Walker Acquisition Fund 86.44)

The unresolved tension between an abstract and figurative reading of the cubistic *Red Queen* bows to the anthropomorphic in its title, suggested to the artist by a friend, who observed that the work reminded him of an illustration of the Red Queen in *Alice's Adventures in Wonderland*. While the work may be seen as a female twisting on point and builds on its associations with the human form, it began in the artist's mind as an abstract shape[1] and its reference to geometry is equally strong.

Like its later companion piece, *Marlin Blue* (1985), *Red Queen* is formed from a double cylinder which has been sliced and then reconstructed into a spiral format. The top cylinder has been cut in half and then glued together; the lower three sections fit together to form the second cylinder. Cast in fiberglass, the resulting surface imperfections, including wood that has adhered from the mold, pockmarks, and occasional holes, remain. Duff painted most of the inner surface of the sculpture in colors ranging from bright orange to blue to black. The effect is a translucent surface that casts mystery and doubt on the weight and density of the piece. One sees a big form but does not experience it as such because it has no resonance as mass.

As provocative as the discrepancy between the size and mass in *Red Queen*, is the seeming irreconcilability of its vastly different appearances from different vantage points. The fullest views, surprisingly, are from either side rather than from the front, but *Red Queen*'s basic roundness places it in precarious relationship to the wall to which it affixes at just two points. Its dramatic, twisting gesture refers to organic processes of transformation and growth and actively contradicts its geometric aspects. As Donald Kuspit described the effect, "Duff has found a way to sail between the Scylla and Charybdis of contemporary sculpture, between the Minimalist preoccupation with holistic simplicity and gestalt and the old assemblage Constructivist strategies of accretion. He has reinvented tension as an absolute goal of art."[2]

M.G.

1. Conversation with the author, 4 September 1986.
2. Donald Kuspit, "John Duff's Perfect Sculpture," *Artforum*, vol. 23 (April 1985), p. 80.

Lyonel Feininger

Barfüsserkirche II (Church of the Minorites II)   1926

American, 1871–1956

oil on canvas

42⅝ x 36⅝
(108.3 x 93)

**upper left, *Feininger/
1926*; on original
stretcher (replaced 1959),
*L. Feininger 1926 /
Barfüsserkirche II***

**acquired from the artist by
the Angermuseum, Erfurt,
1926; Buchholz Gallery,
New York, by 1941;
acquired from the
Buchholz Gallery, 1943
(gift of the T.B. Walker
Foundation, Gilbert M.
Walker Fund 43.20)**

Although he was born in the United States, Lyonel Feininger was a vital participant in the evolution of early twentieth-century European modernism. At age sixteen he followed his parents, who were professional musicians, from New York City to Germany. There he soon decided to forego a planned musical career in order to study art. By 1911, attracted to Cubism and to the art stemming from related developments, such as Orphism and Futurism, Feininger began evolving his own distinctive pictorial style—marked by faceted and fractured planes of light and color—which he was later to characterize jokingly as "Prismism."[1] Over some forty years, he created crystalline images of medieval churches as well as poetic landscapes and seascapes.

In 1919 the architect Walter Gropius appointed Feininger to the faculty of the Bauhaus, his newly established school of art, architecture, and design in Weimar. Although he was primarily inclined toward a spiritual vision of art, Feininger came to join Gropius in his goal of uniting art and craftsmanship for socially useful ends. Gropius held up as his ideal the medieval craftsman and builder who, he believed, had linked labor and art in a single activity that served both social and spiritual functions. Indeed, he chose Feininger's 1919 woodcut *The Cathedral of Socialism* for the cover of the printed version of the Bauhaus manifesto.

In 1923 Feininger was given studio space at the Angermuseum in the town of Erfurt, a dozen miles west of Weimar. *Barfüsserkirche II* is his second work combining the interior and exterior of Erfurt's Gothic church; the first was painted in 1924. In the Walker's version, he enlarged the image and modified the composition, expanding the area of brilliant light striking the buttressed exterior wall of the long sanctuary. The windows were clearly articulated in the 1926 canvas, and Feininger added a hint of blue to suggest stained glass. Finally, the hues of the yellow and red foreground figures were intensified, and a complementary green figure was added at the lower right.

In *Barfüsserkirche II*, Feininger joined aspects of an almost scientific precision with a romanticism reminiscent of the visionary paintings of Caspar David Friedrich and J.M.W. Turner—artists whom he admired. Pairing sharply faceted forms and taut linear structures with a soft palette of diaphanous reddish browns and cool blue-greens, he gives the image a haunting, otherworldly quality. His vision of sublime spirituality is reflected in the vast scale of the Erfurt church, which towers over the people in the painting. Though they are dwarfed by the soaring architecture, the colorful foreground figures are nonetheless integral to the work: the lines of the composition seem to originate from the figures, and to extend outward to shape pictorial space. Throughout, the juxtaposition of intricately layered, interpenetrating transparent and opaque planes to indicate solids and voids works to dematerialize form and unify space and architecture. *Barfüsserkirche II* thus becomes a harmony fusing the material and the immaterial.

A.B.

1. Quoted in Jan van der Marck et al., *In Quest of Excellence: Civic Pride, Patronage, Connoisseurship*, exh. cat. (Miami: Center for the Fine Arts, 1984), p. 127.

Jackie Ferrara

Belvedere   1988

American

cedar

**126 x 506 x 407
(320 x 1,285 x 1,033.8)**

**commissioned by
Walker Art Center, 1987
(gift of the Butler Family
Foundation 88.377)**

Since the early 1970s Jackie Ferrara has explored relationships between sculpture and architecture in her wood constructions, which have evolved from indoor pieces to increasingly large-scale outdoor works. Her investigations began as a response to the rigidity of Minimalist form and theory. Though she shared the Minimalist penchant for modular form fabricated of commonly available building materials, she took her sculpture in a decidedly different direction. She filled it with oblique but still recognizable references to standard architectural elements such as doors, stairs, towers, and ramps.

In the early 1980s Ferrara began making public sculptures motivated in large degree, she says, by the knowledge that "the piece will be used, that is, entered, climbed in, sat on."[1] A prime example of this approach is *Belvedere*, which she designed for a specific site in the Minneapolis Sculpture Garden. As its classical title suggests, this work was intended to serve as a place where visitors could take their ease while enjoying vistas of the Garden. Ferrara's expansive wood plaza has a T-shaped configuration—its wide end incorporates two wooden "couches"[2] that serve as casual seating. These couches are also intended to accommodate some of the audience for informal musical and theatrical events that will occur on *Belvedere's* wooden deck; the rest of the audience can be seated on the stairs around the deck. At its narrow end, the sculpture contains two tall pylons that serve as a passageway. The pylons, whose stepped outer walls slope, are perforated by narrow windows that counter any sense of confinement resulting from the closeness of the walls to each other.

In this stylized architectural work, Ferrara offers the visitor two strong spatial experiences: an open, public one associated with the seating area in the plaza itself, and a more solitary experience afforded by the passageway between the pylons.

Far from being purely functional, *Belvedere* is a finely crafted sculpture whose large planar volumes are in elegant equilibrium. Overlaying its masses are lively complex patterns created by the varying lengths of wood that make up the structure. These irregular patterns, which Ferrara describes as "drawings," provide an elegant counterpoint to the symmetrical solid geometry of the sculpture itself, and serve to lighten its massive forms. Though references to historical architecture are present—in this case to Egyptian temple architecture—Ferrara thinks of her wooden sculptures as timeless forms. "If I wanted to evoke anything, it would be something you couldn't place, something ahistorical.... I'd like my sculpture to imply forms so ancient they precede recorded history or belong 3,000 years in the future. Or come from Mars."[3]

L.R.

1. Quoted in The Aspen Art Museum, *Sculpture/Aspen*, exh. cat., 1986, n.p.
2. The artist refers to these seats as "couches" because their measurements are derived from a couch in her home.
3. Quoted in Carter Ratcliff, Lowe Art Museum, Coral Gables, *Jackie Ferrara: An Architecture of Intent*, exh. cat., 1982, p. 9.

Barry Flanagan

Hare on Bell on Portland Stone Piers   1983

British, b. Wales, 1941

bronze, limestone

**102 x 112 x 75
(259.1 x 284.5 x 190.5)**

**Pace Gallery, New York
(gift of Anne Larsen
Simonson and Glen and
Marilyn Nelson 87.63)**

Throughout his career as a sculptor, Barry Flanagan has sought to oppose the artistic status quo. "Rejection has always been a motivation for me," he once said.[1] As a student at St. Martin's School of Art in London from 1964 to 1966, he was an early innovator in process art, sculpting with such then-unorthodox materials as sand, burlap, felt, and plastic in ephemeral configurations. These transitory and pliant sculptures expressed a concern for the process, rather than the product, of art-making, and challenged the conventional understanding of sculpture as a rigid and permanent art form.

In his more recent work, Flanagan has turned from the no longer avant-garde aesthetic of reductive formalism, to figuration, crafted with markedly traditional media and techniques, including lost-wax bronze casting, gilding, and workshop-executed stone carving. *Hare on Bell on Portland Stone Piers* employs bronze casting in a conflation of disparate images: a bell-shaped form, standing on granite blocks, serves as the base for a monumental leaping rabbit.

The bounding hare is a recurrent motif in Flanagan's recent oeuvre. Lankily supple and loosely structured, these animals exude a sense of spontaneous vitality, playfulness, and fecundity. By contrast, the bell, also a common motif in Flanagan's work, is a rigid and aesthetically orthodox conformation, evoking centuries of bronze casting tradition. As one author wrote: "Perfection in casting is the essence and the myth of bell founding."[2]

The bell presents a formal allusion to the fertility of an abundant breast or, inversely, to the vulva. This sexual analogy serves to pair the bell and the hare (a symbol of masculine prolificacy) as reproductive counterparts. Nevertheless, the exact nature of the animal and the object's relationship remains opaque; and this figurative disjunction subverts the conventionality of the sculpture's representational elements.

N.H.

1. Graham Beal and Mary Jane Jacob, in Museum of Contemporary Art, Chicago, and San Francisco Museum of Modern Art, *A Quiet Revolution: British Sculpture Since 1965*, exh. cat., 1987, p. 92.
2. Michael Compton, in the Pace Gallery, New York, *Barry Flanagan: Recent Sculpture*, exh. cat., 1983. p. 15.

Dan Flavin

untitled   1966

American, b. 1933

fluorescent tubes and
fixtures

96 x 96 x 8
(243.8 x 243.8 x 20.3)

acquired by Irving Blum,
Los Angeles, from the
Nicholas Wilder Gallery,
Los Angeles, 1967;
acquired from the Irving
Blum Gallery, 1969[1]
(gift of the Northern
States Power Company
69.11)

Flavin does not view his enterprise as the production of "works of art," "sculpture," or "environments," but rather as the demonstration of certain propositions or proposals through the medium of fluorescent or incandescent lights.[2] Availing himself of existing fabricated elements that have a particular transformative capacity, he designs these in qualitatively identical and interchangeable drawings for "light in situations;" in so doing, he raises questions regarding the issues of perception through and of light, and of the definition of place, line, and space, omitting the complicating factors of individual gesture and emotional involvement that typify what he disdainfully calls "overwrought tactile fantasies spread over yards of cotton duck."[3] According to Flavin, each "proposal" represents the application of a conceptual system, not a step in a teleological artistic development.

The fundamental situation in this untitled work is the corner, conceptually and optically closed off by a four-sided outline raised 15 inches above the floor (according to the assembly instructions that accompany the work), proposing a penetrable wall. Between the glowing lines of fluorescent light a squarish atmospheric plane or cloud is defined and partly contained, appearing to bow forward, brighter toward its center, i.e., the corner of the room, the area most distant from the imaginary barrier of the plane defined by the fixtures. Despite the evocation of a flat plane, the corner line continues to mark a symmetrical spatial division and to suggest recession. The system of attachment, with the verticals behind the horizontals, allows indirect and reflected light from the side tubes to balance those at the top and bottom, creating a positive-negative syncopation. The reflections on the floor expand the light's impact. Both the shadows and light are subtly graded, dissolving the boundaries of the thing seen.

The paradoxical fusion of flatness and spatial extension is clarified if the work is seen in relation to Flavin's drawing of a corner, composed of three lines converging within the sheet.[4] All shadowing absent, the flat rectangular plane of the paper remains visually intact. Nevertheless, it is conceptually dematerialized by the effects of the converging lines that suggest the meeting of obliquely viewed planes. The sense of recession is understood through signs rather than described in terms of light and dark. In the three-dimensional work these notions are adapted, with

the additional irony of light itself rather than absence of shadow dispelling perspective. The fluorescent lights, however, while efficient in providing both line and atmosphere, present logistical difficulties. Flavin acknowledges that the fixtures can be clumsy and are particularly difficult to attach where they are not flush with a flat surface. As first conceived, the rectangular configuration of works such as this one was visualized not in corners but attached to the floor, walls, and ceiling of a corridor, either singly or in a sequence, permitting a passage into and through light that the corner arrangement only intimates.

L.F.G.

1. The Walker work, which differs somewhat from the version shown at the Wilder Gallery, is "a practically assembled substitute," authorized by Flavin; letter to the author, 2 June 1987.
2. Quoted in Dan Graham, "Flavin's Proposal," *Arts Magazine*, vol. 44 (February 1970), p. 45.
3. Dan Flavin, "… in daylight or cool white," *Artforum*, vol. 4 (December 1965), p. 24.
4. The 1965 drawing is reproduced in The St. Louis Art Museum, *Drawings and Diagrams 1963–1972 by Dan Flavin*, exh. cat., 1973, no. 56, as is a drawing dated "11/5/63", no. 17, and labeled "the complete fluorescent system."

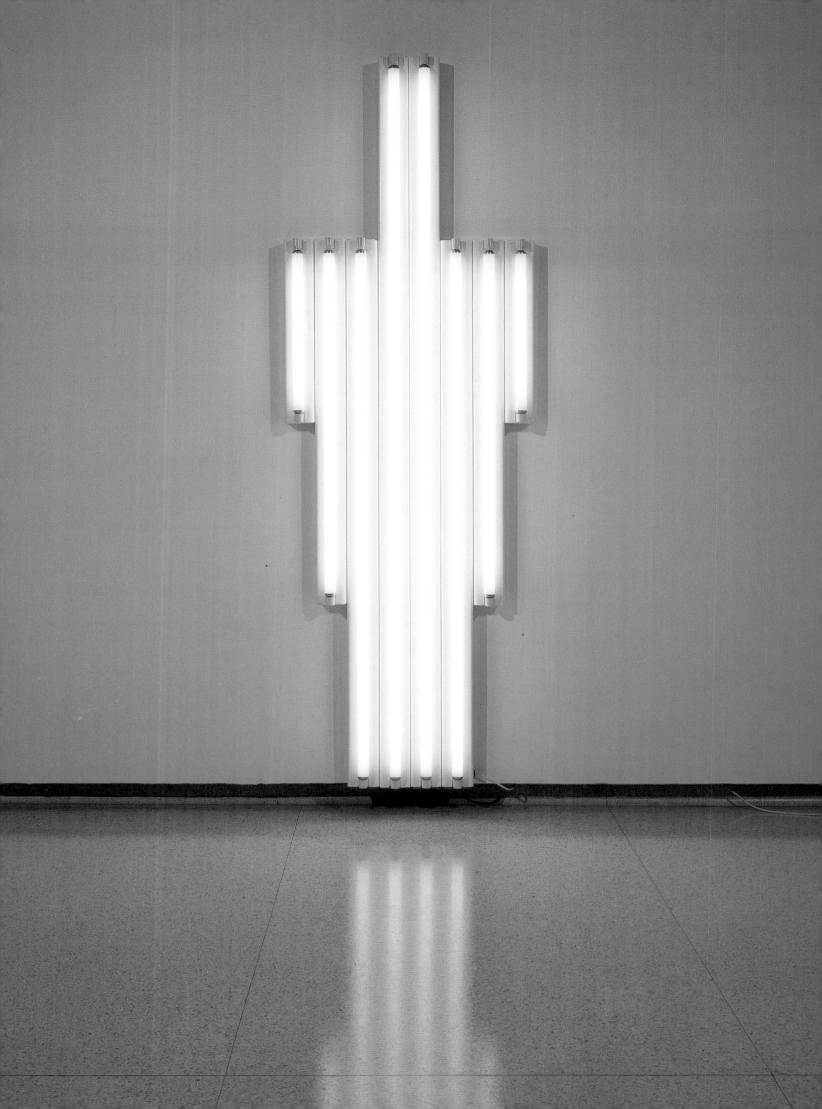

Dan Flavin

"monument" for V. Tatlin   1969

American, b. 1933

fluorescent tubes and
fixtures

96¹⁄₁₆ x 32¹⁄₁₆ x 4¾
(244 x 81.4 x 12.1)

acquired from the Leo
Castelli Gallery, New York,
1981 (gift of Leo Castelli
Gallery 81.25)

About the first untitled *"monument" for V. Tatlin* of 1964 Flavin has explained that the cool white fluorescent light "memorializes Vladimir Tatlin, the great revolutionary, who dreamed of art as science. It stands, a vibrantly aspiring order, in lieu of his last glider which never left the ground."[1] Tatlin (1885–1953), a leading figure of the Russian avant-garde in the teens and 1920s, began in 1929 to develop a flying machine he called "Letatlin," a pun on the Russian verb "to fly," and his own name.[2] Although Tatlin's "air bicycle" never took off, he had confidence that he could combine artistic and engineering aims in an object that would function equally well in both spheres. When first conceiving the monuments in drawing form, Flavin not only considered putting them on the floor, but also raising them to the wall or ceiling, perhaps in reference to Tatlin's hopes of getting his glider off the ground.[3] The configurations of some of the nineteen Tatlin monuments, completed by 1969, approximate gliderlike shapes.

Although he shares Tatlin's aspirations to unite art with technology, Flavin is not concerned with the elegant crafting of a functional object like the Russian's machine. He is sensitive to design, but is indifferent to the aesthetic qualities of the lights that function as both subject and object—lighting, being lit, and being light at the same time. "The equipment which I deploy seems to me to be neither ugly nor handsome."[4] Despite his matter-of-fact approach to his medium, and his bluntly witty protestation that the light carries no mystical overtones ("there is no room for mysticism in the Pepsi denigration"[5]), commentators frequently describe the effect of his work as otherworldly. In this work, the contours of the massed lights suggest a medieval crucifix. The details of industrial fabrication are obscured by the glow of light on the wall, and its expansion and reflection on the floor transform the room in a way that brings to mind the sifted, filtered atmosphere of light through stained glass. Flavin gives the iconic nature of his works a secular interpretation that refers to the hierarchical relationship between light and the rectangular space it illuminates from various directions and in various ways. To undercut spiritual associations he uses standard colors and warmths of light and openly displays the light source. Likewise, his use of the term "monuments," which he insists be spelled in lowercase letters, is ironic rather than presumptuous. He has also called the series "pseudo-monuments,"[6] because of the utilitarian, ephemeral nature of the materials used, contemporary substitutes for traditional bronze and stone.

L.F.G.

1. Dan Flavin, "The Artists Say," *Art Voices*, vol. 4 (Summer 1965) , p. 72.
2. See Troels Andersen in Moderna Museet, Stockholm, *Vladimir Tatlin*, exh. cat., 1968, pp. 9–12.
3. Flavin noted these intentions on an early drawing for the series, reproduced in The National Gallery of Canada, Ottawa, *Fluorescent Light, etc. from Dan Flavin*, exh. cat., 1969, fig. 13, pp. 242, 243. Installed, all the monuments rest on the floor, as specified in the detailed installation instructions that accompanied the Walker work on acquisition.
4. Dan Flavin, "Some Other Comments ...," *Artforum*, vol. 6 (December 1967), p. 21. Flavin has provided details on the materials he uses and their sources; WAC questionnaire prepared by Tiffany Bell and Robert Skolnik, p. 1.
5. Ibid.
6. Quoted in The National Gallery of Canada, *Fluorescent Light*, p. 218. The *"monuments"* are all in editions of five. A signed certificate of authenticity that accompanied this work indicates that it is 3/5.

Helen Frankenthaler

Alloy 1967

American, b. 1928

acrylic on cotton duck

118 x 64 1/16
(299.7 x 162.7)

in pencil, on top horizontal stretcher member, right, *Helen/118 x 64/#11/ Alloy*/arrow/*TOP*/ diagram of reverse of work

acquired from the Andre Emmerich Gallery, New York, 1971 (gift of the grandchildren of Archie D. and Bertha H. Walker 71.11)

Frankenthaler sees her work as primarily derived from the planar preoccupations of Cubism, but freed of its spatial restrictions. By dissolving the Cubist grid, she provokes the coincidence of two contradictory visual events: "different areas, colors, portions, lines, corners, sides, can move in space miles back and forth, while clearly, at the same time, they are resting smack flat next to each other."[1] In *Alloy*, each color area, with the exception of the anchoring blue triangle, abuts all of the others; the central warm ocher, lightened with splattered white dots, is pressed between boulders of pink and tan, pliantly accommodating their encroaching edges. Despite this lateral sandwiching of color areas soaked into the plane of the canvas, the colors appear simultaneously to move forward and back within a nebulous pictorial space.

The twofold movement of shapes in Frankenthaler's work was made possible through her influential staining technique. About 1962–1963, she switched from oil to acrylic, which seeps less into the weave of the unsized, unprimed canvas, but permits sharply delineated contours that were conducive to the simplification of form and increased denseness of image in her work of the late 1960s.[2] Frankenthaler's delicate, sharp line appears where two color areas are joined or as the edge of a single area. At discrete points the contours are blurred and softly exploded, particularly in the central ocher. In discussing her formulation of line she has observed that the function of line as a divider of form has persisted, but it is not drawn as a separate element or used as the graphically channeled trail of the subconscious.[3] The modulations of her unevenly translucent veils in *Alloy* recall the luminous nuanced fields of Miró, which had also been reinterpreted by Baziotes, Rothko, and Motherwell, among others. The veils interact with the bare canvas, which increases the legibility of edge as line and frees the forms in space: "When a picture needs blank canvas to breathe a certain way I leave it."[4]

Like Pollock, whose choreographic, multileveled involvement with the act of painting made a deep impression on her, Frankenthaler generally works on an unrolled length of cotton duck tacked to the floor. She pours paint out of a pail into a Rorschach-like splotch, then manipulates it with a squeegee, brush, or her hands. As with Pollock, working on the floor liberated her from concern about the edge of the canvas and its orientation:

"What was the real top and the real bottom, which way did it work best?"[5] In fact, the orientation of *Alloy* has apparently undergone a change—indications on the stretcher suggest that it was originally intended as a horizontal, with the tan at the bottom. Frankenthaler has also referred to the multidirectional, aerial view that results from the process of working on the canvas from above and around.[6] The continuation of the composition around the edges of the stretcher reflects her practice of deciding the limits of the work after it has been painted.

L.F.G.

1. Quoted in Cindy Nemser, "Interview with Helen Frankenthaler," *Arts Magazine*, vol. 45 (November 1971), p. 54.
2. E.C. Goossen, in Whitney Museum of American Art and the International Council of The Museum of Modern Art, New York, *Helen Frankenthaler*, exh. cat., 1969, p. 13.
3. See Gene Baro, "The Achievement of Helen Frankenthaler," *Art International*, vol. 2 (September 1967), p. 34.
4. Quoted in Henry Geldzahler, "An Interview with Helen Frankenthaler," *Artforum*, vol. 4 (October 1965), p. 38.
5. Quoted in Baro, p. 34.
6. Barbara Rose, *Frankenthaler* (New York: Harry N. Abrams, 1970), p. 73.

Frank Gehry

Standing Glass Fish 1986

American, b. Canada, 1929

wood, glass, steel, silicone

264 x 168 x 102 (670.6 x 426.7 x 259.1)

acquired from the architect, 1986 (gift of Anne Pierce Rogers in honor of her grandchildren, Anne and Will Rogers 86.68)

Originally shown in the Walker Art Center as the introductory element of a retrospective exhibition of Frank Gehry's architecture, S*tanding Glass Fish* was commissioned to be the centerpiece in the Cowles Conservatory of the Minneapolis Sculpture Garden. The conservatory, designed by Edward Larrabee Barnes/John M.Y. Lee & Partners, consists of three industrially glazed greenhouses; the central unit is a 65-foot-high cube, and Gehry's 22-foot-high glass fish is suspended on invisible supports over a rectangular pool of water planted with water lilies and flowering lotus. Twelve giant Washingtonias—palm trees whose fronds create a fan-shaped feather duster at the top of a slender trunk—surround the pool.

In his architecture, Gehry carries on a unique dialectic between the modernist traditions of Wright, Schindler, and Neutra and his own inventive responses to today's complex formal and programmatic needs. Routinely transforming the banal into the extraordinary in his architecture—for example, in his use of ordinary materials such as chain-link fencing, raw plywood, and corrugated cardboard—he performs a similar magical metamorphosis in his obsessive use of fish as recurring formal elements in his work.

The first fish made its appearance in Gehry's studies for the Smith House, an unbuilt 1981 remodeling for which he proposed a colonnade of fish and birds. Later, in a visionary collaboration with Richard Serra for a 1981 exhibition, he made a model of glass fish scales as part of a proposed project in Manhattan.[1] In 1983, for the *Follies* exhibition at the Leo Castelli Gallery in New York, Gehry designed a witty, scaley duo—a coiled brick snake and a glass and wood fish that together were called *The Prison*. Ever since, fish have been swimming in and out of Gehry's work either as notations indicating missing or unresolved architectural elements in drawings, or materially as fish lamps made of laminated plastic shards.[2]

For the interior of Rebecca's, a restaurant in Venice, California (1984–1986), Gehry created a colorful bestiary of crocodiles, octopuses, and two 4-foot-high fish made with glass scales. At that same time he was designing elements for his exhibition at the Walker; he wanted to make a giant transparent fish with glass scales. Through the beneficence of a generous patron his hopes were realized with the commission for the Cowles Conservatory.

A number of complex study models were created by Gehry's collaborator for the project, Joel Stearns. A rugged wood armature was designed, over which the glass-scaled fish was built. Various glues were tested, forms were tried and their curves plotted in computer-generated drawings. Gehry studied and restudied the flip of the tail, the characteristics of the eyes, and the shape of the scales in a series of Plexiglas models. The form was analyzed by a structural engineer, for this fish out of water had to withstand many of the same stresses as the architectural enclosures routinely analyzed by such experts. Finally, a team of artisans from California arrived at the museum for a four-week marathon building session in September 1986. The fish was constructed in sections over wood lath and chicken wire forms. The diamond-shaped scales were joined with silicone, a slow drying substance that retains some flexibility even when it is completely cured. As the sections dried they were removed from the wire structure and bolted in place on the wood armature.

Permanently installed in the Cowles Conservatory, the giant fish seems to leap expectantly toward the sunlight overhead.

M.S.F.

1. Influenced by and in turn influencing, Gehry has often brought artist friends into his projects as collaborators. For example, he has worked with Claes Oldenburg and Coosje van Bruggen on a building in Venice, California, for the Chiat/Day advertising agency. There, Oldenburg's sculptural binoculars will be transformed into a building element to house a conference room and office. The binoculars will create a baroque entryway to the tripartite office complex.
2. In the early 1980s, the Formica Corporation developed a uniformly colored plastic laminate called Colorcore. In an effort to promote its use by designers, the company offered samples to architects, asking them to create something for interior use. Gehry's efforts were frustrated until he realized that broken pieces of the warm colors were translucent, thus lending themselves to his idea for a lamp in the shape of a fish.

Alberto Giacometti

Buste de Diego   circa 1954

Swiss, 1901–1966

bronze

**15¹⁄₁₆ x 13⅛ x 7⁵⁄₁₆
(38.3 x 33.4 x 18.6)**

**rear, lower right, *1/6/
Alberto Giacometti*; rear,
lower left, *Susse Fondeur
Paris***

Susse Fondeur, *Paris*

**acquired from the artist by
the Pierre Matisse Gallery,
New York; acquired from
the Pierre Matisse Gallery,
1957 (gift of the T.B.
Walker Foundation 57.1)**

This bust, one of numerous images of
Giacometti's brother Diego, conveys Alberto's
sensation of the immateriality of things as perceived visually: "I have often felt in front of living
beings, above all in front of human heads, the
sense of space-atmosphere which immediately
surrounds these beings, penetrates them, is
already the being itself; the exact limits, the
dimensions of this being become indefinable."[1]
He frequently expressed his agony at what he
saw as the Sisyphean task of trying to express
the ambiguous limits of the human being's
physical self in the permanent, immobile analogies of rendered images.

In order to convey this sensation of indeterminate boundaries, Giacometti has used pictorial
devices in sculptural terms. This translation becomes clear when *Buste de Diego* is compared
with the painted portrait and drawn studio scene
that followed it.[2] The bronze shows space gnaw-
ing at the sitter's volume in the way that the paper or canvas on which Giacometti drew emerged
between the strokes of pencil or brush that
defined an object; the lines are characterizing
marks rather than literal descriptions of planes
and volumes. As in pictorial representation,
Giacometti presents the bust from single vantage
points—full face and profile—with virtually no
transition in between. The two "drawings in
space" show dramatically different aspects of the
character of the figure, each one varying in nu-
ance in response to the quality and direction of
the light falling on the sculpture. Viewed in
profile, Diego communicates the solemn dignity of
a Roman patrician; viewed frontally, he has a pos-
sessed, hallucinatory look intensified by his
unblinking gaze.

Giacometti shaped, gouged, and molded the
original clay, the most physical of materials, with
the freedom and expressiveness of pen, pencil,
or brush. In consequence of this expressionistic
treatment, the viewer must stand at a certain distance from the work in order to focus on the
image as a whole and at the same time be close
enough to enter into a direct relationship with it.
As is common with Giacometti's figures, as one
approaches *Buste de Diego* it seems to come
forward, but as one gets closer it begins to
recede until, at very close range, the features
dissolve altogether.[3] Giacometti thus implicitly
controls the actual distance between viewer and
sculpture as the painter illusionistically fixes
the distance from picture plane to sitter.

The atmosphere between real and represented
person is equivalent to the fictitious space within
the canvas.

In his explorations of the perplexities of
scale, distance, space, and the very nature of
being, Giacometti turned again and again to the
faces he knew most intimately. Diego (1902–
1985), a highly regarded maker of furniture and
decorative objects, was also Alberto's chief assistant, critic, helpmate, and friend. It was Diego
who would have made the plaster mold from the
clay, and could well have patinated the cast
bronze in his studio near Alberto's in Montpar-
nasse.[4] The bust appears to have been done
from life—the portraits from memory tend to have
a greater degree of distortion and stylization. The
clay original was very likely made in 1954, since
the bust appears on the floor of the artist's
studio in a photograph reproduced in early 1955.[5]

L.F.G.

1. Quoted by David Sylvester in The Arts Council of Great
Britain, *Alberto Giacometti*, exh. cat., 1965, n.p.
2. The painting formerly belonged to Aimé Maeght, Saint
Paul, and is reproduced in Jean-Paul Sartre, "Giacometti in
Search of Space," *Art News*, vol. 54 (September 1955), p.
65. The drawing, showing this bust and another on a
tabletop, is dated 1954 in Galerie Maeght, Paris, *Alberto
Giacometti: Zeichnungen und Druckgraphik*, exh. cat.,
1981, no. 71.
3. Ibid. Sartre also noted this phenomenon.
4. James Lord, letter to the author, 16 October 1985.
5. James Lord, "Alberto Giacometti, sculpteur et peintre,"
L'Oeil, no. 1 (15 January 1955), p. 16.

Sam Gilliam

Carousel Merge   1971

American, b. 1933

acrylic on canvas

**120 x 900
(304.8 x 2286)
dimensions variable with
installation**

**acquired from the artist,
1971 (gift of the Archie D.
and Bertha H. Walker
Foundation 71.14)**

After seeing the shaped canvases of Frank Stella in 1965, Gilliam began thinking about eliminating the rectangular format from his own work.[1] About 1969 he eliminated flatness as an essential quality of painting by removing the canvas from its stretcher to manipulate it expressionistically. He spread thinned paint over folded, crushed, and peaked canvas (bought in 900-inch lengths, 120 inches wide, the largest size he could get up his stairway), creating uneven densities, lines, crumpled passages, poolings, transferred color areas, and lightly washed expanses. He first nailed the swagged material to walls, beams, and pillars, but later allowed it to hang more freely through bunching, which created the curves he associates with the baroque.[2] He then became intrigued with the interaction of the work and the spaces it occupied.

Although the origins of his ideas relied on the thinking of contemporaries such as Held, Stella, Newman, Pollock, and Albers, Gilliam was interested as well in "pre-industrial art" and objects from his environment, such as clotheslines weighted down and propped up.[3] As in clothes dripping dry, the dampened flat planes of Gilliam's "carousels" convey volume through folds that are gravitationally determined. He has made other visual comparisons with curtains, banners, and flags from life and art: "In front of a Dürer arch in which someone stands with a banner, the banner is blown by a breeze that immediately arcs the banner perfectly, schematically, so that it is for me the illusion of a two-dimensional structure being pushed."[4] In The Metropolitan Museum of Art one day he suddenly understood the term "unfurled," designating a kind of work by Morris Louis, in connection with unfurled flags, whose sequence of stripes curved by the breeze reminded him of the "rolling relationship" in his own work.[5] By replacing the rectilinearity and flatness of the painted stripes in his earlier work with the curves and three-dimensional swags of canvas, Gilliam made his own interpretive response to Louis's concerns.

Gilliam has recently explained that the title of this work arose from his use of a slide projector to transfer colors and images onto the canvas, which served as a kind of screen.[6] The seriality of the slides in a carousel reflected the notion of "multiple ideas" projected onto canvas like evanescent preliminary drawings.

L.F.G.

1. Philip Larson, conversation with Gilliam, 23 March 1971.
2. LeGrace G. Benson, "Sam Gilliam: Certain Attitudes," *Artforum*, vol. 9 (September 1970), p. 57.
3. See Donald Miller, "Hanging Loose: An Interview with Sam Gilliam," *Art News*, vol. 72 (January 1973), p. 42.
4. Ibid., p. 43.
5. Ibid.
6. Letter to the author, postmarked 14 October 1986.

Charles Ginnever

Nautilus 1976

American, b. 1931

Cor-Ten steel

approximately 132 x 264 x 408 (335.3 x 670.6 x 1036.3); dimensions variable with installation[1]

Milgo, Inc., Long Island City, New York

commissioned from the artist through Sculpture Now, New York, 1976 (acquired with funds from Dr. and Mrs. John S. Jacoby in memory of John Dixon Jacoby; Suzanne Walker and Thomas N. Gilmore; Art Center Acquisition Fund, and National Endowment for the Arts 76.17)

The configuration of Ginnever's 1975 *Daedalus*, which immediately preceded *Nautilus*, prompted his colleague Richard Serra to ask if he had designed it with a nautilus form in mind.[2] Although he had not, Ginnever agreed that the structure resembled that of the mollusk's shell and used the title for his next work. Coincidentally, the word has a Greek root like the names used for other examples of his Hellenic series, such as *Daedalus* and *Icarus* (also of 1975), in which he associated the sculptures' bent planes with the wings constructed in that mythological attempt at flight. Once he had made the analogy with Greek mythology, an interest influenced by his "world tour of the great sites of antiquity" in 1974,[3] Ginnever appropriated the term "Hellenic" to designate the ongoing series of works based on bent parallelograms resting against one another in a curved linear arrangement. At present, the series comprises twelve full-scale works, ranging from two- to eight-plane sequences.

As with Tony Smith's *Amaryllis* (see p. 486), the relationships among the components of *Nautilus* are confounding if the sculpture is seen from a single point of view. Because of its scale and sprawl, the process of interpreting is a physical activity. Circling the structure, the viewer traces its spiraling motion and experiences its penetrations, to discover that the elements are based on duplicated planar units folded and welded together to produce a spatially complex, unitary form.[4]

By varying at a regular rate the angle to which each parallelogram is folded (from 110 to 150 degrees in 10-degree increments) and welding it to its neighbor, Ginnever produces a gyrostatic structure that is stable but suggestive of collapsing rotational movement. Each form seems to have a gravitational precariousness that increases from one end to the other, while the piece as a whole appears to have a general slow rising, coming apart, and opening, or falling and compressing, along its length. The artist has recently confirmed that the folding of sheets of metal to build a three-dimensional abstract but associative form derives from Japanese origami, the decorative art of cut and folded paper.[5]

The structure of *Nautilus* first appeared in Ginnever's *4 the 5th (Beethoven)* (1968–1972), in which I-beams delineate the contours in a skeletal, linear way: "The linear works create a charged residue of negative space that invites transformation in the next work into positive material. What's left out of one work will eventually appear in another—so the linear and planar works feed one another."[6] The outline planes were given planar volumes in the Walker work, in which Ginnever attempted to soften "the somewhat geometric and rigid elements through folding and balancing."[7]

Although *Nautilus* had originally been planned for the concourse between the Walker Art Center and the Guthrie Theater,[8] its ultimate siting outdoors is consistent with Ginnever's awareness of the environment:

> My works seem to need a lot of sun because what they talk about [are] the changes that occur seasonally and ... where the sun is at any point in the day.... After I moved to Vermont ... I began to observe the pieces through the seasons and make adjustments in my thinking and in the way I designed pieces to take into account all of the conditions that you get through natural sunlight and shade and foggy days, etc., etc.[9]

L.F.G.

1. As presently installed, *Nautilus* has been secured by 12- to 18-inch long pipes welded to it and driven into the earth (memorandum from Carolyn C. DeCato, Walker Art Center, 11 May 1983). When moved it is disassembled and when reassembled it changes somewhat in dimensions. A Cor-Ten model of *Nautilus* was given to Walker Art Center by Linda Filippi in 1977. The original cardboard maquette no longer exists, and there were no preparatory drawings.
2. Letter to the author, postmarked 10 September 1986. *Daedalus* varies in being "composed of four sections that bend in on one another as they ascend, while the five [sic] forms of the *Nautilus* do the opposite—they spiral outward, away from one another."
3. Ibid.
4. The planes were folded by Milgo, Inc., in Long Island City, and welded together in situ by the artist.
5. Letter to the author, 10 September 1986.
6. Ibid.
7. Martin Friedman, interview with the artist, 19 May 1977.
8. See Philip Larson, in Walker Art Center, *Sculpture Made in Place: Dill, Ginnever, Madsen*, exh. cat., 1976, n.p.
9. Friedman, 1977.

Fritz Glarner

Relational Painting, Tondo #40 1955–1956

American, b. Switzerland,
1899–1972

oil on board

42 (106.7) diam.;
on wood strainer 45
(114.3) diam.

lower center, *F. Glarner—
56*; on reverse, center
left, *Fritz Glarner/Paris
55*; on reverse, top center,
*Relational Painting/
Tondo/#40/1955*

acquired from the artist,
1956 (gift of the T.B.
Walker Foundation 56.14)

Glarner sought to translate essential qualities of life, "its duality, its pulsations, its rhythms, its exact recurrences," into abstract terms.[1] Unconsciously maintaining the convention of figuration, he aligned the dominant motif vertically in the great majority of his nonobjective compositions. Although this painting is in many ways representative of his concerns, its orientation is unusual in that the darkest and most prominent color block rests horizontally. The implied rotation of the tondo, itself internally mobilized by diagonal edges and advancing and retreating colors, suggests experimentation with concepts of motion.[2]

Glarner made substantial changes in the disposition of colors in this panel, probably early in 1956,[3] as cracks in the paint film and intervals between color areas reveal. These changes may have been required because of the gravitational consequences of his departure from a basically vertical format. The red area at the upper left, formerly white, prevents the composition from sinking or separating into sky and earth regions. The weightiness of the blue block may also have necessitated the change of the upper red's black rim to blue and the thin central vertical band from yellow to blue. Because any change of color could upset the dynamic balance of the entire composition, the readjustments of the image in coloristic terms were extensive—there are visible substitutions in various areas of blue for yellow, red for white, blue and yellow, black for blue, yellow and gray. Although the hues were changed, the contours of each color area do not appear to have been altered.

The composition reflects Glarner's characteristic mixture of rational and intuitive principles. It is essentially a triptych, the central panel of which is composed of a blue block abutting a narrower yellow block, each buffered from the opposite sides by a gray block that extends to the canvas edge. The yellow and blue are bordered on the left by a curved and straight black strip, respectively, and on the right by straight and curved red strips. Where they meet, the straight red and black strips deferentially halt. One side of each of the main color blocks constitutes an oblique, another a horizontal, the third a vertical, and the fourth a curve related to the board's edge. Above and below this central "panel" are wedges fragmented into a greater number of parts, which interact in variations on the themes established in the central panel.[4]

L.F.G.

1. Glarner in "What Abstract Art Means to Me," *The Museum of Modern Art Bulletin*, vol. 18 (Spring 1951), p. 10.
2. The concept of rotation may have been influenced by Suprematist artists such as Malevich, who frequently inverted his images from exhibition to exhibition.
3. It is conceivable that the changes were undertaken after he had dated the painting "1955" on the reverse. The indication there that it was executed in Paris suggests the possibility that he may have painted it for a show at the Galerie Louis Carré in 1955. Before dating it "1956" on the front he may have altered the work in the early months of the year in preparation for the *12 Americans* show at The Museum of Modern Art, which opened in March.
4. See Dore Ashton, "Fritz Glarner," *Art International*, vol. 7 (January 1963), pp. 49–55, for quotations from Glarner about his development and intentions.

Adolph Gottlieb

Blue at Noon 1955

American, 1903–1974

oil on canvas

**60 x 72¹⁄₁₆
(152.4 x 183)**

lower right, *Adolph Gottlieb*; on reverse, upper right quadrant (in artist's hand), *Adolph Gottlieb/ "Blue at Noon"/60" x 72"/1955/#5501*

acquired from the artist, 1963 (gift of the T.B. Walker Foundation 63.34)

Gottlieb described *Blue at Noon* as representing a transitional phase in his work as he moved from his earlier Pictographs toward his Imaginary Landscapes. He has retained the rectilinear, compartmentalized infrastructure of the Pictograph, which, by his own account, was inspired by his "great fondness for early Italian paintings of the thirteenth and fourteenth centuries, altarpieces in which the life of Christ was depicted in a series of chronological sequences."[1]

In the Pictograph, the Gothic grid, though stripped of its narrative function, continued to suggest the separation of two-dimensional images, which Gottlieb referred to as "symbols." They had no fixed meaning and were arranged according to principles of irrational juxtaposition influenced by French Surrealism. In *Blue at Noon* the "symbols" appear to have evaporated, escaping their enclosure; calligraphic marks and smoky black and white ribbons float behind, through and in front of the grid, itself laid over or situated within a pale blue atmosphere. By introducing the element of depth, however enigmatic and abstract, Gottlieb recapitulates the development of spatial illusionism by artists such as Duccio and Giotto during the period of art he so much admired.

Two vestiges of Gottlieb's symbology, the arrow and the sun form, provide a focal point that challenges the decentralizing effect of the grid. When asked about the significance of the arrow, he pointed to its ready availability in the environment, and its mutability as a pictorial sign in his work: "Cubists made use of it, Stuart Davis made use of it, you see it in signs and billboards all around, you see it in blueprints, diagrams.... [Arrows] are directional, and sometimes in the pictographs an arrow will become a nose,[2] and it will have a double meaning. It ... implies threat, and so forth."[3] Likewise, the circle with radiating lines, whose connotation of sun is reinforced by the title, holds a variety of possible associations, many of which had been earlier used to advantage by Picasso and Miró.

L.F.G.

1. Martin Friedman, interview with Gottlieb, August 1962.
2. For example, *The Seer* (1950).
3. Friedman, 1962.

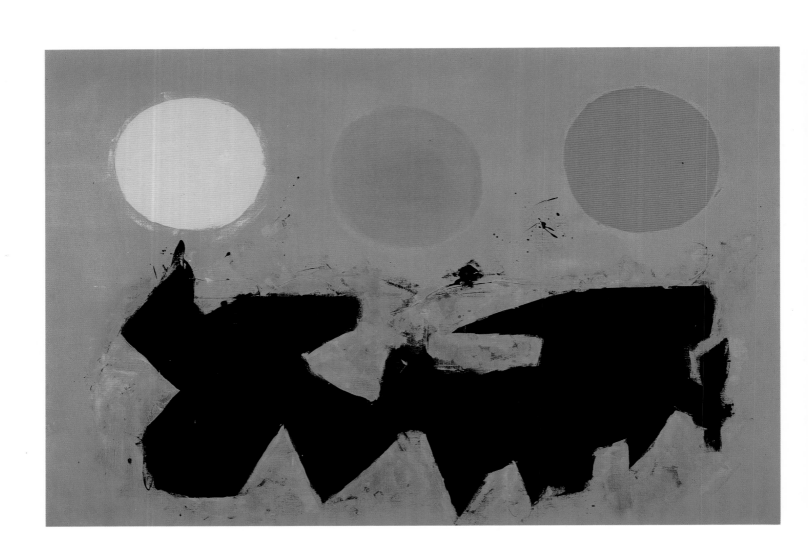

Adolph Gottlieb

Trio 1960

American, 1903–1974

oil on canvas

60 x 90 (152.4 x 228.6)

on reverse, lower right, *Adolph Gottlieb/"Trio"/ 60" x 90"/*1960; lower left, *6014*

acquired from the artist's wife, 1963 (gift of Esther D. Gottlieb 63.36)[1]

The liberated lines and expressive forms of transitional works such as *Blue at Noon* were brought back into partial containment in the Imaginary Landscapes. The notion of a distinct separation of parts was reemphasized by the division of the canvas into top and bottom, with an implied horizon line that suggested to Gottlieb the otherwise arbitrary term "landscape."[2] In *Trio*, the separation of parts is not a simple horizontal division. The yellowish brown surface or space continues along the periphery of the picture, dissipating the association with sky and earth that other, less open examples of the series elicit, and declaring the integrity of the pictorial field. The nature of this space-surface is self-contradictory and changeable. The tan, blue, and red in the upper register simultaneously appear to hover in front of the ground as disks, and to retreat behind it as planes viewed through rounded apertures; or, they can be read as two-dimensional forms impossible to locate in real or invented depths. The massive gravitational form occupying the lower half of the composition seems to have been as much carved into by the encroaching color as conceived as an integral shape, to be as much a product of subtraction as construction. Its crude, hewn contours and the scumbled, obliterative areas that surround it provide a sharp contrast to the uninflected, rounded forms above, whose luminosity increases from left to right. This intensification of luminosity is complemented by an analogous progression in surface treatment, from the thick, knife-spread tan on the left to the gesture-free red on the right.

In a statement that he acknowledged to be oversimplifying, Gottlieb attributed the extreme disparities of form in his work to his internal psychic disparities:

> I have an urge toward serenity and calmness and peace; I am also inclined to be nervous and energetic—I have certain aggressions.... In my painting I try to resolve these conflicts and to bring together and harmonize, to find some equilibrium for these opposing tendencies.[3]

Gottlieb during this period usually used equal parts of turpentine, linseed oil, and varnish, sometimes adding stand oil, and applied his paint with a "large spatula or stick or squeegee" in addition to brushes.[4] He frequently "fooled around" [his term] with medium and technique—

in disregard of possible conservation consequences. As a result, *Trio* unfortunately suffers from multiple physical problems that have drastically altered its appearance. Because of its matte surface, it is nearly impossible to treat the damages without their becoming apparent.[5]

L.F.G.

1. The presence of a Sidney Janis label bearing the number 8763 and the credit line of "Sidney Janis Gallery" in a 1961 exhibition catalogue suggest that the picture passed through the gallery, probably on consignment. However, the inventory card for the work is missing from the gallery, and it has not been possible to establish the details: Donna Harkavy, Walker Art Center, conversation with staff member, Janis Gallery, 30 December 1985.
2. Martin Friedman, interview with Gottlieb, August 1962, transcript of tape 2B, p. 11.
3. Ibid., tape 2A, p. 8. This duality finds an interesting expression in a group of postcards of works of art altered by Gottlieb, published in *Location*, vol. 1 (Summer 1964), pp. 19–26. Gottlieb overlays his own compositions, which respond to those of the postcard images. The reproductions all contain human figures; almost invariably, Gottlieb has painted his characteristic orbs over the faces, thinly enough to allow the features to be legible. The agitated graphic marks cover hands, torso, and, most often, genital areas.
4. Ibid., tape 2B, p. 6, and tape 3B. p. 45.
5. These problems are described in conservation reports by Perry Huston and Foy Casper of July 1970, May and December 1973, and September 1976.

Robert Graham

No. 1 Mirror   1971–1973

American, b. Mexico, 1938

bronze

11⅞ x 35¾ x 27½
(30.2 x 90.8 x 69.9)

acquired from the artist,
1976 (Art Center
Acquisition Fund 76.11)

In the late 1960s, Robert Graham began making Plexiglas boxes containing scenes of small nude figures and architectural or furniturelike structures. The figures in these early pieces were made of wax and, no matter how diminutive, were precisely detailed to give a highly naturalistic appearance. Their idealized nudity alluded to the youth culture prominent in Graham's southern California environs, but the figures remained inaccessible—frozen in their miniaturized, self-enclosed environments.

No. 1 Mirror, Graham's first bronze sculpture, is an extension of ideas explored earlier in his wax pieces. By substituting bronze, with its opaque and reflective qualities, he lent a rich solidity to his compositions. In this work, a pair of small female nudes reclines on either side of two vertical mirrors in an otherwise spare environment. Although the figures are similarly posed below the waist, one sits up, resting on her elbows, while the other lies flat, hands clasped behind her head. Graham positioned the mirrors between them in a way that appears to cause either figure to "sit up" or "lie down" as the spectator moves around the sculpture. The mirrors thus draw attention to each figure and give the illusion of successive motion.

Graham's bronze nudes derive from numerous reference photographs taken from a live model. As accurately as possible, he transposes the model in his studio into permanent form. These figures, nonetheless, cannot be viewed as individuals. Encased in controlled, hermetic environments, their anonymous forms are variations of a type, participants in a carefully composed visual exercise. By creating such generic, idealized beings, Graham diminishes their importance as subjects, focusing our attention instead on such abstract concerns as the mechanics of the human body in motion and the relationship of figures to space.

E.A.

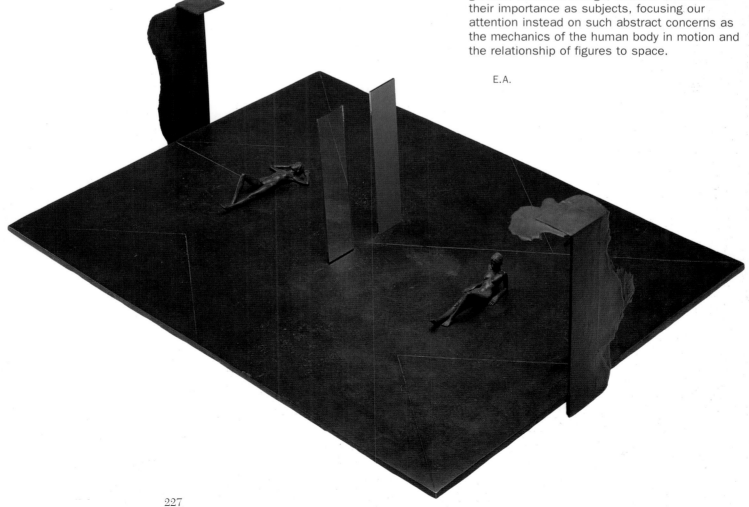

227

Robert Grosvenor

Untitled 1967

American, b. 1937

painted plywood, steel

**105½ x 469½ x 207
(268 x 1,192.5 x 525.8)**

**acquired from the Paula
Cooper Gallery, New York,
by M.A. Lipschultz, 1969;
acquired from M.A.
Lipschultz, 1976 (gift of
M.A. Lipschultz 76.14)**

In the mid-1960s Robert Grosvenor created a
series of dramatic, extraordinary, large-scale
ceiling-hung sculptures that hovered over the floor
in apparent suspended animation. Through these
compelling, seemingly precarious works, he
probed the expressive possibilities of Minimalist
sculpture. Having trained as an architect in
France in the late 1950s, Grosvenor sought to
invest simple forms with a sense of drama
through his audacious engineering.

Regarding his works of this period as "ideas
that operate between the floor and ceiling,"
Grosvenor said he liked to begin with "a very
impractical idea," then find a way to bring it to
fruition.[1] By exploring the interaction of three
horizontal planes—the floor, the ceiling, and eye
level—these pieces served as dynamic intermedi-
aries between the viewer and the architectural
space they inhabited.

Like other Grosvenor sculptures from this
time, *Untitled* was conceived as a site-specific
installation. It was created for the Haags
Gemeentemuseum's 1968 exhibition *Minimal
Art*.[2] Constructed of black-painted plywood anchored to the ceiling by a steel plate, the work
consists of two linear elements with triangular
profiles, one dropping at a thirty-degree angle
from the ceiling, the other crossing it like a "T"
parallel to the floor. The horizontal element
stretches some 40 feet across at a height of 35
inches, roughly the same elevation as a tabletop.
By giving the base of this horizontal beam a slight
tilt, rather than making it perfectly parallel to the
floor, Grosvenor endows the work with a subtle
lifting sensation. The piece thus seems to drop
from the ceiling and then pull up, as if ready to
take off.

Despite the rigid geometry, formal simplicity,
and flat, industrial-looking finish of his work,
Grosvenor draws a distinction between it and that
of Minimalists such as Donald Judd and Robert
Morris, contending he is more interested in
structure than in surface or distilled form. The
gestural dynamism, immense scale, and heroic
defiance of gravity inherent in a piece such as
Untitled reflect a romantic sensibility ultimately
derived from Abstract Expressionism, a debt
Grosvenor freely acknowledges.

To Grosvenor's knowledge, *Untitled* and
Tenerife (1966) are the only two ceiling-hung
pieces from this period still extant.[3]

P.B.

1. All quotations are from a conversation with Martin
Friedman, May 1969. Typescript in the Walker Art Center
Library.
2. The Walker is fortunate to have a gallery whose beam
height is precisely that of the ceiling of the
Gemeentemuseum gallery in which this piece was first
installed.
3. Conversation with the author, 10 July 1989.

Marsden Hartley

Storm Clouds, Maine 1906–1907

American, 1877–1943

oil on canvas

30⅛ x 24¹⁵⁄₁₆
(76.5 x 63.4)

lower right, *Edmund
Marsden Hartley*

Anderson Galleries,
New York, *Seventy-five
Pictures by James N.
Rosenberg and 117
Pictures by Marsden
Hartley,* 17 May 1921, lot
48b, purchased by Mr.
and Mrs. Otto D. Steiner;
acquired from the Bertha
Schaefer Gallery, New
York by Ione and Hudson
D. Walker, Forest Hills,
New York, 1948; acquired
from the Walkers, 1954
(gift of the T.B. Walker
Foundation, Hudson D.
Walker Collection 54.8)

One of the earliest known mature works by Hartley, *Storm Clouds, Maine*, combines a dramatic, baroque handling of light with a controlled divisionist technique derived from illustrations in the periodical *Jugend* of the work of the Swiss-born Giovanni Segantini (1858–1899), whom Hartley credited with having taught him all that he knew about mountains. In the undated, unpublished manuscript "On the Subject of the Mountain: Letter to Messieurs Segantini and Hodler," Hartley wrote:

> It was you [Segantini] who gave me my first true insight into the mountain in general, and my own mountains in particular, and if I have not been able to go all the way with you in your symbolistic and mystical interpretations in connection with your own Engadine [the mountain area depicted in Segantini's *L'aratura in Engadina*, 1886], I have at least felt that you understood so thoroughly the THING-ness of things.[1]

Hartley also acknowledged his indebtedness to Segantini's discovery of the effects of refracted light on the side of a mountain, "the sense of air in all places at all times, the shadows as luminous as the spaces in clear light."[2]

Not only was Hartley responsive to Segantini's topographical accuracy and painterly virtuosity, but he felt that the European shared his empathetic feelings for the overwhelming power and the "profound loneliness" of the mountain. Hartley's Emersonian sense of identification with his natural surroundings permeates much of his poetry and painting; he was particularly preoccupied with the quality of "nativeness," which he felt lent authenticity and allowed for transcendence in the artist's relationship with his subject. In the fall of 1906 he returned to his native Maine to establish a studio in Lewiston, near the southern coast, with the hopes of conveying in painting the character of the country he knew so intimately. On 25 December he wrote his friend Seumas O'Sheel that he had been interviewed for the local newspaper and that a photograph of his most recent painting would appear.[3] *Storm Clouds, Maine*, captioned "*A Study of Speckled Mountain, Lovel,* [sic] *Maine,*" was reproduced in the newspaper several days later; though it was substantially finished, Hartley evidently made some minor changes after this date. This was one of the last instances in which he signed his name "Edmund Marsden Hartley;" he was soon to delete "Edmund" and use his stepmother's maiden name as his first name.

The painting is an autumnal view of Speckled Mountain (2877 feet high), part of the group known as the Center Lovell Mountains of the Appalachian range. The warm rusty color of the foliage is produced by the juxtaposition of short, thick vertical strokes of lilac, orange, yellow, green, and deep blue. The regular pattern of the "stitched" surface à la Segantini is cut through by the jagged outlines of the area of illumination corresponding to the break in the clouds. The smoky, voluminous forms of the clouds sending whipping diagonals of rain toward the land suggest an affinity with Albert Pinkham Ryder's tenebrous sea- and landscapes, which were soon to influence Hartley's work.

This view suggests that Hartley saw the mountain from a higher site. Since Royce Mountain (3202 feet high), about three miles northwest, would provide the only higher vantage point, it seems plausible that he followed one of the logging roads that existed at the time, up from the eighteenth-century Brickett House.[4]

L.F.G.

1. Hartley Papers, Beinecke Rare Book and Manuscript Library, Yale University, New Haven. Segantini's *L'aratura in Engadina* is reproduced by Barbara Haskell, in Whitney Museum of American Art, New York, *Marsden Hartley*, exh. cat., 1980, no. 42, p. 13.
2. Hartley Papers, Beinecke Rare Book and Manuscript Library, Yale University, New Haven.
3. Peter C. Freeman, who found the reference, noted the incomplete state of the painting (letter to Graham Beal, 26 October 1979, Walker Art Center files) and suggested the date 1906–1907. It had previously been dated 1908 or "before 1909."
4. Author's visit to site. If the view is from Royce Mountain, Speckled Mountain is presented as being much closer than it actually is.

Marsden Hartley

Movement No. 9 1916

American, 1877–1943

oil on paper on wood panel

24 x 20¹⁄₁₆ (61 x 51)

on reverse, not in artist's hand, *Stieglitz #5*; formerly visible (according to Elizabeth McCausland, Hartley Papers, AAA, Reel D272), *Movement No. 9*

Alfred Stieglitz, New York, by 1944; acquired from the Stieglitz estate by Ione and Hudson D. Walker, Forest Hills, New York, 1949; on extended loan to the University Art Gallery, University of Minnesota, 1950–1971; Bertha H. Walker, by 1962; acquired from Mrs. Walker, 1971 (gift of Bertha H. Walker 71.45)

After completing *Storm Clouds, Maine* in 1907, Hartley continued painting Maine landscapes and flower studies in a style that became increasingly expressionistic and Fauvist over the years. In 1911 he began to explore abstraction, largely in response to works of the European avant-garde, especially as interpreted by his friend Max Weber. These were available to him at Alfred Stieglitz's 291 gallery and through a visit Hartley made to the Havemeyer collection in New York. He traveled to Europe for the first time in 1912, and there further absorbed the structural and stylistic impact of works by Cézanne, Picasso, Gris, Kandinsky, Marc, Delaunay, and others.

By late 1912 Picasso and Braque had developed what came to be known as Synthetic Cubism, in which figures and objects were described in broad areas of uninflected color bounded by sharp contours, often producing an effect like that of collage, a technique Braque invented about the same time. The influence of this phase of Cubism predominates in *Movement No. 9*, painted probably between late July and October of 1916 in Provincetown, Massachusetts. A group of artists, performers, and writers had formed a loose community there; two of them, Carl Sprinchorn and Charles Demuth, became close friends of Hartley. Hartley wrote to Stieglitz that "we are doing good work both Demuth and I … I have worked quietly and soberly."[1]

During that summer of 1916, Hartley developed a series of hard-edged abstractions based on the motifs of sailboats he observed off the coast, compositions closely related to the abstract portraits of German officers he painted during a sojourn in Europe in 1914–1915. Using a subdued palette, he built the composition of *Movement No. 9* from shapes resembling collaged cutouts overlapping and abutting one another. The "movement" of the title, which is used to distinguish one painting in the series from another, as if each were a section of music, may also signify motion here—the bobbing of the

boat is conveyed by the tilt of its body and the angle of the rudder. The activization of the surface is produced not through optical effects as in *Storm Clouds, Maine*, but by the properties of the paint itself; its grainy, ridged surfaces show Hartley's preoccupation with the medium, which he applied in swirls, feathery strokes, slashes, and zigzags.

L.F.G.

1. Hartley to Stieglitz, 19 September 1916, Stieglitz Papers, Beinecke Rare Book and Manuscript Library, Yale University, New Haven. Hartley described the milieu in his unpublished manuscript "The Great Provincetown Summer," which he incorrectly remembered as being in 1915 (Hartley Papers, Beinecke Rare Book and Manuscript Library, Yale University, New Haven). Hartley had already met Demuth in Paris in 1912–1913.

Marsden Hartley

Cleophas, Master of the "Gilda Grey" 1938–1939

American, 1877–1943

oil on board

28 x 22 (71.1 x 55.9)

on reverse, *Cleophas—/ Master of the "Gilda Grey"/ Marsden Hartley/ 1938–39*

acquired from the artist by Ione and Hudson D. Walker, 1941; on extended loan to the University Gallery, University of Minnesota, 1950–1971; acquired from Bertha H. Walker, 1971 (gift of Bertha H. Walker 71.44)

Francis Mason, the "Cleophas" of this portrait, headed the family with which Hartley boarded during the summers of 1935 and 1936 on an island across from Eastern Points, Lunenberg County, Nova Scotia. Hartley described Mason in 1935 as "a very grand soul. So majestic. The most beautiful man's face I have ever seen. Complete purity and nobility in every line + look of it—has fought the sea for 50 years—and knows of its terrors and cruelties—and the sea is cruel up that way."[1] The cruelty of the sea was made manifest for Hartley the next fall, when Mason's two sons, one of whom the artist particularly adored, died in their punt during a storm. Hartley felt the loss acutely for the rest of his life, and in the summer of 1938, while living on the island of Vinalhaven in Maine, he began a study for a large group portrait of the family and "archaic" portraits of individual members. He continued to work on these into the early part of 1939.

In his unpublished story "Cleophas and His Own: A North Atlantic Tragedy," finished by November 1936, Hartley described the family and the events that befell them, using French-Canadian pseudonyms. He described Cleophas, whom he supposes to be of Norman fisherman ancestry, as "very tall—broad, strong, deep-chested and deep-voiced ... pious and deeply in earnest."[2] Cleophas is seventy years old, over six feet tall, "like an equi-distant quadrangle in all of his behaviors, squarish at all times.... His body is as hard as the rocks and his hands being huge look as if they could take trees in twos and twist them into rope...." In a letter to Stieglitz, Hartley wrote that "Cleophas's face [is] lightness + darkness like a great stone when the sun strikes or leaves it ... palpitating with inner warmth and fire."[3] In the portrait, Hartley's formal means have provided a visual analogy to his impressions of the sitter. The form is flattened, primitivized, and heavily contoured, much in the manner of José Clemente Orozco, whose work Hartley not only respected, but which he had recently seen at Hudson Walker's gallery in New York.

The physical and spiritual fortitude and "plain powerful" personality of Cleophas are expressed in the brutally declarative treatment of the figure, while the lyrical, tender aspect of his nature is conveyed by the sky-blue background and the rose. In a suggestive passage in Hartley's story, Cleophas, in the company of the narrator, pauses to pick a newly opened wild rose, "rich in its first rose-flush" and inserts the petals in his mouth. The rose seems to have homoerotic implications for Hartley; in an unpaginated leaf accompanying the story, the son, whom he calls Etienne, puts flowers in the hand of the older male friend "he loved. You must have a flower he would always say."

Gilda Grey, the Masons' boat,[4] was named after the dancer and actress known particularly for her performance in the 1926 film *Aloma of the South Seas*.

L.F.G.

1. Letter to his niece Norma Berger, 14 December 1935; Hartley Papers, Beinecke Rare Book and Manuscript Library, Yale University, New Haven.
2. Hartley Papers, Beinecke Rare Book and Manuscript Library.
3. Stieglitz Papers, Beinecke Rare Book and Manuscript Library.
4. Gerald Ferguson, Nova Scotia College of Art and Design, conversation with the author.

Marsden Hartley

Roses   1943

American, 1877–1943

oil on canvas

**40 x 30⅛
(101.6 x 76.5)**

**estate of the artist;
A.P. Rosenberg & Co.,
New York, by 1944;
acquired by Hudson D.
Walker, New York, 1948;
acquired from Ione and
Hudson D. Walker, 1971
(gift of Ione and Hudson
D. Walker 71.47)**

Hartley left New York for Corea, Maine, soon after 4 July 1943. He continued to paint during the summer, but his health rapidly declined. Describing Hartley's final days, Louise Young (in whose house he boarded) wrote:

> At times Mr. Hartley could not even tie his shoes, and after he staret [sic] his fift [sic] picture his feet began to swell, and one day he asket [sic] me to walk to his studio and wait for him. I could see it was rather difficult to walk over the ledges. (our place is so rocky) when we got back to the house he seemed so tired and sleepy. After a few days he had to give up painting, and would sleep, and fall out of his chair.... Dr. told us he knew it was getting to the end.[1]

The fifth painting she mentions is probably *Roses*: a photograph of his studio taken soon after his death shows the picture propped up on a table covered with paint supplies; tacked to the wall beside it is a preparatory drawing.

Although *Roses* has been seen as a "splendid efflorescence of glory,"[2] it could equally well be viewed as a deeply unsettling image—the central motif is compressed and flattened, and rears up mysteriously against an azure, cloud-spotted sky. The leaves in the drawing have been transmogrified into voracious, spectral white claws in the painting, which are in sharp contrast to the deep blackish green of the foliage behind or among them. Nervous tendrils and jagged edges form the contours of the massed forms, whose details are submerged in agitated brushwork and blunt scraping. Though the flowers are painted in rich creams, white, pink, and raspberry, their presentation here does not adduce the tenderness and sensuality that Hartley usually brought to his roses in paintings and poems.

His poetry suggests that Hartley also perceived roses as symbols of mourning.[3] He was preparing for his own death as early as August 1940, when he wrote to his niece Norma Berger from Corea: "I want to either be put in the sweet little cemetery inhabited by imaginary beings and wild roses up the road here or scattered on these waters—and a stone of pink granite to say merely—here lived one who did the best he could with what there was and all in all liked the struggle."[4] In August 1943 he drew up a document identifying his nephew Clifton Newell, Norma Berger, and Hudson Walker as persons to be informed in the event of his death, which occurred on 2 September.

L.F.G.

1. Letter to Hudson D. Walker (McCausland Papers, AAA, Reel D267 transcribed by McCausland).
2. Elizabeth McCausland, *Marsden Hartley* (Minneapolis: University of Minnesota Press, 1952), p. 58.
3. Hartley used the image of roses as a tribute to gulls lost at sea in at least one poem. Gerald Ferguson kindly drew the author's attention to a letter in which Hartley refers to the annual service for fishermen lost at sea, which includes the strewing of flowers.
4. Hartley Papers, Beinecke Rare Book and Manuscript Library, Yale University, New Haven.

Marsden Hartley's studio interior, Corea, Maine
n.d.
Elizabeth McCausland papers
Archives of American Art
Smithsonian Institution,
Washington, D.C.

Brower Hatcher

Prophecy of the Ancients   1988

American, b. 1942

cast stone, stainless
steel, steel, bronze,
aluminum

202 high, 246 diam.
(513.1, 624.8)

on steel rim surmounting
columns, *Brower Hatcher/*
©/*1988*

commissioned with
Lannan Foundation
support for the exhibition
Sculpture Inside Outside,
1988; acquired from the
artist, 1989 (gift of the
Lilly family 89.34)

Brower Hatcher's stone and steel-mesh construction *Prophecy of the Ancients* combines an engineer's devotion to structure and logic with a visionary's impulse to transcend time and place. In this celestial garden folly he knits together a series of oppositions—logic and reverie, past and future, public and private, symbol and image, heaven and earth—in an effort to "build an inclusive model ... of the diversity of things as we know them."[1] Such exalted ambition, particularly in combination with the sculptor's incorporation of abstract, geometric architectural forms, recalls the designs of the eighteenth-century French visionary architect Etienne-Louis Boullée, or, in our own era, Buckminster Fuller.

Hatcher evokes the transcendence of time through the work's title and through the juxtaposition of mock-Egyptian columns with a futuristic dome,[2] whose openwork hemisphere is created from thousands of flexible wire polyhedrons, held together by stainless steel and aluminum hubs. Hatcher likens this filigreed construction technique to "geometric clay" and has employed it to fashion a startling array of monumental forms.[3]

Just as the dome and columns symbolize the language of building through their evocation of ancient and modern architectural styles, the objects and abstract forms imbedded in the dome of *Prophecy of the Ancients* exemplify a variety of visual languages. These range from straightforward representation—recreations of a ladder, a turtle, a human figure, a house and more—to abstract signs such as letters, numbers, discs, and dashes. Floating in "galaxies" and "streams" within the network of the dome, these forms are vehicles of communication waiting to be pieced together into meaningful constructs. "I am trying to get to a point where there is an integration between symbol and structure," Hatcher says. "It has to do with the fundamental nature of language. When you write a sentence, you have words which are fragments, but it's through structure that they work upon one another and generate significance and meaning."

Hatcher's imagery is distilled from a personal iconography that has developed over a number of years. Though individual images may hold private significance for him—turtles and alligators, for example, appeal to him because of the similarity of their gridded hides to the pattern of the dome—his intention is to stimulate viewers to bring their own associations and interpretations to the complex of images. By employing a diverse, open-ended iconography, Hatcher strives to create an art that is at once personal and universal, developed from a store of images that have a private significance yet are accessible to all.

P.B.

1. All quotations are from a conversation with Walker Art Center curatorial associate Donna Harkavy, 28 June 1987.
2. Although the columns symbolize the ancient process of carving and stacking thick stone elements, the expense of using such techniques forced Hatcher to resort to a more modern alternative. The individual elements of the columns are cast in resin-bound aggregate, then slipped over a steel pipe that runs through the center of each column, holding them together.
3. In addition to *Prophecy of the Ancients*, these include a behatted head in the *Adirondack Mountain Guide* (1984); the huge figure of a robed judge in *The Principle of Justice* (1986); and an elongated comet tail in *Starman* (1987–1989).

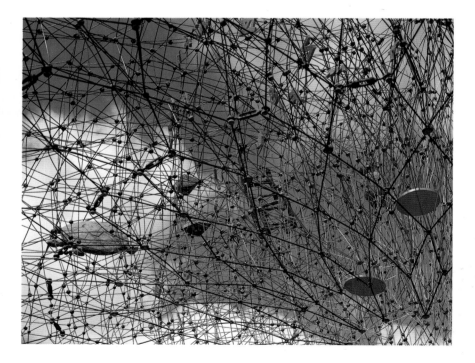

Barbara Hepworth

Figure: Churinga   1952

British, 1903–1975

Spanish mahogany

48⁷⁄₁₆ x 12¼ x 12⁵⁄₁₆
(123 x 31.1 x 31.3)

acquired from the Martha
Jackson Gallery, New
York, 1955 (gift of the
T.B. Walker Foundation
55.14)

Hepworth said in a statement prepared a couple of years after this piece was executed:

> There are fundamental shapes which speak at all times and periods in the language of sculpture.... The forms which have had special meaning for me since childhood have been the standing form (which is the translation of my feeling towards the human being standing in a landscape); the two forms (which is the tender relationship of one living thing beside another); and the closed form, such as the oval, spherical or pierced form (... which translates for me the association and meaning of gesture in landscape).[1]

In *Figure: Churinga*, Hepworth combines the standing and the pierced closed forms, in her terms "translating" a gesturing being in a landscape. The meaning is given additional complexity by virtue of the subtitle, which she added sometime between 1952 and 1954. *Churinga* is a word of Austral derivation referring to a wood or stone object, carved by aboriginal tribes in central Australia, and believed to be sacred. Hepworth could have been aware of the word and its meaning from a description in Freud's essay "Totem und Tabu" (for example, in the English translation published by Routledge & Kegan Paul, London, 1950).

The *churinga* in aboriginal usage represents the bond between an individual and his or her totem ancestor, a figure from a mythical past who may have been transformed into an animal, plant or stone, and who is reincarnated as a child within a pregnant woman. The mystical animation of inert matter as a specific human spirit is a notion that finds expression in Hepworth's acknowledgment of a personal, mystical identification with her own sculpture: "From the sculptor's point of view one can either be the spectator of the object or the object itself. For a few years I became the object."[2] Although she was not referring to this particular sculpture, one is encouraged nonetheless to interpret it as a kind of abstract spiritual self-portrait.

The maternal, procreative aspect of the *churinga* is suggested by the pierced interior of the sensuous mahogany block. Viewed from one side, the penetration is a simple, round-edged slit; from the other, the piercing describes a keyhole contour, and a hollowed-out cavity within resembles a womb or a shrouded concave head. The opening up of the sculpture in the manner of Moore not only has a symbolic function, but acts formally to disrupt the monolithic volume of the trunk and to permit the environment to interact with the sculpture in a participatory way.

Hepworth made at least two other *churinga* sculptures in the early 1960s—a walnut *Stringed Figure (Churinga)* and a lignum vitae *Hollow Form (Churinga III)*.

L.F.G.

1. Quoted in Walker Art Center, *Barbara Hepworth: Carvings and Drawings 1937–1954*, exh. cat., 1955, n.p.
2. Quoted in Herbert Read, *Barbara Hepworth: Carvings and Drawings* (London: Lund Humphries, 1952), n.p.

Jene Highstein

Untitled 1987–1988

American, b. 1942

granite

**three elements
108 x 48 x 28
(274.3 x 121.9 x 71.1)
75 x 61 x 43
(190.5 x 154.9 x 109.2)
30 x 90 x 51
(76.2 x 228.6 x 129.5)**

**commissioned with
Lannan Foundation
support for the exhibition
Sculpture Inside Outside,
1988; acquired from the
artist, 1989 (acquired
with funds provided by
Martha and John Gabbert,
Joanne and Philip Von
Blon, and the National
Endowment for the Arts
89.62)**

Jene Highstein's three granite monoliths hover in a twilight state between nature and artifice, seeming as much to have been found as created. Simultaneously familiar and enigmatic, they resemble totems carved in homage to an animistic universe or meteors cast down from the sky.

When asked about the difference between his stone sculptures and boulders found in nature, Highstein replies that boulders "are a product of their process…. They are the result of a natural force. They have no intent." Highstein's intent, by contrast, is to endow his compact, rounded forms with a variety of associations by providing each granite mass with a series of subtly irregular profiles that shift as the viewer walks around them. As a result, these fabricated boulders "relate to a whole vocabulary of forms: to animal forms, to fish forms, to phallic forms, to a whole spectrum of associations. And that's what makes them work. I prefer that they suggest a really broad range of things. If it comes down to one image, then there's something wrong."[1]

Highstein began working in stone in 1980. Before that he had fashioned massive iconic forms from cement troweled over steel armatures. He found that in making these cement pieces he focused principally on issues of mass, scale, and silhouette, taking what he termed "the long view." By contrast, the slow process of carving, of chipping, of evaluating and chipping again, made him highly attuned in "the short view" to surface and the inherent structure and texture of his materials, be they wood or stone. As a result, his work evolved from simple forms endowed with a bristling, assertive energy to complex, subtly allusive masses.

Untitled is Highstein's fourth outdoor work in stone.[2] The three elements are made from blocks of Pennsylvania granite that the artist worked on simultaneously, so that each stone was shaped in relation to the other two. Their graduated heights and masses, from recumbent to firmly upright, evoke stages of organic growth.

Highstein first roughed out their shapes using pneumatic tools, then scored their surfaces with a diamond-tipped circular saw, creating a series of parallel lines slightly less than an inch apart. Next, using a chisel, he broke out the stone between the saw cuts. This technique allowed him to expose the crystalline structure of the stone. By retaining the stone's natural surface quality, Highstein minimized his own intervention and enhanced the perception of his

boulders as found objects. At the same time, however, the parallel saw lines underscore the contours and so add to their expressiveness.

P.B.

1. All quotations are from a conversation with the author, 25 June 1987.
2. The others are: *One* and *Blackfish* (1980–1981), *Ptah* and *Tem* (1985), and *Untitled* (1987). The first two are each made up of two stones, while the last is a single stone.

David Hockney

Hollywood Hills House   1980

British, b. 1937

oil, charcoal, collage on canvas

three panels
60 x 120
(152.4 x 304.8) overall

acquired from the artist
(gift of Penny and Mike
Winton 83.5)

Since the 1960s, Hockney has allowed his personal interests to serve as the subjects of his art, particularly the people and places of importance to him. Through his drawings, paintings, prints, and photographs, one can trace his wanderings in Egypt, France, Japan, England, and the United States, especially southern California. Although still a British citizen, Hockney's preferred home is Los Angeles, which he has extensively documented.

Hollywood Hills House is a highly subjective image of the house in California where Hockney has lived since 1979. It was painted from memory while he was in London for Christmas in 1980. Depressed by the cold gray of the English winter, he says he made the painting to cheer himself up. Rather than providing a single view of his house, he depicted it from various perspectives. The left panel of this large-scale triptych shows the inside of Hockney's living room, while the outside of the house is shown in the two other panels. At the time Hockney made this painting he was also working on set designs for *Parade*, a series of three works of twentieth-century French musical theater by Poulenc, Ravel, and Satie. Two of his models for these sets are depicted on the living room floor, which, with its dangerous upward tilt, is itself painted in the style of a stage set. Among the many painted images on the back wall of this room are two collaged elements: a postcard reproduction of Rembrandt's portrait of his mother,[1] and a photograph of a portrait of Laurel and Hardy painted by Hockney's father. In contrast to the details of the interior, the outside of the house is described by Hockney in simple, abstract shapes laid out like a Matisse *papier collé*.[2] The scene is dominated by the palm tree in Hockney's backyard, a curved brick wall, a portion of his pool and, above it all, yellow rays of sunshine and blue sky.

The unusual juxtapositions of images and perspectives in the painting reveal the artist's longstanding interest in photography. In the late 1960s, he had begun using photographs as well as drawings as studies for his paintings. He would take dozens of Polaroids of his subject and later use them to jog his memory while he painted. While not based on photographs, *Hollywood Hills House* anticipates Hockney's thorough exploration of photocollage, an activity in which he immersed himself between 1981 and 1983.[3] In one of his earliest photocollages, *My*

House, Montcalm Avenue, Los Angeles, Friday, February 26th, 1982, Hockney again focused on his California house. Like the painting, but in greater detail, this rectangular collage of thirty individual Polaroids takes the viewer from the living room, to the sliding glass door leading outside, across the deck and down to the pool.

In his work of the 1980s, Hockney has sought to provide a more intimate view of his subject than he believes possible with the traditional one-point perspective of a photograph or with a single vantage point. In its free juxtaposition of interior with exterior, *Hollywood Hills House* is an early example of Hockney's use of multiple perspectives to change the nature of representation. By incorporating views from memory, he confounds the logical sequence of space and captures the essence of his recollections and feelings for this place.

E.A.

1. Gary Schwartz, *Rembrandt: His Life, His Paintings* (New York: Viking, 1985), p. 66.
2. Martin Friedman, in Walker Art Center, *Hockney Paints the Stage*, exh. cat., 1983, p. 56.
3. See Lawrence Weschler, *Cameraworks* (New York: Alfred A. Knopf, 1984), p. 8.

David Hockney

Large-scale painting with separate elements based on a design for the opera,
Les mamelles de Tirésias (The Breasts of Tirésias)   1983

British, b. 1937

oil on canvas

**132 x 228 x 120
(335.3 x 579.1 x 304.8)**

**acquired from the artist,
1984 (gift of the artist
84.7)**

The painting reproduces at approximately one-fifth scale the essential elements of the stage design Hockney made for the Metropolitan Opera's 1981 production *Parade*, under the direction of John Dexter. The triple bill opened with the title work by Erik Satie, continued with Francis Poulenc's *Les mamelles de Tirésias*, and concluded with Maurice Ravel's *L'enfant et les sortilèges*. Many important decisions about the production and particularly about the set design were directed toward achieving a unity of message and mood among the three works. All were set against the background of French culture during World War I, specifically emphasizing French patriotism, a sense of the absurdity of war, and a very pronounced interest in children as the one remaining hope for the future.[1]

Although Poulenc did not compose the score of *Les mamelles* until 1947, the play by Guillaume Apollinaire on which it was based was written in 1917, thus tying the work to the period in question. The story is set in the imaginary village of Zanzibar, on the Mediterranean coast. As the opera opens, Tirésias has tired of her housewifely and motherly tasks and she opens her bodice to reveal two balloons, which then

float away. Tirésias decides to switch places with her husband, and promptly—having lost her breasts—turns into a man. By the end of the story, however, a series of astonishing events has led her back to her original identity, and she happily resolves to raise her family with her husband in a conventional way.

In the interests of creating a lively, childlike ambience suitable both to the story and this production, Hockney drew on the styles of early twentieth-century French painters. He acknowledges especially the influence of Henri Matisse and Raoul Dufy, although the role of Picasso, important in Hockney's work generally, has perhaps been underestimated for this particular painting.[2]

Executed specifically for the exhibition *Hockney Paints the Stage*, the Walker painting reproduces Hockney's answers to the special needs of the Met production, i.e., the three simple sets of backdrops in keeping with Dexter's wish to suggest the ambience of a French music hall, or the painted floor, an accommodation to the steep pitch of the Met's tiered seating. In adapting the image to a gallery installation, however, Hockney made important changes. He added seven columns of small paintings—a total of forty-three—to represent the main characters in the opera. Each small painting, although it depicts just one segment of a figure—a head, shoulders, or legs, for example—seems complete in itself, and thus interchangeable with the other depicted parts. This solution stays within the framework of early twentieth-century French painting by making reference to the Cubist breakdown of images into component parts; it also reiterates the theme of "adjustable parts" that recurs so often in Poulenc's opera. Generally, although physically much smaller than the original set design, the finished painting is considerably more comprehensive in scope, attempting not to simply "set a stage," but to convey the flavor of the whole theatrical production in one image.

N.R.

1. See Martin Friedman, in Walker Art Center, *Hockney Paints the Stage*, exh. cat., 1983, pp. 125, 126.
2. Kenneth E. Silver, "Hockney, Center Stage," *Art in America*, vol. 73 (November 1985), p. 156.

Edward Hopper

Office at Night   1940

American, 1882–1967

oil on canvas

22³⁄₁₆ x 25³⁄₁₆ (56.4 x 64)

lower right, *Edward Hopper*

acquired from the artist by the Frank K.M. Rehn Galleries, New York, by 1941; acquired from Rehn, 1948 (gift of the T.B. Walker Foundation, Gilbert M. Walker Fund 48.21)

In 1948 Hopper discussed the genesis of his ideas for *Office at Night*:

> The picture was probably first suggested by many rides on the "L" train in New York City after dark and glimpses of office interiors that were so fleeting as to leave fresh and vivid impressions on my mind. My aim was to try to give the sense of an isolated and lonely office interior rather high in the air, with the office furniture which has a very definite meaning for me. There are three sources of light in the picture: indirect lighting from above, the desk light and the light coming through the window. The light coming from outside and falling on the wall in back made a difficult problem, as it is almost painting white on white; it also made a strong accent of the edge of the filing cabinet which was difficult to subordinate to the figure of the girl. I was also interested in the sombre richness of the furniture against the white walls. Any more than this, the picture will have to tell, but I hope it will not tell any obvious anecdote, for none is intended.[1]

In denying any "obvious anecdote," Hopper clearly wished to discourage a narrative or biographical reading of the image. What the picture does "tell" is of psychological, probably sexual, tension between the two figures in the depersonalized work environment. Hopper's wife, Jo, who posed for the female figure,[2] alludes to this element in the subtitle "Confidentially Yours," which she appends below Hopper's drawing in his record book.[3] The double-entendre plays on a secretary's relationship with her boss, her knowledge of sensitive information meant for someone else's eyes only. This kind of ostensibly neutral witnessing of private exchanges forms a parallel with the inadvertent voyeurism of the artist on the elevated train, and that of the viewer of the picture.

Solitude and the invasion of privacy are recurrent themes in Hopper's work. Jo's second subtitle, "Room 1005," implies that she fanta-sizes that the two figures are on the tenth floor of the office building, remote from the rest of the world, as Hopper suggests in his commentary. The boundary between day and night activities, between professional and personal roles, is maintained only by an effort of the will. The possibility of intrusion is implicit in the open window, through which light and breeze enter, the partly open door, and the presence of the telephone.

Although Hopper was greatly concerned with formal issues, as his notes on the structure, colors, and textures of the picture attest, his pictorial effects contribute to the metaphoric content. The conventional young man (somewhat similar in appearance to that in Hopper's early self-portraits) is pinned within the irrationally compressed space of the room, fixed stiffly in place by the letter he reads, the light of his desk lamp, and the visual frame created by the file cabinet, window frame, and the solid mahogany desk. Conversely, the secretary, whom Jo called Shirley and described as wearing "plenty of lipstick," is mobile and exposed, having left her desk to work in the files.

Hopper's sources for this picture have been persuasively identified in works of Degas, such as *The Cotton Exchange, New Orleans* (1873); the argument is supported by Hopper's professed admiration of the French Impressionist, the internal evidence in the finished work, and in two of the preparatory drawings.

L.F.G.

1. Statement accompanying a letter dated 25 August 1948, sent to Norman A. Geske, Walker Art Center, from Hopper's summer home in Truro, Massachusetts.
2. Gail Levin, "The Office Image in the Visual Arts," *Arts Magazine*, vol. 59 (September 1984), p. 101. Levin quotes from Josephine Hopper's diary entry of 1 February 1940: "I'm to pose for the same [female fishing in a filing cabinet] tonight in a tight skirt short to show legs—Nice I have good legs and up and coming stockings."
3. Published in Gail Levin, "Edward Hopper's 'Office at Night,'" *Arts Magazine*, vol. 52 (January 1978), p. 137.

Edgar Degas
The Cotton Exchange, New Orleans 1873
oil on canvas
28¾ x 36¼ (73 x 92)
Collection Musée des Beaux-Arts, Pau, France

Rebecca Horn

The Little Painting School Performs a Waterfall   1988

German, b. 1944

metal rods, aluminum, sable brushes, electric motor, acrylic on canvas

228 x 143 x 95 (579.1 x 363.2 x 241.3) approximate overall

acquired from Marian Goodman Gallery, Inc., New York, 1989 (T.B. Walker Acquisition Fund 89.63)

Thirteen feet above the floor on a gallery wall, three fan-shaped paintbrushes mounted on flexible metal arms make their slow, fluttering descent into cups filled with blue and green acrylic paint. After a few seconds' immersion they snap backward, spattering paint onto the wall, the ceiling, the floor, and onto a cascade of small canvases projecting from the wall below. The brushes immediately resume their descent, and the cycle is repeated until each canvas bears a richly dappled coating of paint.[1]

Entitled *The Little Painting School Performs a Waterfall*, this work was created by the German artist and filmmaker Rebecca Horn. In recent years she has gained prominence through her strangely poetic installations in which mechanized objects perform simple, repetitive actions that suggest the frustrations and dramas of daily life. In the present work, Horn has employed the traditional implements of painting—brushes, canvas, and paint—to comment on the nature of art and the role of artists in contemporary culture.[2]

On one level, *The Little Painting School Performs a Waterfall* makes wryly humorous references to the idea of the accident or chance in painting, which has appeared at various times in the history of modern art. Early in the century Dada artists produced collages "according to the laws of chance,"[3] and during the 1920s many Surrealists practiced self-hypnosis to make what they called "automatic" paintings and drawings. Horn's installation also alludes to the more recent Abstract Expressionism, and to the Swiss artist Jean Tinguely's painting machines, which also poke gentle fun at "action painting."

In a less lighthearted vein, Horn's work in the Walker collection encourages reflection on modern man's estrangement from nature, and seems to imply that contemporary art has suffered profoundly from this separation. Though the somewhat sentimental title suggests the classic genre of landscape painting,[4] its accumulation of canvases does not depict the *appearance* of a waterfall but rather documents its *action*. Several shades of blue and green acrylic paint stand for water, and the members of the painting school, represented by identical mechanized paintbrushes, are portrayed as automatons. In Horn's disquieting vision no physical trace of either man or nature can be found; humanity has all but evaporated from this art. And though its absence is unsettling, Horn ironically suggests that human presence in a work of art—including that of the artist—may not be necessary after all; invoking the ideas of Duchamp, she suggests that aesthetic significance may lie not in the realm of the senses but rather in the realm of the mind.

J.R.

1. Installation of this work at the Walker, including the painting of the canvases, took place over a period of three days and was directed by Horn's assistant Hasje Boegin. The artist has stated that, after the canvases have been covered with paint, the piece may be exhibited either "at rest" with its motor turned off, or in action but without paint in its cups.
2. In a related Horn work entitled *The Little Painting School* (1989), the canvases have been replaced by empty stretcher frames. Other works by her that address the theme include *Pollinating Brush Machine* (1987), *An Art Circus* (1988), and *Brush Wings* (1988).
3. The phrase comes from the titles of works by Dadaist Hans Arp.
4. It also refers to the work's commission for and installation in *Waterworks*, an exhibition organized by Visual Arts Ontario and held at the R.C. Harris Water Filtration Plant, Toronto, from 22 June through 20 September 1988. See *ArtViews*, vol. 14, no. 2/3 (Spring/Summer 1988) (published by Visual Arts Ontario), an issue devoted entirely to the exhibition.

Vilmos Huszár

untitled 1924

Hungarian, 1884–1960

wood, nails, oil paint

7⅝ x 6¾ x 4⅞
(19.4 x 17.2 x 12.4)

on bottom, in light blue
paint, lower left, *VH*;
lower right, *24*

acquired from a private
dealer in The Netherlands
by Annely Juda Fine Art,
London; acquired from
Annely Juda Fine Art,
1985 (given in memory of
Fred Weil, Jr., from his
family and friends 85.24)

By the time Theo van Doesburg used Huszár's work to demonstrate the aesthetic principles of De Stijl in an article of 1919, the Hungarian painter was already a fluid practitioner of the art—its intuitive, geometrically motivated method of composition, where the precise diversities in shape, size, position, proportion, and color of seemingly similar forms establish a balanced visual relationship.[1] For De Stijl artists, harmony, whose implications were ethical and spiritual as well as aesthetic, was to be attained not through any correspondence with natural form, but through the impersonal, non-allusive dialogue of rectilinear color areas on a flat surface. Like van Doesburg, Huszár was not content with limiting that surface to single-planed, rectangular easel-scale canvases, and participated in several architectural collaborations in which he was designated "colorist." As he had written in the first volume of *De Stijl*, the artist "demands an active part in society through his work,"[2] achievable through his application of painting concerns to architecture, design, and craft.

In his earliest architectural projects, Huszár adhered to the approach Mondrian used in applying colored rectangles to the walls of his studio, i.e., treating each wall as an independent plane. In interior architectural design projects of 1923 and (probably) 1924,[3] Huszár, like Piet Zwart before him, rejected this pronouncement, carrying some color rectangles over the edges of corners, and thereby handling the entire interior as one pictorial surface.[4] According to Mondrian's stringent dogma, this departure would have been as much an assault on the supremacy of the plane as the diagonal was a betrayal of orthogonal composition. In fact Huszár, by inviting a reading of the room as a single pictorial arena, implicitly introduces the diagonal, which results from the foreshortening of rectangles seen from an angle. The color planes, viewed obliquely as well as frontally, are not absolute in their configuration, but are subject to change in the eyes of the viewer passing through space.

Although the Walker box is a small, rather crudely fashioned object of unknown function,[5] it serves as a consummate exposition of Huszár's treatment of the right-angled juncture of two planes in space in the architectural projects. The box is like the model for a room turned inside out, the floor ignored and the wall behind the viewer removed.[6] The design is a synthesis of theme and variation within and among the four painted sides. The top and front planes of the box as presently exhibited are mirror images, a device related to those used in the design for De Leeuwerik of 1918 by Bart van der Leck, whose work had influenced that of Huszár.[7] The other two sides are almost mirror images with respect to the grid created by the edges of each color block, but they differ from each other in the selection and placement of colors, which show a response to the activity of adjacent planes. In certain instances, Huszár observes the change of plane by ending a color block along the edge of the box, while in others he disregards it by folding a rectangle over the edge. Throughout the box, each color area serves a multiple purpose, acting with equal authority as a discrete part of a single flat plane and as an element in a complex compositional exchange within a three-dimensional planar system. The process of adjustment is reflected in the overpainted changes of color and shape visible on close examination. Although the dynamic equilibrium of the piece is sensed immediately, the means by which it is achieved are absorbed over time, through analysis and intuition.

L.F.G.

1. Theo van Doesburg, "Over het zien van nieuwe Schilderkunst," *De Stijl*, vol. 2 (February 1919), pp. 42–44.
2. Huszár, "Aesthetische Beschouwingen," *De Stijl*, vol. 1 (May 1918), p. 80.
3. Plans and models for these projects, *Spatial Composition for an Exhibition* and *Spatial Composition in Gray* are reproduced and discussed in Nancy J. Troy, *The De Stijl Environment* (Cambridge, Massachusetts: M.I.T. Press, 1983), pp. 46, 129–131, fig. 59, and Troy, "De Stijl's Collaborative Ideal: The Colored Abstract Environment, 1916–1926," Ph.D. dissertation, Yale University, New Haven, p. 70.
4. For Mondrian's notion of architectural interior space, see Michel Seuphor, *Mondrian* (New York: Harry N. Abrams, 1956), p. 339.
5. The box may have been decorative: in an old photograph provided by Huszár's widow, it is placed horizontally on a tabletop, against the wall.
6. The designs for rooms by De Stijl artists were frequently shown as boxes with their sides flattened out to form a cross—the exploded box plan.
7. Van der Leck painted designs that were nearly identical on walls opposite each other; Troy, "De Stijl's Collaborative Ideal," p. 66.

Robert Indiana

The Green Diamond Eat and The Red Diamond Die 1962

American, b. 1928

oil on canvas

two panels
85¹⁄₁₆ x 85¹⁄₁₆
(216.1 x 216.1) each

**The Green Diamond Eat,
on reverse, on upper right
edge of canvas, stenciled
in green and red paint,
Eat•Robert Indiana•
1962•Coenties Slip•NYC;
on stretcher members at
their juncture, 85 x 85; on
reverse, lower left edge of
canvas, USA; on reverse,
top, UP/arrow. Same
inscriptions on The Red
Diamond Die, except at
upper right edge, which is
obscured by length of red
tape**

**acquired from the Stable
Gallery, New York, 1963
(gift of the T. B. Walker
Foundation 63.45)**

The integration of words and forms in Indiana's work was inspired by stencils he collected, the first being a plate containing the insignia of The American Hay Company.[1] The letters spelling the name of the company formed a circle around an inscribed diamond shape, a conjunction that was to appear in works such as the Walker canvases. In 1962 Indiana took a pencil rubbing of the plate, substituting for the diamond a cross composed of the word EAT written vertically and horizontally.[2] He considers the word one of his "primary signs," recalling the childhood memory of "the EAT signs that signalled the roadside diners that were usually originally converted railway cars.... In similar cheap cafés my Mother supported herself and son by offering 'home-cooked' meals for 25 cents when Father disappeared behind the big 66 sign in a westerly direction out Route 66."[3] The original company colors of Phillips 66, where his father was employed, were the red and green of the Walker Eat. Indiana's choice of palette was, by his own admission, indebted as well to that of his friend Ellsworth Kelly, who also lived at Coenties Slip, Manhattan, during the early 1960s.[4]

Indiana keeps biographical references on the surface, recognizing that his mother and father were "conspicuously crucial to my life and my becoming an artist." He paid homage to his parents in the nostalgic diptych Mother and Father, 1963–1967, in which they are portrayed alongside the family car, as he perceived them— his mother nurturing and vibrant and his father gray and remote. Something of the same contrast of nurturance and denial is implicit in the juxtaposition of the words "EAT" and "DIE" in the two panels: "the most personal aspect of the matter was that the word 'Eat' was the last word my mother said before she died."[5] The association of love, cars, consumption, disposability, and death in American culture was imprinted in his work with the force of personal psychology. Referring again to his mother, he wrote that his father "wooed her on wheels ... until she became fat and middle-aged when he ditched her and went shopping for a newer model—built-in obsolescence Yankee-style."[6] The cautionary causal connection between eating and dying was also suggested in the title of another work of 1962, The Dietary in which the word "DIE" circles the perimeter of numbered wedges, as if on a roulette wheel. The presence of the word "eat"

within the word "death" may not have escaped Indiana.

In the first version of Eat/Die, the words are painted in circles that float at the top of two abutting oblong panels. The lozenge orientation of the Walker version suggests warning in the convention of road signs; the green and red backgrounds are the colors of semaphore signals for "go" and "stop," the equivalent in driving of "eat" and "die." Legitimate though these connections are, Indiana is concerned that the reading of the picture not be limited by them, asserting that Eat/Die "doesn't have too much to do with American road signs. This is a very personal jump across a very peculiar gap and there's no doubt there was that influence, but I painted words for reasons other than that." Likewise minimizing the significance of the graphic qualities of his painted words, he says that they are primarily evocative of things in his life.[7]

Indiana first used letters attached to wooden beams, whose width permitted only short words. The fact that "those beams came very, very close to the width of a tombstone and that I should have been early preoccupied with 'Eat' and 'Die' in that context isn't so unusual."

L.F.G.

1. Reproduced by John W. McCoubrey, in Institute of Contemporary Art, University of Pennsylvania, Philadelphia, Robert Indiana, exh. cat., 1968, p. 10.
2. Reproduced in Art in America, vol. 53 (April 1965), p. 106.
3. Institute of Contemporary Art, p. 25.
4. Donald B. Goodall, "Conversations with Robert Indiana," in University Art Museum, University of Texas at Austin, Robert Indiana, exh. cat., 1977, p. 27.
5. Ibid., p. 33.
6. Ibid., p. 36.
7. Ibid., p. 33.

Robert Irwin

untitled 1963–1965[1]

American, b. 1928

oil on canvas on bowed
wood veneer frame

82⅜ x 84½ x 5¹¹⁄₁₆
(209.3 x 214.6 x 14.5)

acquired from the Pace
Gallery, New York, by Mrs.
Albert A. List, New York,
1966; on extended loan to
the Walker Art Center
from Mrs. Albert A. List,
1968–1972 (gift of the
Albert A. List Family 72.6)

This is one of the Dot paintings that Irwin made between 1963 and 1967 in Los Angeles, in which he continued the rigorous examination of the premises of art he had undertaken about 1959. Divesting his surface of conventionally bounded painted form and line, he substituted a dot pattern that reads from the customary viewing distance as a glow or, in his term, a "physical-phenomenal field," emanating from the canvas. At first glance, the canvas appears utterly devoid of perceptible form. After the viewer has become accustomed to it, however, a central, vaguely greenish square can be sensed, so evanescent that its borders cannot be located. This area seems to be surrounded by a pinkish halo that interpenetrates and fuses with the outside border of the white painted canvas, which takes on a warm yellowish cast.

The color is so insubstantial that one doubts one's eyes, entertaining the possibility that an optical confusion has occurred and that the canvas is actually of a uniform neutral color with a slightly lower value at the center. A closer examination shows that the effect is produced by a grid pattern of thousands of evenly staggered, hand-painted bright green and red dots, densely clustered in the center and progressively less so toward the periphery. Although the two complementaries neutralize each other in the central area, where they form a complete screen of alternating rows, the gradual dropping out of green and consequent preponderance of pinkish-red produce the coloristic halo described above. The reds, too, become fragmented, paler, and less frequent as they merge with the edges of the canvas.

The pulsing advance of these color mists and the retreat of the canvas border are abetted by the almost imperceptible swelling of the canvas, laboriously produced with a concealed strutting system covered with a wood veneer, resembling that used for airplane wings.[2] Viewed from the side, the strut system bows the front and back surfaces in convex curves, making the work a three-dimensional object projecting from the wall. Recognizing the paradoxes of perception, Irwin made the canvas slightly off-square in order to give the illusion of a square.[3] He was soon to dispense with the problem of the square altogether by introducing the disk. The conjunction of imageless but active painting surface and subtly adjusted three-dimensional structure transforms the realm of experience from picture-viewing to that of perception itself.

To ensure the desired viewing, Irwin provided lighting instructions that detailed the number of fixtures, their distance from the work and placement in relation to it, and the quality and wattage of the bulbs.

L.F.G.

1. Irwin assigns no titles to his paintings. The dates given refer to the beginning of the series and the completion of this particular work: "I began the series on the first date and worked at the singular format. At one point a single painting would be better than the rest, so I would throw all of the earlier ones away and begin again, and so on, until I could not improve them further;" letter to the author, 26 April 1986.
2. See Irwin's description, recorded sometime between 1976 and 1979, in Lawrence Weschler, *Seeing Is Forgetting the Name of the Thing One Sees: A Life of Contemporary Artist Robert Irwin* (Berkeley: University of California Press, 1982), p. 90. The artist has provided detailed information on his materials and procedures in a letter to the author, 26 April 1986.
3. Weschler, p. 89.

Robert Irwin

untitled   1965–1967

American, b. 1928

acrylic automobile
lacquers sprayed on
prepared, shaped
aluminum surface, with
metal tube, four 150–watt
floodlights

60 (152.4) diam.

acquired from the Pace
Gallery, New York, 1968
(purchased with a
matching grant from the
Museum Purchase Plan,
National Endowment for
the Arts and Art Center
Acquisition Fund 68.33)

Irwin's Disks of late 1965 to 1967 developed directly from his Dot paintings, and expand on his concepts of perceptual experience. While continuing to retain painting's most elemental attributes—surface, paint, and light—he has denied, subverted, and literalized other features traditionally associated with the activity in order to draw attention away from the object and toward the act of apprehending it.

Like other of his contemporaries, Irwin uses an unconventional medium (automobile lacquer), support (convex aluminum disk), and technique (spraying and construction). He departs further from traditional painting by elaborating on the devices that customarily supply the illusion of an isolated, illuminated surface floating against the wall while remaining inconspicuous themselves. The means of attachment is clearly visible from the side—a tubular "arm" holds the disk about 18 inches from the wall. The lights trained on the disk, two on the floor and two on the ceiling, are not variable, extraneous elements, but integral, controlled aspects of the work.[1]

Irwin uses these devices not only to dispute the conventional relationships among art object, wall, and illumination, but also to set up an alternative event. The shadows that are created by the positioning and quality of the lights and the distance of the disks from the wall are not the irrelevant strips on the wall that a flat canvas casts. Instead, they are four equal, diaphanous, geometrically interlaced disks, physically derived from the primary surface and aesthetically and conceptually responsive to it. His intention is to "marry the 'figure' (object) with its 'ground' shadow/space."[2] As he notes:

> Visually it was very ambiguous which was more real, the object or its shadow. They were basically equal. I mean, they occupied space very differently, but there was no separation in terms of your visual acuity in determining that one was more real than the other. And that was the real beauty of those things, that they achieved a balance between space occupied and unoccupied in which both became intensely occupied at the level of perceptual energy.[3]

This balance is achieved as well within each sprayed disk, whose "empty" center is as occupied as its faintly colored periphery: "I discovered that if you spray at just the right distance, lacquer dries on hitting the surface, and you start getting a fine grainy build-up, very

texturey, so that the center of the disc becomes very strong in a tactile sense."[4] Graceful and radiant though they are, the sprayed halos of evanescent color dissipate the focus, just as the emphasis on the behavior of things in response to physical laws broadens the field of interest from the aesthetic appeal of the painted surface.[5]

L.F.G.

1. See John Coplans, in Pasadena Art Museum, *Robert Irwin*, exh. cat., 1968, for a detailed physical description of the disks and their ideal environment. Lawrence Weschler, *Seeing Is Forgetting the Name of the Thing One Sees: A Life of Contemporary Artist Robert Irwin* (Berkeley: University of California Press, 1982), pp. 102,103. Weschler quotes from Irwin's discussion of the lights he used. He specified Sylvania floods, which are the coolest and hence do not mute the pale colors at the edge of the circle as much as warmer lights; even so, he added a pale blue filter to further minimize the "bias inherent in incandescent light;" letter to the author, 26 April 1986. In Irwin's undated instructions to Walker Art Center, and in an installation drawing, he indicated that the four fixtures were to be placed at approximately the same distance from the painting, two on the ceiling, two on the floor, for "lighting to accomplish equalizing edge of painting and surrounding shadows." He feels that the disks "work best in natural light when the conditions are available;" letter to the author, 26 April 1986.
2. Ibid.
3. Quoted in Weschler, p. 104.
4. Ibid., p. 103.
5. Unfortunately, as Irwin observes, the absence of imagery makes photography, which "records imagery and distorts all physicality," inadequate, a fact that prompted him to forbid reproductions for several years.

Robert Irwin

untitled   1971

American, b. 1928

synthetic scrim, wooden frame, double-stripped fluorescent lights, floodlights

96 x 564 (243.8 x 1,432.6) dimensions of scrim may vary with installation

acquired from the artist, 1971 (gift of the artist 71.17)

Having discarded or transformed the elements of the pictorial tradition that he felt had limited inherent meaning, Irwin realized that painting was no longer germane to his inquiry into the act of perception. In 1970 he began constructing scrim environments that more directly addressed the question of how we see and understand phenomena.

Like his other Scrims, this untitled environment was conceived specifically for the space it was to occupy. Having studied the scale, proportions, and architectural features of the Walker gallery for which it was commissioned, Irwin drew up detailed drawings, instructions and plans, carefully orchestrating the elements of the piece to achieve the visual and pedagogical effects he sought.[1] He itemized the materials he required— the synthetic Tergal scrim material imported from Amsterdam (where he had first encountered its use in curtains and on ceilings),[2] the light fixtures, the industrial bonding agent, and wood and wire to affix the scrim and lights. He specified the height of the scrim, its treatment at the edges, and the number, placement, and coolness or warmth of the fluorescent tubes and floods. The deeply ribbed precast concrete ceiling of the Walker gallery led Irwin to use the scrim as a space divider rather than as a ceiling,[3] an innovation he had explored in his studio in Los Angeles in 1970. The recesses of the ceiling also enabled him to conceal the light fixtures, minimizing the utilitarian aspect of the hardware acknowledged by other artists working with light, such as Dan Flavin.

By enclosing the space at the end of the gallery, Irwin created two areas, one accessible to the viewer and the other separated by the oblique plane of the scrim. Because of the immateriality of the media and the elusiveness of their interactions, the boundary between these two realms is indistinct, resistant to resolution. As one nears the scrim to look through it, its dimensions and angle in relation to the room cannot be grasped; the plane dissolves, becoming a hazy, luminous mist, pinkish or greenish according to the light reflected on it, which seems to fill the end of the room beyond. When one steps back and to the side to gauge the angle of recession and the scale of the work, the scrim reconstitutes itself, losing its quality of transparency and visually sealing up parts of the area behind. At the same time, its reflection on the floor expands the field of its presence into the

space the viewer occupies. By making simultaneous apprehensions of the piece impossible and provoking illusionistic effects, Irwin encourages recognition of the paradoxes, relative truths, and durational aspect of perception. The cooperative viewer, suspending pragmatic techniques for rationalizing experience, enters into an unprejudiced engagement with the power of pure visual sensation.

L.F.G.

1. These plans, preserved in the Walker files, reveal that Irwin had originally envisaged a concrete "sidewalk" for the piece, but withdrew the proposal because of cost and engineering problems.
2. Irwin's use of Tergal and its source in Amsterdam are discussed in Lawrence Weschler, *Seeing Is Forgetting the Name of the Thing One Sees: A Life of Contemporary Artist Robert Irwin* (Berkeley: University of California Press, 1982), p. 170.
3. Letter to Martin Friedman, 12 May 1970.

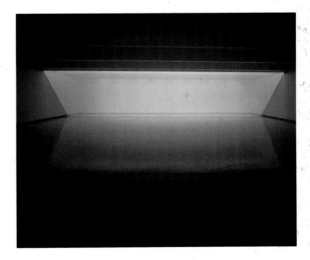

Donald Judd

untitled 1965

American, b. 1928

lacquer on galvanized
steel

14¹¹⁄₁₆ x 76⁹⁄₁₆ x 25⅝
(37.3 x 194.5 x 65.1)

acquired from Richard
Bellamy, New York, 1966
(Harold D. Field Memorial
Acquisition 66.44)

During the early 1960s Judd moved rapidly from painting on canvas to visualizing and drawing three-dimensional objects for fabrication, which he distinguished carefully and precisely from sculpture.[1] The Walker's red Progression, to use his term, derives in part from Judd's systematic elimination of painting's limitations without a complete rejection of all its physical properties: "Finally, a flat and rectangular surface is too handy to give up."[2]

Among the limitations Judd identified were the tendencies of the painted field to create the almost inescapable distinction of figure and ground, the illusion of spatial extension, and the parallel relationship between picture plane and wall. In 1961 he tried to break from these conventions by curling the canvas away from the wall at top and bottom. He soon replaced the canvas with a composite structure made of a rectangle of painted plywood bordered top and bottom with curled strips of galvanized iron.[3] Important features of the Progressions were incipient in this piece, particularly the notion of a rectangular plane parallel to the wall supporting projecting curves that simultaneously detached themselves from it and formed part of it.

Although still attached to the wall as paintings, the Progressions do not hang passively but are assertively cantilevered. Made entirely of metal, they no longer have disparate elements. It is as though the wooden rectangle of the 1961 work had changed substance, been compressed on its horizontal axis and extended out from the wall into a three-dimensional block, and the scrolled top and bottom iron fringes had met and merged to complete a round-ended holistic projection. The planes implied by coordinate edges have been filled in, literalized.

The primary shape of the Progression is an implied circle merged with a rectangle, visible as such when the piece is viewed from either end; these two-dimensional forms have been extended into three-dimensional volumes of box and crenellated cylinder. This perception is clarified when the work is viewed from the front, where the curved edge is cut into segments that imply its derivation from a cylinder.

The Walker example is a single irreducible form with features varying in a predictable, unified, mathematically ordained way: the protrusions increase from left to right in 1½-inch increments, the ratio of the intervals increasing similarly from the opposite direction; the regular,

systematic, predetermined rhythm does not establish a composition in which major and minor parts interrelate in an orchestral way. Presumably the work, like a Brancusi column, could have been extended further, since it implies its own growth.

Judd disclaims the title of sculptor because he considers such pieces to be three-dimensional renderings of his discourse on painting, although removed from the activity itself. At the same time, the objects that concretize his thoughts about art are things complete in themselves, carrying what has been called "a beauty and authority which is nowhere described or accounted for in the polemics of object-art."[4] The strength of this example derives in part from the allure of the shimmering rococo patterning of its red surfaces sprayed with transparent Harley-Davidson "Hi-Fi Red," set against the puritanism of crisp silhouettes.[5]

L.F.G.

1. John Coplans, "An Interview with Don Judd," Artforum, vol. 9 (June 1971), p. 43.
2. Donald Judd, "Specific Objects," Arts Yearbook 8 (1965), p. 75.
3. See Dudley Del Balso, Roberta Smith, and Brydon Smith, "Catalogue Raisonné of Paintings and Objects, 1960–1974," in The National Gallery of Canada.
4. Rosalind Krauss, "Allusion and Illusion in Donald Judd," Artforum, vol. 4 (May 1966), p. 24.
5. For details on the fabrication and precise dating of the Walker work, see Dudley Del Balso, Roberta Smith and Brydon Smith, "Catalogue Raisonné of Paintings and Objects, 1960–1974," in The National Gallery of Canada.

Donald Judd

untitled   1968

American, b. 1928

stainless steel, Plexiglas

33 x 67⅞ x 48
(83.8 x 172.4 x 121.9)

Bernstein Bros., Long
Island City, New York

acquired from the Irving
Blum Gallery, Los Angeles,
1969 (Art Center
Acquisition Fund 69.9)

Three years after the Walker Progression of 1965, Judd was perceiving still more limitations in painting, and abolishing them in his objects: now the work has left the wall altogether to rest directly on the floor; it is an inert shape, conveying no implied directional movement, bearing no accommodating relationship to the height of the viewer, offering no advised orientation. As in the category-resistant work of Lee Bontecou, which Judd much admired and championed in his reviews in *Arts*, the structure of the work is identical with its form. His description of Bontecou's work could be adapted to apply to his own:

> The image, all the parts and the whole shape are coextensive. The parts are either part of the hole or part of the mound which forms the hole. The hole and the mound are only two things which, after all, are the same thing.[1]

Opening up his work more radically than Bontecou, Judd pierces his box literally and visually to allow as complete an understanding of its structure as an isometric drawing could give— every single surface of the work can be seen or measured or analyzed functionally. The only departure from its transparent self-declarativeness occurs when it is viewed end on, where it appears to be a solid steel block with an open rectangular core. From other angles, Judd's construction becomes, alternatively, a weightless Plexiglas box anchored at the ends by steel plates, a metal H, or a hollow rectangular pillar resting on its side, supported by projecting capitals and surrounded

by a Plexiglas screen. All of the readings are equally persuasive, which makes the experience of viewing the piece complex and paradoxical. Judd's description gives little hint of these difficulties: "The whole scheme has to do with defined ends and open body."[2]

The central lengthwise void on the inside is seen as a closed volume through the Plexiglas, which itself creates another void around the core. Judd liked Plexiglas because, he said, it "has a hard, single surface and the color is embedded in the material. In some cases it also gives access to the interior."[3] Although this Plexiglas permits the viewing of the exterior of the inner "box," it also constitutes four sides of the larger box, thus achieving the same status as the stainless steel despite its comparative flimsiness. The opacity of the steel denies complete viewing but it does permit a strong definition of planes and an expression of weight, which the more insubstantial Plexiglas cannot supply.

An earlier version, identical except in the amber color of its Plexiglas, was first exhibited in February 1968, and was preceded by at least one drawing. Judd had originally intended to make a box about 5 x 7 x 11 or 12 feet, of ½-inch aluminum sheets, but the problem of sagging forced him to reduce the dimensions and increase the thickness of the aluminum to ¾-inch.[4]

L.F.G.

1. Donald Judd, "Specific Objects," *Arts Yearbook 8* (1965), p. 80.
2. Quoted in John Coplans, "An Interview with Donald Judd," *Artforum*, vol. 9 (June 1971), p. 50.
3 Ibid., p. 45.
4. Untitled statement, *Art Now: New York*, vol. 1 (January 1969), n.p.

Donald Judd

untitled   1971

American, b. 1928

anodized aluminum

six cubes
48 x 48 x 48 (121.9 x
121.9 x 121.9) each,
placed at intervals of 12
(30.5)

acquired by exchange
from the artist, 1971
(gift of the T.B. Walker
Foundation 71.10)

Judd's systematic divestment of the conventional properties of painting and, incidentally, of sculpture, continued in works such as this row of boxes. The parts are not components of a single monolithic.object, but literally individuated. Identical, isolated from one another by the interruption of the floor and the space above and between them, all secondary aspects expunged, their sum equals the whole. Because he does not "compose" but rather organizes parts in his stacks and rows in a nonsuggestive, nonjudgmental, instantly assimilable and unpuzzling way, it does not matter to Judd if the sequence contains four or six, or as in the case of the prototype, eight stainless steel or galvanized iron elements. He explained that "there is the premise that the piece fits into the space."[1] The aspects of the parts do not need to be adjusted to suit the changed whole. Where the boxes stand in the neutrally organized row and whether a box has one or two boxes beside it varies from installation to installation. The qualities of the piece are, in Judd's word, coextensive. By placing the parts relatively close together in a standard foot-long measurement aligned in a basic single file, he assures that the work will be seen as a single whole in parts rather than as six individual pieces. The large scale, weight, and proximity of the units prohibit free passage to the viewer and thus bluntly declare the work's physical presence. Two sides of each box are recessed $3\frac{1}{2}$ inches, remaining perpendicular to the floor and parallel to each other. By means of these recessions, Judd gives a sense of the interior planes of the box, shows the thickness of the plates, and emphasizes the construction of each box—how it was assembled and how it could be dismantled.

> It occurred to me if you took one of the sides and pushed it in, it would open the top surface up. I was always interested in edges and flanges.... It defines what the boxes are made of by showing the thickness of the sheet metal, and thus becomes less arbitrary, more rigorous.... So it shows, or makes, or emphasizes, the edge more clearly.[2]

The anodic film of the surfaces makes color even more integral than it was in the red Progression.[3] Each object was assembled from plates already colored on all sides, as examination of the areas revealed by the recessed planes confirms, and thus is not a single constructed form whose exterior is painted blue.

L.F.G.

1. Quoted in John Coplans, "An Interview with Don Judd," *Artforum*, vol. 9 (June 1971), p. 45.
2. Ibid., p. 50.
3. Anodizing, the process by which the blue of this piece was achieved, involves coating electrolytically with an oxide. For information on the fabrication and dating of the work, see Dudley Del Balso, Roberta Smith, and Brydon Smith, "Catalogue Raisonné of Paintings and Objects, 1960–1974," in The National Gallery of Canada, Ottawa, *Donald Judd*, exh. cat., 1975, pp. 230, 231, and Ronald Alley, *The Tate Gallery's Collection of Modern Art, Other than Works by British Artists* (London: The Tate Gallery, 1981), p. 378.

Anish Kapoor

Mother as a Mountain   1985

Indian, b. 1954

gesso, powder pigment on wood

55 x 91½ x 40½ (139.7 x 232.4 102.9)

acquired from the Lisson Gallery London Ltd., 1987 (T.B. Walker Acquisition Fund 87.117)

Born in Bombay, Anish Kapoor moved to London at the age of seventeen to attend art school. He first enrolled at the Hornsey College of Art and later graduated from the Chelsea School of Art. Although his work is often associated with that of British sculptors such as David Nash, Tony Cragg, and Bill Woodrow, Kapoor's evocative biomorphic and architectonic forms and saturated primary colors distinctly reflect the influences of his Indian roots.

Returning to India for the first time in 1979, Kapoor was fascinated by the mounds of colored, natural powders he saw ritually placed outside temples as well as by the symbolic forms of Indian religious and popular sculpture. Upon his return to England he created a series of installations—individually and collectively entitled 1,000 Names—each of which contained a number of elements that have since recurred in his work. In these works, three-dimensional abstract forms were laid out carefully on the gallery floor, dusted with bright powdered pigments, and juxtaposed with drawings executed directly on the wall.

Since the early 1980s, Kapoor has been involved in creating larger-scale, individual sculptures, of which *Mother as a Mountain* is an example. As its title suggests, this work invites a range of geological and biological readings. Rising up dramatically from the gallery floor, it suggests an erupting volcano; however, with its slitlike opening it also resembles a womb or an overgrown cocoon. The piece thus becomes a metaphor for birth and nurturing, growth, endurance, and death.

Its rich red folds form a metaphorical cloak that enshrouds a dark, mysterious chasm, creating a highly sensual and alluring piece. The viewer is at once drawn to the dark core and overwhemed by the brilliant red pigment that surrounds it—symbolic, in Kapoor's mind, of earth and blood. Counteracting this tactile attraction is the apparent fragility of the pigmented surface and the narrowness of the opening, which prevents entry and even discourages close investigation.

Appearing to be a carefully sculpted mass of powdered pigment, the sculpture looks as if it might collapse at the slightest touch. However, despite its apparent preciousness, *Mother as a Mountain* is composed of common, sturdy materials. The basic form is carved wood coated with gesso, to which a layer of powdered red pigment

has been affixed. A dusting of loose pigment around the base of the sculpture creates a nimbus of color that obscures the boundary between object and environment. The blurred contours of the piece operate in concert with the rich, light-absorbing character of the pigment and the obscurity of the seemingly bottomless cavity, visually dematerializing the sculpture. This work seems to exist in an almost metaphysical realm, hovering between spirit and matter.

C.B.

273

Ellsworth Kelly

Red Green Blue 1964

American, b. 1923

oil on canvas

90 x 66 (228.6 x 167.6)

on reverse, upper edge of canvas, visible from reverse, *332 EK 1964*; upper right horizontal stretcher member, *Kelly 1964*; upper left horizontal stretcher member, *#332 90 x 66"*

acquired from the Ferus Gallery, Los Angeles, 1966 (gift of the T.B. Walker Foundation 66.9)

Kelly first conceived this work in a pencil drawing of 1955[1] in which he divided a vertical rectangle with three horizontal lines at different points. He then drew a diagonal from the lower left corner to the upper right of each new rectangle thereby defined. Using these rectangles as reference points, he drew two pairs of right-angled lines that created three abutting shapes (one rectangle at the lower left and two L shapes around it), a configuration that was to become the basis for colored paper collages of 1962 and oil sketches for two square canvases of 1963, and for *Red Green Blue* of the following fall. This process reflects Kelly's intention "to divide the space and not to arrange the forms. I am not interested in composing."[2] The development of this work represents an additive process; Kelly does not see the color areas as fragments of concentric squares in the manner of Albers or Stella, but rather as independent rectangular and L-shaped areas.[3]

Given the rigor of images such as *Red Green Blue*, Kelly's working method is surprisingly flexible: "When enlarging [the studies] into paintings, I solve the size, color, etc., changing as I go along."[4] The proportions of one of the three colored rectangles in *Red Green Blue* are different from those of the other two; a diagonal from lower left to upper right hits the upper right corner of the red, but not that of the green.

The process of shifting and realigning coordinate points and internal scale in these works is extended to the adjustment of color. According to Kelly, the red of the rectangular "kernel," as a primary color, has a kinship with the blue, while the more "subtle" secondary green (being derived from blue mixed with the third and "palest" primary, yellow) enters into a dialogue with the blue. Through this relationship, the blue and green make the red "stand out."[5] The reciprocal influence of Kelly's colors produces a curious effect. The vivid red collides with its complementary, green, which in turn abuts vibrantly with its neighbor on the color chart, blue. An illusionary after-image band of yellow hovers along the edge of the boundaries between red and green, and more subtly between green and blue, paradoxically rendering these "hard" edges optically dematerialized. The effect was not deliberate—Kelly's intention was to "make the painting with rich colors, not vibrating colors"—but it was inevitable, as Albers understood.[6]

Kelly began *Red Green Blue* in New York in September 1964 and finished it in October at Miró's graphic studio at Levallois outside Paris.[7] He made five related oil sketches that same year in different sizes and formats and with different blues, including one on newspaper.

L.F.G.

1. "Since 1951 I had done horizontal and vertical groupings of panels. This drawing (page 31 of Kelly's Sketchbook #26) is a loose example of a combination of the two or 'angle panels;'" letter to the author, postmarked 2 October 1986.
2. Quoted in John Coplans, *Ellsworth Kelly* (New York: Harry N. Abrams, 1971), p. 25.
3. Letter to the author, 23 June 1986.
4. Ibid.
5. Ibid.
6. Josef Albers, *Interaction of Color* (New Haven and London: Yale University Press, 1963), p. 65. For Kelly's remarks, see his letter to the author, 23 June 1986. Kelly claims not to have seen *Interaction of Color* and considers Albers's didacticism antithetical to his own concerns. He relates an incident in which Albers asked what color theory he had applied, to which he replied that he used none; conversation with the author, 12 June 1986.
7. Kelly, in WAC questionnaire, 2 April 1974, p. 2.

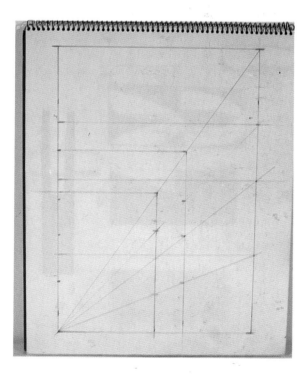

Ellsworth Kelly
Sketchbook #26, page 31
1955
Collection the artist

Ellsworth Kelly

Green Rocker 1968

American, b. 1923

painted aluminum

**20¼ x 97¾ x 112
(51.4 x 248.3 x 284.5)**

**Lippincott, Inc., North
Haven, Connecticut**

**acquired from the Irving
Blum Gallery, Los Angeles,
1969 (purchased with a
matching grant from
Museum Purchase Plan,
National Endowment for
the Arts and Art Center
Acquisition Fund 69.4)**

This sculpture is the third in a series of seven initiated in 1959. Kelly described the conception of the first version:

> I happened to be having breakfast with Agnes Martin in her studio. I made a model for the piece called Pony from the top of a coffee container we used at breakfast. I folded it and cut it and it rocked. Agnes said you ought to do that.... I did it almost without thinking, almost as if I didn't decide; as if they just happened.[1]

The folding and cutting led naturally to a drawing and collage Kelly made while ruminating on a cover design for an exhibition of his work at Arthur Tooth & Sons Ltd., London, in 1962, which later served as studies for *Green Rocker*.[2] Cutting an arc through a piece of folded paper produced a shape, when the paper was unfolded, which was not a smooth oval, but which had a slight point at the crease on one of the long sides.

Although the first two works in the Rocker series were two-colored, one color on the top, another on the underside, Kelly decided on a monochrome scheme for *Green Rocker*. He was also interested in the work in its unpainted state, and photographed it extensively that way. However, because unfinished aluminum did not age well at that time,[3] in the end he painted it. Although the forms have an inferred rocking capacity, Kelly is not in fact interested in the notion of the works moving. As he points out, because the Walker version is so close to the ground, it would in any case produce only a "silly, funny little motion." He is no longer using the word "rocker" in recent related sculptures, and the larger of these must be bolted down for safety reasons.[4]

Green Rocker does not have the same self-revealing quality as the earlier Rockers because it is flattened out to a greater degree. Yet this flattening permits an intimate relationship between the work and its green reflection on the white terrazzo gallery floor. The reflection intrigued Kelly, perhaps carrying with it a memory of Paris bridge arches and their reflections.[5] The green color, bisected flat oval form, and lowered positioning also suggest a connection with Kelly's water lily drawings,[6] whose linear contours bounding unmarked planes translate literally into the sculpture. These in turn may be at least in part inspired by his expressed admiration for Monet.[7] Kelly had visited Giverny in 1952 while living in France, and painted a green monochrome as a tribute to the French Impressionist.[8] Kelly is also indebted to Calder, whose planar stabiles support their own weight and whose mobiles are frequently related to plant forms.

Having completed a small oil on cardboard model in 1967, Kelly had *Green Rocker* fabricated according to his specifications, submitting a template to Lippincott and overseeing all stages of fabrication and finishing.[9]

L.F.G.

1. Quoted in Henry Geldzahler, "Interview with Ellsworth Kelly," in Washington Gallery of Modern Art, Washington, D.C., *Paintings, Sculpture, and Drawings by Ellsworth Kelly*, exh. cat., 1964, n.p.
2. The collage, EK no. 62.93, is reproduced by Patterson Sims and Emily Rauh Pulitzer, in Whitney Museum of American Art, New York, *Ellsworth Kelly*, exh. cat., 1982, p. 97.
3. Conversation with the author, 12 June 1986. Kelly has been able to achieve the successful translation of the rocker form into weathering and stainless steel in works of the 1980s.
4. Letter to the author, 23 June 1986.
5. For example, Kelly's *White Plaque: Bridge Arch and Reflection* of the early 1950s. For Kelly's interest in *Green Rocker*'s reflection, see Martin Friedman, in Walker Art Center, *14 Sculptors: The Industrial Edge*, exh. cat., 1969, p. 23.
6. Sims and Pulitzer, p. 97.
7. Ellsworth Kelly, "Notes from 1969," in Stedelijk Museum, Amsterdam, *Ellsworth Kelly: Paintings and Sculptures 1963–1979*, exh. cat., 1979, p. 32.
8. Barbara Rose, "The Focussed Vision," in ibid., p. 18.
9. Kelly's catalogue number for *Green Rocker* is S418; details regarding its manufacture and finishing were provided by the artist in a questionnaire of 2 April 1974.

Ellsworth Kelly

Double Curve   1988

American, b. 1923

bronze

**two elements
216 x 40 x 4½
(548.6 x 101.6 x 11.4)
each**

**commissioned for the
Minneapolis Sculpture
Garden, 1988 (gift of Judy
and Kenneth Dayton
88.380)**

Although he is perhaps better known for his austere Minimalist paintings, Ellsworth Kelly has also produced a large body of sculpture throughout his career; his works in both media often address similar issues of form and space. Like his paintings, Kelly's sculptures employ abstract, geometric shapes whose carefully constructed relationships activate the surrounding spaces. The forms of his paintings and his sculptures are distillations of both natural and man-made objects; they recall the evocative abstractions of earlier modernists, from Constantin Brancusi and Hans Arp to Alexander Calder.

In *Double Curve*, an imposing pair of eighteen-foot-high bronze totems installed in the Minneapolis Sculpture Garden, Kelly has employed the flattened, rigidly frontal forms common to much of his production. He has explored this imagery in his Minimalist paintings and drawings since the mid-1950s; among these are a series of Brooklyn Bridge canvases of the 1960s and the 1959 painting *Rebound*. A sculptural antecedent of the Walker's piece is *Curve XV* (1975), which is part of an extensive series of freestanding single curves begun in 1974.[1]

The wide arcs of *Double Curve* are insistently two-dimensional, and, like any silhouetted image, they depend on their surroundings for much of their impact. Like all outdoor sculptures, Kelly's pair of totems are transformed under changing conditions of light. In the Garden, under the morning sun, their deep brown surfaces glow; by late afternoon, they become almost black silhouettes.

Despite its resolutely formalistic character, *Double Curve* at times seems to have figurative associations. Unlike most Minimalist sculpture in which irreducible geometry dominates, Kelly's pair of arc-shaped sentinels are benign, symmetrical presences serenely dominating their surroundings. There is a strong gestural quality to this work; the matched arcs seem to bend gently toward each other in graceful balletic motion. Studies for the piece show that Kelly experimented with varying the distance between the two elements, finally settling on a configuration that both maintains their separateness and assures that they are perceived as elements of a whole.[2]

M.G.

1. The artist in conversation with the author, 13 November 1989.
2. Kelly originally thought that the two elements of *Double Curve* might touch, in a similar fashion to those in a collage he produced in 1958 for the French journal *Derrière le Miroir*. He says this collage figured importantly in the development of *Double Curve*. The artist in conversation with the author, 13 November 1989.

279

Mel Kendrick

Large Walnut with Teeth   1985

American, b. 1949

walnut

**54⁷⁄₁₆ x 20 x 20
(138.3 x 50.8 x 50.8)**

**underneath top of stool,
*Mel Kendrick 1985***

**Margo Leavin Gallery, Los
Angeles, 1985; acquired
from the Margo Leavin
Gallery, 1986 (Butler
Family Fund and T.B.
Walker Acquisition Fund
86.7)**

As a graduate student at Hunter College in the early 1970s, Mel Kendrick studied with Robert Morris and Tony Smith, leading practitioners of Minimal Art. Although initially influenced by Minimalist doctrine, he later rejected the severe, reductivist format in favor of more expressive sculpture. The angular, animated forms of Kendrick's sculpture are more closely linked to such early twentieth-century styles as Cubism and Futurism as well as to African sculpture.[1]

Cut and reassembled from a block of wood formed by laminating three pieces of walnut, *Large Walnut with Teeth* twists and turns as it unfolds along a double spiral. Jagged edges abut smooth, rounded forms. Since each component of the sculpture comes from the same block, one shape often echoes another. Sawed-out voids interacting with solid forms generate a lively play between positive and negative space, between inside and outside, and give the work an emphatic three-dimensional presence.

The surfaces of *Large Walnut with Teeth* have been left raw. Saw marks, like drawn lines incised into the wood, animate the surface, as do the lines of dark glue which have seeped through the cracks of the laminated wood. These marks, along with actual pencil lines, record the artist's choices. Kendrick has compared his work to that of the painter Cy Twombly, whose canvases record the continous process of drawing and erasing.[2]

The base, also made of walnut and resembling a simple stool, is an integral part of the sculpture. Whether to use a base or not has been an important issue in twentieth-century sculpture, and many artists have abandoned it altogether. Kendrick, however, integrates it into his work in order to bring the work to eye level, directly engaging the viewer, and to define the sculpture as an object.[3]

D.H.

1. Affinities have been noted between Kendrick's sculpture and that of Picasso, Boccioni, and Brancusi; see Wade Saunders, "Mel Kendrick at John Weber," *Art in America*, vol. 71 (Summer 1983), p. 156; Kate Linker, "Mel Kendrick," *Artforum*, vol. 22 (September 1983), p. 78. Kendrick has cited Picasso and Oceanic art as important influences; see Betsy Siersma, "Conversation with Mel Kendrick," in University Gallery, University of Massachusetts, Amherst, *Mel Kendrick Recent Sculpture*, exh. cat., 1986, p. 18. In a conversation with the author on 16 July 1986, the artist mentioned Picasso and Robert Mangold as major influences.
2. Conversation with the author, 16 July 1986.
3. Siersma, p. 22.

Anselm Kiefer

Emanation   1984–1986

German, b. 1945

oil, acrylic, wallpaper paste, lead on canvas

161⅛ x 110¼ (409.3 x 280)

acquired from Heiner Bastian by exchange (gift of Judy and Kenneth Dayton 90.22)

Because Anselm Kiefer believes art should "ask the important questions,"[1] his paintings confront some of the eternal enigmas of human existence: life, love, God, death, and redemption. In his grandly scaled, mixed-media canvases he alludes to mythological and historical sources, including alchemy, Nordic myth, the Bible, Wagnerian opera, folk music, and modern German history. By suggesting correspondences among them, Kiefer encourages us to look anew at ancient symbols and ponder their relevance to contemporary problems.

Emanation is typical of Kiefer's synthesizing approach to subject matter. On one level—in its capacity as a monumental, transcendent landscape—*Emanation* follows in the tradition of the works of the German Romantic painter Caspar David Friedrich (1774–1840), for whom untrammeled nature was the purest manifestation of the divine and the means by which man could achieve union with God. In Kiefer's hands, however, Friedrich's glorious vistas become ravaged battlefields bearing the wounds left by man's ceaseless quest for power.

Emanation can also be linked to several textual sources associated with Judaism.[2] Most important among these is the Old Testament Book of Exodus, which relates how God helped guide the Israelites through the wilderness by appearing to them "by day in a pillar of cloud ... and by night in a pillar of fire."[3] In *Emanation* this divine manifestation is represented by an expanse of molten lead that descends from the scorched heavens to a turbulent sea, uniting the separate realms of God and man.

In addition to the Bible, the painting has been linked to the collection of mystical Jewish texts now known as the Cabala, which encompasses such concepts as creation through emanation and the pouring forth of divine attributes from heaven to earth.[4] By making lead the central element in this work, Kiefer also alludes to the esoteric science of alchemy, whose practitioners sought a metaphorical spiritual transformation through the conversion of a base metal (lead) into a precious substance (gold).

Kiefer's paintings are celebrated for their brutally beautiful surfaces, which are formed of unorthodox materials, such as straw and lead, as well as dense layers of paint. The surface of *Emanation* is built up with wallpaper paste and linseed oil mixed with pigment, which Kiefer then scraped, peeled, hacked, and burned.[5] Flattened lumps of sand and glue make up the round "blisters" in the sky, and two small photographs depicting flames are affixed to the bottom of the canvas. Into the center of this apocalyptic storm flows the molten-lead pillar, which functions not only as a representation of the divine but also as a conduit for communion between God and man.

J.R.

1. Quoted by John Hallmark Neff, in Marian Goodman Gallery, New York, *Anselm Kiefer: Bruch und Einung*, exh. cat., 1987, p. 8.
2. Kiefer has named the Bible, the Cabala, and the Babylonian Talmud as textual sources for *Emanation*. Correspondence with Martin Friedman, September 1989.
3. Exod. 13:21
4. Gudrun Inboden has pointed out that this work is related to the Cabalistic writings of Isaac Luria, in particular his notion of the *sefiroth*. See her essay in Galerie Paul Maenz, Cologne, *Anselm Kiefer*, exh. cat., 1986, pp. 11–16.
5. Correspondence with Martin Friedman, September 1989.

Anselm Kiefer

Die Ordnung der Engel (The Hierarchy of Angels)   1985–1987

German, b. 1945

oil, emulsion, shellac,
acrylic, chalk, lead
propeller, curdled lead,
steel cables, band-iron,
cardboard on canvas

134 x 220½ x 21½
(340.4 x 560.1 x 54.6)

acquired from the artist,
1987 (gift of Penny and
Mike Winton, 87.11)

Anselm Kiefer has emerged as the preeminent German painter of the postwar era. His brooding landscapes and interiors reflect a modern artist's attempt to come to grips with history.

Kiefer studied in the early 1970s with the German artist Joseph Beuys and first gained prominence with a series of paintings that dealt with German cultural history as seen in the wake of the catastrophic excesses of Nazi ideology. Many of these featured barren, ravaged landscapes viewed from a bird's-eye perspective and inscribed with names from German history and legend. Frequent biblical references added to the epic, even apocalyptic, tone of his work. *Die Ordnung der Engel* continues this tendency to combine religious and historical themes in an effort to place the dilemmas of the present in a larger context.

Die Ordnung der Engel refers to a sixth-century text on the hierarchy of heavenly beings erroneously attributed to a first-century Athenian, Dionysius the Areopagite.[1] According to the text, the heavenly host was organized into nine orders—angels, archangels, seraphim, cherubim, virtues, powers, principalities, dominions, and thrones. In Kiefer's painting these nine orders are represented by lead "stones" that hang on steel cables from the top of the painting. Above them is suspended a large lead propeller, symbolic of the proposed spiral structure of the heavens. The beach scene in the background makes reference to the eternal rhythm of the universe.

Conflict and paradox lie at the heart of much of Kiefer's work, and this painting is no exception. The weight of the lead propeller and stones is at odds with the celestial elements they supposedly represent. The hanging objects also inevitably suggest the flight of a bomber over the landscape, an allusion to Germany's fate during the war.

As Kiefer points out, Dionysius's text was written at a time of great theological conflict. In this painting the artist makes a connection between the yearnings for a clearly ordered universe and the brutality men are willing to employ to bring about their own vision of an earthly order.[2]

Die Ordnung der Engel is one of several Kiefer paintings dealing with the theme of the celestial hierarchy. It is also one of three paintings featuring the propeller motif, the others being at the Fundació Caixa de Pensions, Barcelona—also entitled *Die Ordnung der Engel*—and at the Art Gallery of New South Wales, Sydney, where the propeller has three blades rather than two.

P.B.

1. At the top of the canvas the artist has written "Dionysius Aeropagita," undoubtedly misspelling the Athenian name as a play on the prefix "aer" referring to airplane and to the propeller that is the central object in the painting. See Charles Werner Haxthausen, "Kiefer in America: Reflections on a Retrospective," *Kunstchronik*, vol. 42 (January 1989), p. 9.
2. Anselm Kiefer, conversation with Martin Friedman, 7 January 1987.

Edward Kienholz and Nancy Reddin Kienholz

Portrait of a Mother with Past Affixed Also   1980–1981

American, b. 1927 and 1943, respectively

mixed media environment

99⅞ x 94⅝ x 81 (253.7 x 240.4 x 205.7)

acquired from the L.A. Louver Gallery, Venice, California, 1985 (Walker Special Purchase Fund 85.12)

The viewer approaches this work to encounter a closed door, marked with a K, identifying it as the Kienholz residence, lit by a porch light. Opening the door, the interior overhead light comes on, illuminating the room inside behind a Plexiglas threshold dripping with Ed Kienholz's signature fiberglass resin. According to the Kienholzes' statement of purpose,[1] the viewer should scan the interior from left to right to parallel the artists' conception of movement from past to future. The kitchen is the past, a re-creation of that room in the farmhouse on the ranch where Ed Kienholz was born and raised outside Fairfield, Washington. A view of the ranch is frozen in time and space "through the window" in the form of a photograph[2] above the sink; the sink is a wooden washbasin modeled on the original Kienholz helped his father build when the farmhouse was being expanded.[3] The exterior and center of the work, signifying the present, represent the house where Kienholz's mother, a former Sunday school teacher, now lives, which she and his father built in the hamlet of Hope, Idaho, in the Bitterroot foothills of the Rockies. In a generationally removed reenactment, Edward and Nancy Kienholz made this piece together in Hope, where they live part of each year.[4]

The figure is a "portrait" of Kienholz's mother in 1980–1981, her photographed head framed and mounted on a body cast from life, made of plaster bandages covered with wallboard mud, then oil paint and finally fiberglass resin. The hand-tinted photograph she holds is of herself as a child. Nancy Reddin Kienholz has explained that the doll arms "represent the young wanting to grow up and the old looking back at herself when young." Again, the appointments of the room detail the character of the home: plastic flowers in a star-shaped vase rest on a table set for two with flowered plates, cups, and tablecloth. On the mirrored wall is a poem called "Resignation" by Kienholz's mother typed on a flowered note sheet. A display case in the corner carries sentimental, patriotic, homiletic and Christian knickknacks; on its exterior, the Lord's Prayer hangs from an American eagle. A swan bowl, a kerosene lamp decorated with a porcelain couple, and family snapshots from the recent and distant past rest on a ledge.[5] An empty plastic wastebasket sits by a television whose stand holds a 23 November 1981 issue of *U.S. News & World Report* with a cover story on "U.S. Defense Policy," and a December 1981 issue of *Our Daily Bread*.

An oval frame on the rightmost wall, which in the temporal scheme of the piece occupies the place of the future, holds a deeply inset photograph of Kienholz's aged father in a wheelchair after his stroke.[6] Beneath is a photograph of the young Lawrence Kienholz, beside a crucifix and imitation flowers. The photographs allude to past moments in the life of a man who in death, according to the Kienholzes, resides in the future, "waiting for his wife to join him." The three pairs of portrait and landscape photographs memorializing moments in the parents' lives from the teens to the 1980s reflect the sequential nature of the piece as a whole—the mother regards the past, the present is recorded (however quickly receding), and the father occupies the future. Intertwined with the chronological intricacies, which will become compounded with the further passage of time, is the absent consciousness of the father and mother, available to the viewer through the objects they made or acquired and through the projected vision of the artists. The piece holds so much personal meaning for Kienholz that he evidently was reluctant to exhibit it at first.[7]

Through an ingenious management of space and manipulation of the proportions of the elements within it, an extraordinary number of full-scale objects have been introduced into the interior, illusionistically expanding a space measuring only about 4 x 8 feet square. The 1100-pound tableau folds up like an outsize crèche, a form Kienholz knew from his childhood,[8] its galvanized metal exterior forming a protective shell that serves as a packing crate.

L.F.G.

1. Information on the piece and its motivations are largely derived from a WAC questionnaire prepared by Nancy Reddin Kienholz, 1 October 1985, from which all unattributed quotations are taken.
2. This photograph was taken by Giancarlo Bocchi in 1974; letter to the author from the artists, 14 October 1986.
3. Lawrence Weschler, "The Subversive Art of Ed Kienholz," *Artforum*, vol. 83 (September, 1984) p. 102.
4. The two artists have officially collaborated since 1981 and sign every work jointly.
5. Although slightly rearranged by the artists, the family photographs were already in the flip holder when they got it from Ed's mother. The wedding picture is of Ed's sister Shirley and her husband Dick White; letter to the author, 14 October 1986.
6. Weschler, p. 102.
7. Ibid.
8. He made crèches and religious dioramas with his mother; Ibid., p. 105.

Georg Kolbe

Junge Frau (Young Woman)   1926

German, 1877–1947

bronze

50⅝ x 14⅝ x 12¼
(128.6 x 37.2 x 31.1)

top rear of base,
monogram; stamped rear
side of base, *H. NOACK,
BERLIN*

acquired from Fine Arts
Associates, New York,
1958 (gift of the T.B.
Walker Foundation 58.35)

During the mid-1920s Georg Kolbe gained widespread popularity in Europe for his rhythmic, lyrical sculptures of female dancers and lithe, supple nudes, of which *Junge Frau* is a masterly example. In these works, Kolbe organizes the proportions of the human figure in order to describe an ideal of balance and harmony; this approach reflects the influence of late nineteenth- and early twentieth-century French academic classicism.

In the Walker's sculpture, the model stands frontally in an attitude of hesitant withdrawal. A solitary and vulnerable figure, Kolbe's young woman is a particularly romanticized vision—a quiet, long-limbed, coltish girl captured on the threshold of womanhood. While such elements as the slightly tilted and turned head, the pivoting arm and open left palm, and the barely bent knees suggest that the model is poised to move, the figure's stance is curiously rigid. It is probably this quality that makes the figure, for all the specificity of its rendering, seem depersonalized and even generic.

The work is a subtle synthesis of naturalistic depiction and classicism. Kolbe departs from tradition, however, in his emphasis on the material, seen in the sculpture's richly worked surface. He allows the bronze cast to show the effects of the modeling process, and the final sculpture retains the liveliness and spontaneity of the original plaster. The work's rough texture creates an evocative play of light and shadow that dapples and softens the forms of the figure. This texture also recalls the impressionistic freshness and vigor that distinguished the broken, variegated surfaces of sculptures by Rodin, who was an early influence on Kolbe. The young artist paid homage to the master by visiting his Paris studio in 1909.

A.B.

291

Jannis Kounellis

Untitled 1982

Italian, b. Greece, 1936

Feather River travertine, cast plaster, steel

86½ x 59 x 16 (219.7 x 149.9 x 40.6)

acquired from the Donald Young Gallery, Chicago, 1987 (Walker Special Purchase Fund 87.28)

Of central significance to Kounellis's art is his belief that postwar Europe is fundamentally a fragmented culture that needs to regain a cohesive social outlook. "Since the war," he has said, "our culture has operated through contradictions, we have only contradictions."[1] In his art, therefore, Kounellis works with materials from his immediate environment to deal with themes of history, fragmentation, paradox, renewal, and revision. The 1980s have seen him striving to integrate these multiple themes in individual works.

Untitled was originally installed in a doorway of the Staatliche Kunsthalle in Baden-Baden, West Germany; it was reconstructed in 1986 using its current steel frames and travertine rock from California. The sculpture brings together a pair of recurrent motifs in Kounellis's work: the walled doorway and the use of fragmented plaster casts of classical sculpture.

The blocked passage first became a component in Kounellis's art in 1969, when he used rough stones to fill in a doorway as part of a museum installation. His blockading of doorways and windows, means of access both physical and visual, has been interpreted as a comment on obstructed vision and, since these blocked passages often occur in galleries and museums, as a critique of the art world. This practice in his work has also been likened to the Mediterranean habit of sealing off abandoned buildings with masonry to preserve the interiors from the elements.

Kounellis himself has emphasized his intention to identify the doors, windows, and rocks as forms of human-related measurement. The dimensions of the openings relate to the human figure; the size of the rocks acts as a measure of what one person can grasp and lift, a size closely related to that of the human head. The stones, representing ancient building techniques and measures, are brought into conjunction with a modern structure.[2] In its current manifestation, *Untitled* would seem to support this interpretation more than the theme of blocking something in or out.

Fragments of plaster casts, generally heads, have recurred in Kounellis's work since the early 1970s. These remnants clearly evoke a sense of division and disunity. Since they involve the head in particular, they seem to allude to a lack of conceptual or perceptual wholeness, of understanding suppressed, denied, or missing. Kounellis

also employs the casts to evoke history, particularly as a resource from which to draw in creating new orders. In the Mediterranean area, for example, fragments from cultures have frequently been stripped from their original context and used to build new structures. The fragments thus are double-edged in their implications, at once connoting loss, the debasement of a past golden age, and renewal, the reuse of the past in the creation of the new.

P.B.

1. Quoted in Thomas McEvilley, "Mute Prophecies: The Art of Jannis Kounellis," Museum of Contemporary Art, Chicago, *Jannis Kounellis*, exh. cat., 1986, p. 173.
2. Ibid., p. 87.

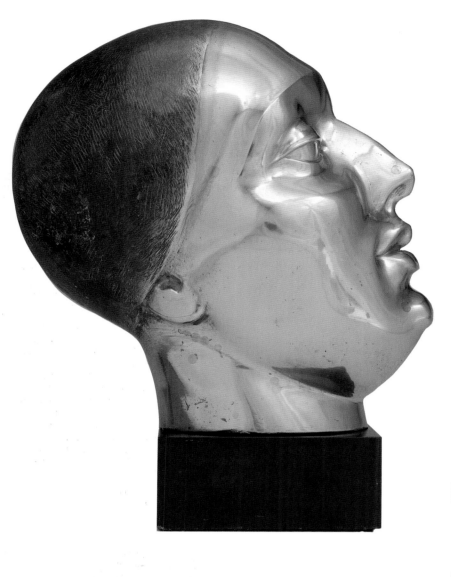

Gaston Lachaise

Head circa 1928

American, b. France,
1882–1935

**bronze, formerly nickel-
plated**

**13¾ x 9⁹⁄₁₆ x 13¾
(34.9 x 23 x 34.9)**

**acquired from the artist
by Morris R. Werner, New
York, immediately upon
completion; acquired from
Werner, 1955 (gift of the
T.B. Walker Foundation
55.5)**

In 1928 Lachaise wrote: "At twenty, in Paris, I met a young American person who immediately became the primary inspiration which awakened my vision and the leading influence that has directed my forces. Throughout my career, as an artist, I refer to this person by the word 'Woman.'"[1] This person was the Canadian-American Isabel Dutaud Nagle (d. 1957), whom he married in 1917. If one examines photographs of his wife, it is clear that the features of the *Head* are hers: the thin expressive eyebrows over heavily lidded eyes; the slightly curved nose with long, flaring nostrils; the pronounced cleft between nose and upper lip; the thick lower lip, squarish jaw, and rounded, double chin. Not only does the *Head* correspond physically with Isabel's features, but it also captures her personality as described by those who knew her: "She carried herself proudly, head high, chin slightly raised, exuding a sense of poised self-esteem."[2]

The face appears again and again atop Lachaise's obsessive depictions of the tiny-footed, big-bosomed standing nudes for which he is best known. A particular physiognomy is transformed through repetition into a generalized, iconic description of Lachaise's notion of "Woman." According to Morris R. Werner, the previous owner of this piece, Lachaise told him once that

> he had thought of it originally as the head for a large figure about seven feet or more high which would be with arms outstretched and body bent backwards. As Lachaise expressed his conception to me in his own words: "A sort of crucifixion without the cross."[3]

In the second and only other cast of the *Head*, which belongs to the Whitney Museum of American Art, New York, and is signed and dated 1928, the flesh areas are plated in nickel and highly polished; the bronze is exposed at eyes and lips, producing a polychromatic effect. The Walker cast originally was plated in a similar but not identical way, though the nickel now appears only as a narrow band along the hairline.[4] Though coloristic distinctions between surfaces have thereby been diminished, the textural variation from the dark, feathery helmet of hair to the lustrous, smooth skin of the face has been preserved.

L.F.G.

1. "A Comment on My Sculpture," *Creative Art*, vol. 3 (August 1928), p. xxiii.
2. Gerald Nordland, *Gaston Lachaise: The Man and His Work* (New York: George Braziller, 1974), p. 9.
3. Typed, undated and unpaginated memorandum to Mrs. Robert J. Morgan. Werner first saw the original plaster in Lachaise's studio on 8th Street in New York about 1926.
4. Letter from Morris R. Werner to Walker Art Center, 27 December 1954; in this letter he also wrote that Lachaise had lamented the high degree of polish on the Whitney Museum cast. In Werner's memorandum to Mrs. Morgan, he noted that Lachaise preferred the "less dramatic quality of my copy," although he "did like the nickel patina." According to Robert Schoelkopf (letter to the author, 11 December 1984), the plating would probably have been accomplished at a jewelry factory, where large acid baths for silver and nickel plating could be used to produce a surface a few thousandths of an inch thick. The process of plating involves the application of grease or another non-porous substance to areas which are to remain patinated bronze, leaving the rest of the surface open to the metal skin applied through electrolysis.

Isabel Lachaise
n.d.
Collection The Lachaise
Foundation, Boston,
Massachusetts

John Latham

Painting Is an Open Book 1961

British, b. Mozambique,
1921

**books, plaster, wire, wire
mesh, wood, ceramic tile,
glass, burlap mounted on
board**

**63 x 36 x 7½
(160 x 91.4 x 19)**

**acquired from the Lisson
Gallery London Ltd., 1987
(T.B. Walker Acquisition
Fund 87.118)**

Painting Is an Open Book is one of a number of book constructions produced from the late 1950s through the late 1960s by the British artist John Latham. It typifies his investigation into the relationship between language and representation, an investigation that began in the mid-1950s and continues in his current work.

In this as in other such pieces, Latham utilizes assemblage and collage "to assault an object emblematic of traditional cultural values."[1] Twenty-eight books of varying description are torn, cut, burned, and affixed with plaster along with sundry other materials—a fragment of ceramic glass, wire mesh, and strands of cut wire—to a burlap-covered wooden panel. Some of the books are attached face-in to the burlap backing, their contents never to be revealed; others seem to have burst from wire bindings and are splayed open to the viewer's gaze, though so defaced as to be unreadable.

Unlike American Pop Art, in which various cultural icons were lifted from their contexts and re-formed by means of techniques borrowed from advertising graphics and Hollywood, Latham's book pieces are accumulations across a surface rather than iconic images. Indeed, they have ties to art made in the late 1950s and early 1960s by the so-called New Realists, Europeans such as the Swiss Daniel Spoerri and the Frenchman Arman, who juxtaposed a vast array of everyday objects in assemblages in order to question traditional compositional methods and cultural assumptions. The books Latham uses—volumes of all sizes, shapes, and classifications—are, once incorporated into his constructions, denied their initial function or meaning. Though at the most basic level they refer to communication, their ability to communicate is disrupted by the artist's manipulation of their contents. Latham, in effect, wipes the slate clean in order to suggest possibilities for seeing the book in new ways. According to one critic, these assemblages "are the residue of former communication, an inert heap which Latham revitalizes by discovering a potential for non-verbal meaning within it."[2]

Latham's way of jarring our fixed perceptions about familiar objects has much in common with the approach of American artists such as Robert Rauschenberg and Jasper Johns, whose assemblages of the 1950s—consisting of actual objects incorporated within paintings on canvas—bridged the conceptual gap between Abstract Expressionism and Pop Art. For Latham, in works such as *Painting Is an Open Book*, as for the Americans, the canvas is a runway for the collision of events.

C.B.

1. Edward Lucie-Smith, *Art Now: From Abstract Expressionism to Superrealism* (New York: Morrow, 1977), p. 173.
2. Lawrence Alloway in Kasmin Ltd., London, *John Latham,* exh. cat., 1963, n.p.

Jack Levine

The Neighborhood Physician   1939

American, b. 1915

oil on panel

47⅞ x 29¾
(121.6 x 75.6)

lower right, *Levine*

acquired from The
Downtown Gallery, New
York, 1943 (gift of the
T.B. Walker Foundation,
Gilbert M. Walker Fund
43.11)

Like many American artists who emerged during the Depression era, Jack Levine began his career under the sponsorship of the federally funded Works Progress Administration program, which not only supported the creation of many publicly oriented works of art but also encouraged studio activities such as easel painting. Levine's association with the Massachusetts branch of the WPA began in 1935, when he was only twenty. From the outset his paintings bore the stamp of urban regionalism, taking as their topics the streets and people of Boston's rough-and-tumble South End, the environment in which he had grown up and to which he long remained emotionally attached.

Despite the immediacy of his subject matter, Levine's technique was decidedly traditional. His fluent brushwork and rich, sensuous palette demonstrate that Rembrandt, Rubens, and Titian were his ideals. Although Cubist-inspired abstraction and Surrealism were beginning to transform American art and challenge its regionalist bias, Levine apparently saw himself as working within a continuum whose spirit reflected centuries-old traditions of genre and narrative painting. But while he felt a kinship with high art of the past, he was nonetheless susceptible to some aspects of modernism, notably its expressionistic manifestations as seen in the lavishly brushed canvases of Oskar Kokoschka and Chaim Soutine—artists who exaggerated form to the point of distortion as they probed the essences of their subjects. Levine's work, like theirs, is filled with oddly distorted forms, figures, and objects and is typically taken to the verge of caricature.

Levine's eccentric drawing style and mastery of traditional painting techniques are especially evident in *The Neighborhood Physician*, a portrait drawn from his memories of youth. In the artist's words, the subject of this painting is "a general practitioner [seen] after a delivery," whom he characterizes as "a Boston anarchist and whiskey drinker—a pill-rolling Don Quixote."[1] He is rendered in a representational style that Levine described as "taffy-pull," in which bodily proportions are radically altered. His elongated head, with its prominent nose and juglike ears, and large pawlike hands make him almost grotesque. But for all its distortion, the old doctor is portrayed as a sympathetic, even vulnerable, figure.

The work started out, Levine wrote, "as a sketch of a man standing in front of his home—a dual portrait with a chance to show a family resemblance between them."[2] Soon, however, the subject matter broadened to include a striped pole, a traffic marker, and segments of street signs, and Levine arrived at an urban vignette that vividly synthesizes memory and imagination.

A.B.

1. From a letter to Daniel Defenbacher, Walker Art Center, 14 September 1943.
2. Ibid.

Sol LeWitt

Cubic Modular Piece No. 2 (L-Shaped Modular Piece) 1966

American, b. 1928

baked enamel on steel

109⅛ x 5⅞ x 55⅞
(277.2 x 141.9 x 141.9)

acquired from the John
Weber Gallery, New York,
1974 (Purchased with a
grant from Museum
Purchase Plan, the
National Endowment for
the Arts and Art Center
Acquisition Fund 74.7)

In LeWitt's gridded structures the ubiquitous verticals and horizontals are locked in an uncompromisingly logical sequence whose limits are predetermined. Intimated in the repetition of modular form is the potential for an ever expanding three-dimensional grid system that, if unrestrained, would obliterate everything in its path, replacing organic matter with the impersonal logic of mathematical progression. The limits LeWitt imposes to restrain the grid and produce a configuration follow from numerical, geometrical or linguistic propositions. The grid becomes a medium through which a defined idea, such as "L-shaped," can take visible form in whatever scale he determines.[1]

The materials are neutral—blandly white, fabricated, uninflected in surface—making the module, his "grammatical device," inexpressive in itself. His skeletal, dematerialized cubes, lacking the fundamental characteristics of actual cubes (six equal sides, twelve edges), are, rather, descriptions of cubic spaces. The LeWitt module resembles a perspective drawing of a cube in which all edges have been included, even those that cannot be seen from a single point of view. In such a description, qualities of opacity or solidity are disregarded. If this cubic "idea" is extended into a grid, space loses its active function, becoming only the interval between lines. LeWitt has pointed out that the division of space into identical parts produces "a kind of negation of space."[2] Grids, as opposed to cubes, are lines and intervals, measuring distance rather than defining space. Volume disappears in the transparencies, linear overlappings, penetrations, and perspectival effects of the grid.

In this piece, space is actually occupied only by the "lines" that constitute the grid. As physical realizations of the drawn line, these rectangular rods are inescapably three-dimensional. While the drawn line is composed of an infinite series of connected points, LeWitt's "lines" are an infinite series of connected squares, thus remaining faithful to his cubic premise.

Despite the rigorous clarity of the form as conceived, the effect is what LeWitt calls perceptual chaos. If one were to attempt to describe this perfectly intelligible, simple structure, one would be faced with many ambiguities: Where exactly is the L-shape? Is the structure one wall of cubic spaces interpenetrated by a second? If so, where does each begin and end? Is it one rank of three columns of cubic volumes with two similar columns projecting from one end at right angles? Or a column of six cubes forming a corner, with identical arms coming out at right angles? A pruned endless grid, or a viscerated cube? Composition has been eliminated as an organizing principle, and identical formal ideas have replaced individualized motifs, but relationships are epistemologically complex, changeable and contradictory.[3]

L.F.G.

1. The idea of an "L" can take many forms at any scale. For this work, LeWitt increased the number of modules stacked vertically from five to six and reduced the relative thickness of the "line" from the original maquette.
2. Quoted in Lucy R. Lippard, "Sol LeWitt: Non-visual Structure," Artforum, vol. 5 (April 1967), p. 46 n. 2.
3. Donald Kuspit has suggested a philosophical purpose in LeWitt's work, the "cognitive intuition of the abstract essence of art," an ordered realm that does not reside within the art object but cannot be apprehended without it; "Sol LeWitt: The Look of Thought," Art in America, vol. 63 (September–October 1975), p. 44. LeWitt himself has called Conceptual artists "mystics rather than rationalists;" "Sentences on Conceptual Art," O to 9, no. 5 (January 1969), p. 3.

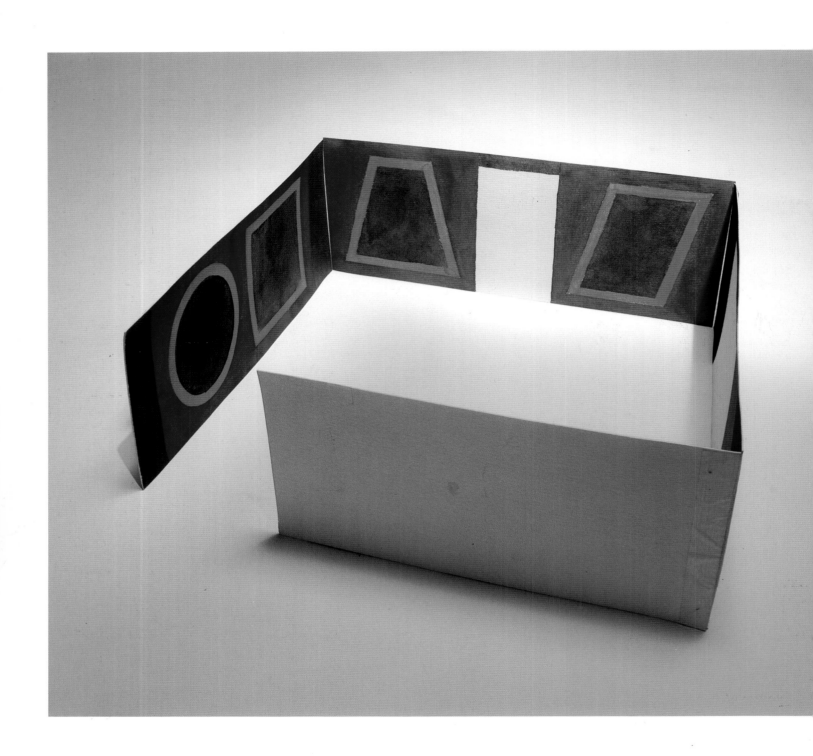

Sol LeWitt

Four Geometric Figures in a Room   1984[1]

American, b. 1928

ink on latex paint on
gypsum board

102 x 1,112
(259.1 x 2823) overall

commissioned from the
artist, 1984
(Commissioned by the
Art Center with funds
provided by Mr. and Mrs.
Julius E. Davis 84.8)

In an explanation of the genesis, intentions, and characteristics of his wall drawings, LeWitt wrote that he wanted to make a work of art that was as two dimensional as possible.[2] In doing so, he brought under control much of the "perceptual chaos" that his declarative three-dimensional grids paradoxically had produced. Independently taking the Greenbergian imperative of the close identification of medium and support to its logical conclusion, he made the ink-painted surface indistinguishable from the wall on which it appears. Shunning the use of canvas and painting materials, he favors the term "drawing" for these works because it implies for him a more "direct and simple concept" than that of painting.[3]

LeWitt provides detailed instructions for each wall drawing. In the Walker's mural, the geometric figures—circle, square, trapezoid, and parallelogram are described in lines 4 inches wide, with the spaces inside and outside painted blue and red. According to his plan, the blue and red may be exchanged so long as inside and outside are consistently coded. The plan was then carried out by assistants who function as collaborators in the final manifestation of the idea. Four layers of flat white paint were applied to the walls to provide a stable surface to receive the ink. A team of artists—Jo Watanabe, Kate Hunt and Owen Osten—worked from a model and written instructions, under LeWitt's supervision. They applied the ink wash with a small brush or swab, allowing it to dry before making another application, and smoothing uneven gradations with a damp cloth rubbed in circular motions. LeWitt recognizes and appreciates the inflections that result from the individual sensibilities of each executor.[4] Like a musical score, with which he frequently compares his work, or an architectural blueprint, the plan awaits animation by others. However, although the instructions exist outside the execution, which can be carried out at any time, he emphasizes that the ideas of wall drawings alone are "contradictions of the idea of wall drawings."[5] The idea presupposes, requires, and depends upon its execution.

The color areas marking changes in the architecture of the Walker room—e.g., a corner or a doorway—are painted in the same gray that was added to the yellow, blue, and red primaries, to mute and harmonize them. LeWitt has explained that he prefers primary colors because they are used in printing.[6] This claim, in turn, raises the issues of reproducibility, mechanical

re-creation, collaboration, and his implicit allegiance to democratic principles, as well as intimates a conceptual rather than entirely aesthetic premise. Yet, the precise quality of these subdued variations was arrived at empirically, through the preparation and careful study of color samples.

The use of gray, apart from clarifying the constitution of the other colors, allows for a symmetrical ordering: four figures are complemented by four colors. The figures have some of the same ambiguity as the grayed "primaries." The circle and square are forms that imply frontality, but demonstrate it only when the viewer is standing directly in front of them. Although the less "basic" (to use LeWitt's term[7]) forms of the parallelogram and trapezoid can be viewed as frontal presentations, they can also be seen as figures that describe the distortions of perspective, the consequences of the oblique gaze. Viewed from an angle, the square can become a parallelogram or trapezoid, as photographs demonstrate.[8]

L.F.G.

1. Because of his conceptual bias, LeWitt does not consider the date of a particular execution of his plan the date of the work. However, a conventional date is used here to record the present execution, completed 21 April 1984.
2. First published in "Documentation in Conceptual Art," Arts Magazine, vol. 44 (April 1970), p. 45.
3. "Excerpts from a Correspondence, 1981–1983," in Stedelijk Museum, Amsterdam, Sol LeWitt: Wall Drawings 1968–1984, exh. cat., 1984, p. 24.
4. Sol LeWitt, untitled statement, Art Now: New York, vol. 3 (June 1971), n.p.
5. Ibid.
6. LeWitt, in "Documentation in Conceptual Art," p. 45.
7. Stedelijk Museum, p. 18.
8. Photographic distortion, particularly that produced by the wide-angle lens needed to encompass the room, complicates one's understanding of the relationship between the ideal form (the perfect circle or square) and its material analogue (the depicted and viewed circle or square).

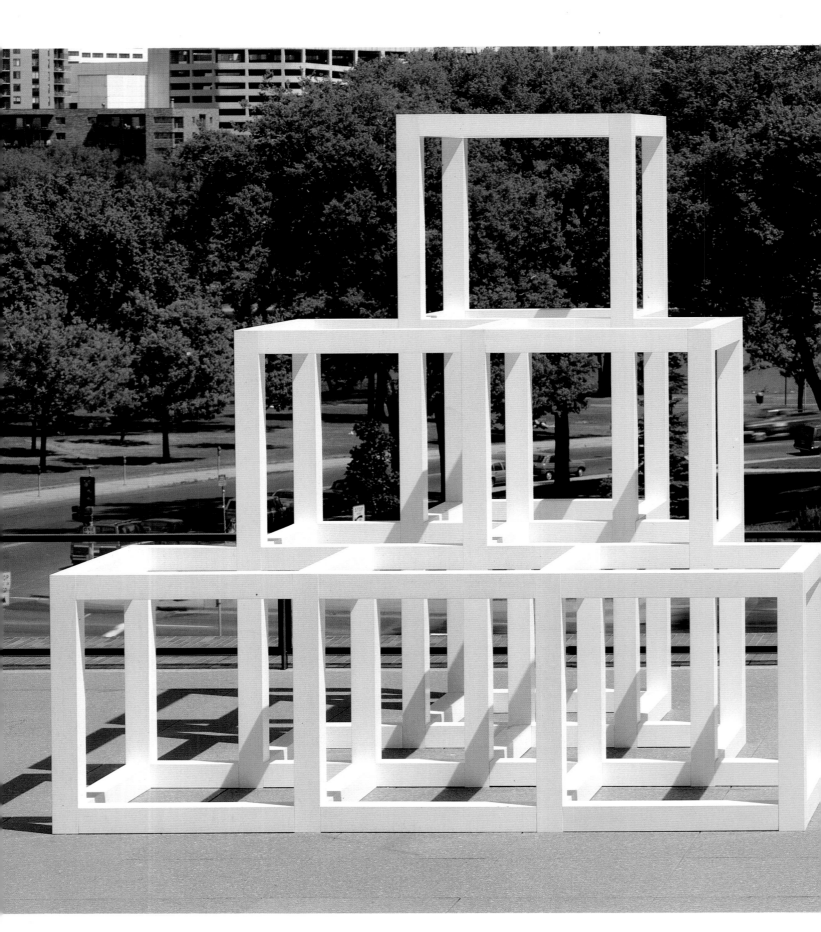

Sol LeWitt

Three x Four x Three   1984

American, b. 1928

white enamel on aluminum

**169 x 169½ x 169¼
(429.3 x 430.5 x 429.9)**

**acquired from the John
Weber Gallery, New York,
1987 (Walker Special
Purchase Fund 87.12)**

Three x Four x Three offers another variation on
the cube, a longstanding theme that LeWitt first
introduced in his work in the early 1960s. He
explains his gravitation to this form as follows:

> The most interesting characteristic of the cube is that
> it is relatively uninteresting. Compared to any other
> 3-D form, the cube lacks any aggressive force, implies
> no motion, and is least emotive. Therefore, it is the
> best form to use as a basic unit for any more
> elaborate function, the grammatical device from which
> the work may proceed.[1]

The format for this particular sculpture was
initially explored in a series of works begun in
1969, which were also made out of 6-inch square
steel or aluminum tubing that LeWitt had manufactured in The Netherlands. This work maintains
the ratio of 8:5:1 between the material and the
space in between that he had first established in
about 1965, the same time he began painting his
structures white, a change that the artist felt
"mitigated the expressiveness of the earlier black
pieces."[2] As in previous works, the cubic unit is
intended to be eye level (63 inches) and the
joints are readily visible, so the viewer can see
how the piece is assembled.

A work whose height and scale suggest it is
intended for the outdoors, and whose structure
recalls a jungle gym, *Three x Four x Three* functions in part like an orderly series of windows,
through whose frames the colorful and more
chaotic world can be seen. Its form clearly
speaks of architecture, an abiding interest of the
artist. LeWitt has written specifically on the
appeal of ziggurat office buildings in midtown
Manhattan,[3] whose setback profiles are echoed
in this work. LeWitt points out that the ziggurat
buildings came about as a result of zoning codes,
"just as an idea might give any work of art its
outer boundaries and remove arbitrary and
capricious decisions."[4]

M.G.

1. Quoted in The Museum of Modern Art, New York, *Sol
LeWitt*, exh. cat., 1978, p. 172.
2. Ibid., p. 59.
3. Sol LeWitt, "Ziggurats," *Arts*, vol. 41 (November 1966),
pp. 24, 25.
4. Ibid.

Roy Lichtenstein

Artist's Studio No. 1 (Look Mickey)   1973

American, b. 1923

oil, acrylic on canvas

96 x 128 (243.8 x 325.1)

acquired from the Leo Castelli Gallery, New York, 1981 (gift of Judy and Kenneth Dayton and the T.B. Walker Foundation 81.3)

Best known as the artist who transformed comic strips into paintings, Roy Lichtenstein populated his canvases of the early 1960s with such well-known cartoon characters as Donald Duck and Mickey Mouse. Since then, he has raided not only the comics, but also other popular culture sources, including advertisements, commercial catalogues, postcards, and art reproductions, both for imagery and technique. In this painting, he brings together familiar elements from his own oeuvre.

Artist's Studio No. 1 (Look Mickey) is a virtual compendium of Lichtenstein's iconographic interests, incorporating major themes that have recurred in his work since the early 1960s. The painting even contains a partial depiction of his well-known 1961 *Look Mickey, I've Hooked a Big One*, in which Donald Duck is caught in the act of "catching" himself. The picture of a cartoon bubble filled with cartoon text is another allusion to Lichtenstein's fascination with the comic strip.

Other self-quotations in the painting include the mail-order couch from his office furniture series, grapefruit and bananas typical of his academic still lifes, a telephone table with legs like one of his recent sculptures, a painting of the back of a canvas, a simplified landscape painting, and, on the far left, a mirror painting. The molding along the ceiling is yet another self-reference—to his Entablature paintings.

In addition to being highly autobiographical, Lichtenstein pays homage here to Henri Matisse, whose radical reduction of form and use of color as a major compositional element shocked viewers early in the century. Lichtenstein's single object pictures of the early 1960s were, in their own way, raw simplifications that also elicited the scorn of many critics when first shown. They incorporated the restrictive means of commercial printing, especially its flat primary colors and the Benday dots of mechanical reproduction that quickly became the hallmark of Lichtenstein's style.

Matisse was also known for his paintings of the studio. In fact, one of four other large-scale studio interiors painted by Lichtenstein during 1973–1974, *Artist's Studio: "The Dance,"* is closely related to Matisse's *Still Life* with the "Dance" (1909).[1] Matisse also populated depicted interiors with his own paintings.

Lichtenstein's paintings are generally based on carefully composed drawings from which he deviates very little. For *Artist's Studio No. 1 (Look Mickey)* he made a small, preliminary study and then projected it to make a larger drawing that is very closely aligned to the painting in its color and composition.[2] Unlike the painting, however, it reveals the artist's hand freely working and reworking compositional elements.

E.A.

1. Jack Cowart in The St. Louis Art Museum, *Roy Lichtenstein 1970–1980*, exh. cat., 1981, p. 72.
2. Both studies for the painting are reproduced in Bernice Rose, The Museum of Modern Art, New York, *The Drawings of Roy Lichtenstein*, exh. cat., 1987, pp. 39, 102.

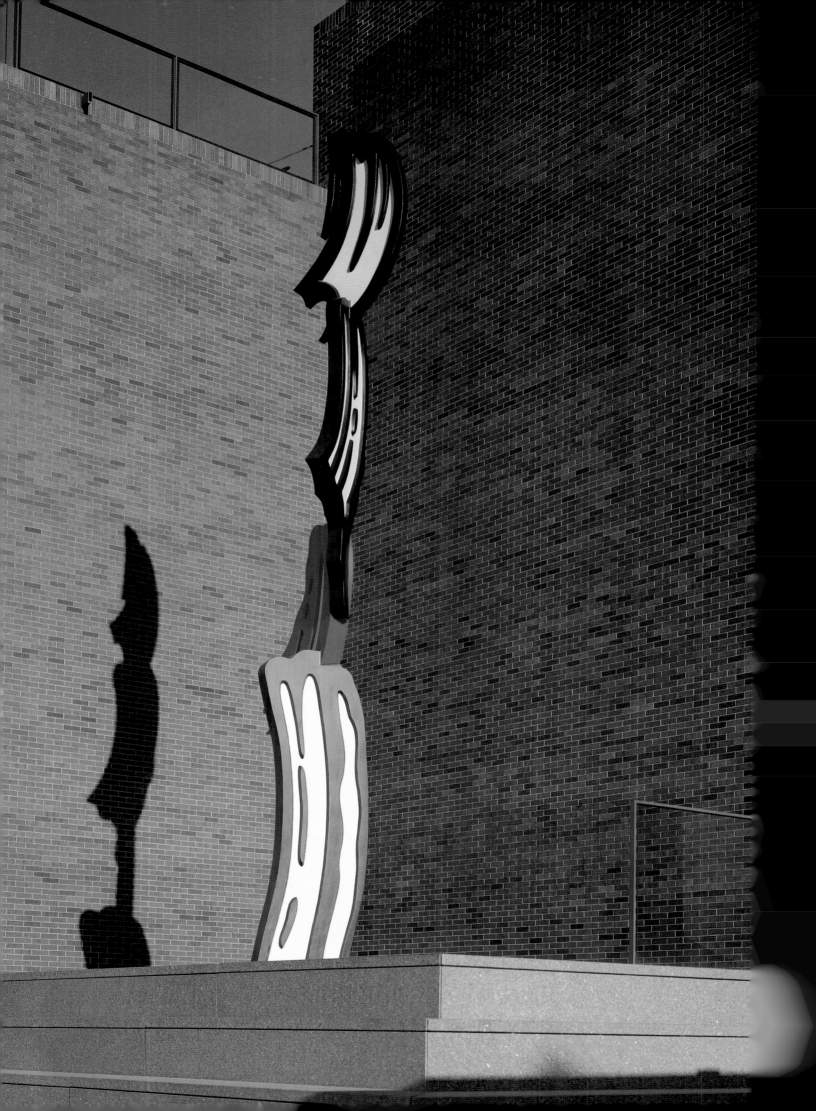

Roy Lichtenstein

Salute to Painting   1985–1986

American, b. 1923

painted aluminum

300 (762)

Tallix, Inc., Peekskill, New York

commissioned by Walker Art Center, 1984; acquired through the Leo Castelli Gallery, 1985 (given in honor of Martin Friedman by past and present members of the Walker Art Center Board of Directors 85.31)

Commissioned by Walker Art Center for the museum's front entrance, Roy Lichtenstein's *Salute to Painting* is a witty monument to modern art. From a distance, its four abstracted brushstrokes—splashes of red, white, pink, and yellow, arranged vertically one over the other—appear to wave like fluttering pennants. Up close, one is struck by the fluid grace of the refined 25-foot aluminum sculpture welcoming visitors to the Walker.

Primarily known as a painter, Lichtenstein has periodically turned his attention to sculpture. In recent years, he has explored this medium with particular exuberance, transforming many of his best-known images into three-dimensional form. The subject of the brushstroke first shocked viewers when it appeared as early as 1965 in Lichtenstein's Pop paintings. At the time, the brushstroke made ironic reference to Action Painting, in which each gestural painting mark suggested a revelation of self. In contrast to the intense subjectivity of these paintings, works by Pop artists such as Lichtenstein seemed startlingly neutral, even impersonal. In the brushstroke paintings, Lichtenstein's methodical way of working, in which he outlined and then carefully filled in his forms, was anathema to the very nature of his subject.

Built-in contradictions abound in Lichtenstein's work. As a concrete symbol of the ephemeral, the brushstroke not only expresses the artist's underlying interest in visual paradox, but also his fascination with the play between abstraction and realism. Lichtenstein's reductive approach to representation, in which "unessential" elements are eliminated from his paintings, tends to make the subject matter of his sculptures even more abstract. Thus, a sculpture in the form of a painted brushstroke takes on particular irony.

Martin Friedman, who commissioned the sculpture for the museum, first showed the artist's work at the Walker in 1967. Intrigued by Lichtenstein's transformation of the brushstroke theme into sculpture, Friedman invited the artist to plan a large-scale version for the museum's front terrace. Lichtenstein had recently pursued the theme in another large-scale outdoor work titled *Brushstroke in Flight* at the Port Columbus International Airport in Ohio. In preparation for the Walker project, he made a prototype of painted wood standing nearly 4 feet high. Lichtenstein and Friedman used this maquette to help determine the final colors and placement of the larger work. The model was also used by the craftsmen at Tallix, Inc.

During the reception for Lichtenstein at the Walker Art Center in February 1986, the museum's Board of Directors announced that they had secretly purchased *Salute to Painting* as a surprise tribute to Friedman on his twenty-fifth anniversary as the Walker's director.

E.A.

Roy Lichtenstein on the Walker's Terrace, February 1986, with the model for *Salute to Painting*.

311

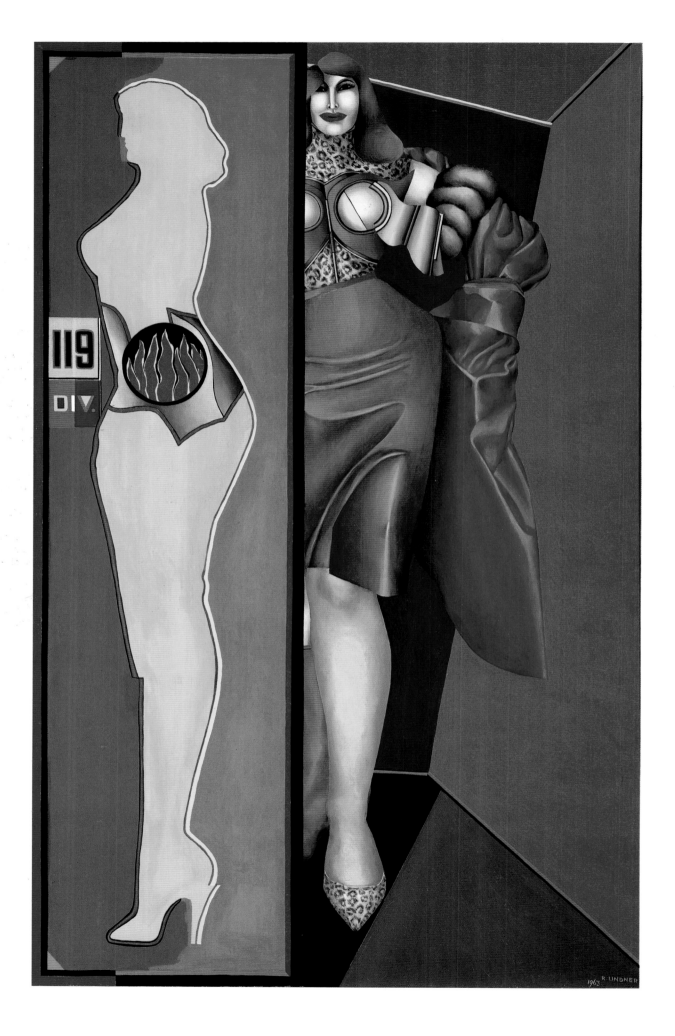

Richard Lindner

119th Division 1963

American, b. Germany,
1901–1978

oil on canvas

79⅞ x 50 (202.9 x 127)

**lower right, *R. Lindner
1963***

**acquired from Cordier &
Ekstrom, New York, 1967
(gift of the T.B. Walker
Foundation 67.31)**

Standing in front of this canvas, whose title refers to a military division, Lindner commented:

> Soldiers are all alike.... In the barracks, soldiers talk constantly of the women they will have when they go into town. But, it never happens. That blank, burning form is what they want; the other is what they find.[1]

Lindner's view of women as complex, empowered, fortified, unassailable yet achingly desirable may have been conditioned to some extent by an experience he had at about age eleven, when an actress he remembered as being about twenty abducted him, creating a scandal in Nuremberg.[2] The fascination with women as sexual objects rendered hard and predatory by their own lasciviousness continued to influence his work throughout his life. Here a vampish Brunhilde, her face a mask of heightened pallor with painted features, poses with hip thrust out, dressed in leopard skin—which Lindner calls "almost a 'Playboy' symbol for women"—edged with red to form a collar, and repeated in her single pointed shoe.

Lindner told Larry Rivers that he used to spend time in the department stores of New York watching women go through and try on undergarments.[3] He analyzed his erotic fascination with clothing:

> The nude is asexual.... It's clothes that create sexual appeal. Erotic curiosity plays an important part. Although we know perfectly well what is under the garments, they still make us want to see what they conceal.[4]

What they conceal according to the *119th Division* is not the body, which itself becomes a carapace, but inner flames.

Lindner theorized that the complexity of women's sexuality, which he saw as secret and dangerous, set it apart from the relatively simple responses of men.[5] He attributed the threatening power of the twentieth-century woman to her new right to pleasure and her rejection of the myth of manhood, a "19th-century concept that's been fed and nurtured and swallowed by generations of women who, in the meantime, have had all the time and years to strengthen and deepen their own mystery and power."[6] The consequence as he describes it is the theatrical aspect of social and sexual exchange that characterized both Germany of the 1920s and America of the 1960s, with roles played and costumes

assumed, "always two levels of conversation going on at the same time.... We are always on stage."[7]

L.F.G.

1. Quoted in Don Morrison in "Books and the Arts," *The Minneapolis Star*, 13 August 1969, p. 68.
2. "A Conversation with Richard Lindner and Stephen Prokopoff," in Museum of Contemporary Art, Chicago, *Richard Lindner: A Retrospective*, exh. cat., 1977, n.p.
3. Larry Rivers, "A Send-off for Richard Lindner," *Art in America*, vol. 66 (November–December 1978), pp. 149, 150. For a convincing discussion of the psycho-sexual implications of the corset and its use in Lindner's work, see Roland Penrose, "Richard Lindner," *Art International*, vol. II (20 January 1967), p. 32.
4. Quoted in Museum of Contemporary Art.
5. Dean Swanson, "Interview with Richard Lindner," in University Museum, University of California, Berkeley, with the Walker Art Center, *Lindner*, exh. cat., p. 11.
6. Quoted in John Gruen, "Richard Lindner: 1901–1978," *Art News*, vol. 77 (Summer 1978), p. 77.
7. Quoted in Museum of Contemporary Art. He saw his work as being influenced not only by the decadence, cruelty, and bizarre social environment of German cities in the 1920s, but also by the Dada inventiveness of artists such as Oskar Schlemmer, whom he admired for the "simplicity and precision" of his forms; see Nancy Schwartz, "Oskar Schlemmer: An Interview with Richard Lindner," *Arts Magazine*, vol. 44 (November 1969), p. 23.

Jacques Lipchitz

Prometheus Strangling the Vulture II   1944/1953

American, b. Lithuania,
1891–1973

bronze

91¾ 90 x 57
(233 x 228.6 x 144.8)

base, *J. Lipchitz 1944 2/2*
and thumbprint

probably Modern Art
Foundry, New York

acquired from Lolya
Lipchitz through the artist,
1956 (gift of the T.B.
Walker Foundation 56.17)

Paul Gauguin
*Jacob Wrestling with the
Angel*   1888
oil on canvas
28¾ x 36¼ (73 x 92.1)
Collection National Gallery
of Scotland, Edinburgh

Lipchitz first proposed the mythical hero as a personification of human progress in paper and clay sketches of 1933, in which the "guardian of the flame" is triumphantly unchained, and the vulture, according to the sculptor, "barely alive."[1] In 1936, when he was invited to submit a work to the *Paris Exposition Internationale* of 1937, he again modified the subject for the wall above one of the entrances to the scientific pavilion, the Palais de la Découverte. In this approximately 30-foot version cast in plaster, the figure of the wounded but superior Prometheus, "coifed [sic] with a Phrygian bonnet," which Lipchitz interpreted as a symbol of democracy,[2] is locked in combat with the vulture. After the sculpture was removed from the wall in the fall of 1937 and placed in front of one of the entrances near the Champs-Elysées, it was the victim of "xenophobic" attacks in the press and within the artistic community, and finally was smashed and the pieces carried to the state warehouse.[3] In 1939, Lipchitz made a new model, which he intended to show at the Brummer Gallery, New York, but the outbreak of war made it impossible to ship the work; Lipchitz fled France for New York, leaving the contents of his studio behind, recovering them only years later.

In 1943, the Brazilian government became interested in a Prometheus for its new Ministry of Education and Health building in Rio de Janeiro, designed by Oscar Niemeyer with an exterior auditorium wall planned to support a sculptural project.[4] Lipchitz made studies, one of which shows the base system he was to use for the Walker work. "This sculpture," he wrote, "was so important to me that I made many different studies of it."[5] From January to August of 1944 Lipchitz worked on a model 7 feet high in plastilene, the plaster cast of which he sent to Rio with the understanding that it would be enlarged three times to approximately 20 feet in height, as shown in his scale sketch, and cast under his supervision. Due to some "fantastic mistake" the work was cast without enlargement and without his involvement, and Lipchitz disassociated himself from it.[6]

In the earliest version of the Prometheus theme, Lipchitz had the hero strangling the vulture with both hands, but decided that this "warped the ensemble:"

I then tried to overcome this by having him choke the vulture with one hand only, and use the other to

defend himself against the claws of the bird. In this way, my composition became more eloquent, at the same time that it opened up space and permitted one to see the depth.[7]

The work for Brazil and the Walker variant reflect this change of conception. The spread wings, bare feet, fluttering robes, and restraining gesture recall the contestants in Gauguin's *Jacob Wrestling with the Angel* of 1888.[8] The view of the contest is intended to be not only from a distance as in the Gauguin, but from below rather than above. Since the sculpture was designed originally to float on a wall, the frontality and foreshortening that Lipchitz struggled to achieve is explained. Recognizing that it would not always be installed that way, he attempted to rework it with attention to all sides,[9] but did not alter the foreshortening.

A plaster belonging to Lipchitz was exhibited in the Pennsylvania Academy's annual exhibition. Upon its return, he retouched it, added a base and made one bronze cast for the Philadelphia Museum of Art and one (in 1953) for himself, which he kept in his garden in Hastings-on-Hudson until its acquisition by Walker Art Center.

L.F.G.

1. Jacques Lipchitz, "Lipchitz Writes 'The Story of My Prometheus,'" *Art in Australia*, ser. 4 (Summer 1942), p. 29.
2. Lipchitz, "The Story of My Prometheus," pp. 29, 30.
3. Ibid. pp. 34–35.
4. See John Rewald, "Jacques Lipchitz's Struggle," *The Museum of Modern Art Bulletin*, vol. 12 (November 1944), p. 9. Philip Goodwin, planning the exhibition *Brazil Builds* for The Museum of Modern Art, commissioned a plaster sketch from Lipchitz. Nine studies were shown in The Museum of Modern Art's *Modern Drawings* show in the spring of 1944.
5. Jacques Lipchitz with H.H. Arnason, *My Life in Sculpture* (New York: The Viking Press, 1972), p. 167.
6. See Lipchitz, quoted in Irene Patai, *Encounters: The Life of Jacques Lipchitz* (Funk & Wagnall's Co., 1961), p. 383.
7. Lipchitz, p. 35.
8. He had seen the Gauguin in Paris as a young man (see Hammacher, p. 75), and in 1932 made a sculpture of the same title which anticipates the composition of the final version of *Prometheus*. He expressed his admiration for Gauguin several times; see Katherine Kuh, "Conclusions from an Old Cubist," *Art News*, vol. 60 (November 1961), p. 73.
9. Lipchitz, p. 139.

Robert Lobe

Killer Hill C.W. 1985

American, b. 1945

anodized aluminum

**100 x 192 x 27
(254 x 487.7 x 68.6)**

**lower right, *Bob Lobe
1985 Killer Hill***

**acquired from the Willard
Gallery, New York, 1986
(Justin Smith Purchase
Fund 86.80)**

Since 1976, Robert Lobe has been fabricating sculpture by covering trees and rocks in situ with aluminum sheets and hammering them until he captures the shape and volume of the natural elements underneath. He then removes the aluminum and reassembles it in his studio by riveting or welding the seams together. The result is a hollow skin of metal, either a wall relief or freestanding sculpture, in which the process of fabrication is recorded.

The character of Lobe's sculptures is determined, in large part, by the original site. *Killer Hill C.W.* was made at Chesterwood, the Stockbridge, Massachusetts home and studio of Daniel Chester French, creator of the Lincoln Memorial. The title comes from the spot where it was made, dubbed "Killer Hill" by the local children. As in much of his work, Lobe here records the convergence of stone and tree, in this instance a large shale rock bordered by fir and maple trees. Pairing both elements invests the work with contrasting formal ingredients: the boulder is horizontal and massive, while the trees are vertical and linear. Mounted on the wall, these shapes seem to float above the floor, denying their original mass and weight.

For *Killer Hill C.W.*, Lobe required several types of tools. Since shale is a soft material, he chiseled the aluminum so as not to destroy the actual rock. For the trees, however, he hammered the surface with a power tool, piling up the metal to simulate the patterning of the bark. (Lobe often uses power tools that enable him to work quickly. "It's an interesting way of working because it permits a lot of expression and a lot of decision making while I'm in the action of doing it."[1])

In all, Lobe estimates that the sculpture received between three and six million blows. The result is a surface rich in texture. The aggressively chiseled rock, presents a matte surface in contrast to the more reflective, sinuously patterned trees. Lobe calls his works "industrial artifacts." In extracting natural forms from their usual context and rendering them in an industrial material, the artist comments on man's encroachment into the environment.

Lobe likes to use aluminum because of its artificial associations and its inert quality. The metal shells fix a particular moment in time and transform living, natural elements into ghostly images that are at once easily recognizable and abstract. His use of a monochromatic material visually unifies the disparate natural elements into an overall composition, and his decision to re-create only fragments of the original source emphasizes formal properties such as shape, density, and surface.

D.H.

1. Conversation with the author, 19 June 1987.

Richard Long

Minneapolis Circle 1982

British, b. 1954

red slate

264 (670.6) diam.

commissioned by the Walker Art Center through Sperone, Westwater, Fischer, New York, 1982 (Justin Smith Purchase Fund 82.161)

Richard Long
Circle in Alaska: Bering Strait Driftwood on the Arctic Circle 1977
photograph
34⁷⁄₁₆ x 48¼
(87.5 x 122.5)
Collection Anthony d'Offay Gallery, London

Minneapolis Circle can be understood in the context of the walks Long has been taking, since 1967, through landscapes that are preferably "extreme, neutral, uncluttered."[1] He marks his passage through a place by arranging natural materials he finds to make sculptures that are directly and exclusively related to that place, and by photographically recording these "three-dimensional traces." One such photograph is of his Circle in Alaska: *Bering Strait Driftwood on the Arctic Circle* (1977). Traveling to the Arctic Circle—itself a conceptual, man-made circle—Long imposed his own circle, randomly arranging within its circumference pieces of driftwood formed by the actions of a specific place, the Bering Strait. Other walks have resulted in texts that combine precise information on the ordained course, distance, and duration of an individual walk with vignettes of unassociated sensations that have the poetry of the keenly felt, unexpectedly encountered fact. Long wrote recently about the different manifestations and processes of his work:

> A sculpture feeds the senses directly at a place. A photograph or text feeds the imagination by extension to other places. Each work is simple and contemplative. A sculpture orders and concentrates materials. A walk is a simple way to pass and order time.[2]

Long's indoor works refer to these questions of place, imagination, contemplation, and order but, having no visible natural context, exist in a more traditional sculptural realm than the outdoor works. He notes that the "outdoor works are about the landscape of that place—outward looking. Indoor works are about themselves, concentrated and inward looking."[3] *Minneapolis Circle*, composed of slate elements ordered precut by the artist from a favorite quarry, then repeatedly and variably assembled by others according to specifications, does not record a single artistic episode taking place in the natural world. Despite its self-sufficiency, however, it can be seen as alluding to the outdoors Long traverses by virtue of having been made of a natural material unique to a particular place,[4] and evoking the kind of landscapes to which he is drawn.

The surface of the piece resembles the mineral skin of the earth rent and fragmented by geological action and by human intervention, producing the changing random order of topography. Lines, positive and negative areas, and changes in depth created by the arbitrary placement of individual pieces of slate occur within a prescribed form, the circle, in much the same way that the events on his walks seem unpredictable and random while following an intellectually conceived program related to mapping, recording, and charting. Just as the texts he writes about his walks describe a precise plan combined with unexpected events, so the Walker work proposes a specified, predetermined boundary that encloses a configuration that, according to the written instructions that accompany the work, is changeable.

Unlike Carl Andre, Long does not intend the viewer to walk on his work,[5] indicating a fundamental conceptual difference: "Andre makes (indoor) sculptures which are transportable places, which can be walked on, where I make sculpture by the act of walking itself."[6]

L.F.G.

1. Quoted in Michael Craig Martin, "Current and Forthcoming Exhibitions." *The Burlington Magazine*, vol. 122 (November 1980), p. 791.
2. Letter to the author, 26 October 1986.
3. Ibid.
4. When the commission was first being discussed in the fall and early winter of 1980, the possibility of Long's using granite from the Cold Spring quarry in Minnesota was suggested by Martin Friedman; this apparently was not feasible, either because of the nature of the blocks that could be quarried or the onset of the Minnesota winter, and Long used a standard size and cut of red slate pieces he had gotten from Sheldon Slate Products, Middle Granville, one of his preferred quarries in upstate New York. The piece was first installed 16 October 1982.
5. As has been noted, the fact that he lays the stones on the gallery floor "without embedding them into any medium which would fix them and make it possible for us to walk safely on them suggests that he really does not want us to walk on those stones except in our minds;" see John T. Paoletti, "Richard Long," *Arts Magazine*, vol. 57 (December 1982), p. 3.
6. Letter to the author, 26 October 1986.

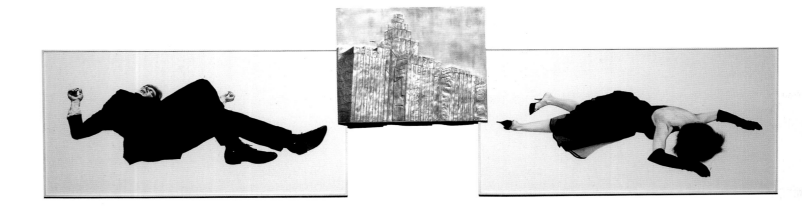

Robert Longo

National Trust 1981

American, b. 1953

charcoal, graphite on paper, aluminum bonded to cast fiberglass

48 x 93¾ (121.9 x 238.1) each drawing; 37¾ x 47¾ (95.9 x 121.3) relief; 62 x 235¼ x 63 (157.5 x 597.5 x 160) overall

on reverse, right and left panels, *Robert Longo 1981*

acquired from Brooke Alexander, New York, 1981 (Art Center Acquisition Fund 81.54)

National Trust forms part of Longo's Men in the Cities series of 1979–1982, in which chic young urbanites are drawn in contorted poses on a blank background, frequently accompanied by cast aluminum panels depicting architectural structures. Here the building in the center is The Tombs,[1] a courthouse and prison in lower Manhattan not far from the nightclubs patronized by Longo's subjects. Viewed from below, the architecture rises and projects over the flat renderings of the prone figures, as if to assert its solidity and unassailability and to dramatize the figures' vulnerability. Yet, at the same time, the building is dwarfed by the figures' monumental scale. The National Trust is the government agency responsible for preserving historical landmarks, and the title probably puns ironically on contemporary cynicism about America's institutions.[2] On notebook sketches of the piece Longo has inscribed the phrases "modern tomb" and "sound government" by the image of fallen people and looming government buildings.

The ensemble of images was carefully worked out in a series of twelve sketches and drawings. During the evolution of the piece, Longo attempted to achieve "corporate propor-tions," comparing the overall configuration with a battleship, fighter plane, and eagle with wings spread, all predatory images, the latter reminis-cent of shots of the Napoleonic eagle spread over three screens in Abel Gance's 1927 film *Napoleon*. The theme of attack is fused with that of self-destruction in the ambiguous gestures of Longo's figures, suggestive of foul play, terrorist assault, or chemically induced collapse; they resemble media images. Longo is concerned with mirroring his own time and culture, not only by describing its fashions and socio-political struc-tures, but by the very gestures of the figures. As he notes, there is a fashion in movement as well as in clothing.[3]

Longo depicts the figures as dead, and in the sketches compares the male with ancient sculptures of the Dying Gaul and the mortally wounded warrior from the east pediment of the Temple of Aegina. "They all die the same," reads an inscription. He associates the extremism of the poses in this and other pictures with the effects of the "corporate wars," a phrase in-scribed on one of the studies. The corporate war is a bloodless, contemporary urban combat, a kind of stylized brutality that leaves no physical wounds. The ambiguity concerning the figures'

actual state—perhaps they're just posing—diminishes the sensation of horror and reflects the theatricality of the artist's image-making process, which begins with the acting out of extreme states: his friends assume poses that are photographed in slide form and projected onto a screen to be drawn by Longo and his assistants. The absence of context and the scale disparity further defuse the image. The figures are linked with a "landscape" rather than integrated in it, producing a disjunctive relationship compa-rable to that of a movie, in which a close-up of a character cuts to a long shot of the environment.

    L.F.G.

1. Richard Price, in *Men in the Cities 1979–1982: Robert Longo* (New York: Harry N. Abrams, 1986), p. 98. For an interpretation of the relationship between the figures and the architecture, see Carter Ratcliff, *Robert Longo* (New York: Rizzoli, 1986), pp. 17, 18.
2. Robert Hobbs, in The University of Iowa Museum of Art, Iowa City, *Robert Longo:Dis-Illusions*, exh. cat., 1985 , n.p. The Tombs has not, in fact, been designated a historic landmark by the National Trust.
3. In Barry Blinderman, "Robert Longo's 'Men in the Cities': Quotes and Commentary." *Arts Magazine*, vol. 55 (March 1981), p. 92.

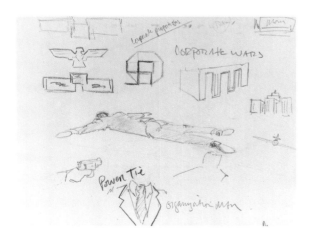

Robert Longo
untitled study for *National Trust* 1981
pencil on paper
8⁷⁄₁₆ x 10¹⁵⁄₁₆
Collection Walker Art Center
Gift of the artist, 1982

Morris Louis

Dalet Chaf 1958

American, 1912–1962

acrylic resin on canvas

**92⅛ x 134
(234 x 340.4)**

estate authentication on reverse, sideways, lower left, in pencil, *M. Louis #111*

on extended loan from the estate of the artist, since 1978 (intended gift of Marcella Louis Brenner)

In recalling the impact of his and Louis's historic visit to Helen Frankenthaler's studio in 1953, Kenneth Noland said that "we were interested in Pollock but could gain no lead from him. He was too personal. But Frankenthaler showed us a way—a way to think about, and to use, color." Louis added, "She was the bridge between Pollock and what was possible."[1] Louis followed Pollock's lead by implementing the gravitational flow of liquid paint as a force to be directed by the artist, requiring of him, in Michael Fried's phrase, "an apparent abdication of certain executive faculties."[2] In this kind of painting, the physical instigator of the mark on the canvas is not Louis's hand or wrist alone, but his entire body, as he pours paint and lifts, turns, creases, bows, and lowers the support to guide precisely the streams of color.[3] From Frankenthaler he learned the technique of staining with thinned paint, which permitted the picture plane to become identical with the canvas weave, and color to be embodied in the cloth support rather than in a layer of paint.[4]

In the works known as Veils,[5] including *Dalet Chaf*, Louis departed from Frankenthaler by merging currents of hues along their contours and washing scrims of darker incorporeal color over these; the effect is like that of the residual moisture held and absorbed by sand on a beach as overlapping waves recede. The fusing rather than layering of pigment constitutes a veritable pun on the term "mixing color." The individual character of each wash of color is visible at its point of origin: in *Dalet Chaf* hems of pale yellow (in the center) and orange (to the edges) luminously inflect the central region, while a dark blue and a soft green edge the top left and right, respectively. Other coloristic episodes take place throughout—a mauve peeks out at the bottom left, a black where orange is subsumed by grayish blue and gray. A brown strip appears to have been brushed on later to add definition to the outermost edges of the stained area. These softly ragged edges reiterate the diagonals of the two clefts formed by the bifurcated flow of paint. The overall configuration mimics the funneling and pooling behavior of a poured liquid.

The central vertical line along which the paint streams diverge may have resulted from the folding of the cotton duck, but it may have been a consequence of the canvas sagging under the weight of the wet paint from members of the supporting frame Louis used.[6] The work was probably cropped and stretched after Louis's death, at the instructions of the estate under the supervision of Clement Greenberg.[7]

The title *Dalet Chaf* was given to the painting by Marcella Louis Brenner, the artist's widow, when it left the studio. For the Veil series, she used letters from the Hebrew alphabet, doubling them after she had run through the alphabet once.[8]

L.F.G.

1. Quoted by James McC. Truitt, "Art—Arid D.C. Harbors Touted 'New' Painters," *The Washington Post*, 21 December 1961, p. A20.
2. Michael Fried, "Some Notes on Morris Louis," *Arts Magazine*, vol. 38 (November 1963), p. 25.
3. John Elderfield has suggested that the Veils may not have been simply poured, but applied with a swab, with intact color areas having been masked; see The Museum of Modern Art, New York, *Morris Louis*, exh. cat., 1986, p. 41. For a detailed description of the composition and properties of Leonard Bocour's synthetic medium trade-named Magna, which Louis was among the first to use, see Angelica Rudenstine, in Museum of Fine Arts, Boston, *Morris Louis: 1912–1962*, exh. cat., 1967, Appendix 1, p. 79.
4. Clement Greenberg, "Louis and Noland," *Art International*, vol. 4 (25 May 1960), p. 28, was the first to comment on the significance of the fusion of paint and canvas.
5. The term Veil, which came to identify a whole body of work Louis produced in 1954 and 1958–1959, was first used in print by William Rubin in "Younger American Painters," *Art International*, vol. 4 (1960), p. 27.
6. See Diane Upright [Headley], in the Walker Art Center, *Morris Louis: The Veil Cycle*, exh. cat., 1977, p. 24.
7. Greenberg explained his procedures in "Letters," *Arts Magazine*, vol. 47 (December 1972–January 1973), p. 94. Although Louis had experimented with leaving a greater expanse around the stained areas, in Veils exhibited in 1959 he soon reduced the borders. According to Diane Upright, *Morris Louis: The Complete Paintings* (New York: Harry N. Abrams, 1985), p. 43, although some Veils of 1954 were exhibited inverted, the 1958–1959 group was always shown by Louis as illustrated here, i.e., oriented as the paint fell.
8. This arbitrary system was inspired by Louis's having used the Greek alphabet to title two works (Upright, *Morris Louis*, p. 37). Chaf is Brenner's spelling of the Hebrew letter usually transliterated as *kaph*.

Morris Louis

#28 1961

American, 1912–1962

acrylic on canvas

91 x 78 ⁵/₁₆
(231.1 x 198.9)

estate authentication on reverse, lower right, *M. Louis #28*

acquired from the André Emmerich Gallery, New York, 1964 (gift of the T.B. Walker Foundation 64.9)

The sfumato veil subduing the limpid streams of color in *Dalet Chaf* was lifted by the time Louis undertook the so-called Stripe or Pillar pictures in the last year of his life.[1] The structure of #28 alludes but does not strictly adhere to principles of geometric form and hard edge. Superficially more direct than the Veils, the Stripes show Louis's continued preoccupation with the effects of staining, overlapping, fusion, separation, edge, proportion, and angle, with an increased attention to the expressive power of saturated color.[2] The lengths of color are less stripes than lambent color columns motivated and channeled by the artist. By late 1961 he had abandoned the symmetrical format and introduced double stacks.[3] The palette used in the compact stacks of *#28* is surprisingly comprehensive, including the three primaries and two of the three secondaries (with the exclusion of violet), black and a family of yellows. The qualities of each hue and value are brought into relation with all others through disparity, similarity, harmony, or dissonance. The color lines shift back and forth optically, sometimes forming alliances with near and sometimes with distant neighbors, and intermittently distinguishing themselves as isolated entities. The thinness of the bled paint prevents them from becoming tactile or volumetric forms, and hence they hover outside the ambit of the figure-ground relations. Furthermore, the separation of the two groups, which permits the activation of the bare canvas as a completely dematerialized "invisible" color column, simultaneously contributes to the two-dimensional design by balancing the rectangle of bare canvas to the right.[4]

The slightly diagonal journey of the leftmost blue creates an upward swelling, like the entasis of a classical column, while the drips and poolings at the top give the illusion of an inversion of top and bottom, lending an anti-gravitational sensation to the experience of the painting.[5] Louis originally intended to fold the canvas through the pillars and hide the tops from view, and did so in other instances; here the line of the fold around his work stretcher creates "heads" on the top of each shaft, except in the case of the green at the right, which apparently dripped down the back of the supporting frame. The slight change in direction at the bottom of this strip may have resulted from the same gesture of tilting the support that produced the bend at the top. Clement Greenberg, Louis's longtime friend and champion, persuaded him to anchor the stripes at the bottom and leave an empty expanse at the top,[6] in a more extreme variation on the handling of these peripheral areas in the Veils.

L.F.G.

1. The term Pillar originated with Clement Greenberg, who used it in a letter of 3 May 1961, quoted in Diane Upright, *Morris Louis: The Complete Paintings* (New York: Harry N. Abrams, 1985), p. 27. After Louis's death the works became known, often derogatorily, as Stripes.
2. Technical innovations about 1960 included a lighter canvas, no additional sizing, and the use of a thinner Magna; see Angelica Rudenstine in Museum of Fine Arts, Boston, *Morris Louis: 1912–1962*, exh. cat., 1967, p. 79.
3. Upright, p. 29.
4. Like *Dalet Chaf*, the work was stretched at the instruction of the estate under the supervision of Clement Greenberg.
5. Louis experimented with the orientation of the Pillars, and since his death there has arisen some confusion about the proper hanging. According to Upright, p. 44, Clement Greenberg, André Emmerich, and the artist's widow concurred that his intention in the vertical canvases was always to anchor the paint at the bottom.
6. See Upright, p. 42.

Louis Lozowick

New York 1925–1926

American, b. Russia,
1892–1973

oil on canvas

**30⅛ x 22⅛
(76.5 x 56.2)**

**lower right, *Louis
Lozowick*; on reverse,
upper center (visible
through lining), *Louis/
Lozowick***

**acquired for the Walker
Art Center by Hudson D.
Walker from the artist,
1961 (gift of Hudson D.
Walker 61.17)**

Responding to the Walker Art Center's request for
information on *New York*, Lozowick wrote:

> When I was at the National Academy (1912–1915)
> I used to pass daily an elevated line on W 109th St,
> making a sharp turn a couple of blocks west of Central
> Park. It was probably the tallest elevated line in NY.
> It towered above the street and was tremendously
> impressive as it turned the corner. After the Academy
> I went to college, then into the army and to Europe.
> I began to paint again in the '20s and it was then,
> curiously, that the memory of that line came to me.
> I made a painting of it adding a memory impression of
> Brooklyn Bridge and several skyscrapers (1903 [*sic*],
> sketch I). About a year later I did the same subject
> with quite a number of modifications (II). I changed the
> directional lines of the buildings, lowered the bridge
> and treated the right hand side in a futurist technique.
> After that I did one more painting and two drawings all
> of the same subject. Yours is the fourth painting and
> the final version.[1]

The first three canvases form part of a group
of American city subjects Lozowick painted in
Europe in the early 1920s.[2] The final two paintings depart abruptly and radically from the first
two, where the colors are vivid and saturated. The
later versions are nocturnal, a choice influenced
perhaps by Lozowick's interest in the monochromatic scheme of his prints. In comparison with
the others, they are moody and atmospheric,
albeit in the clipped, chic mechanomorphic
vocabulary of the *style moderne*.[3] The three
elements of bridge, skyscrapers, and elevated
tracks have been integrated in a swooping but
tightly rhythmic composition. At the right, the
curves of the multiplied train tracks are punctured
by the rigid vertical and horizontal lines of the
buildings, which halt their movement like a
sudden application of brakes.

The American cityscapes Lozowick painted
abroad were exhibited in the early 1920s in
Berlin, where they attracted the attention of the
European artistic community, particularly the
Russian Constructivist and German Expressionist
artists with whom he associated before his return
to the United States in 1923. Shortly before his
death he reminisced about the success of these
pictures in Berlin, which he attributed as much to
their being American as to their intrinsic quality.[4]

L.F.G.

1. Letter to Martin Friedman, 12 October 1961. The first
two oils, of 1922, are in private collections; the third
appears to be lost; Virginia Hagelstein Marquardt, letter to
the author, 26 September 1985.
2. The Walker canvas is one of a series of replicas he
painted after his return to the United States in 1924. The
"two drawings" seem to be one drawing and a lithograph
related to the third painting, the original version of the
Walker *New York*. It is likely that he began work on the
fourth painting in late 1925, completing it before his
exhibition at the New Art Circle in January 1926. Virginia
Hagelstein Marquardt, conversation with the author, 7 June
1987.
3. For a discussion of Lozowick's formative stylistic
influences during this period, including the work of Léger,
Moholy-Nagy, El Lissitzky, Gabo, and Van Doesburg, see
Virginia Hagelstein Marquardt, "Louis Lozowick:
Development from Machine Aesthetic to Social Realism,
1922–1936," Ph.D dissertation, University of Maryland,
College Park, 1983.
4. Seton Hall University, South Orange, New Jersey, *Louis
Lozowick 1892–1973*, exh. cat., 1973, p. 3.

George Luks

Breaker Boy of Shenandoah, Pa. 1921

American, 1866–1933

oil on canvas

30⅛ x 25⅛
(76.5 x 63.8)

lower left, *george luks*;
on reverse in black paint
(recorded by J. Roth,
1971; not visible through
lining), *Breaker Boy of
Shenandoah Pa, George
Luks 1921*

John F. Braun, Merion,
Pennsylvania, by 1923;
Babcock Galleries,
New York, 1943; The
Milch Galleries, New York,
1947; Mrs. Jacob H.
Rand, New York, 1947;
acquired from the
Babcock Galleries, 1949
(gift of the T.B. Walker
Foundation, John T.
Baxter Memorial
Collection of American
Drawings 49.13)

When asked for a characterization of Luks's work
soon after his death, his colleague John Sloan
wrote:

> He seemed to be of the direct line of Hals and Goya
> and related to George Morland. The mutual phobia
> between Luks and the Academy and all its works set
> him apart from the average artist.... Like other notable
> painters of his time he reacted to the creative
> inspiration of Robert Henri without any degree of
> imitation.[1]

Although the debt to Henri, which irritated
Luks,[2] is in strong evidence in *Breaker Boy*, the
authenticity of the image results from Luks's
personal involvement with the subject. Luks was
raised in the coal-mining town of Shenandoah,
Pennsylvania, where his father was a doctor.
Breaker boys were employed in the coal breakers,
where the anthracite was crushed; their job
generally was to sort coal from slate. As an adult
Luks visited the cottages, churches, mine shafts,
and the residents of this central Pennsylvania
region, and sketched and painted (in watercolor
and oil) numerous images, a number of which
were exhibited at the Rehn Gallery in New York in
1925.

By evoking art of the past—the swift descriptions of Hals's energized brushstrokes, the
nocturnal light of Caravaggio and Goya, the
penumbra of Rembrandt, and the modernist
planes of Manet—Luks dignifies the laborer, who
looks out appraisingly from the dark maroon
recesses of his eyes. The figure prompted the
following commentary:

> Hard of eye, confident, a little swaggering, he gazes
> back at the spectator, the image of a life which never
> polished, but hardened. The canvas has been
> projected in a clot of emotion, and accordingly it stirs
> our feelings—or at least burns and assaults them—
> while the handling has an undeniable brilliance. Luks
> could paint. He knew it too. "Art my slats! Say, listen,
> you, it's in you or it isn't. Who taught Shakespeare
> technique? ... Guts! Guts! Life! Life! That's my
> technique."[3]

The quotation is consistent with recorded
descriptions of the artist as a hard-drinking, hard-
talking, irascible, and sentimental powerhouse, a
personality that can be sensed in the depiction,
both blunt and tender, of the nonchalant and
haughty breaker boy.

L.F.G.

1. Quoted in The Newark Museum, *George Luks
1867–1933: Paintings and Drawings*, exh. cat., 1934,
p. 12.
2. Mahonri Sharp Young, *The Eight: The Realist Revolt in
American Painting* (New York: Watson-Guptill, 1973),
p. 112.
3. Jerome Mellquist, *The Emergence of an American Art*
(New York: Charles Scribner's Sons, 1942), p. 136.

Stanton Macdonald-Wright

Synchromy in Green and Orange   1916

American, 1890–1973

oil on canvas

34⅛ x 30⅛
(86.7 x 76.5)

on stretcher, upper
member, not in artist's
hand, *Property/Alfred
Stieglitz/Stieglitz*

Alfred Stieglitz, New York,
by 1935; acquired from
Hudson D. Walker, 1953
(gift of the T.B. Walker
Foundation, Hudson D.
Walker Collection 53.49)

The Synchromists' intention was to make color the subject of their paintings in the way that music is the subject of symphonic compositions. Macdonald-Wright and Morgan Russell based their notions of "harmonic" relationships on principles of nineteenth-century color theory[1] and on the empirical discoveries they themselves made about the behavior of hue, tone, and value. Although the title of this painting mentions only green and orange, the "dominant chord" emblazoned on the figure's torso includes purple as well. This combination of the three secondaries, each 120 degrees apart on the chromatic wheel, satisfies Ogden Rood's prescription for harmonious color relations as well as Michel-Eugène Chevreul's law of the harmony of contrast.

Given the greater warmth of orange and green (due to their yellow component), these colors tend to advance, while the cooler purple, muted here with blues and grays, seems to recede. Macdonald-Wright commented on the importance of blue for him "from the standpoint of spatial extension," an issue raised in his reading of Leonardo da Vinci's *Trattato della Pittura*.[2] Compensation for the tendency of the violet and blue hues to recede is made by the judicious application of a muted yellow at four points of an imaginary rectangle overlaying the figure. The yellow, opposite purple on the color chart, tends to pull it forward. The care Macdonald-Wright took to modulate the purple bears out his statement that he preferred harmonic to complementary colors: "If you take yellow, violet is a complementary. I never use a violet in a thing where I have yellow, I use a blue violet or a red violet."[3] Macdonald-Wright also uses the contrast of values for spatial effect: the lighter values occur in the areas of leg and arm that are closest to the picture plane and the darker values in the areas of the body that are farther away.

In contrast to the Cubist method that influenced this work, the sculptural volume of the figure remains intact rather than being fragmented and reconstructed architectonically. The iridescent interpenetrating planes of color do not substitute for the traditional devices of modeling, foreshortening, and the implication of an essentially continuous contour. The figure, an amalgam of Michelangelo's *David*, *Adam*, the Medici Chapel figures, and the Sistine *ignudi*, supports Macdonald-Wright's statement that "every particle of composition that I have ever used is based on Michelangelo,"[4] although the casualness of the pose suggests that the model might have been drawn from life.

L.F.G.

1. See William C. Agee in M. Knoedler & Co., New York, *Synchromism and Color Principles in American Painting 1910–1930*, exh. cat., 1965.
2. See Frederick Wight in The University of California, Los Angeles Galleries/The Grunwald Graphic Arts Foundation, *Stanton Macdonald-Wright: A Retrospective Exhibition*, exh. cat., 1970, n.p.
3. Ibid.
4. Ibid.

Aristide Maillol

Study for La Méditerranée   circa 1905

French, 1861–1944

sand-cast bronze

**27⅞ x 17½ x 11¼
(70.8 x 44.5 x 28.6)**

**left lower edge,
M (inscribed in circle)
2/6/•Alexis Rudier•
/ •Fondeur•Paris**

**Alexis Rudier Fondeur,
Paris**

**acquired from the
Fine Arts Associates,
New York, 1960 (gift of
the T.B. Walker
Foundation 60.30)**

Aristide Maillol
La Méditerranée
1902–1905
bronze
41 (104.1) high
Collection The Museum of
Modern Art, New York
Gift of Stephen C. Clark

This bronze torso is closely related to Maillol's La Méditerranée, the plaster of which was received with great critical acclaim when first exhibited at the Salon d'Automne in 1905.[1] The original conception had been a clay piece called simply *Femme accroupie* (*Crouching Woman*), enlarged from a statuette, one of Maillol's earliest sculptures. He had taken the work in the spring of 1900 from Banyuls to Paris, where Matisse helped him make a plaster cast.[2] Numerous studies in clay followed as Maillol developed and refined the figure; the process culminated in at least two highly finished plasters.[3] From one of these he made a stone version, carving and chiseling for the first time in his life, for Count Kessler. A bronze proof of this work was erected by the city of Perpignan in the patio of its Hôtel de Ville and a marble replica of 1923 (not carved by Maillol) is in the Jardin des Tuileries in Paris. It has also been cast in bronze.

It is difficult to know exactly where in the sequence of studies the Walker torso belongs. It does not have the variations and provisional qualities of a preparatory study, but seems rather to represent a late stage in the evolution of the image.[4] The pose of the torso—with back and neck bent forward, right shoulder and juncture of leg and torso lowered and the corresponding parts on the left raised—clearly replicates that of the full figure. *La Méditerranée* sits on a ground, resting her left elbow on her lifted left knee, buttressing her weight through her straightened right arm, her right leg lowered to the ground and bent at the knee with the ankle resting behind the ankle of the left leg. The pose is a variation of that of *La Notte* on Michelangelo's tomb of Giuliano de' Medici at San Lorenzo in Florence, which Maillol knew from reproductions and passionately admired, preferring it to ancient Greek sources for its air of melancholy.[5]

The difference between the Walker torso and the full figures related to *La Méditerranée* is the torso's slight twist above the waist, which Maillol may have abandoned in favor of the more static rectilinear pose. He said in an interview that "I construct my figures according to a geometric plan, but I choose this plan myself. My Mediterranean is enclosed in a perfect square."[6] He may have felt that axial rotation detracted from the geometric authority of the square. The raw edges of the otherwise highly resolved form suggest that it was part of a larger figure that Maillol dismembered. He was particularly concerned with the trunk of the body, and criticized Rodin for concealing the beauties of his *Penseur* behind the arms of the figure.[7] He also described the felicitous effect of the absence of arms in the *Venus de Milo*, which he considered the most beautiful statue in the world:

> If she had her arms, which perhaps would hold a shield, she would be less beautiful. There is a mystery there: the arms would have an explanatory, anecdotal gesture, while in her present state—it is pure beauty.[8]

It is said that Maillol used no armature to build his forms, which therefore are skins supported and balanced by their own weight distribution.[9]

L.F.G.

1. André Gide, "Promenade au Salon d'Automne," *Gazette des Beaux-Arts*, vol. 34 (1905), pp. 478, 479, gives a rapturous description of La Méditerranée, which he reproduced as *Femme*.
2. Judith Cladel, *Maillol: sa vie, son oeuvre, ses idées* (Paris: Grasset, 1937), p. 73, recounts Maillol's admiration from an interview with the artist.
3. For these plasters, see Waldemar George, *Maillol: 24 Phototypies* (Paris: Les Albums d'Art Druet [1930]), n.p., under the title *Baigneuse accoudée, I,* and Gide, "Promenade," p. 479, a *Femme, statue en plâtre,* which George called *Baigneuse Accoudée, II.* For three preliminary studies, see John Rewald, *Maillol* (London, New York: The Hyperion Press, 1939), p. 52; Musée National d'Art Moderne, Paris, *Hommage à Aristide Maillol,* exh. cat., 1961, no. 7; and Staatliche Kunsthalle Baden-Baden, *Maillol,* exh. cat., 1978, no. 24.
4. Although the Walker bronze has been variously dated 1902–1905, 1905, and 1908, both Dina Vierny and Linda Konheim Kramer (conversation with the author, 9 May 1984) feel that the model from which it was made was probably a late study for *La Méditerranée,* although it may have been another, unfinished piece. In either case, it is doubtful that the bronze was cast during Maillol's lifetime.
5. Cladel, p. 37: "Je pense constamment à sa [Michelangelo's] Vièrge, à La Nuit, aux Tombeaux."
6. Ibid., p. 148.
7. Henri Frère, *Conversations de Maillol* (Geneva: Pierre Cailler Editeur, 1956), p. 173.
8. Cladel, p. 141.
9. Denys Chevalier, *Maillol* (Lugano: Bonfini, 1970), p. 55.

Robert Mallary

The Parachutist   1962–1963

American, b. 1917

polyester, tuxedos,
Rustoleum, umbrella,
fiberglass, sand, metal
rods, ceramic and wood
understructure[1]

90 x 108 x 42
(228.6 x 274.3 x 106.7)

acquired from the Allan
Stone Gallery, New York,
by Mrs. Albert A. List,
1963; acquired from Mrs.
List, 1972 (gift of the
Albert A. List Family 72.7)

Soon after completing *The Parachutist* Mallary discussed the series to which it belongs. He sees the figures implied by the misshapen, disjointed tuxedos impregnated with plastic as paradigms of contemporary man in a society dominated by machines:

> ... assailed, harassed, confused, frustrated, befuddled, desperate and hysterical. As lonely, isolated, afraid and alienated. As tragic, comic and tragi-comic. The attitude is ironic, sardonic, sarcastic and just plain hateful. The figures are smashed, torn, shredded, twisted, lacerated, maimed and broken. They are being clouted, clobbered, jabbed, manacled, tripped, crushed, run over, caught ... and are taking pratfalls. They are involved in vague happenings, mysterious projects and rush about madly in pursuit of uncertain goals. The images are those of shock, crisis, peril, the "extreme situation"—and the absurd.[2]

Here the unfortunate parachutist has only a broken, inverted umbrella to ease his fall earthward, and his limbs thrash anarchically.[3] The image may have been inspired by an incident in Mallary's childhood, when his father, holding an umbrella, jumped off their barn in Iowa, and broke a leg. Mallary does not remember witnessing the accident, but it was part of the family lore.[4] The tuxedo for Mallary is a substitute for

the human figure in stiff poses from "painting, sculpture, slapstick comedy, vaudeville, the dance, the animated cartoon, the theater, puppetry, and pantomime."[5] He compares the passivity of the fabric being formed into tuxedos to the docility of an artist's medium being manipulated, and to the submission of organisms to natural forces.

Mallary has been motivated in these works by a desire to purge anxiety and self-resentment to make a more objective statement on the ominous trends of current history.[6] While comparing his brutalization of the human figure to that of de Kooning and Dubuffet, he has stated that visual aspects of the forms remind him of his friend Franz Kline's black-and-white Action paintings.[7] He produced the tension of his "strokes" by stretching the material, using clamps and dozens of taut ribbons of inner tubes tied to ropes that were attached to the four walls of his studio in New York. By moving individual ropes he could change the angle of a limb, developing the form in an improvisatory way, without preparatory drawings. He felt that the contrast between the great tension of the ropes and the loose, dangling quality of the fabric was analogous to the character of the human body.[8] The incorporation into the piece of the cable from which the figure is suspended is intended as a play on the concept of the pedestal [9]

L.F.G.

1. A mixture of polyester and fiberglass was used to reinforce sections out of view, and to attach a welded steel reinforcement. Sand was added for a "dusty, dirty quality, part of the junk think." Mallary estimates that he used about four or five fragmented tuxedos for this piece; conversation with the author, 29 September 1986.
2. "Robert Mallary: A Self-Interview," *Location*, vol. 1 (Spring 1963), p. 61.
3. *The Parachutist* actually did fall on 27 October 1984, sustaining serious injuries that required extensive reconstruction by the artist. The restoration, documented in letters from Mallary to Martin Friedman, 12 June and 28 October 1985, was complete by January 1986, and included a new old umbrella.
4. Conversation with the author, 29 September 1986.
5. "Robert Mallary: A Self-Interview," p. 61.
6. Ibid., p. 62.
7. Ibid., pp. 63 and 65.
8. Martin Friedman, interview with Robert Mallary and Peter Agostini, 9 March 1964, typescript, p. 7.
9. "Robert Mallary: A Self-Interview," p. 66.

Robert Mangold

Pink X within X   1980

American, b. Canada,
1937

acrylic, colored pencil on
canvas

112½ x 112
(285.8 x 284.5) overall

on reverse, center,
*R. Mangold 1980–81/
Pink X within X/should be
hung/so that the drawn X
is/square on wall/
diagram of work*

acquired from the Paula
Cooper Gallery, New York,
1983 (Justin V. Smith
Purchase Fund 83.199)

By slight departures from rigidity within a geometrically generated format, Mangold suggests a dialectically active Constructivism in works that are lyrical though hard-edged, complicated though reductive. In this painting, the "X within" is that marked by the black colored pencil lines that run along the edges of the four canvases. The two left arms of this X are determined by the right-angled meeting of the two left-hand canvases, scored with the drawn lines. In order for the upper right arm of the drawn X to be the same length, the upper right identically contoured canvas had to be dropped, as if filling in the central vacancy. As a result, the lower right arm of the drawn X has to be depicted as independent of the canvas that supports it, the only alternative to overlapping the canvases and thus destroying the essential flatness of the painting. The discontinuous line leaves the implication of an imaginary square at the end of the lower right canvas, which is identical with that suggested at the center of the piece, rationalizing the irregularity of the overall contours. The drawn edges taken as boundaries set up proportional relationships as compelling as those established by the canvas edges.

Although the drawn lines set up these interactive dramas with the canvases as an allover configuration, the X they stand for is not formed of continuous lines that ignore the passage from one plane to another. Taken separately, each canvas has its own "private" linear activity. Mangold is interested in the idea of a form being complete in itself while functioning simultaneously as a fragment of a larger whole.[1] His rational, mathematical manipulations create an optical illusion, that of the upper right arm appearing to be shorter than the others, an irony extended to the ambiguous way the panels, differentiated by the drawn marks, seem at the same time to be identical. The sameness or difference in forms are concepts contingent on subjective choices of the viewer.

The asymmetry that Mangold's devices induce by upsetting the static balance of echoing forms gives a gravitational sense to the work, suggesting a potential for movement that brings it into relation with Malevich's rotational compositions. The lyricism of the floating angular forms is derived as well from the soft color, the acrylic brushed on and sealed with a matte varnish applied with a roller.[2] Mangold has said of his color:

> ... it plays an important, but controlled role in the works. It identifies and separates the individual work, and gives the surface an assertive presence. In most cases, the color is kept somewhat subdued to prevent it from dominating the piece since I want the work to be a total unity of color-line-shape.[3]

L.F.G.

1. "I liked the idea of a section of something implying more and yet being a complete thing;" Rosalind Krauss, "Robert Mangold: An Interview," *Artforum*, vol. 12 (March 1974), p. 36.
2. WAC questionnaire, 2 February 1984, p. 1.
3. Quoted in Krauss, p. 37.

Sylvia Plimack Mangold

Carbon Night 1978

American, b. 1938

acrylic, oil on canvas

60 x 73 (152.4 x 185.4)

on central horizontal stretcher members, in black felt-tip pen, left, *Sylvia Plimack Mangold*; right *"Carbon Night" 8* (changed from "7")/ *78 Ac + oil/canvas*

acquired from the Droll/ Kolbert Gallery, New York, 1979 (purchased with the aid of funds from the Justin V. Smith Memorial Fund and the National Endowment for the Arts 79.164)

Mangold first began using masking tape to mark the particular board she was copying in paintings of her floors; she could thereby locate it quickly as she shifted her gaze between subject and canvas.[1] Her attention was then drawn to the tape itself, both as an object in its own right (having qualities of translucency and texture, and functions of securing and marking) and as delineator of the visual limits of the particular segment of the perceived environment she wished to represent. In the gridded drawings in her book *Inches and Field*,[2] rectangular sections of the landscape outside her home in Washingtonville, New York, are isolated by blank framing strips whose contours resemble those of masking tape torn in lengths and applied.

Carbon Night was the first nocturnal view in a series of landscapes of that Washingtonville scene. "My primary concern ... has been that they have the appearance of becoming and that despite all the deliberate choices, they should look casual."[3] Mangold's painterly choices and the technical means with which she enforced them can be surveyed through an examination of five preparatory studies and the final canvas. Discussing the study she gave to the Walker to accompany the painting,[4] she explained that she was primarily concerned about the color line between the similarly valued and hued passages of land and sky, a problem she resolved by varying the ground rather than changing the color.

Mangold began *Carbon Night* in Liquitex acrylic, but, unable to achieve the desired degree of luminosity in the dark colors, changed midway to oil paint, the medium she continues to use. Textural variation has resulted from the combination of masking tape and oil on sanded layers of acrylic, the velvety blue field, and the landscape.[5]

It appears that actual tape was applied to the surface to serve as a model for its painted replication before being removed, as what appears to be adhesive residue seems to remain at the edges, but the illusion of the reality of the tape is so overwhelming that the naked eye can not be trusted.[6] The borders of the central landscape are painted unevenly, imitating the effects of tape having been carelessly removed so as to drag out the edge of the paint layer. Stains and drips vividly and immediately convey the behavior of uncontrolled liquid color, while simultaneously posing as carefully depicted subjects themselves. The drip can be seen as a painting of a drip, the deliberate rendition of

accident. That the tape should be so exquisitely rendered contributes to the sense of disjunction between the concreteness of the materials of painting and the subjectivity of painterly decisions, most blatantly demonstrated in abstract or impressionistic painting but present in all image making. The tape almost incidentally serves as a compelling compositional element on a flat, formalist surface, as the indicator of a geometric grid on a darkly atmospheric color cloud, and as a definer and interpreter of spatial relations. It can be read as outlining a window onto a reality beyond or as restraining a painted icon with illusionistic depths on a flat sheet. Overlapping itself, the tape forms a sandwich of imagined planes. Being painted, like the landscape, it comments on the different degrees of persuasiveness of illusionistic means.

L.F.G.

1. Lisa Lyons, "Sylvia Plimack Mangold," in *Design Quarterly 111/112, Eight Artists: The Elusive Image* (1979), p. 37.
2. Sylvia Plimack Mangold, *Inches and Field* (New York: Lapp Princess Press, 1978).
3. Ibid.
4. Study for *Carbon Night*, oil on canvas, 9 x 12 inches; four other studies, one of these dimensions and three others of 11 x 14 inches, were shown with the finished painting at the Walker Art Center exhibition, *Eight Artists: The Elusive Image*, 1979.
5. Detailed technical information was provided by the artist in a WAC questionnaire of 18 July 1980.
6. The story circulates that Sol LeWitt once tried to pry off the tape on a Mangold; K[im] L[evin], "Midtown," *The Village Voice*, 21 January 1980, p. 80.

Franz Marc

Die grossen blauen Pferde (The Large Blue Horses)[1] 1911

German, 1880–1916

oil on canvas

41⁵⁄₁₆ x 71¼
(104.9 x 181)

acquired by J.E. Wolfensberger, Zurich, from Maria Marc, 1919[2]; sold to F.J. Weck, Zurich; Mr. Tanner, Zurich; Karl Nierendorf, New York, by 1940; acquired from the Nierendorf Gallery, New York, 1942 (gift of the T.B. Walker Foundation, Gilbert M. Walker Fund 42.1)

Painted at Sindelsdorf, in Upper Bavaria, *Die grossen blauen Pferde* depicts a subject that was already predominant in Marc's work by 1911. Maintaining that animals had a purer, more sublime relationship with the world than did human beings, he not only represented them, but also sought to experience their world view empathetically. He wrote: "How does a horse see the world…? How wretched and how soulless, is our convention of placing animals in a landscape which belongs to our eyes, instead of sinking ourselves in the soul of the animal in order to imagine his perceptions."[3] Abstraction, Marc felt, was the means of expressing the exalted state of a spirit in harmony with nature.

Marc's admiration of the horse manifested itself as early as 1905, in sketches from life. In 1908 he executed anatomical studies of the horse and painted *Grosses Pferdebild Lenggries I,* in which a group of horses is disposed in the foreground of a landscape in an exaggeratedly horizontal format. In 1911 he returned to this composition in sketchbook drawings, introducing the circular rhythms that typify *Die grossen blauen Pferde*. In a letter of 2 October 1910, Marc described the incompatibility of his previous style with the large scale of the surface and the forms within it in the *Lenggries* picture, and by the summer of 1911 exclaimed that he has at last found the proper style in the "large one," presumably the Walker painting.[4] In this work Marc has replaced the pale tonalities of the 1908 canvas with a vivid palette deriving from his theory of the correspondence of certain colors with particular concepts. In 1915 he wrote from the war front that "blue is the only color with which I feel comfortable and which does not bore me; all other colors exist only to awaken the longing for blue."[5] According to his programmatic color symbolism, outlined in a frequently cited letter to August Macke of 12 December 1910, blue represents the spiritual, male principle. Red represents intractable matter (appropriately applied here to the landscape), and yellow suggests the comfort of the female principle. Green, the combination of blue and yellow, is used here primarily for vegetation; Marc felt that green served to activate red.

Marc presents his equine group as a fusion of charged physicality and transfigured spirituality. The animals, colored in cool, anti-material blue, are posed with their heads bowed, forming enclosed, rounded volumes; they are removed, private, and introspective. The sense of confinement is emphasized by the two white stalks, which appear to continue beyond the limits of the canvas, in the manner of Marc's friend Kandinsky, who lived in nearby Murnau. Comparison with an earlier drawing suggests that these are abstract representations of trees that serve the formal function of providing a sweeping linear contrast to the rolling forms of the horses and echoing hills.

L.F.G.

1. The title *Die grossen blauen Pferde*, by which the work has come to be known, was apparently not Marc's (see n. 2), and probably originated with a questionnaire prepared by Maria Marc, Alois Schardt, and Frau Schardt in early 1936, to distinguish the work from a smaller version, the so-called *Kleinen blauen Pferde*.
2. On p. 23 of Marc's *Werkbuch*, transcribed on the author's behalf by Klaus Lankheit, the artist indicated that *Bl. Pferde*, which is thought to be the Walker picture, was purchased by a Dr. Glaser from the Blaue Reiter exhibition of 1911–1912. However, Wolfensberger, in conversation with Jan van der Marck, stated that he purchased the work directly from Maria Marc.
3. Excerpted from Franz Marc, *Briefe, Aufzeichnungen und Aphorismen*, 1920, translated by Robert J. Goldwater in Buchholz Gallery, New York, *Franz Marc*, exh. cat., 1940, n.p.
4. Klaus Lankheit provided a copy of the 1936 questionnaire prepared in connection with Schardt's 1936 monograph, *Franz Marc*, which included this information.
5. Quoted by Klaus Lankheit, in University Art Museum, University of California, Berkeley, *Franz Marc: 1880–1916*, exh. cat., 1979, p. 49.

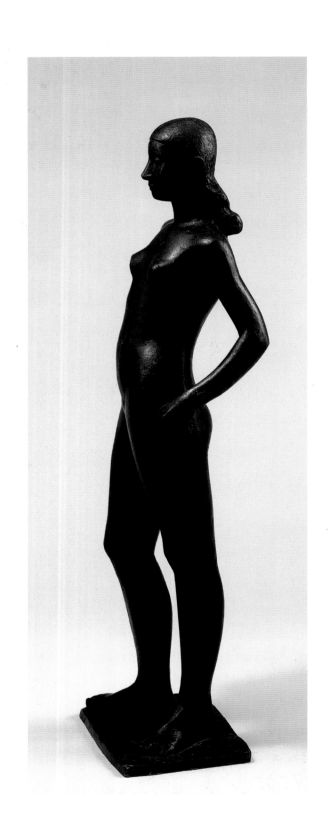

Gerhard Marcks

Mélusine III   1949/1951

German, 1889–1981

bronze

43½ x 13⅜ x 11 (110.5 x 34 x 28)

front top of base, monogram; interior of base, 1/Pisulla/51

Giesserwerkstatt der Landeskunstschule, Hamburg

acquired from the Curt Valentin Gallery, New York, 1953 (gift of the T.B. Walker Foundation 53.48)

Like Kolbe, Marcks sought inspiration in early Western sculptural traditions, particularly those of ancient Greece and medieval Germany. Although his attitude toward sculptural form was relatively conservative, his work was considered advanced enough to be condemned by the Nazis, and many of his prewar works were melted down for munitions or lost.

The nude *Mélusine III* was completed two years after the clothed *Mélusine I* and *II* and is, in comparison, more naturalistic and fluid. The model for all three works, Esther von König, daughter of the painter Leo von König,[1] also appeared as a prepubescent in a 1940 mother-daughter group, and as a fully developed woman in 1950. The name Mélusine is that of a mythical figure in French folklore whose laments of loss and pain gave rise to the traditional phrase "cries of Mélusine." She became the embodiment of victimized but heroic femininity for André Breton, who describes the "child-woman" resisting the domination of men:

> Even that which strikes her strengthens her, makes her flexible, refines her, and, in a word, realizes her, like the chisel of a visionary sculptor submissive to a preestablished harmony, who never fully finishes because he treads on the path to perfection, without being permitted a single false step, and that path knows no end.[2]

The model poses here with hips thrust forward in a relaxed contrapposto, accentuated by the left hand resting on the raised hip, while the backward bend of her left arm balances the forward bend of her right leg. The lightly textured but essentially smooth surfaces of the sculpture allow for subtle transitions from light to dark to indicate solid volumes.

In a 1951 exhibition catalogue,[3] the original plaster of *Mélusine III* is dated 1949, with the indication that casts had not yet been made. A man named Pisulla cast the Walker piece in 1951 at the short-lived foundry Marcks established at the Landeskunstschule in Hamburg, where he had been invited to teach in 1946.

L.F.G.

1. Martina Rudloff, Gerhard-Marcks-Stiftung, Bremen, letter to the author, 15 March 1985, identified the model and provided information on the casting of the edition. See her entry in *Gerhard Marcks: Das plastische Werk* (Frankfurt: Propyläen Verlag, 1977), no. 535.
2. André Breton, *Arcane 17* (New York: Brentano's, 1945), p. 98.
3. Galerie Rudolf Hoffmann, Berlin, *Gerhard Marcks: Bildwerke in Bronze 1946–1950*, exh. cat., 1951.

Brice Marden

Untitled 1971–1972

American, b. 1938

beeswax, oil on canvas

three panels
90 x 96
(228.6 x 243.8) overall

acquired from the Bykert
Gallery, New York
(gift of the T.B. Walker
Foundation 72.10)

Brice Marden has been characterized as the last Abstract Expressionist painter—following in the tradition of Mark Rothko and Barnett Newman—as the "most important abstract painter to emerge during the Minimalist era...."[1] In fact, his art embodies both of these styles, just as it represents his intensely personal inquiry into the nature and traditions of painting.

Marden studied art as an undergraduate at Boston University and then as a graduate student at Yale. After finishing his schooling in 1963, he returned to New York and took a job as a guard at the Jewish Museum. During his stint there he had the opportunity to study firsthand the paintings of Jasper Johns, whose work was the subject of a major exhibition at the museum and appears to have had an influence on Marden, especially in its eccentric colors and richly textured surfaces. Marden's colors are unnameable and, as Roberta Smith has observed, "Ultimately, they are too subtle and complex, too intricately and ironically related to each other to be anything but artificial and non-referential, the products of an artist's painstaking attention."[2]

Marden, who began mixing his paint with beeswax in 1965, applies the paint with a brush and then smooths it over with a palette knife. He has only about thirty minutes to work before the mixture dries and thus he must scrape it off and start anew if he is not satisfied. The result is a taut surface that reveals the process of its creation at the edges and a painting that somberly asserts its identity as such, an object without illusionism.

Marden's paintings have always been concerned with squares and rectangles. Initially he made square monochrome paintings; gradually he began experimenting with contiguous vertical, then horizontal bands. The Walker work, divided into three horizontal bands of color of equal value, forms a near square. The upper panel, slate blue, is barely distinguishable in color from the lower panel, rich gray. They tend to pinch the central panel, giving the painting the impression of being smaller than it actually is and demonstrating the way in which color affects our perception of scale. Like Ellsworth Kelly, with whom Marden is frequently compared, his paintings explore the relationship between color and shape. Marden adds a third element—texture—to the equation and this painting, like those which preceded, considers the delicate balance among the three.

M.G.

1. Peter Schjeldahl, Art of Our Time: The Saatchi Collection, Book 1 (London: Lund Humphries, 1984), p. 27.
2. Roberta Smith, "Brice Marden's Paintings," Arts Magazine, vol. 47 (May–June 1973), p. 38.

John Marin

Rocks, Sea and Boat, Small Point, Maine   1932

American, 1870–1953

watercolor, charcoal on paper

15⅜ x 20⅞ (39.1 x 53), mounted on paper 20³⁄₁₆ x 25¹³⁄₁₆ (51.3 x 65.6)

lower right, *Marin 32*

acquired from The Downtown Gallery, New York, 1947 (gift of the T.B. Walker Foundation 47.56)

According to Marin, the artist should serve as a kind of medium who transmits the qualities of nature in paint: "Water you paint the way water is and moves—Rocks and soil you paint the way they were worked for their formation—Trees you paint the way trees grow."[1] In the Walker watercolor, the effects of wind are described in the feathery diagonals of the trees and the broader slanted strokes of the water. The rocky arms of the coastline, rendered in washes heightened with charcoal, suggest the action of the sea. Marin, however, also uses anti-naturalistic devices whose source is the pictorial tradition—the juncture of boat and water is defined by an incised line; areas of unpainted paper are put to descriptive use, as foam and cloud edges and as compositional elements in the manner of Cézanne, whose work Marin knew from Stieglitz's 291 gallery. The significance of the two Xs between the boat and the lower rock outcropping remains uncertain.

Correspondence with Stieglitz indicates that Marin visited Small Point for the first time in 1915, when he bought one of the small islands that punctuate the Maine shoreline.[2] The view shown in this watercolor is from a bluff a short walk from the former Aliquippa Hotel, where he stayed: Goose Rock is on the right, Hermit Island on the left, and Wood Island beyond.[3] As his writings, drawings, and paintings reveal, Marin had profound feelings for the landscape of Maine, particularly the rocks, beaches, ocean, and boats of its coast. In characterizing the state for Stieglitz in a letter written during the summer he painted this watercolor, Marin commented on the transformation from "an unforgettable loveliness" when the weather is serene to a sudden fierceness when it is not: "Turns masculine—borders big and mighty—against—the big and mighty Atlantic. Tremendous shoulders to brace against his furious brother."[4]

Marin's custom of visually framing his own composition, although common in works of the European avant-garde, was considered a radical innovation in American painting at the time.[5] In the Walker work, he first painted the green and orange borders on a larger sheet, and then inserted the painted composition from a smaller sheet. On the reverse of the smaller sheet are numbered drawings of sailboats;[6] on the reverse of the larger sheet is a wide, uneven grayish green painted frame with the number "(8)" written in pencil.

L.F.G.

1. Letter to Stieglitz, 28 August 1931, quoted in MacKinley Helm, *John Marin* (Boston: Pellegrini & Cudahy in association with the Institute of Contemporary Art, 1948), p. 67.
2. Letter to Stieglitz published in Dorothy Norman, ed., *The Selected Writings of John Marin* (New York: Pellegrini & Cudahy, 1949), p. 20.
3. Author's visit to the site, July 1986; Nick Sewell, a local resident, identified the location. Marin painted in a way that was pictorially satisfying but that did not literally portray the scene.
4. Quoted in Norman, p. 144.
5. See Herbert J. Seligmann, "Frames: with Reference to Marin," in the unpaginated brochure *It Must Be Said*, no. 3, published by An American Place in 1934.
6. These sketches predate the Walker watercolor, and do not appear to have been made in connection with it. They are clearly sketched from life, while the boat on the recto is clumsily drawn. Although such a boat could have negotiated the passage—John Marin, Jr. recalls that there were "one or two master schooners around Small Point in 1932" (letter to the author, 27 March 1986)—as depicted it is grossly out of scale.

Marino Marini

Cavaliere (Horseman) circa 1949

Italian, 1901–1980

bronze

70⅝ x 45½ x 32
(179.4 x 115.6 x 81.3)

rear center of base, *MM*;
on edge of base, foundry
stamp

Fonderia d'Arte M.A.F.,
Milan

acquired from the Curt
Valentin Gallery, New
York, 1953 (gift of the
T.B. Walker Foundation
53.50)

In Marini's early explorations of the horse and
rider theme in the 1930s, the figures were poised
and formal, clear evocations of the classical
tradition. Gradually they became more stylized
and active. Marini interpreted the obsessive development of the theme in his work after the war:

> If my equestrian statues are considered one by one ...
> one can see that each time the rider is less able to
> control his mount and that the animal, in its anguish,
> becomes wilder and wilder, and more rigid.... My
> equestrian statues express the torment caused by
> events of this century.... My wish is to reveal the final
> moment of the dissolution of a myth, the myth of the
> heroic individual, the humanists,' "man of virtue."[1]

Cavaliere belongs to the middle phase of the
theme, when Marini was still celebrating the
heroic myth, but beginning to announce its even-
tual dissolution. In *Angelo della città* of the
previous year, the rider sits with arms rapturously
spread and phallus erect; the line from the
horse's neck to tail is perpendicular to the
staunch legs. In the Walker work, the horseman
has drawn his outstretched hands together as if
manacled, pulling up the horse's straining head,
which rises at an improbable angle, with mouth
open and contorted. The erotic symbolism
graphically displayed in the earlier work is
sublimated, implicit only in the raised and turgid
neck and vestigial tail of the horse. In later
versions the horse falls and the rider tumbles.
The process of sexual excitation and consummation serves as an apocalyptic metaphor for the
rise and fall of civilized states. Marini saw Italy's
past upheavals, the decline of the Roman Empire
and the destruction of Pompeii, as harbingers of
a modern collapse: "I myself seriously believe
that we are heading toward the end of a world."[2]

Marini began working on the original plaster
of *Cavaliere* in 1949, as corroborated by a
photograph of the artist in his studio.[3] In the
photograph the plaster is identifiable, although
the horse's neck and head have not yet been
attached. The date of the first two casts is not
known, but one was available for an outdoor
exhibition of sculpture in London in 1951.[4]

During this year Marini completed a polychromed
wood version of the same size, begun in 1949.
He worked on each bronze individually after it was
cast, explaining: "It is said that Donatello
attacked the bronze directly. It is certainly a joy to
work such a hard, dense surface, to chisel it, to
give life to a form which is practically dead when
it comes out of the foundry.... The more you
strike it, the more alive it becomes."[5]

L.F.G.

1. "Pensées de Marino sur l'art et sur les artistes," in
Hommage à Marino Marini (special issue of *XXe Siècle*,
Paris: 1974).
2. Ibid.
3. Enzo Carli, *Marino Marini* (Milan: Ulrico Hoepli Editore,
1950), n.p. The photograph is by Valeska.
4. *Sculpture: An Open Air Exhibition at Battersea Park*,
presented by the London County Council in association with
the Arts Council of Great Britain, May-September 1951, no.
30 (as *Horseman*, 1949, lent by the artist). This was
probably the first cast, which entered the collection of R.
Sturgis Ingersoll, Penllyn, Pennsylvania. The Walker cast is
the second, and definitely existed by 1953. The third cast,
made in 1953–1954, belongs to The St. Louis Art Museum
(letter from Curt Valentin to Perry T. Rathbone, 16
December 1953, Archives, The St. Louis Art Museum).
5. "Pensées de Marino."

Agnes Martin

Untitled No. 7 1977

American, b. 1912

India ink, graphite, gesso
on canvas

72 x 72 (182.9 x 182.9)

on reverse, upper left,
a. martin/1977

acquired from the artist by
the Pace Gallery, 1979
(purchased with the aid of
funds provided by The
Butler Family Foundation,
Mark B. Dayton, Roderick
McManigal, Dr. and Mrs.
Glen D. Nelson, Mr. and
Mrs. Miles Q. Fiterman,
Art Center Acquisition
Fund, and the National
Endowment for the Arts
79.34)

Martin's descriptions of her work adumbrate her mystical conception of the "untroubled mind" in relation to nature: "My paintings have neither objects, nor space, nor time, not anything—no forms. They are light, lightness, about merging, about formlessness, breaking down form."[1] She sees the rectangular alternation along each strip of her penciled grid not as a regimental geometric system but, on the contrary, as a mollification of the authority of the square:

> My formats are square, but the grids never are absolutely square; they are rectangles, a little bit off the square, making a sort of contradiction, a dissonance, though I didn't set out to do it that way. When I cover the square surface with rectangles, it lightens the weight of the square, destroys its power.[2]

Significantly, in the Walker work, as in Martin's grids of the early 1960s, the vaporous, fragile grid floats unanchored to its surround, stopping about one-half inch short of the canvas edge. Thus, the edges of the canvas are not allowed to function as virtual lines completing the grid and the support is declared as an independent field. The distinction between support and grid creates a tension between real object and drawn mark comparable to the tension between the assertive physical presence of the canvas, removed from the wall by a thick stretcher and hence disassociated from it, and the field of activity within or on top of its surface.

The rectangles that "cover the square surface" are simply the consequence of intersecting orthogonal lines, in the same way that the fabric of the canvas is woven with warp and woof. The graphite lines, thickening and thinning along their courses, mimic the threads of the canvas. The irregularity of the linen's own grid is exploited by the frottagelike effects produced by thin washes of gray ink rubbed or pulled over the textured gessoed surface. The washes have a generally horizontal movement that coincides with the emphasis of the grid, an emphasis produced by the slightly greater strength of the horizontal lines. The vertical lines, like those of Mondrian's Pier + Ocean series of the teens, check this expansiveness by balancing the horizontal accent through their relative frequency—they are separated by half the space that the horizontals are—and by the regularity of their intermittent syncopated rhythm.

The proliferation of nearly identical units, and the situation of small elements (the shapes formed by the grid) within a large field (the canvas) are Martin's means for attempting to transmit the therapeutic benefits of her pantheistic vision: "In a big picture a blade of grass amounts to not very much/worries fall off you when you can believe that."[3] The immeasurable extension of the washed, nebulous atmosphere is intended to provide another, equally revivifying experience that she compares to communion with the natural world: "There's nobody living who couldn't stand all afternoon in front of a waterfall."[4]

L.F.G.

1. Quoted in Ann Wilson, "Linear Webs," *Art and Artists*, vol. 1 (October 1966), p. 48.
2. Quoted in Lucy R. Lippard, "Homage to the Square," *Art in America*, vol. 55 (July–August 1967), p. 55.
3. Agnes Martin, in"The Untroubled Mind," in Institute of Contemporary Art, University of Pennsylvania, Philadelphia, *Agnes Martin*, exh. cat., 1973, p. 20.
4. Quoted in Wilson, p. 48.

Alfred Maurer

Self-Portrait with Hat   circa 1927

American 1868–1932

oil on panel

39⅛ x 23¹⁵⁄₁₆
(99.4 x 60.8)

upper left, *A.H. Maurer*

estate of the artist; purchased from Eugenia Maurer Fuerstenberg by Hudson D. Walker, New York, 1941; acquired from The American Federation of Arts, 1946 (gift of the T.B. Walker Foundation 46.50)

This image was painted during a period of crisis in Maurer's artistic life, when he temporarily returned to naturalistic drawing from the model, after years of attempting a more experimental pictorial language. In April 1928, he presented two anomalous subjects, the nude and the self-portrait, in his annual exhibition at the Weyhe Gallery in New York. Although he later effectively destroyed the nudes by painting abstractionist compositions over them, the self-portraits survive as visual records of the profound self-doubt of an artist who, according to his friend Mahonri Young, never fully resolved his struggles with modernism.[1]

By the time this self-portrait was completed, Maurer had moved his studio from the family brownstone owned by his father, Louis, a renowned Currier & Ives lithographer who wept in dismay in front of his son's work, to the Lincoln Square Arcade Building at the corner of Broadway and 66th Street.[2] At about the same time Maurer began to suffer from a painful prostate condition, which he endured almost until his death by suicide in 1932. Despite Maurer's physical and emotional difficulties, however, his craggy good looks were not as impaired at the age of sixty as the *Self-Portrait* would suggest. Comparisons with photographs show that he brutalized and exaggerated his own features.

In this and another contemporary self-portrait, Maurer stares at the viewer (i.e., himself) with huge unswerving liquid eyes, his brow deeply furrowed, eyebrows jutting forward, lips grimly set and face haggard and puffy. In the Walker picture he has opened his shirt collar; his jaunty polka-dot bow tie flops listlessly below the droop of his shoulders. Behind is a field of frenzied slashing paint strokes interacting with the exposed board to produce a darkly luminous, expressionistic matrix. Maurer's direct, unsentimental approach to his own image met with a mixed response from contemporary critics. While the reviewer for the *Chicago Evening Post* (3 April 1928) called it "a

new departure, a psychological document as well as a marvelous piece of painting," Virgil Barker, who was generally sympathetic to Maurer, wrote for *The Arts:*

> To me Mr. Maurer's greatest danger, to which he has succumbed in the large Self-Portrait, seems to be overemphasis—a danger which he shares with a whole age of headlines and electric signs and jazz. It would be silly to urge restraint upon those who have nothing to restrain: but where real power exists there is still some virtue in understatement.[3]

The mottled discoloration of the surface is attributable to the inferior grade of linseed oil Maurer used as a varnish, a practice he was soon to abandon. Despite repeated conservation efforts, the painting, like many in Maurer's oeuvre, remains somewhat disfigured by the yellowed oil.[4]

L.F.G.

1. Mahonri Sharp Young, *Early American Moderns: Painters of the Stieglitz Group* (New York: Watson-Guptill Publications, 1974), p. 114.
2. Elizabeth McCausland, in *A.H. Maurer* (New York: A.A. Wyn for the Walker Art Center, 1951), p. 193. McCausland surmises from interviews with Maurer's friends that he must have rented the studio in the fall of 1927.
3. V[irgil] B[arker], "The Month in the Galleries," *The Arts,* vol. 13 (May 1928), p. 321.
4. For a still relevant discussion of the conservation issues Maurer's work presents, see McCausland, pp. 271–274.

Joan Miró

Tête et oiseau (Head and Bird)   1967

Spanish, 1893–1983

bronze

24½ x 28⁹⁄₁₆ x 11
(62.2 x 72.5 x 27.9)

Incised, lower left rear,
miró 3/5

Parellada, Barcelona

acquired from the Pierre
Matisse Gallery, New
York, 1970 (gift of the
T.B. Walker Foundation

During the second half of the 1940s, Miró made about ten sculptures—of heads, birds, female figures—including the prototypes for *Tête et oiseau* and *Femme debout*.[1] He carved the granite stone on which the head is based in 1949 or 1950 during a fallow period in his collaborative work in ceramics with his old friend José Llorens Artigas. After 1953, when they resumed work at Artigas's house in the Catalan village of Gallifa, the ceramicist produced a clay replica of the head, precisely duplicating its stone surface. Two variations were fired and mounted on elongated triangular and rectangular bases or "bodies" in 1955–1956.

The clay model from which the head in *Tête et oiseau* was cast closely resembled the granite source except in the addition of pupils in the eyes, a feature that appears in Miró's painted work. Casts of other natural found objects are assembled totemically to form a combination of Miró's obsessive subjects—head, figure, bird. According to his own account, he never considered forms "abstract" but always signs for human beings, animals, and so on.[2] The squat proportions and natural folds in the rock as he found it may have suggested the features of the head, which he then accentuated with heavily incised outlines to describe a stylized, pre-Columbian face.

From about 1939 on, Miró frequently included forms he designated as birds in his paintings—hovering above or around female figures; in his sculpture, perched on their heads. The association is so recurrent that the bird acquires the status of amulet or attribute. In *Tête et oiseau,* the bird is based on a stalk of elegantly proportioned and curved weed. The tripartite stalk, while signifying "bird," also resembles the pitchfork and rake used in other of Miró's assembled sculptures. The witticism of creating the figure's "trunk" from a chopped segment of a tree branch had occurred to him as early as 1937, when he painted a sign for female genitalia on the exposed stump of *L'Objet du couchant.* In *Tête et oiseau,* the shaft of the tree stump combines with the head in a phallic configuration. When asked about the image of the bird, Miró responded that "a human being is like a tree, planted in the ground. Birds fly into space—they can carry us away, off the ground into higher things, into the world of fantasy and imagination that is not earthbound."[3]

The forms selected from nature for this piece have been assaulted with varying degrees of violence by man—the stem is torn, the log chopped, the stone incised in the artist's effort to "incorporate myself in the elements of that landscape by marking them with my imprint."[4] The imprint is explicitly made in the thumb-sized holes at the back of the head. The multiple equations (branch=bird=pitchfork; stone=head; stump=torso=base), and the various materials and disparate parts of this work are unified by their metasomatosis,[5] through casting by José Parellada, and by the perfectionism of the artist who, Artigas recalled, would spend hours adjusting the angle at which a head was joined to a body.[6]

L.F.G.

1. Jacques Dupin, *Joan Miró: Life and Work* (New York: Harry N. Abrams, 1962), pp. 464, 466.
2. See James Johnson Sweeney, "Joan Miró: Comment and Interview," *Partisan Review,* vol. 15 (February 1948), p. 208.
3. Quoted in translation by Barbara Rose, in Museum of Fine Arts, Houston, *Miró in America,* exh. cat., 1982, p. 120.
4. Quoted in Rosamond Bernier, "Miró ceramiste," *L'Oeil,* no. 17 (May 1956), p. 46.
5. A geological term used by Hugo Weiss in "Miró—Magic with Rocks," *Art News,* vol. 55 (Summer 1956), p. 57.
6. See Georges and Rosamond Bernier, *The Selective Eye,* II (New York: Reynal & Co., 1956–1957), p. 13.

Joan Miró

Femme debout (Standing Woman)   1969

Spanish, 1893–1983

bronze

75½ x 46¼ x 42¼ (191.8 x 117.5 x 107.3)

lower center back, *Susse Fondeur, Paris*; lower right back, *Miró 2/4*

Susse Fondeur, Paris

acquired from the Pierre Matisse Gallery, New York, 1973 (gift of the Pierre Matisse Gallery and the T.B. Walker Acquisition Fund 73.1)

Miró's ponderous female figure is an idiosyncratic version of one of sculpture's most ancient subjects—the earth goddess. Her stylized, symmetrical forms and exaggerated female attributes are evocative of archaic Mediterranean and Mesopotamian fertility figures and African tribal sculpture. Yet for all her overwhelming femininity, Miró's great goddess would seem to possess the power of self-fertilization. Within her swelling anatomy are male as well as female sexual elements: the scooped-out womb-vagina, prominent breasts, and buttocks coexist with phallic protuberances from the forehead and shoulders. This sexual duality is repeated in the play between swelling and hollow forms. *Femme debout* is an expression of metamorphosis, replete with forms that have multiple meanings. The figure's breasts and vagina, for example, can also be read as eyes and mouth. Such dualism, especially with respect to the depiction of the female figure, is characteristic of classical Surrealism, and can also be found in the metaphysical imagery of Dali and Magritte.

Thus, despite her archaic character, Miró's serene, dark goddess is decidedly a twentieth-century personage. Her sleek biomorphic form—simultaneously monstrous and maternal, gentle and demonic—seems to have emerged full-blown from one of the fantastic surrealistic universes Miró was so fond of painting. Here in three dimensions are the smooth ballooning ovals and fantastic shapes that characterized his repertoire of abstract figures from the 1920s through the 1950s.

Even though its configuration is closely related to the animated shapes in Miró's painting, *Femme debout* was actually developed over a long period as a sculptural idea. In 1948, Miró made a small bronze figure, *Femme*, in a conical shape, with prominent sexual elements, and, two years later, reworked this into a small-scale sculpture that clearly foreshadowed the Walker piece. In the late 1960s, he returned to this figure and had her "pointed-up"[1] to a large plaster model. In a second plaster version, the womb-vagina of this by now iconic figure was elongated into a sinuous groove that reached to the base of the neck. It was from this variation on the goddess theme that *Femme debout* came into existence.

Miró's sculptural production consisted of two seemingly antithetical styles. Perhaps best known are his assemblages—relief and full-volume sculptures—in which a diversity of natural forms is combined, such as rocks and fragments of wood, with "found," man-made objects. In his later years he frequently had such improvised constructions cast in bronze, some of which he patinated in subtle gray and earth tones, others of which he painted in lively primary colors. Another aspect of his sculpture is revealed in the smooth, seamless volumes of *Femme debout*. This figure, along with two preceding works, *Oiseau solaire* and *Oiseau lunaire,* both of 1966, represent the artist's efforts to deal with form as dense, highly compressed mass. In *Femme debout,* Miró has elegantly synthesized richly anatomical associations with spare, highly reduced forms. The result is a stately iconic presence which, though the product of Miró's singular imagination, projects a sense of universality and timelessness.

L.R.

1. "Pointing-up" is a technique for producing an exact, enlarged-scale version of a sculpture. It involves taking from a small model a large number of measurements from a series of verticals around it, and drilling holes to corresponding depths in a larger block of plaster or stone. The material is then chiseled away to the depth of the drilled holes.

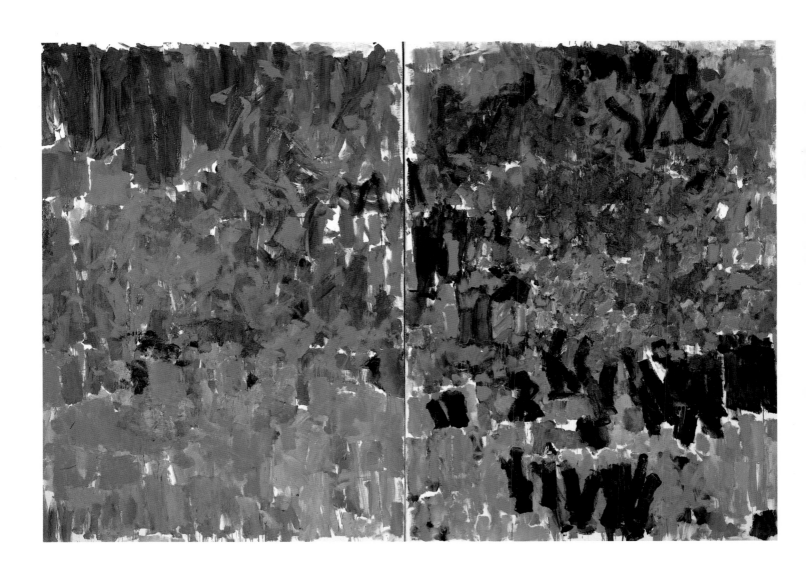

Joan Mitchell

Posted 1977

American, b. 1926

oil on canvas

**110 x 157½
(279.4 x 400)**

**acquired from the Robert
Miller Gallery, New York,
and Bernard Lennon, Inc.,
New York (gift of Joanne
and Philip Von Blon
89.61)**

Over the course of a career that has spanned four decades and dozens of artistic "isms," Joan Mitchell has been unflagging in her commitment to the nonrepresentational, gestural style that is the hallmark of Abstract Expressionism. She has remained equally devoted to her subject matter, the landscape. In her sensuously lyrical paintings, which she likens to poems, she has sought to make tangible her empathy with the natural world.

Mitchell's source of inspiration is the landscape around Vétheuil, France, a rural area some forty miles north of Paris where she has lived and worked since 1968. Her two-acre estate includes the cottage in which Claude Monet resided from 1878 to 1881, but Mitchell's approach to landscape painting is quite distinct from his. While the Impressionist master sought to render nature by distilling its visual essence, Mitchell concentrates on her emotional responses to a scene. "I paint from remembered landscapes that I carry with me," she has written, "and remembered feelings of them, which of course become transformed. I could certainly never mirror nature. I would like more to paint what it leaves me with."[1]

Mitchell painted *Posted*, a large diptych, in Vétheuil in 1977. Its horizontally banded composition evokes a landscape space, and her palette of rich blues, greens, and ochers suggests sky, trees, and fields. The surface of the painting is a dense panoply of strokes ranging from heavy patches of scumbled pigment to broad, flat strokes created with a palette knife. This heavy curtain of thickly applied paint seems to bar entry into the overgrown, verdant landscape and creates a shallow pictorial space that feels closed, almost airless.

The notion of being denied entry is also suggested by the work's title, a term sometimes used to designate a place of sanctuary where hunting is forbidden and animals can find safety from their human predators.[2] The haven depicted in *Posted* may also be for Mitchell a visual metaphor for the act of painting, an act she has described as "what allows me to survive."[3]

J.R.

1. Letter from the artist, quoted in John I. H. Baur, Whitney Museum of American Art, *Nature in Abstraction: The Relation of Abstract Painting and Sculpture to Nature in Twentieth-Century American Art*, exh. cat., 1958, p. 75.
2. Judith E. Bernstock, *Joan Mitchell*, (New York: Hudson Hills Press in association with the Herbert S. Johnson Museum of Art, Cornell University, 1988), exh. cat., p. 151, and discussion of a related work, p. 129.
3. Quoted in Marcia Tucker, Whitney Museum of American Art, *Joan Mitchell*, exh. cat., 1974, p. 7.

Henry Moore

Time/Life Screen—Working Model 1952

British, 1898–1986

bronze

14⅞ x 38¾ x 1¹¹⁄₁₆
(37.8 x 98.4 x 4.3)
(depth variable)
base, 1¾ x 43 x 5
(4.5 x 109.2 x 12.7)

on bottom of wooden
base, in pencil, *Base for
Time/Life Screen/Henry
Moore*

the artist until at least
1954; acquired from M.
Knoedler & Co., New York,
1957 (gift of the T. B.
Walker Foundation 57.11)

While considering possibilities for a freestanding sculpture for the terrace of the Time/Life building overlooking Old Bond Street in the West End area of London, Moore was asked by the architect of the building, Michael Rosenauer, to judge the relative merits of a group of proposals for a sculpture to be mounted on the retaining wall at the Bond Street side of the terrace.[1] Dissatisfied with the submissions, Moore worked up his own ideas and was given the commission.

Moore's concept was to integrate the sculptured image completely with the architecture of the building by making the wall into a perforated screen holding a group of abstract figures worked on both sides; the piercing declares the nature of the wall as a screen with empty space beyond, allows light to pass through, and permits the figures to function essentially in the round. Moore said that he decided against a pictorial bas-relief because it would be "like using the position only as a hoarding for sticking on a stone poster."[2]

Moore made four small maquettes in plaster, which were cast in bronze editions. In these maquettes, he grappled with the issue of achieving a harmony of sculptural and architectural forms, gradually moving toward the final solution:

> The first of the four maquettes I rejected because I thought it too obvious and regular a repetition of the fenestration of the building. In the second maquette I tried to vary this and make it less symmetrical but in doing so the rhythms became too vertical. In the third maquette I tried to introduce a more horizontal rhythm but was dissatisfied with the monotony of the size of the forms. The fourth maquette I thought was better and more varied and so this became the definitive maquette, although a further working model produced other changes.[3]

The Walker cast was made from the plaster working model[4] and reveals an aspect of the project that Moore was forced to abandon for reasons of safety. He had hoped that each "motif" or figure could rotate, perhaps on the first of each month, to display it completely and to serve as an event for the Time/Life employees.[5] After carving the four big stones in his garden without the frame, he realized that the frame was unnecessary. The screen was already in place, however, and the only thing he could do was to enlarge the openings as much as structural considerations would allow. His more ambitious conception would have required a turntable for each form, so that they would "project from the

building like some of those half animals that look as if they are escaping through the walls in Romanesque architecture. I wanted them to be like half-buried pebbles whose form one's eye instinctively completes."[6] Although he was not entirely pleased with the immovable screen, he explained that the consummation of his idea would have necessitated prohibitively expensive reinforcement. He hoped that one day the rotational idea would bear fruit in architectural sculpture.

L.F.G.

1. Moore described the history of the project in David Finn, *Sculpture and Environment* (New York: Harry N. Abrams, 1976), p. 224; it is also recapitulated in John Russell, *Henry Moore* (New York: G. P. Putnam's Sons, 1968), p. 139.
2. Quoted in London County Council, *Sculpture in the Open Air,* exh. cat., 1954, n.p.
3. From a text prepared by Moore for *Henry Moore: Volume Two: Sculpture and Drawings Since 1948,* rev. ed. (London: Percy Lund, Humphries & Company, 1955), p. XV.
4. The plaster appears in the reproduction of a photograph taken of the artist's studio in a book published not long before his death: Henry Moore and John Hedgecoe, *Henry Moore: My Ideas, Inspiration and Life as an Artist* (San Francisco: Chronicle Books, 1986), color spread, pp. 98, 99.
5. *Henry Moore: Volume Two: Sculpture and Drawings Since 1948,* pp. XV, XVI.
6. Statement of 1955 reprinted in Philip James, ed., *Henry Moore on Sculpture* (London: Macdonald & Co., 1966), p. 238.

Henry Moore
Time/Life Screen
1952–1953
Portland Stone on building
facade, Bond Street,
London

Henry Moore

Reclining Mother and Child 1960–1961

British, 1898–1986

bronze

**90 x 35½ x 52
(228.6 x 90.2 x 132.1)**

**right edge, side of base,
Guss: H. Noack Berlin; top
of base, at right rear,
*Moore 3/7***

H. Noack, Berlin

**acquired from the artist
through Marlborough Fine
Art, London, and M.
Knoedler & Co., New York,
1963 (gift of the T. B.
Walker Acquisition Fund
63.11)**

In an interview the year the plaster of this work was completed, Moore acknowledged that the themes fused in it—the mother and child and the reclining figure—had each been an "absolute obsession" with him at one time.[1] He explained that the isolation of a single theme did not reflect an absence of interest in other subjects, but on the contrary, was the only plausible response to limitless possibilities. In order to make anything at all, he felt, the artist had to select a subject that would encompass all aspects of his thinking. Of the "fundamental human poses" that fulfilled this aspiration—standing, sitting, and lying down—he considered the latter the most flexible in practical, compositional, and spatial terms, as it was "free and stable at the same time."[2]

Moore had brought the two themes together in several drawings of the 1920s. It has been suggested that a drawing of a reclining figure from a sheet called *Ideas for Sculpture in Metal* of 1939 anticipates the Walker work.[3] That same year he carved in wood a recumbent female figure whose essentially rectangular outline, softened volumes, and grottolike apertures provided the formal prototype for the mother.[4] It is possible that the memory or renewed viewing of one of these images triggered memories of the other, integrated with the formal discoveries of his "internal and external" combined forms of the early to mid-1950s.

In the Walker bronze, the rounded, hollowed, and enclosing mother, whose forms suggest not only female procreative parts but also rocks, caves, and other landscape phenomena, protects the stocky child, whose head resembles a section of bone. Moore hoped that his sculpture would project energy from its own depths in the way that bone appears to jut through space underneath skin:

> … bone is the inner structure of all living form. It's the bone that pushes out from inside; as you bend your leg the knee gets tautness over it, and it's there that the movement and the energy come from…the knee, the shoulder, the skull, the forehead, the part where from inside you get a sense of pressure of the bone outward—these for me are the key points.[5]

The child's figure could be interpreted as the bone striving outward from the mother's elastic aperture in imitation of the birth process.

Moore aggressively manipulated the plaster, carving hatchings and striations on its hardened surfaces. The plaster was colored before being cast, to give an idea of its future appearance.[6] After receiving the bronze from the foundry, where it was cast by the lost-wax process, Moore spent several days putting finishing touches on the patina, including further superficial markings.[7]

L.F.G.

1. Vera and John Russell, "Conversations with Henry Moore," *The Sunday Times,* 17 December 1961, Magazine Section, p. 17.
2. Quoted in John D. Morse, "Henry Moore Comes to America," *Magazine of Art,* vol 40 (March 1947), p. 101.
3. David Sylvester, *Henry Moore* (New York: Frederick A. Praeger Publishers, 1968), p. 22, fig. 34; Philip James, ed., *Henry Moore on Sculpture* (New York: The Viking Press, 1966), fig. 150a.
4. Moore attributed the open character of his recumbent figures to the possibilities of wood: "I have always known and mentioned how much easier it is to open out wood forms than stone forms, so it was quite natural that the spatial opening-out idea of the reclining figure theme first appeared in wood," quoted in David Sylvester, "The Evolution of Henry Moore's Sculpture: I," *The Burlington Magazine,* vol. 90 (June 1948), p. 164.
5. Quoted in Warren Forma, *5 British Sculptors (Work and Talk)* (New York: Grossman Publishers, 1964), p. 59.
6. Letter from Henry Moore to Harry [Brooks], 5 June 1962.
7. Letter from Harry A. Brooks to Martin Friedman, 16 November 1962, where he quotes a letter dated 14 November 1962 he received from Moore: "The *Reclining Mother and Child* for Minneapolis arrived yesterday and there is two or three days work on it touching up the patina, but it looks a jolly good cast." As Brooks had explained in another letter to Friedman, 25 October 1962, "When a big Moore is cast the artist then does considerable work on it with regard to the patina which he can change by burnishing and by the use of acids to mark highlights and coloration. He also does considerable work with abrasives, polishing the roughness which may be left by casting. In some cases he also incises lines on a piece to bring up its form. In other words, when it leaves the caster it is still in an embryo state and the piece achieves its personality only when worked on personally by the artist." See Donald Hall, "An Interview with Henry Moore," *Horizon,* vol. 3 (November 1960), pp. 102–115, for Moore's own discussion of his involvement in bronze casting.

Henry Moore

Standing Figure: Knife Edge   1961

British, 1898–1986

bronze

111 x 45½ x 24
(281.9 x 115.6 x 61)

on base, *Moore 3/7*

**acquired from the artist
by Bruce Dayton through
Marlborough Fine Arts,
London, for Dayton's,
Minneapolis, 1963 (gift of
Dayton's 87.20)**

Victory of Samothrace
circa 200 B.C.
marble
90 (243.8) high
Collection The Louvre,
Paris

This standing figure, once titled by the artist *Winged Figure,* in reference to the Greek figure *Victory of Samothrace,* was actually inspired by the breast bone of a bird.[1] In fact, an early maquette for the piece incorporated the bone itself; clay was added to the base and the figure's neck and arms.[2] The 1961 bronze *Seated Woman (Thin Neck)* incorporated the forms of the upper section of this study and later in the same year Moore completed *Standing Figure: Knife Edge,* which extended the "knife-edge thinness"[3] of the bone throughout a whole figure. In this work, Moore has retained the bone's rough surface, emphasizing particularly the honeycomblike texture that runs down one of the sides and across the front.

Moore wrote of this work: "Since my student days I have liked the shape of bones, and have drawn them, studied them in the Natural History Museum, found them on the sea-shores and saved them out of the stewpot."[4] He responded to skeletal forms because they inherently possess what Moore felt to be sculpture's most important qualities—complexity and dynamism in the round. In his words, a sculpture should have "a full-form existence, with masses of various size and section conceived in their air-surrounded entirety, stressing and straining, and thrusting and opposing each other in spatial relationship."[5] *Standing Figure: Knife Edge* presents just such a variety of impressions when seen from different vantages: from one view the figure's neck, head, and body seem tenuously thin and dangerously sharp; from another they widen to a billowy fullness. Seen from below, the sculpture's contours create a rhythm of sinuous curves arching upward.

L.R.

1. Statement of 1965 reprinted in Philip James, ed., *Henry Moore on Sculpture* (New York: The Viking Press, 1967), p. 278; rev. ed., 1971, p. 299.
2. Alan G. Wilkinson, *The Moore Collection in the Art Gallery of Ontario* (Toronto: Art Gallery of Ontario, 1979), p. 174, fig. 145.
3. Statement of 1965 in James, p. 278; rev. ed., p. 299.
4. Ibid.
5. Henry Moore, "The Sculptor's Aims," in Herbert Read, ed., *Unit One* (London: Cassel & Co. Ltd.), p. 128.

Robert Morris

untitled   1968

American, b. 1931

felt, metal grommets

144 x 114
365.8 x 289.6)

Leo Castelli Gallery, New
York; acquired from the
Gordon Locksley Gallery,
Minneapolis, 1969
(gift of the T. B. Walker
Foundation 69.19)

This soft sculpture by Robert Morris consists of a stack of eight rectangles of commercial felt sliced through with fourteen parallel horizontal cuts that stop short of the edges, at a distance equal to that between the cuts themselves. When suspended from the wall by grommets attached to the upper right and left corners, the sculpture falls in loose strips, revealing the colors—green, black, pink, blue, gold, yellow, red, and pale peach—of the layered felt. The use of colorful material—unusual in Morris's sculpture of this period—resulted from its relative availability, the artist says, as opposed to the much heavier, gray industrial material that he was to obtain for his later felt pieces. If the use of color in the Walker piece was arbitrary, Morris, nevertheless, in

retrospect, has noticed its relationship to other works he made during the late 1960s, particularly a 1968 "dispersal" piece consisting of masses of multicolored thread deployed in seemingly random fashion over a floor. In this work, as in the Walker felt piece, Morris says, the sculpture involves using "a multiplicity of color that approaches no color."[1]

The arbitrary use of color in the Walker felt sculpture complements its partially random form. Given the soft material that composes it, the shape of the piece varies from one installation to another, its form to some extent controlled by chance. In a 1968 article, "Anti Form," Morris expounded on his interest in the use of indeterminacy as an art-making principle:

> The focus on matter and gravity as a means results in forms which were not projected in advance. Considerations of ordering are necessarily casual and imprecise and unemphasized. Random piling, loose stacking, hanging give passing form to the material.[2]

However, despite their somewhat free-form installation, Morris's felt sculptures carry echoes of the spare, boxlike wood and metal sculptures characteristic of the Minimalist style he had helped pioneer in the early 60s, and which he continued to produce throughout that decade. His felt sculptures, when laid out on the floor prior to installation, are also simple rectilinear forms; it is only when they are suspended that their straight lines, right angles, and precise layering disappear in favor of dynamic new configurations of interweaving loops and curves.

L.R.

1. Conversation with the artist, 23 February 1988.
2. Robert Morris, "Anti Form," *Artforum*, vol. 4 (April 1968), p. 33.

Robert Motherwell

Untitled 1971

American, b. 1915

acrylic on oil-sized cotton
duck

108 x 144
(274.3 x 365.8)

on reverse, upper right, *R.
Motherwell / 1971*

acquired from the artist,
1972 (gift of the T. B.
Walker Foundation 72.22)

In everything in his work that is even remotely rectangular, Motherwell has identified a subtle reference to the French door or window, a "classical theme of modern art."[1] The structure was familiar to him from the Spanish- and French-style homes of his childhood in California,[2] and as a pictorial subject in works by Caspar David Friedrich, the Impressionists, Bonnard, Matisse, Picasso, and others. He is intrigued by the window's function as the mediator between inside and outside spaces that can be differentiated as much or as little as the artist chooses.

In the Walker painting two approaches to the internal versus external problem are taken, in the black and ocher motifs, respectively, which contribute to the sense of unresolved contradiction or ambivalence Motherwell sees as the subject of the picture.[3] The ragged black rectangle, held in place by two faint light blue vertical lines, interrupts the yellowish gray wall. Comparison with a small acrylic and crayon painting on board that Motherwell entitled *The White Window*, made about the same time and including a white version of the motif, shows that it was conceived as a window.[4] The blackness in the Walker painting makes the window pane an opaque assertive plane, literally and paradoxically pierced by inscribed bars.[5] Whether the window is black itself or revealing blackness beyond is not disclosed, making the relationship between inside and outside enigmatic.

In the upper right-hand corner the other "window," outlined by an L-shape of smudged ocher lines, marks off a corner of the evocative field, but leaves inside and outside indistinguishable in character. While suggesting the combined palpability and transparency of a pane of glass, the demarcated area is empty and seemingly inaccessible. Motherwell recognizes a link between aspects of his work and certain Eastern art, particularly in relation to his discovery of how slight a mark is required to animate the "metaphysical void."[6] He wrote admiringly of the expanses of expressive ground on which Miró added his minimal signs: "When Miró has made a beautiful, suggestive ground for himself, emotionally the picture is half-done."[7]

Motherwell has recently compared his paintings to the wall paintings of ancient Egypt, and his collages to old posters and torn bits of papers on walls.[8] In the Walker work, a shred of the ocher color clings to the lower right edge of the black rectangle, as if the ocher pane had been wrenched away from the subject it framed. Formally this effect suggests the procedures of his collages of torn shapes.[9] Here the black form resembles a ripped and pasted scrap, while the uneven edges of the ocher lines are like the remains of a sheet of paper glued along the periphery. Motherwell was to return to collage, which he had largely abandoned, when he finished the Open series, to which this work belongs, in 1972.

Motherwell had been considering various ideas for a monumental painting for the Walker Art Center by 10 July 1971.[10] In the fall of that year Martin Friedman was in Motherwell's Greenwich, Connecticut, studio, when the artist's summer work arrived from Cape Cod. When the crates were unpacked, Friedman was so struck by what he saw that he proposed showing them as they were, before Motherwell had undertaken his usual reworkings. After the exhibition, he did in fact rework most of the summer paintings, and probably would have modified the Walker work if it had not been purchased.[11]

L.F.G.

1. In an interview with Irmeline Lebeer, "Robert Motherwell," *Chroniques de l'Art Vivant*, no. 22 (July–August 1971), p. 10. H. H. Arnason discussed the motif in "Motherwell: The Window and the Wall," *Art News*, vol. 68 (Summer 1969), p. 48.
2. Letter to the author, 15 October 1986; his mother was an avid collector of eighteenth-century French country furniture.
3. Ibid.
4. Motherwell, ibid., wrote that this work is not a study for the Walker painting, but perhaps an offspring.
5. In a WAC questionnaire, 15 May 1974, p. 2, Motherwell emphasized the somberness of the palette of this painting, instructing that it not be over lit. Interview with Martin Friedman, August 1972.
6. Quoted in Jack D. Flam, "With Robert Motherwell," in Albright-Knox Art Gallery, Buffalo, *Robert Motherwell*, exh. cat., 1983, p. 23.
7. Robert Motherwell, "The Significance of Miró," *Art News*, vol. 58 (May 1959), p. 65.
8. Letter to the author, 15 October 1986.
9. For the artist's comments on his use of collage, see Vivien Raynor, "A Talk with Robert Motherwell," *Art News*, vol. 73 (April 1974), p. 51.
10. Letter to Martin Friedman, 10 July 1971, written from Motherwell's seaside studio "Sea Barn," in Provincetown, Massachusetts, where he painted the picture.
11. Letter to the author, 15 October 1986, in which Motherwell adds that "usually, I am better off living with a work for a long period before letting it out into the world."

Elizabeth Murray

Sail Baby   1983

American, b. 1940

oil on canvas

three panels
126 x 135
(320 x 342.9) overall

on reverse, right panel,
top center, *Sail Baby /
springfall, 1983 /
Elizabeth Murray*

acquired from the Paula
Cooper Gallery, 1984
(Walker Special Purchase
Fund 84.813)

Elizabeth Murray is considered by many to be one of the most important American painters of her generation. As Richard Armstrong has observed, "her influential work has come to symbolize the reinvigoration of painting that occurred, largely unheralded, through the second half of the 1970s."[1] More rambunctious than refined, recently more figurative than abstract, her work is distinguished for its formal inventiveness and adventurousness.

Sail Baby is the final work in a series of approximately eight paintings that feature a large floating cup. The image is fragmented into three separate but overlapping canvases. "[They] seemed to represent three children to me uniting as one image" and the "yellow cup somehow for me is a reference to my mother and childhood."[2] The title itself refers to the blue lake implied by the liquid in the cup,[3] and to a lullaby the artist's mother sang to her as a child.[4] In an earlier statement Murray confirmed the reference to her mother: "Cup is a specially meaningful symbol for me—it has a hard exterior and a soft interior—it is a container, it is open, it is feminine."[5]

Murray began introducing recognizable images into her work in 1980, at about the same time she began to construct paintings from several parts. She makes paper templates from which a carpenter then fabricates shaped stretcher bars. When the piece is fully assembled, she begins painting. *Sail Baby* has a truly sculptural surface, whose tension derives from the fit of the interlocking sections rather than the viewer's attempt to reassemble the individual components as in a puzzle, which was true of Murray's previous "shattered" paintings.

The painting thrives on the contrasts between the geometric and biomorphic, between the yin and yang of the blue and pink "birth shapes" (oppositions which also characterize her earlier work), as well as the overlay of cup image on human shape. The green ribbon of paint echoes the painting's scalloped edges as it cheerfully wends its way across the canvases to tie the elements together in a tidy package.

M.G.

1. Richard Armstrong, in Whitney Museum of American Art, New York, *Five Painters in New York*, exh. cat., 1984, p. 46.
2. Murray, in WAC questionnaire, December 1984.
3. Interview with Murray, January 1988.
4. WAC questionnaire.
5. Quoted in Mark Rosenthal, "The Structured Subject in Contemporary Art: Reflections on Works in the Twentieth-Century Galleries," *Philadelphia Museum of Art Bulletin*, vol. 79 (Fall 1983), p. 21.

Robert Murray

Track 1966

Canadian, b. 1936

steel and aluminum plate

**56¾ x 35 x 176⅛
(144.2 x 88.9 x 447.4)**

**stamped on plate on base,
*Robert Murray/1966***

**S.Q.R. Division of David
Smith Steel Co., South
Plainfield, New Jersey,
under supervision of the
artist**

**acquired from the Betty
Parsons Gallery, New
York, 1969 (gift of the T.
B. Walker Foundation
69.20)**

In his fabricated work of this period, Murray's aim was to use metal plate to suggest volume without enclosing it.[1] *Track* functions as a skeletal demarcator of a wedge-shaped volume of space whose lower plane is defined by the ground on which the sculpture rests. Despite the unitary impression the monochrome work gives, it is composed of six parts that are separable.[2] A pair of lengths of hollow tubing are maintained on a parallel "track" by a flattened U-shaped bar curving into them at their lower extremities; this bar serves no other structural function. Two flat vertical supports folded up from a rectangular base that stabilizes the form curve into the tracks to support them. These supports are bolted to the inside of the lower lip of the tracks, raising them higher than natural gravitational pull would permit, giving them a lift-off, diagonally ascending quality. Writers frequently associate Murray's interest in inclined planes with his command of flying. Although he acknowledges it as a contributory factor, he relates the tracks in the Walker work more immediately to trajectories in parabolic geometry, the subject of *Track* being "length and direction."[3]

Sketchbook drawings of 1965–1966 show that Murray considered resting the two tracks on a single rectangular vertical plane, and on a squared U-shaped plane. One sketch shows the U-shape rising from tracks resting on the ground. He thought about making one track one width lower than the other, but decided in the end to respect the plane they established. He also considered putting the tracks farther apart to permit passage between them. Numerous decisions concerning the thickness of plate, the method of attachment and the angle were made intuitively during the course of the piece's construction.[4]

Murray usually has works fabricated from sketches and cursory models. This piece, however, was made from a finished aluminum study painted red, 14 x 42 inches, which was translated into a detailed working drawing by George Trainor, the fabricator. In order to have access to the equipment Murray requires—brake-presses for bending plate, torches and saws for cutting it, welding equipment to attach joins, grinders and sand-blasting tanks to smooth and

clean it—he has used a number of industrial shops since 1958–1959; he was, in fact, one of the first artists to employ such fabricators.

L.F.G.

1. Barbara Rose, "An Interview with Robert Murray," *Artforum*, vol. 5 (October 1966), p. 45.
2. The detachable nature of the parts arose from the practical problem of getting the work into the Betty Parsons Gallery. The artist provided advice and information on installation of the work, as well as permission to repaint it to maintain the original red (WAC questionnaire, 20 February 1982).
3. Conversation with the author, 27 October 1986.
4. Letter to the author, 24 October 1986.

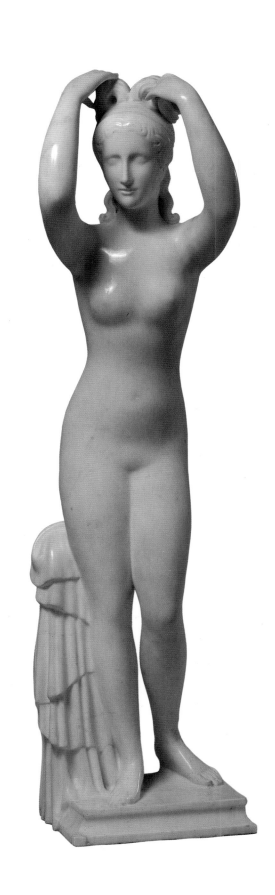

Elie Nadelman

Figure   circa 1925[1]

American, b. Poland,
1882–1946

marble

**37⅜ x 10⁹⁄₁₆ x 11⅞
(94.9 x 26.8 x 30.2)
including base**

**acquired by Mrs. A.
Stewart Walker from
Ferargil Gallery, New York,
circa 1948; acquired from
Mrs. Walker through the
Edwin Hewitt Gallery, New
York, 1955 (gift of the
T.B. Walker Foundation
55.12)**

Statuette—Aphrodite or a
woman, perhaps holding a
garland
fourth century B.C.
bronze
18 (45.7) high
Collection The Metropolitan
Museum of Art, New York
Gift of Mr. and Mrs. Francis
Neilson, 1935

Self-taught as an artist, Nadelman had visited the
art capitals of Munich and Paris before emigrating
from Poland to the United States in 1914 at the
outbreak of World War I. During the 1920s he
worked on two types of sculpture simultaneously—doll-like wooden figures of fashionable
men and women, influenced by American folk art,
and marble heads and figures conceived in response to the classical tradition he had absorbed
in Europe.

Nadelman's classicizing works seem to have
derived to a great extent from clippings, postcards, and other printed reproductions of classical Greek and Hellenistic subjects that he had
collected.[2] The Walker figure appears to be an
amalgam of several possible sources. The face,
in its proportions, expression and modeling, is
very similar to that of a fifth-century B.C. Greek
male head belonging to the Metropolitan Museum
of Art in New York, of which Nadelman had a
postcard. In a drawing apparently of the same
period, the addition of a chignon at the back of
the head feminizes the face, as do the long curls
of the Walker piece. The body echoes in reverse
the pose and structure of figures such as the
Hellenistic standing female figure reproduced in
another of his postcards. Other cards illustrate
fragments of Greek drapery like that supporting
the figure. The use of drapery or a tree stump to
buttress a marble freestanding figure was, of
course, a common device in classical sculpture.
Here it also serves to offset the precarious
forward tilt of the body. The boneless, swollen
arms, which look like those of Nadelman's folk
art types, may have been invented rather than
appropriated from ancient sources.

Though relying on and paying homage to
ancient prototypes, Nadelman has attenuated the
proportions of the classical ideal, softening the
angles in languid contours and polishing the
marble so highly that it has the appearance of
porcelain. Combined with the under-life-size scale
of the work, the shine imparts a decorative, anti-
monumental effect.

L.F.G.

1. Although a dating of ca. 1920–1925—which the artist's
son, E. Jan Nadelman, and late widow, Viola M. Nadelman,
have favored on stylistic grounds—is provisionally accepted
here, it is possible that the work may date as early as
1916. The similarity with works such as *Sur la plage,*
exhibited in January 1917 at Scott and Fowles, and the
possibility of a correspondence between the Walker work
and the *Femme rue, debout,* no. 21 in the same show,
makes this doubt plausible, as Lincoln Kirstein recently
agreed: letter to the author, 17 December 1985.
2. Lincoln Kirstein, *Elie Nadelman* (New York: Eakins Press,
1973), figs. 152, 175, 183.

Reuben Nakian

Goddess with the Golden Thighs   1964–1965/1987

American, 1897–1987

bronze

84 x 150 x 42
(213.4 x 381 x 106.7)
overall

on plate inset into right
back of sculpture, *Nakian
SC 1965 ¾ 1987* ©⊼

cast posthumously for
Walker Art Center, 1987
(gift of Dolly J. Fiterman
87.62)

Reuben Nakian was one of a generation of pioneering American sculptors whose work paralleled the development of Abstract Expressionist painting. Although he was studio apprentice to the well-known American sculptor Paul Manship from 1916 to 1920, and later shared a studio with the French-born sculptor Gaston Lachaise, Nakian forged a personal style inspired by heroic Greek and Roman art and classical mythology.

Nakian's early sculptures were sleek animal figures in bronze, wood, and marble. In the 1930s he began making realistic portrait busts of fellow artists and political personalities. His work in portraiture culminated in the 8-foot-high, full-length statue of Babe Ruth.

Through his friendships with Arshile Gorky and Willem de Kooning, whom he met in the 1930s, Nakian was introduced to modernist ideas in the work of Cézanne and Picasso. His work consequently became more abstract. By the late 1940s, Nakian was working in terra-cotta, both in three-dimensional form and as drawings incised into the surface of terra-cotta slabs. Along with numerous fluid ink drawings on paper, these "stone drawings" were both exercises in composition and the genesis of new subject matter: earth goddesses, nymphs, and centaurs. During the next several decades these arcadian themes evolved into an obsession with the classic erotic myths of the Judgment of Paris, the Rape of Lucretia, Leda and the Swan, and Europa and the Bull.

Goddess with the Golden Thighs is an ambitious work synthesizing expressionist technique and heroic subject matter. Created concurrently with a large sculptural ensemble, *Judgment of Paris, Goddess* is related to the individual figures of Juno, Venus, and Minerva—the three Roman goddesses who vie for the attention of Paris. Because the *Goddess with the Golden Thighs* has no specific identity, she assumes archetypal significance. With her massive, cylindrical thighs splayed and supported on an altar of heavy vertical elements recalling the rough-hewn formations of Stonehenge, she is a formidable image of female sexuality and fertility. The artist has said this work symbolizes "the birth of the universe; like coming out of a woman, all life comes out of the female."[1] Nakian's use of mythological subject matter and the grandeur of his vision place this work within a heroic tradition. The disposition of the goddess in a triangular format recalls classical pedimental sculpture. The figure seems to rest on the ruins of an ancient temple. At the same time, Nakian seeks to render the past modern; the ravaged, expressionistic surface and the transformation of the figure into fragmented, abstract forms, link this work to the Rodinesque tradition in modern sculpture.

For Nakian, as for many of his Abstract Expressionist peers, myth was essential to his art. Whereas the Abstract Expressionist painters for the most part created personal mythologies, primordial landscapes of the mind based on Jungian themes, Nakian's subjects were the erotic myths of the Greeks and Romans, which he realized in specific, voluptuous terms. Through myth, Nakian imbued his work with content: "Myths are good because they give you form and a grand story. I don't want only form; I want philosophy, love."[2] In his monumental, sensuous figures such as the *Goddess*, passion and sexuality function as metaphors for the creative process.

D.H.

1. Quoted in "Sculpture: Demigods from Stamford," *Time*, 30 June 1967, p. 50.
2. Ibid.

David Nash

Standing Frame 1987

British, b. 1945

white oak

**172 x 209¾ x 209½
(436.9 x 532.8 x 532.1)**

**acquired from the artist,
1987 (gift of *Star Tribune*
and Cowles Media
Foundation 87.75)**

Since the late 1970s, British artist David Nash has been making sculpture from hewn trees. An ardent environmentalist who refers to trees as "earth and sky woven together,"[1] he works principally with trees that are past their prime or otherwise slated to come down. A given tree will generally yield a series of sculptures; Nash is careful to use as much of the wood as possible, including making charcoal from twigs and scraps to use in his drawings.

Standing Frame was commissioned by the Walker in September 1987. Consisting of an open square "frame" held some ten feet aloft by three sinuous legs, the work was fashioned from two white oaks growing near the St.Croix River at Taylors Falls, Minnesota. The three major sections, each made up of a long, thick branch and a six-foot section of trunk, came from a single tree. Working with a team of local assistants, Nash squared off the trunk portion of each piece with a chain saw to yield the three sides of the frame. A two-inch layer of sapwood was then hacked off the branches by hand, exposing the durable, rot-resistant heartwood. Nash had hoped to make the entire piece from this one tree, but the fourth, or top, side of the square had to be carved from a second oak.

After the four pieces that comprise *Standing Frame* had been shaped, they were assembled in tongue-and-groove fashion, with each joint held together with two wooden pegs. Once the sculpture was placed upright, the three legs were trimmed to allow the square frame to stand level. The sculpture was then coated with a solution of linseed oil and wood preservative.

The sculpture's height and the size of the square opening were calculated to match those of Sol LeWitt's *Three x Four x Three* (1984), which is installed on the Walker roof terrace where Nash's piece was originally placed.[2] The artist's appreciation for LeWitt's rigorously geometric work is not surprising considering Nash's stated desire "to return geometry to its original home as one of the seven liberal arts 'under the protection of the goddess Natura.'"[3] To the artist, *Standing Frame*, with its combination of organic material and ideal geometric form, symbolizes the harmonic unity of man and nature.

P.B.

1. Conversation with the author, 21 September 1987.
2. From the first, *Standing Frame* was intended to be placed in the Minneapolis Sculpture Garden. As the Garden was only under construction at the time Nash finished his piece, the sculpture was displayed for several months opposite the LeWitt on the museum's middle roof terrace.
3. Graham Beal, "David Nash: Respecting the Wood," in Museum of Contemporary Art, Chicago, and San Francisco Museum of Modern Art, *A Quiet Revolution: British Sculpture since 1965*, exh. cat., 1987, p. 136.

Jud Nelson

Hefty 2-Ply 1979–1981

American, b. 1943

marble

26¾ x 26½ x 18
(67.9 x 67.3 x. 45.7)

on bottom, *Nelson 79–81*

commissioned by the Walker Art Center, 1979 (purchased with the aid of funds from Mr. and Mrs. James K. Wittenberg, the Art Center Acquisition Fund, and the National Endowment for the Arts 79.26)

In January 1979, Nelson met with Isamu Noguchi for advice on locating the best marble for this work, commissioned by Walker Art Center.[1] Noguchi told him about Cooperativo, a stone-carving shop near the Carrara quarry that had earlier provided him with *bianco puro* marble. By late July, Nelson was working on the conception and wrote, "I have been copying MacDonalds [*sic*] trash bags from up the block [in lower Manhattan], which prove to be the most sensitive for the sculpture's surface."[2] In September he attended an international exhibition of marble and industrial equipment in Valpolicella and obtained a block of Carrara marble and the diamond tools needed for the project.[3] A month later, at work on the piece in his studio, he described the brown plastic two-ply, forty-gallon trash bags that were serving as models: "A Mobil oil product. It comes like this with all of these folds that sort of make a grid, and there's this birthmark seam that runs all around. A heat seal. All these years I've been paying attention to all the process marks."[4] Nelson spent three months preparing the models, filling each plastic bag with a different assortment of trash, and spraying it white. Finally, one was selected:

> It is sprayed white, battered, and patched with masking tape. After some months of work on the block of marble, Nelson's model suddenly split open—the overstuffed plastic bag collapsed. And all the original tension was released. "It's as though I had a female model and I'm halfway through and she dies."[5]

In its carved rendition, the bag holds the shapes of discarded products from Coca-Cola, General Electric, Proctor and Gamble, Ajax, Ivory, Kitty Klean, Joy, and Dutch Boy, among others, all of which the artist can identify in the bulges and corners of marble.[6] A piece of masking tape from the model's repair has been preserved, and even lettering from the label for Clorox can be discerned.

Working the two-ton rectangular block with chisel and hammer and a dentist's drill, and then rubbing it by hand, Nelson delighted in the anomaly of classical, reductive carving in the manner of Michelangelo taking place in the "space age."[7] The work was originally called *Holos Series 9, No. 1*, the word "holos" used throughout his series of veristic carvings to allude to holographic reproduction, as well as to holistic perception.[8]

Nelson has explained that his work has required the rigorous training of his mind to see things as precisely and fully as humanly possible, rather than in the shorthand generalizations that constitute ordinary perception.[9] He also dispenses with the qualities of native color and weight. This and the fact that the trompe l'oeil representation is a meticulous, virtuoso performance in carving rather than a cast, distinguishes his work from the polychromed verbatim molds of John de Andrea or Duane Hanson.[10]

L.F.G.

1. Letter to Martin Friedman, 13 January 1979.
2. Letter to Martin Friedman, 24 July 1979.
3. Letter to James Dean, National Air and Space Museum, Washington, D.C., 21 July 1979.
4. Quoted in Kim Levin, "Jud Nelson: Sculpture Is His Bag," *Arts Magazine*, vol. 56 (October 1981), p. 108.
5. Ibid., pp. 108, 109.
6. Ibid., p. 109, for an interpretation of the meaning of the garbage bag as social commentary.
7. Ibid. He had a color reproduction of Michelangelo's *Pietà* on his studio wall, gridded by its folds like a new garbage bag.
8. Patricia Ensworth, "Jud Nelson," *Arts Magazine*, vol 51 (June 1977), p. 7, and Lisa Lyons, "Jud Nelson," *Design Quarterly, 111/112, Eight Artists: The Elusive Image* (1979), p. 48, confirmed by the artist in a letter to the author postmarked 22 September 1986. In this letter he explains that he changed the title because he wanted the sculpture to remain unique rather than form part of a series.
9. Both Lyons, "Jud Nelson," p. 47, and Michael Klein, "Jud Nelson: Sculpture as Seeing," *Arts Magazine*, vol. 54 (September 1979), p. 136, have discussed the importance for Nelson of Aldous Huxley's *The Art of Seeing* (1942), a text on the improvement of vision for physical and psychological health through techniques of "analytical looking," "central fixation," "shifting," and the use of memory and the imagination; Nelson has read it closely and annotated his copy.
10. Nelson's first cast was a black-patinated bronze made from the sculpture *Hefty 2-Ply* rather than from the original garbage bag model.

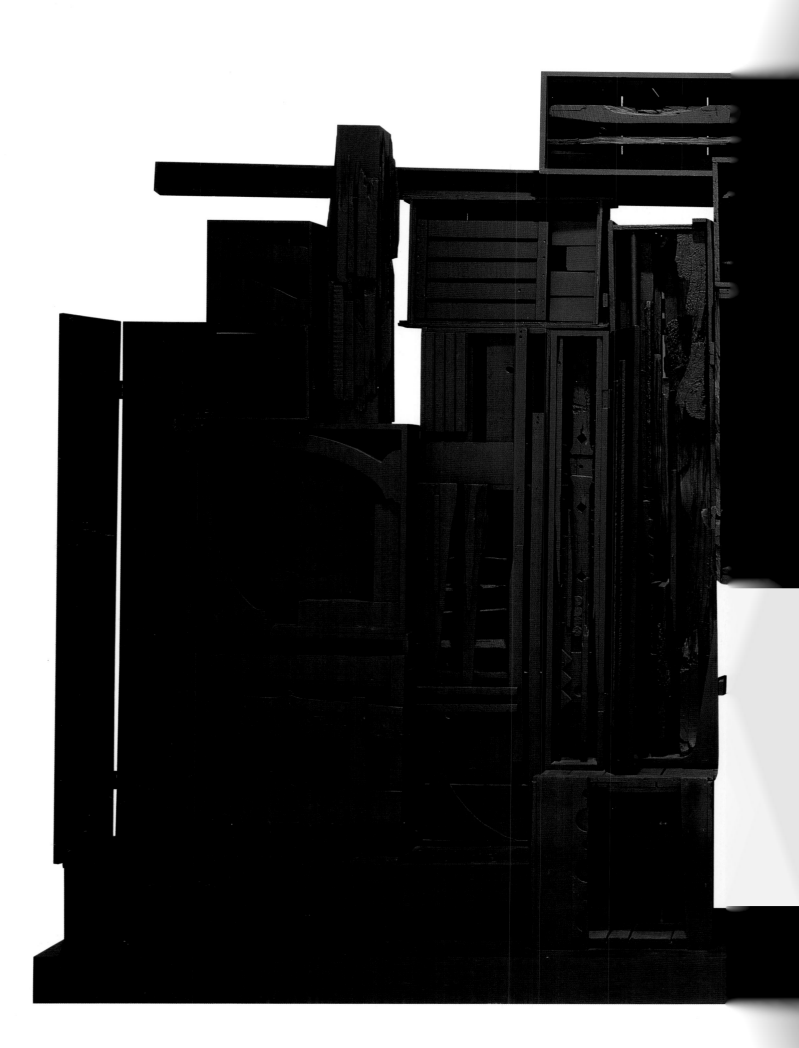

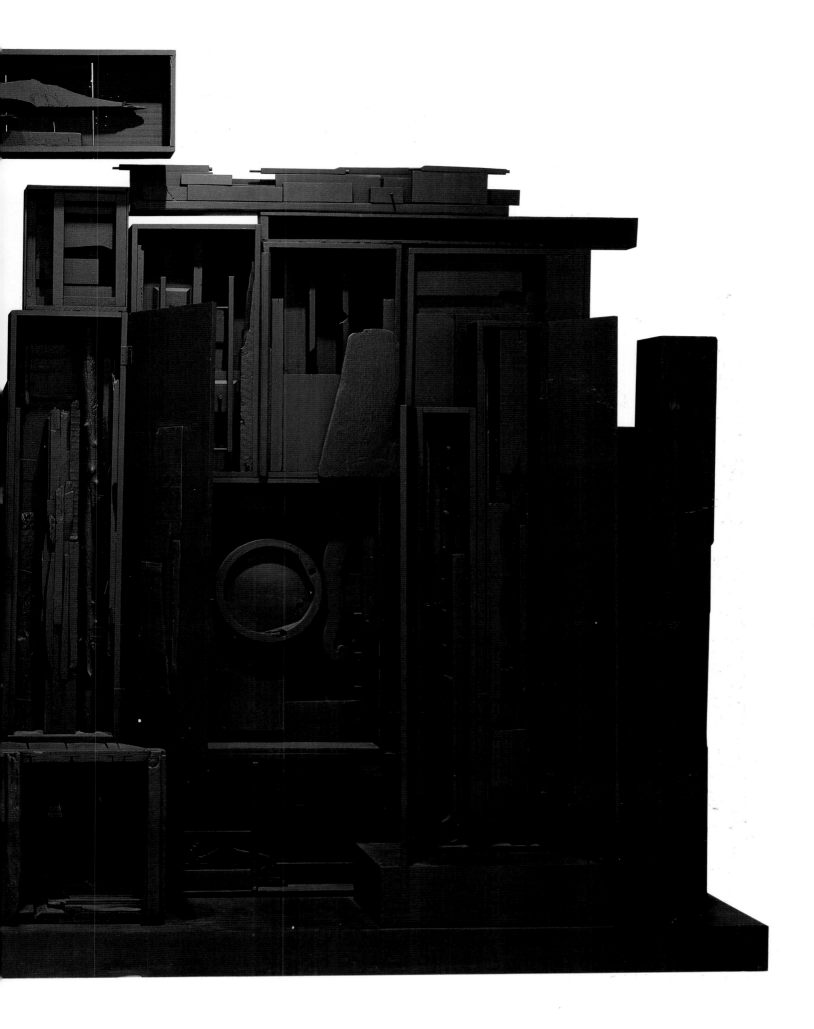

Louise Nevelson

Sky Cathedral Presence   1951–1964

American, b. Russia,
1900–1988

painted wood

**122¼ x 200 x 23⅞
(310.5 x 508 x 60.7)**

**acquired from the Pace
Gallery, New York, 1969
(gift of Judy and Kenneth
Dayton 69.5)**

When Louise Nevelson first exhibited her large, black wooden "walls" in the late 1950s, critics recognized in the engulfing size, intricacy, and mysterious presence of the work a significant new vision in American sculpture. In retrospect, it is also clear that the walls represented the artist's mature style. The environmentally scaled images that she produced between about 1958 and 1975, including *Sky Cathedral Presence*, constitute her most characteristic and influential body of work. She used other materials from time to time, and she worked in other colors and scales. But she consistently returned to black, to wood, and to the working patterns established in the walls. She gathered such objects as architectural fragments, crates, cast-off furniture, and assembled them into rectilinear units to be painted. From these square or rectangular units she built an infinite variety of forms in space, a "kingdom," as she often described it.

The boundaries of Nevelson's individual works are unusually fluid. She thought of her creative activity as a continuous flow of energy which could be channeled into several works at once, turned back by revising or recombining existing works, or, as in the case of *Sky Cathedral Presence*, by recycling segments of unfinished pieces begun many years earlier. For this reason, specific objects are not so much singular or superlative specimens, or even landmarks in the artist's development, as they are unique aspects of one huge, multifaceted work, the work of Nevelson's lifetime. *Sky Cathedral Presence* was thus in the artist's mind one element in a much larger project which was, in turn, bound up with Nevelson's artistic personality, the image of an enormously energetic, loquacious, and thoroughly independent woman.

"I attribute the walls to this," Nevelson said,

> I had loads of energy.... If I'd had a city block it wouldn't have been enough because I had this energy that was flowing like an ocean into creativity.... There is great satisfaction in seeing a splendid, big, enormous work of art. I'm fully aware that the small object can be very precious and very important. But to me, personally, there is something in size and scale.[1]

Nevelson's long-standing attraction to pre-Columbian art and architecture, nourished through her travels to Mexico and her friendship with the Mexican painter Diego Rivera in the 1930s, is widely considered a primary influence on the walls. Her acquaintance with Surrealism, her great admiration for the work of Picasso, particularly, has been proposed as a source for the idea of combining objects in unfamiliar, suggestive ways. Nevelson's well-established interest in dance and theater, pursued most actively before she had determined to become a sculptor, seems to bear on the dramatic, staged ambience of much of her work. Perhaps an even more critical factor, however, was a drive—shared by many prominent New York artists in the 1950s—to create a personal terrain, a full-scale environment, an alternative "place" in which to exist. More recently, Laurie Wilson has proposed certain internal psychological pressures related to the idea of place, which the walls may have helped Nevelson to resolve.[2] In particular, Wilson refers to a house the artist had owned since 1945, her first permanent residence after some fifteen years of frequent moves. In 1954, the City of New York notified her of its intention to buy the property, and by 1958, just at the time Nevelson was working steadily with wood constructions, she was forced to move once again: materials, tools, and works-in-progress had to be stacked together. "She had managed," Wilson writes, "just before departing, to crate her own imaginary habitation with the detritus of the world that was forcing her out of her real home."[3]

Nevelson denied any direct religious intention in her Cathedral works, preferring to think of a cathedral as "man's temple to man." From the time of the first *Cathedral in the Sky* of 1958, she produced large Sky Cathedrals, and Cathedral Presences, as well as three works entitled *Sky Cathedral Presence*, numbered I, II, and III.

N.R.

1. Louise Nevelson, *Dawns and Dusks: Taped Conversations with Diana Mackown* (New York: Scribner, 1976), p. 138.
2. Laurie Wilson, *Louise Nevelson: Iconography and Sources* (New York: Garland Publishing, 1978), pp. 108 ff.
3. Ibid., p. 116.

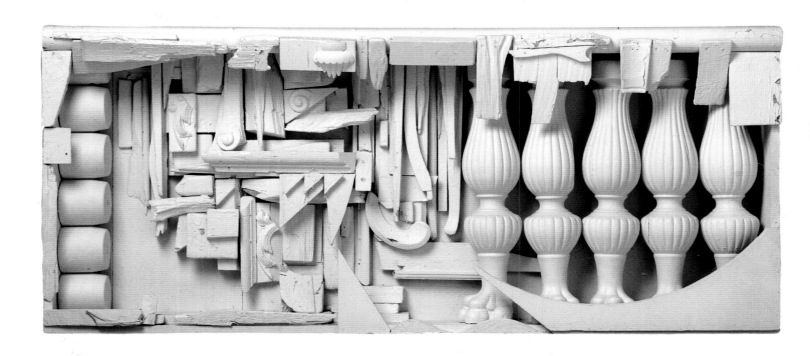

Louise Nevelson

Case with Five Balusters   1959

American, b. Russia,
1900–1988

painted wood

**27⅝ x 63⅝ x 9½
(70.2 x 161.6 x 24.1)**

**Martha Jackson Gallery,
New York, to 1980; Mr.
and Mrs. Peter M. Butler,
1980; acquired from Mr.
and Mrs. Peter M. Butler,
1983 (gift of Mr. and Mrs.
Peter M. Butler 83.124)**

If you paint a thing black or you paint a thing white, it takes on a whole different dimension. A state of mind enters into it. Now white is what was on my mind. I feel that the white permits a little something to enter. I don't know whether it's a mood.... The white is more festive. The forms have just that edge. For me, the black contains the silhouette, the essence of the universe. But the whites move out a little bit into outer space with more freedom.[1]

In 1959, Nevelson was steadily gaining recognition for her all-black wooden constructions made of such found architectural elements as moldings, cornices, and balustrades. Invited by curator Dorothy Miller to participate in the exhibition *Sixteen Americans* at The Museum of Modern Art in New York, she immediately decided to fill one gallery with an ambitious environment—all in white. In order to heighten the surprise value of such a dramatic change, she secretly rented a second studio exclusively for the production of "white work." The result, an installation entitled *Dawn's Wedding Feast*, was a complex arrangement of some eighty-five separate reliefs, boxes, and columns set up in various configurations with such names as *Dawn's Wedding Chapel*, *Dawn's Wedding Cake*, *Dawn's Wedding Mirror*, and *Case with Five Balusters*. This, Nevelson's first exhibition in a major museum—at the age of sixty—was cause for celebration. It was, as she later told Diana Mackown, "a wish fulfillment, a transition to a marriage with the world."[2]

The exhibition closed with no prospects of a permanent home for the whole environment. *Dawn's Wedding Feast* was dismantled, and a number of its component parts sold to various collectors. Nevelson later made an effort to reunite as many of the parts as possible. One such effort, shown at the 1962 Venice Biennale, was named *Voyage*. In that configuration, *Case with Five Balusters* occupied a more prominent position than it had in *Dawn's Wedding Feast*; however, Nevelson, who had personally supervised the installation both at The Museum of Modern Art and in Venice, decided to place it "upside down," that is, reversed from the position in which it had originally been shown two years before.

Case with Five Balusters is one of only three reliefs first made for the 1959 installation of *Dawn's Wedding Feast* that are still in existence.[3]

N.R.

1. Louise Nevelson, *Dawns and Dusks: Taped Conversations with Diana Mackown* (New York: Scribner, 1976), p. 144.
2. Ibid., p. 138.
3. Arnold Glimcher, letter to Martin Friedman, 25 April 1980: "Several of the pieces in that exhibition [*Sixteen Americans*] were later destroyed, and *Case with Five Balusters* is one of the 3 reliefs that I know are still in existence."

Barnett Newman

The Third   1962

American, 1905–1970

oil on canvas

101 x 121
(256.5 x 307.3)

lower right, *Barnett Newman 1962*

acquired from the artist by Dolly Bright Carter, 1964; acquired from Mrs. Carter through Xavier Fourcade, Inc., New York, 1978. (gift of Judy and Kenneth Dayton 78.3)

Although Newman intended to convey a state of exaltation in his work, he differentiated this carefully from the expression of transitory personal emotions: "My concern is with the fullness that comes from emotion, not with its initial explosion, or its emotional fall-out, or the glow of its expenditure."[1] He wanted to find in modern painting an equivalent to the Gothic communion with the absolute, as distinguished from the Greek and Renaissance equation of ideal beauty with truth. In order to be a pure expression, according to Newman, art had to relinquish symbol, myth, legend, object, and form. With the extinction of form he was left with space, interpreted in his work as color, and painted in a scale through which the viewer physically experienced its resonance. For the authentic modern expression of the plenitude of being or the secular sublime, Newman felt that several requirements had to be met: equal light intensity, an expressed acknowledgment of the frontal planarity of painting, scale (meaning the congruence of form and size rather than size alone), elimination of all anecdote and detail and their replacement by a single, holistic image and, above all, passion, intensity, and boldness.

In the "zip" Newman discovered a device that would lend scale to the single image without isolating itself as a form. He specified that the thin vertical channels were not intended to divide space but rather to declare it. Intruded on at their edges by the deckled border of the orange field, the zips in *The Third* do not lie on top like a line; nor, as the activity at the left implies, do they represent a field below. They are not substantial enough, or shaped strongly enough, to displace the space of the orange atmosphere.[2] The effect illustrates his comments on his intended psychological effects: "I hope that my painting has the impact of giving someone, as it did me, the feeling of his own totality, of his own separateness, of his own individuality, and at the same time of his connection to others, who are also separate."[3] In addition to the issue of identity is that of creation, the primordial differentiation of realms, which Newman perceived as biblical in its absoluteness. He alerts the viewer to his own creation of this elemental space by showing the space dematerialized at the left edge, which clarifies its origin as brushstrokes laid on canvas,[4] and by the prominent signature and date, which confirm that the painting was made by a particular person at a particular moment.

The Third belongs to a group of paintings in which Newman resumed the use of color after the black and white Stations of the Cross series. Several subsequent orange paintings allude to the number three in their titles, including *Tertia* of 1964 and *Triad* of 1965.

L.F.G.

1. Quoted in Dorothy Gees Seckler, "Frontiers of Space," *Art in America*, vol. 50 (Summer 1962), p. 83.
2. The painting had just been finished when it was shown at the Allan Stone Gallery, New York, in 1962, and Stone assigned the title *Orange Colossus* without Newman's approval. Newman changed it immediately after it appeared in the catalogue; Stone in conversation with Matthew Dixon Cowles, July 1986.
3. From a 1967 statement, quoted in Harold Rosenberg, *Barnett Newman* (New York: Harry N. Abrams, 1978), p. 246.
4. Although Newman sometimes rolled the first coats of paint, he apparently always used a brush for the top layers; see editorial note in Jeanne Siegel, "Around Barnett Newman," *Art News*, vol. 70 (October 1971), p. 60.

Ben Nicholson

February 12, '52 (Carafe) 1952

British, 1894–1982

oil, graphite on canvas

34 1/16 x 18 1/16
(86.5 x 45.8)

on top edge of canvas folded over stretcher, visibel from reverse, *Ben Nicholson Feb 12–52 (carafe)*

acquired from Durlacher Brothers, New York, 1953 (gift of the T.B. Walker Foundation 53.6)

The tabletop still-life theme Nicholson treated throughout his work was a preferred subject of the French Cubists. In a 1948 review of Daniel Henry Kahnweiler's then recently published monograph on Juan Gris, Nicholson explained that the very banality of the theme made it the most suitable for an exploration of essential pictorial issues: "Subject matter is at last free to be utterly trivial...." Portraiture, and "even landscape, dependent on transitory impressions, on association, on the play of wind and rain, cannot be sufficiently divested of ... drama to be appropriated by the canvas."[1] In Cubism, he maintained, imagery emerges within the continuum of the picture, carrying no greater meaning than the other elements of structure, space, color, volume, and light. In writing about Gris he seems to have touched on the issues that most concerned him in his own still-life work:

> Out of the circles, quadrilaterals, crescents traced on his canvas, emerges almost by accident the semblance of a flower-vase, half buried behind some complementary shape—a pipe-stem, is it?... No matter. The objects have lost their significance in the general scheme. Rhythms have taken charge.[2]

In *February 12, '52* the linear arabesques and angles resolve only fleetingly into carafe, goblets, mug, and pitcher. Some of the lines underlying the uneven washes of paint were reworked for formal reasons alone, strengthened by the oily black pencil on top of the washes. Nicholson felt that color likewise should be freed of its descriptive function: "Blue exists in a painting in its own right—no sea, no sky, no 'key,' is required to experience this blueness." Color constitutes "the inner core of an idea and this idea cannot be touched physically any more than one can touch the blue of a summer sky."[3] Within the predominantly neutral palette of this picture the light blue areas serve as a chromatic theme offset by black accents and anchored by a red wedge.

In the non-objective reliefs Nicholson pursued concurrently with still lifes such as this one, he demonstrates a commitment to modernist principles that makes any subject matter, however neutral, seem recidivist. His inability to relinquish the still life may have arisen from factors more personal than he generally professed and is generally recognized. In an interview of 1963 he revealed that:

> I owe a lot to my father—especially to his poetic idea and to his still-life theme. That didn't come from Cubism, as some people think, but from my father—not only from what he did as a painter but from the very beautiful striped and spotted jugs and mugs and goblets, and octagonal and hexagonal glass objects which he collected. Having those things throughout the house was an unforgettable early experience for me.[4]

It seems likely that at least some of the numerous bottles, jugs, carafes, and pitchers visible in photographs of Nicholson's studio taken about the time this painting was made[5] came to him after the death of his father, Sir William Nicholson, in 1949. The play of transparency and opacity that intrigued him may have derived in part from these glass and ceramic objects, imaginatively reconstructed as the fragmentary motifs of this canvas.

L.F.G.

1. Benedict Nicholson, "Selected Notice: Cubism and Juan Gris," *Horizon*, vol. l7 (March 1948), p. 227.
2. Ibid.
3. Ben Nicholson, "Notes," in The Tate Gallery, London, *Ben Nicholson*, exh. cat., 1955.
4. "The Life and Opinions of an English 'Modern:' Ben Nicholson in Conversation with Vera and John Russell," *The Sunday Times*, 28 April 1963, p. 28.
5. Reproduced in Maurice de Sausmarez, *Ben Nicholson* (London and New York: Studio International, 1969), frontispiece; see also photographs of his Ticino studio reproduced in Marco Valsecchi, "A Visit to Ben Nicholson," *Metro*, no. 1 (December 1960), pp. 22, 23.

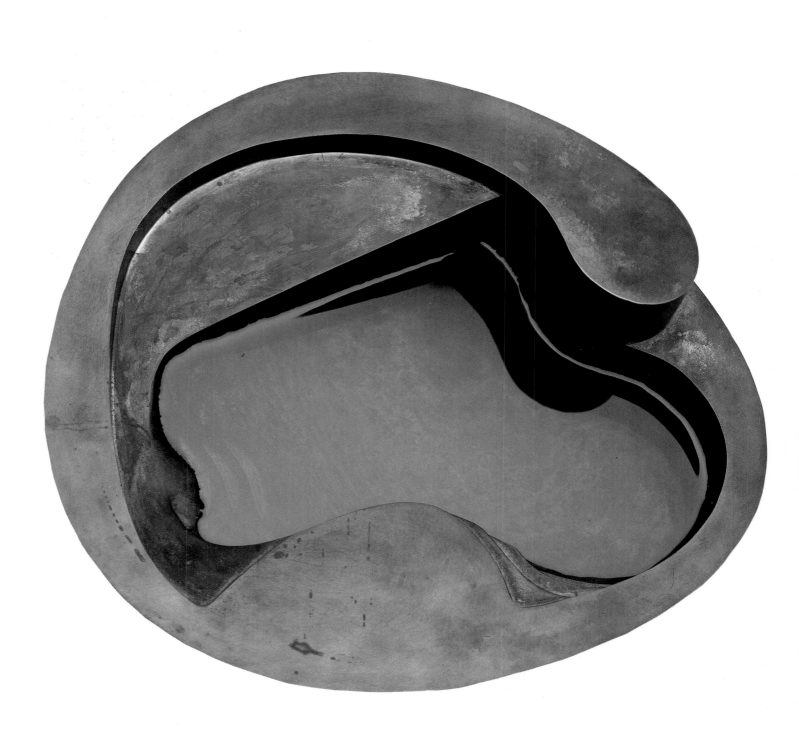

Isamu Noguchi

Swimming Pool for von Sternberg   1935/1980

American, 1904–1988

bronze

6⅜ x 14¼ x 15¼
(16.2x 36.2 x 38.7)

on rim, *I.N. 2*

Modern Art Foundry, Inc., Long Island City, New York

recast for the Walker Art Center at the request of the artist, 1980 (gift of the artist 80.14)

Swimming Pool for von Sternberg represents a very early statement, in model form, of ideas about sculpture and function that would occupy Noguchi throughout his career. Not only the characteristically simple, economical form, but more specifically the sweeping, helical gesture of the piece appears repeatedly in later works in a variety of sizes and materials. *Swimming Pool* further reflects Noguchi's broad conception of sculpture as functional object, a belief that led him to devote a significant proportion of his career to the design of public parks and plazas.

In his monograph on Noguchi,[1] Sam Hunter selects 1933 as the year the sculptor embarked on two different, but closely related paths; visionary landscape architecture and the design of imaginative functional objects. As Noguchi himself later put it, he was seeking "other means of communication—to find a way of making sculpture that was humanly meaningful without being realistic, at once abstract and socially relevant."[2] His new efforts were directed largely toward playground design, which had a special meaning for him:

> When the adult would imagine like a child he must project himself as a primer of shapes and functions; simple, mysterious, and evocative: thus educational. The child's world would be a beginning world, fresh and clear. The sculptural elements … have the added significance of usage—in actual physical contact—much as is the experience of the sculptor in the making.[3]

Noguchi designed the swimming pool as part of architect Richard Neutra's plans for the house of the film director Josef von Sternberg.[4] Neutra later changed his design, and, as a result, the swimming pool was never built. Much to the sculptor's disappointment, in fact, none of his playground designs of the period 1935–1942 was realized.[5] Noguchi, however, was able to implement his more general ideas, and even some very specific aspects of the earlier work, in a variety of public projects. The same pared-down spiral shape and steps seen in the *Swimming Pool*, for example, appear again in slightly different proportions in a full-scale marble playground slide entitled *Slide Mantra*, created for the 1986 Venice Biennale.[6]

N.R.

1. Sam Hunter, *Isamu Noguchi* (New York: Abbeville Press, 1978), p. 55.
2. Isamu Noguchi, *A Sculptor's World* (New York: Harper & Row, 1968), p. 21.
3. Ibid., p. 161.
4. Information from Carol Vaughn, former assistant to Isamu Noguchi.
5. Noguchi independently approached New York City's Parks Commissioner, Robert Moses, with one of his playground designs, *Play Mountain*, in 1935. Moses's sarcastic rejection of the piece was one of the incidents that prompted Noguchi to leave the United States in 1935 in search of an opportunity to create public sculpture.
6. The Walker cast of *Swimming Pool* is the second of three.

Isamu Noguchi

Cronos   1947

American, 1904–1988

balsa wood, string, metal

**86¼ x 22 x 31
(219.1 x 55.9 x 78.7)**

**incised on mobile
element, *1***

**acquired from the artist,
1979 (gift of the artist,
79.30)**

After a thirteen-year absence from New York's commercial galleries, Noguchi, at the urging of his friend Willem de Kooning, agreed to show his recent work at the Egan Gallery in 1948. The critical response to the exhibition was generally favorable; the influential critic Clement Greenberg, however, writing in *The Nation*, objected to the high finish—the exhibition consisted almost entirely of marble sculpture—of most of the works. Greenberg pinned his hopes for Noguchi's future development specifically on one work, *Cronos*, carved in feather-light balsa wood and left with a rough, wood-grain finish.[1]

The delicately suspended organic volumes in *Cronos*, as in *Avatar*, suggest the Surrealist bone forms familiar especially from the slightly earlier work of Picasso and Tanguy. They may also bear some direct connection to the stage sets Noguchi had designed for the choreographer Martha Graham, which incorporated skeletal shapes.

Noguchi included three balsa wood pieces in a 1961 exhibition at Cordier and Warren Gallery, New York, which consisted mainly of his large recent pieces in aluminum. He called the exhibition *Weightlessness*. But soon, as he wrote in his autobiography,

> ... my preoccupation with weightlessness changed. Now [1962] I wanted the tension of levitation, but not weightlessness as such; on the contrary, I wished to stress weight in the elements composing the sculptures, so that their weight would enhance the effect of floating in a gravitational field.... I realized that lightness added to lightness does not add tension, but diminishes it. I decided to have the [balsa] sculptures cast in bronze, letting bronze supply the extra element of weight.... the balsa wood pieces that I cast in bronze did indeed gain weight in more ways than one. The change of medium seemed to give authority, or finality as works of art.[2]

N.R.

1. Clement Greenberg, "Art," *The Nation*, 19 March 1949, pp. 341, 342; cited in Sam Hunter, *Isamu Noguchi* (New York: Abbeville Press, 1978), p. 87.
2. Isamu Noguchi, *A Sculptor's World* (New York: Harper & Row, 1968), pp. 37, 38.

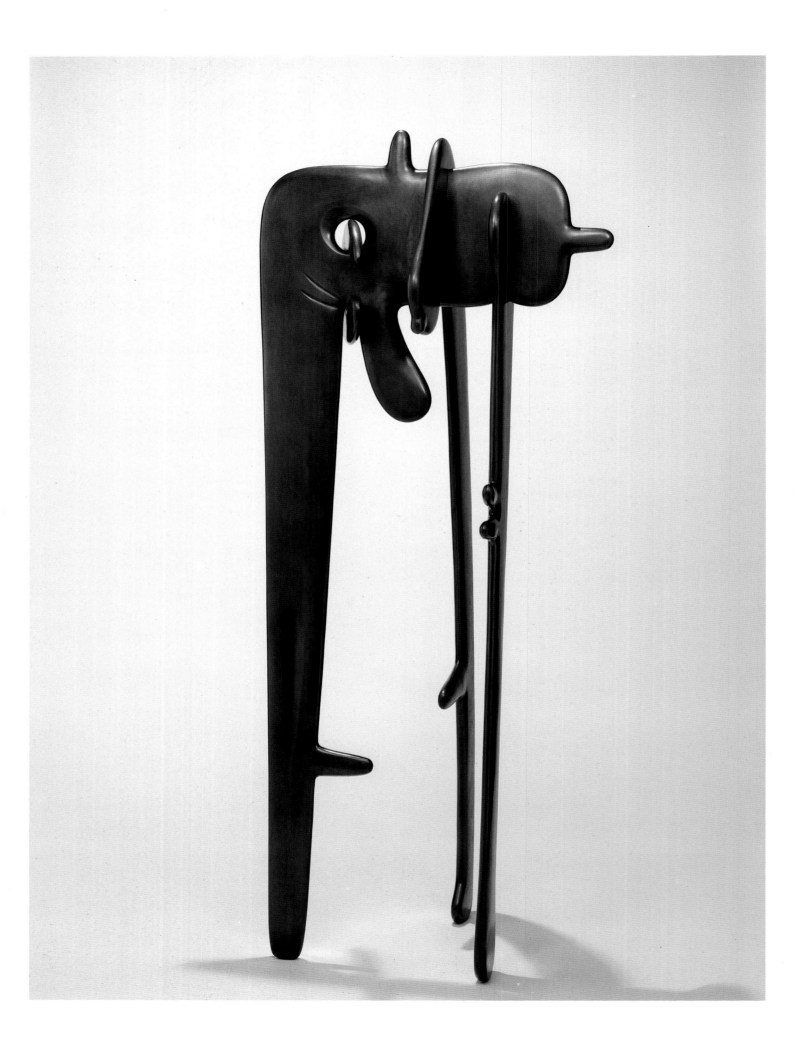

Isamu Noguchi

Avatar 1947/1980

American, 1904–1988

bronze

78½ x 33 x 23 (199.4 x 83.8 x 58.4)

recast for the Walker Art Center at the request of the artist, 1980 (gift of the artist 80.20)

Noguchi began to carve in stone in 1942, shortly after spending a year voluntarily interned with his fellow nisei in Poston, Arizona. In part as a result of his camp experience, he determined to be "an artist only," that is, to give up the lucrative portrait commissions that had earlier been his primary source of income. His new interest in stone—particularly marble—presented a substantial financial problem. Therefore, marble sheeting, a construction material used to face buildings and readily available at the time at low cost, proved a workable solution. Making a virtue of necessity, he produced between 1944 and 1947 a series of sculptures, including *Avatar*, in which the flat shape of the original marble sheet is still apparent. This group of works assured Noguchi's place as a major figure in American art.

Since his two-year association with Constantin Brancusi in Paris in the late 1920s, Noguchi had pursued a clean, pared-down, essential form in sculpture; the work of the mid-1940s, however, introduced a new tension between abstraction and figuration. *Avatar* strongly suggests organic, erotic shapes without ever quite making the identification clear. By this time, too, Noguchi had reestablished contact with his Japanese father and his father's side of the family, and had consciously adopted certain of the aesthetic values of Japanese culture. He admired, in particular, the economy and beauty of the traditional Japanese house, whose parts fit together so perfectly that no nails or glue are needed, and which can, consequently, be taken apart, moved, and reassembled with ease. In a similar fashion, the finely finished planes of *Avatar* are joined in an intricate system of slots and joints, and can be disassembled when the work is to be moved.

Speaking years later, Noguchi stressed the delicacy of the work of this period. "It defies gravity, defies time in a sense. The very fragility gives a thrill; the danger excites. It's like life—you can lose it at any moment."[1] Largely because the marble originals were so dangerous to ship, Noguchi had a number of his earlier works, including *Avatar*, cast in bronze for the first time in 1962.[2] Since then, five other casts of the work have been made.

N.R.

1. Isamu Noguchi, *A Sculptor's World* (New York: Harper & Row, 1968), p. 84. Although Noguchi is here discussing a slightly earlier work, *Kouros*, the remarks seem equally applicable to *Avatar*.
2. Martin Friedman, videotaped interview with Noguchi, 24 October 1977.

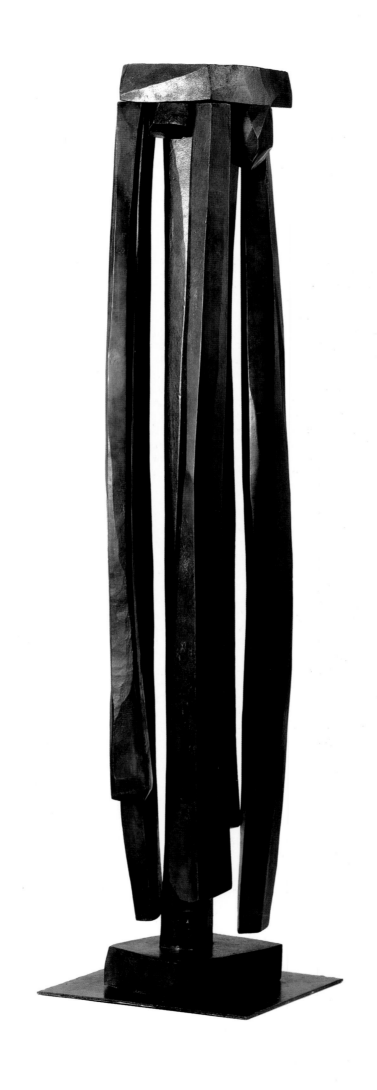

Isamu Noguchi

Mortality 1959/1962

American, 1904–1988

bronze

75⅞, width and depth variable (192.7)

on lower trunk,
I. Noguchi °62

acquired from the Cordier & Ekstrom Gallery, New York, 1964 (gift of the T.B. Walker Foundation 64.1)

In 1963, Noguchi's exhibition at the Cordier & Ekstrom Gallery consisted of earlier works (1946–1959) recently cast in bronze and a second group of what Noguchi called "studies based upon a concern for gravity and man's relation to the earth."[1] *Mortality* was installed with the first group. The original had been made in 1959 in balsa wood and shown in a 1961 exhibition entitled *Weightlessness*, in which Noguchi also introduced fifteen of his large aluminum sculptures. In bronze, however, the stately, somber form and very dark patina of *Mortality* clearly had a literal and figurative gravity that linked it to the second group as well. The work consists of a tall central shaft with a lintel, from which five strongly vertical elements, shaped vaguely like long bones, swing freely, though in a close configuration. Any motion causes the elements to bump together, producing musical sounds reminiscent of a Chinese wind chime.

Sometime in 1961, Noguchi's ideas about the role of physical weight in his sculpture changed abruptly. He had long been interested in a paradoxical play of opposites between the appearance and the fact, that is, in heavy things that look light, or conversely, light things—balsa wood or aluminum—made to look heavy. Quite suddenly, however, he began to want things that look heavy to in fact be heavy; the paradox became their delicate balance in the sculptural context. The decision to have his balsa wood sculptures cast in bronze thus had quite a different motivation from the decision to have a number of marble pieces—including *Avatar*—similarly cast at the same time. With the marble, the casting won a measure of durability at the expense of a desirable surface quality;[2] with the balsa, it actually brought the works to completion.[3]

N.R.

1. Quoted in Dore Ashton, "Isamu Noguchi," *Arts and Architecture*, vol. 80 (June 1963), p. 7.
2. Martin Friedman, videotaped interview with Noguchi, 24 October 1977.
3. The Walker's *Mortality* is the first of five known casts.

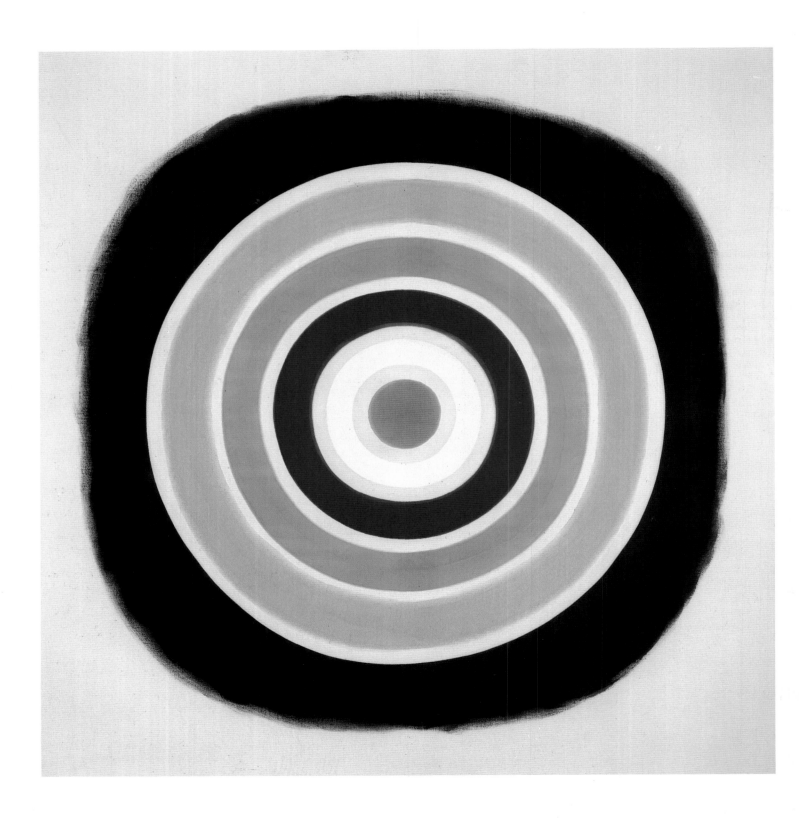

Kenneth Noland

Cantabile 1961

American, b. 1924

acrylic on raw cotton duck

**66¹³⁄₁₆ x 64⁷⁄₈
(169.7 x 164.8)**

**on reverse, upper right, in
blue ballpoint pen,
Kenneth Noland / 1961
(recorded 1965; obscured
by cotton edges added by
1974)**

**acquired from Kasmin
Limited, London, 1965
(gift of the T.B. Walker
Foundation 65.35)**

In order to dispense with certain traditional compositional issues, Noland made a series of paintings from 1957 to 1963 in which a circle is centered on the canvas and surrounded by concentric rings: the width, number, texture, edges, and, most significantly, color of the circular areas are the variables. This solution reflects his ruminations on Pollock's success in eliminating hierarchical composition in his webs of paint. Noland decided that in an equally viable alternative to the all over distribution of color, the "almost inevitable result," would be to start at the most logical point on the canvas and work out from there toward the edges.[1] He did not intend to provoke the associations with targets, cosmic bodies, or symbolic concepts that have been made in critical writings about these works.[2]

Frankenthaler's technique of staining thinned acrylic into raw canvas had shown Noland a way to eliminate the spatial actuality of overlapping physically dense paint, permitting him to liberate color from matter: "Above all, no *thingness*, no *objectness*. The thing is to get that color down on the thinnest conceivable surface, a surface sliced into the air as if by a razor. It's all color and surface, that's all."[3] Although rejecting the physicality of paint, Noland acknowledges the physical relationship between the artist's body and the work of art, citing de Kooning's statement that "he only wanted to make gestures as big as his arm could reach."[4] This sense of identification with physical, human activity applies too to the handling of the paint: the path of the paint in *Cantabile* mimics the artist's movement around the square canvas.[5] Given the thinness of the paint, the viewer correctly infers that the regularity could be achieved only if the paint had been applied to a horizontally placed canvas, hence mentally reconstructing the artist's act of making the work.

In *Cantabile*, Noland has used the properties of turpentine to vary the qualities of surface in different color areas. Although the outer edge of the inner blue band is crisp, it is optically softened by a cloudy aureole of spreading turpentine; the peachy orange is also diffused at its inner and outer periphery; the central dot, thinned at its edge, is matte and dull, again due to the quantity of turpentine added. Noland has stated that a "contrast of tactility can keep [two colors of unequal value] visually in the same dimension ... adjacent,"[6] a phenomenon he much admires in the work of Hans Hofmann.

He has commented on the different emotional responses that qualities of denseness, fuzziness, warmth, and clarity elicit. The contrast of value likewise introduces optical illusions, which "can be expressive and dramatic, like the difference between high or low volume or the low keys and the high keys on the piano. But normally a composer doesn't go just from one extreme to the other. There are ranges of things, two notes being hit side by side, for example. Either or both are possible."[7] Noland's analogy with music is reinforced by the title of this picture, a musical term describing a lyrical, flowing line. The warm ocher and peach, the cool blue and the dead black in *Cantabile* appear to gently pulsate, as a consequence of their own qualities as hues, their interactions, the variation in the treatment of their edges, and the doubling of the "negative" spaces of bare canvas as positive, unifying color areas.

L.F.G.

1. Statement quoted in *Newsweek*, 16 April 1962, p. 108. The story that Noland conceived this series of Circle paintings suddenly after circling a 6-foot square canvas on the floor until he lost track of its top and bottom (see "Painting: Bold Emblems," *Time*, 18 April 1969, p. 74) was denied by the artist; conversation with the author, 4 November 1986. It probably arose from the fact that he painted the pictures by moving around them, and only later determined their orientations.
2. See, for example, reviews of the first exhibition in which this work was shown: Edwin Mullins, "In Search of a Line," *Apollo*, vol. 77 (May 1963), p. 416, and Norbert Lynton, "London Letter," *Art International*, vol. 7 (25 May 1963), p. 58.
3. Quoted in Philip Leider, "The Thing in Painting Is Color," *The New York Times*, 25 August 1968, p. D22.
4. Quoted in Diane Waldman, "Color, Format and Abstract Art: An Interview with Kenneth Noland," *Art in America*, vol. 65 (May 1977), pp. 104, 105.
5. In a more somatic way than Stella, Noland thereby buttresses Michael Fried's theory of deductive structure, or, as amended, structure that acknowledges the edges of the support. Kenworth Moffett, *Kenneth Noland* (New York: Harry N. Abrams, 1977), p. 50, notes also that the Circle painting relates to the square by a shared central point.
6. Quoted in Waldman, p. 104.
7. Ibid.

Georgia O'Keeffe

Lake George Barns 1926

American, 1887–1986

oil on canvas

21¼ x 32 (54 x 81.3)

on original stretcher, in artist's hand, recorded in photograph, *Barn—Lake George/1925 O'Keeffe*[1]

The Intimate Gallery, New York, 1927; An American Place, New York, to at least 1946; acquired from The Downtown Gallery, New York, 1954 (gift of the T.B. Walker Foundation 54.9)

Alfred Stieglitz first took O'Keeffe to Oaklawn, his family's estate in the Adirondacks at Lake George, New York, in 1918. The Stieglitz family had acquired what had been a pig farm upwind of the house, whose farmhouse replaced Oaklawn as the summer home after his mother's death in 1922. O'Keeffe spent part of each year at Lake George with Stieglitz (whom she married in 1924) until his death in 1946. Late in life, she reminisced about the barn across from the house:

> There was a fine old barn at the Lake George farmhouse. You could see it from the kitchen window or from the window of Stieglitz's little sitting room. With much effort I painted a picture of the front part of the barn. I had never painted anything like that before. After that I painted the side where all the paint was gone with the south wind. It was weathered grey—with one broken pane in the small window. A little of the stone foundation was visible above the grass. I have looked at the barn in summer and have looked at it in winter when the snow was deep. Lake George had many grey days. When I painted the back of the barn there was a grey cloud over it toward the lake.[2]

Stieglitz had photographed the two left windows on the front barn in 1920 (*Barn, Lake George*); about 1923 he enlarged the field to include all three windows (*Barnside*).[3] In comparing the photographs with the painting, one observes both O'Keeffe's fidelity to and transformation of objective fact. While Stieglitz emphasizes the contrasts and harmonies of texture and tonal value in the shingles, clapboards, and irregular foundation stones, O'Keeffe eliminates all such surface distinctions, and imaginatively alters the scale and proportions of windows and buildings. Stieglitz shot the barn from a slight angle, creating a diagonal thrust in the lines of boards and shingles. O'Keeffe's view is direct and emphatically frontal.[4] The implied grid, the flattened planes, and the geometric rhythms of the buildings and their perforations produce an austere structure unusual in relation to the voluptuous flowers and abstractions she was painting at the same time.[5] The characteristic sensuality of O'Keeffe's work is expressed not in the subject matter, but in the application of soft, moody color in fugitive, deft brushstrokes.

L.F.G.

Alfred Stieglitz
Barnside 1923
gelatin silver print
3⅝ x 4⅝ (9.2 x 11.8)
National Gallery of Art, Washington, D.C.
Alfred Stieglitz Collection, 1949

1. The "1925" inscription contradicts the 1926 date given in O'Keeffe's records (letter from O'Keeffe to Lynda Hartman, Walker Art Center, 19 June 1974) and in the catalogue of the first exhibition in which it appeared: The Intimate Gallery, New York, *Georgia O'Keeffe: Paintings, 1926*, January–February 1927. Although O'Keeffe suggested in 1974 that she may have painted it in 1925 and first exhibited it in 1926, thus explaining the discrepancy, it is clear that it was not shown until 1927. Stieglitz customarily showed only new work, and it can safely be assumed that the 1926 date in his catalogue is accurate. The Whitney Museum of American Art artists' file holds a card, probably prepared for the American Art Research Council, which indicates that when the work was examined at An American Place in March 1946, the backing carried a label reading "Lake George Barns 1926."
2. Georgia O'Keeffe, *Georgia O'Keeffe* (New York: Viking Press, 1976), opp. pl. 45.
3. Sixteen photographs by Stieglitz of the Lake George barns, dating from 1920 to 1923, are in the Alfred Stieglitz Collection, National Gallery of Art, Washington, D.C.
4. The frontal view initiating the Barn series of paintings, *Red Barn* (1921 or 1922), shows the main barn with the small shed abutting it at the lower left. O'Keeffe continued the series with an oblique view, the *Ends of Barns*. In the summer or fall of 1926, she took up the side view in the small version she mentions and in two paintings of the same size, designated *The Side of the Barn, No. 1* and *No. 2* when exhibited at Stieglitz's Intimate Gallery at the beginning of the next year. One of these two is the Walker canvas. (The card in the Whitney Museum artists' file identifies the Walker painting as No. 2 in the Intimate Gallery show, but evidence is not given for distinguishing it from No. 1). About 1933–1934 she painted *Barn with Snow* from a slightly different vantage point.
5. There is evidence of some competitive feelings on O'Keeffe's part toward Stieglitz (as well as other male artists of the period whom he supported and whom she referred to as "the boys"): "Once Stieglitz got ahead of me. He shot a door before I could paint it;" quoted in Laurie Lisle, *Portrait of an Artist: A Biography of Georgia O'Keeffe* (New York: Seaview Books, 1980), p. 103.

Claes Oldenburg

Upside Down City 1962

American, b. Sweden,
1929

muslin, enamel,
newspaper, wood,
clothespins, hangers

118 x 60 x 60
(299.7 x 152.4 x 152.4)
variable

acquired from the artist,
1979 (purchased with the
aid of funds from the
National Endowment for
the Arts and Art Center
Acquisition Fund 79.24)

Upside Down City is a prop salvaged from the theatrical event *World's Fair II*, which took place in Oldenburg's Ray Gun Theater at 107 East 2nd Street in New York on 25, 26 May 1962.[1] At the end of the Happening—a sequence of events and objects linked by association rather than narration—the participants hung fabric buildings upside down from a web on the ceiling. The environment that resulted served as a monumentalized mirror of an image that had been created earlier in the piece, when objects were organized under and on top of a cloth on a table to form a miniature man-made landscape.

After the event, Oldenburg rehung the buildings with clothes hangers and pins in rows on a wooden frame, as if they were freshly dyed garments dripping dry on a line. To Oldenburg, they resembled letters,[2] similar to those in the soft alphabet he had made the same year, which also called for a linear arrangement. The organization of *Upside Down City* further suggests the city blocks of New York. Elsewhere Oldenburg slurs the name of the city as "Nug Yar," which in reverse spells "Ray Gun," one of the artist's primary icons, whose potent right angle dominates many of the *Upside Down City* buildings. Viewed from the side, the city's grid structure and hollow canyons are suggested; from the front they appear as a skyline of fantastic skyscrapers and townhouses scrawled with graffiti, the public art of the urban anarchist.

The unfinished look of the paint dabs that indicate windows appealed to Oldenburg, who remembers rushing to get ready for the performance.[3] Although he attributes no particular significance to the color red staining the "top" edges of the buildings, viewers who attended the Happening *Store Days II* the previous March could have associated it with the pervasive blood imagery of that piece. The drafts of the script include descriptions of buckets, sinks, and mouthfuls of blood, and blood dripping and being swept up with a broom.[4] A more benign interpretation of the crimson staining in *Upside Down City* is that it simulates the effects of the setting sun on building tops; in fact, the buckets in *World's Fair II* contained not blood but lights illuminating the city from below, i.e., "above."

In the second draft of *Store Days II*, one of the performers is "above on a shelf with a bunch of toys sewn on muslin, a ship, a sailboat, the city of NY upside down etc."[5] Other images from the earlier piece that are related to *Upside Down City* are pillows being painted, shoes filled with paper meat hanging from the ceiling, sausages being stuffed, and a giant man descending from the ceiling. Such correspondences illustrate the interrelatedness of Oldenburg's entire repertoire of images—through the application of his "system of iconography" each of his objects can systematically metamorphose into a multitude of other objects.

According to Oldenburg, the piece ideally is hung in a room about 11 or 12 feet high, so that the tallest building almost touches the floor. The viewer would then have an interactive relationship with the forms comparable to that of the performers and audience in the Happening.

L.F.G.

1. For a transcription of the script of *World's Fair II* and a description of the production, see Michael Kirby, *Happenings* (New York: Dutton, 1965), pp. 220–233.
2. Conversation with the author, 21 October 1985.
3. Ibid.
4. Claes Oldenburg and Emmett Williams, ed., *Store Days. Documents from The Store* (1961) and *Ray Gun Theater* (1962) (New York: Something Else Press, 1967), pp. 71, 123, 130, 131.
5. Ibid., p. 132; the *Freighter and Sailboat* is another hanging inverted sculpture that originated in *Store Days II*.

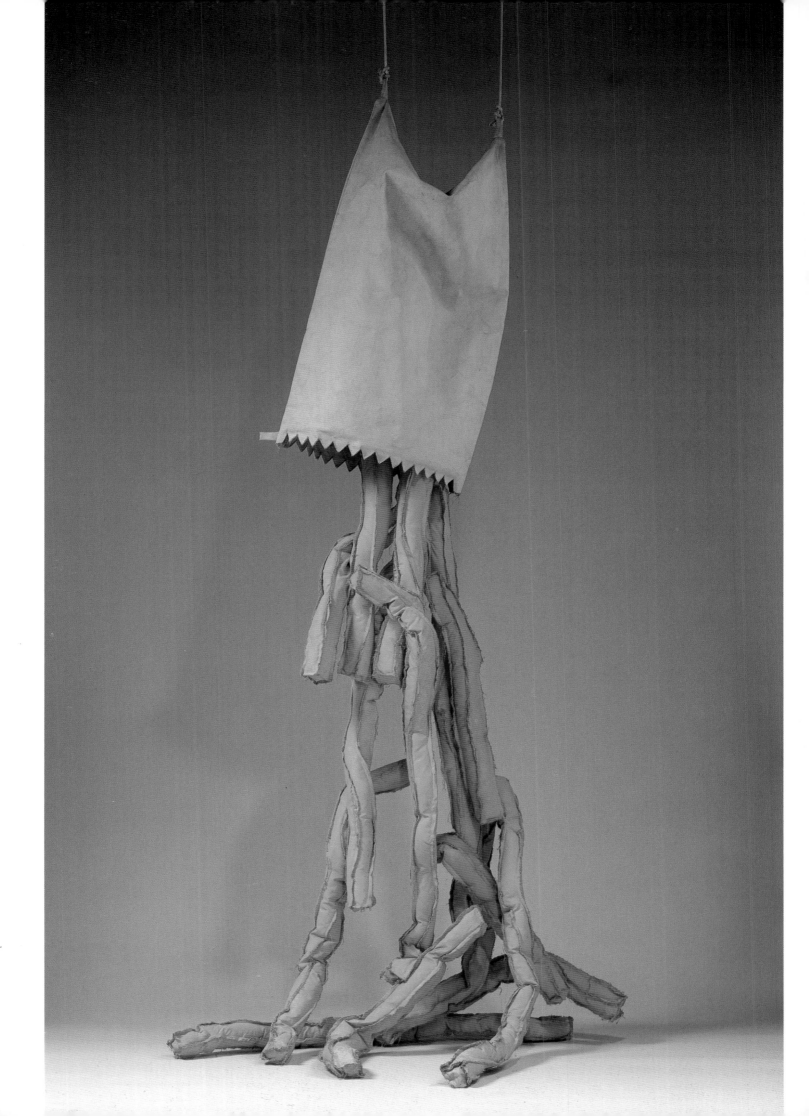

Claes Oldenburg

Shoestring Potatoes Spilling from a Bag 1966

American, b. Sweden, 1929

canvas, kapok, glue, acrylic

108 x 46 x 42
(274.3 x 116.8 x 106.7)
variable

inside edge of bag, *Claes Oldenburg / 1966*

acquired from the Sidney Janis Gallery, New York, 1966 (gift of the T.B. Walker Foundation 66.46)

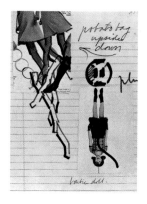

Claes Oldenburg
Notebook Page #292: Working Collage for Shoestring Potatoes and Plug 1965
ballpoint pen, felt pen, paper clippings on paper, mounted on paper
Collection the artist

Oldenburg's usual procedure is to submit an ordinary object to unaccustomed treatment, transforming it through changes of scale, color, material, orientation, and situation. In the case of the *Shoestring Potatoes*, the object itself has already undergone a series of comparable ordeals before its ultimate transfiguration into art. The creation of the fast-food French fry begins with the peeling of a potato and its fragmentation into "shoestrings," which are then frozen and later lowered into boiling oil, where they are softened on the inside and hardened on the outside. Finally, the grease-covered potatoes are over-spilled into a small serving bag.

Oldenburg's potatoes encapsulate this process, but the gnarled, twisting, glue-stiffened forms also emphasize the process of making the sculpture. With his usual witticisms and puns, Oldenburg uses canvas, historically assigned to painting, to make sculpture. He leaves the container, or support, unpainted, and colors the contents, or figures, in a parody of "realistic" painting. He restores the character of canvas as cloth by having it cut from a pattern and stitched, and alludes to the activity of sewing by pinking the edges of the bag (which here simulate the serrated top of the wax bag), reversing the seams of the fries, and leaving their edges frayed. The way in which flat pieces of cloth are joined and treated to form volume-enclosing skins to cover flesh or space is analogous to the way Oldenburg visualizes the conversion of drawings into three-dimensional forms: the contour awaits its volume.

Shoestring Potatoes and an accompanying upside down *Giant Soft Ketchup Bottle* (1967) were derived from an advertisement in a 1965 *Life* magazine, which Oldenburg clipped, altered, and titled *Shoestring Potatoes, Ketchup Bottle and 'Coke' Glass.*[1] The use of the clipping compounds the levels of removal from the original object, distanced exponentially by the techniques of commercial photography, retouching, montage, and reproduction. Oldenburg's notes on the clipping reflect his thinking as he considered transforming the images into sculpture, in terms of technique ("Sandcast," "carve," "Calipers"); material ("styro" and plaster," "FIBERGLAS," "METAL," "TIN," "WAX"); color ("orange"); and associations: tripartite ensembles in Pisa and in his own work. Typically, he suggests inverting the image to add the factor of gravity, his "favorite form creator,"[2] and to draw attention to new sets of morphological similarities.

The inverted shoestring potato image appears in another altered clipping of 1965, showing the overlapping legs of fashion models. The miniskirts of two of the figures, pressed out in stiff folds, are outlined as one form, marked "potato bag upside down." Oldenburg has overscored the legs and reiterated them as a cascade of angular fries. In a second clipping pasted below on the same sheet, he inverts the figure of a woman he has labeled "barbie doll," whose skirt becomes the cover of a plug and her legs its prongs, to be inserted in an outlet Oldenburg has drawn above.[3]

As always, the forms in Oldenburg's sculpture suggest innumerable others, both in his own work and in the viewer's visual memory. Oldenburg sees the bag as a mask, the fries as "hairy" and "tangled," and recently has described the entire piece as resembling a huge squid or man-of-war.[4]

L.F.G.

1. Reproduced in Claes Oldenburg, *Notes in Hand* (New York: Something Else Press, 1971), no. 9. In his commentary on the reproduction Oldenburg adds: "The image is trimmed so that on its side it forms a 'Ray-Gun' shape—the string potatoes become triggers." The projected Coke glass was never made.
2. A phrase Oldenburg published in his "Extracts from the Studio Notes (1962–64)," *Artforum*, vol. 4 (January 1966), p. 33.
3. The relationships among plug, skirt with legs and upside-down shoestring potatoes are also explored in the drawings *Studies for Hanging Electric Cord*, reproduced in Basel Kunstmuseum and Tübingen Kunsthalle, *Zeichnungen von Claes Oldenburg*, exh. cat., 1975, fig. 164, and *Plug = Legs = Shoestring Potatoes*, 1966.
4. Conversation with the author, 21 October 1985. In order to expand the range of implications, Oldenburg has tried visualizing the piece lying on its side. The associations this work and others provoke are governed by their installation. When the third tab at the lower edge of the French fry bag is used to pull it up, as in early photographs of the piece in the artist's studio, the distinction between "spilling" and "falling," which he established when he formalized the title in 1969, is more pronounced. The material is now so stiffened that it is difficult to achieve the original effect.

Claes Oldenburg

Geometric Mouse—Scale A   1969/1971

American, b. Sweden, 1929

steel, aluminum, automotive paint

145 x 143 x 73 (368.3 x 363.2 x 185.4)

stamped on yellow tear drop, *No. 4 OPC/GM1-A 1971/Claes Oldenburg/ ©/work executed by/ Lippincott/North Haven Conn.*

acquired from the Leo Castelli Gallery, New York, by Mr. and Mrs. Miles Q. Fiterman, Minneapolis, 1974 (intended gift of Mr. and Mrs. Miles Q. Fiterman)

Claes Oldenburg
Notebook Page #2560 A: Self-Portrait as Mystical Mouse 1969
ballpoint pen on paper
image 5 x 3 (12.7 x 7.6)
mounted on paper 11 x 8½ (27.9 x 21.6)
Collection the artist

The evolution of the *Geometric Mouse*, one of Oldenburg's fundamental icons, began with the shapes of Mickey Mouse's head and that of the early film camera.[1] These appeared together in the performance of Oldenburg's *Moveyhouse* (December 1965), in which a projector and geometric mouse head figured prominently. The shape of the *Geometric Mouse* is also that of a double Ray Gun, which "shoots but does not kill; it is a device of 'illumination,' not aggression."[2] The colder contours of the mechanical mouse-camera, in comparison with Mickey Mouse's rounded and genial features, recall the "murderous" camera in Oldenburg's 1961 performance *Fotodeath*.[3]

As Oldenburg almost obsessively developed the mouse image, it became increasingly remote from Mickey Mouse (itself a dubious relative of an actual mouse), and took on the qualities of a logo, which the artist used for a letterhead and banners. In 1967 it became a building in the form of a proposal for a facade for the Museum of Contemporary Art in Chicago, where its eyes are windows and the lids are shades with pulls attached, a feature that finds its way into the *Geometric Mouse* sculpture.

As a sculpture, the logo poses an engineering problem, having essentially no volume and hence no self-sufficient means of support. A solution is found in a drawing from Oldenburg's notebooks (published as a lithograph in 1968 by Gemini G.E.L.), in which the flat mouse head tumbles down a hill, bending at its points of stress.[4] The sculptural translation of the head is similarly bent, as if falling or fallen, permitting the work to rest in stable balance on three points, two of which are bent, giving the *Mouse* the appearance of being partially submerged. The angle at which the head rests recalls Brancusi's *Muse*, to which Oldenburg alludes with the word "M(o)use" inscribed on a notebook sketch. An Easter Island head at Lippincott suggested a sculpture composed entirely of a head.[5]

In the lower right corner of the same drawing, the mouse head floats on water as if dead,[6] the pulls of its shade-eyes elongated in a way that evokes a sequence in the notes for *Moveyhouse*, in which one of the performers would attach strings from his eyes to the screen, in a concrete representation of "lines" of sight.[7] In the sculpture, the disks are attached to the lids by chains that to Oldenburg resemble tears coursing down a face.[8]

The *Geometric Mouse* was made in various scales, four of which are illustrated in a drawing of 1971. Of the edition of Scale A, begun in 1969, two were painted blue and yellow, the colors of the Swedish flag.[9] These were destined for Stockholm and for Minneapolis, many of whose inhabitants—like Oldenburg—have Swedish roots.

The autobiographical aspects of Oldenburg's contrived mouse form are confirmed by his *Self-Portrait as Mystical Mouse* (1969), in which the disks or reels on his head are marked as the right and left brains. Given the associations with camera, projector, and self-portrait, the *Mouse* represents the activity of the artist using all his intuitive and analytic powers to absorb, create, reflect, and regard his own imagery.

L.F.G.

1. For a description of the history and content of the *Geometric Mouse*, see Coosje van Bruggen, in Rijksmuseum Kröller-Müller, Otterlo, *Claes Oldenburg: Mouse Museum/Ray Gun Wing*, exh. cat., 1979, and Martin Friedman, interview with Oldenburg, Walker Art Center, *Oldenburg: Six Themes*, exh. cat., 1975, pp. 25–33.
2. Letter to the author, 28 August 1987, in reference to van Bruggen, p. 8.
3. Oldenburg remarked on the connection in his *Raw Notes* (Halifax: University of Nova Scotia Press, 1973), p. 84. In *Fotodeath*, the camera's capacity figuratively to stop life was compared to the literal capacity of a pistol, via the account of a murderer who always photographed his victims before killing them; see van Bruggen, p. 8.
4. This lithograph, no. 7, is from a series titled *Notes*.
5. Letter to the author cited above. The connection was first noted in print by Ellen H. Johnson, "Oldenburg's 'Giant 3-Way Plug,'" *Arts Magazine*, vol. 45 (December 1970– January 1971), p. 43,
6. For a discussion of Oldenburg's association of the mouse with death, see Walker Art Center, p. 25.
7. Oldenburg, *Raw Notes*, p. 55.
8. Conversation with the author, 21 October 1985.
9. The Walker's work is 5/6 in the edition.

Claes Oldenburg

Three-Way Plug—Scale A, Soft, Brown   1975

American, b. Sweden,
1929

Naugahyde, Masonite,
wire mesh, padding, wood,
foam rubber, zipper, rope,
chain, cleat, pulleys

144 x 77 x 59
(365.8 x 195.6 x 149.9)
variable

acquired from the artist,
1979 (gift of the artist
79.120)

In a drawing of 1965 Oldenburg posits a colossal three-way plug as a cathedral floating on water; above the surface, its identical, symmetrical facades, based on interpenetrating cylinders, rise grandly in an architectural equivalent of the art of Mondrian and the compositions of Debussy.[1] In contrast, the portion under water is distorted and evanescent, as if dissolved. The paradoxical nature of the water-borne building is fundamental to Oldenburg's plug sculptures—buoyant is heavy, hard is soft, wet is dry. Because of its scale and material, the Naugahyde plug is a particularly ponderous, sodden, lumpy, and lethargic form; its skin sags from the hard armature as if it had just been hoisted out of the water.

Oldenburg first built a cardboard *Three-Way Plug* the same year as the drawing: "I was just thinking of reconstructing the plug in an ideal way. I wanted to change it from the original, to simplify it, to make it look more the way I wanted it to look."[2] He made a Masonite and wood version, followed by mahogany and cherrywood examples,

> ... which became the basis for the set of blueprints that led to the steel plug. Out of that grew the soft ones—the rest of the family, so to speak. Once I had the patterns for the steel one, I made patterns for sewing soft versions. One set of patterns went to ... Liz de Blanc for sewing.[3]

As in all of Oldenburg's work, ghosts of his other objects inhabit the plug: the drooping elephant mask with trunk, human legs resembling prongs, the Good Humor bar with body and legs, Swedish knäckebröd with soft indented slits, the ubiquitous Ray Gun, even the shoestring potatoes. In an article Oldenburg wrote in October 1966, he describes his process of "rhyming," the intuitive identifying of connections among forms.[4] Among the illustrations of the process are drawings of *Geometric Mouse* ears extended and filled in to make toast, which when elongated and inserted into toaster slots suggest the prongs of the plug. The prongs also resemble Oldenburg's ping-pong paddles inflated and put side by side. In the *Three-Way Plug*, "the 'ear' disk [of the *Geometric Mouse*] takes the place of the 'face' rectangle, so that the 'eyes' are contained in the 'ears.' The result gives the appearance of a pig's nose ... and that includes the element of smell."[5] Another drawing from a 1965 notebook page

compares the plug with Brancusi's *Torso of a Young Man*.[6]

Referring to his image of the floating plug, Oldenburg recently remarked on the shared vocabulary applied to water and electricity (e.g., "flow," "current," "outlet," "draining").[7] As he perceives it, "plugging in, or establishing contact is a theme—which goes beyond the merely sexual to the contact of the person with his surroundings. Many of the objects also refer to masturbation or forms of touching oneself instead of another...."[8] The hermaphroditic three-way plug, with male and female elements, has such onanistic implications, though it is not ungenerous, and can also "receive the observer into itself"[9] through its apertures; ideally, the plug and the cleat holding the ropes that raise it should be low enough so that the spectator could imagine interacting with the object directly.

L.F.G.

1. In the drawing, which is also in the Walker collection, the words "Mondrian" and "Englouti" are written in the water. Oldenburg makes a connection between the floating plug and architectural projects by Mondrian and associates the word "Englouti" with Debussy (conversations with the author, 21 October 1985 and 26 February 1986), who wrote the prose-poem "La Cathédrale engloutie" ("swallowed cathedral"). Oldenburg recalls that in the poem, villagers attend a cathedral floating in water after a flood. He may have been aware of Mondrian's plan for the *Salon de Madame B à Dresden* of 1926, in which rectangles, squares, truncated cylinders, and ovals constitute the architecture and furniture of a private room.
2. Martin Friedman, interview with Oldenburg, in Walker Art Center, *Oldenburg: Six Themes*, exh. cat., 1975, p. 37. For the history of the plug image, see pp. 37, 45.
3. Ibid., p. 45.
4. See Barbara Rose, in The Museum of Modern Art, New York, *Claes Oldenburg*, exh. cat., 1970, pp. 195–198.
5. Ibid., p. 197.
6. Reproduced in Ellen H. Johnson, "Oldenburg's 'Giant 3–Way Plug,'" *Allen Memorial Art Museum Bulletin*, vol. 28 (Spring 1971), p. 229. See p. 230 for the artist's additional associations.
7. Conversation with the author, 21 October 1985.
8. Rose, p. 198.
9. Friedman, in Walker Art Center, p. 37.

Claes Oldenburg and Coosje van Bruggen

Spoonbridge and Cherry 1985–1988

Oldenburg, American, b.
Sweden, 1929;
van Bruggen, Dutch,
b. 1942

stainless steel, painted
aluminum

354 x 618 x 162
(899.2 x 1,569.7 x 411.5)

Lippincott, Inc., North
Haven, Connecticut
subcontractors, spoon:
Merrifield-Roberts, Inc.,
Bristol, Rhode Island
cherry: Paul E. Luke, Inc.,
East Boothbay, Maine

commissioned by Walker
Art Center, 1985 (gift
of Frederick R. Weisman
in honor of his parents,
William and Mary
Weisman 88.385)

Claes Oldenburg and Coosje van Bruggen's large-scale fountain sculpture, *Spoonbridge and Cherry*, provides an impressive conclusion to the principal north-south axis of the Minneapolis Sculpture Garden.[1] It is one of only two fountain projects undertaken to date by these artists, who have been collaborating on large-scale public sculptures since 1976, the other being *Dropped Bowl with Scattered Slices and Peels*, in Miami, Florida.

Plans for the sculpture began in 1985 when Walker Art Center approached the two artists with a proposal to create a work for a large pool designed by architect Edward Larrabee Barnes for the new Sculpture Garden. Sketches and notes indicate that the artists considered at least two different concepts before arriving at the final design. Among the early considerations were a trio of related forms, one vertically oriented, one diagonally, and one more solidly earthbound. Another idea, stimulated by Minnesota's Scandinavian and Native American heritages, involved the prow of a Viking ship or of a canoe pulled up onto the shore.

Ultimately, the artists proposed a spoon form whose bowl rises to suggest a boat prow or even a duck rising from the water. The provocation of multiple associations from the abstracted forms of common objects has been a staple of Oldenburg's art since the 1960s.

Van Bruggen revised the architect's original design for the pool—two semicircles joined on their flat sides but having different centers—into the abstracted shape of the seed of a linden tree, as lindens are planted along the two main allées of the Garden. She also provided the idea of the cherry placed in the spoon's bowl. Water rises from the base of the stem and flows over the cherry, running down into the spoon and pool.

The spoon motif has been an ingredient in Oldenburg's work since 1962, when he bought a novelty spoon from which fake chocolate sauce dripped to form an "island" under the bowl. This inspired a 1967 drawing comparing Chicago's Navy Pier to an enormous dessert spoon jutting out into Lake Michigan. The comparison was made even more appropriate by Oldenburg's observation that Lake Michigan itself is vaguely spoon-shaped.[2] The motif reappeared in a preliminary study for a sculpture commission for the Social Security Administration building in Chicago, where Oldenburg envisioned embedding a large vertical spoon into the ground. By the time of the final design, the upright spoon handle had been transformed into an inverted baseball bat.[3]

P.B.

1. An expansion of the Garden to the north is planned for the near future, which will place the fountain as the central element in an eleven acre site.
2. See Coosje van Bruggen, in Rijksmuseum Kröller-Müller, Otterlo, *Claes Oldenburg: Mouse Museum/Ray Gun Wing*, exh. cat., 1979, pp. 34,35.
3. See Coosje van Bruggen, R.H. Fuchs, and Claes Oldenburg, *Claes Oldenburg: Large-Scale Projects, 1977–1980* (New York: Rizzoli International Publications, 1980), pp. 12, 13.

Claes Oldenburg and **Coosje van Bruggen**
Model for *Spoonbridge and Cherry* (detail) 1986 wood, paint, plastic, graphite, felt pen (acquired in connection with the construction of the Minneapolis Sculpture Garden 86.62)

Amédée Ozenfant

The Sleeping Canyon 1945–1946

French, 1886–1966

oil on canvas on Masonite

52 x 38¹⁵⁄₁₆
(132.1 x 98.9)

lower right, *Ozenfant 45*;
on original stretcher
(recorded in a
photograph), *Arizona 1,
second version/ozenfant
1945/The Sleeping
Canyon*

acquired from the artist by
the Passedoit Gallery,
New York; acquired from
Passedoit, 1946
(gift of the T.B. Walker
Foundation, Gilbert M.
Walker Fund 46.22)

In 1946, in response to a question from the Walker Art Center about the location of the actual "sleeping canyon" depicted, Ozenfant stated that it

> ... exists nowhere, except on your canvas. "The Sleeping Canyon" is the synthesis of a long series of emotions received before many Colorado and Arizona scenes in 1938 and 1939. I was moved by the drama of the clifs [sic] and by the contrasting peaceful Pueblo villages. I tried to reconcile those opposites mainly by using light as a [sic] organizing agent.[1]

On Ozenfant's first visit to the United States in 1938, he taught summer school at the University of Washington in Seattle. At the end of the session he took a Greyhound bus down the Pacific coast, across to the Grand Canyon, through the Painted Desert to Santa Fe, returning to Chicago by way of Denver. He went back to Europe, but immigrated to the United States in February 1939. After teaching at the University of Washington that summer, he again traveled by bus through America, ending up in New York.[2] Memories of the images he absorbed during those travels became the subject of his imaginary Surrealist-influenced landscape *The Sleeping Canyon*, executed in New York, where he was teaching at his Ozenfant School of Fine Arts (founded in 1939).[3]

Ozenfant had developed Purism in the late teens with Charles-Edouard Jeanneret (Le Corbusier). They drew on pre-1914 Cubism, but dismissed its subsequent evolution as too decorative and unordered. According to the principles of Purism, the artist could find formal and coloristic equivalents to the emotions he experienced that would have a predictable effect on the viewer:

> My emotion, I "shaped" it, using the knowledge of the effects on us of forms and colors that I gained through my long purist analysis and synthesis. I think I know what certain types of forms and colors impose on us (in a word, which are the sound "plastic words" capable of expressing each category of emotions). There was no guess work but use of the knowledge of keyboards of forms and colors for expressing what I intended to communicate. That is science serving emotion, that is knowledge helping emotion to express itself.

A critic writing at the time was convinced, stating that "the warm-colored *Sleeping Canyon* ... lighted with the last flash of setting sun on the topmost hump, and shrouded by the gloom of slow twilight, is less an ode to nature than one to flesh and blood."[4]

L.F.G.

1. Letter to Daniel S. Defenbacher, 9 October 1946.
2. J.J. Sweeney, "Eleven Europeans in America," *The Museum of Modern Art Bulletin*, vol. 13 (1946), pp. 7, 8.
3. According to his dealer, Georgette Passedoit, the canvas was begun in 1945 and completed in 1946 (letter from Georgette Passedoit to Daniel S. Defenbacher, 20 September 1946), suggesting that he reworked it after inscribing the "1945" date, perhaps in preparation for his March 1946 show at the Passedoit Gallery. The inscription on the original stretcher, in the artist's hand, suggests that Ozenfant may have first called this work *Arizona 1*, and that there may have been another, earlier version of the same or a similar composition.
4. A.C., "New York Exhibitions," *MKR's Art Outlook: A Critical Commentary on People and Events in Art*, vol. 1 (February 1946), p. 3.

Martin Puryear

Ampersand 1987–1988

American, b. 1941

granite

**east column, 163 x 36 x
36 (414 x 91.4 x 91.4);
west column, 167 x 36 x
38 (424.2 x 91.4 x 96.5)**

**commissioned by Walker
Art Center; acquired
through the Donald Young
Gallery, Chicago, 1987
(gift of Margaret and
Angus Wurtele 88.388)**

Martin Puryear
For Beckwourth 1980
earth, wood
40 x 34 x 34
(101.6 x 86.4 x 86.4)
Collection the artist

Flanking the entrance to the Minneapolis
Sculpture Garden are two 14-foot-high columns
by Martin Puryear, fashioned from huge blocks of
granite found at the Cold Spring Granite quarries,
which are located seventy-five miles northwest of
Minneapolis. At one end of each column Puryear
has maintained the essentially rectangular shape
and craggy surface of the found stones, while
using a machine lathe "like a pencil sharpener"
to shape the other end of each column into a
smooth, truncated cone.[1] The overlapping of
these two areas within each column creates an
elegant pattern of scalloped curves. Puryear
emphasizes these visual and textural contrasts
by installing the vertical columns in opposite directions; one rises from a smooth, cylindrical
base to a thick rectangular top; the other rises to
a round pinnacle from a rough-hewn rectangular
base.

The interplay of square and conical forms has
been a major theme in Puryear's work for many
years. Among significant early examples was *Box
and Pole*, (1977), his first large-scale landscape
sculpture, temporarily installed at Art Park in
Lewiston, New York; it consisted of a tapering
100-foot pole standing alongside a densely built
wooden box. Another predecessor of the Walker
columns is *For Beckwourth*, (1980), a wood
square topped by a conical earthen mound. In the
Walker piece, as in many of his other sculptures,
formal and textural contrasts suggest thematic
oppositions such as organic versus machinelike
and primitive versus modern.

In siting his granite columns, Puryear worked
closely with the Minneapolis Sculpture Garden's
architect, Edward Larrabee Barnes. The sculpture
simultaneously relates to and asserts its independence from the site. His stone sentinels
define the entrance to the Garden, framing its
symmetrical panorama of tree-lined sculpture
courts. By turning one of the columns on its end,
Puryear challenges the formal purity of the
Garden's classical design "by standing symmetry
on its head."[2] The dark color and physical density
of the stone verticals reflect an emotional gravity
that further distinguishes them from the cool
symmetrical layout of the Garden.

L.R.

1. Conversation with the author, 18 August 1987.
2. Ibid.

Martin Puryear

To Transcend   1987

American, b. 1941

Honduran mahogany,
poplar

169 x 13 x 90
(429.3 x 33 x 228.6)

acquired from the Donald
Young Gallery, Chicago,
1988 (Walker Special
Purchase Fund 88.4)

To Transcend is an unusual sculpture in Martin Puryear's oeuvre in that it relies on both wall and floor for support. Its base is a dense, podlike form; rising gracefully from this weighty terminus is a long, curved mahogany shaft that culminates, high above the viewer's head, in a delicately fashioned disk whose razor-thin edge rests gently against the wall. The sculpture seems to mediate between two predominant types of Puryear motifs: linear wallpieces, many of which resemble oversized necklaces, and volumetric objects that rest solidly on the floor.

In this work, Puryear weds a series of oppositions—organic and geometric, line and volume, high and low, stability and instability—within an unexpectedly simple configuration. The gourdlike form at its base and the long curving shaft at first appear to be objects taken from nature, with only slight modification by the artist; yet close inspection reveals them to have been carefully constructed from laminated poplar and mahogany sections that were then carved into their final forms. Through these subtle contradictions, Puryear effectively slows down the viewing process; what seems at first to be simple and straightforward turns out to be complex and elusive.

Puryear's meticulous craftsmanship derives in large part from his admiration for the African craft traditions he was first exposed to in the mid-1960s while a Peace Corps volunteer in Sierra Leone. He has long been interested in ethnography, biology, and history and is fascinated by "the way different cultures have resolved the same problems."[1] Many of the shapes he uses are therefore adaptations of familiar forms, such as architectural domes, jewelry, and household implements, which he subjects to sharp changes in scale that render them new and unfamiliar. Others are variations on forms he has previously used but reworks in an effort to mine them for new resonances. The podlike base in *To Transcend*, for example, recurs in a much larger mesh-and-tar version in an untitled sculpture from 1987.

Puryear belongs to the generation of sculptors who, in the early 1970s, inherited the reductivist aesthetic of Minimalism, yet sought to invest their work with a greater range of references than could be found in that movement's impersonal, industrial style. Although he credits Minimalism with legitimizing in his own mind a belief in "the power of the simple, single thing,"[2]

he also asserts that after experimenting with Minimalism during his graduate-student days he found that it "had no taste, so I spat it out."[3] Because of their particular blend of formal simplicity and allusive richness, Puryear's sculptures appear, paradoxically, to be at once reticent and profoundly resonant.

P.B.

1. The artist in a conversation with the author, 5 December 1987.
2. The artist quoted in Hugh M. Davies and Helaine Posner, "Conversations with Martin Puryear," in University of Massachusetts, Amherst, *Martin Puryear*, exh. cat. 1984, p. 32.
3. The artist quoted in "New Cultural Worlds," *U.S. News and World Report*, vol. 105, no. 25 (26 December 1988–2 January 1990), p. 101.

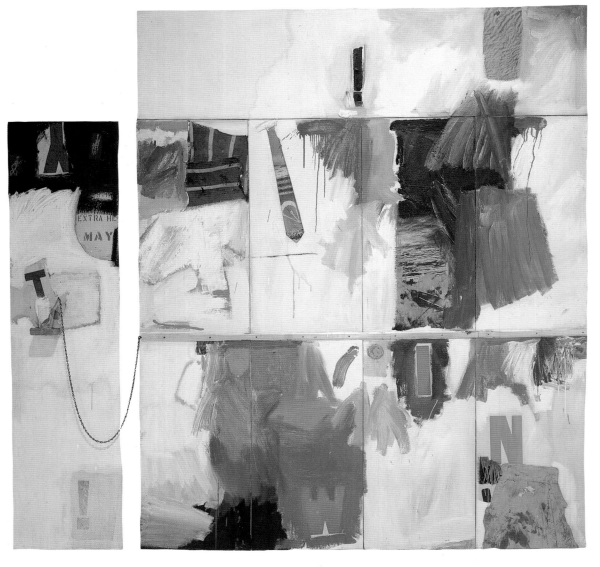
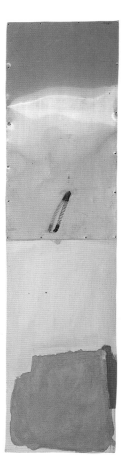

Robert Rauschenberg

Trophy II (for Teeny and Marcel Duchamp) 1960

American, b. 1925

oil, charcoal, paper, fabric, metal on canvas, drinking glass (not original), metal chain, spoon

seven panels
72 x 18
(182.9 x 45.7) each
height when assembled
90 (228.6)

on reverse of each panel, in the artist's hand, with felt-tip green and black pen, *Trophy II/ Rauschenberg/1960/#1* (leftmost), *#1/Teeny/ Trophy II/(for Teeny + Marcel Duchamp)/* diagram of front of work showing placement of numbered panels, with indication metal strip flush with *#5/Rauschenberg/ 1960/put spoon in glass/ keep glass filled with clear water*, panel #7 (rightmost), *#7 Marcel/ Trophy II/(for Teeny + Marcel/Duchamp).*

the artist until at least 1968; acquired from the Leo Castelli Gallery, New York, January 1970 (gift of the T.B. Walker Foundation 70.1)

Rauschenberg considers Duchamp, whom he met through Nicolas Calas the year he began this multipaneled Combine painting,[1] the only artist of the past who has had a significant impact on him: "I find his life and work a constant inspiration.... His 'Bicycle Wheel' has always struck me as one of the most beautiful pieces of sculpture I've ever seen."[2] Like Duchamp, Rauschenberg disassociates beauty in art from taste and from the tradition of hierarchically disposed referential forms on canvas, an attitude that Duchamp described in himself with customary wit as "complete anesthesia." It has been observed that Rauschenberg manages to trap objects from the external world in his pictorial field much the same way that Duchamp pressed images between panes of glass, a procedure whose effect is to "materialize the image, to make a representation read as though it were a corporeal thing."[3]

Rauschenberg's objects, being left intact enough to be recognizable, do not lose their identity as things with independent functions when reassigned to the context of art; on the contrary, they draw attention to the materiality of the artist's traditional means. As Rauschenberg stated in early 1961: "Paint itself is an object, and the canvas as well. In my opinion, there is no emptiness waiting to be filled."[4] This coincides with Duchamp's statement made later that year that "since the tubes of paint used by the artist are manufactured and readymade products, we must conclude that all the paintings in the world are Readymades, and also works of assemblage."[5]

Rauschenberg wants his work to be regarded as having a value neither greater nor less than that of ordinary perceptual experience. "I would like for my work to be as clear, as interesting and as vivid as the fact that you wore that tie today instead of another."[6] As in newspapers or the experience of daily urban life, one item is juxtaposed with another without connections other than those made by viewers based on their own memories, experiences, and predilections. The five Trophies, begun in 1959 and dedicated to artists Rauschenberg admires—Merce Cunningham, Duchamp, Jean Tinguely, John Cage, and Jasper Johns—suggest a random but deliberate order. While it has previously been thought that only *Trophy I* bore the image of its conferee (Cunningham), an examination of the reverse of *Trophy II* shows that the leftmost panel is identified as "Teeny," and the rightmost as

"Marcel." Rauschenberg refers to Teeny's name by integrating a T and a Y on the front of her panel.[7] The reflective sheet of aluminum on the upper half of the Marcel panel may refer to Duchamp's move from canvas to glass and to the themes of reflection, transformation, and narcissism that run through his work. The coiled spring, while paying homage to Duchamp's concept of the found object, also serves as a mechanomorphic phallic motif. The central panel contains images that can be associated with the American competitive ethos: the letters W, I, N, a silkscreened view of a baseball game on a tie, moonscapes, a newspaper fragment in which the word "Record" is legible, a helmeted pilot in a racing boat. However, these and the other objects—the stencil on canvas masked to read "9 x 12 / EXTRA HE[AVY] / MAY," the glass of water with a spoon resting in it, attached by a chain to the metal strip dividing the central panels, the exclamation marks, sleeve parts, tin can top, and painted surfaces—can trigger a complicated network of personal associations in the viewer.

L.F.G.

1. The details of Rauschenberg's meeting with Duchamp are given in National Collection of Fine Arts, Smithsonian Institution, Washington, D.C., *Robert Rauschenberg*, exh. cat., 1976, p. 38.
2. Quoted in Calvin Tomkins, "Profiles: Moving Out," *The New Yorker*, 29 February 1964, p. 104. Rauschenberg acquired a replica of Duchamp's *Bottle Dryer* in 1960, about the time he was working on the Walker's *Trophy II*; see Alan R. Solomon, in The Jewish Museum, New York, *Robert Rauschenberg*, exh. cat., 1963, n.p.
3. Rosalind Krauss, "Rauschenberg and the Materialized Image," *Artforum*, vol. 13 (December 1974), p. 39.
4. Interview by André Parinaud, *Arts* (Paris), no. 821 (10–16 May 1961), p. 18. The concept was demonstrated in his uniformly white, multipaneled White paintings of 1951, one of which was dismantled, painted over to form *Trophy II*, and replaced by a replica; for further discussion, see Roberta Bernstein, in Larry Gagosian Gallery, New York, *Rauschenberg: The White and Black Paintings 1949–1952*, exh. cat., 1986, n.p.
5. "Art of Assemblage Symposium," held at The Museum of Modern Art, New York, 19 October 1961; typescript at The Museum of Modern Art library, p. 20.
6. Quoted in Parinaud, p. 18.
7. The T and Y were not part of the original scheme, as can be seen from a photograph of Rauschenberg in front of the work in progress, where the only letter on the panel is an S, which was later removed; reproduced in *Metro no. 2* (25 May 1961), p. 35.

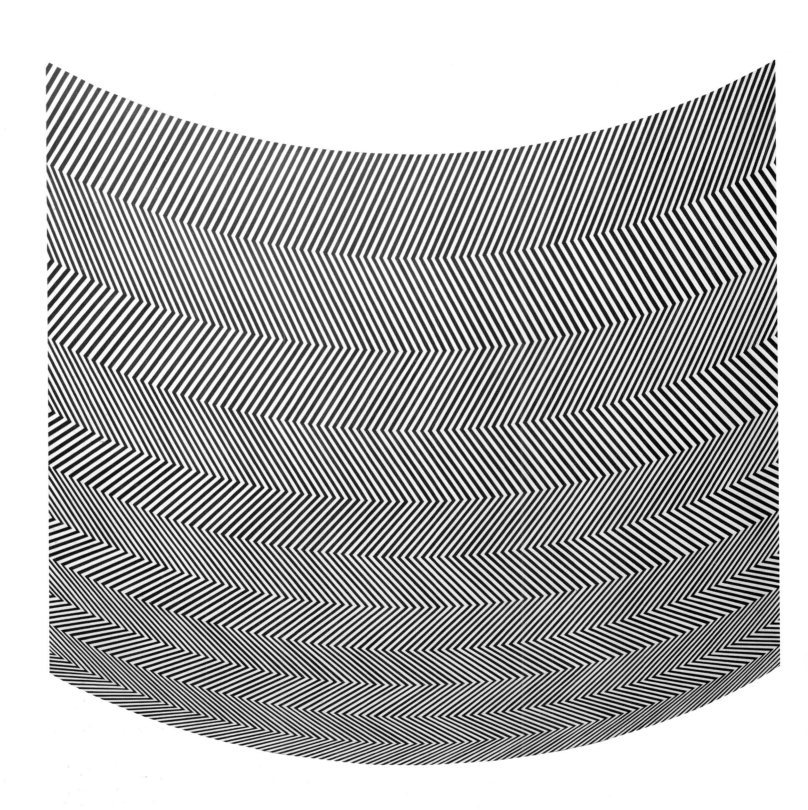

Bridget Riley

Suspension 1964

British, b. 1931

emulsion on wood

45¾ x 45⅞
(116.2 x 116.5)
projected 2¼ (5.7)
from wall by wooden cross
braces

lower left edge, within
thickness of panel, in
white paint, *Riley '64*; on
reverse, *Riley/1964/
Suspension/Emulsion on
wood/46 x 46 ins*

acquired from the Feigen
Palmer Gallery, Los
Angeles, 1965, by Mr. and
Mrs. Stanley Freeman, Los
Angeles; acquired by the
Rowan Gallery, London, at
Sotheby's London, 1971;
acquired from the Rowan
Gallery by Mr. and Mrs.
Julius E. Davis, 1981 (gift
of Mr. and Mrs. Julius E.
Davis 81.50)

Discussing the ideas that led to her work of the 1960s, Riley wrote in 1986:

> One of the things—or principles perhaps—which fascinated me and which must be part of common understanding, although I realized it for myself ... is that movement is change; change cannot be experienced without reference to that which does not change. So that which is constant or static is an inseparable part of that which changes or moves—in a painting they have to be experienced simultaneously. This I recognized in the studies I was making at the time.[1]

Riley experienced a vivid demonstration of this concept while traveling in Italy, when the interlocking pattern of black and white marble stones in a piazza was visually fragmented and put into motion by a violent storm.[2] The regularly iterated, rigid black and white patterning of *Suspension* is likewise dynamically charged, producing the distressing or stimulating "visual prickles"[3] that suggest a field of activity rather than an observed form. Although Riley's painting reflects the non-figurative, allover, anti-compositional principles assumed by many artists of the generation following Pollock, her intentions are symbolic rather than abstract. Through the multiplication of line carefully calibrated in terms of scale, dimension, angle, and frequency, she attempts to suggest a parallel with the structure of human emotion—its "repetition, contrast, calculated reversal and counterpoint."[4] Within a hard-edged, gesture-free vocabulary, Riley uses strategies of contradiction and ambiguity to create her analogy of the rhythms and paradoxes of human psychology. The reduction of scale from top to bottom gives *Suspension* a rearing quality, but the absence of shading contradicts such a perspectival reading. While the changes in direction of the lines construct the illusion of a staircase, it is negated by the isometric rendering of the "steps," the shaping of the panel and the implied continuation of the flat, non-allusive pattern ad infinitum. The shape of the board introduces another contradiction: the contour imitates a suspended, sagging rectangle, but the panel is solid and the lines of the painting taut. Yet another element in this oppositional arena derives from peculiarities of vision: the field pulsates with the pale spectral hues of afterimages running diagonally across the black and white lines.

Riley has described her approach as a series of "empirical analyses and syntheses," and has made it clear that her mathematical procedures are "confined to equalizing, halving, quartering and simple progressions."[5] She frequently does her preparatory drawings on graph paper, which provides a simply adjustable system of regularization.[6] In *Suspension*, variations in the thickness of the hand-painted lines and the angles at which they meet, arrived at through trial and error, disrupt the uniformity of progression as well as suggest the shadings of human intention and feeling.[7] The condensation or attenuation of lines automatically propels the eye, which is simultaneously pulled in contrary directions by the alternation of direction and the peripheral awareness of other clusters of lines, causing a disorienting effect. In formal terms, the illusion of motion projected by primary oppositions is an aggressive interpretation of Mondrian, who claimed that his own paintings were faster than if they actually moved. In her interest in dynamic motion, Riley responds to Futurism, which she knew and admired from trips to Milan in 1959 and Venice in 1960.[8]

The psychological symbolism of Riley's work has been generally overlooked, and she is usually characterized as a leading practitioner of Op Art, a term coined in the mid-60s to describe works whose impact derives from peculiar or powerful optical effects.

L.F.G.

1. Letter to the author, 15 July 1986.
2. The episode is recounted in John Russell, "The Cogency of Bridget Riley," *The New York Times*, 28 June 1979, p. D27.
3. A term used by Riley in an interview with David Sylvester, *Studio International*, vol. 173 (March 1967), p. 134.
4. Bridget Riley, "Perception is the Medium," *Art News*, vol. 64 (October 1965), p. 33.
5. Ibid., p. 32.
6. In this case, eleven rows of ninety-two lines descend in a regularly diminishing sequence; the top row is 7 inches high, the bottom 1½. The angle at which the lines meet becomes increasingly acute from top to bottom, though the rate of their diminution obeys no detectable mathematical or arithmetical imperative.
7. The hand of the artist is not crucial in the painting of Riley's work: *Suspension* was completed by assistants working under her supervision from drawings she prepared; letter to the author, 15 July 1986.
8. "Bridget Riley and Maurice de Sansmarez," *Art International*, vol. 11 (20 April 1967), p. 37.

Thomas Rose

Watchtower 1983

American, b. 1942

oil on wood

96⅜ x 50½ x 3⅜
(244.8 x 128.3 x 8.6)

on reverse, top center,
Rose 83

acquired from the
Thomson Gallery,
Minneapolis, 1984
(Justin Smith Purchase
Fund 84.23)

Tom Rose has evolved a limited vocabulary of easily recognizable, often domestic images, including doors, windows, ladders, and stairs, which he uses to maximum effect. Often "emblems of place,"[1] these images, which function both literally and allusively, make his work instantly familiar and curiously ambiguous. The enigmatic quality is reinforced by abrupt changes in scale within a single work as well as by shifts in perspective, which create an indeterminate space. Rose has said that one of his goals is to "force the observer into a situation which requires new or altered consciousness of a known object or situation."[2]

Although *Watchtower* incorporates many of the themes and devices of Rose's earlier small-scale tableaux, drawings, and set designs, it also looks forward to his subsequent glass sculpture. His long-standing interest in sculpture is evident here in the strong play between two and three dimensions. Rose uses both physical construction and painterly illusion to create, as he says, "mental space."[3] An actual 2 x 2-inch raw lumber strip jutting out of the surface not only emphasizes the handmade quality of the work, but it also acts as a wall or corner behind which the trompe l'oeil stairway seems to disappear. This illusion is reinforced by the actual cutout area, which represents a doorway. Further play between two and three dimensions is evident in the orange wall, which appears to recede at the top of the work, only to read as a flat element, flush with the bottom of the painting.

Painted shortly after Rose returned from a trip to the south coast of England, *Watchtower* is both specifically a memory of that trip and, more generally, a meditation on the theme of transition. Each of the images underlines this theme. The doorway and the windows suggested by lines gouged out of the surface are, as Rose has said, between places; they are neither inside nor out.[4] The stairway, too, is neither here nor there, but a way of getting from one level to another. And the ship, collaged onto the surface of the painting, symbolizes transition and passage. Alone on an expanse of blue, it moves silently toward an unknown place.

D.H.

1. Miranda McClintic, in Hirshhorn Museum and Sculpture Garden, Smithsonian Institution, Washington, D.C., *Directions 81*, exh. cat., 1981, p. 50.
2. Ibid.
3. Conversation with the author, 14 August 1986.
4. Ibid.

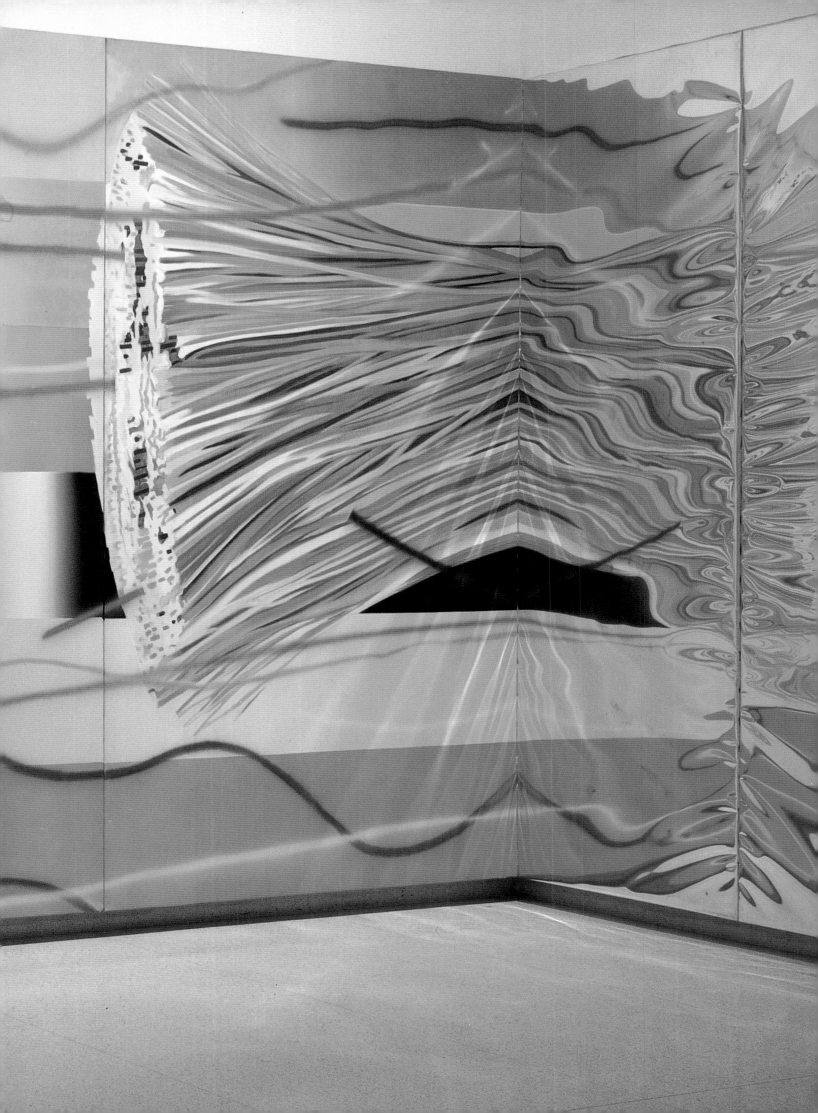

James Rosenquist

Area Code 1970

American, b. 1933

oil on canvas, Mylar

four canvas panels
114 x 69⅛
(289.6 x 175.6) each
Mylar panels
114 x 37½
(289.6 x 95.3) each,
varying in number with
installation

central horizontal
members of stretchers of
canvas panels, not in
artist's hand, 1 (or 2, 3,
4, respectively)
–AC–LC–81/ Castelli/
Gallery/Rosenquist;
central horizontal
members of each Mylar
panel, Castelli Gallery /
Rosenquist LC 81

acquired from the Leo
Castelli Gallery, New York
1971 (gift of the T.B.
Walker Foundation 71.8)

After his notorious *F–111* of 1965, Rosenquist made a group of five monumentally scaled paintings with projecting wings at either end— *Horse Blinders, Area Code, Flamingo Capsule, Slush Thrust,* and *Horizon, Home Sweet Home*— in which he attempted to re-create the heightened awareness of the peripheral vision he experienced during his days working for Artkraft-Strauss as a billboard painter in Times Square.[1] The areas at the corners of one's vision are activated in these works by the Mylar panels whose rippling surfaces sinuously distort color forms in a way that reminds Rosenquist of fun-house mirrors.[2] Mylar also offered an expressive and conceptual capacity distinct from that of canvas.[3]

The Mylar panels serve to extend the painting by reflecting it, refuting the finality of its outermost painted edges. As early as 1963, Rosenquist was concerned about "purging myself of devices that would put boundaries on my pictures."[4] The fragmentary images seen in the Mylar panels tacitly explain that the painting is just a fragment. The continuity of air-brushed, softly crackling lines of color across the central void similarly contradict the finality of the snipped bunch of wires.

Referring again to *F–111*, Rosenquist observed that bright fluorescent colors visually dissolve the corner, rendering it curved.[5] Here the reflectiveness produces the duplication of the wing shape at the upper left, while at the right it creates an extension of the telephone wire paint. The nebulous, colorless central area is like a fog in which information becomes uncoded. This haze foretells the actual fog created by the dry ice he used to dissolve color in front of the panels of *Horizon, Home Sweet Home* in 1970.

One hesitates to make more than formal connections between the two "images," in the multi-paneled picture: the bunched color-coded wires of the communication system resemble the (also coded) feathers of a bird's wing. Rosenquist has frequently expressed his interest in mass media and communication, and sees "a closer tie with technology and art and a new curiosity about new methods of communication coming from all sides."[6] The connections between the objects depicted in Rosenquist's work have the quick, unpredictable changeability of the ordinary urban experience, and the immediacy intensified by the "vulgar" colors of advertising softened with a

white-lead base. As close inspection shows, the painting was the subject of repeated modifications and rethinkings.

The scale of the work helps to evoke the mixed feelings of numbness and exhilaration Rosenquist felt while working on billboards.[7] The effect of the scale disparity between objects within the work and between them and the viewer was summarized astutely by one writer in 1965:

> Traditional implications of illusionism are reversed. The disproportionate scale of Rosenquist's images forces them out rather than back into the painted distance, envelops the spectator in an elephantine trompe l'oeil…. In the process of the attack [the "assault on normality" by the gigantism], the object loses its identity and becomes form.[8]

L.F.G.

1. Jeanne Siegel, "An Interview with James Rosenquist," *Artforum*, vol. 10 (June 1972), p. 33.
2. Ibid.
3. Rosenquist was no doubt aware of this, as his commentary on the metal sheets of *F–111* would suggest: "The physical feeling that [metal] gave … is something different from canvas, a brittle feeling;" quoted in "The F–111: An Interview with James Rosenquist by G.R. Swenson," *Partisan Review*, vol. 32 (Fall 1965), p. 596.
4. Quoted in The Museum of Modern Art, New York, *Americans 1963*, exh. cat., 1963, p. 87.
5. Siegel, p. 33.
6. "The F–111," p. 601.
7. Siegel, p. 30.
8. Lucy R. Lippard, "James Rosenquist: Aspects of a Multiple Art," *Artforum*, vol. 4 (December 1965), p. 41

Theodore Roszak

Cradle Song Variation No. 2 1957–1960

American, b. Poland,
1907–1981

steel, bronze

**64¹¹⁄₁₆ x 21⁹⁄₁₆ x 35³⁄₁₆
(164.3 x 54.8 x 89.4)**

**on plaque inside larger
crescent, *Theodore*
(remainder obscured by
molten metal); plaque on
upper rear of smaller
crescent, *Theodore
Roszak***

**commissioned by Walker
Art Center, 1957;
acquired 1960 (gift of the
T.B. Walker Foundation
60.9)**

According to Roszak, the title of the work refers
to the birth of his daughter Sara Jane in 1947,
while the content derives from his memories of
her childhood:

> At the age of two, she had several dreams in which
> she saw a cradle in the stars. She'd tell me about this
> object that she clearly saw and we'd work at it and
> then she'd tell me more, and I'd work more at it and
> this is the result. Something of the exploding star form
> has appeared in this, too…. Children ask extraordinary
> questions, sometimes not wanting an answer. One
> night at Cape Ann, my daughter turned to me and
> asked: "Why is the moon so sharp?" and this
> reminded me of other naive and anxious questions
> she had asked, such as "We do have the biggest army
> in the world, don't we, daddy?" Later, out of this,
> came a sudden desire on my part to create something
> that would embody, side by side, the soft, probing
> quality of the child-mind and the terrible menace that
> surrounds it everywhere.[1]

In formal terms the piece would seem to owe
a debt to Julio González's wrought iron *Head* of
1935, already in The Museum of Modern Art, New
York, when Roszak began the sculpture. He
evidently first conceived it in 1952 and worked on
various versions of it during the next seven years.
As was his custom, he elaborated the image fully
in numerous sketches and detailed drawings
(many of which he later destroyed) before producing a small sculptural study in 1955. Two other
studies were made before the Walker version.
Commissioned in 1957, the Walker work was
completed by 24 December 1959, although
finishing touches were not made until May of the
following year.[2] Several modifications were
introduced in this version, such as the deletion of
a central star motif, the doubling of the lower
point of the crescent, and the addition of two
diagonal spikes projecting at the lower rear.

Roszak's procedure was to build a steel
armature, and, with an oxyacetylene torch, to
weld the protuberances, molten flow forms, and
plates of steel together on it; i.e., the work was
made free form rather than from a mold. The flux
added to the molten metal to prevent oxidation
and to improve its flow leaves a chalky residue
that is visible in crannies and depressions.

These craggy, encrusted surfaces are highlighted
with smoother, shinier areas. According to Sara
Jane Roszak, her father was not concerned with
achieving a pristine finish, but intended to
provoke associations with primordial matter or
with an ancient artifact fresh from the dig.[3]

L.F.G.

1. Quoted in Howard Griffin, "Totems in Steel," *Art News*,
vol. 55 (October 1956), p. 34.
2. The dating details given here are supported by
correspondence from 1956 to 1959 between the artist and
the Walker Art Center, and the artist and Arnold H.
Maremont; the latter in the possession of Sara Jane
Roszak.
3. Conversation with the author, 27 December 1984.

Julio González
Head circa 1935
wrought iron
17¾ x 15¼ (45.1 x 38.7)
Collection The Museum of
Modern Art, New York
Purchase

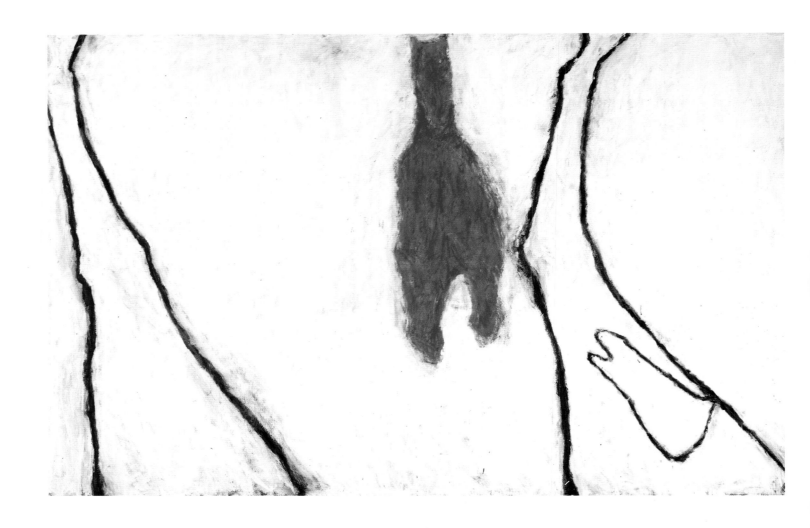

Susan Rothenberg

Tattoo 1979

American, b. 1945

acrylic, flashe on canvas

67 x 103 (170.2 x 261.6)

acquired from the Willard Gallery, New York, 1979 (purchased with the aid of funds from Mr. and Mrs. Edmond R. Ruben, Mr. and Mrs. Julius E. Davis, the Art Center Acquisition Fund, and the National Endowment for the Arts 79.50)

Susan Rothenberg's abiding interest in portraiture is obvious only in retrospect, for when she first started painting seriously in 1974 her subject was horses, shown in profile. In 1979, these horses took on a more disembodied presence, as in *Tattoo*. It is only in recent years that she has featured the figure in a direct way. But Rothenberg has since acknowledged that "The horse was a way of not doing people, yet it was a symbol of people, a self-portrait, really."[1]

In a different sense, horses were Rothenberg's vehicle for reintroducing the representational imagery that had been banished from the canvas during the hegemony of abstraction in the preceding decades. Her work was first seen by a wide public in a Whitney Museum exhibition *New Image Painting* (1978), which featured a number of younger American artists who were returning to representational painting. That same year, Rothenberg had her first one-artist museum exhibition, at the Walker Art Center, and *Tattoo*, executed shortly thereafter, was purchased in 1979.

Rothenberg's sources for this work, a characteristic late horse painting, range from the cave paintings of Lascaux to Jasper Johns, whom the artist has frequently cited as an important influence. Her debt to Johns is evident in the milky white field, beaten with black, whose rich and expressive texture recalls his work. The blue horse coming toward the viewer looks like a creature lost in a blinding snowstorm, the pathways on either side, other facets of itself, its only bearings. The title, *Tattoo*, refers to the horse's head drawn within the outline of its leg, "a tattoo or memory image," as the artist describes it, a format as illogical as the oddly hollow and upside-down legs. Rothenberg, who often contrasts hollows with solids, presents one version of the horse as solid at center but with ill-defined boundaries, whereas its ghost image, hollow at the core, is firmly outlined in heavy black. It is a many-sided self-portrait, suggesting some of the different ways one negotiates the world.

M.G.

1. Quoted in Grace Glueck, "Susan Rothenberg: New Outlook for a Visionary Artist," *The New York Times Magazine*, 22 July 1984, p. 20.

Susan Rothenberg

Night Ride 1987

American, b. 1945

oil on canvas

93 x 110¼ (236.2 x 280)

on reverse, lower right, *S. Rothenberg 1987 Night Ride*

acquired from the Sperone Westwater Gallery, New York, 1987 (Walker Special Purchase Fund 87.78)

It was in the mid-1970s that Susan Rothenberg's paintings of horses and spiritlike human figures began attracting attention in the art world. Her elemental linear images—chiefly monumental side views of horses and fragments of humans—had an insistent presence and, notwithstanding their modernist sensibilities, were richly evocative of prehistoric cave-wall paintings and the totemic imagery of aboriginal societies. These paintings, of which the Walker's *Tattoo* (1979) is a prime example, possess a riveting immediacy, a sense of locked-in energy.

In 1987 Rothenberg's painting took a significant new turn: both surface and subject matter assumed a powerful agitation. The human figure remained a regular theme, but no longer did she represent it in disembodied parts. Instead, she began portraying full figures, often the same one defined in successive layers so that the results were dense, vibrant tangles of overlapping contours. Like her earlier work, these richly gestural canvases seem to be evocations of dream states that, in their agitation, verge on the demonic.

Rothenberg is hardly the first artist who has sought to express motion through overlays of sequential imagery. Eadweard Muybridge's stop-action photographs of speeding horses and leaping athletes from the 1870s and 1880s, as well as paintings by Giacomo Balla, Umberto Boccioni, and other Futurists that depict velocity and power, probably helped inspire her pursuit of similar themes. But unlike that of such predecessors, Rothenberg's imagery is not even remotely analytical. It is more a portrayal of febrile nerve endings than of corporeal forms. While her earlier totemic images reflect a timeless calm suggestive of universal myth, her newer works, such as the spectral *Night Ride*, appear to probe the darker recesses of the unconscious. Its subject is a single figure—a ghostly bike rider, defined in roughly scrawled, luminous lines; it emerges in three stages, one overlapping the other, from the blackness of night. Her figure, which echoes itself, is a dematerialized presence, volumeless and phantomlike—an image of fear.

Working to convey a sense of powerful dynamism, Rothenberg has turned to figures of action for her painting themes. In addition to bicyclists[1] she depicts whirling dancers, pole vaulters, and high jumpers, all of whom charge through pictorial space.

M.G.

1. The bicyclist made his first appearance in *Biker* (1985) and has also been the subject of several drawings made during the same period as *Night Ride*.

Mark Rothko

Ritual circa 1944[1]

American, b. Russia,
1903–1970

oil, graphite on canvas

**53¹⁵⁄₁₆ x 39½
(137 x 100.3)**

**lower right, *Mark Rothko*;
on reverse, in red paint,
upper left, *Mark Rothko/
Ritual*; in black chalk,
*1944***

**bequeathed by the artist
to The Mark Rothko
Foundation, New York;
acquired from The Mark
Rothko Foundation, 1986
(gift of The Mark Rothko
Foundation, Inc. 86.1)**

Ritual constitutes a virtual homage to Joan Miró, whom Rothko himself acknowledged as a powerful influence on his work and thinking during the early 1940s.[2] Clearly in Miró's spirit are the use of a straight horizon line to divide the picture plane into two parts, a mottled ground resulting from technical manipulations, and the frontal presentation of flat forms.[3] Specific shapes appropriated from Miró's repertoire, particularly that of the 1920s, include scrolled threads, udderlike digits, sinuous lines, transparent volumes, irregular geometric cutouts, scale disparities, and triangles floating freely in the upper regions of the composition.

Also like Miró, Rothko intimates the presence of a "personage"[4] composed of abstract signs that bear a remote relationship to features of the human form. In the Rothko picture, the torso is rendered as a dematerialized rounded volume delineated by curving lines against a blank rectilinear support. The effect is also similar to that achieved by Picasso in his 1927 etching *Painter with a Model Knitting*, an illustration for Balzac's *Le chef d'oeuvre inconnu*, exhibited at The Museum of Modern Art in its 1939 Picasso retrospective. In the print, an abstract painter transforms an ordinary woman into a web of unbroken, swooping lines. The image serves as a concise demonstration of the independence of the work of art derived from nature but imaginatively abstracted from it. Rothko likewise felt that

> the familiar identity of things has to be pulverized in order to destroy the finite associations with which our society increasingly enshrouds every aspect of the environment.

He claimed that his shapes

> are unique elements in a unique situation. They are organisms with volition and a passion for self-assertion. They move with internal freedom, and without need to conform with or to violate what is probable in the familiar world. They have no direct association with any particular visible experience, but in them one recognizes the principle and passion of organisms. The presentation of this drama in the familiar world was never possible, unless everyday acts belonged to a ritual accepted as referring to a transcendent world.[5]

The smudges that Rothko applies between the multiple lines of the torso contribute to the sense of whirling motion in the ritualistic realm of the picture. The element of sound is introduced emblematically with the replacement of the head by an enlarged ear, a motif borrowed from several Miró works, such as *La terre labourée* of 1923–1924.

Although Rothko's admiration for Picasso, Klee, Ernst, Miró, Masson, Matta, and others pervades his work of this period, *Ritual* is unusual in showing so direct and incontestable a relationship with European forerunners.

L.F.G.

1. The work is dated 1944 on the reverse in an unknown hand, but was assigned to 1945 when first published by Oscar Collier, "Mark Rothko," *The New Iconograph* (Fall 1947), p. 44. Rothko and his assistants did not add dates for works in his possession until 1968–1969, so the inscriptions are not always accurate; Bonnie Clearwater, letter to the author, 24 April 1986.
2. See Diane Waldman in the Solomon R. Guggenheim Museum, New York, *Mark Rothko*, exh. cat., 1978, p. 45.
3. Perhaps in an emulation of Miró's effects in paintings of the mid-1920s (see Angelica Z. Rudenstine, *Peggy Guggenheim Collection, Venice* [New York: Harry N. Abrams and the Solomon R. Guggenheim Foundation, 1985], p. 537), Rothko produced a scumbled effect by manipulating his surface, scraping, leaving impasto in scattered areas and incising lines. It was typical of Rothko to draw in the composition with pencil directly on the canvas; by 1943 he rarely used preparatory sketches for his work and none are known for *Ritual*; Bonnie Clearwater, letter to the author, 24 April 1986.
4. Rothko used the plural form of Miró's term "personage" as the title of a watercolor reproduced in *The Tiger's Eye*, no. 1 (October 1947), p. 69.
5. The three preceding quotations are from Mark Rothko, "The Romantics Were Prompted," *Problems in Contemporary Art: Possibilities I* (Winter 1947–1948), p. 84.

Joan Miró
The Tilled Field
1923–1924
oil on canvas
26 x 36½ (66 x 92.7)
Collection Solomon R.
Guggenheim Museum,
New York

Mark Rothko

untitled   1953

American, b. Russia,
1903–1970

oil on canvas

93$\frac{13}{16}$ x 47$\frac{7}{8}$
(238.3 x 121.6)

on reverse lower left
quadrant, in brown paint,
Mark Rothko/1953; on
reverse, upper right
quadrant, *5063.53*[1]

bequeathed by the artist
to The Mark Rothko
Foundation, New York;[2]
acquired from The Mark
Rothko Foundation, 1986
(gift of The Mark Rothko
Foundation, Inc. 86.3)

By the time this untitled work was painted, Rothko, like other artists imprecisely grouped in the designation Abstract Expressionist, had moved out of the phase he described as Surrealistic (as in *Ritual)* and established his characteristic format of a vertical field occupied by broad nebulous color areas, frequently separated by narrower horizontal strips of cloudy color. About this time he strengthened and warmed his palette, often favoring the oranges and yellows used here.

Rothko believed that the painting and viewing of his work should be seen in spiritual rather than formal terms.

> I'm not an abstractionist.... I'm not interested in relationships of color or form or anything else.... I'm interested only in expressing basic human emotions— tragedy, ecstasy, doom and so on.... The people who weep before my pictures are having the same religious experience I had when I painted them.... And if you ... are moved only by their color relationships, then you miss the point![3]

Due to the vehemence of his views, many critics since the 1950s have avoided formal and technical discussion to concentrate on the transcendent, emotional or, to use Rothko's word, "poignant" aspects of the work. However, given the subjectivity of direct communion between spectator and painting, this discussion will be confined to the means by which this experience is precipitated in a particular picture, rather than address the issue of content.

In this canvas, the pale grayish-yellow that underlies the entire composition shows through the dryly applied red (thinned perhaps with linseed oil rather than turpentine, and sponged on with a piece of fabric), creating the illusion of a pulsing alternation of receding and advancing light. In the lower section of the canvas, a pale yellow is unevenly applied over a yellowish-green, producing a form scarcely distinguishable from the ground out of which it seems to rise, or in which it is embedded. However vague its limits, the integrity of this form is declared, most conspicuously in the ragged edge completed just above the bottom edge of the canvas.

While acknowledging the rectangular format of the canvas by his choice of shapes, Rothko resisted its absolute authority by blurring and feathering the horizontal and vertical edges of his forms. He unified the canvas not only through the consistent ground and the autumnal palette, but also by highlighting the right and left edges of the large red rectangle with the orange of the lower horizontal strip. This device also prompts an optical vibration around the cloud of color that distinguishes it from the more passive yellow cloud below. Although the luminosity of this yellow cloud allows it to hold its own against the more active red, an anti-gravitational sensation results from the relationship between the two colors. The "figure" of the red is anchored by the black and appears to float above a void.

The black strip, which on close inspection reveals itself to be glazes of brown, blue, and violet, is painted over the lower part of the red cloud, and hence takes on some of its qualities, as well as those of the yellow beneath. Its containment in the red is made explicit by the slight overlapping of red at its lower edge. The orange strip below, more thickly painted, has greater independence, solidity, and detachment. It hovers between the black-rimmed red and the yellow cloud, surrounded by the base coat of yellow. The interval of ground around the orange band is consistent with the space left along the periphery of the canvas, compounding the sense of its isolation as a form. Despite its coloristic weakness, it is thus able to compete with the optically denser and more assertive black rim.

L.F.G.

1. The inventory number was inscribed by Rothko or his assistants in 1968–1969; Bonnie Clearwater, letter to the author, 24 April 1986.
2. This painting was among the group returned to the estate by Marlborough Gallery upon settlement of a lawsuit against the executors in 1970; Rothko Foundation records.
3. Selden Rodman quoting Rothko from what he describes as a chance encounter at the Whitney Museum of American Art; the passage is probably a paraphrase. See Rodman, *Conversations with Artists* (New York: Devin-Adair Co., 1957), pp. 93, 94.

Mark Rothko

untitled (#2)[1]   1963

American, b. Russia,
1903–1970

oil, acrylic, glue on canvas

80¼ x 69⅛
(203.8 x 175.6)

on reverse, upper left
quadrant, in black paint,
Mark Rothko/1963; on
reverse, upper right
quadrant, *5037.63*;[2] on
reverse, upper left
quadrant, not in artist's
hand, *1963 #2/Orange
Stripe/Black Rect/Dk
Grey Bottom on dk Red*

bequeathed by the artist
to The Mark Rothko
Foundation, New York;
acquired from The Mark
Rothko Foundation, 1985
(gift of The Mark Rothko
Foundation, Inc. 85.16)

Like Newman and Still, Rothko sought to provoke ineffable, transcendental states of awareness through an unprecedented conception of the possibilities of painting. More reticent in his pictures than they, he categorically rejected the notion of the self-expressive gesture held by those colleagues Harold Rosenberg termed the Action Painters. The dark palette and large scale of this painting are characteristic of the work Rothko produced in the relatively inactive period between the completion of a series of murals for Harvard University in 1962 and the beginning of his mural cycle for Dominique and John de Menil's chapel in Houston in 1964. The low-key color has commonly been attributed to Rothko's growing emotional and physical difficulties. One critic wrote in 1963: "More recently, of course, the artist, his light going out, has descended into the darkness, and at times, the bleakest of harmonies. The colors, more heavily sheathed and scrimmed, have almost morbid ceremonial associations."[3]

It is reported that at this time Rothko executed his paintings directly and spontaneously after a long period of consideration and study. He apparently spread a powdered pigment dissolved in a heated rabbit-skin glue over the entire surface, then applied acrylic or oil paint thinned to the texture of consommé. After the composition was determined, he fastidiously altered specific areas with a brush or sponge to establish precise relationships among parts.[4] Although this painting has a uniformly matte, stained surface, uneven chromatic layering creates varying degrees of reflectiveness that give the field a flickering or pulsing quality. Black is spread over an orange ground to produce an atmospheric purple or wine red, on or in which the discrete color clouds are located. The central brown color zone is darkened by a blacker brown layer underneath it, while the lower brown area is lightened with white. Despite their tonal differences, these clouds of color appear almost to merge below the sharply punctuating orange bar at the top.

L.F.G.

1. This number was inscribed by Rothko or his assistants in 1968–1969; Bonnie Clearwater, letter to the author, 24 April 1986.
2. Inventory numbers were given by Rothko and his galleries for purposes of identification.
3. Max Kozloff, "Letter to the Editor," *Art International*, vol. 7 (25 June 1963), p. 91.
4. See Thomas B. Hess, "Rothko: A Venetian Souvenir," *Art News*, vol. 69 (November 1970), p. 72; Hess relies on descriptions of Rothko's procedures from Oliver Steindecker, Rothko's assistant in his final years.

Edward Ruscha

Steel 1969

American, b. 1937

oil on canvas

**60 x 54 x 1⅝
(152.4 x 137.2 x 4.1)**

**center right horizontal
stretcher member, in
artist's hand, in pencil,
*this is Ulrikes'/Edward
Ruscha/1974***

**acquired from the artist by
Ulrike Kantor, Los
Angeles, circa 1972;
acquired from the Leo
Castelli Gallery, New York,
1980 (purchased with the
aid of funds provided by
The Clinton and Della
Walker Accessions Fund
and the National
Endowment for the Arts
80.24)**

About 1961 Ruscha began a series of word depiction works. As if analyzing two ordinary physical procedures in writing—the depositing of dry graphite and the spilling of wet ink on paper—Ruscha formed letters in gunpowder or oil paint. The gunpowder letters appear to be made of ribbons of paper balancing on their edges, while the oil paint letters look like pools of a liquid substance spilled on a flat surface. He has recalled that seeing the image of kidney beans "dumped out" triggered his idea of studying liquids and their behavior.[1] Sabotaging reason through the devices of Surrealist incongruity and the Dada non sequitur, he objectified words in liquid in a manner that has no apparent relation to their meaning, provoking a cognitive tremor in the viewer's consciousness. A Tanguy-like recession of the space surrounding the word helps to remove it from trompe l'oeil illusionistic painting.

Here the word "steel," unusually soft and sibilant for Ruscha,[2] is written in what appears to be chocolate syrup, axle grease, or some other common viscous substance. The associations can be industrial (lubricating a car) or childish (playing with food), both of which are confirmed in Ruscha's published statements. When asked about the content of the gas station images he has painted, Ruscha answered, with a Duchampian inflection, that what interested him most were the oil drippings left by the cars.[3] Habits of thought may prompt a viewer to see the blue circle to the left of the word as a water drop, but this only provides an ironic commentary on the arbitrariness of meaning: although closer in color to steel, and sharing its qualities of reflectiveness and smoothness, is water any more like steel than syrup or oil, given its fundamental difference in state? The artist himself does not wish to limit the associations of the drop by identifying its substance, but in casual conversation alluded to it as a ball bearing, closer to the word spelled than the material spelling it. The dubious identity of the materials depicted raises questions about the criteria by which one is persuaded of metaphor, and whether anything rendered in paint can have a significant connection with things in the world.

Ruscha himself discounts interpretations based on the meaning of the words he chooses, hoping for a detachment from content: "I separate myself from the English definition of the word."[4] If the words are considered as divested of meaning the letters themselves can be seen as forms with personality, as in Oldenburg's soft and hard three-dimensional alphabets. Ruscha explains:

> My "romance" with liquids, came about because I was looking for some sort of alternative entertainment for myself—an alternative from the rigid, hard-edge painting of words that had to respect some typographical design.[5] These didn't—there were no rules about how a letter had to be formed. It was my sandbox to play in. I could make an "o" stupid or I could make it hopeless or any way I wanted and it would still be an "o."[6]

While concerned with respecting the scale of actual objects (such as the carefully measured and accurately depicted beans and ants he sometimes mired in the liquid words), Ruscha amusedly exploits the scale-free nature of language: "We see [a word] on billboards, in four-point type and all stages in between."[7]

L.F.G.

1. Conversation with the author, 24 September 1986.
2. David Bourdon has noted that "Ruscha generally prefers short words with a blunt or brusque sound, such as 'chop,' 'egg,' 'honk,' or 'hey;'" "A Heap of Words About Ed Ruscha," *Art International*, vol. 15 (20 November 1971), p. 26.
3. See Patricia Failing, "Ed Ruscha, Young Artist: Dead Serious about Being Nonsensical," *Art News*, vol. 81 (April 1982), p. 80.
4. Quoted in Bourdon, p. 25.
5. Ruscha studied industrial and graphic design at the Chouinard Art Institute in Los Angeles in the late 1950s.
6. Quoted in Failing, p. 79.
7. Ibid., p. 78.

No. 59

No. 226A

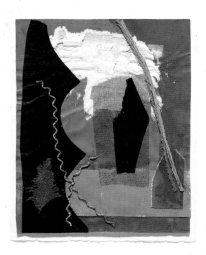

No. 237

No. 308

Anne Ryan

four collages   1948–1954

American, 1889–1954

No. 59: fabric, paper

6⅞ x 4⅞ (17.5 x 12.4)

lower right, in pencil,
A. Ryan; on reverse, lower
left, *#59*

No. 226A: fabric, paper,
string

6 x 4¾ (15.2 x 12.1)

lower right, in pencil,
A. Ryan; on reverse, in
pencil, *No. 226*; on paper
backing, lower left, *#226A
/(astrological sun sign)*

No. 237: fabric, paper,
embossed paper, postage
stamp, thread

6⅜ x 4⅞ (16.2 x 12.4)

lower right, *A. Ryan*; upper
left, in pencil, *No. 237*;
on reverse, lower left, in
pencil *(astrological sun
sign)/No. 237*

No. 308: fabric, paper

6⅜ x 5¼ (16.2 x 13.3)

lower right, in pencil,
A. Ryan; on reverse, lower
left *(astrological sun sign)
/#308*; lower right,
A. Ryan

estate of the artist;
acquired from Elizabeth
McFadden, 1979
(gift of Elizabeth
McFadden 79.3; 79.8;
79.9; 79.14)

In early 1948 Anne Ryan was living with her daughter in New York in a cold-water flat at 826 Greenwich Street, trying to establish herself as an artist working in the woodcut medium. Her daughter recalled that it might have been at a party about this time at the home of Ruth and John Steffan, who published the literary-artistic periodical *The Tiger's Eye,* that they heard about Kurt Schwitters's show at Rose Fried's Pinacotheca uptown.[1] When they first visited the gallery,

> Mother went from one collage to another in a passion of delight. She knew instantly and completely that she had found her métier. And she was practically exalted. She had a great capacity for joy but I never saw her so consumed by it.… We went home and before she put water on for supper, she was at her work table making collages. During the following weeks she visited the Fried Gallery a couple of times and we saw it together the day it closed, taking tea at Rumpelmayer's on 58th Street. Of course, she put several cubes of hard sugar in her pocket: their wrappers showed up in collages.[2]

Her daughter's description of Ryan's character, "a strange and marvelous mixture of mid-Victorian and ultra modern," characterizes her collages as well. On the one hand, they show the seamstress's sensitivity to the textures, design, and weight of fabric, respect for the individual thread and sense of nostalgia for remnants of past wholes;[3] on the other, a strong structural sense reflecting the impact of Cubism, Constructivism, De Stijl, Klee, and, of course, Schwitters.

The dating of the collages, all executed during the last six years of her life, is problematic. She evidently completed at least the first hundred by February 1949 and numbered them herself before assembling them in French pastel books, where they could be looked at without being handled.[4] The Walker's No. 59 no doubt belongs to this group. However, she then became bored with punctually numbering the works, and returned to enumeration only intermittently. After her death, her daughter completed the cataloging without attempting to reconstruct a chronological sequence.[5] Demonstrating the problem of the numbering system, the Walker's No. 226 is one of three so numbered (the addition of "A" indicates that this one was classified as a small collage at one of the galleries). Dating the works on stylistic grounds could be treacherous.

Internal evidence can give more certain cutoff dates: the cancellation mark on the postage stamp on No. 237 indicated that the collage was made after that date of 15 January 1949.[6] Further research will be required before other dates can be securely attached to specific works.

No. 59 is supported by a cream-colored paper made by Douglass Howell, who was trained in papermaking in Florence before returning to the United States after the war. He settled in Levittown, where he made "exquisite papers" from laundry fragments he collected from establishments throughout New York City.[7] Ryan supplied him with other scraps of linen[8] and drew his work to the attention of Jackson Pollock, who did a series of ink drawings on Howell paper.

L.F.G.

1. Letter from Elizabeth McFadden to the Assistant Director of the Montclair Art Museum, Robert Koenig, 7 February 1979. Schwitters had died in January. The memorial exhibition at the Pinacotheca, which closed on 28 February, included twenty-six collages from 1920 to 1947; an extensively illustrated article on his work by Carola Giedion-Welcker, "Schwitters: or the Allusions of the Imagination," was published in the *Magazine of Art* vol. 41 (October 1948), pp. 218–221.
2. McFadden to Koenig, 1979.
3. Ryan made many of her own clothes and quilts, and bought trunkfuls of Victorian clothes at an antique shop in Brooklyn; see Donald Windham, "Anne Ryan and Her Collages," *Art News,* vol. 73 (May 1974), p. 76.
4. McFadden to Koenig, 1979.
5. Ibid.
6. About this work, Elizabeth McFadden has indicated that the thread is probably "an intrinsic part of a piece of Chinese tea paper;" letter to Gwen Bitz, Walker Art Center, 27 January 1979.
7. McFadden to Koenig, 1979. Ryan's notebook cites the inclusion of Howell's papers in individual works.
8. Windham, p. 78. She used Howell papers first as support only, but gradually incorporated them fully into the collages.

447

Lucas Samaras

untitled   1965

American, b. Greece, 1939

pin chair: wood, pins, glue

35⅜ x 19¼ x 35¾
(89.9 x 48.9 x 90.8)

yarn chair: wood, yarn,
glue

35⅜ x 18 x 26⅝
(89.9 x 45.7 x 67.6)

under seat of pin chair, in
ink, *May '65/LS*

acquired from the Pace
Gallery, New York, 1966
(Art Center Acquisition
Fund 66.2)

In an interview of 1966 Samaras suggested that the psychological motivation for works such as the two chairs might be his alienation from others:

> Sometimes I feel that I want to eliminate people, so that I can just live by myself with things and memories ... often, I suppose, I put dialogues that I have with myself into the things that I make, but I don't call them that. I mean, for example, I made these two chairs, one leaning against the other ... it's like ... one person sort of leaning against another person, but I don't call them *Two People* and I don't even call them *Chairs*, I don't want people to be concerned with the fact that they're chairs.... It should be visual: visual-emotional, not verbal-emotional.[1]

By associating the chairs with people,[2] Samaras confers on them a fetishistic intensity connected with a narcissistic awareness of his own body and its relation to "a highly erotic reality called beauty."[3] The sado-masochistic overtones of an object covered with pins accompany Samaras's description of his relationship with materials. After working with "aggressive"objects for a time, their associations with pain were replaced for him by the seductiveness of their power to ignite the sense of touch. The compelling attraction of assertive materials gave rise to his fantasy of a magnetized building covered with pins to which various creatures are fatally drawn.[4]

While provoking a confusion of pain and pleasure in the viewer's visceral response, Samaras also offers the work as an intellectual investigation into the properties of painting and sculpture. In its rectilinear structure, the prototypical chair imitates the shapes of canvas and stretcher, or the flat surfaces and squared bars of Minimalist sculpture. In an indirect comment on the authority of the rectangle, he points out in connection with the Walker work that "as long as you have a rectangular perimeter all sorts of unbalances that you can create inside it get supported by its perpendicularity. The leaning chairs do not have that benefit. Movement is suggested but a soar into the wild blue yonder is clearly not intended. It's the start of a horizontal collapse."[5]

Samaras prevents the chairs from implying a collapse from three-dimensional sculpture to two-dimensional painting by his use of the pins and yarn, which give features of painting and drawing three-dimensional, concrete form. He observes

that the pin is, in formal terms, a line and a point, and describes the yarn as lines of color related to his liquid aluminum and pastel stripes.[6] These pictorial effects, however, are achieved in three-dimensional substances. There are, according to Samaras, two kinds of space in visual perception traditionally applied respectively to sculpture and painting: "objective *real space*, the interval between two points or objects, and subjective illusive space, the surface of objects, also known as color." While we habitually trust that surfaces are finite and impenetrable, he continues, their irregularity and texture can be subtly apprehended by touch: "when we touch we feel what we touch touching us."[7] Only color remains unsusceptible to understanding through any sense except sight. By contrasting the tactility but untouchability of the pins with the immateriality but three-dimensional extension of the spectral color of the yarn, Samaras ironically sets forth the difficulties of perceptual understanding.

L.F.G.

1. Quoted in Alan Solomon, "An Interview with Lucas Samaras," *Artforum*, vol. 5 (October 1966), p. 41.
2. The connection is made explicit in the body-shaped chairs he imagined in notes he wrote on 31 December 1961 for a Happening; see Kim Levin, *Lucas Samaras* (New York: Harry N. Abrams, 1975), p. 69. Elsewhere he has described chairs as being "like the molds people leave when they get up;" quoted in Robert Hughes, "Nowhere to Sit Down," *Time* (9 November 1970), p. 62.
3. Statement in the Pace Gallery, New York, *Samaras: Selected Works 1960–1966*, exh. cat., 1966, pp. 39, 40.
4. This would seem to be directly connected to his memory of playing with pins and a horseshoe magnet in the dressmaking shop of a cousin; Samaras has noted other biographical influences on his choice of materials: his father's occupational nailing of shoes and, at another time, nailing of stretched furs; the Christian iconography of nails; and his early and intense memory of seeing an Indian fakir sitting on a bed of nails in a *World Book Encyclopedia*; Levin, pp. 40, 45, 46.
5. Quoted in Whitney Museum of American Art, New York, *Lucas Samaras by Lucas Samaras*, exh. cat., 1972, n.p. Samaras has suggested that this collapse may have been inspired in part by a snapshot taken from his window of one house leaning away from the next; Levin, *Samaras*, p. 65. The precariousness of the chairs has made it necessary to screw them into the floor or base. The vitrine that generally covers them is not an integral part of the work.
6. See his 1968 statement, quoted in Paul Cummings, *Artists in Their Own Words. Interviews by Paul Cummings* (New York: St. Martin's, [1979]), p. 216.
7. Lucas Samaras, "An Exploratory Dissection of Seeing," *Artforum*, vol. 6 (December 1967), p. 2.

Egon Schiele

Two Figures   1917

Austrian, 1890–1918

charcoal, watercolor, gouache on paper

17⅜ x 11⅛ (44.1 x 28.3)

lower left, *Egon Schiele 1917*

(gift of Elizabeth and Donald Winston, Los Angeles 73.29)

Drawn with a masterful brevity of line and sure command of complex perspective, Egon Schiele's *Two Figures* of 1917 demonstrates the virtuosity of the artist's fully mature draftsmanship. In the course of his brief career, Schiele executed several thousand works on paper, which together illustrate an anxious and angularly brittle calligraphic style. This late drawing, however, reveals a soft and tender quality found in many of the paintings and drawings made in Schiele's last years, before his sudden death at the age of twenty-eight. With their rounded fullness and placid quietism, these nudes represent a departure from his earlier, characteristically emaciated and often contorted images of the human form.

Two Figures presents two nude women lying gently encircled in each other's arms. Set against an empty, shadowless background, their forms register simultaneously as material volumes in space and as an elegant graphic configuration on the page. The loosely drawn contours of the figures are bestowed with three-dimensionality through a minimal application of gouache and watercolor. Although Schiele's palette is restrained in *Two Figures*—employing only a few somber tones of raw and burnt sienna, cobalt blue, and black—the artist painted with a wide vocabulary of brushstrokes, varying from opaque, dry scumbles on the bony hands, feet, and elbows to delicate, translucent washes of color over the softer throat, thighs, and breasts. Schiele thus varied the quality of his brushstrokes to intrinsically express the complex curvaceous and angular surfaces of the nudes he was describing.

The homoerotic theme of *Two Figures* is a recurrent one in Schiele's oeuvre. Notably similar depictions of embracing nude or partially nude women include *Two Friends, Reclining* of 1913, and *Two Girls Lying Entwined* of 1915. While the latter two drawings display couples engaged in overtly sexual encounters, however, this work of 1917 seems simply to portray a tender embrace. Such images, which earned Schiele notoriety for their "pornography" and even led to a twenty-four-day imprisonment for immorality in 1912, bear the influence of Gustav Klimt, Aubrey Beardsley and Auguste Rodin, whose titillating and daringly specific drawings met an eager market for erotica at the turn of the century. Nevertheless, Schiele's expressionistic imagery, often brutally anguished and nakedly unsparing, has none of the fin-de-siècle decadence of Klimt's sumptuous, unabashed sensuality or Beardsley's sybaritic carnality.

N.H.

Sean Scully

To Want 1985

American, b. Ireland, 1945

oil on canvas

96¼ x 118½
(244.5 x 301) overall
depth of panels, left to
right, 2¾ (7); 9½ (24.1);
4½ (11.4)

left canvas, on reverse, *To
Want 1/3*; center canvas,
on reverse, *Sean Scully/
To Want/1985*

acquired from the David
McKee Gallery, New York,
1985 (Justin Smith
Purchase Fund 85.399)

After having lowered his aesthetic voice to a "whisper" in the horizontally striped monochromatic paintings he began making after his move to New York in 1975, Scully raised it again in works of the early and mid-1980s. While the information in the earlier work disclosed itself slowly, requiring the approach and close scrutiny of the viewer, these multileveled paintings literally step forward to introduce themselves.[1]

In *To Want*, three panels are unevenly stepped out and painted to form a complex and paradoxical set of spatial relations whose constant unit is a length of modulated color bounded by roughly straight, parallel lines, which continues until it meets an orthogonal obstacle, whether the edge of a stretcher or a painted line. Through a technique of applying broad, halted, translucent strokes of wet paint into wet paint, Scully creates a luminously layered, suggestive denseness influenced by Rothko's nebulous color fogs.[2] He describes each of his works as having a separate personality, its colors, structure, and internal relations combining to express particular states of mind and emotion. *To Want* touches on the sense of longing, the emotional urge to "get at something that's not really there," expressed in the compression of elements "being pushed out or trying to get in."[3]

The juxtaposition of panels whose stripes vary in color and direction has been frequently associated with visual sources from Scully's experience—Moroccan tents, Matisse, doorways in Lower Manhattan. Such juxtaposition suggests to him the essential duality of the horizontal and vertical and their connotations as the passive and active principles, connotations that Mondrian distilled from the objective world and presented in a dematerialized, abstract way. Scully, conversely, while wanting to give form to profound concepts, seeks to infuse his pictures with the qualities of life and nature as lived, an approach that Mondrian would have found overly materialistic: "I would describe myself as a hunter moving through a forest, appreciating its natural beauty but looking for something deep inside it."[4]

Scully's transcendental aspirations and material means coincide with an intellectual interest in issues of depiction, illusion, and fact. In *To Want*, the stripes are painted along their lengths: in the rightmost panel, the blue and white areas are painted with horizontally directed strokes, as if to clarify that they are fragments of stripes on their sides rather than blocks of color.

Weakened coloristically through the recessive white and blue, they are strengthened by physical advancement and broad scale. In their contours they echo and balance the block of stripes inset at the lower left of the work. Being depicted rather than projecting, the strength of this block is pictorial rather than sculptural. While subordinate to the broad stripes above it, which are closely allied with the strong, projecting central panel, the small group breaks up the phalanx above it, which would otherwise unbalance the blue and white column. Physical units both compete and collaborate with pictorial units.

Within this diplomatic adjustment of vying elements, Scully introduces events at different scales. Each stripe moves forward and back and up and down, interacting fugally through rhythms established by color, interval, and degree of recession. A blue-gray lead primer ground unifies the panels, revealed in slivers between stripes, and felt as a presence beneath or beyond the dominant overlaid color.

L.F.G.

1. The multileveled works were arrived at accidentally in 1980 when Scully cut off the end of a painting on a board he felt was too long, and, not wanting to waste it, attached it to the picture, "and then the painting had a step in it." See Judith Higgins, "Sean Scully and the Metamorphosis of the Stripe," *Art News*, vol. 84 (November 1985), p. 108.
2. Ibid. p. 107.
3. Conversation with the author, 11 November 1986.
4. Quoted in Steven Henry Madoff, "A New Generation of Abstract Painters," *Art News*, vol. 82 (November 1983), p. 82.

George Segal

The Diner 1964–1966

American, b. 1924

plaster, wood, chrome, laminated plastic, Masonite, fluorescent lamp

98¾ x 144¼ x 96 (250.8 x 366.4 x 243.8)

acquired from the Sidney Janis Gallery, New York, 1966 (gift of the T.B. Walker Foundation 66.47)

Segal's "situation" sculpture, peopled with white plaster figures, has become widely accepted as emblematic of the tension, anxiety, boredom, and loneliness of modern life. The style emerged between 1958 and 1961, as the artist was becoming increasingly dissatisfied with his achievements as a painter. Admiring the profound emotional content of Abstract Expressionist painting and striving for a comparable emotional impact in his own work, he nevertheless found the process of Action Painting too detached from ordinary experience. At first Segal set roughly modeled figures against paintings in three-dimensional environments; later, he developed his characteristic way of casting figures from life and setting them into environments fashioned from found materials. The parts for *The Diner*, for example, came from a restaurant that went out of business in New Brunswick, New Jersey.

Like all of Segal's situations, *The Diner* stems from a specific event in the artist's memory:

> I suppose the piece is a self-portrait. In those years I was farming, which is a physical activity, with very little mental—I was extremely restless. I was running into New York all the time and forever seeing friends or driving home at midnight or 1:00 a.m. and almost invariably stopping at a diner for coffee so I could stay awake to finish the last leg of that journey, which always became painful. After midnight in a diner, when you're the only customer, there's both fatigue and electricity. The waitress behind the counter is always sizing you up, either wondering is this guy going to rob me or rape me? Am I going to be dangerous or sexually attracted? So that there would be this careful avoidance of eye contact. Two people alone in a diner after midnight—you know—there's that electric danger. It's always present.[1]

Segal discusses his sculpture, however, not as a representation or reconstruction of this experience, but to a considerable extent as a solution to formal problems. His choices for *The Diner*, for example, were governed largely by considerations of color and shape.

> It was the essence of every New Jersey diner. I'm forever running into New York to see the art galleries and this exalted, delicate, elitist stuff. I have that hunger. Then I have mixed feelings. When you drive into New York you see those factories lined endlessly, horizontally on the ground like feeder cables into the New York skyline. It was like a zap of electric energy. The forms reminded me of Léger paintings. What it was in industrial forms that Léger loved I thought was absolutely radiating in the Esso refineries. And when I look at a New Jersey diner, you know one of those stainless steel jobs, vast expanses of pure, broken color, exactly the stainless steel machinery that serves the diner, I thought that they were imposing, sinful, erect, austere, minimal forms. I thought they were marvelous sculptures.[2]

After *The Diner* was first shown in 1965, Segal changed the disposition of the two figures in order to heighten the tension between them.

> Originally I had separated them and then when I moved the waitress and the urn much closer to the customer at the counter, it increased the psychological distance between them, which astounded me. I couldn't understand it. I still don't understand what happens when you do that. I don't care about the specific soap opera that's taking place—like everybody's got a story. Is there a relationship? Do they know each other, blah, blah, blah. It's enough to see two people and if you've lived long enough you can imagine forty-eight different plots.[3]

Because it is figurative and concerns industrial culture, Segal's work from this period is sometimes discussed in the context of 1960s Pop Art. More often, however, the spare configuration, use of clear expanses of color—as, for example, the 4 x 8-foot sheet of clear red in *The Diner*—links this work with the Minimalist sensibility of the same period.

N.R.

1. Martin Friedman, interview with Segal, 5 June 1978.
2. Ibid.
3. Ibid.

George Segal

Embracing Couple 1975

American, b. 1924

plaster

33¾ x 31½ x 13
(85.7 x 80 x 33)

acquired from the Sidney
Janis Gallery, New York,
1979 (gift of Mr. and Mrs.
Julius E. Davis 79.168)

Starting in 1969, Segal began to work with cast fragments—details of hands, shoulders, breasts—that had accumulated in his studio in the course of his other work, forming them into independent pieces. "The fragments," he later told Phyllis Tuchman, "must have begun from some kind of erotic or sensual impulse, to define bits of lips, fingers, breasts, folds of flesh, intricate lines.... When I walk down a street and I notice something, I notice it in a glimpse.... I thought, what happens if I do a piece of the body and try to catch that piece of the gesture that moves me?"[1]

Quite abruptly in 1971, Segal also altered his well-established process of casting full-scale figures from life. He continued to build up layers of plaster-impregnated gauze in sections around live models. But instead of then reassembling these rough sections into whole finished figures, he used them as negative molds, casting a positive in hydrostone on the inside of the plaster pieces. Using this method, he achieved not only much more durable work, but also much more exact, well-defined images. The greater specificity in the new work was balanced against a new generalization in its content:

> The fuller surface detail opened the door to a more "hyper-realist" phase that re-established new relationships to classical themes and even to academic sculpture, thus transcending Segal's obsessive slice-of-life subject matter with its limited implications of a specific locale and imagery. At the same time, relieved of certain descriptive obligations, Segal could now suggest through an abbreviated body language more universal values and attitudes than he had heretofore been able to articulate through rich and specific environmental and gestural detail. The new approach proved particularly effective in his wall pieces....[2]

The fragments became gradually more and more sensuous and erotic in content until, by the mid-1970s, Segal produced a group of works, including *Embracing Couple*, that seems more like close-up glimpses than fragments. Parallels have often been drawn between Segal and Rodin, in that both have attempted to represent a complete physical gesture by means of one particularly telling part, one moment.[3] In the Lovers series, which includes *Embracing Couple*, Segal is specifically concerned with the physical expression of tenderness. He himself saw the series as an antidote, "inevitable ... and

necessary, after dealing with the hallucinatory glare and menacing voids [of earlier work]."[4]

As in his earlier work, however, Segal has concentrated on giving very specific, naturalistic representations a broader meaning. In the Lovers series, this is effected through the alternation between the very sharp detail of physical forms achieved in the new casting method and the indistinct background.

> In their play between the explicit and the vague, the body fragments fluctuate as consciousness itself does during sex. Where they emerge, they evoke that clarity of perception that ascends, then disappears, when, making love, one relapses into pure and silent pleasure. Where they recede, they suggest the fading of sexual memory itself, so that the whole collection of reliefs seems a display of pungent, remembered moments surrounded on all sides by an immaterial ethos.[5]

N.R.

1. Phyllis Tuchman, *George Segal* (New York: Abbeville Press, 1983), p. 71.
2. Sam Hunter and Don Hawthorne, *George Segal* (New York: Rizzoli International Publications, 1984), p. 58.
3. Albert Elsen, "'Mind Bending' with George Segal," *Art News*, vol. 76 (February 1977), p. 34.
4. Hunter and Hawthorne, p. 65.
5. Leo Rubinfien, "On George Segal's Reliefs," *Artforum*, vol. 15 (May 1977), p. 44.

George Segal

Walking Man 1988

American, b. 1924

bronze

72 x 36 x 30
(182.9 x 91.4 x 76.2)

commissioned for the
Minneapolis Sculpture
Garden, 1988 (gift of the
AT&T Foundation and the
Julius E. Davis family in
memory of Julius E. Davis,
88.389)

George Segal has long been committed to making human-scale sculptural works whose themes are readily accessible to the viewer. His bronzes created for outdoor sites are scenes of everyday existence, depicting figures on park benches, seated at tables, and walking. Segal's sculptures are anti-monumental in subject and scale. "Most sculpture," he remarks, "is up on a pedestal in a psychologically different space." He notes that he is "determined" to have his own outdoor work "inhabit ordinary space."[1] He wants people to walk around and among his figures.

Represented in the Walker's collection by such classic early works as *The Diner* (1964–1966), Segal was invited in 1988 to propose a work for the then new Minneapolis Sculpture Garden. After visiting the site he decided to make a single figure in bronze for placement along one of the Garden's tree-lined walkways. Now installed at the intersection of two paths, *Walking Man* is a focal point of considerably greater force than its scale would suggest. Visitors are drawn to this lonely figure who seems to be deep in thought.

For his sculptures, Segal prefers to work with "everyday people" rather than professional models. "When I started casting people," he says, "I discovered that ordinary human beings with no great pretensions of being handsome were somehow singing and beautiful in their rhythms."[2] Though modeled on an artist-friend, *Walking Man* transcends the specificity of conventional portraiture to emerge as an Everyman—but one placed in contemporary context by the long shapeless coat he wears and the fragment of concrete sidewalk he occupies.

The sculpture also strongly reflects Segal's fascination with art history. Asked if his bronze for the Garden evokes the long tradition of the striding figure, he says it does, and singles out early examples. "My favorite is Egyptian—those walking men right at the transition between Egypt and Greece." The tradition, he observes, "goes on and on through Rodin and Giacometti."[3] His enduring interest in the relationship between painting and sculpture is particularly evident in the richly modeled and textured surface of *Walking Man*. He applied the patina by hand and states that he "made it drip and tried to make it as complicated as an Abstract Expressionist painting."[4] In making sculpture, Segal combines the seemingly opposite elements of meticulous realism and gestural expressionism to create poignant vignettes of daily life.

A.B.

1. Sam Hunter and Don Hawthorne, *George Segal* (New York: Rizzoli International Publications, 1984), p. 114.
2. Phyllis, Tuchman, *George Segal* (New York: Abbeville Press, 1983), p. 115. Walker Art Center, *Public Sculpture 1988* symposium, 10 September 1988.
3. Dialogue with Donna Harkavy, Walker Art Center, *Public Sculpture 1988* symposium, 10 September 1988.
4. Ibid.

Richard Serra

Five Plates, Two Poles 1971

American, b. 1939

Cor-Ten steel

96 x 276 x 216
(243.8 x 701 x 548.6)

acquired from the Leo
Castelli Gallery, New York,
1984 (gift of Judy and
Kenneth Dayton 84.1147)

Since 1967 Richard Serra has been making works dealing primarily with the fundamental sculptural properties of mass and gravity. The earliest of these were made of flat or rolled sheets of lead. *Prop* (1968; p. 552), for example, consists of a 60-inch-square sheet of lead held flat against the wall and some three feet off the ground by a rolled lead cylinder that leans against it. In 1969 Serra came "off the wall," placing his lead sheets on edge on the floor and keeping them vertical either by propping them against each other or by ingeniously balancing rolled sheets along their top edges. The precariousness of the compositions underscored the weight of the sheets and simultaneously asserted and defied the force of gravity.

These works are the direct predecessors of *Five Plates, Two Poles*. Serra began working with steel in 1969 when, as part of the Art and Technology Program at the Los Angeles County Museum of Art, he created a series of works at the Kaiser steel yard in Fontana, California. Steel offered him a greater rigidity than lead, allowing for different configurations and permitting him to radically enlarge the size of his work. Its durability also made it more appropriate for outdoor installations.[1]

Unlike the earlier, smaller lead pieces, *Five Plates, Two Poles* cannot be taken in and under-stood from a single point of view. As it is essen-tially a two-sided composition, one side is always screened from view and the complete configura-tion of the work must be pieced together in the viewer's mind. This emphasis on perambulation, gradual discovery, and memory is due in part to a 1970 trip Serra made to Japan, where he visited the temples at Myoshin-ji, with their complex interplay of buildings, gardens, and pathways.

In *Five Plates, Two Poles*, Serra runs the two poles along the ground, using them to tip the plates into each other, quite unlike earlier pieces in which the poles are elevated and separate the plates. As a result, the tenuous stasis and regularity cf the earlier work is replaced by a dynamic interplay of line, space, and silhouette, the forms seeming to jostle roughly against one another. The impressive mass of the steel pieces and the tilting of the plates heighten the viewer's awareness of gravity and suggest a certain imbalance. But this precariousness is purely visual. By wedging the poles against notches in the plates and precisely calculating the thrust of the counterbalanced plates, Serra has made the piece extremely stable.[2]

Like the best Minimalist art, Serra's work, in spite of its austerity and apparent impersonality, is based on physical sensation, creating an intimate experiential bond between the artwork and the viewer.

P.B.

1. It should be noted that Serra worked in steel mills to put himself through high school and college: "I was exposed to steel being rigged and structured all my life so I have a certain deference and respect for the potential of steel;" reprinted in The Hudson River Museum, Yonkers, *Richard Serra: Interviews, Etc. 1970–1980*, exh. cat., 1980, p. 62.
2. For the installation of *Five Plates, Two Poles* in the Minneapolis Sculpture Garden, however, the steel elements have been spot-welded together.

Joel Shapiro

Untitled 1975

American, b. 1941

cast iron, wood

**20 x 22 x 29½
(50.8 x 55.9 x 74.9)
with base**

**acquired from the Paula
Cooper Gallery, New York,
1976 (purchased with the
aid of funds from Mr. and
Mrs. Edmond R. Ruben,
Mr. and Mrs. Julius E.
Davis, Suzanne Walker
and Thomas Gilmore, and
the National Endowment
for the Arts 76.4)**

Joel Shapiro first began making the small-scale houses for which he has become so well-known in 1973. This 1975 work is the first version that both situates the house on a field and sets it atop a spindly base. Shapiro lifted the work up off the floor to create the impression that the house is floating and to make it, in his words, "independent of context,"[1] in contrast to his earlier houses, which sat directly on the floor and were dependent on engaging the space around them. Unlike a number of the subsequent versions, which feature two or three houses on a field in an unspoken dialogue with one another, this work conveys a sense of profound isolation.

The tiny house sits a bit like an animal on its haunches, head high, rear stooped. The peak of the collapsed roof curves ever so slightly to the right from front to back. The overall irregularity of the form humanizes the house. It makes reference to the activity of the artist and distinguishes the sculpture from its Minimalist antecedents, often industrially fabricated, with their emphasis on regularity of design.

Of the many artists who were drawn to the image of the house during the 1970s, Shapiro was perhaps the keenest on psychologizing the form. Shapiro's house, so small that one readily has a complete overview, is ultimately a metaphor for one's experiences in the world. The facticity of the dense, black mass suggests the past; the surrounding space, the present.

M.G.

1. Conversation with the author, March 1986.

Judith Shea

Enduring Charms   1986

American, b. 1948

iron, copper

**iron piece
36 x 14 x 10½
(91.4 x 35.6 x 26.7)**

**copper piece
4 x 6 x 6
(10.2 x 15.2 x 15.2)**

**acquired from the Willard
Gallery, New York, 1986
(Clinton and Della Walker
Acquisition Fund 86.63)**

Judith Shea's sculptural shells of felt, bronze, or cast iron reveal her beginnings as a clothing designer. These simplified elements are a synthesis of figurative art and Minimalism's pared-down aesthetic. Shea works with clothing forms because they are at once familiar and a way to represent the human figure using the most economical of means: "It eliminates the need to have arms, legs, hands, fingers, toes ... all the things that seem extraneous to me."[1] Devoid of detail, these anonymous figures assume archetypal significance.

In the mid-1980s, Shea began pairing figures to give the work greater complexity. The addition of a second figure created formal and psychological relationships. However, to minimize an exclusively narrative reading of her work, and to lessen the interpretation of her garments as male and female, in 1985 Shea decided to juxtapose figurative and geometric elements within specific works, thus establishing dialogues between dissimilar entities.

Enduring Charms is composed of a standing, full-length iron skirt and a copper pyramid. The title of this work refers to the idea of magic, as historically, both the female form and the pyramid were believed to possess mysterious powers. Like other Shea works from this period, the figure is more anatomical than in earlier examples. The hollow shape seems animated from within as the bent knee and draping skirt suggest movement toward the pyramid. Rich in associations for the artist, these geometric forms are "symbols, either symbols of history, of a specific period, or a specific place, or time."[2]

Each element animates the other through a dialogue of opposition: the skirt is organic, emotional, and figurative; the pyramid is geometric, cool, and abstract. These dichotomies are underscored by the contrasting colors of the two metals. Though it recalls Egyptian and Greek statuary, the figure is nevertheless strongly contemporary; like other simplified dress forms used by Shea, it is based on an evening dress that belonged to the artist's mother. By contrast, the pyramid alludes to ancient art and architecture. Thus the work bridges time and culture, establishing a nexus between contemporary art and its precedents.

D.H.

1. Conversation with the author, 15 June 1987.
2. Ibid.

Judith Shea

Without Words 1988

American, b. 1948

**bronze, cast marble,
limestone**

**78 x 80 x 118
(198.1 x 203.2 x 299.7)**

**Johnson Atelier,
Princeton, New Jersey**

**commissioned by Walker
Art Center, 1987 (gift of
Jeanne and Richard Levitt,
88.391)**

In *Without Words*, three symbolic presences—
a rumpled man's overcoat, a slim elegant dress,
and a fragment of a classically modeled ancient
head—engage in a silent interplay that encompasses art, history, and contemporary gender relationships. Employing clothing forms as human
surrogates, Shea creates spiritual icons that transcend corporeal presence and individual identity.
Viewers can metaphorically slip into the hollow
forms and assume the roles of the male and
female protagonists in this mysterious narrative.

The sculpture amplifies ideas tentatively introduced in Shea's earlier, more abstract works,
such as *Enduring Charms* (1986; p. 464). In a
1989 conversation she said that while formal
concerns had dominated her work up to that
point, she now felt open to exploring the more
narrative and metaphorical potential of her
imagery.[1] Whereas *Enduring Charms* deals in
large measure with the reconciliation of her
proclivity for description and her respect for
Minimalist abstraction—the short, skirtlike form
and the copper pyramid equivocating between
representation and abstraction—the dress,
overcoat, and head in *Without Words* are more
emphatically descriptive and figural. Speaking of
the head in particular, Shea contends that the
work reflects her desire "to get involved technically in something that was more explicitly figurative; to truly understand traditional figurative
sculpture through the process of re-creating it."[2]

As a result, *Without Words* demonstrates a
definite sense of narrative, though it is an
ambiguous narrative operating on several levels.
"I'm much more interested in what you can
imagine is about to happen," she states, "than in
'this is what is happening here.'"[3] Shea establishes a temporal dialogue through the juxtaposition of the ancient head fragment—modeled after
an Egyptian Eighteenth Dynasty sculpture of
Queen Tiye—and the unmistakably contemporary
overcoat.[4] Mediating between them is the slender
dress form, evocative at once of ancient Greek
Kore sculptures and of mid-twentieth-century
couture. Shea describes this simultaneously
timeless and contemporary figure as "an ideal
female image that is specific to our times."[5]
Consequently, *Without Words* serves as a
meditation both on historical modes of representation and on the relation of the present to
history.

Supplementing these artistic and historical
concerns is the purely psychological interplay
among the figures. The closed, self-contained
dress turns away from both the overcoat and the
head, creating a sense of aloofness and insular-
ity. By contrast, the rumpled, open overcoat is
actively engaged in contemplation of the head.
Though the male-female counterpoint is clearly
apparent, Shea contends that these two garments also represent two facets of her own
persona: the composed, controlled public face
and its more informal, disheveled, and inquisitive
alter ego.

P.B.

1. Conversation with Donna Harkavy, Walker Art Center, 15
June 1987.
2. Ibid.
3. Ibid.
4. The yellow jasper fragment now in The Metropolitan
Museum of Art, New York, is dated circa 1417–1379 B.C.
5. Harkavy, ibid.

Charles Sheeler

Buildings at Lebanon 1949

American, 1883–1965

tempera, graphite on
pressed board faced with
sized drawing paper

14⁵⁄₁₆ x 20¼ (36.4 x 51.4)

lower right, *Sheeler.
1949*; on reverse, in blue
ink, upper left, *Charles
Sheeler 1949*

acquired from The
Downtown Gallery, New
York, 1952 (gift of the
T.B. Walker Foundation
52.5)

Buildings at Lebanon, uncannily similar in style and composition to Georgia O'Keeffe's 1926 *Lake George Barns*, (p.402), presents a cropped view of the three-part barn complex at the Shaker community in Hancock, Massachusetts. Sheeler also visited, photographed, and painted the community in New Lebanon, New York, and evidently confused the two when titling this work.

The first part of the barn complex in Hancock, the long concrete and stucco barn, was built in 1879–1880 and reconstructed after a fire in 1910, when it was roofed with polychromed New Hampshire slate.[1] The dairy building to the right and the shed to the left (which has since been demolished and replaced), were also in place when Sheeler visited the site. With the aid of a ruler, he precisely penciled in the composition before painting it. He drew the scene much as he saw it, maintaining the proportions and disposition of the buildings, but he simplified the multicolored roof by rendering it as a uniform, unarticulated slice of gray.

Sheeler's characteristically utilitarian, unromanticized attitude toward his subject complements the Shakers' puritanical sensibility; he describes the buildings in luminous, broad expanses of color sharply bounded by rectilinear edges, rhythmically perforated by the rectangles of the windows. The Millennial Laws of the early nineteenth century that govern the behavior of Shakers expressly forbids ornamentation, or any "odd or fanciful styles of architecture."[2] The unadorned, harmonious congruence of form and function of the buildings erected according to these dictates produced an aesthetic that predated reductivist modernist values by over a century. However, Sheeler's interest was not historical, but philosophical and aesthetic. He wrote that the Shaker communities "understood and convincingly demonstrated that rightness

of proportion in a house or a table, with regard for efficiency in use, made embellishment superfluous. Ornament is often applied to forms to conceal uncertainty—and this applies to painting too...."[3] Interested in Shaker design since the late 1920s, he photographed examples of Shaker architecture and appointed his home with Shaker furniture. "I don't like these things because they are old but in spite of it. I'd like them still better if they were made yesterday because then they would afford proof that the same kind of creative power is continuing."[4]

L.F.G.

1. John H. Ott, *Hancock Shaker Village: A Guidebook and History* (Hancock, Massachusetts: Shaker Community, 1976), p. 103. Ott was the first to recognize the Hancock barn complex as the subject of Sheeler's painting; letter from Ott to Gwen Bitz, Walker Art Center, 22 December 1977. Robert A. Guffin of the Hancock Shaker Village provided further details on the history of the complex; letter to the author, 29 July 1985.
2. Quoted in Edward Deming Andrews, "The Shaker Manner of Building," *Art in America*, vol. 48 (1960), p. 40.
3. Quoted in Constance Rourke, *Charles Sheeler: Artist in the American Tradition* (New York: Harcourt Brace and Co., 1938), p. 133.
4. Ibid., p. 136.

A 1974 photograph of the barn complex at Hancock Shaker Village.

Charles Sheeler

Midwest 1954

American, 1883–1965

oil on canvas

17¹⁵⁄₁₆ x 32 (45.6 x 81.3)

lower right, in red paint,
Sheeler–1954

acquired from The
Downtown Gallery, New
York, 1955 (gift of the
T.B. Walker Foundation
55.6)

Although Sheeler never painted on location, he was always alert to the surrounding environment, and frequently recorded it in sketches and photographs. He encountered the source for *Midwest* during one of his visits to his friend and patron Otto Spaeth, a founder of the Pabst Brewing Company, who had a plant in Cedarburg, Wisconsin, not far from Milwaukee.[1] At Spaeth's urging, Sheeler accompanied one of the salesmen on a daylong trip into the Wisconsin countryside, where he saw the Midwestern farm subject that he later integrated with memories of previously viewed rural scenes.[2]

In works such as *Midwest*, Sheeler describes an optical phenomenon he found intriguing—the momentary persistence of an image after the retina has registered another. He has compared this effect to the activity of memory, which overlays recollections, transforming and synthesizing them into composite images. The technique of overlapping in the context of the aesthetic of this canvas results in features that are shared with Cubism—a shallow picture plane, the intersection of transparent planes moving forward and back to create dynamic tensions, spatial ambiguity, fragmentation of form, and the use of non-local color to define independent pictorial areas. Unlike the Cubists, however, Sheeler never fully disintegrated his forms to reassemble them as new structures. His admiration for the objects constructed by builders, fabricators, and craftsmen compelled him to preserve their integrity, which he renders through realistic details, precise lines and proportions, and descriptive modeling.

The fused layering of two clearly lit and realistically drawn images emulates the effect of a double exposure on film. Photography, as an efficient, direct, and relatively non-expressionist means of producing an image, was a medium to which Sheeler responded with great enthusiasm and skill, and one that informs his painting. His aversion to self-expression through painterly gesture is reflected in his working procedures, which assured that all sense of process was expunged from the final image. From the early 1950s on, he often made preparatory sketches in miniature in tempera on paper before transferring the image onto Plexiglas of the same size. After enlarging the composition in oil on canvas, he sometimes returned to the tempera on paper and modified it to correspond with the finished work.[3]

A 4½ x 8-inch tempera sketch, dated 1954 and entitled *Mid-West #2*, differs only slightly from the oil.[4]

Sheeler's use of glass and then, at the instigation of his friend William Lane, plastic as a support for his preparatory sketches enabled him to easily sponge away dissatisfying strokes or passages. Describing his resistance to composing on an opaque surface, Sheeler commented that

> it would be objectionable because there would be so much evidence of the material. You just keep piling color on top of color, when you want several successive changes, maybe just in one area, which proves puzzling to you until you feel you have it.... I'm always going back to my last remark—that an efficient army buries its dead.

In photography, no evidence of reworking exists on the final negative—the history of the image is distributed over separate surfaces. For Sheeler, the successful painting would be the fulfillment of his aims as a photographer: a single, unlabored image in which all parts appear to be instantaneously resolved. The limpid composition of works such as *Midwest* registers these conceptual preoccupations as well as the technical consequences of his interest in photography.

L.F.G.

1. Bartlett Cowdrey, interview with Charles Sheeler, 9 December 1958, transcript on deposit at the AAA.
2. Factual information and all quotations in this entry are taken from Martin Friedman's interview with Charles Sheeler at the artist's home in Irvington-on-Hudson, New York, 18 June 1959. A transcript of the interview is on deposit at the AAA, which published a portion in the *Archives of American Art Journal*, vol. 16, no. 4 (1976), pp. 15–19.
3. See Abigail Booth in the National Collection of Fine Arts, Smithsonian Institution, Washington, D.C., *Charles Sheeler*, exh. cat., 1968, pp. 26, 28.
4. A photograph of this study is in The Downtown Gallery Papers, AAA. Although the existence of a Plexiglas version has not been verified, it is likely that there was one.

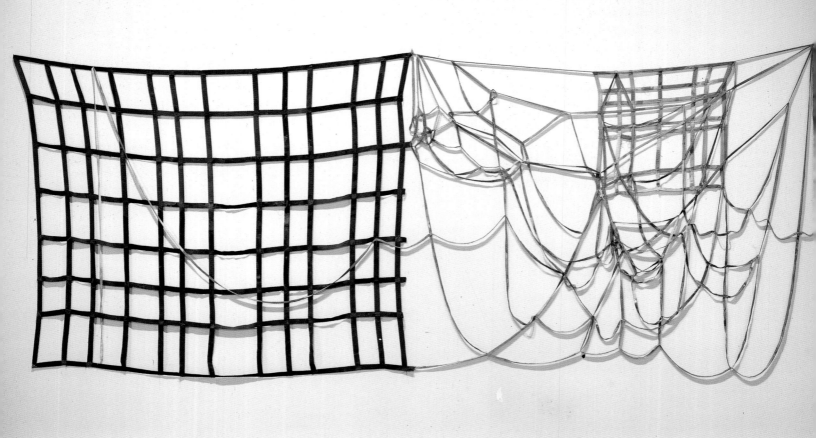

Alan Shields

Zig Zag 1976

American, b. 1944

acrylic, cotton thread,
cotton canvas, glass
beads

65 x 153¾
(165.1 x 390.5) variable

acquired from the Paula
Cooper Gallery, New York,
1978 (purchased with the
aid of funds provided by
the Art Center Acquisition
Fund and the National
Endowment for the Arts
78.1)

To free canvas from its traditional artistic role as the support for painting, Shields first used a sewing machine to "draw" stitched lines on cotton in art class in Kansas. By rejecting the artifice of the taut stretching of canvas over a rectangular frame, he allows canvas to behave like the fabric it is, existing in a symbiotic rather than subservient relationship with the color he ebulliently stains into it. The form of the work is as much contingent on internal tensions related to the actual fixing of the structure's parts and the action of gravity as on the application of paint and changes from one installation to the next.

Although his aesthetic is not hard-edged or reductive, Shields sees connections between his work and Minimalism, primarily in the "interest in systems and the possibilities of systems" and the focus on intervals.[1] The grid, quintessential system of intervals, is both defended and challenged in *Zig Zag*. (The title refers to a sewing stitch, as well as to the brand name of cigarette rolling papers.) The dark grid on the left side of the work is countered with a more expressive, freer form in the right half, in which the line is slackened into festooned curves. Bright colors project from the light ground of the fabric and mutually interact along the length of the bars and across the voids, and organic form crawls over geometry.

Unlike purist Minimalists, Shields did not discover the grid as a neutral, elemental organization of non-expressive lines. He has said that he first used it as a didactic aid in understanding space through subdivision,[2] as in the device of the cartoon, which permits the renderer to see the two-dimensional effects of spatial relations and transfer these to a different scale: "From one of the grids within the painting, your eye can expand out to the whole thing."[3] This function of the grid is acknowledged in *Zig Zag* in the contrast between the relatively small square enmeshed in the upper right of the relaxed right-hand grid, and the large square to the left, to which it is attached by one swooping and one tense line.

Although other of Shields's grids are colored on both sides, and on occasion hang from the ceiling in the middle of exhibition spaces, the contrast in *Zig Zag*, he notes, is between right and left rather than front and back. He began the work with the systematized left side, made of ready-cut strips of material bought at an awning and ribbon store in São Paulo, then produced the miniaturizing version on the right with lighter weight fabric, and finally drew them together with the free lines. He recently explained that this work was in part inspired by a grid he made and hung in a boat he was sailing to Florida in 1974 or 1975, that rocked back and forth; he describes the left side of *Zig Zag* as the "landlubber," and the right as "sea-going."[4]

On inspection one finds a decorative band of Italian glass beads tacked at the juncture of the two grids. In order to see the surface clearly, the viewer has to approach to a point where the outside edges of the piece are no longer visible. Backing away to contain the entire image in the field of vision, the viewer can no longer perceive the inner activity. Shields intended that the alternate telescoping and magnification of detail contribute to a dialectical understanding of the work.[5]

L.F.G.

1. Conversation with the author, 6 November 1986.
2. In Emily Wasserman, "A Talk with Alan Shields," *Artforum*, vol. 9 (February 1971), p. 60.
3. Ibid.
4. Conversation with the author, 6 November 1986.
5. Wasserman, p. 59.

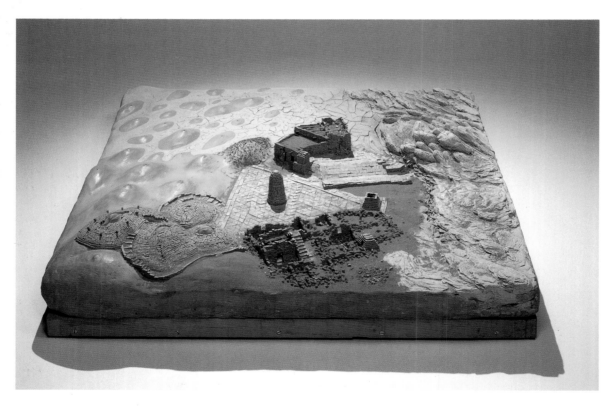

Charles Simonds

△ **Early** and △ **Later** 1977

American, b. 1945

△ Early
clay, sand, glue, twigs on wood base

7⅜ x 33¾ x 34½
(18.8 x 85.7 x 87.6)

acquired from the artist, 1977 (purchased with the aid of funds provided by the Art Center Acquisition Fund and the National Endowment for the Arts 77.71)

△ Later
clay, sand, glue, twigs on wood base

5 x 34⅝ x 34
(12.7 x 87.9 x 86.4)

acquired from the artist, 1977 (purchased with exhibition funds for *Scale and Environment: 10 Sculptors* 77.68)

In 1971 Simonds was building tiny architectural environments on the dilapidated exteriors of Lower East Side, New York buildings, using tweezers to lay courses of diminutive unfired bricks cut from rolled-out clay with a mortar of thinned Elmer's glue. He made these dwellings, he explained, in the service of an imagined race of Little People whose attitudes he inferred from the structures that seemed to come into being through him. The Little People's vulnerable environments of organic and architectural forms were subject to cyclical changes during which they inevitably reverted to the primary matter—clay. The action of man and the elements gradually or abruptly destroyed the civilizations whose history seemed to be compressed in proportion to their miniaturization. As the habitations decayed or were destroyed, others appeared elsewhere, their forms altered in consonance with the new circumstances. Some of Simonds's environments, such as the two Walker pieces, were not presented within the gigantic urban context of New York, but built on plywood bases and examined in isolation. Although some of the levels of wit and observations concerning scale, the relations to the city, actual time, and the social activity of building are sacrificed in the decontextualized objects, pairing facilitates a more systematic, synchronic study of the development of societies.

In △ *Early*, a rudimentary civilization has been established on the arid landscape by an organizing intelligence. A fence or barricade marks a boundary, stones line a riverbed, a four-legged structure with ritualistic overtones supports a pile of burnt sticks. Facing this "altar" is a cavelike mound resembling female genitalia, an extension of the sexual analogies of the topography in which swelling forms resemble breasts. The identification of the body with the contours, substances, and activities of the earth has been made manifest in Simonds's filmed Happening *Landscape↔Body↔Dwelling* of 1970, in which he built dwellings on his own nude body. The implication of the action is that the earth generates and sustains life forms, including the human organism that designs and builds social and architectural structures to protect its own momentary survival and to perpetuate the species. Simonds is interested in the primitive, evolutionary implications of "dwelling:" "I've learned more from watching the small-brained genius of the Caddisfly larva building its house by attaching

blade after blade in an ascending spiral around its body as it grows than by studying the works of large-brained architects."[1] Unlike the larva, the Little People make structures designed at a scale that permits social use; this sense of monumentality, however, is inverted by the miniaturization of the dwellings in relation to the artist who constructs them. This magnification of the human being is in turn counteracted by the outscale proportion of the buildings of New York City, which "makes us all feel like Little People sometimes."[2]

This relative, variable set of scale relationships also applies to the actual and imagined time that has elapsed between △ *Early* and the vaguely comparative △ *Later*, which the artist made in Maine. In △ *Later*, the scattered "trees" or sticks have disappeared, presumably put to the use of the society that has built more substantial, but in the end equally perishable, structures. The natural forms and the primitive dwellings that dominated the "early" view have for the most part been respected, fortified, or exploited; seldom are they entirely erased. The flat land has been worked, part of the hills covered with pavings and plantings. The triangular layout of the settlement referred to in the title has been formalized with the diamond-patterned plaza surrounding the phallic cairn that replaces the vulvular mound. The "altar," now a stepped, truncated tapering brick structure, marks the apex.

Because Simonds's primary concern seems to be the behavior of natural forms, the visible effects of intelligence, and the process of organic and circumstantial change that transforms simple life forms into a complex society, the viewer tends not to make formal comparisons between the two objects. Conventional observations on the development of an artistic theme, the physical realities of the art object, the integrity of the medium, or its allusive and descriptive powers, seem incidental to Simonds's pursuit.

L.F.G.

1. Quoted in Nancy Foote, "Situation Aesthetics: Impermanent Art and the Seventies Audience," *Artforum* vol. 18 (January 1980), p. 29.
2. Quoted in Phil Patton, "The Lost World of the 'Little People,'" *Art News*, vol. 82 (February 1983), pp. 84, 87.

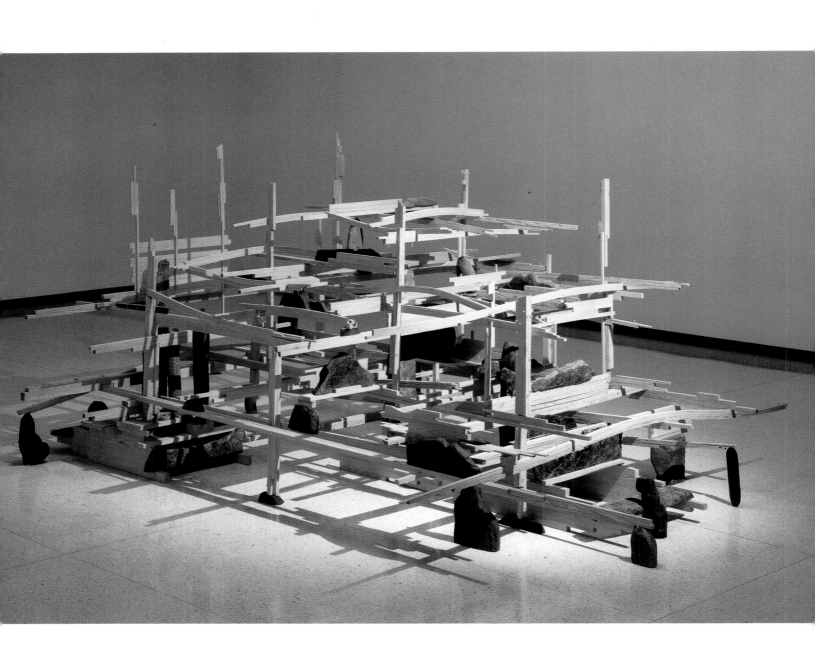

Michael Singer

Cloud Hands Ritual Series 1982–83 1982–1983

American, b. 1945

wood, stone, metal clamps

149 x 112¾ x 72 (378.5 x 286.4 x 182.9)

acquired from the Sperone Westwater Gallery, New York, 1986 (Walker Special Purchase Fund 86.43)

Michael Singer's interior works such as *Cloud Hands Ritual Series* maintain the strong reference to nature that characterized his earlier pieces, located out-of-doors in marshes and bogs. The organic materials and intricate systems of structural support of *Cloud Hands* allude to ecological systems, although the precision cuts made in various stones suggest man's interventions in the landscape. Singer's interior works refer to architecture as well. Among the many sculptors of his generation who share this concern, he is the most metaphorical, suggesting the idea of shelter by giving us the barest outlines rather than constructing something that could be functional.

In particular, *Cloud Hands* brings to mind architectural references to shrines, with the elegant combination of wood and stone giving the work a distinctly Asian cast. In its extreme deliberateness—each stone painstakingly chosen and set just so against carefully bent wooden slats—the work seems to be the product of an elaborate ritual. The harmony and balance that define *Cloud Hands* evoke a feeling of timelessness and transcendence. The partial concealment of certain stones and the inaccessibility of those located at the center suggest both the sacred and the unknowable.

Singer first developed *Cloud Hands* in pine, which is easier to shape and cut than the ash in which he finally realized the work. The result is a three-dimensional drawing in space, with a lyricism and sense of airiness not generally associated with sculpture. *Cloud Hands Ritual Series* is one of approximately thirteen similar constructions made thus far, and takes its poetic name from a movement in t'ai chi. It is a transitional piece, which Singer worked on at the same time he began making sculptures entirely in stone. He clarified here the use of stone as support, enabling himself to concentrate on exploring the volume and weight of stone in subsequent works.

M.G.

John Sloan

South Beach Bathers   1907–1908

American, 1871–1951

oil on canvas

26 x 31¾ (66 x 80.7)

lower left, *John Sloan–'08*;
on reverse, upper left,
South Beach Bathers; on
original stretcher frame,
in pencil, recorded when
work was restretched in
1971, *South Beach—
Sunday—Sloan*; on
canvas, top and bottom
edges of painting within
depth of stretcher, in
paint, *South Beach*

acquired from the artist
through Kraushaar
Galleries, 1948 (gift of the
T.B. Walker Foundation,
Gilbert M. Walker Fund
48.27)

It has been possible to precisely date Sloan's
South Beach Bathers on the basis of notes from
the diary he kept between 1906 and 1913. On
Sunday, 23 June 1907, he wrote:

> Dolly [his wife] and I went to Staten Island, South
> Beach this afternoon by Municipal Ferry and Train.
> Our first visit and we found the place quite to our
> liking. Reminds one of Atlantic City years ago. It is
> not so touched by the "Refinements" as Coney Island.
> We walked along the beach on the little board walks
> and came home in time to have dinner about eight
> o'clock.[1]

The next day Sloan "started to make a memory of South Beach;" he recorded working on it on
the 26th, 27th, and 29th. On 14 August he wrote
that he had been considering his selection of
works for the Chicago showing of the now historic
group exhibition of The Eight and had decided to
include *South Beach Bathers*.

Sloan, who had an apartment-studio on West
23rd Street in New York, was an attentive observer of the gestures, movements, glances, and
interactions of urban dwellers and the environment they inhabited, and he generated his
imagery from daily memories. Although he and
other members of The Eight were criticized in the
press for their prosaic subject matter and
uninhibited manner of execution, works such as
South Beach Bathers may now be seen as controlled orchestrations of light, movement, color,
design, and structure depicting a particular
moment in a specific culture.[2] The composition
demonstrates Sloan's ability to create a dramatic
focus despite the proliferation of incident.
A diagonal line of movement through the group of
figures at the lower right intersects with the diagonal of the shoreline. The point at which they meet
is marked by the "belle," whose glance connects
her with the "beau" at the lower left. Three
spectators behind and to her left complete the
circle of figures enclosing her. The rest of the
crowd fills a triangular section at the upper right
that balances her monumental presence. The peculiar double nature of the urban seashore, the
interplay that occurs within it between the ordinary and the mythical, the contemporary and the
classical, is wittily epitomized in the menu of hot
dogs and shellfish.

L.F.G.

1. Published in Bruce St. John, ed., *John Sloan's New York
Scene* (New York: Harper & Row, 1965), pp. 138, 167,
234, 235, 237. An additional diary entry alluding to the
work, written on 27 July 1908, does not appear in this
publication.
2. Commenting on the period-piece quality of the work,
Sloan wrote in his *Gist or Art* (New York: American Artists
Group, 1939), p. 218: "It is amusing to recall how very chic
the bathing costume seemed at the time."

David Smith

The Royal Bird 1947–1948

American, 1906–1965

welded steel, bronze, stainless steel

22⅛ x 59¹³⁄₁₆ x 8½ (56.2 x 151.9 x 21.6)

on support attaching bird to base, *David Smith/ 1948*

acquired from the Willard Gallery, New York, 1952 (gift of the T.B. Walker Foundation 52.4)

Photograph of fossil skeleton of *Hesperornis regalis* at American Museum of Natural History, New York
David Smith papers
Archives of American Art
Smithsonian Institution, Washington, D.C.

The Royal Bird is based on the skeleton of a prehistoric diving bird of the Cretaceous period, the *Hesperornis regalis* (royal evening bird) in the collection of the American Museum of Natural History, New York, of which Smith had at least one, if not two photographs.[1] The imaginative additions to the skeleton's forms were developed in sketchbook drawings of the mid-1940s. Some of the changes in the figure may have derived from information Smith acquired about the prehistoric bird. A page of sketches of bird skeletons from the period 1944–1954, exploring both details and the general layout of *The Royal Bird*, are accompanied by his notes: "Hispornis [sic] fat tail ... diver."[2] He concentrated on the development of the bulbous tail, and streamlined the figure so that it would resemble the taut body of a diving bird. The drawings show the notching of the esophagus, the clustering of the tail feathers, the resolution of the scissorlike beak, hammerheaded teeth, and perforated skull planes, and the derivation of the pyramidal support from the stick legs of a bird. Treated as separate problems, these individual elements were brought together to form a complete figure only after the work was modeled three dimensionally.

Clement Greenberg in 1958 noted the pictorial aspect of certain of Smith's sculptures, illustrating his argument with a reproduction of *The Royal Bird*: "sculpture can confine itself to virtually two dimensions (as some of David Smith's pieces do) without being felt to violate the limitations of its medium, because the eye recognizes that what offers itself in two dimensions is actually (not palpably) fashioned in three."[3] Smith himself detailed the advantages of linear structure: "The line contour with its variations and its comment on mass space is more acute than bulk shape. In vision the overlay of shapes seen through each other not only permits each shape to retain its individual intent but in juxtaposition highly multiplies the associations of the new and more complex unity."[4] Another result is the integration of form not only with empty space but also with the environment viewed through it, suggesting an interpenetration of the world and the art object. On the last page of the handmade booklet Smith fashioned in 1949 of photographs of his work at Bolton Landing, he mounted a shot of *The Royal Bird* resting on a ledge over Lake George with trees in the background;[5] elsewhere it appears in front of a rock wall, lending it a fossil-like look.

Smith knew that the *Hesperornis regalis* was a diving carnivore. His writings show that he was intrigued by the evolutionary metamorphosis of fish into bird,[6] which in connection with this work adds cannibalistic overtones to a creature whose aggressiveness is implied by the spiky protuberances on its head and its prominent teeth and talons: the bird pursues its own evolutionary prototype. The sense of violence inherent in the image was characteristic of his works of the period. Problems in his marriage and the fresh memory of World War II have been proposed as contributing factors to his obsessive treatment of the themes of predation, dead birds, and the perversion of Darwinian survival laws in the form of the unnatural belligerence of what he saw as warmongering, imperialist, capitalist powers. Smith himself, however, only said about *The Royal Bird* that "I worked for a certain kind of perfection in it that I have not been inspired to put in most of my work."[7]

L.F.G.

1. For the photographs, see Cleve Gray, ed., *David Smith by David Smith* (New York: Holt, Rinehart and Winston, 1968), p. 98, and Edward Fry, in the Solomon R. Guggenheim Museum, New York, *David Smith*, exh. cat., 1969, p. 53.
2. Reprod. in Gray, p. 99. One of the drawings on this page is similar to two others related directly to *The Royal Bird*. See Fry, p. 53; although Fry dates them "ca. 1948," they appear to be preparatory and hence more likely date from 1947.
3. Clement Greenberg, "Sculpture in Our Time," *Arts*, vol. 32 (June 1958), p. 2.
4. Quoted in The Museum of Modern Art, New York, "The New Sculpture: A Symposium," 12 February 1952, moderated by Andrew C. Ritchie.
5. "Selections from Recent Work, 1948–1949," given by the artist at an unspecified date to The Museum of Modern Art.
6. See Hirshhorn Museum and Sculpture Garden, Smithsonian Institution, Washington, D.C., *David Smith: Painter, Sculptor, Draftsman*, exh. cat., 1983, p. 136.
7. Letter to H.H. Arnason, Walker Art Center, 16 June 1952.

481

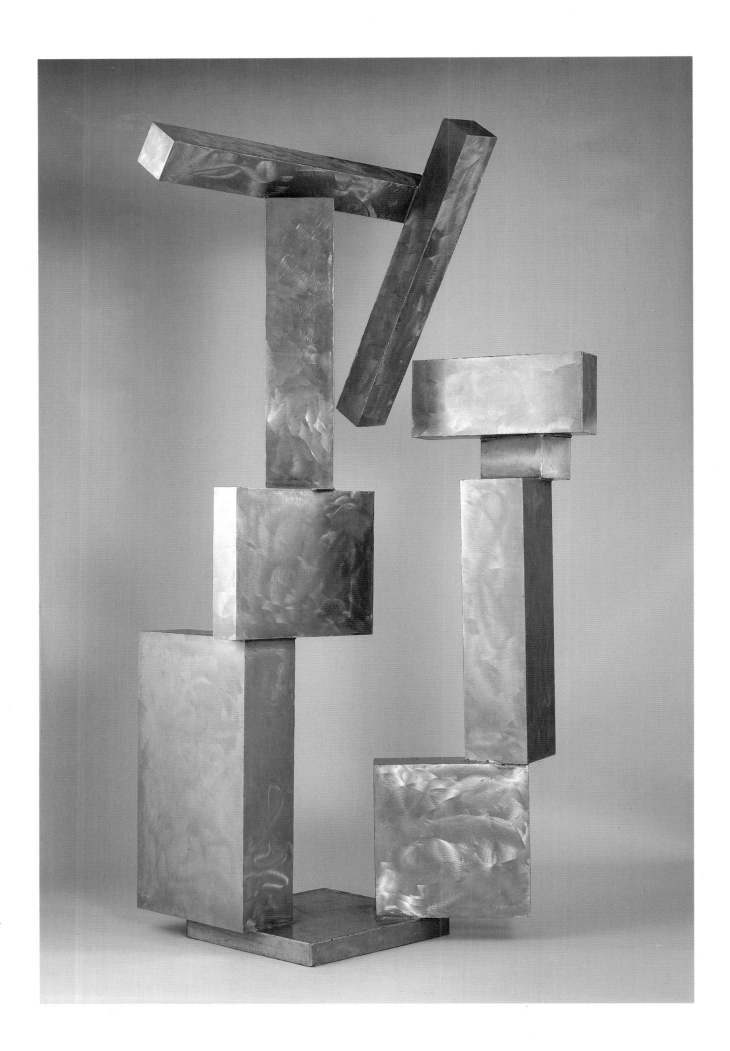

David Smith

Cubi IX   1961

American, 1906–1965

stainless steel

105¾ x 58⅝ x 43⅞
(268.6 x 148.9 x 111.5)

on two edges of top plane
of base, in raised cursive
script, *Cubi IX/David
Smith Oct. 26. 1961*

acquired from the estate
of the artist through the
Marlborough-Gerson
Gallery, New York, 1966
(gift of the T.B. Walker
Foundation 66.20)

In 1961 Smith ordered over three and one half tons of steel from Ryerson Steel Fabricators, to be cut according to templates he provided.[1] Four hundred and sixty-nine pounds of this order were used to complete *Cubi IX* at Terminal Iron Works, his studio at Bolton Landing, New York, in October 1961. In the spring of 1962 he sent the work to Spoleto for inclusion in the Festival of Two Worlds,[2] before deciding to make a trip to Voltri, near Genoa, to make a new series of sculptures for the occasion. The core group was shown at the Roman amphitheater in Spoleto, with *Cubi IX* and five other sculptures distributed throughout the city. According to Smith's recollections, Giovanni Carandente placed *Cubi IX* high on a six-foot tufa-block pillar in the lower part of the town in front of a fourteenth-century church with seventeenth-century restorations, which pleased the sculptor: "Its stainless cubes in a different way held with the soft variables of the church wall stones."[3]

Cubi IX bears no resemblance to the "rod-and-disk," works produced in Voltri, but rather, like *Cubetotem* and *Cubi III* of 1961, signals the beginning of a series of large-scale assemblages of box-shaped elements that Smith produced from 1963 until his death. He had been concerned with monumental scale since 1957, when he began using stainless steel for large sculpture designed for the outdoors,[4] and ultimately took the "defiant position" of vowing to make his works so big they couldn't be moved.[5] In placing broad-planed steel sculptures outdoors, he was faced with the problem of too much sunlight on the metal, which made it look "like car chrome."[6] In order to diffuse the steel's reflectiveness and to develop illusions both of surface and depth, he and his assistant, Leon Pratt, burnished the planes, "creating coloristic effects responsive to the changing surroundings." Specifying that his works were not designed for "modern buildings" but for siting in nature, Smith polished them so they would take on the colors of the sky, the sun, water, and trees.[7]

Radically different interpretations of the intentions and effects of the Cubi series have been put forward. It has been argued that the structures are dematerialized and optical and that they are massive and strongly sculptural. They have been seen as anthropomorphic, heraldic, totemic, architectural, gestural, corporeal, or exclusively geometric.[8] Smith had an inclusive attitude that admitted such disparate readings:

"My world was the Dutch movement De Stijl; it was Russian Constructivism; it was Cubism; it was even Surrealism. Or even German Expressionism. Or even Monet…. They all fitted in to me."[9] The tension or interplay among sculptural, pictorial, and graphic properties reflects his continued involvement with all three modes. Trained in painting rather than sculpture, he commented several times that the flat planes of his work had their primary origins in montage and Cubism.[10] He was not tied to representation as the Cubists were, but approached form abstractly, in an augmentative, concrete way, "rarely the Grand Conception, but a preoccupation with parts [that have] unities and associations and separate afterimages—even when they are no longer parts but a whole."[11]

L.F.G.

1. See Stanley E. Marcus, *David Smith: The Sculptor and His Work* (Ithaca and London: Cornell University Press, 1983), p. 117.
2. See David Smith, "Report on Voltri," in Garnett McCoy, ed., *David Smith* (New York and Washington: Praeger Publishers, 1973), pp. 156, 157.
3. Ibid., p. 163.
4. See Marcus, pp. 162, 163, for detailed discussion of the properties of stainless steel and its use by Smith.
5. Quoted in Marlborough-Gerson Gallery, New York, *David Smith*, exh. cat., 1964, n.p.
6. David Smith, "Notes on My Work," *Arts*, vol. 34 (February 1960), p. 44.
7. See Marlborough-Gerson Gallery, *David Smith*.
8. See William Rubin, "David Smith," *Art International*, vol. 7 (5 December 1963), p. 48; Donald Judd, *Arts Magazine*, vol. 39 (December 1964), p. 62; Jane Harrison Cone, in Fogg Art Museum, Harvard University, Cambridge, Massachusetts, *David Smith: 1906–1965*, exh. cat., 1966, p. 9; Hilton Kramer, in Los Angeles County Museum of Art, *David Smith*, exh. cat., 1966, p. 7; Edward Fry, in the Solomon R. Guggenheim Museum, New York, *David Smith*, exh. cat., 1969, p. 154; Rosalind E. Krauss, *Terminal Iron Works: The Sculpture of David Smith* (Cambridge, Massachusetts: The MIT Press, 1971), pp. 177–181.
9. From an interview with David Sylvester, 16 June 1961, for the BBC, published in *Living Arts* (April 1964).
10. See Katharine Kuh, *The Artist's Voice: Talks with Seventeen Artists* (New York: Harper & Row, 1960), pp. 221, 229, and Smith, "Notes on My Work," p. 44. Fry, in *David Smith*, p. 154, singles out *Cubi IX* and two other early Cubis as unusual in having no "compositional focus, or principle of organization derived from the cubist-constructivist tradition."
11. Smith, "Notes on My Work, " p. 44.

Richard Smith

Quartet 1964

British, b. 1931

oil on canvas

56 x 72 x 20½
(142.2 x 182.9 x 52.1)

acquired from the Green
Gallery, New York, 1964
(Art Center Acquisition
Fund 64.37)

The source for the primary motif in this three-dimensional painting—the reiterated, projecting rectangle—was strips of film showing advertisements for cigarettes, with identical images repeated in a vertical piling of stills.[1] Smith's interest in systems of representation, mass communication, and the ubiquity of consumer products, which attracted him to Marshall McLuhan's thinking,[2] led him to an understanding that in merchandising, the packaging of goods comes to replace the goods themselves: "You don't buy cigarettes, only cartons. The box is your image of the product."[3] *Quartet* is an object representing a film strip representing a photograph representing a cigarette pack representing cigarettes. Not only does Smith allude to this multiple processing activity, but he appropriates the advertising device of exploiting color to convey sensations that the advertiser wishes to identify with the product: "There is a kind of colour that I find especially attractive: pale green with pale yellow, which makes a reference to something cool, a 'hint of mint'—as in menthol-Cool. I like this artificiality, and … in using it I am already halfway away from reality or from specific representations that I want to avoid." It is important to Smith that the image and its metaphoric palette have their own history within the world of consumerism and do not spring meaningfully from his unconscious or personal experience.

In earlier works, Smith had represented projecting boxes or their silhouettes illusionistically on a flat, shaped surface. In the three-dimensional pieces, in which the "drawing is done by the stretcher," sculptural issues were introduced that create incompatible relationships between representational and actual form. The projecting element in *Quartet* is a parallelogram whose top is perpendicular to the wall. In order to make the box painted on its lower right corner line up with the boxes projecting illusionistically on the recessed canvas below to form a Judd-like "stack," or the strip of film, the viewer has to stand at a particular angle to the piece. From that vantage point, the angle at which the real top recedes toward the wall is inconsistent with the illusory recession of the boxes and hence reports on the artifice, as does the difference between the real shadows cast by the overhanging and the stylized shadows within the painted image.

While the disjunction between the work as painting and the work as object draws attention to Smith's notions of representation, it weakens the visual impact of the piece. After he had returned to two-dimensional canvases, he voiced his own uncertainty about the success of these three-dimensional works: "When you paint across something that is three-dimensional, the third dimensional reality is too strong for any extra play with added illusion." Subsequent works were simplified, reduced in color and more clearly holistic, more consonant with Minimalist theory.

L.F.G.

1. Letter to the author, 3 November 1986. For examples of these film strips, see the illustratlons in Richard Smith, "Trailer: Notes Additional to a Film," *Living Arts*, vol. 1 (1963), p. 35.
2. For Smith's familiarity with McLuhan's *Mechanical Bride*, see Barbara Rose in The Tate Gallery, London, *Richard Smith*, exh. cat., 1975, p. 10.
3. Quoted in Bryan Robertson, "Dialogue with the Artist," in Whitechapel Gallery, London, *Richard Smith: Paintings 1958–1966*, exh. cat., 1966, n.p. All subsequent quotations are taken from this source.

Tony Smith

Amaryllis 1965/1968

American, 1912–1980

Cor-Ten steel

133⅞ x 107⅝ x 144½
(340 x 273.4 x 367)

engraved on stainless
steel plaque imbedded in
Cor-Ten plate underneath
sculpture, *Tony Smith/
65/68–2/3*

Industrial Welding,
Newark, New Jersey

acquired from the
Fischbach Gallery, New
York, 1968 (gift of the
T.B. Walker Foundation
68.34)

In 1965 Smith began work on a project that derived from his 1962 *Gracehoper*, a many-legged, angular, monumental sculpture: "I didn't have the model of *Gracehoper* to work from, so I had to begin with a few separate units."[1] While assembling the maquette from the tetrahedra and octahedra that form the basis of most of his work, he realized that his concept was too complicated and abandoned it, but not without having composed *Amaryllis* along the way. Having settled on "components made up of clusters such as the one I already had, I made another as a whole unit and stuck it to the first. Needless to say, the result was symmetrical. I thought it looked a little bit like Brancusi, and was so stunned by this that I stopped." The particular Brancusi he had in mind could well have been the marble *Leda* of 1920, a work he probably had known since at least 1936, when it was loaned by Katherine Dreier to The Museum of Modern Art's historic *Cubism and Abstract Art* exhibition; Smith was studying at the Art Students League at the time.

This comparison with Brancusi, which Smith may not have felt was to his advantage, may partly account for his initial unease about *Amaryllis*. In an interview published in 1979 he acknowledged:

> When I did the sculpture *Amaryllis*, I had the sense that it looked so ungainly and unbalanced. It also seemed rather classical from one view, but then taken from another, it seemed some kind of a caricature of form. We're all born with a sense of rightness of form, and this seemed to be some kind of desecration of all that, just as the amaryllis plant seems to me a kind of orchid made out of wood or some terrible aberration of form.... When it was actually built, I was quite terrified by it. You know I have such a Hellenistic view of things that when I see something that strikes me as abortive, it terrifies me. That's how I thought of *Amaryllis*, but then, after a while I began to see that it had some kind of presence. The qualities which I thought so strange actually pulled themselves together into a kind of contemporary expression of form which although novel wasn't just frivolous. I think now of it as a somewhat formidable piece of sculpture.[2]

The structure of *Amaryllis* is economical: two identical irregular polyhedra are fused at an angle to produce a physically stable but visually dynamic single form. Despite its structural clarity and linear simplicity, the work's topological aberrations produce bafflingly complex and changeable profiles as the viewer circles it. The jutting corners and extended planes geometrically displace space like a faceted stone.

Smith used Cor-Ten in this piece at the request of the Walker Art Center, though it was not a material with which he felt particularly comfortable;[3] the rust brown distinguished this version from the more characteristic black of the other two in the edition. The initial maquette of 1965, measuring about 10 inches high, was made of heavy black paper taped together; the 1966 full-size mockup was made of plywood and painted black.[4] The Walker's sculpture is now painted black, to conform with the artist's original conception.

L.F.G.

1. This and the subsequent quotation are taken from Wadsworth Atheneum, Hartford, *Tony Smith: Two Exhibitions of Sculpture*, exh. cat., 1966, n.p.
2. Quoted in Sam Hunter, "The Sculpture of Tony Smith," in the Pace Gallery, New York, *Tony Smith: Ten Elements and Throwback*, exh. cat., 1979, p. 6.
3. William J. Schmidt of Industrial Welding, Newark, conversation with the author, 12 June 1985.
4. Jane Smith, the artist's widow, resolved questions about the various versions of *Amaryllis*.

Constantin Brancusi
Leda 1920
marble on plaster base
26 x 7½ (66 x 19)
Collection The Art Institute
of Chicago
Katherine S. Dreier
Bequest, 1953

487

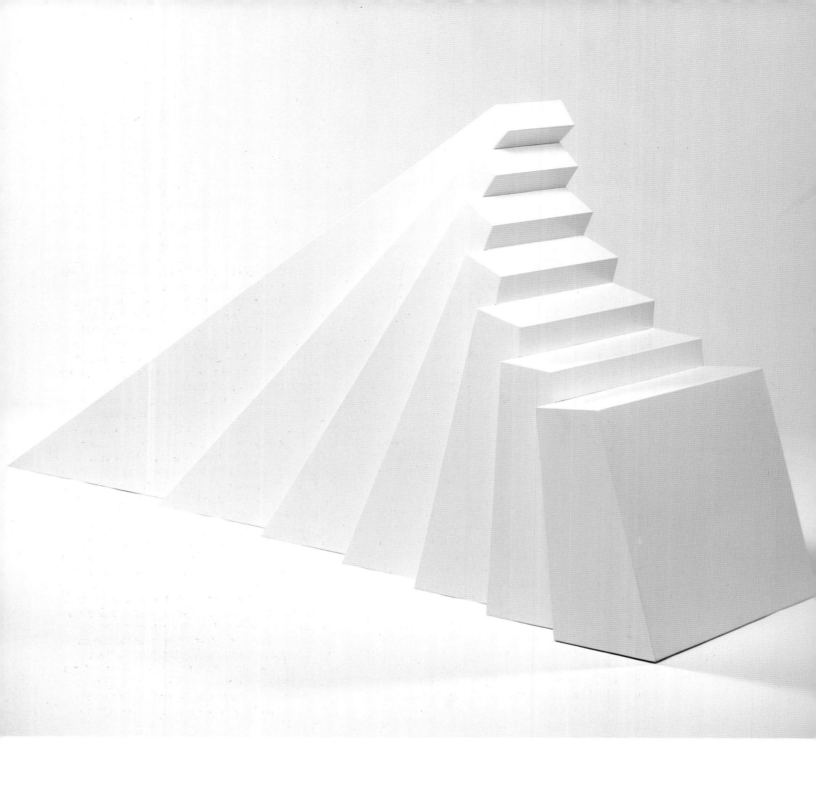

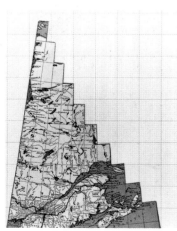

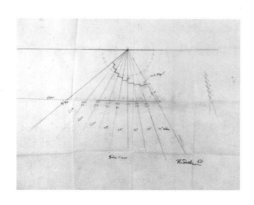

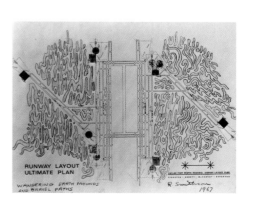

Robert Smithson

Leaning Strata 1968

American, 1938–1973

painted steel

105 x 49⅛ x 30
(266.7 x 124.8 x 76.2)

Dwan Gallery, New York;
acquired from Virginia
Dwan, 1985 (gift of
Virginia Dwan 85.761)

Leaning Strata is the visual manifestation of an extensive set of interrelated investigations Smithson was conducting during the mid-1960s bearing on geology, astronomy, systems of perspective in art, mapping, and the nature of time and matter. Clues to the implications of the work can be found in an untitled collage of circa 1966, for which Smithson cut a conic map projection of the world along the grid of latitudinal and longitudinal lines from the Arctic to upper New York State, one edge stepped in the manner of Leaning Strata. The grid, which he calls "a kind of mental construct of physical matter,"[1] is the universal organizing system for the mapping of the globe, the structure of the city and farmland: "In short, all air and land is locked into a vast lattice."[2] The segments of Leaning Strata are in one sense three-dimensional extensions of the cartographic trapezoids whose diagonals represent an acknowledgment of the spherical nature of the earth's surface, suggested in the sculpture by the curve in the line joining coordinate points at the top of the piece. This curve was fashioned, as can be seen from an examination of three preparatory drawings, by the intersection of concentric circles with a one-point perspective grid system emanating from their center. In the sculpture itself the center is present by implication: "I found that I was dealing not so much with the center of things but with the peripheries. So that I became very interested in that whole dialogue between ... the circumference and the middle...."[3] The incomplete circle (the arc formed at the top of the piece) is a mate to the missing vanishing point (the titular subject of another piece of the same period to which Leaning Strata is closely related[4]) toward which the lines of the sides of the elements are converging.

On one of the preparatory drawings the distance between the circles and hence the height of each "step" of the sculpture is marked as "3," the distance in inches by which the elements progressively vary in depth. The stepping of the elements in the form, if continued according to the system established (i.e., moving at a regular rate away from the implied center) would eventuate in a spiral, Smithson's elementary crystallographic structure, which attained its greatest scale in his Spiral Jetty of 1970, now buried under the Great Salt Lake in Utah. Given the anchoring of the units on a horizontal plane, and their resultant attenuation from one end to the other, the spiral would soon become invisible despite its infinite extendability.

The possibility of infinity and the disintegration of time are suggested as well within the drawing by the simultaneous presentation of fragments of a perspectival system, cross-section, plan, and elevation, in a systematized Cubist conflation. This probably refers, too, to the geological stratification alluded to in the title, more concretely realized in the sculpture. In geology, a cross-section provides a vertical display of horizontal expanses; the distinctive features of geological strata reflect different conditions at different times, but are present in a single perceptual field at a single moment. Likewise, as Smithson has written, aerial photography and viewing resolve the changing appearance of the landscape into a single image comparable to a mapped site.[5] The aerial perspective is central to the conception of the Aerial Map—Proposal for the Dallas-Fort Worth Regional Airport Layout Plan, (1967), a formal forebear of the Walker piece.

Smithson's regression to the most undifferentiated primal realities of infinite space and the crystalline structure of matter within it through mapping devices demonstrates a philosophical quest disguised as geology. Despite its hard edges, neutral white surfaces, and clarity of form, Leaning Strata summarizes his "tendency toward primordial consciousness, a kind of tendency toward the prehistoric after digging through the histories."[6]

L.F.G.

Robert Smithson
from left:
untitled collage, circa
1966, from conic map
projection of the world with
one edge stepped in the
manner of Leaning Strata

Drawing for Leaning Strata
(side view), 1968

Drawing of earth mound-
sand gravel paths on an
Aerial Perspective of the
Dallas Fort Worth Regional
Airport Layout Plan, 1967
Courtesy John Weber
Gallery, New York

1. Quoted in an interview by Paul Cummings for the AAA, 14 and 19 July 1972, transcribed and published in Nancy Holt, ed., The Writings of Robert Smithson: Essays with Illustrations (New York: New York University Press, 1979), p. 149.
2. Robert Smithson, "Towards the Development of an Air Terminal Site," Artforum, vol. 5 (June 1967), p. 37.
3. Quoted in Holt, p. 155.
4. Smithson originally planned to show five diminishing Pointless Vanishing Points, providing a serial regression of perspective, at the Walker Art Center in 1968 (letter to Martin Friedman). An early preparatory drawing for Leaning Strata shows that he first conceived it in relation to this series, which was never realized.
5. Robert Smithson, "Aerial Art," Studio International, vol. 177 (April 1969), p. 180.
6. Smithson, quoted in Holt, p. 155.

T.L. Solien

The Bricklayer's Tender   1982

American, b. 1949

oil, enamel, beeswax on canvas

66⅛ x 90¼ (168 x 229.2)

acquired from the Getler/ Pall/Saper Gallery, New York, 1984 (Jerome Foundation Purchase Fund for Emerging Artists 84.24)

T.L. Solien's first paintings, pictographic symbols against flat fields of color, were more abstract than figurative. They led to works such as *The Bricklayer's Tender*, in which the pictographs are fleshed out, given color, dimension, and specific identities. A self-portrait dominates the upper left portion of the painting. Primitively drawn and painted, his half-yellow, half-black elongated face represents his good and evil sides. The black form beneath, though disconnected from the head, is meant to suggest his back,[1] with the camera slung around his neck, so he appears to be looking over his shoulder. He is surrounded by objects that have personal meaning and recur frequently in his work, including the tools, wheelbarrow, diamond, and candle. The candle, a symbol of knowledge, recalls for Solien a song he sang as a child in Bible class, likening faith to a candle one must allow to shine. The beehive refers to the actual making of the painting, for which he mixed homemade beeswax with oil and enamel paint.

In his youth, Solien worked summers assisting his uncle as a bricklayer's tender, and the painting also includes the tools of that trade—a wheelbarrow and a three-pronged trowel, specially designed to carry bricks. The title puns on the meaning of tender, referring both to the artist's wife, here depicted as a geisha[2] in the upper right-hand section of the canvas, and to currency. The painting itself represents potential earnings or tender. The autobiographical tone of *The Bricklayer's Tender*, one of the last two paintings Solien made prior to a long sojourn in France, is consistent with many of his paintings and works on paper of that time.

The work is still somewhat tentative, relying as much on drawing as painting. But the many objects crudely rendered against the flat, blue backdrop combine to form a whole greater than the sum of the parts, a portrait of two people that is both subjective and universal, resonating with the complexity of our conscious and unconscious selves.

M.G.

1. Conversation with the author, August 1986.
2. Solien, in WAC questionnaire, 1986.

Niles Spencer

Wake of the Hurricane   1951

American, 1893–1952

oil on canvas

30⅛ x 36⁷⁄₁₆ (76.5 x 92.6)

lower left, *Niles Spencer*—; lower right, copyright sign; on top edge of canvas, visible from reverse, *Wake of the Hurricane Niles Spencer 1951*; above this date, *42*

acquired from The Downtown Gallery, New York, 1953 (gift of the T.B. Walker Foundation 53.8)

Spencer finished this painting in early 1951 in time for an exhibition at The Downtown Gallery in early April. There is evidence of considerable reworking of the composition, which may conceivably have been originally laid out during the war years.[1] The repainting, confirmed by examination with ultraviolet light,[2] is partially visible to the naked eye—colors and contours have been shifted and replaced, sometimes more than once, in a graphic demonstration of Spencer's slow, revisionary method.

Using the title as an interpretive clue, one can read the image as a description of the heightened silence that seems to follow momentous natural events. The structure of the picture, based on two triangles meeting at the horizon line, fronted by retreating rectilinear planes, is one of asymmetrical but static balance. The sense of equilibrium is reinforced by the judicious arrangement of the earth-colored pigments, thickened to a stuccolike texture; the abstract planes seem to be as soundly built as the architecture they represent. The searchlight beams close off the central masses of the composition. The only agitation occurs in the brushstrokes; the artist's hand becomes the natural force disturbing the clean geometry of the scene.

Although Spencer's title may be metaphorical or poetic, the idea of the hurricane could have evolved during the storm season of 1950, which witnessed the greatest number of hurricanes ever recorded. *The New York Times* followed the course of a particularly vicious hurricane named "Dog" up the Atlantic coast from 3 to 12 September, when it veered away from New England toward the open sea. Spencer was then renovating a house he had just purchased in Sag Harbor, Long Island.[3] Although the hurricane never came close enough to cause serious damage, it did produce high winds and breakers in coastal areas. It may have been Spencer's anticipation that inspired the picture's subject, producing what has been described as "an almost suppressed excitement" that "invaded what had been the lyric calm of his classicism."[4]

L.F.G.

1. The work has been dated 1942–1951 in the literature on Spencer, but the basis for this has not been established. The "42" above the inscribed date on the painting's reverse may refer to 1942. No preparatory studies or handwritten records emerged to support it, however.
2. Conservation report, Foy C. Casper, Jr., April 1974.
3. Richard B. Freeman, in University of Kentucky Art Gallery, Lexington, *Niles Spencer*, exh. cat., 1965, p. 16.
4. Ibid., in reference to this and other very late paintings.

493

Richard Stankiewicz

Grass 1980–1981

American, 1922–1983

steel

151 x 104 x 37
(383.5 x 264.1 x 94)

acquired from the
Zabriskie Gallery, New
York, 1988 (gift of Judy
and Kenneth Dayton
88.10)

Stankiewicz emerged in the 1950s as an exemplar of what was then frequently characterized as "junk" sculpture. His works from that period often took the form of outlandish anthropomorphic figures assembled from fragments of old boiler tanks, chains, wire, machine parts, and other discarded metal objects. In the early 1960s he gradually moved toward a more abstract vocabulary, and in 1969 he abandoned the use of cast-offs in favor of prefabricated steel components.

Stankiewicz's use of junk materials has a logical history. As a child he lived next to a scrap yard and frequently made toys for himself from the materials he found there. Determined to pursue a career as an artist, he studied painting at the Hans Hofmann School of Fine Arts in New York City from 1948 to 1950 and spent 1950–1951 in Paris studying with Fernand Léger and the Russian sculptor Ossipe Zadkine. He made his first welded-steel constructions upon his return to New York in 1951, using pieces of scrap metal he unearthed while converting his backyard into a garden. Noticing that the found objects often had figural associations, Stankiewicz assembled them into bizarre, often humorous personages. Although these welded-steel images suggest the influence of David Smith, their whimsical character also calls to mind the sculptures Pablo Picasso created from found objects and the Surrealist images of Max Ernst, such as *The Elephant of the Celebes* (1921).

Stankiewicz's narrative impulses gave way, during the 1960s, to a more purely formal orientation. An example of this shift is his highly linear untitled work of 1962 (p. 554); though vaguely headlike, the piece defies a simple descriptive reading. During a visit to Australia in 1969, he began using prefabricated industrial materials such as plate steel, I-beams, angle irons, and pipe. As his materials became more standardized, Stankiewicz's work in the 1970s became increasingly simple and geometric, featuring compact, often cylindrical, masses rather than the gestural line of his earlier work.

Shortly before his death in 1983, Stankiewicz began reintroducing found materials and representational elements into his sculpture; it is to this period that *Grass* belongs. The work features two arched hoops at the base from which several linear pipes sprout upward. Cylindrical elements welded to these pipes give the piece a resemblance to a weedy tuft, presumably accounting for

its title. As in his earliest works, Stankiewicz here utilizes industrial materials to suggest organic forms, though in this sculpture the theme is landscape rather than figural forms. While his sculptures from the 1970s are often quite massive, *Grass* is distinguished by an elegant linearity. In this monumental work he seems effectively to have reconciled the formal simplicity and iconic character of his mid-career work with the representational allusions and calligraphic gesture of his early sculpture.

P.B.

Frank Stella

Sketch Les Indes Galantes   1962

American, b. 1936

oil on canvas

71½ x 71⅝
(181.6 x 181.9)

acquired from the Leo
Castelli Gallery, New York,
1964 (gift of the T.B.
Walker Foundation 64.26)

This work is one half of an intended pair of twin grisaille and colored Mitered Maze images forming part of a series conceived in 1962.[1] An extant sketch of the other half as planned[2] shows how the six primary and secondary colors were to be disposed along the maze in a programmatic translation of the progression of six consecutive gray-scale values that appear in the Walker work. Once Stella saw how the colors lined up he disliked the effect of emphatically repeated triangles and, after completing the grisaille version, abandoned the pendant concept for this work.[3] He continued to struggle with color as a structural element in the maze format but, as he himself realized, the lucidity of his scheme was threatened by the peculiar qualities of hues, which misleadingly complicated the work: "Thinking about color abstractly hasn't done me any real good."[4]

In the austere, declarative but richly complex grisaille version, spatial issues dominate. The tension between shallow depth and surface is heightened by the presence of the flat, unprimed canvas into which the edges of the bands physically bleed, in contrast to the illusory back-and-forth movement of the graded and alternated non-colors. A slight sense of recession from periphery to center is subtly provoked by the quarter-inch increase in width of the four outer-most bands. The spatial paradoxes in these works are precipitated by Stella's device of jogging the diagonal running from lower left to upper right, which leaves the vertical white band at the right with an open orthogonal end, like the entrance to a maze. Stella was interested in mazes for their structural rather than psychological implications, and he dispels the illusion of an open path spiraling through space in various ways: he systematically alters the values of the mitered bands, separates them with negative "lines" of raw canvas, and organizes them to function as distinct units contained in one of four discrete triangular fields, thereby emphasizing them as individual "meanders" of color.[5] As hard-edged, visually projecting and receding parts of a whole, the bands also suggested sculptural possibilities to Stella, which materialized in studies for a ceiling based on the mitered maze in which polychromed plaster bands were designed to progressively descend to form an inverted coffer.[6]

Stella has compared the pictorial space of this work to that of a stage. The title refers to an opera-ballet by the composer Jean-Philippe Rameau, first performed in 1735, which Stella has described as "a Frenchman's idea of the new world."[7] He felt that the black and white palette of the Walker study not only alluded to the harpsichord keyboard, but also captured "the rhythm" and "ordered sense" of Rameau's music.[8]

L.F.G.

1. Frank Stella drew a series of about eleven pairs of concentric square and Mitered Maze studies for paintings whose stretchers he ordered all at once; (information from Barbara Rose, published by Ronald Alley in his *Catalogue of The Tate Gallery's Collection of Modern Art Other than Works by British Artists* (London: The Tate Gallery in association with Sotheby Parke Bernet, 1981), p. 707.
2. Colored pencil on graph paper, 1964 (collection Jonathan D. Scull, New York).
3. Stella, in conversation with Kay Bearman of the Leo Castelli Gallery, who conveyed his comments to Jan van der Marck, Walker Art Center, letter of 2 July 1965. In the sketch, opposite triangles are closely related, sharing the same colors and value rhythm (A-B-C laterally and A-B-B vertically).
4. From a 1966 interview, quoted by William Rubin in The Museum of Modern Art, New York, *Frank Stella,* exh. cat., 1970, p. 80.
5. The Museum of Modern Art, p. 46.
6. Martin Friedman, videotaped interview with Stella, 22 February 1982.
7. Ibid.
8. Ibid.

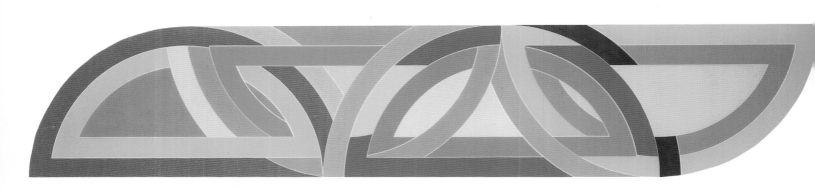

Frank Stella

Damascus Gate Stretch Variation 1968

American, b. 1936

acrylic on canvas

60 x 300¾
(152.4 x 763.9)

on reverse, central
vertical stretcher member,
F. Stella '68

acquired from the
Lawrence Rubin Gallery,
New York, 1969 (gift of
Mr. and Mrs. Edmond
R. Ruben, 69.6)

The Protractor series represented a significant departure for Stella: for the first time, limited and self-contradictory overlapping complicated the spatial activity in his work. He had conceived the Protractor series about 1965 as three versions with thirteen variations each; by 1969, he had projected thirty-one formats in three versions.[1] He named these works, derived from serially linked protractor elements, after ancient circular plan towns in Asia Minor that he knew from an archaeological text[2] and from a trip to Iran with Henry Geldzahler at the invitation of Stanley Woodward, an art collector and retired diplomat:

> The trip was a very big experience for me.... There's all that interlacing, or interweaving, in barbarian decoration.... I'd touched on it in my thesis at Princeton [on Hiberno-Saxon manuscript illumination]. Things doubling back on themselves, like snakes swallowing their tails. This came out in the Protractor pictures.[3]

The non-imagistic, ornamental aspects of Middle Eastern architectural reliefs also appealed to Stella. One of his primary concerns has been to elevate so-called decorative art to the status of abstract painting by strengthening its structure: "I would like to combine the abandon and indulgence of Matisse's *Dance* with the overall strength and sheer formal inspiration of a picture like his *Moroccans*."[4] The arched contours, swooping rhythms, lateral extension, and architectural scale show a clear connection with the two versions of Matisse's *La Danse* of the early 1930s.

In its exaggerated length, the picture evokes the mid-nineteenth-century panoramas of the Mississippi River exhibited at the time as continous visual travelogues unscrolled between two spools, a reference that Stella intended. In an undated page of his notes, he mentions John Banvard's 440-yard canvas and Henry Lewis's 1,325-yard work,[5] two of the most well-known panoramas. Not only the size but the idea of movement were inspirations for the Protractors: "the color should travel here ... like a rolling hoop ... having the energy and the resilience to spring itself along."[6] Stella's painting process was similarly continuous: once he had applied the tape to control the edges, he painted the work uninterruptedly, not rethinking the colors but only reinforcing some with a second or third coat.[7]

L.F.G.

1. According to Frederick Castle, "What's That, the '68 Stella? Wow!," *Art News*, vol. 66 (January 1968), p. 64, Stella first conceived the series while working on his eccentrically shaped canvases about 1965; William S. Rubin, in The Museum of Modern Art, New York, *Frank Stella*, exh. cat., 1970, p. 127, stated that they first date from 1967.
2. Castle, p. 64.
3. Quoted in Calvin Tomkins, "Profiles: The Space Around Real Things," *The New Yorker*, 10 September 1984, p. 84.
4. Quoted in Rubin, p. 149.
5. The notebook page was published by Christian Geelhaar, in Kunstmuseum Basel, *Frank Stella Working Drawings / Zeichnungen 1956–1970*, exh. cat., 1980, p. 70. Several books on the subject of the panoramas would have been available to Stella, including one by John Francis McDermott, *The Lost Panoramas of the Mississippi* (Chicago: The University of Chicago Press, 1958).
6. Quoted in Martin Friedman, videotaped interview with Stella, 22 February 1982.
7. Ibid.

Henri Matisse
La Danse II 1931–1933
oil on canvas
140½ x 564
(356.9 x 1,432.6)
Collection The Barnes
Foundation, Merion
Station, Pennsylvania

Frank Stella

Loomings 3X 1986

American, b. 1936

ink, oil on etched
magnesium and aluminum

142⅞ x 162½ x 44
(361 x 412.8 x 111.8)

acquired from M. Knoedler
& Co., 1987 (gift of Joan
and Gary Capen 87.8)

Loomings 3X is the first of a proposed series of eleven works by Frank Stella to be titled after the chapter headings in Herman Melville's *Moby Dick*. In this piece Stella continues a trend established in the mid-1970s, when he began using honeycomb aluminum—a product commonly used in airplane fuselages—to create relief compositions that protrude from the wall.

In spite of its three-dimensionality and relative lack of applied color, the artist still thinks of this work in terms of painting rather than sculpture. The central ribbonlike form is conceived as a brushstroke freed from the surface of a canvas. "I consider such work my effort to make painting more fluid. Indeed, my interests are fluidity and surface deformations."[1] In his recent work, Stella has sought to reintroduce a sense of spatial density and drama that he believes has been absent from modern painting since the advent of Cubism.[2]

Stella did not set out to create a fundamentally monochromatic work, but once the elements were installed on the wall he was impressed by the silver tones of the unpainted aluminum and magnesium parts and decided to retain this quality.[3] He did, however, create subtle variations in tone and effect by lacquering, polishing, and etching the diverse elements.

In *Loomings*, Stella continues a practice that has typified his career: achieving a new expression—in this case, of monumental grand drama—while building logically upon the foundation of earlier work. He utilizes a number of favorite motifs that can be found in other series: the French curve from the Exotic Birds and Indian Birds series of the 1970s; the column from the Pillars and Cones series of the 1980s; the triangle from the recent Malta series; and the evenly spaced parallel lines from his Stripe paintings of the late 1950s and early 1960s. The presence of unpainted metallic surfaces was a feature of the South African Mines series of the mid-80s and is also reminiscent of earlier works like the aluminum and copper paintings of the early 1960s.

For this and other proposed pieces in the series, Stella began by making a number of paper models. The most successful of these were translated into lightweight metal compositions made three times larger than the paper originals. Some of these scale models, including the model for *Loomings*, were then cast in bronze. *Loomings* is the first work in the series to be realized in full scale.

As has been Stella's usual practice, the work was titled after it was created. The title did not therefore influence the content or the form of the work, but it does provide it with an added element of associative resonance.

P.B.

1. Martin Friedman, conversation with Stella, February 1987.
2. See Frank Stella, *Working Space* (Cambridge, Massachusetts: Harvard University Press, 1986).
3. Martin Friedman, conversation with Stella.

Joseph Stella

American Landscape 1929

American, b. Italy,
1877–1946

oil on canvas

79⅛ x 39⁵⁄₁₆ (201 x 99.9)

on reverse, lower right,
photographed in 1957
before relining, partly
visible through lining, in
the artist's hand, *Joseph
Stella/New York March/
1929*; on central member
of original stretcher,
*Cooperative Gallery—
Newark/June 1937*[1]

Cooperative Gallery,
Newark, 1937;
acquired by Arthur F.
Egner; acquired from the
Knoedler Gallery, New
York, 1957 (gift of the
T.B. Walker Foundation
57.15)

The Brooklyn Bridge, designed by John Roebling
and completed in 1883, was euphorically celebrated by artists, poets, and photographers
working in the United States during the first
decades of the twentieth century. The contrast
between the monumental neo-Gothic construction
of its granite towers and the technological
wizardry of its cable suspension system provided
a subject that was rich with visual and metaphorical possibilities. In his essay "The Brooklyn
Bridge (A Page of My Life),"[2] Stella describes his
first impressions of the structure, a "shrine containing all the efforts of the new civilization of
AMERICA," which awakened his passionate
desire to challenge the engineering achievements
of modern technology with the "gigantic art" of
his paintings. In his autobiographical notes he describes his nocturnal visits to the bridge when he
was living in the Williamsburg section of Brooklyn
during the last years of World War I. Calling on
"the soaring verse of Walt Whitman and ... the
fiery Poe's plasticity," he confronted his subject
on canvas:

> Upon the swarming darkness of the night, I rung all
> the bells of alarm with the blaze of electricity
> scattered in lightnings down the oblique cables, the
> dynamic pillars of my composition, and to render more
> pungent the mystery of the metallic apparition, through
> the green and red glare of the signals I excavated here
> and there caves as subterranean passages to infernal
> recesses.[3]

Stella's complex, Wagnerian vision of the
bridge was explored in paintings such as *Brooklyn
Bridge,* circa 1919, and *New York Interpreted* of
1920–1922. He had hoped to include one of
these in his 1930 show at the Galerie Sloden in
Paris, but apparently substituted *American
Landscape.*[4] This version departs from the earlier
ones in that the axis is off center, with the
eastern tower in the foreground cropped, one of
its archways revealing the distant western tower.
The elongation of the archway produces an
outline that echoes the silhouettes of the
skyscrapers to the right, and intimates the
spiritualizing content of the painting; extreme
variations of texture, from thick impasto and
grainy drops of paint to thin, scraped areas and
exposed primed canvas, heighten the expressionism of the work.

L.F.G.

1. Stella's handwriting was identified by his nephew Sergio
Stella, in conversation with the author, 18 March 1987. As
it is known that Stella moved from Paris to Italy in
December of 1928 (from a letter to Carl Weeks, 1 June
1929, Whitney Museum of American Art Papers, AAA), it
seems more likely that "New York" refers to the subject,
rather than to the place of execution as it ordinarily would
in Stella's inscriptions. It may be that the Walker work was
the *New York, 1929,* shown at the Valentine Gallery in a
1931 one-man show called *Paintings Done in Africa and
Europe during 1929–1931* (no. 1). In a letter of 7
December 1931 (Whitney Museum of American Art Papers,
AAA, Reel 346), Pierce Williams expressed to Stella his
delight in the latter's ongoing interest in the problems set
out by the Brooklyn Bridge as demonstrated at his
Valentine Gallery show; as *New York* is the only title in the
show referring to an American subject, it seems plausible
that this was the work in question, sent over by Stella from
Europe.
2. The essay was first published by Stella himself in a
monograph prepared during the mid-1920s; it was reissued
in the Paris periodical *Transition,* nos. 16–17 (June 1929),
pp. 86–88.
3. "Autobiographical Notes by Joseph Stella," typescript
given to Lloyd Goodrich by Stella in February 1946, p. 6
(microfilmed copy in the Whitney Museum of American Art
Papers, AAA, Reel N689).
4. See Irma B. Jaffe, *Joseph Stella* (Cambridge,
Massachusetts: Harvard University Press, 1970), no. 91,
p. 190 n.1.

Clyfford Still

Untitled 1950

American, 1904–1980

oil on canvas

117 x 81¾
(297.2 x 207.7)

lower left, in white paint,
Clyfford 1950; on reverse,
lower left, in blue crayon
or pencil, *Clyfford/1950-C
/82 x 116*

Bert Kleiner, Beverly Hills;
Sam Levin; acquired by
Noah Goldowsky for Jason
Art Investments Corp.,
Chicago, while on loan
from Levin to the Los
Angeles County Museum
of Art, 1961–1963;
returned to Goldowsky on
consignment; acquired
through Noah Goldowsky,
Inc., 1972 (Art Center
Acquisition Fund and gift
of Judy and Kenneth
Dayton, Suzanne Walker
and Thomas N. Gilmore,
Mr. and Mrs. Richardson
B. Okie, and Mr. and Mrs.
Hall J. Peterson 72.9)

Explaining the notations that serve as titles for his work (in this case, 1950-C [PH-337]), Still compared the single painting to an entry in a journal recording his interior experience.[1] He described his artistic process as a solitary ethical journey,[2] and each painting as an "instrument of thought," an extension and exaltation of his self and its contradictions. As in contemporaneous pictures by Newman and Rothko, color replaced form as the bearer of meaning in his work. In diary notes of 11 February 1956, he wrote of his identification with color in typically passionate, grandiose terms:

> Like Belmonte weaving the pattern of his being by twisting the powerful bulls around him, I seem to achieve a comparable ecstasy in bringing forth the flaming life through these large responsive areas of canvas. And as the blues or reds or blacks leap and quiver in their tenuous ambience or rise in austere thrusts to carry their power infinitely beyond the boundaries of the limiting field, I move with them.[3]

Still's aim was to relieve color of its traditionally "pleasant, luminous, and symbolic" aspects,[4] and to heighten its expressive potential through selection, juxtaposition, and method of application—he laid his paint down in craggy slabs with a palette knife to animate the picture's surface without suggesting recognizable shapes. He delighted in the sensible and evocative qualities of color, and was acutely attuned to variations of hue and value. Color corrections he submitted to a magazine reproducing this work provide a revealing and useful document of such responses. In these instructions he specified that the red was not "alizarine but slightly sharper than deep cadmium," the blue was an "intense ultramarine—rather bright for it has some white in it," the ocher at the upper right "an intentional minor note." The black was "all black. Much of it is heavy impasto so there is some textural reflection in places. But it is an intense lamp black."[5] The large body of mineral orange pigment, which varies in warmth over the canvas, was "redder than a cadmium orange. It has a fiery quality." The light cadmium red line on the left which trickles down almost to the bottom was intentional. Synopsizing the color relations, he wrote that "the colors and values are crisply differentiated and the contrasts between the

orange, the red and the ochre are sharply clear, the black acting as a binder or unifier of images and color-chords."[6]

As in an orchestral composition, to which he often compared his work,[7] variation, combination, and repetition occur within an instantaneously apprehended totality that is artificially bounded, whether by the walls of the concert hall or the edges of the canvas. Still rejected the concept of pictures as windows, considering them infinitely expansive in themselves, and avoided the use of frames as artificially limiting.[8]

L.F.G.

1. J. Benjamin Townsend, "An Interview with Clyfford Still," *Albright Art Gallery Notes*, vol. 24 (Summer 1961), p. 9. The date, number, and letter titles, as Still frequently explained, are arbitrary designations intended to facilitate identification; the "PH" number refers to his photographic archive.
2. See his letter to Gordon Smith in The Buffalo Fine Arts Academy, Albright Art Gallery, *Paintings by Clyfford Still*, exh. cat., 1959, n.p.
3. Quoted in Townsend, p. 14.
4. From a letter to Thomas B. Hess, communicated by Patricia A. (Mrs. Clyfford) Still in a WAC questionnaire, 27 October 1981. In this questionnaire she also supplied Still's lengthy analysis of the physical properties of his pictures and his conservation recommendations for them.
5. Quoted in San Francisco Museum of Modern Art, *Clyfford Still*, exh. cat., 1976, p. 14.
6. In this detailed analysis, he does not mention the crucial band of yellow at the lower right, which had no doubt already been cropped from the reproduction of the photograph. The dabs of red vivifying the lower edge of the black, remnants of an underlying red field that now shows through cracks in the black, likewise go unregistered in the reproduction and unmentioned by Still.
7. See Mrs. Still's questionnaire, cited above.
8. Information sent to Michael R. Klein, Walker Art Center, by Mrs. Clyfford Still, 6 July 1977.

Michelle Stuart

Niagara II, Niagara Gorge   1976

American, b. 1938

shale on muslin-mounted
rag paper

156 x 62 (396.2 x 157.5)

acquired from the artist,
1983 (McKnight
Acquisition Fund and Art
Center Acquisition Fund,
83.16)

This work belongs to a group of huge drawings made by Stuart in the 1970s, which are often referred to as scrolls. Ten to twenty feet in length, they have a sensual, majestic presence that borders on the sculptural. They appear to be slices out of the earth itself and are, indeed, derived from the earth's pigments. Stuart's medium is, literally, the earth, which she has excavated on-site and then, back in the studio, methodically beaten and rubbed into the surface of heavy, muslin-backed paper. Through this process of grinding large chunks of shale, rocks, and loose soil, the paper is embossed and tinted by the earth.

Niagara II, Niagara Gorge is named for the place that the shale came from, Niagara Gorge in Lewiston, New York. (Both the red Queenston and gray shales used come from this site.) Stuart spent time there in 1975 working on an on-site piece, *Niagara Gorge Path Relocated*, where she laid 460 feet of her standard width paper (62 inches) down a cliff face that had been the original site of the nearby falls.[1] This earth-encrusted work has a shimmering verticality that could be said to evoke a waterfall.

Underlying the strong formal qualities of Stuart's work are her various interests in geological history, Neolithic societies, myth, and ritual. Her art derives from visits to the Southwest, Central America, the Galapagos Islands, Morocco, and other places whose history and geology are of particular interest. At Niagara Gorge, the earth has a substratum of red iron oxide that has been hidden by time but is brought to the surface—fossilized, so to speak—in the work. "I've always been interested in things that exist but are not a part of our tangible reality. They are incredibly important in determining our pattern of existence," Stuart has said.[2] The artist's working process, in which she pounds, rubs, and fuses the earth's pigment with the fiber of the paper, takes on a meditative, ritualistic character. She quarries not only the earth, but cultural patterns hidden in its layers—investing the paper, in a sense, with a kind of "memory."

E.A.

1. Lawrence Alloway, in Hillwood Art Gallery, Long Island University, C.W. Post Center, Greenvale, New York, *Michelle Stuart: Voyages*, exh. cat., 1985, p. 50.
2. Quoted in Walker Art Center, *Viewpoints: Michelle Stuart: Place and Time*, exh. brochure, 1983.

George Sugarman

Yellow Top 1959

American, b. 1912

acrylic on laminated wood

**89 x 46 x 34
(226.1 x 116.8 x 86.4)**

**acquired from the Stephen
Radich Gallery, New York,
1966 (gift of the
T.B.Walker Foundation
66.19)**

In order to more completely separate the forms he was using to clarify space, Sugarman introduced color in his wood multiform sculptures for the first time with *Yellow Top*.[1] Like Stuart Davis, for whom he has expressed his admiration, he understood that "what is important is that two colors are not in the same place," that color determines spatial relations by its inherent power to suggest advancement and retreat. He uses store-bought colors, generally unmixed, sharing Davis's opinion that it is not the exoticism or subtlety of the colors but how they are put to use as spatial definers that should concern the artist. Sugarman recently explained that he arrived at the color relations of *Yellow Top* empirically, having applied a dozen different layers of paint,[2] beginning from the top and working down in an inversion of the way he built up the forms. By distinguishing the base coloristically he enabled it to work as a constituent formal element rather than simply an engineering device.

The cantilevered spreading and rising of this column of fluttering forms, suggesting instability, weightlessness, and motion, create a structure more frequently encountered in painting than in sculpture. The forms in *Yellow Top* can be seen as magnified skins of paint shredded, cut, folded, stiffened, and bent, propped up and apart by white braces, layering space rather than filling it. Although the denseness of the laminated wood is suggested by the hewn light-capturing and reflecting surfaces, other qualities of the material are concealed.

Sugarman was not content to have color serve as the sole demarcator of form, and has remembered that immediately after finishing *Yellow Top* he realized that he was only distinguishing forms of the same family.[3] The other attachment to traditional sculpture was the persistence of the figural reference. Despite the subtly engineered, Cubistic floating of planes in all directions, and the absence of a central core, a sense of figure or growing organism persists in the overall vertical clustering complex. Sugarman was soon to disrupt this monolithic unity by varying elements more fundamentally, and more radically subverting the subordination of parts to the whole.

L.F.G.

1. He did not, as some authors have suggested, originally conceive the work as unpainted; conversation with the author, 29 October 1986.
2. See Holliday T. Day, in Joslyn Art Museum, Omaha, *Shape of Space: The Sculpture of George Sugarman*, exh. cat., 1982, p. 29.
3. Interview by Sidney Simon, "George Sugarman," *Art International*, vol. 11 (20 May 1967), p. 22.

Donald Sultan

Forest Fire, April 13, 1984   1984

American, b. 1951

latex, tar, vinyl on Masonite

**four panels
96 x 96½
(243.8 x 245.1) overall**

on reverse, lower right panel, *Forest Fire April 13 1984 DS*

acquired from the Blum Helman Gallery, 1984 (T.B. Walker Acquisition Fund 84.1152)

Sultan is one of a group of artists who, since the late 1970s, has been looking for a new way to bring recognizable imagery back into art. His large paintings feature massive, weighted images of simplified shapes such as tulips, smokestacks, and lemons. These forms are often manipulated by his use of scale and materials, placing emphasis on their abstract qualities. Although the images border on the abstract, they are meant to be recognizable and, to reinforce this idea, Sultan gives them simple descriptive titles.

Forest Fire, April 13, 1984 deals with one of Sultan's favorite themes: the difficult relationship between man and nature. In this painting, the heavy, static forms of the cypress trees in the foreground are contrasted with leaping, gestural flames burning out of control in the trees behind. The viewer's vantage point is uncertain, but could be from a car. Sultan, in fact, remembers driving through a forest fire on a road in Georgia and seeing the flames light up the trees close to the road.[1]

This painting is one of a series of Forest Fire paintings that Sultan evolved from earlier imagery of factories and smokestacks; these, in turn, had come out of his flower imagery. The branchlike structures on fire in the background of *Forest Fire, April 13, 1984*, which look like burning ship masts, later developed into a mysterious painting of silhouetted masts at dusk.[2] The metamorphosis that occurs as Sultan moves from one picture to the next has an internal logic, a natural flow which allows room for free association and chance. By incorporating into the title the date on which he finishes each work, he keeps a running record of his imagery.

The thick surfaces of Sultan's paintings are composed of vinyl tiles—portions of which he leaves untouched. The parts that he covers are first drawn upon; he then softens specific areas with a blowtorch, scraping away the surface and filling it in with either tar or plaster, then painting it over. The tiles are affixed to Masonite, backed by heavy plywood and attached by steel rods to rectangular stretcher bars. With their built-in density, reinforced by the mass of Sultan's simplified forms, the paintings have a powerful, emphatic presence.

E.A.

1. Marge Goldwater, interview with Sultan, 2 May 1984.
2. Carolyn Christov-Bakargiev, "Donald Sultan," *Flash Art*, no. 128 (May–June 1986), pp. 48–50.

Robert Therrien

No Title 1986

American, b. 1947

lacquer, electroplating
with gold on bronze

35½ x 16 x 16
(90.2 x 40.6 x 40.6)

acquired from the Leo
Castelli Gallery, New
York, 1987 (Walker
Special Purchase Fund
87.54)

Robert Therrien's work plays on the related themes of memory and abstraction. Much as memory abstracts incident according to its most psychologically compelling aspects, Therrien pares form down to its essential components. Since the mid-1970s he has restricted himself to a limited lexicon of forms which he continually reworks in an effort to coax new implications from familiar subjects. Despite their apparent simplicity, his sculptures abound in paradox. Whether rendered in relief or as freestanding works, they fluctuate between two and three dimensions, between representation and abstraction, between object and image. At once laconic yet resonant, they are personal icons elevated to the level of archetypal symbols, their warm, glowing surfaces echoing the richness of their associations.

Many of Therrien's motifs are rooted in childhood experience: "I try to stay with themes or objects or sources I can trace back to my personal history. The further back I can trace something as being meaningful to me in some way or another ... the more I am attracted to it."[1] The snowman is rooted in memories of his boyhood in Chicago, when building snowmen provided him with his first glimmer of sculptural awareness.

Therrien's simplified rendering of the image—three stacked balls of diminishing size—strengthens the allusion to childhood. But this reductive tendency is also a legacy of his education in the early 1970s when Minimalist aesthetics were dominant. It was the elemental nature of the snowman that appealed to him: "The first sculpture ever made for decorative purposes might have had that structure—a pile of three rocks."[2]

Therrien has, however, sought to reinvigorate what he views as the excessively cerebral and restrictive Minimalist canon by infusing his work with allusion. He tinkers endlessly with his images, altering their dimensions, weight, color, surfaces, proportions, and materials, in an effort to come up with the "perfect" image, one that can absorb the widest variety of associations. In this way, he strives on the one hand to achieve a paradigmatic image and on the other to rediscover the unexpected in the familiar. For Therrien, the true content in any given work lies in what that image stirs up in the mind and memory of the viewer, hence his affinity with Surrealism and Symbolism as well as Minimalism.

The snowman first appeared in Therrien's work in 1981 as a drawing of three stacked circles.[3] As with most of his other images, he has rendered it in drawing, relief, and freestanding sculpture. There are currently five freestanding versions of the snowman, the earliest of which dates from 1984. All are silver in color except for the Walker's, which is golden.

P.B.

1. Quoted in Wade Saunders, "Talking Objects: Interviews with Ten Younger Sculptors," *Art in America*, vol. 73 (November 1985), p. 136.
2. Ibid.
3. Michael Auping, "Robert Therrien," in Albright-Knox Art Gallery, Buffalo, *Structure to Resemblance: Work by Eight American Sculptors*, exh. cat., 1987, p. 55.

Jantje Visscher

Horizon 1982

American, b. 1933

acrylic, graphite, mica, fiberglass

88 x 161 (223.5 x 408.9)

acquired from the C.G. Rein Galleries, 1986 (Walker Special Purchase Fund 86.27)

Jantje Visscher created the subtle and elegant *Horizon* in an elaborate process that took nearly a year's time and involved the fabrication of three layers of fiberglass veil to which a layer of fabric is affixed from behind. To the fiberglass, she meticulously applied many yards of auto-striping tape and spray-painted those areas that remained uncovered. Using a precise working drawing to guide her, the artist began the painting by drawing a series of horizontal rules one-half inch apart that span the entire surface of the painting, and then drawing a series of lines that radiate from a center point at the top. All of these lines are still visible. At every point of intersection, she drew a line at a right angle connecting the horizontals. She then taped along the pencil lines and sprayed a light blue paint, which, when applied to the fiberglass, gives a velvety texture. Darker at the center and lighter at the perimeter, the soft blue provides a distinctly heavenly cast.

This work, the second in Visscher's Moiré series, is her first large-scale fiberglass painting and was inspired by a similar drawing she had done directly on the walls of the WARM Gallery in downtown Minneapolis in 1980 in the manner of Sol LeWitt, who, along with Agnes Denes, has been an important influence. When *Horizon* first was exhibited Visscher accompanied it with a line by the Spanish poet Federico García Lorca, "I've lost myself many times at sea." The strong suggestion of a horizon line in combination with the blue overtones in this abstract work argues for an alternate reading as seascape, which the citation implies. The undulating surface further promotes this interpretation of the work.

The meditative spirit of the painting recalls the aspirations of a previous generation of artists as well as composers. Its seriality invites comparison not only with such artists as LeWitt, but also with contemporary composers such as Steve Reich and Philip Glass. Eleanor Heartney has observed: "This creation of music out of repetition of simple building blocks of sound is a startling analogue to Visscher's procedure. [Glass and Visscher] build hypnotic fields whose perceptual complexities belie their simple constructions."[1]

By working on a large scale, Visscher creates a vast surface in which viewers can become immersed and lose themselves in what has been described as a "meditative net." The discrepancy between the undulating waves one sees in this painting and what Visscher has actually drawn and painted is part of her ongoing inquiry into the nature of perception and the relationship between nature and geometry.

M.G.

1. Eleanor Heartney, in The Minneapolis Institute of Arts, Minnesota Artists' Exhibition Program, *Jantje Visscher: Harmonic States*, exh. cat., 1984, n.p.

Ursula von Rydingsvard

Five Mountains 1989

American, b. Germany,
1942

graphite, stained cedar

**61¼ x 102 x 70
(155.6 x 259.1 x 177.8)**

**acquired from the Lorence
Monk Gallery, New York,
1990 (T.B. Walker
Acquisition Fund 90.71)**

In characterizing her work, Ursula von Rydingsvard resists too close an alliance with the formal tradition of wood sculpture. While she acknowledges deep respect for Constantin Brancusi's geometric abstractions of nature and for Louise Nevelson's monumental wooden assemblages, she finds a genuine kinship with artists of obsessive vision and deep commitment to the exploration of materials. Among direct inspirations for her massive wooden constructions she cites Alberto Giacometti's surrealistic abstractions and Louise Bourgeois's sensually infused biomorphic forms. Von Rydingsvard works with milled, four-by-four-inch cedar boards specifically because they are distanced from their origin in nature. She is interested in wood because it is a pliable medium, one that yields readily under her hand.

Five Mountains originated, as does much of von Rydingsvard's sculpture, from fragments of unfinished works. In this case, she used an extraneous element discovered in her studio as a base from which she built up the final form in an improvisational manner.[1] As she had done previously, she first carved the ends of the individual boards, then laminated them together and performed finish carving to unify the piece. Because the sculpture is wrought at near human scale, the viewer responds to the forms comprising it almost as if they were figures. Nonetheless, *Five Mountains* is filled with earthbound allusions. It can be seen to evoke a cluster of mysterious miniature burial mounds, or perhaps a group of primitive sanctuaries and dwellings.

One critic has characterized the disorientation the viewer feels when confronted with these shifts in scale: "In their modest theatricality [von Rydingsvard's sculptures] put us in the world of *Gulliver's Travels*, reversing the relationship to which we are accustomed.... It is like the world of a child, without the promise that we will grow up to dominate it."[2]

Von Rydingsvard's uncomplicated respect for her materials and forms is indeed like that of a child. Her simple approach to weight, mass, scale, and the evocative power of forms comes, in part, from her upbringing in rural Germany. Utilitarian objects with which she was familiar during her childhood, such as spoons, instruments, and furniture, are savored and juxtaposed to form quiet, poetic abstractions such as *Mandolin Shovel*, *Spoon Altar*, and *Confessor's Chair* (all 1989). The viewer is led to respond empathetically to such works, partaking in the reverential feelings with which they are imbued.

C.B.

1. Conversation with the artist, 7 May 1990.
2. Saul Osterow, "Blow by Blow: A Working Metaphor," in Lorence Monk Gallery, New York, *Ursula von Rydingsvard*, exh. cat., 1990, n.p.

Andy Warhol

16 Jackies 1964

American, 1928–1987

acrylic, enamel on canvas

sixteen panels
20 x 16 (51 x 40.6) each
80⅜ x 64⅜
(204.2 x 163.5) overall

**acquired from the Leo
Castelli Gallery, New York,
1968 (Art Center
Acquisition Fund 68.2)**

Although Warhol was already impressed with the glamour of Jackie Kennedy by 1962,[1] he was unmoved by the news of John Kennedy's assassination the following year. He later recalled:

> I heard the news over the radio when I was alone painting in my studio. I don't think I missed a stroke. I wanted to know what was going on out there, but that was the extent of my reaction.... Henry Geldzahler wanted to know why I wasn't more upset, so I told him about the time I was walking in India and saw a bunch of people in a clearing having a ball because somebody they really liked had just died and how I realized then that everything was just how you decided to think about it. I'd been thrilled having Kennedy as president; he was handsome, young, smart—but it didn't bother me that much that he was dead. What bothered me was the way the television and radio were programming everybody to feel so sad. It seemed like no matter how hard you tried, you couldn't get away from the thing.... John Quinn, the playwright ... was moaning over and over, "But Jackie was the most glamorous First Lady we'll ever get."[2]

For Warhol, the visual means for expressing detachment from emotions, an attitude he regarded as characteristic of the 1960s in general,[3] was through the replication of images. Like the droning repetition of newscasts, the device dissipates meaning, and with it the capacity of images to move or disturb: "The more you look at the same exact thing, the more the meaning goes away and the better and emptier you feel."[4]

The sixteen faces of Jackie Kennedy in Warhol's painting were blown up from four news photos that appeared ubiquitously in the media after the assassination. From top to bottom, the images are of Jackie smiling at Love Field on arrival in Dallas; stunned at the swearing-in ceremony for L.B.J. on Air Force One after the president's death; grieving at the Capitol; and in the limousine before the shooting. The top three appeared in the 24 November and 6 December 1963 issues of *Life* magazine: the first by an unidentified photographer; the second and third by Cecil Stoughton and Fred Ward, respectively; the source for the bottom one has not been identified, although a U.P.I. photograph similar to it was reproduced in *Newsweek*. Eventually, in Warhol's view, these images became so familiar that neutral identification is all that the viewer experiences.

Warhol makes this point by repeating each of the four images of Jackie four times, in a simple, well-designed non-sequential alternation of strips of "before and after" pictures. The high-contrast, low-information pictures, each as different from the others as one reproduction from another, are cropped to focus on Jackie's face, rhythmically directed one way along one row and then the other along the next. A deliberately careless look gives the painting a sense of chance and hurry, suggesting the quick duplication and dissemination of images.[5] Additionally, expressivity is, in a sense, absent from the images themselves. Public expectation forces the face of the politician's wife into a perpetual, meaningless smile, while shock renders the widow as inexpressive and numb as one of Warhol's somnambulant superstars. The two faces, perceived by Warhol as equally unreal, have been further sapped of meaning by the mythologizing American culture and the techniques of reproduction, and are finally emptied of meaning by the artist's stylization.

L.F.G.

1. See Andy Warhol and Pat Hackett, *PoPism: The Warhol '60s* (New York and London: Harcourt Brace Jovanovich, 1980), p. 36.
2. Ibid., p. 60.
3. Andy Warhol, *The Philosophy of Andy Warhol* (New York and London: Harcourt Brace Jovanovich, 1975), p. 27.
4. Warhol, *PoPism*, p. 50. It is interesting to note that *16 Jackies* ignited the passion of a vandal who inscribed the words "HOGWASH/USA" on the panel third from the top on the leftmost column and "BLACK" on the panel second from the top on the rightmost column in ballpoint pen in November 1967; the inscriptions were successfully removed by Daniel Goldreyer in New York by late January 1968.
5. Warhol describes the silkscreening process he used, which allowed him to turn the work of reproducing the design over to Gerard Malanga and other assistants: "You pick a photograph, blow it up, transfer it in glue onto silk, and then roll ink across it so the ink goes through the silk but not through the glue. That way you get the same image, slightly different each time. It was all so simple—quick and chancy;" Warhol, *PoPism*, p. 22.

H.C. Westermann

A Piece from the Museum of Shattered Dreams 1965

American, 1922–1981

cedar, pine, ebony, rope, twine

28⅞ x 23½ x 15½
(73.4 x 59.7 x 39.4)

in incised anchor contours, top of base, *HCW/SF/65*; on right edge, in thickness of base, *A PIECE FROM THE MUSEUM OF SHATTERED DREAMS MADE OF PINE-CEDAR & EBONY. OIL FINISH.*; on bottom of base, *PIECE REPAIRED & REFINISHED/IN 1970—H.C.W.*[1]

acquired from the Allan Frumkin Gallery, New York, 1966 (gift of the T.B. Walker Foundation 66.45)

Although generally reticent about discussing his work, Westermann described the ideas that generated the Walker sculpture with particular intensity:

> Everybody has marvelous illusions and dreams.... And [for] so many people, it just never happens. It's a real tragedy, you know. Their dreams just never come true.... It's a very, very sad thing and it's been bugging me for years. You know how many people have these magnificent dreams, and everybody does, and so few people realize them. It's a terrible thing.

He went on to envision a museum of "god-damned great buildings for everybody that had dreams that never came true, some kind of memorial to them."[2] Westermann nevertheless would not apply these ideas specifically to the iconography of the work, insisting that his aim was simply "to make a beautiful piece."[3] The scroll-ended ornamental motifs attached to the central shaft were "purely functional elements" with "vaguely classical" features. The topmost form "isn't really any shape of anything." However, his comment that this shape "is supposed to look like something tied up,"[4] suggests that his disavowal of symbolic intention may be somewhat disingenuous. Elevated above a wooden sea on which the passage of sharks is indicated by their fins and by the motion lines in the wood, the ambiguous form may be construed as the victim of "shattered dreams"—a stranded, threatened, bound, mute, immobilized, and bloated body whose options are suicide or stagnation.[5]

The natural media Westermann used show his interest in the paradoxical mutation of substances. Here, the liquid, agitated nature of the sea is contradicted, though the qualities of density and flatness of the wood that represents it are respected. Conversely, the ambiguous bound object is carved to appear elastic in a way that wood is not. The artist takes advantage of the varieties of wood to distinguish forms by color and texture, as if they were indeed made of different substances: ebony is used for the shark's fins, and laminated, oil-stained cedar for the sea, the architectural motif, and the bound form.

The incised anchor that bears data on the execution of the work is Westermann's Kilroy, accompanying his signature on letters and recurring throughout his work. Not only is it a memory of the three crucial years he spent as a Marine on the U.S.S. Enterprise in the Pacific during World War II,[6] but it can also be read as a grinning face and as a full figure in an acrobatic pose that Westermann, as a trained acrobat, could assume.[7]

L.F.G.

1. The right shark's fin, which had been broken, was replaced with a new one, sunk and glued into a depression in the "sea;" the replacement is slightly thicker and not exactly the same shape as the original. Westermann took advantage of the occasion to make structural changes (letter to Martin Friedman, 30 September 1970, in which he humorously comments: "I refinished 'the Museum,' that would be something wouldn't it."). A big bolt in the center now attaches the trunk of the piece to the base, four screws hold the laminated wood of the base together, and two strips of wood lift the work just above the surface on which it sits.
2. Martin Friedman, interview with Westermann, 28 June 1966.
3. Ibid.
4. Ibid.
5. Suicide was another subject that touched a passionate chord in the artist; ibid.
6. Ibid.
7. The animation of the anchor shape as a figure he calls a "phantom"—with round head, outstretched arms, and bowed legs on several later pieces (e.g. *The Jock Strap*, 1966–1967)—supports these autobiographic associations.

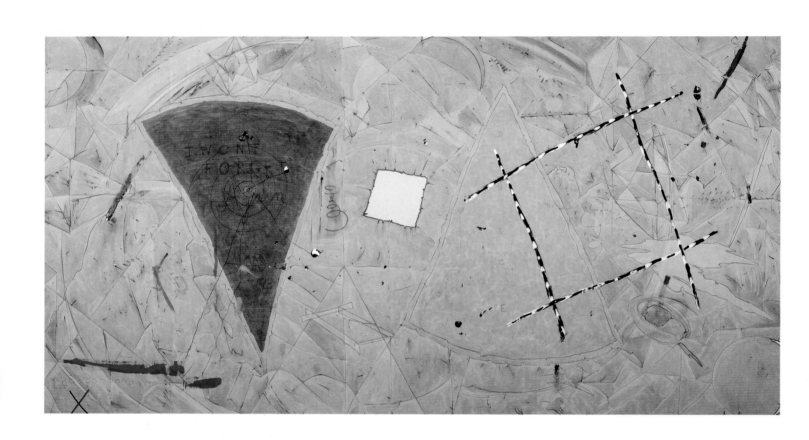

William T. Wiley

I Won't Forget Again One Jillion Times 1973

American, b. 1937

acrylic, charcoal, ink on
canvas

78½ x 149
(199.4 x 378.5)

acquired from the
Hansen-Fuller Gallery,
San Francisco, 1974
(purchased with a
matching grant from
Museum Purchase Plan,
the National Endowment
for the Arts, and Art
Center Acquisition Fund
74.6)

I Won't Forget Again is a compendium of words, abstract forms, and marks that recur throughout Wiley's work and usually have autobiographical referents.[1] His works, however, while open to investigation and interpretation for their associative possibilities, are not intended to be limited by analytic compulsion. The illogically linked images occupy the psychic territory of the imagination, enlisting fantasy, wit, the subconscious, whimsy, and biographical experience in the service of a kind of figurative nonobjectivity. Wiley has found kindred notions about the imaginative realm in the writings of James Hillman, who has described its operations as alchemical.[2] The activity of the imagination, according to Hillman, is anarchic, transformative, and unrestricted, beginning and ending at any point, without definite boundaries or goals. The power of the unconscious against the aims and commitment of the intellect is epitomized in Wiley's vain avowal in this piece: "I WONT FORGET Again 1,000000… [zeros continue from the lower left to the upper right of the canvas, culminating in the word] Times." The title word "jillion" is a child's hyperbole, the attempt to express the infinite in a number that sounds like a known, vast quantity, but is enlarged and intensified through the nonsensical rhyme with "million." Wiley vainly struggles to assert his will, here against the power of forgetfulness. He described the work as "a kind of homage to the promise of not forgetting again—and then forgetting *again*."[3]

The central square and the crescent at the lower right appear to be perforations through a creased and crumpled paper or bark sheet map that also emulates a topographic surface interrupted by geometric forms and mystical emblems as well as hills and bodies of water. Wiley has compared art with mapping, a process of creating a reference point from which an exploration can take place: "When you paint or draw you're charting a course."[4] Hillman notes that the term "charting" is used in psychology to describe the urge for exploration of the internal, psychic world which will always be sabotaged by the imagination.

The explorer who often appears in Wiley's work is Mr. Unatural [*sic*], a Janus-like composite of magus and fool, whose accoutrements—the striped pole and conical hat, here marked "DUNCE"—serve as talismanic motifs.[5] Dislocated from their possessor, Mr. Unatural, as they are in this work, these forms are, nonetheless,

suggestive of meaning: they become, to borrow Hillman's phrase, "alien even while familiar." The viewer's consciousness should be disoriented, stymied in trying to make sense of what it apprehends. With puns, clichés, and folksy, whimsical, good-humored phrases, as in the nonsensical spellings of "DYE A NIECE SEA IN" [Dionysian] and "CAP EARN A KIN" [Copernican], Wiley suggests two polarized approaches to the world, one accepting the irrational as a primary principle and the other fixing reality immutably and scientifically. His implicit recommendation is that the viewer loosen the fetters of rational interpretive thought to allow the image to reverberate fully. Interpretations, in his mind, are equally fantastic and no more significant than the pristine image devoid of allegory, symbolism, and metaphor.

L.F.G.

1. See Graham W.J. Beal, "The Beginner's Mind," in Walker Art Center, *Wiley Territory*, exh. cat., 1979, p. 29; Wiley, interviewed by George Tooker, "How to Chart a Course," *Artscanada*, vol. 31 (Spring 1974), p. 82; and Emily Wasserman, "William T. Wiley and William Allen: Meditating at Fort Prank," *Artforum*, vol. 9 (December 1970). p. 63.
2. James Hillman, *Re-Visioning Psychology* (New York: Harper & Row, 1977), p. 40.
3. Letter to the author, 2 October 1986.
4. Quoted in Tooker. p. 82.
5. For the history of Mr. Unatural, see Beth Coffelt in "Beyond the Flesh, Beyond the Bone," in University Fine Arts Galleries, University of Florida, Tallahassee, *William T. Wiley*, exh. cat., 1981, p. 12.

Christopher Wilmarth

Trace 1972

American, 1943–1987

glass, steel, wire rope, copper crimp fittings

60 x 60⅛ x 35¼ (152.4 x 152.7 x 89.5)

incised, lower right edge of steel, *TRACE 1972/ Christopher Wilmarth*

acquired from the artist, 1976 (purchased with the aid of funds provided by Mr. and Mrs. Edmond R. Ruben, Mr. and Mrs. Julius E. Davis, Suzanne Walker and Thomas Gilmore, and the National Endowment for the Arts 76.8)

The pairing of steel with etched glass in Wilmarth's work originated in 1971, when Mark di Suvero suggested that he and Wilmarth collaborate on a piece; di Suvero made a steel framework and Wilmarth added glass.[1] Wilmarth had been combining glass with other materials for several years, etching it with acid to produce a scumbled surface and bring out its natural green color. He thought that the inspiration for treating the surface of a smooth plane may have arisen out of his experience of painting the surfaces of Tony Smith's sculpture for two years.[2] Wilmarth's interest in glass revolved around its capacity for activating light; through the variety of superficial incident, light is absorbed, reflected, and refracted. Form viewed through the etched areas becomes dematerialized, fractured at its edges, and appropriated into the fictitious space of the glass, in abrupt contrast to the sharp outlines and cohesive volumes occupying the real space framed by the cutout square in the center. Wilmarth enjoyed the contrast between the smooth geometric forms made of industrial materials and the evocative, transcendent aura light creates. The wires that attach metal to glass add a linear element marking the center of the hypothetical line from outside to inside corner and fulfilled Wilmarth's wish to show the entire structure by integrating rather than concealing the method of attachment.[3]

While the flatness of the glass is respected in this piece, the steel plate that echoes its contours is folded back like a flayed skin that releases the possibilities of the glass while serving as its support. Metaphorically, the work, according to the artist, "concerns the survival of the spirit," the release of creativity from oppression and confinement.[4] The centering of the aperture, unique in Wilmarth's freestanding work, and the directional thrust of the diagonals headed toward its center, graphically illustrate his descriptions of moments of realization, in which understanding occurs through the convergence and compression of events he experienced.

L.F.G.

1. Maurice Poirier, "Christopher Wilmarth: 'The Medium is Light,'" *Art News*, vol. 84 (December 1985), p. 72.
2. Robert Pincus-Witten, "Christopher Wilmarth: A Note on Pictorial Sculpture," *Artforum*, vol. 9 (May 1971), p. 55.
3. Grace Glueck, "New York," *Art in America*, vol. 59 (March–April 1971), p. 46. The glass in *Trace* broke in early July 1984 and was replaced by Wilmarth. The surface etching of the new glass differs somewhat and the blackened cord is slightly narrower than in the original work.
4. Wilmarth in WAC questionnaire, 24 November 1981.

Terry Winters

Montgolfier   1987

American, b. 1949

oil on canvas

96 x 120 (243.8 x 304.8)

on reverse, upper left,
T. Winters

acquired from the
Sonnabend Gallery, New
York, 1987 (Walker
Special Purchase Fund
87.56)

Like a number of painters who began showing in
the mid-70s, Terry Winters has sought to reinvest
painting with the emotion and expression that he
felt was lacking in the work of the previous generation. But unlike many of his contemporaries,
he has generally pursued a more or less abstract
point of view. *Montgolfier* develops in part with
elements such as the colored orbs that were first
introduced in the series of Schema drawings
made by the artist just prior to this painting. It is
one of a series of works that utilize the pigment
asphaltum, whose somber expanse of dark, rich
brown contrasts rather strikingly with the colorful
spheres that are clustered in the upper half of
the canvas.

Suggestive of late nineteenth-century
American trompe l'oeil painting in its color and
feel, *Montgolfier's* background closely resembles
a peeling wood wall, and brings to mind the work
of Winters's close friend Carroll Dunham, who
often paints directly on veneer. In the foreground,
geometric spheres replace the more organic
forms characteristic of Winters's earlier paintings,
though they spin out from one another like cells
dividing in a reproductive process that imitates
nature.

The painting's title, *Montgolfier*, a reference
to the French hot air balloonists of the late nineteenth century, encourages a reading of the work
as an aerial view in which spheres are hovering
above the earth. And the painting's gridlike
surface resembles plats of land as seen from
the air.

As in Winters's earlier paintings, once again
the history of the painting's creation is neatly incorporated into the structure of the work. Its
central image of spinning orbs, in its implication
of time passing, suggests both the activity of
making the painting and of viewing it over time.

M.G.

Additional Works from the Collection

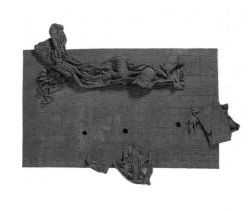

Nicholas Africano
American, b. 1948

Ironing   1978
acrylic, wax, oil on canvas
83½ x 65 (212.1 x 165.1)
(purchased with the aid of funds from Ann Hatch
and the National Endowment for the Arts 78.17)

Peter Agostini
American, b. 1913

Winter Wall   1962
bronze
62 x 78 x 6 (157.5 x 198.1 x 15.2)
(gift of the T.B. Walker Foundation 64.13)

Pierre Alechinsky
Belgian, b. 1927

Referendum   1963
ink on paper and canvas
50½ x 59¼ (128.3 x 150.5)
(gift of Collectors Club of Minnesota 64.4)

William Anastasi
American, b. 1933

Untitled from Continuum series   1986
gelatin silver print mounted on aluminum
60 x 48 (152.4 x 121.9)
(gift of Virginia Dwan 85.755)

Shusaku Arakawa
Japanese, b. 1936

Hard or Soft   1969
oil on canvas
72 x 48 (182.9 x 121.9)
(gift of Virginia Dwan 85.756)

Shusaku Arakawa
Japanese, b. 1936

"No!" says THE SIGNIFIED NO. 2   1973
acrylic on canvas, Styrofoam
74⅝ x 106 (189.5 x 269.2)
(intended gift of Mr. and Mrs. Miles Q. Fiterman)

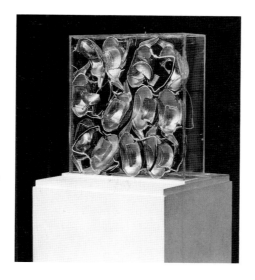

Alexander Archipenko
American, b. Russia, 1887–1964

Turning Torso   1921/1959
bronze
20½ x 9¾ x 10½
(52.1 x 24.8 x 26.7) with base
(gift of the T.B. Walker Foundation 60.25)

Arman
French, b. 1929

Accumulation of Teapots   1964
metal, plastic
16 x 18 x 6 (40.6 x 45.7 x 15.2)
(gift of the T.B. Walker Foundation 64.40)

Robert Arneson
American, b. 1930

Brick at Sea   1974
ceramic
3 x 20 x 13 (7.6 x 50.8 x 33)
(gift of Mr. and Mrs. Russell Cowles, II 79.63)

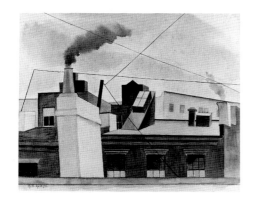

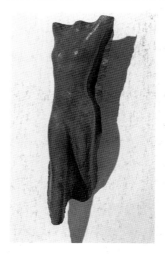

George Ault
American, 1891–1948

Village Roofs   1931
watercolor on paper
10 x 12 (25.4 x 30.5)
(gift of Mrs. George Ault 61.11)

Milton Avery
American, 1893–1965

Nude Resting   1948
ink on paper
13⅝ x 16¾ (34.6 x 42.5)
(gift of American Association of University
Women 59.24)

Saul Baizerman
American, 1889–1957

Nike   1949–1952
copper
67½ x 21½ x 18
(171.5 x 54.6 x 45.7)
(gift of the T.B. Walker Foundation 53.1)

531

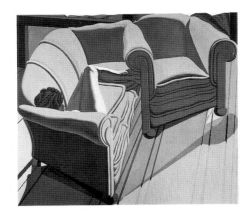

Joost Baljeu
Dutch, b. 1925

Synthesist Construction W XIV 2d   1964–1966
acrylic on mahogany plywood
28½ x 16 x 8¼ (72.4 x 40.6 x 21)
(gift of the artist 66.15)

Jennifer Bartlett
American, b. 1941

Fire/Nasturtiums   1988–1989
oil on canvas, enamel on wood
two elements
84 x 60¼ (213.4 x 153);
32½ x 35¼ x 30¾ (82.6 x 89.5 x 78.1)
(T.B. Walker Acquisition Fund 89.66.1-2)

Jack Beal
American, b. 1931

Nude on Sofa with Red Chair   1968
oil on canvas
70 x 78 (177.8 x 198.1)
(purchased with matching grant from
Museum Purchase Plan/National Endowment
for the Arts and Art Center Acquisition Fund
69.3)

Max Beckmann
German, 1884–1950

Woman Reading at the Beach   1939
oil on canvas
23¾ x 35¼ (60.3 x 89.5)
(gift of Mr. and Mrs. John Cowles, Sr. 64.15)

Lynda Benglis
American, b. 1941

Excess   1971
purified beeswax, damar resin, pigments
on Masonite and pine wood
36 x 5 x 4 (91.4 x 12.7 x 10.16)
(Art Center Acquisition Fund 72.11)

Joseph Beuys
German, 1921–1986

Filzanzug (Felt Suit)   1970
felt
two elements
45 x 38½ x 7 (114.3 x 97.8 x 17.8);
31 x 49½ x 5 (78.7 x 125.7 x 12.7)
(Walker Special Purchase Fund 87.121)

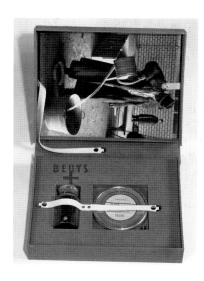

Joseph Beuys
German, 1921–1986

Celtic + ~~   1971
linen, cardboard box, cotton, metal, glass, cork,
beeswax, gelatin, celluloid film, wood, foam
core, body fluids, gelatin silver prints
16¾ x 20½ x 4½ (42.6 x 52.1 x 11.4) closed
37 x 20½ x 4½ (94 x 52.1 x 11.4) open
(gift of Sheldon and Claire Sparber 88.435)

Ilya Bolotowsky
American, b. Russia, 1907–1981

Metal Column B   1966
painted aluminum
36 x 2½ x 2½ (91.4 x 6.4 x 6.4)
(Art Center Acquisition Fund 66.11)

Richard Bosman
Australian, b. India, 1944

Crossing   1984
oil on canvas
96 x 96 (243.8 x 243.8)
(Justin V. Smith Purchase Fund 84.1095)

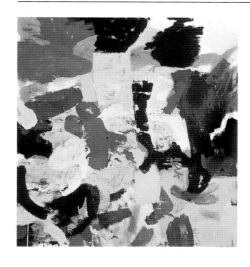

James Brooks
American, b. 1906

Karrig   1956
oil on canvas
79 x 73½ (200.7 x 186.7)
(gift of the T.B. Walker Foundation 60.4)

Charles Burchfield
American, 1893–1967

Blackbirds in the Snow   1941–1945
watercolor on paper
20¼ x 29½ (51.4 x 74.9)
(gift of the T.B. Walker Foundation, Gilbert M.
Walker Fund 46.21)

Tom Butter
American, b. 1952

A.A.   1985
painted fiberglass, resin
88¼ x 28 x 24 (224.2 x 71.1 x 61)
(gift of Grace Borgenicht Brandt 86.65)

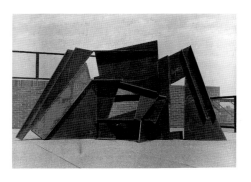

Alexander Calder
American, 1898–1976

Mobile   circa 1948
painted sheet iron
17½ x 25 x 10 (44.5 x 63.5 x 25.4)
(gift of Mr. and Mrs. Samuel H. Maslon 55.11)

Steven MacMillan Campbell
Scottish, b. 1953

Two Humeians Preaching Causality to Nature
1984
oil on canvas
115 x 94 (292.1 x 238.8)
(Jerome Foundation Purchase Fund for Emerging
Artists and McKnight Acquisition Fund 84.4)

Anthony Caro
British, b. 1924

Straight Flush   1972
steel
78 x 145 x 52 (198.1 x 368.3 x 132.1)
(gift of Judy and Kenneth Dayton 73.2)

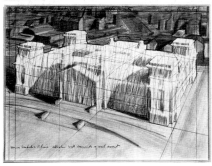

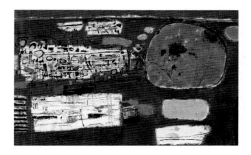

Christo (Javacheff)
Bulgarian, b. 1935

Wrapped Reichstag (project for Berlin)   1980
pastel, charcoal, fabric, twine, paper
two elements
11¼ x 28¼ (28.6 x 71.8);
22¼ x 28¼ (56.5 x 71.8)
(gift of Mr. and Mrs. David Z. Johnson 80.29)

Chryssa (Mavromichaeli)
American, b. Greece, 1933

Times Square Sky   1962
neon, aluminum, steel
60 x 60 x 9½ (152.4 x 152.4 x 24.1)
(gift of the T.B. Walker Foundation 64.14)

Corneille
Belgian, b. 1922

**Souvenir d'une terre lointaine (Memory of a
Distant Land)**   1959
oil on canvas
30 x 46 (76.2 x 116.8)
(gift of Howard Wise 67.38)

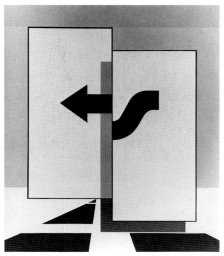

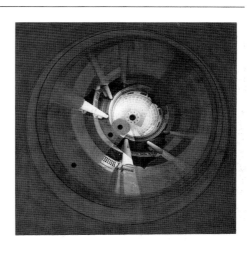

Allan D'Arcangelo
American, b. 1930

Proposition #9 1966
acrylic on canvas
65 x 54 (165.1 x 137.2)
(Art Center Acquisition Fund 67.16)

Arthur B. Davies
American, 1862–1928

Home n.d.
oil on canvas
14⅛ x 10¼ (35.9 x 26)
(gift of the T.B. Walker Foundation 62.44)

Gene Davis
American, 1920–1985

See Saw 1979
acrylic on canvas
72 x 92½ (235 x 182.9)
(gift of Judy and Kenneth Dayton 89.55)

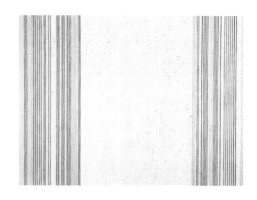

Tony DeLap
American, b. 1927

Saros 1964
painted aluminum, board, lacquer, Plexiglas
11¾ x 23½ x 8⅝
(29.8 x 59.7 x 21.9)
(gift of the T.B. Walker Foundation 65.2)

Donna Dennis
American, b. 1942

Station Hotel 1974
papier-mâché, metal, fluorescent and
incandescent lights, acrylic on wood and
Masonite
75 x 72 x 13½ (190.5 x 182.9 x 34.3)
(gift of Donald S. Dworken 82.166)

Jan Dibbets
Dutch, b. 1941

Cupola 1985–1986
color photographs, watercolor, graphite,
glass pencil on paper mounted on chipboard
72⅛ x 72⅛ (183.2 x 183.2)
(Walker Special Purchase Fund 88.12)

Preston Dickinson
American, 1891–1930

Still Life with Demijohn   1930
pastel on paper
17⅜ x 18⅛ (44.1 x 46)
(gift of Edith Halpert 54.10)

Rosalyn Drexler
American, b. 1926

Sorry About That   1966
acrylic on canvas
48 x 72 (121.9 x 182.9)
(gift of the T.B. Walker Foundation 66.3)

Jean Dubuffet
French, 1901–1985

Tour (Tower) 1975
polyurethane on laminated panel
107 x 47 x 1⅜ (271.8 x 119.4 x 3.5)
(gift of the artist 76.9)

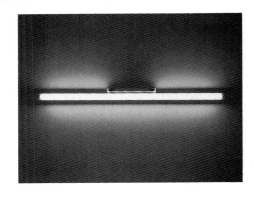

Philip Evergood
American, 1901–1973

Woman on Couch   1948
ink on paper
15⅛ x 20½ (38.4 x 52.1)
(gift of American Association of University
Women 59.23)

Herbert Ferber
American, b. 1906

**Calligraph in Cage with Cluster No. 2, II
(with Two Heads)**   1962
brass, copper
46 x 32 x 36 (116.8 x 81.3 x 91.4)
(gift of the T.B. Walker Foundation 62.50)

Dan Flavin
American, b. 1933

untitled   1963
glass, metal, fluorescent light gas
8 x 96 x 4 (20.3 x 243.8 x 10.2)
(gift of Mrs. Harold Field 86.103)

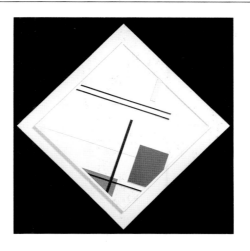

Lucio Fontana
Italian, 1899–1968

Concetto Spaziale "Natura" 1961
bronze
33 x 38½ x 34 (83.8 x 97.8 x 86.4)
(gift of the T.B. Walker Foundation 66.4)

Peter Forakis
American, b. 1927

Hyper-Cube 1967
aluminum
35⅞ x 36⁷⁄₁₆ x 36⅛
(91.2 x 92.6 x 91.8)
(gift of Virginia Dwan 85.757)

William Glackens
American, 1870–1938

Fourth of July 1896
pencil, watercolor, ink on paper
17 x 10½ (43.2 x 26.7)
(John T. Baxter Memorial Collection of
American Drawings 49.9)

William Glackens
American, 1870–1938

The Swing 1910
oil on canvas
26 x 32 (66 x 81.3)
(gift of the T.B. Walker Foundation 58.12)

Jean Albert Gorin
French, b. 1899

Composition #37 1937
oil on wood
52 x 52 (132.1 x 132.1)
(gift of Archie D. and Bertha H. Walker
Foundation 67.7)

Morris Graves
American, b. 1910

Scream Laughter Cup 1940
graphite on paper
13⅛ x 9⅝ (33.3 x 24.4)
(gift of American Association of University
Women 59.19)

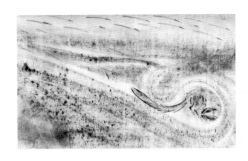

Morris Graves
American, b. 1910

Hibernation 1954
ink on paper
21½ x 34¾ (54.6 x 88.3)
(Art Center Acquisition Fund 57.14)

Nancy Graves
American, b. 1940

Hindsight 1986
steel, wood, polychromed bronze
31 x 35 x 14 (78.7 x 88.9 x 35.6)
(Walker Special Purchase Fund 87.64)

George Grosz
German, 1893–1959

The Long Way 1930
ink, watercolor on paper
25 x 18¾ (63.5 x 47.6)
(John T. Baxter Memorial Collection of
American Drawings 49.24)

Philip Guston
American, 1913–1980

Winter 1961
oil on paper mounted on aluminum core panel
30 x 40 (76.2 x 101.6)
(gift of the T.B. Walker Foundation and the
Longview Foundation 64.11)

Richard Haas
American, b. 1936

Gertrude Stein in Her Living Room n.d.
Masonite, wood, non-skid paint, paint,
Plexiglas, ceramic, electric light bulb and cord;
ink, graphite, paint, colored pencil, watercolor
on paper and wood
15½ x 15 x 18⅝ (39.4 x 38.1 x 47.3)
(gift of Mr. and Mrs. Steven Gano 82.168)

Richard Haas
American, b. 1936

Apollinaire in His Bedroom 1968
Masonite, wood, non-skid paint, paint,
Plexiglas, cotton, mirror, tinfoil, electric
light bulb and cord; ink, graphite, colored
pencil, conté crayon on paper and wood
15 x 15 x 16½ (38.1 x 38.1 x 41.9)
(gift of Mr. and Mrs. Steven Gano 83.173)

538

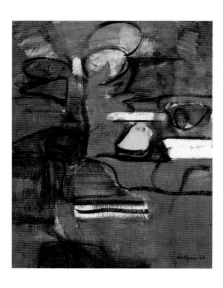

Grace Hartigan
American, b. 1922

Human Fragment   1963
oil on canvas
81¾ x 63¾ (207.6 x 161.9)
(gift of Alexander M. Bing 63.44)

Marsden Hartley
American, 1877–1943

Still Life   1920
oil on canvas
32¼ x 24 (81.9 x 61)
(gift of Mr. and Mrs. Edgar W. Davy 75.27)

Marsden Hartley
American, 1877–1943

Masks   1931–1932
oil on Masonite
36 x 20 (91.4 x 50.8)
(gift of Mrs. Joshua B. Cahn 73.37)

Marsden Hartley
American, 1877–1943

Maine Coast Still Life   1941
oil on Masonite
40 x 30 (101.6 x 76.2)
(gift of Mrs. Archie D. Walker, Josiah Bell
Hudson Memorial 46.49)

Marsden Hartley
American, 1877–1943

Still Life with Flowers   n.d.
oil on mat board
23⅝ x 17⅝ (60 x 44.8)
(gift of Bertha H. Walker 72.2)

Marsden Hartley
American, 1877–1943

Beaver Lake, Lost River Region   1930
oil on canvas
35 x 30 (88.9 x 76.2)
(gift of Bertha H. Walker 71.43)

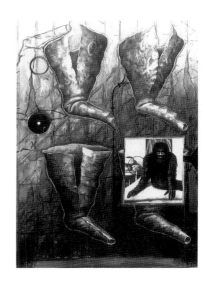

Jann Haworth
American, b. 1942

The Maid   1966
nylon, cotton, satin, kapok, human hair,
plastic, paint, wood, overstuffed chair, floor lamp
43 x 38 x 58 (109.2 x 96.5 x 147.3)
(Art Center Acquisition Fund 70.32)

Al Held
American, b. 1929

Hidden Fortress   1961
acrylic on canvas
108 x 60 (274.3 x 152.4)
(gift of the T.B. Walker Foundation 64.18)

Edward Henderson
American, b. 1951

One Dances, the Other Doesn't   1984
metal, slate, paper, oil, epoxy on canvas
84 x 60 (213.4 x 152.4)
(T.B. Walker Acquisition Fund 87.3)

Robert Henri
American, 1865–1929

Big Rock and Sea   n.d.
oil on wood panel
7½ x 9½ (19.1 x 24.1)
(Art Center Acquisition Fund 60.23)

Hans Hofmann
American, 1880–1966

Elegy   1950
oil, plaster on wood
40 x 59½ (101.6 x 151.1)
(gift of the T.B. Walker Foundation, Gilbert M.
Walker Fund 51.16)

Lester Johnson
American, b. 1919

Figures with Columns   1965
oil on canvas
78 x 92 (198.1 x 233.7)
(gift of Mr. and Mrs. David Anderson 78.2)

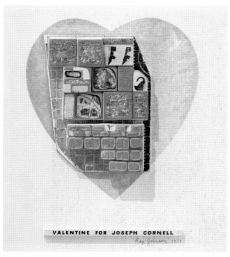

Ray Johnson
American, b. 1927

Valentine for Joseph Cornell   1971
cardboard, paint on paper
24½ x 17¹³⁄₁₆ (62.2 x 45.2)
(gift of Betty Parsons Foundation 85.41)

Howard Jones
American, b. 1922

Time Column Two   1966
aluminum with light and sound
96 x 10 x 10 (243.8 x 25.4 x 25.4)
(gift of Northern States Power Company 67.18)

Donald Judd
American, b. 1928

Untitled-10 Stacks   1969
anodized aluminum
ten elements
27 x 24 x 6 (68.6 x 61 x 15.2) each
(gift of Mr. and Mrs. Edmond R. Ruben 81.26)

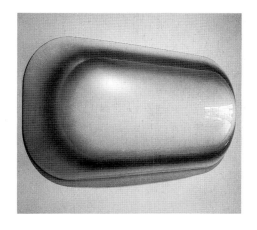

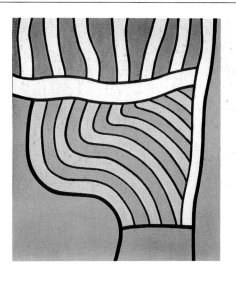

Craig Kauffman
American, b. 1932

Untitled   1969
Plexiglas, acrylic lacquer
43 x 89¼ x 16 (109.2 x 226.7 x 40.6)
(Art Center Acquisition Fund 69.18)

James Kielkopf
American, b. 1939

Untitled   1971
latex paint on canvas
66 x 108 (167.6 x 274.3)
(Art Center Acquisition Fund 71.20)

Nicholas Krushenick
American, b. 1929

Battle of Candy Stripes   1964
Liquitex on canvas
84 x 70 (213.4 x 177.8)
(Art Center Acquisition Fund 64.36)

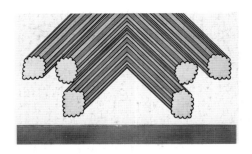  

Nicholas Krushenick
American, b. 1929

Steeplechase   1967
acrylic on wood
97 x 189 (246.4 x 480.1)
(gift of Pace Gallery 68.5)

Yasuo Kuniyoshi
American, 1893–1953

Nude in Grey Chemise   1929
oil on canvas
14 x 22 (35.6 x 55.9)
(gift of Dr. and Mrs. Malcolm McCannel 53.43)

Yasuo Kuniyoshi
American, 1893–1953

Lay Figure   1938
oil on canvas
38⅛ x 58¼ (96.8 x 148)
(gift of the T.B. Walker Foundation, Gilbert M.
Walker Fund 48.22)

Kay Kurt
American, b. 1944

Weingummi II   1973
oil on canvas
72 x 72 (182.9 x 182.9)
(purchased with the aid of funds from the
National Endowment for the Arts and the Butler
Family Foundation 81.2)

Jacob Lawrence
American, b. 1917

Shooting Gallery   1941
gouache on paper
21¾ x 29½ (55.2 x 74.9)
(gift of Dr. and Mrs. Malcolm McCannel 53.40)

Fernand Léger
French, 1881–1955

**Plongeurs sur fond noir (Divers on a Black
Background)**   1941
oil on canvas
25½ x 36¾ (64.8 x 93.3)
(gift of Dr. and Mrs. Malcolm McCannel 53.42)

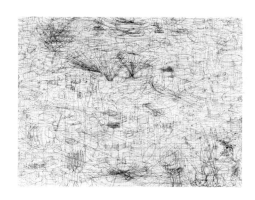

Frantisek Lesák
Czechoslovakian, b. 1943

Untitled 1975
graphite on paper
59½ x 79 (151.1 x 200.7)
(Art Center Acquisition Fund 80.19)

Alfred Leslie
American, b. 1927

Baby's Curse 1959
oil on canvas
72 x 84¼ (182.9 x 214)
(gift of the T.B. Walker Foundation 60.12)

Jacques Lipchitz
American, b. Lithuania, 1891–1973

Theseus 1942
bronze
24 x 24 x 18 (61 x 61 x 45.7)
(gift of the T.B. Walker Foundation 61.33)

Donald Lipski
American, b. 1947

Untitled #89–23 1989
stainless steel, steel, plastic, Plexiglas, water
78 x 33½ x 27 (198.1 x 85.1 x 68.6)
(T.B. Walker Acquisition Fund 90.20)

Richard Long
British, b. 1945

A Line of Flint 1983
flint
60 x 480 (152.4 x 1,219.2) variable
(gift of Penny and Mike Winton 88.11)

George Luks
American, 1866–1933

Peddler n.d.
graphite on paper
10 x 7¾ (25.4 x 19.7)
(John T. Baxter Memorial Collection of
American Drawings 49.4)

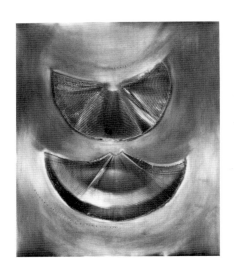

Heinz Mack
German, b. 1931

Wings of an Angel   1963
aluminum on wood
63 x 29½ x 1 (160 x 74.9 x 2.5)
(gift of the T.B. Walker Foundation 65.1)

Paul Manship
American, 1885–1966

Europa and the Bull   1924
bronze
9 x 11 x 6½ (22.9 x 27.9 x 16.5)
(gift of the T.B. Walker Foundation 57.13)

Giacomo Manzù
Italian, b. 1908

La grande chiave (The Large Key)   1959
bronze
96½ x 36 x 14¾ (245.1 x 91.4 x 37.5)
(anonymous gift 63.10)

Conrad Marca-Relli
American, b. 1913

The Joust   1959
acrylic, oil, cotton, linen on canvas
57 x 77 (144.8 x 195.6)
(gift of the T.B. Walker Foundation 60.5)

John Marin
American, 1870–1953

New York, Downtown No. 7   1936
ink on paper
26 x 20 (66 x 50.8)
(gift of the T.B. Walker Foundation, Gilbert M.
Walker Fund 47.57)

Reginald Marsh
American, 1898–1954

Coney Island   n.d.
oil on Masonite
18 x 24 (45.7 x 61)
(gift of the estate of Felicia Meyer Marsh 79.98)

Reginald Marsh
American, 1898–1954

Girl Walking   1948
watercolor, ink on paper
10½ x 7⅝ (26.7 x 19.4)
(John T. Baxter Memorial Collection of
American Drawings 49.3)

Walter Martin
American, b. 1953

Old Fleece Preaching to the Sharks
1985–1986
plaster, metal, steel, rubber
36 x 72 x 84 (91.4 x 182.9 x 213.4)
(Clinton and Della Walker Acquisition Fund
86.81)

**Roberto Antonio Sebastian Matta
Echaurren**
Chilean, b. 1911

Cat for Piano   1951
oil on canvas
48½ x 59 (123.2 x 149.9)
(gift of Mr. and Mrs. Donald Winston 77.7)

Ann Messner
American, b. 1952

Meteor   1987
steel
five elements
300 x 300 (762 x 762) variable
(Butler Family Fund 90.74)

Joan Mitchell
American, b. 1926

Painting 1953   1953
oil on canvas
52 x 55 (132.1 x 139.7)
(gift of the T.B. Walker Foundation 56.2)

Henry Moore
British, 1898–1986

Mother and Child No. 3: Child on Knee   1956
bronze
8¼ x 4 x 5 (21 x 10.2 x 12.7)
(gift of Mrs. Phoebe H. Hanson, in memory of
Robert Eugene Hanson 56.49)

Ed Moses
American, b. 1926

ILL. 245 Hegemann 1971
powdered pigment, acrylic resin on canvas
95 x 146 (241.3 x 370.8)
(gift of Archie D. and Bertha H. Walker
Foundation 71.15)

Louise Nevelson
American, b. Russia, 1900–1988

End of Day Nightscape III 1973
painted wood
111 x 92½ x 3½ (281.9 x 235 x 8.9)
(gift of the artist 73.34)

Louise Nevelson
American, b. Russia, 1900–1988

Owl 1947
terra cotta
10½ x 8¼ x 11 (26.7 x 21 x 27.9)
(gift of the artist 73.6)

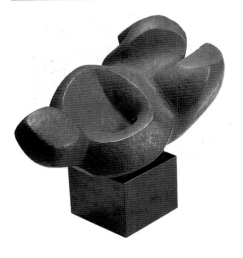

Louise Nevelson
American, b. Russia, 1900–1988

Mother and Child 1947
terra cotta
7½ x 10 x 7½ (19.1 x 25.4 x 19.1)
(gift of the artist 73.10)

Louise Nevelson
American, b. Russia, 1900–1988

Figure 1947
terra cotta
21 x 11 x 8 (53.3 x 27.9 x 20.3)
(gift of the artist 73.8)

Louise Nevelson
American, b. Russia, 1900–1988

Relief 1956
painted wood
35 x 24 x 6 (88.9 x 61 x 15.2)
(gift of the artist 73.11)

Louise Nevelson
American, b. Russia, 1900–1988

Rain Forest Column XXXI 1967
painted wood
83¼ x 12⅛ x 12⅛ (211.5 x 30.8 x 30.8)
(gift of the artist 73.12)

Louise Nevelson
American, b. Russia, 1900–1988

Young Tree II 1971
painted wood
24 x 7 x 6 (61 x 17.8 x 15.2)
(gift of the artist 73.13)

Louise Nevelson
American, b. Russia, 1900–1988

Young Tree VI 1971
painted wood
23¾ x 9¾ x 7 (60.3 x 24.8 x 17.8)
(gift of the artist 73.14)

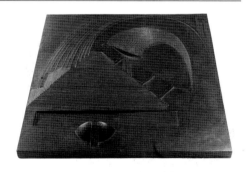

Louise Nevelson
American, b. Russia, 1900–1988

Young Tree XIX 1971
painted wood
24¾ x 8 x 8 (62.9 x 20.3 x 20.3)
(gift of the artist 73.15)

Don Nice
American, b. 1930

Grapes 1967
acrylic on canvas
108 x 72 (274.3 x 182.9)
(Art Center Acquisition Fund 67.29)

Isamu Noguchi
American, 1904–1988

Model for **Play Mountain, New York** 1933
bronze
4 x 29³⁄₁₆ x 25¹¹⁄₁₆ (10.2 x 74.1 x 65.3)
(gift of the artist 80.15)

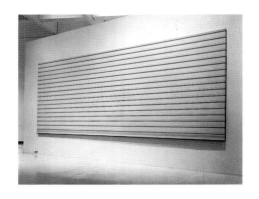

Isamu Noguchi
American, 1904–1988

Shodo Shima   1978
granite
eight elements
12 x 66 x 69 (30.5 x 167.6 x 175.3) overall
(gift of the artist 78.14)

Isamu Noguchi
American, 1904–1988

Theater set piece from **Judith**   1950/1978
bronze
four elements
108 x 109 x 54
(274.3 x 276.9 x 137.2) assembled
(purchased with the aid of funds from the Art
Center Acquisition Fund and the National
Endowment for the Arts 78.6)

Kenneth Noland
American, b. 1924

Track   1969
acrylic on canvas
90 x 240 (228.6 x 609.6)
(gift of Mr. and Mrs. Julius E. Davis 69.14)

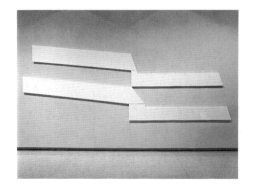

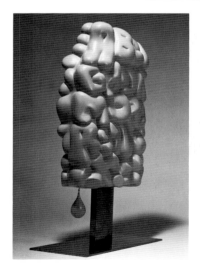

Richard Nonas
American, b. 1936

Razor-Blade   1977
steel
96 x 102 x 6 (243.8 x 259.1 x 15.2) overall
(Art Center Acquisition Fund 77.45)

David Novros
American, b. 1941

4:20   1966
acrylic lacquer on canvas
four elements
73½ x 187¼ (186.7 x 475.6) overall
(gift of Virginia Dwan 85.759)

Claes Oldenburg
American, b. Sweden, 1929

Alphabet/Good Humor, 3-Foot Prototype
1975
painted fiberglass, bronze, wood
35½ x 20 x 11 (90.2 x 50.8 x 27.9)
(gift of Mr. and Mrs. Julius E. Davis 80.28)

George Ortman
American, b. 1926

Rites of Love   1961
painted wood, Masonite, ping-pong balls,
oil on canvas
96 x 32 (243.8 x 81.3)
(gift of the T.B. Walker Foundation 63.9)

Jerry Ott
American, b. 1947

Carol and the Paradise Wall   1972
acrylic on canvas
84 x 108 (213.4 x 274.3)
(Art Center Acquisition Fund and Mr. and Mrs. C.
David Thomas 72.15)

Sir Eduardo Paolozzi
British, b. Scotland, 1924

Silk   1965
chrome-plated steel
31¼ x 45¾ x 36 (79.4 x 116.2 x 91.4)
(gift of the T.B. Walker Foundation 67.14)

Raymond Parker
American, b. 1922

Red Over Blue Beside Red   1962
oil on canvas
74 x 85 (188 x 215.9)
(gift of the T.B. Walker Foundation and the
Longview Foundation 64.10)

I. Rice Pereira
American, 1907–1971

Rose Planes   1945
oil on parchment
21⅞ x 25⅞ (55.6 x 65.7)
(gift of the T.B. Walker Foundation, Gilbert M.
Walker Fund 46.24)

Pablo Picasso
Spanish, 1881–1973

Le fou (The Jester)   1905
bronze
15¼ x 13¼ x 9 (38.7 x 33.7 x 22.9)
(gift of the T.B. Walker Foundation 56.5)

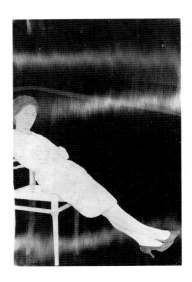

Otto Piene
German, b. 1928

Electric Flower 1967
chromed steel, aluminum, 100 incandescent
lamps with timer box
41½ x 18 x 18 (105.4 x 45.7 x 45.7)
(gift of Northern States Power Company 68.4)

Michelangelo Pistoletto
Italian, b. 1933

Seated Woman 1963
paper, graphite, adhesive on stainless steel
71 x 47¼ (180.3 x 120)
(gift of the T.B. Walker Foundation 66.8)

Joseph Raffael
American, b. 1933

Water Painting VII 1973
oil on canvas
90 x 83 (228.6 x 210.8)
(gift of Dr. Jack E. Chachkes 77.10)

Odilon Redon
French, 1840–1916

The Sybil circa 1900
oil on paper mounted on linen
23 x 14½ (58.4 x 36.8)
(gift of Alexander M. Bing 53.53)

Ad Reinhardt
American, 1913–1967

M 1955
oil on canvas
47⅞ x 11⅞ (121.6 x 30.2)
(gift of Virginia Dwan 87.111)

Germaine Richier
French, 1904–1959

Don Quixote of the Forest 1950–1951
bronze
93 x 35 x 25 (236.2 x 88.9 x 63.5)
(gift of the John and Elizabeth Bates Cowles
Foundation 56.50)

George Rickey
American, b. 1907

Two Planes Horizontal   1966–1967
stainless steel
25 x 65 x 40 (63.5 x 165.1 x 101.6)
(gift of the T.B. Walker Foundation 67.30)

Auguste Rodin
French, 1840–1917

**Le baiser du fantôme à la jeune fille
(Girl Kissing a Phantom)**   circa 1895
marble
12 x 23 x 10½ (30.5 x 58.4 x 26.7)
(gift of the T.B. Walker Foundation 56.3)

Thomas Rose
American, b. 1942

**I Think Today Is Wednesday But What If It Isn't
Who Cares**   1975
porcelain
16 x 20 x 4 (40.6 x 50.8 x 10.2)
(purchased with the aid of funds from the
National Endowment for the Arts and gifts from
Mr. and Mrs. Edmond R. Ruben, Mr. and Mrs.
Julius E. Davis and Suzanne Walker and Thomas
Gilmore 76.3)

Harry Roseman
American, b. 1945

Room with a View of Hoboken   1976
painted wood, plaster
19¼ x 39 x 27 (48.9 x 99.1 x 68.6)
(purchased with the aid of funds from the
Art Center Acquisition Fund and the National
Endowment for the Arts 78.4)

Harry Roseman
American, b. 1945

Bathroom Wall   1977/1978
painted aluminum
21½ x 17½ x 1¾ (54.6 x 44.5 x 4.4)
(purchased with the aid of funds from the
Art Center Acquisition Fund and the National
Endowment for the Arts 78.5)

Charles Ross
American, b. 1937

Prism Wall—Muybridge Window   1970
liquid-filled acrylic
five elements
105⅝ x 48 (268.3 x 121.9) each
(gift of Virginia Dwan, by exchange 88.433)

Mark Rothko
American, b. Russia, 1903–1970

Number 12   1949
oil on canvas
67⁹⁄₁₆ x 42⁵⁄₁₆ (171.6 x 108.1)
(gift of The Mark Rothko Foundation, Inc. 86.2)

Morgan Russell
American, 1886–1953

Synchromy Number 4 (1914) to Form   1914
oil on canvas
23¾ x 19½ (60.3 x 49.5)
(gift of Mr. and Mrs. A. Atwater Kent, Jr. 54.6)

Kay Sage
American, 1898–1963

On the Contrary   1952
oil on canvas
35½ x 27¾ (90.2 x 70.5)
(gift of the T.B. Walker Foundation 53.9)

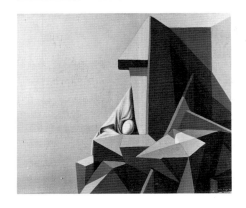

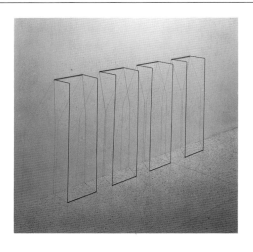

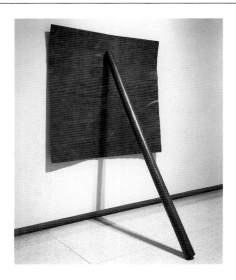

Kay Sage
American, 1898–1963

From Another Approach   1944
oil on canvas
15 x 18 (38.1 x 45.7)
(gift of the estate of Kay Sage Tanguy 64.45)

Fred Sandback
American, b. 1943

Untitled   1968
painted steel
four elements
30 x 6¼ x 9⅛ (76.2 x 15.9 x 23.2) each
(gift of Virginia Dwan 85.760)

Richard Serra
American, b. 1939

Prop   1968
lead antimony
two elements
60 x 60 (152.4 x 152.4);
95½ x 4 diam. (242.6 x 10.2)
(gift of Penny and Mike Winton 77.44)

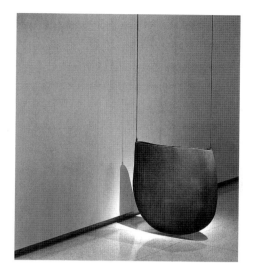

Ben Shahn
American, 1898–1969

Italian Landscape   1943–1944
tempera on paper
27½ x 36 (69.9 x 91.4)
(gift of the T.B. Walker Foundation, Gilbert M.
Walker Fund 44.4)

Peter Shelton
American, b. 1951

Bigflatsack   1984–1986
cast iron
41 x 45 x 5½ (104.1 x 114.3 x 14)
(Butler Family Fund 87.6)

Jonathan Silver
American, b. 1937

Wounded Amazon   1982–1983
bronze
85 x 21 x 16 (215.9 x 53.3 x 40.6)
(gift of Sidney Singer, Jr. 87.79)

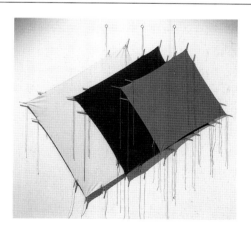

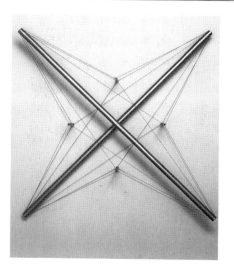

Alexis Smith
American, b. 1949

Golden State   1980
emery paper, chalk paper, paint, U.S. dollar bills,
"roadside refuse"
three elements
14 x 48 (35.6 x 121.9);
14 x 57⁷⁄₁₆ (35.6 x 145.9);
14 x 48 (35.6 x 121.9)
(gift of Audrey Taylor Pretorius Gonzalez 86.108)

Richard Smith
British, b. 1931

The Other Hero   1976
acrylic on canvas with string
three elements
60 x 60 (152.4 x 152.4);
30 x 30 (76.2 x 76.2);
20 x 20 (50.8 x 50.8)
(Art Center Acquisition Fund 79.32)

Kenneth Snelson
American, b. 1927

X-Tetra   1970
steel, aluminum
68 x 68 x 14¼ (172.7 x 172.7 x 36.2)
(gift of Virginia Dwan 86.127)

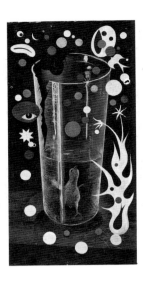

T.L. Solien
American, b. 1949

His Face   1986
pastel, enamel, paper collage on paper
76 x 40 (193 x 101.6)
(Jerome Foundation Purchase Fund for Emerging
Artists 87.7)

Pierre Soulages
French, b. 1919

Painting, 26 December 1955   1955
oil on canvas
38 x 51 (96.5 x 129.5)
(gift of the T.B. Walker Foundation 56.16)

Andrew Spence
American, b. 1947

Light   1987
oil on linen mounted on wood
72 x 36¹⁄₁₆ (182.9 x 91.6)
(purchased with funds from The Prudential
Foundation and Jerome Foundation Purchase
Fund for Emerging Artists 87.84)

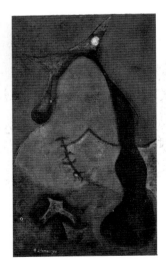

Theodoros Stamos
American, b. 1922

Archaic Release   1946
oil on composition board
48 x 28⅛ (121.9 x 71.4)
(gift of the T.B. Walker Foundation, Gilbert M.
Walker Fund 48.28)

Theodoros Stamos
American, b. 1922

Day of the Two Suns   1963
oil on canvas
60 x 40 (152.4 x 101.6)
(gift of the T.B. Walker Foundation 63.8)

Richard Stankiewicz
American, 1922–1983

untitled   1962
iron, steel
27¹⁵⁄₁₆ x 13½ x 20¼ (71 x 34.3 x 51.4)
(Art Center Acquisition Fund 63.46)

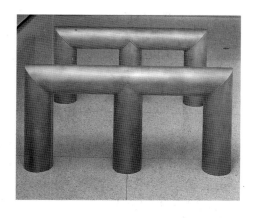

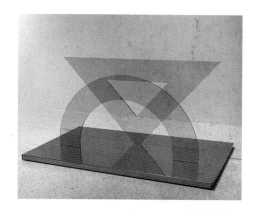

Michael Steiner
American, b. 1945

Untitled 1966
aluminum
two elements
36⅛ x 72⅛ x 11 diam.
(91.8 x 183.2 x 27.9) each
(gift of Virginia Dwan 85.762)

Florine Stettheimer
American, 1871–1944

Still Life with Flowers 1921
oil on canvas
25½ x 29½ (64.8 x 74.9)
(gift of Mrs. Ettie Stettheimer 55.19)

Sylvia Stone
American, b. 1928

Untitled 1971
Plexiglas, aluminum
43⅞ x 47½ x 44 (111.5 x 120.7 x 111.8)
(gift of Mr. and Mrs. Julius E. Davis 77.41)

Michelle Stuart
American, b. 1938

Every Wave Book (For Melville) 1979
earth, sand, sea pebbles, linen
11½ x 31 x 2¼ (29.2 x 78.7 x 5.7) variable
(McKnight Acquisition Fund and Art Center
Acquisition Fund 83.17)

George Sugarman
American, b. 1912

Rorik 1965
painted wood
32 x 26 x 5 (81.3 x 66 x 12.7)
(gift of Penny and Mike Winton 82.165)

Rufino Tamayo
Mexican, b. 1900

Wounded Beast 1953
oil on canvas
31 x 39 (78.7 x 99.1)
(gift of the T.B. Walker Foundation 58.13)

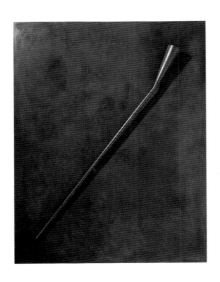

Robert Therrien
American, b. 1947

No Title   1986
bronze
100 x 78½ x 12½ (254 x 199.4 x 31.8)
(Walker Special Purchase Fund 87.34)

Robert Therrien
American, b. 1947

No Title   1987
enamel on bronze
14¹¹⁄₁₆ x 11⅜ x 2¾ (37.3 x 28.9 x 7)
(anonymous gift 87.55)

Joe Tilson
British, b. 1928

LOOK!   1964
oil, acrylic on plywood
73⅝ x 76¾ (187 x 194.9) overall
(Art Center Acquisition Fund 66.12)

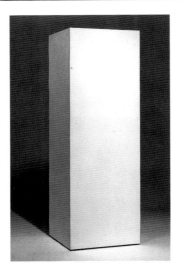

Ernest Trova
American, b. 1927

Study: Falling Man   1965
silicon bronze
60 x 48 x 20¹³⁄₁₆ (152.4 x 121.9 x 52.9)
(gift of the T.B. Walker Foundation 65.36)

Anne Truitt
American, b. 1921

Australian Spring   1972
painted wood
72 x 24 x 24 (182.9 x 61 x 61)
(gift of Mrs. Helen B. Stern 73.16)

William Tucker
American, b. Egypt, 1935

Persephone   1964/1990
painted aluminum
71 x 54 x 42 (180.3 x 137.2 x 106.7)
(gift of the T.B. Walker Foundation 64.42)

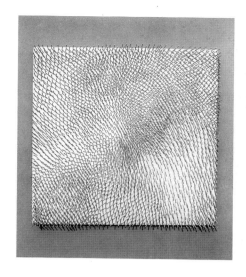

Jack Tworkov
American, b. Poland, 1900–1982

No. 1 Spring Weather   1962
oil on canvas
50½ x 37½ (128.3 x 95.3)
(gift of the T.B. Walker Foundation 64.12)

Jack Tworkov
American, b. Poland, 1900–1982

Sirens   1950–1952
oil on canvas
44 x 36 (111.8 x 91.4)
(gift of Alexander M. Bing 53.52)

Günther Uecker
German, b. 1930

White Field   1964
nails, canvas on wood
34½ x 34½ x 2¾ (87.6 x 87.6 x 7)
(gift of the T.B. Walker Foundation 64.41)

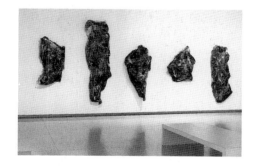

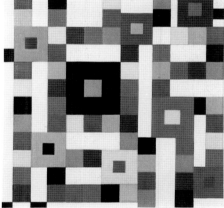

Richard Van Buren
American, b. 1937

Five Reds for Walker   1971
polyester resin, fiberglass, pigments, charcoal,
paper, glass beads, metal
96 x 240 x 12 (243.8 x 609.6 x 30.5) variable
(gift of the T.B. Walker Foundation 71.9)

Charmion von Wiegand
American, 1899–1983

The Great Field of Action or the 64 Hexagrams
n.d.
oil on canvas
27¾ x 27¾ (70.5 x 70.5)
(gift of Mr. and Mrs. Howard Wise 74.41)

Max Weber
American, 1881–1961

Woman Carrying Picture   1944
oil on canvas
50¼ x 31¼ (127.6 x 79.4)
(gift of the T.B. Walker Foundation, Gilbert M.
Walker Fund 46.28)

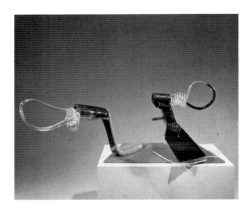

David Weinrib
American, b. 1924

Needle 1962
metal
90 x 74 x 97 (228.6 x 188 x 246.4)
(gift of the Longview Foundation 63.31)

David Weinrib
American, b. 1924

Double Loops 1965
plastic, wood
18½ x 41 x 21 (47 x 104.1 x 53.3)
(gift of Mr. and Mrs. Howard Wise 65.31)

Lynton Wells
American, b. 1940

Untitled (man with jacket) 1969
photo-sensitized linen, urethane foam
73½ x 22 x 9 (186.7 x 55.9 x 22.9)
(gift of Mr. and Mrs. Russell Cowles 70.20)

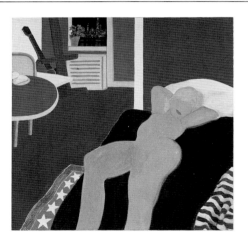

Lynton Wells
American, b. 1940

Untitled (woman in print dress) 1969
photo-sensitized linen, urethane foam
73½ x 22 x 8 (186.7 x 55.9 x 20.3)
(gift of Mr. and Mrs. Russell Cowles 70.21)

Tom Wesselmann
American, b. 1931

Great American Nude #32 1962
oil, polymer enamel, pigments on gelatin silver
print on wood
48 x 48 (121.9 x 121.9)
(gift of Fred Mueller 66.22)

Robert Wilson
American, b. 1944

Beach Chairs 1979
aluminum
two elements
29½ x 82 x 23⅞ (74.9 x 208.3 x 60.6);
21 x 80⅛ x 23⅞ (53.3 x 203.5 x 60.6)
(T.B. Walker Acquisition Fund and Clinton and
Della Walker Acquisition Fund 87.15)

James Wines
American, b. 1932

Frontier Wall 1961
bronze, cement
33½ x 23 x 11 (85.1 x 58.4 x 27.9)
(gift of the T.B. Walker Foundation 63.7)

Adja Yunkers
American, 1900–1983

Foundries of the Night 1954
pastel, wax crayon, graphite on paper
69 x 48 (175.3 x 121.9)
(gift of Howard Wise 67.60)

Michelle Zalopany
American, b. 1955

The Castleton 1987
pastel, charcoal on paper, mounted on canvas
91½ x 120⅝ (232.4 x 306.4)
(Walker Special Purchase Fund and Jerome
Foundation Purchase Fund for Emerging Artists
87.88)

Joe Zucker
American, b. 1941

Pairkeets 1973
acrylic, Rhoplex, cotton balls on canvas
48 x 48 (121.9 x 121.9)
(gift of Chuck Close 81.57)

Selected Bibliography

Note: Listed here are the major works referred to in the preparation of this volume. Numerous other references are cited in the essays and collection entries.

Agee, William C. *The 1930's: Painting & Sculpture in America*, exh. cat., New York: Whitney Museum of American Art, 1968.

Alloway, Lawrence. *Topics in American Art Since 1945*, New York: W.W. Norton & Co., 1975.

Arnason, H. Harvard. *Stuart Davis*, exh. cat., Minneapolis: Walker Art Center, 1957.

_____. *60 American Painters 1960*, exh. cat., Minneapolis: Walker Art Center, 1960.

_____. *History of Modern Art: Painting, Sculpture, Architecture, Photography*, 3rd ed., New York: Harry N. Abrams, Inc., 1986.

Ashton, Dore. *American Art Since 1945*, New York: Oxford University Press, Inc., 1982.

Battcock, Gregory, ed. *Minimal Art: A Critical Anthology*, New York: E.P. Dutton, 1968.

Beal, Graham W.J., et al. *Jim Dine: Five Themes*, exh. cat., Minneapolis: Walker Art Center; New York: Abbeville Press, Inc.,1984.

Bourdon, David. *Carl Andre: Sculpture 1959–1977*, New York: Jaap Rietman, 1978.

Brown, Milton Wolf. *American Painting from the Armory Show to the Depression*, Princeton, New Jersey: Princeton University Press, 1955.

Bruggen, Coosje van, R.H. Fuchs, and Claes Oldenburg. *Claes Oldenburg: Large-Scale Projects, 1977–1980*, New York: Rizzoli International Publications, Inc., 1980.

Coplans, John. *Ellsworth Kelly*, New York: Harry N. Abrams, Inc., 1972.

Cowart, Jack. *Roy Lichtenstein 1970–1980*, exh. cat., Saint Louis: Saint Louis Art Museum; New York: Hudson Hills Press, Inc., 1981.

Dupin, Jacques. *Miró*, New York: Harry N. Abrams, Inc., 1962.

Frascina, Francis and Charles Harrison, eds. *Modern Art and Modernism: A Critical Anthology*, New York: Harper & Row Publishers, Inc., 1982.

Friedman, Martin L. *The Precisionist View in American Art*, exh. cat., Minneapolis: Walker Art Center, 1960.

_____. *Adolph Gottlieb*, exh. cat., Minneapolis: Walker Art Center (for the VII Bienal de Sao Paulo), 1963.

_____.and Jan van der Marck. *Eight Sculptors: The Ambiguous Image*, exh. cat., Minneapolis: Walker Art Center, 1966.

_____, et al. *Charles Sheeler*, exh. cat., Washington, D.C.: National Collection of Fine Arts, Smithsonian Institution, 1968.

_____, et al. *14 Sculptors: The Industrial Edge*, exh. cat., Minneapolis: Walker Art Center, 1969.

_____. *Nevelson: Wood Sculptures*, exh. cat., Minneapolis: Walker Art Center, 1973.

_____. *Oldenburg: Six Themes*, exh. cat., Minneapolis: Walker Art Center, 1975.

_____. *Charles Sheeler*, exh. cat., New York: Watson-Guptill Publications, Inc., 1975.

_____. *Design Quarterly 106/107, Noguchi's Imaginary Landscapes*, exh. cat., Minneapolis: Walker Art Center, 1978.

_____ and Graham W.J. Beal. *George Segal: Sculptures*, exh. cat., Minneapolis: Walker Art Center, 1978.

_____, et al. *Hockney Paints the Stage*, exh. cat., Minneapolis: Walker Art Center; New York: Abbeville Press, Inc., 1983.

Goodrich, Lloyd and John I.H. Baur. *American Art of Our Century*,New York: Praeger Publishers, 1961.

Gray, Cleve, ed. *David Smith*, New York: Holt, Rinehart & Winston, Inc., 1968.

Hammacher, Abraham Marie. *Jacques Lipchitz: His Sculpture*, New York: Harry N. Abrams, Inc., 1960.

Hancock, Jane and Stefanie Poley. *Arp 1886–1966*, exh. cat., Stuttgart, Germany: Württembergischer Kunstverein, 1986.

Hauser, Arnold. *The Social History of Art*, New York: Vintage Books, 1951.

Helm, MacKinley. *John Marin*, Boston: Pellegrini & Cudahy, 1948.

Hess, Hans. *Lyonel Feininger*, New York: Harry N. Abrams, Inc., 1961.

Hockney, David. *David Hockney, Looking at Pictures in a Book at the National Gallery*, exh. cat., London: National Gallery, 1981.

_____ and Lawrence Weschler. *Cameraworks*, New York: Alfred A. Knopf, Inc., 1984.

Hope, Henry Radford. *The Sculpture of Jacques Lipchitz*, exh. cat., New York: The Museum of Modern Art, 1954.

Hunter, Sam. *American Art of the 20th Century*, New York: Harry N. Abrams, Inc., 1973.

James, Philip Brutton, ed. *Henry Moore on Sculpture*, New York: Viking Press, 1967.

Jones, Kellie. *Martin Puryear*, exh. cat., (for the 20a Bienal Internacional De São Paulo 1989), Jamaica, New York: Jamaica Arts Center, 1989.

Judd, Donald. *Complete Writings 1959–1975*, Halifax: Press of the Nova Scotia College of Art and Design; New York: New York University Press, 1975.

Kelder, Diane, ed. *Stuart Davis*, New York: Praeger Publishers, 1971.

Kozloff, Max. *Renderings: Critical Essays on a Century of Modern Art*, New York: Simon & Schuster, Inc., 1969.

Krauss, Rosalind E. *The Originality of the Avant-Garde and Other Modernist Myths*, Cambridge, Massachusetts: MIT Press, 1985.

Kuh, Katharine. *The Artist's Voice: Talks with Seventeen Artists*, New York: Harper & Row Publishers, Inc., 1960.

Lampert, Catherine. *Tony Cragg*, exh. cat., London: Hayward Gallery, 1987.

Lankheit, Klaus. *Franz Marc: Katalog der Werke*, Cologne: DuMont Schauberg, 1970.

Legg, Alicia, ed. *Sol LeWitt*, exh. cat., New York: The Museum of Modern Art, 1978.

Lippard, Lucy R. *Pop Art*, New York: Praeger Publishers, 1966.

Livingstone, Marco. *David Hockney*, New York: Holt, Rinehart & Winston, Inc., 1981.

Lyons, Lisa. *Design Quarterly 111/112, Eight Artists: The Elusive Image*, exh. cat., Minneapolis: Walker Art Center, 1979.

_____.*Close Portraits*, exh. cat., Minneapolis: Walker Art Center, 1980

McShine, Kynaston, ed. *Joseph Cornell*, exh. cat., New York: The Museum of Modern Art, 1980.

Masheck, Joseph. *Christopher Wilmarth: Nine Clearings for a Standing Man*, exh. cat., Hartford, Connecticut: Wadsworth Atheneum, 1974.

Mellquist, Jerome. *The Emergence of an American Art*, New York: Charles Scribner's Sons, 1942.

Moore, Henry and John Hedgecoe. *Henry Moore: My Ideas, Inspiration and Life as and Artist*, San Francisco: Chronicle Books, 1986.

Motherwell, Robert and Ad Reinhardt, eds. *Modern Artists in America: First Series*, New York: Wittenborn Schultz, Inc., 1951.

Ness, June L., ed., Lyonel Feininger. *Lyonel Feininger*, New York: Praeger Publishers, 1974.

Nevelson, Louise. *Dawns + Dusks: Taped Conversations with Diana Mackown*, New York: Charles Scribner's Sons, 1976.

O'Keeffe, Georgia. *Georgia O'Keeffe*, New York: Viking Press, 1976.

Pincus-Witten, Robert. *Postminimalism*, New York: Out of London Press, 1977.

Ratcliff, Carter. *Robert Longo*, New York: Rizzoli International Publications, Inc., 1985.

Rodman, Selden. *Conversations With Artists*, New York: Devin-Adair Publishers, Inc., 1957.

Rose, Barbara. *American Art Since 1900: A Critical History*, New York, Praeger Publishers, 1967.

_____, ed. *Readings in American Art Since 1900: A Documentary Survey*, New York: Praeger Publishers, 1968.

_____. *Claes Oldenburg*, exh. cat., New York: The Museum of Modern Art, 1970.

Rosenberg, Harold. *The Anxious Object: Art Today and its Audience*, New York: Horizon Press, 1964.

_____. *The De-Definition of Art*, New York: Horizon Press, 1972.

_____. *Art on the Edge: Creators and Situations*, New York: Macmillan Publishing Co., Inc., 1975.

Rosenthal, Mark. *Anselm Kiefer*, exh. cat., Chicago: Art Institute of Chicago; Philadelphia: Philadelphia Museum of Art, 1987.

Russell, John and Suzi Gablik, eds. *Pop Art Redefined*, New York: Praeger Publishers, 1969.

Sandler, Irving. *The Triumph of American Painting: A History of Abstract Expressionism*, New York: Praeger Publishers, 1970.

_____. *The New York School: The Painters and Sculptors of the Fifties*, New York: Harper & Row Publishers, Inc., 1978.

Schapiro, Meyer. *Modern Art: 19th and 20th Centuries*, New York: George Braziller, Inc., 1978.

Seitz, William Chapin. *The Art of Assemblage*, exh. cat., New York: The Museum of Modern Art, 1961.

Selz, Jean. *Modern Sculpture: Origins and Evolution*, New York: George Braziller, Inc., 1963.

Shapiro, David. *Jim Dine: Painting What One Is*, New York: Harry N. Abrams, Inc., 1981.

St. John, Bruce, ed., John Sloan. *John Sloan's New York Scene*, New York: Harper & Row Publishers, Inc., 1965.

Stella, Frank. *Working Space*, Cambridge, Massachusetts: Harvard University Press, 1986.

Stooss, Toni. *Rebecca Horn*, exh. cat., Zurich: Kunsthaus Zurich, 1983.

Swanson, Dean and Diane Upright Headley. *Morris Louis: The Veil Cycle*, exh. cat., Minneapolis: Walker Art Center, 1977.

Tuchman, Phyllis. *George Segal*, New York: Abbeville Press, Inc., 1983.

Upright, Diane. *Morris Louis: The Complete Paintings: A Catalogue Raisonné*, New York: Harry N. Abrams, Inc., 1985

Warhol, Andy and Pat Hackett. *POPism: The Warhol '60s*, New York: Harcourt Brace Jovanovich, Inc., 1980.

Wilson, Laurie. *Louise Nevelson: Iconography and Sources*, New York: Garland Publishing, Inc., 1981.

Wye, Deborah. *Louise Bourgeois*, exh. cat., New York: The Museum of Modern Art, 1982.

Young, Mahonri Sharp. *The Eight: The Realist Revolt in American Painting*, New York: Watson-Guptill Publications, Inc., 1973.

_____. *Early American Moderns: Painters of the Stieglitz Group*, New York: Watson-Guptill Publications, Inc., 1974.

Acknowledgments

The preparation of this comprehensive publication of the Walker collection has involved the talents of many individuals, both at the museum and outside of it. Although a catalogue of the Walker's sculpture collection was issued in 1969, this volume is the first thorough analysis of the museum's collection of painting and sculpture; in it over two hundred of the most significant works are discussed in detail and an additional one hundred-fifty are illustrated. To provide a context for these presentations the Walker invited five distinguished authors to write on aspects of the art of this century.

The editorial supervision and in-house production of this catalogue, to date the most detailed and extensive publication issued by the museum, was the responsibility of Mildred Friedman, the Walker's design curator. Carolyn DeCato and Gwen Bitz, the Walker's former and current registrars, provided access to the records on the works of art described in this book. The Walker's exhibition crew gave invaluable assistance in handling objects under study; special thanks are due Owen Osten, whose major assignment this was. For the catalogue's numerous illustrations, many new photographs were made of older works in the collection, as well as of important recent acquisitions, a formidable task handled admirably by Glenn Halvorson, the museum's photographer. The clear and handsome typography and layout of the catalogue was the responsibility of Glenn Suokko, the Walker's senior graphic designer, who was ably assisted by graphic designer John Calvelli. Business details related to the catalogue's publication were handled by David Galligan, the museum's administrative director.

The organization of this catalogue is essentially chronological, with essays by guest authors dealing with many significant thematic and stylistic aspects of twentieth-century art. Special thanks are due William C. Agee, Edward F. Fry, Joseph Masheck, Carter Ratcliff, and Diane Waldman, who have written knowledgeably and fluently about significant currents in the art of this century, utilizing works from the Walker's collection to illustrate many of their ideas. Thanks to their impressive efforts, this publication also serves as a compelling history of Modernism. Lucy Flint-Gohlke, Assistant Director of the Wellesley College Museum, provided the majority of the catalogue entries on individual works of art. In addition, working closely with the Walker staff, she helped develop the research method and presentation style for the entries. Additional characterizations were written by Walker Art Center curators Elizabeth Armstrong, Peter Boswell, and Mildred Friedman, by curatorial associate Joan Rothfuss and curatorial intern Ann Brooke. A number of essays were provided by former staff members Marge Goldwater and Donna Harkavy, by former interns Nora Heimann, Nancy Roth, and Lawrence Rinder, and by Constance Butler, curator of Artists Space, New York.

Manuscript preparation was overseen by curatorial secretary Brian Hassett, working closely with guest editor Sheila Schwartz, whose insights and knowledge of art history were invaluable to the authors of this book; editorial assistance was provided by Walker staff members Phil Freshman and Linda Krenzin.

We are indebted to the staff of Rizzoli International, particularly Gianfranco Monacelli and Solveig Williams, who have collaborated patiently with the Walker on this project from its beginning, some five years ago, to its realization.

Finally, on behalf of the Board of Directors of the Walker Art Center, I wish to express deep appreciation for their generous support of this publication to The Andrew W. Mellon Foundation, The Henry Luce Foundation, Inc., and the National Endowment for the Arts.

Martin Friedman, Director
Walker Art Center   May 1990

Reproduction Credits

Index

566

The text for this book was set in Linotype Franklin Gothic and New Caledonia.
The book was printed at Toppan Printing Co., Ltd., Tokyo, Japan

568